Teacher's Edition

Level 5 • Unit 5

Going West

— Program Authors —

Marilyn Jager Adams
Carl Bereiter
Ann Brown
Joe Campione
Iva Carruthers
Robbie Case
Jan Hirshberg
Anne McKeough
Michael Pressley
Marsha Roit
Marlene Scardamalia
Marcy Stein
Gerald H. Treadway, Jr.

A Division of The ***McGraw-Hill*** *Companies*

Columbus, Ohio

Acknowledgments

Grateful acknowledgment is given to the following publishers and copyright owners for permissions granted to reprint selections from their publications. All possible care has been taken to trace ownership and secure permission for each selection included. In case of any errors or omissions, the Publisher will be pleased to make suitable acknowledgments in future editions.

“Connecting the Country” from BEYOND THE MISSISSIPPI: EARLY WESTWARD EXPANSION OF THE UNITED STATES by Angela M. Herb. Copyright © 1996 Laing Communications. Used by permission of Lodestar Books, an affiliate of Dutton Children's Books, A Division of Penguin Young Readers Group, A Member of Penguin Group (USA) Inc., 345 Hudson Street, New York NY 10014. All rights reserved. From SACAGAWEA by Betty Westrom Skold. Copyright © 1977 by Dillon Press. Reprinted with permission of the author. Copyright © 1988 by Russell Freedman. All rights reserved. Reprinted from BUFFALO HUNT by permission of Holiday House, Inc. SONGS OF THE DREAM PEOPLE: Chants and Images from the Indians and Eskimos of North America. Edited and illustrated by James Houston. Atheneum, New York, copyright © 1972 by James Houston. "The Flower-Fed Buffaloes", from GOING TO THE STARS by Vachel Lindsay, copyright 1926 by D. Appleton & Co., renewed 1954 by Elizabeth C. Lindsay. A Hawthorn Book. Used by permission of Dutton Children's Books, an imprint of Penguin Putnam Books for Young Readers, a division of Penguin Putnam Inc. From THE JOURNAL OF WONG MING-CHUNG by Laurence Yep. Copyright © 2000 by Laurence Yep. Reprinted by permission of Scholastic Inc. From SING DOWN THE MOON by Scott O'Dell. Copyright © 1970 by Scott O'Dell. Reprinted by permission of Houghton Mifflin Company. All rights reserved. "OLD YELLER AND THE BEAR" (SRA excerpt title), pages 32-39 from OLD YELLER by FRED GIPSON. Copyright © 1956 by Fred Gipson. Reprinted by permission of HarperCollins Publishers, Inc. BILL PICKETT: RODEO RIDIN' COWBOY, Text copyright © 1996 by Andrea Davis Pinkney, illustrations copyright © 1996 by Brian Pinkney, reprinted by permission of Harcourt, Inc. MCBROOM THE RAINMAKER TEXT COPYRIGHT © 1973 BY SID FLEISCHMAN. Used by permission HarperCollins Publishers.

www.sra4kids.com

SRA/McGraw-Hill

A Division of The **McGraw·Hill** *Companies*

Send all inquiries to:
SRA/McGraw-Hill
8787 Orion Place
Columbus, OH 43240-4027

Printed in the United States of America.

ISBN 0-07-602769-4

1 2 3 4 5 6 7 8 9 WEB 10 09 08 07 06 05 04

Making the Difference

Welcome to SRA Open Court Reading

Proven Results

Inspire a lifetime love of learning by using research-based instruction.

Open Court Reading is an instructional leader for three key reasons.

1. Research-based instruction that works
2. Teacher-tested lessons that are effective in classrooms like yours
3. Unparalleled support to help you do what you do best—Teach

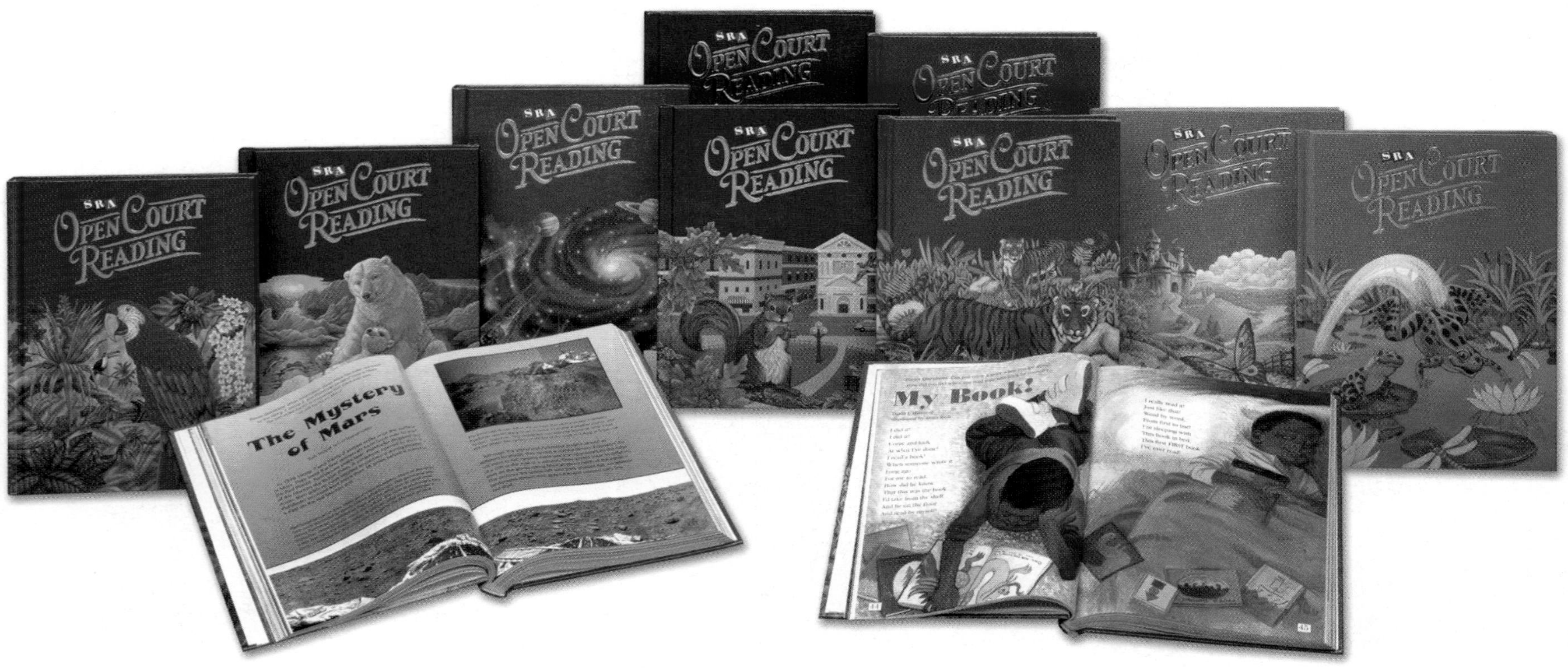

Achieve your classroom goals with *Open Court Reading's* proven approach.

Students attending schools using ***Open Court Reading*** score higher in basic reading skills than students attending schools that do not use ***Open Court Reading*** materials.

"Since using ***Open Court Reading,*** our students have gone beyond even my expectations. ***Open Court Reading*** is by far the best systematic approach to instruction of reading skills that I have taught in my thirty years as an instructor or administrator."

— **Gerald Judd,** 6th Grade Language Arts
Dunbar 6th Grade Center,
Fort Worth, TX

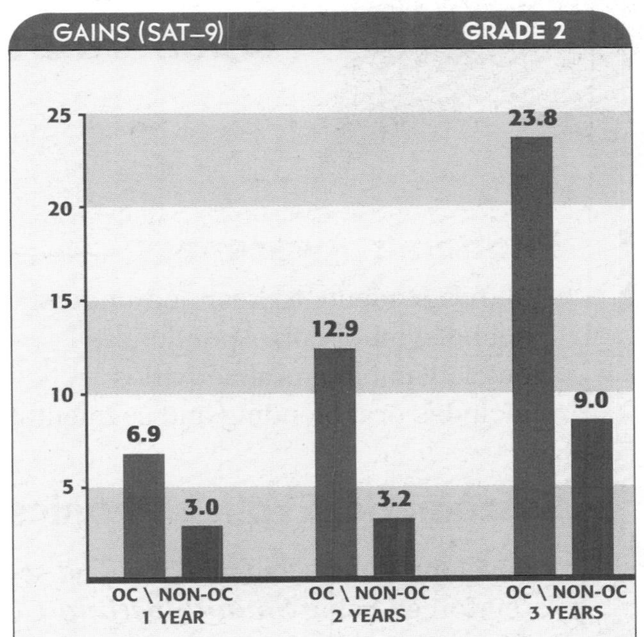

In California schools serving large concentrations of Low Socioeconomic Status students, differences over three years were most impressive.

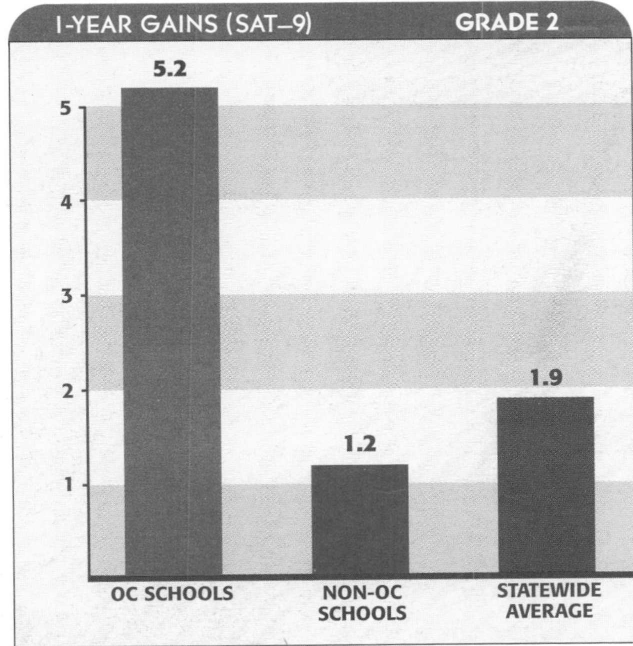

One-year gains for students in more than 700 California schools show that ***Open Court Reading*** schools outgain non-***Open Court Reading*** schools by a factor of four.

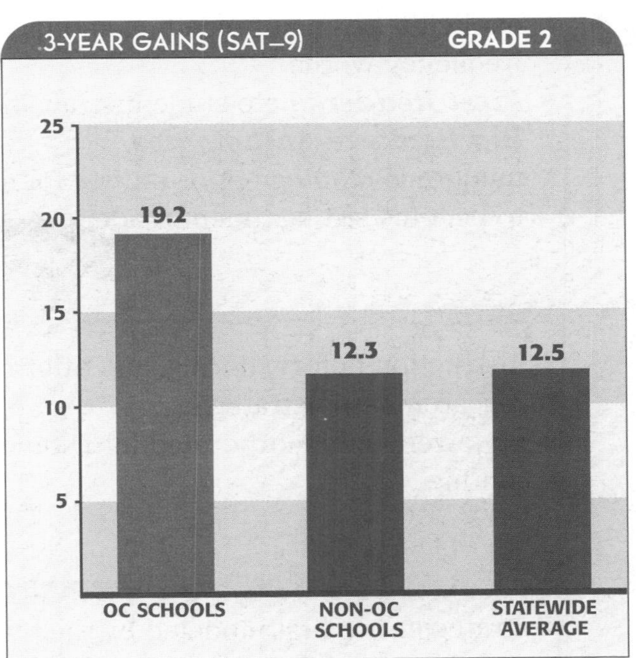

Open Court Reading schools outgain demographically similar non-***Open Court Reading*** schools as well as the statewide average by 50 to 75 percent.

For a copy of the detailed ***Open Court Reading*** **Research Report** and **Results Report**, visit SRAonline.com, or contact SRA at 1-888-SRA-4543.

Effective Instruction

Lead the way in research-based instruction with *Open Court Reading.*

1 Phonemic Awareness

- allows students to hear and understand sound/symbol correspondences
- quick, gamelike oral activities
- includes oral blending and segmentation

connecting letters to their sounds

2 Systematic, Explicit Phonics

- developmental sequence of sound spellings
- reinforced using ***Sound/Spelling Cards***
- ***Decodable Books*** help student apply, review, and reinforce sound/spelling correspondences

applying the links between letters and sounds to printed words

3 Fluency

- explicit teaching of blending and high-frequency words
- ***First Readers*** help students transition from ***Big Books*** to ***Anthologies***
- numerous reading opportunities for students to become strong, fluent readers

reading effortlessly with speed, accuracy, and expression

4 Vocabulary

- instruction before, during, and after reading
- research-based strategies
- reviewed and incorporated into students' writing

learning word meanings to build comprehension

5 Text Comprehension

- strategies are first modeled by the teacher
- graphic organizers can be used to categorize information
- skills are explicitly taught and reviewed

thinking actively before, during, and after reading

Manage instructional time to make the most of your day.

Beginning with a strong foundation in Pre-Kindergarten, ***Open Court Reading*** effectively builds skills and strategies throughout all grade levels.

Comprehensive Program

Grade						
Pre-K	Letter Recognition	Print/Book Awareness		Phonics	Comprehension and Fluency	Writing
K	Letter Recognition	Print/Book Awareness	Phonological and Phonemic Awareness	Phonics	Comprehension and Fluency	Writing
1	Letter/Book/Print Awareness	Phonemic Awareness	Phonics	Comprehension and Fluency	Writing	Language Arts and Vocabulary
2	Phonics/Word Knowledge	Comprehension and Fluency	Inquiry Learning	Writing	Language Arts and Vocabulary	
3	Phonics/Word Knowledge	Comprehension and Fluency	Inquiry Learning	Writing	Language Arts and Vocabulary	
4	Phonics/Word Knowledge	Comprehension and Fluency	Inquiry Learning	Writing	Language Arts and Vocabulary	
5	Phonics/Word Knowledge	Comprehension and Fluency	Inquiry Learning	Writing	Language Arts and Vocabulary	
6	Phonics/Word Knowledge	Comprehension and Fluency	Inquiry Learning	Writing	Language Arts and Vocabulary	

This chart shows the time allocated for skill instruction at each grade level.

Award-Winning Literature

Engage students with great literature to help them become independent readers.

The literature in each theme was thoughtfully selected with the following goals in mind:

- **A variety of literature** provides a full spectrum of fiction and nonfiction.
- **Excellent literature** provides models for student writing and helps students develop their expertise as writers.
- **Award-winning authors** and different styles of writing encourage students to develop a cultural literacy.

Literature in ***Open Court Reading*** is available in a variety of formats, depending on the grade level.

- Big and Little Books
- Anthologies
- Teacher Read Alouds
- Story Time Selections (Kindergarten)
- Leveled Classroom Libraries
- First Readers

Thought-provoking themes in ***Open Court Reading*** span grade levels.

	Pre-K BIG BOOKS	K BIG BOOKS	1 BIG BOOKS	2 STUDENT ANTHOLOGIES	3 STUDENT ANTHOLOGIES	4 STUDENT ANTHOLOGIES	5 STUDENT ANTHOLOGIES	6 STUDENT ANTHOLOGIES
Unit 1	I'm Special	School	Let's Read!	Sharing Stories	Friendship	Risks and Consequences	Cooperation and Competition	Perseverance
Unit 2	Families Everywhere	Shadows	Animals	Kindness	City Wildlife	Dollars and Sense	Astronomy	Ancient Civilizations
Unit 3	All Kinds of Friends	Finding Friends	Things That Go	Look Again	Imagination	From Mystery to Medicine	Heritage	Taking a Stand
Unit 4	Helping Hands	The Wind	Our Neighborhood at Work	Courage	Money	Survival	Making a New Nation	Beyond the Notes
Unit 5	Let's Go!	Stick to It	Weather	Fossils	Storytelling	Communication	Going West	Ecology
Unit 6	Senses	Red, White, and Blue	Journeys	Our Country and Its People	Country Life	A Changing America	Journeys and Quests	A Question of Value
			STUDENT ANTHOLOGIES					
Unit 7	At the Farm	Teamwork	Keep Trying					
Unit 8	Changes	By the Sea	Games					
Unit 9			Being Afraid					
Unit 10			Homes					

"Reading is the basis for all learning. I applaud ***Open Court Reading*** for allowing teachers to spend so much time on reading and yet not miss out on some of the other areas of learning. So much science and social studies is built into the program that it really makes my job as a teacher easier."

— **Deanna Sinift**, Grade 1 Teacher
Woodville Elementary School,
Porterville, CA

Comprehensive Resources

Open Court Reading **materials will help your students expand their knowledge by exploring, discussing, and researching ideas.**

Student Materials

Big and Little Books
- Award-winning authors and illustrators
- Variety of cultures and genres represented

Anthologies
- Award-winning authors and illustrators
- Wide variety of cultures and genres represented
- Concept Connections include vocabulary practice

First and Second Readers
- Transitions Level 1 students from ***Big Books*** to ***Anthologies***
- Reviews skills in Level 2

Decodable Text
- Pre-Decodable and Decodable stories in either book or takehome format
- Practice blending strategies and high-frequency words

Story Time Selections
- Trade books to support Kindergarten unit themes

Leveled Classroom Libraries
- Leveled trade books that support unit themes

Desk Strips
- Miniature pictures of ***Alphabet Sound Cards*** or ***Sound/Spelling Cards***

Language Arts Big Books
- Language arts skills for students in Kindergarten and Level 1

Language Arts Handbooks
- Language Arts conventions and examples for students in Levels 2–6

Practice Books
- Activities to practice and reinforce skills found in all parts of the lesson

Science/Social Studies Connection Centers
- Reinforce reading across the curriculum

Online

Online Phonics
- Interactive multimedia lessons to practice phonics skills
- Includes an assessment tool to monitor student progress

Literacy Launcher
- ***Online Phonics*** and vocabulary instruction
- Assessment and management tools included

CD-ROMs

Alphabet Book Activities
- Interactive activities to accompany ***Alphabet Big Book***

Decodable Book Activities
- Includes interactive activities to practice and review sound/spellings

Spelling Software
- Features a variety of interactive activities to review spelling patterns

Ultimate Writing and Creativity Center
- Activities to reinforce writing process skills

Research Assistant
- Provides forms to help students plan, organize, present, and assess research projects

TechKnowledge
- Technology skills and applications to help students research, write, calculate, and present topics more effectively
- Step-by-step instruction made easy

Leap Into™ Phonics
- Phonemic awareness and phonics activities

Power Vocabulary
- Vocabulary practice for ***Leveled Classroom Libraries*** in Levels 3–6

Audiocassettes/CDs

Listening Library
- ***Big Book*** and ***Anthology*** selections available on audiocassette or compact disc

Alphabet Sound Card Stories
- Appropriate grade-level jingles set to music

Sound/Spelling Card Stories
- Appropriate grade-level jingles set to music

Teacher materials help you make the most of your day.

Teacher's Editions
- Separate books for each unit theme
- Three-part lessons, each containing phonics, reading comprehension, and language arts
- Plans to help differentiate instruction
- Tips to accommodate students learning English

Teacher Read Alouds
- Available in every unit for each grade level

Phonics Packages
- Contain manipulatives necessary for phonics instruction

Home Connection
- Blackline masters to inform and support ***Open Court Reading*** lessons

Part 1 Lesson Cards
- Easy-to-use aid to use while teaching the phonics portion of each lesson (Levels K–3)

Teacher Management
- Printable blackline masters of all practice, ***Reteach,*** and ***Challenge*** books

Assessments to track and meet the needs of all students

Program Assessment
- Includes Pretests, Midyear Tests, and Posttests

Unit Assessments
- Assess skills introduced or reviewed in each lesson
- Include charts to monitor student progress

Test Preparation and Practice
- Prepares students for taking standardized tests

Assessment CD-ROM
- Printable blackline masters of all assessments
- Interactive record charts

Online Assessment
- Helps differentiate instruction
- Correlated to state standards
- Charts progress and monitors instruction
- Reports available at student, class, building, and district level

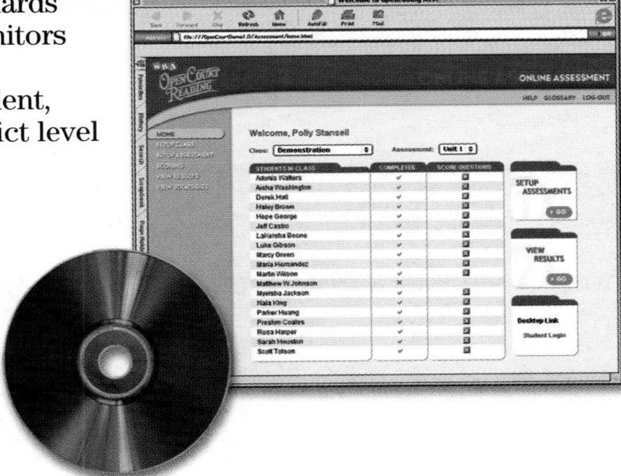

Materials to Differentiate Instruction

English Learner Support Guides and Activities
- Preteach and review ***Open Court Reading*** lessons

Intervention Guides and Workbooks
- Support students who need remediation

Reteach
- Activities for students who need a skill review during the lesson

Challenge
- Activities for students who would benefit from a skill challenge during the lesson

Differentiating Instruction Support Activities
- Quick activities available at the end of the unit to address students who need an additional review before moving to the next unit
- Activites are also available for those students who would benefit from extending a skill lesson

Differentiating Instruction

Meet students' individual needs during Open Court Workshop.

The ***Open Court Reading Teacher's Editions*** provide easy-to-use references to ensure that you have the tools you need to help every student succeed in reading.

English Learner Support

Lessons using English Learner routines to preteach skills and concepts critical to understanding each ***Open Court Reading*** lesson

Reteach lessons

For those students who need extra practice on any of the lesson's skills

Intervention lessons

More intensive support, with controlled vocabulary selections and specific skills lessons to bring students up to grade level

Challenge activities

Continued stimulation for students working at or above grade level

Science/Social Studies Connection Centers

Additional cross curricular support

Differentiating Instruction Support Activities

For students who require extra practice activities to help bolster skills and extend unit instruction

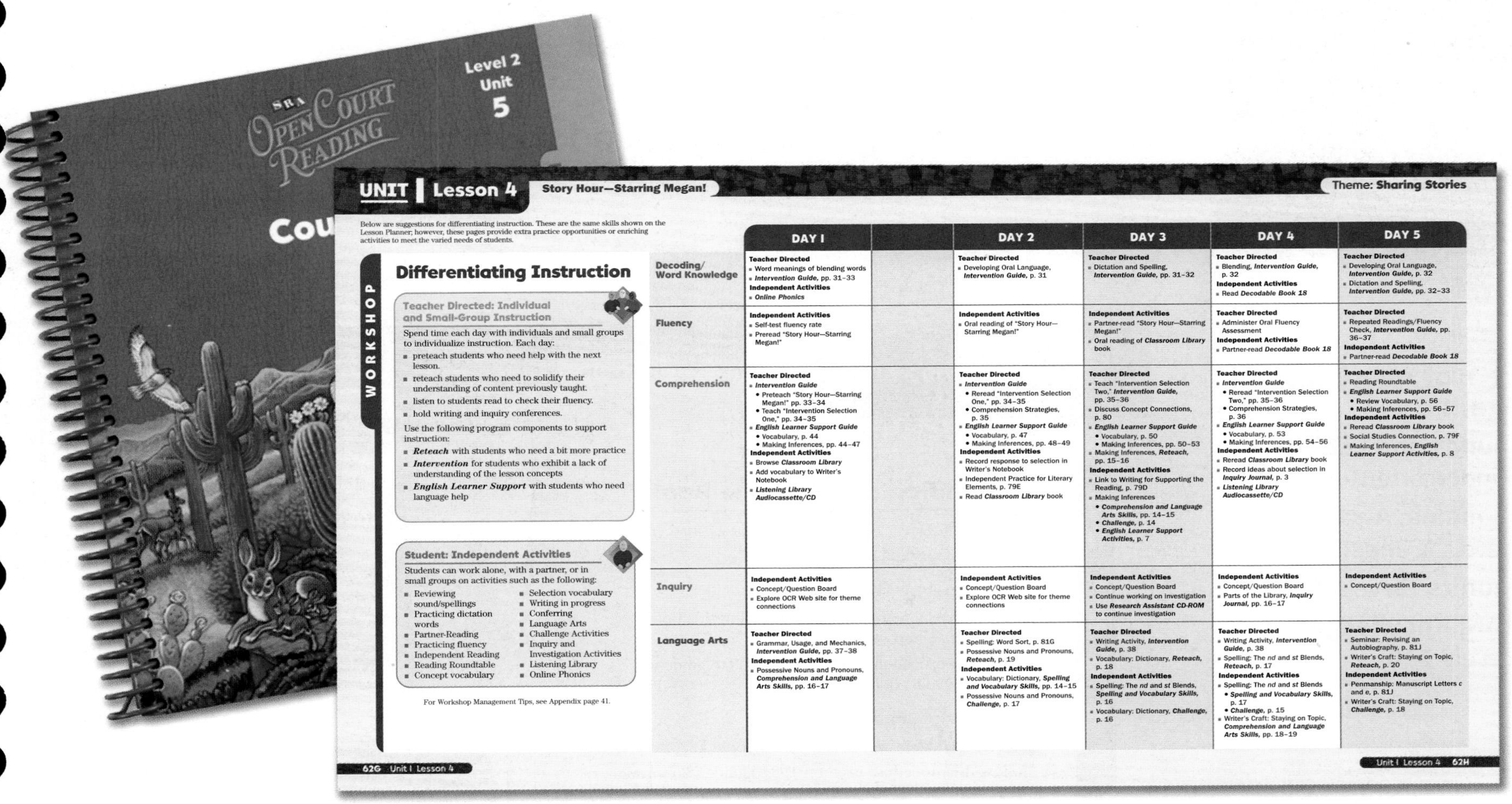

Level 2 Unit 5

SRA Open Court Reading

UNIT | Lesson 4 Story Hour—Starring Megan!

Theme: Sharing Stories

Below are suggestions for differentiating instruction. These are the same skills shown on the Lesson Planner; however, these pages provide extra practice opportunities or enriching activities to meet the varied needs of students.

WORKSHOP

Differentiating Instruction

Teacher Directed: Individual and Small-Group Instruction

Spend time each day with individuals and small groups to individualize instruction. Each day:

- preteach students who need help with the next lesson.
- reteach students who need to solidify their understanding of content previously taught.
- listen to students read to check their fluency.
- hold writing and inquiry conferences.

Use the following program components to support instruction:

- ***Reteach*** with students who need a bit more practice
- ***Intervention*** for students who exhibit a lack of understanding of the lesson concepts
- ***English Learner Support*** with students who need language help

Student: Independent Activities

Students can work alone, with a partner, or in small groups on activities such as the following:

- Reviewing sound/spellings
- Practicing dictation words
- Partner-Reading
- Practicing fluency
- Independent Reading
- Reading Roundtable
- Concept vocabulary
- Selection vocabulary
- Writing in progress
- Conferring
- Language Arts
- Challenge Activities
- Inquiry and Investigation Activities
- Listening Library
- Online Phonics

For Workshop Management Tips, see Appendix page 41.

	DAY 1	DAY 2	DAY 3	DAY 4	DAY 5
Decoding/ Word Knowledge	**Teacher Directed** - Word meanings of blending words - *Intervention Guide*, pp. 31–33 **Independent Activities** - *Online Phonics*	**Teacher Directed** - Developing Oral Language, *Intervention Guide*, p. 31	**Teacher Directed** - Dictation and Spelling, *Intervention Guide*, pp. 31–32	**Teacher Directed** - Blending, *Intervention Guide*, p. 32 **Independent Activities** - Read *Decodable Book 18*	**Teacher Directed** - Developing Oral Language, *Intervention Guide*, p. 32 - Dictation and Spelling, *Intervention Guide*, pp. 32–33
Fluency	**Independent Activities** - Self-test fluency rate - Preread "Story Hour—Starring Megan!"	**Independent Activities** - Oral reading of "Story Hour—Starring Megan!"	**Independent Activities** - Partner-read "Story Hour—Starring Megan!" - Oral reading of *Classroom Library* book	**Teacher Directed** - Administer Oral Fluency Assessment **Independent Activities** - Partner-read *Decodable Book 18*	**Teacher Directed** - Repeated Readings/Fluency Check, *Intervention Guide*, pp. 36–37 **Independent Activities** - Partner-read *Decodable Book 18*
Comprehension	**Teacher Directed** - *Intervention Guide* • Preteach "Story Hour—Starring Megan!" pp. 33–34 • Teach "Intervention Selection One," pp. 34–35 - *English Learner Support Guide* • Vocabulary, p. 44 • Making Inferences, pp. 44–47 **Independent Activities** - Browse *Classroom Library* - Add vocabulary to Writer's Notebook - *Listening Library Audiocassette/CD*	**Teacher Directed** - *Intervention Guide* • Reread "Intervention Selection One," pp. 34–35 • Comprehension Strategies, p. 35 - *English Learner Support Guide* • Vocabulary, p. 47 • Making Inferences, pp. 48–49 **Independent Activities** - Record response to selection in Writer's Notebook - Independent Practice for Literary Elements, p. 79E - Read *Classroom Library* book	**Teacher Directed** - Teach "Intervention Selection Two," *Intervention Guide*, pp. 35–36 - Discuss Concept Connections, p. 80 - *English Learner Support Guide* • Vocabulary, p. 50 • Making Inferences, pp. 50–53 - Making Inferences, *Reteach*, pp. 15–16 **Independent Activities** - Link to Writing for Supporting the Reading, p. 79D - Making Inferences • *Comprehension and Language Arts Skills*, pp. 14–15 • *Challenge*, p. 14 • *English Learner Support Activities*, p. 7	**Teacher Directed** - *Intervention Guide* • Reread "Intervention Selection Two," pp. 35–36 • Comprehension Strategies, p. 36 - *English Learner Support Guide* • Vocabulary, p. 53 • Making Inferences, pp. 54–56 **Independent Activities** - Reread *Classroom Library* book - Record ideas about selection in *Inquiry Journal*, p. 3 - *Listening Library Audiocassette/CD*	**Teacher Directed** - Reading Roundtable - *English Learner Support Guide* • Review Vocabulary, p. 56 • Making Inferences, pp. 56–57 **Independent Activities** - Reread *Classroom Library* book - Social Studies Connection, p. 79F - Making Inferences, *English Learner Support Activities*, p. 8
Inquiry	**Independent Activities** - Concept/Question Board - Explore OCR Web site for theme connections	**Independent Activities** - Concept/Question Board - Explore OCR Web site for theme connections	**Independent Activities** - Concept/Question Board - Continue working on investigation - Use *Research Assistant CD-ROM* to continue investigation	**Independent Activities** - Concept/Question Board - Parts of the Library, *Inquiry Journal*, pp. 16–17	**Independent Activities** - Concept/Question Board
Language Arts	**Teacher Directed** - Grammar, Usage, and Mechanics, *Intervention Guide*, pp. 37–38 **Independent Activities** - Possessive Nouns and Pronouns, *Comprehension and Language Arts Skills*, pp. 16–17	**Teacher Directed** - Spelling: Word Sort, p. 81G - Possessive Nouns and Pronouns, *Reteach*, p. 19 **Independent Activities** - Vocabulary: Dictionary, *Spelling and Vocabulary Skills*, pp. 14–15 - Possessive Nouns and Pronouns, *Challenge*, p. 17	**Teacher Directed** - Writing Activity, *Intervention Guide*, p. 38 - Vocabulary: Dictionary, *Reteach*, p. 18 **Independent Activities** - Spelling: The *nd* and *st* Blends, *Spelling and Vocabulary Skills*, p. 16 - Vocabulary: Dictionary, *Challenge*, p. 16	**Teacher Directed** - Writing Activity, *Intervention Guide*, p. 38 - Spelling: The *nd* and *st* Blends, *Reteach*, p. 17 **Independent Activities** - Spelling: The *nd* and *st* Blends • *Spelling and Vocabulary Skills*, p. 17 • *Challenge*, p. 15 - Writer's Craft: Staying on Topic, *Comprehension and Language Arts Skills*, pp. 18–19	**Teacher Directed** - Seminar: Revising an Autobiography, p. 81J - Writer's Craft: Staying on Topic, *Reteach*, p. 20 **Independent Activities** - Penmanship: Manuscript Letters c and e, p. 81J - Writer's Craft: Staying on Topic, *Challenge*, p. 18

62G Unit 1 Lesson 4

Unit 1 Lesson 4 62H

Built into every ***Open Court Reading*** lesson, Workshop provides the time for you to meet with individuals and small groups to provide individualized, differentiated instruction based on each student's needs. Other students may be working independently on

- conducting inquiry.
- developing listening skills with audio stories.
- discussing selections in Reading Roundtable.
- reading library collections.
- completing computer activities.
- working on their writing.

Preparing to Read

Start by building a strong foundation for reading and fluency.

Part 1 of every lesson contains:

- **Sounds and Letters** (Kindergarten)
- **Phonemic Awareness** (Levels K and 1)
- **Phonics** (Levels 1–3)
- **Word Knowledge** (Levels 2–6)

Use comprehensive, explicit instruction to deliver effective learning routines.

Give added support for differentiating instruction.

1 Preparing to Read | **Song of the Train**

PHONICS

Reading a Decodable Book

Core Set, Book 32: *Zack the One-Man Band*
Phonics Focus: /z/ Spelled *z*

High-Frequency Words

- The high-frequency words introduced in this book are *do*, *here*, *one*, and *start(ed)*.
- Follow the procedure used on page T98 to guide you through this part of the lesson.

Reading Recommendations

- No nondecodable words are in this book.
- Follow the procedure used on T98 to guide you through the lesson.

Responding

- Invite the students to discuss any hard words they encountered in *Zack and the One-Man Band* and how they figured out these words. Have volunteers retell the story.
- Follow the procedure used on T99 to guide you through this part of the lesson.

  Where did Gus and Cass sit? *(Gus and Cass sat on rocks.)*
  Who is on the big red bus? *(A man and a big brass band are on the big red bus.)*
  What does Zack tell Gus and Cass to do? *("Grab tin pots! Grab small sticks! Start a grand band!")*

Differentiating Instruction

If...	Then...
Students need help with high-frequency words	See *Intervention Guide* page 86
English Learners need additional help with vocabulary from the story and comprehension	Preread the story with them. Make sure they understand the story and can define the words used in the story.

Decodable Book 32

Zack the One-Man Band
by Diane Zaga
illustrated by Len Epstein

Gus and Cass sat on rocks.
ZAP! POP! SNAP!
"What is it?" said Cass. 3

"A big red bus has zipped up. It has a man and a big brass band," said Gus. 4

The man on the red bus blasted, "I am Zack the One-Man Band, and here is my big brass band!" 5

BAM! ZAP! BOP!
Zack's band started up.
"Zack, you are a grand band!" called Cass. 6

Zack huffed and puffed.
"I must stop," he panted. 7

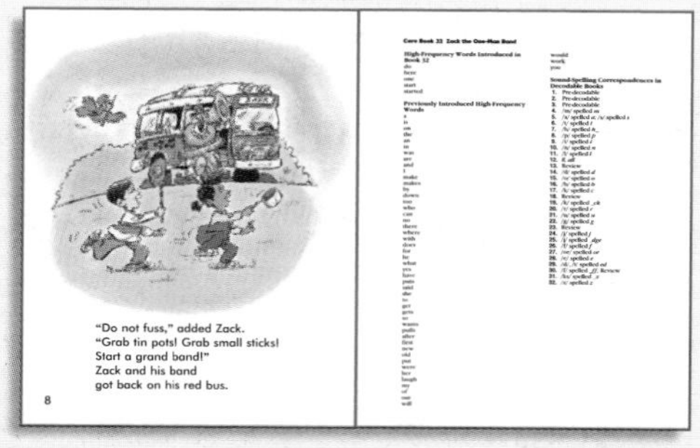

"Do not fuss," added Zack.
"Grab tin pots! Grab small sticks!
Start a grand band!"
Zack and his band
got back on his red bus. 8

T124 Unit 3 Lesson 6

Theme: **Things That Go**

Decodable Book 33

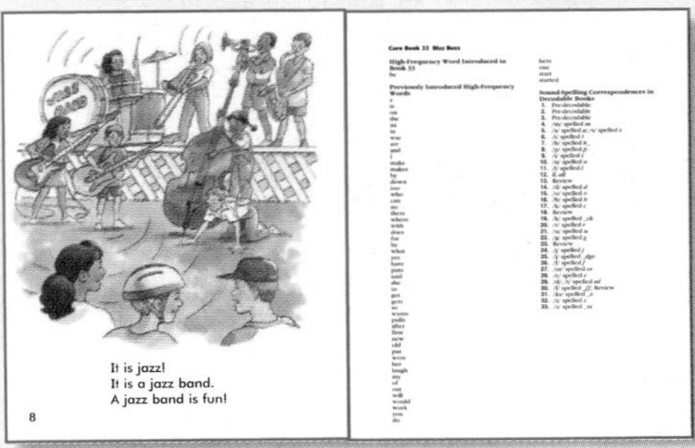

Reading a Decodable Book

Core Set, Book 33: *Bizz Buzz*
Phonics Focus: /z/ Spelled ■zz

PHONICS

High-Frequency Words

- The high-frequency word introduced in this book is *be.* Write *be* on the board and ask students to say it.
- Follow the procedure used on page T98 to guide you through the lesson.

Reading Recommendations

- No nondecodable words are in this book. See page T98 for the Reading Recommendations procedures.

Responding

- Invite the students to discuss any hard words they encountered in *Bizz Buzz* and how they figured out these words. Call on volunteers to retell the story.
- Refer back to page T99 as a guide for this portion of the lesson.

  What kind of buzz is it? *(It is a big buzz.)*
  From where do the children think the noise comes? *(from Dad)*
  What is the buzz? *(It is a jazz band.)*

Building Fluency

Encourage partners to build fluency by rereading ***Decodable Books 32*** and ***33*** of the Core Set. After the second reading, the partners should read ***Decodable Books 24****, Liz,* and ***25****, Fuzz on a Cuff,* of the Practice Set.

Teacher Tip **DECODABLE BOOKS** It is recommended that you send a story home after it has been read several times in class. Stories are available in the ***Decodable Takehome Books.***

Informal Assessment

READING PROGRESS While the students are reading to each other, invite several individuals to read with you so that you can assess their reading.

Routine Card
Refer to ***Routine 5*** to review the procedure for reading a ***Decodable Book.***

Unit 3 Lesson 6 **T125**

Use Decodable Books in Levels K–3 to support systematic phonics instruction.

Focus instruction and make teaching and learning easy by using instructional routines.

Provide multiple opportunities to practice fluency.

Help guide Workshop by using Teacher Tips that suggest varied activities.

Monitor student progress with Informal Assessment tips to meet individual needs.

Reading & Responding

Skills and strategies help students make sense of text.

Part 2 of every lesson contains:

- **Authentic literature**
- **Comprehension strategies and skills instruction**
- **Inquiry and Investigation**

Teach comprehension strategies through teacher modeling.

Use highlighted selection words to build word knowledge or phonics sound/spellings.

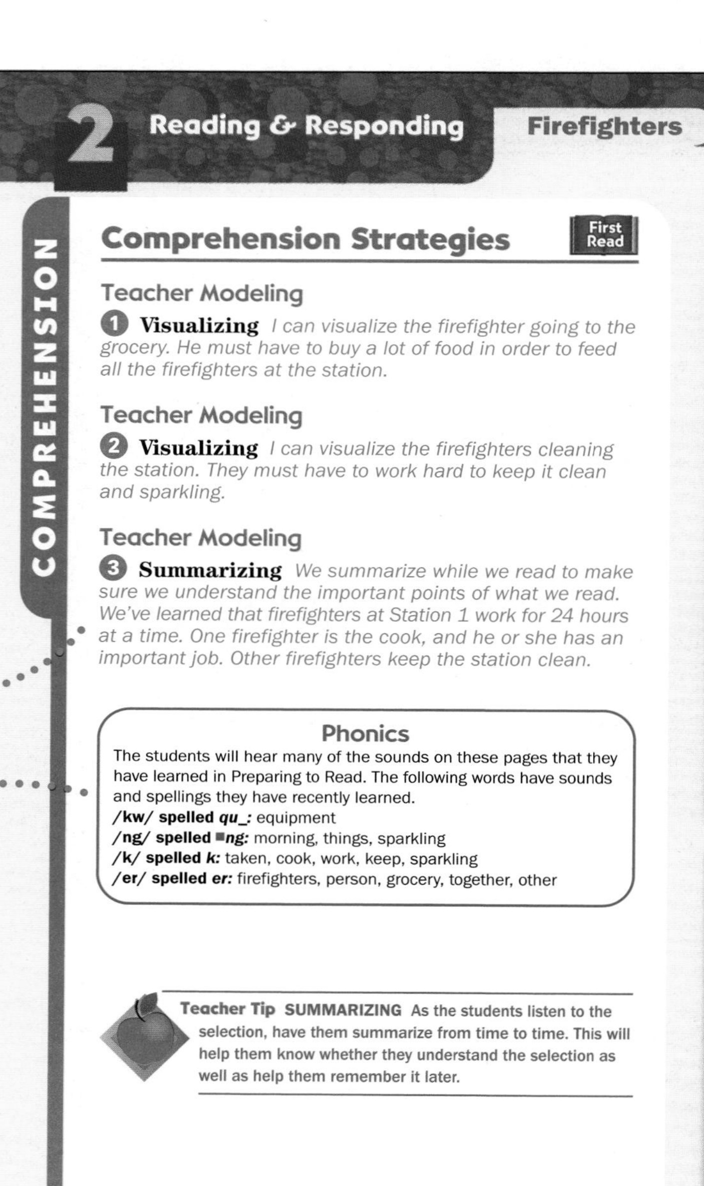

2 Reading & Responding | Firefighters

COMPREHENSION

Comprehension Strategies

First Read

Teacher Modeling

1 **Visualizing** *I can visualize the firefighter going to the grocery. He must have to buy a lot of food in order to feed all the firefighters at the station.*

Teacher Modeling

2 **Visualizing** *I can visualize the firefighters cleaning the station. They must have to work hard to keep it clean and sparkling.*

Teacher Modeling

3 **Summarizing** *We summarize while we read to make sure we understand the important points of what we read. We've learned that firefighters at Station 1 work for 24 hours at a time. One firefighter is the cook, and he or she has an important job. Other firefighters keep the station clean.*

Phonics

The students will hear many of the sounds on these pages that they have learned in Preparing to Read. The following words have sounds and spellings they have recently learned.

/kw/ spelled *qu_*: equipment
/ng/ spelled ■*ng*: morning, things, sparkling
/k/ spelled *k*: taken, cook, work, keep, sparkling
/er/ spelled *er*: firefighters, person, grocery, together, other

Teacher Tip SUMMARIZING As the students listen to the selection, have them summarize from time to time. This will help them know whether they understand the selection as well as help them remember it later.

T128 Unit 4 Lesson 6

Focus Questions What do firefighters do? How do firefighters help your neighborhood?

Firefighters

Jan Mader
photography by Justin Shady

This book is dedicated to hardworking firefighters everywhere. Special thanks to Lt. John Hill.

Inside Station 1 at 8:00 each morning roll call is taken. The firefighters live at the fire station for 24 hours at a time and there are many things to do.

24

Some firefighters think that the cook has the most important job at the station.

26

Review Comprehension Skills explicitly taught through all grade levels.

One of the firefighters is the cook. He collects money from each person and goes to the grocery store to buy enough food for the whole crew. 1

25

Other firefighters work together to keep the fire station sparkling clean. 2 The fire trucks are washed every morning, and the other equipment is cleaned and checked regularly, too. 3

27

COMPREHENSION

Comprehension Skills

Second Read

Main Idea and Details

Have the students tell what they know about Main Idea and Details. Explain that the main idea is one big idea that the author wants you to understand. Details are small pieces of information that help support the main idea.

Point out that the words *there are many things to do* are a clue to the main idea of "Firefighters." The main idea is that firefighters have many things to do at work.

Differentiating Instruction

Intervention Tip

MAIN IDEA AND DETAILS To further help students identify the main idea, say, "Pretend you are the writer of this selection. Tell the class the big idea you would like the readers to learn."

Apply Intervention Tips given throughout each lesson in order to differentiate instruction.

Unit 4 Lesson 6 **T129**

Language Arts

Students make connections using an integrated Language Arts approach.

Part 3 of every lesson contains:

- Spelling
- Vocabulary
- Writing process strategies
- Writer's craft
- Grammar, usage, and mechanics
- Listening, speaking, and viewing
- Penmanship
- TechKnowledge

Present many opportunities to differentiate instruction in every part of the lesson.

Develop word-processing skills while working on the writing lesson.

Connect current research to instruction using Research in Action.

3 Language Arts — Firefighters

Objectives

Word Analysis Vocabulary
- **Compound Words.** Using words from "Firefighters," develop the understanding that compound words derive their meaning from the meanings of two words that are joined together to make one new word.

Writing Process Strategies
- **Personal Writing: Thank-you note.** Building on the theme "Our Neighborhood at Work," learn the form and purpose of a thank-you note as an expression of gratitude.

English Language Conventions
- **End Punctuation.** Understand correct use of end punctuation for declarative, interrogative, and exclamatory sentences.

Materials
- Language Arts Big Book, pp. 43, 150
- Comprehension and Language Arts Skills, pp. 52–53

Differentiating Instruction

Reteach, Challenge, and ***Intervention*** lessons are available to support the language arts instruction in this lesson.

Research in Action
Spelling

Treat spelling as a complex process. Remember that part of the problem with the teaching and learning of spelling has been that we have treated it too simplistically: as a memorization task, as a list to be assigned, as learning that occurs incidentally, or as not important at all. Learning to spell is an important aspect of language and learning to spell is complex. (*J. Richard Gentry and Jean Wallace Gillet*, Teaching Kids to Spell)

OVERVIEW

Language Arts Overview

Word Analysis

Vocabulary The Vocabulary activity focuses on vocabulary from "Firefighters" to discover that compound words are words that combine the meanings of two words that can stand alone, forming a new word. This activity also introduces the use of a dictionary to determine whether student-generated words are compound words or separate words.

Vocabulary Skill Words

firefighters* **fireman** **fireplace** **fireworks** **firefly**
everywhere **everyone** **everything** **everybody**

**Also Selection Vocabulary*

Additional Materials

classroom dictionaries

Writing Process Strategies

The Writing Process Strategies lesson introduces the purpose of a thank-you note, a form of personal writing. A thank-you note is a form of writing that is used to express gratitude for something such as gift, a special time, special help given, or a kind deed.

To develop computer skills for writing, help students start writing a thank-you note by opening a blank word processing document and keying in text. Show students how to create new lines using the **Return** or **Enter** key. ***TechKnowledge*** Level 1 Lessons 20–21 teach these word processing skills.

Professional Development

Teacher Resource Library CD-ROMs or ***Online Professional Development*** provides courses that help you better understand the Writing instruction in ***Open Court Reading.*** For more information about this program, visit SRAonline.com.

English Language Conventions

Grammar, Usage, and Mechanics **End Punctuation.** This lesson develops the understanding of proper use of periods, question marks, and exclamation points.

T136 Unit 4 Lesson 6

Theme: **Our Neighborhood at Work**

Word Analysis

Vocabulary

Compound Words

Teach

- Explain that some words are two words joined together to form a new word. For example, in today's reading selection, the word *firefighters* is a compound word formed by two separate words, *fire* and *fighters*. This new compound word takes its meaning from the words *fire* and *fighters: Firefighters are people who fight fires.*
- Write the word *fire* on the board, and ask students to suggest new compound words by joining *fire* to other words *(fireman, fireplace, fireworks, fireproof, firefly, firearm).*
- Explain that some words, such as *fire truck* and *fire station*, are not compound words, and that you will teach them later on how to use a dictionary to determine whether a word is a compound word or two separate words.

Guided Practice

- Explain that the word *everywhere* is also a compound word as you write it on the board. Ask students to suggest separate meanings of the words *every (all, each)*, and *where (location, place).*
- Explain that they can discover the meaning of *everywhere* in a dictionary.
- **Teacher Model:** Model using a dictionary for them by looking up the meaning of everywhere. *(in all places)*
- Encourage students to create new compound words beginning with *every (everyone, everybody, everything)* as you write their answers under the heading.
- Conclude by discussing the meanings of their new compound words.

Writing Process Strategies

Getting Ideas

Thank-You Note

Teach

Introduce Writing Form

Read ***Language Arts Big Book*** page 43 to introduce the thank-you note writing form. Discuss the page. Point out the parts of a thank-you note, including the commas.

Inspiration

Teacher Model: Model ideas for a thank-you note related to the unit investigation and "Our Neighborhood at Work." *I want to thank someone whose job helps the community. I could thank someone who works in the school, someone who does something for all of us, or a firefighter.*

Brainstorming

- Using how people's jobs help others as a basis for ideas, encourage students to suggest ideas for thank-you notes they could write (thanking the school employee who came to speak to the class or a person in the community who does something for everybody (police officer, trash collector, and so on).
- Discuss ways that firefighters help the community. Have students start thinking about writing a thank-you note to a firefighter. See Inquiry, page T172.

Guided Practice

Have students write their ideas in their Writer's Notebook. Then have each student choose an idea to develop. Make sure the ideas are practical and sincere.

Thank-You Notes

A **thank-you note** is a short letter. It thanks someone for a gift, a nice time, or something special he or she did for you.

Take a Look

Lila wrote this thank-you note to Gracie.

Greeting — Dear Gracie,
Message — Thank you for the puzzle. It looks like fun. I can't wait to put it together.
Closing — Your friend,
Your Name — Lila

Try It! Why did Lila write the note to Gracie?

Reading Your Writing

A thank-you note must tell why you are thanking a person.

Language Arts Big Book p. 43

English Language Conventions

Grammar, Usage, and Mechanics

End Punctuation

Teach

- Explain that there are three kinds of sentences.
  Some sentences tell information.
  Some sentences ask a question.
  Some sentences show strong feelings.
- Each kind of sentence has an end mark.
  A telling sentence ends with a period **(.)**.
  An asking sentence ends with a question mark **(?)**.
  A strong feeling sentence ends with an exclamation point **(!)**.
- Use ***Language Arts Big Book*** page 150 for examples of sentences with proper end marks.

Independent Practice

Use ***Comprehension and Language Arts Skills*** pages 52 and 53 to practice using proper end punctuation.

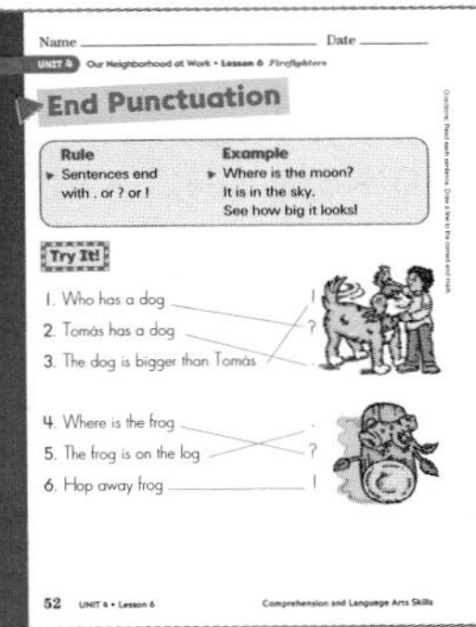

End Punctuation

Rule	Example
Sentences end with . or ? or !	Where is the moon? It is in the sky. See how big it looks!

Try It!

1. Who has a dog
2. Tomás has a dog
3. The dog is bigger than Tomás
4. Where is the frog
5. The frog is on the log
6. Hop away frog

Comprehension and Language Arts Skills p. 52

Offer daily practice activities for Language Arts.

Explicitly teach lessons using the Teach-and-Practice format.

Support the implementation of the writing process using Guided Practice activities.

Professional Development

Partner with SRA/McGraw-Hill to meet reading challenges with confidence.

At SRA/McGraw-Hill, we recognize that high-quality, long-term professional development, combined with an understanding of your needs, is critical to the successful implementation of ***Open Court Reading.*** Our commitment to systematic and sustained staff development has led to unparalleled communication between administrators, teachers, students, and SRA consultants. Our continued commitment to quality, both in product and professional development, is the hallmark of SRA, and we are fully dedicated to working with you to support your needs in the classroom.

SRA's staff development helps you teach all students to read by providing options including

- hands-on, interactive staff development.
- individual classroom demonstration and coaching by classroom-experienced consultants.
- customized workshops to meet district and staff needs.
- staff development for administrators and support staff.
- online staff development to accommodate teachers' needs and schedules.
- summer workshops and institutes.
- CD-ROMs with classroom demonstrations of best practices.

"I love ***Open Court Reading!*** It is so easy to teach (and allows me to incorporate so many creative touches), and my students just soak up the lessons."

— **Laura Ivory,** Grade K Teacher
St. James Catholic School,
Perris, CA

Professional Development Resources

Professional Development Guides

- Explain the research behind ***Open Court Reading's*** Comprehension, Phonics, Writing, Assessment, and Inquiry

Online Professional Development

- Videos showing best-practice instruction at all grade levels
- Practical advice from program consultants helps support teachers and principals

Teacher's Resource Library

- CD-ROMs showing video footage of best-practice instruction

Lesson Model Videos

- Videos showing ***Open Court*** teachers in classroom situations

Meet the *Open Court Reading* Authors

Marilyn Jager Adams, Ph.D.
Cited in the *2000 Politics of Education Yearbook* as one of the most influential people in the national reading policy arena, Dr. Adams has worked closely with a number of agencies to develop reading standards, policies, and staff development strategies.

Carl Bereiter, Ph.D.
An accomplished author, researcher, and professor, Dr. Bereiter has published extensively on teaching and learning. A member of the National Academy of Education, Dr. Bereiter also invented CSILE (Computer Supported Intentional Learning Environments), the first networked collaborative learning environment in schools, with Dr. Marlene Scardamalia; the current version, *Knowledge Forum®*, is in use in twelve countries.

Joe Campione, Ph.D.
A leading researcher on cognitive development, individual differences, assessment, and the design of innovative learning environments, Dr. Campione is currently a Professor in the School of Education at University of California, Berkeley.

Iva Carruthers, Ph.D.
Equipped with both hands-on and academic experience, Dr. Carruthers serves as a consultant and lecturer in both educational technology and matters of multicultural inclusion.

Jan Hirshberg, Ed.D.
Focusing on how children learn to read and write and the logistics of teaching reading and writing in the early grades, Dr. Hirshberg currently works as a language arts resource teacher and consultant in Alexandria, Virginia.

Anne McKeough, Ph.D.
A Professor in the Division of Applied Psychology and Chair of the Human Learning and Development program at the University of Calgary, Dr. McKeough has received a number of research awards and grants.

Michael Pressley, Ph.D.
Most recently honored by the National Reading Conference as the 2000 recipient of the Oscar Causey Award for career contributions to reading research, Dr. Pressley is Professor of Educational Psychology and Teacher Education at Michigan State University. He has authored numerous books and articles about reading instruction and comprehension.

Marsha Roit, Ed.D.
The Director of Professional Development for SRA/McGraw-Hill, Dr. Roit spends considerable time in classrooms developing reading curricula and working with teachers and administrators in effective instructional practices. Dr. Roit has also published in a variety of professional journals, including *Exceptional Children*, *Journal of Learning Disabilities*, and *The Elementary School Journal*.

Marlene Scardamalia, Ph.D.
A Professor at the Centre for Applied Cognitive Science and Department of Curriculum Teaching and Learning, Ontario Institute for Studies in Education, Dr. Scardamalia has conducted research and been published in the areas of cognitive development, psychology of writing, intentional learning, the nature of expertise, and educational uses of computers. She is also a member of the U.S. National Academy of Education.

Marcy Stein, Ph.D.
An Associate Professor and founding faculty member of the education program at the University of Washington, Dr. Stein currently coordinates At-Risk and Special Education graduate programs and teaches in the teacher certification program. She has served as consultant to departments of education on the translation of reading research to instructional practice.

Gerald H. Treadway, Jr., Ph.D.
Professor at San Diego State University, Dr. Treadway teaches classes on reading methods, balanced reading programs, bilingual methods, and reading comprehension. He is the Director of Research and Development for the California Reading & Literature Project.

UNIT 5 Table of Contents
Going West

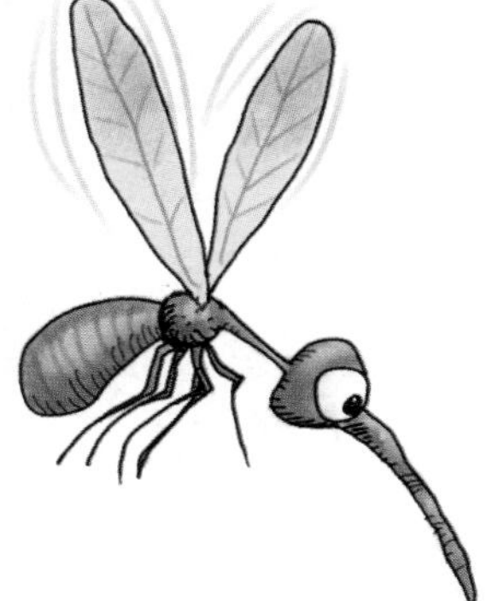

National Advisory Board

Sheree Bryant
Curriculum Director
Covington, GA

Karen Hansill
Teacher
Savannah, GA

Georgana Johnston
Consultant
Hatteras, NC

Mary McAdoo
Consultant
Fenwick Island, DE

Karen McKenna
Reading Coordinator
Cloquet, MN

Joyce Pulley
Principal
Jackson, MS

Jill Strange
Teacher
Lawrenceville, GA

Tricia Trucker
Teacher
Monmouth Beach, NJ

Sharon Van Vleck
Principal
Sacramento, CA

Contributing Author

Michael Milone
Assessment Specialist
Placitas, NM

Literature Consultants

Dr. Sylvia Hutchinson
Professor, University of Georgia
Athens, GA

Dr. Helen Foster James
Lecturer, San Diego State University
San Diego, CA

Program Reviewers

Ann Adams
Chair, Teacher Education
Mobile, AL

Judy Alexander
Teacher
Grand Ridge, FL

Arlene Amodei
Curriculum Coordinator
Sierraville, CA

Pam Barret
Teacher
Murrieta, CA

Charlotte Bennett
Reading Coordinator K-5
Sweeny, TX

Mita Bhattacharya
Teacher
Inglewood, CA

Charlene Bigelow
Teacher
West Valley City, UT

Carol Bishop
Principal
Tallahassee, FL

Virginia Blount
Principal
Sneads, FL

Mary Brandenburg
Teacher
Gainesville, FL

Jennifer Bray
Teacher
Jefferson, GA

Frances Brown
Teacher
Shalimar, FL

Shayla Brown
Teacher
Long Beach, CA

Angela Burkard
Teacher
Dallas, TX

Carolyn Cappleman
Headmaster
Windermere, FL

Linda Carle
Teacher
Roanoke, VA

Jennifer Charles
Teacher
Irvine, CA

Kris Charlton
Head of School
Coral Gables, FL

Beverly Chernoff
Reading Coordinator
Fremont, CA

Susan Clarabut
Principal
Grass Valley, CA

Karen Cooksey
Director of Curriculum
Santa Barbara, CA

Kathy Degi
Reading Specialist
Denver, CO

Suzanne Delaware
Assistant Superintendent
Atwater, CA

Court DeSpain
Principal
Salt Lake City, UT

Kerri Doyle
Teacher
Charlotte, NC

Joan Draper
Teacher
Ogden, UT

Susan Drew
Teacher
Lemoore, CA

Dr. Mary Fritz
Principal
Westbury, NY

Diane Garland
Teacher
Cartersville, GA

Stuart Greenberg
Director, Broward County Schools
Ft. Lauderdale, FL

Nancy Hanssen
Reading Specialist
San Diego, CA

Ann Harvey
Reading Specialist
San Diego, CA

Victoria Holland
Teacher
Santa Ana, CA

Michelle Holman
Teacher
Sonora, CA

Judy Hughes
Teacher
Media, PA

Barbara Johnson
Curriculum Coordinator
Salinas, CA

Barbara Jones
Teacher
Baltimore, MD

Linda Kehe
Teacher
Tualatin, OR

Ray King
Principal
Tallahassee, FL

Lucy Kozak
Teacher
Bradenton, FL

Linda Kramer
Teacher
Grass Valley, CA

Sandy Loose
Consultant
Media, PA

Mickey Manning
Reading Coordinator
Santa Barbara, CA

David Maresh
Teacher
Yucca Valley, CA

Sharon Massingill
Teacher
Lemoore, CA

Anne McKee
Teacher
Tualatin, OR

Ann McMillen
Teacher
Ringgold, GA

Barbara Miles
Teacher
North Tonawanda, NY

Nancy Mitchell
Consultant
Grass Valley, CA

Jennifer O'Donnell
Teacher
San Diego, CA

Jeff Ohmer
Teacher
Baltimore, MD

Bethany Payne
Consultant
Ft. Lauderdale, FL

Becky Player
Teacher
Grand Ridge, FL

Sharon Preston
Teacher
Hortonville, WI

Billie Reeves
Principal
Perris, CA

Dolores M. Roberts
Teacher
Monterey, CA

Gretchen Rogers
Teacher
Lakeland, FL

Kathryn Scozzari
Teacher
Union Springs, NY

Aundrea Sellars
Teacher
Marianna, FL

Suzanne Slaughter
Teacher
Ocala, FL

Cherry Mae Smith
Teacher
Rupert, ID

Heather Stephens
Teacher
Marianna, FL

Vicki Thomas
Teacher
Los Angeles, CA

Margaret Tomko
Teacher
Johnstown, NY

Dr. Sandy Trinca
Director of Professional Development
Ft. Lauderdale, FL

Maria Wentworth
Educational Consultant
Union, NH

Elaine Wiener
Teacher
Villa Park, CA

Brenda Williams
Teacher
Ft. Lauderdale, FL

Lois Zercher
Assistant Superintendent/Curriculum
Lemoore, CA

Robin A. Zimmerman
Teacher
Grass Valley, CA

Level 5 • Unit 5

Going West

Exploring the Theme

Introduction

For centuries, the American West inspired curiosity and excitement among early explorers and settlers. Various cultural groups, such as Native Americans, peoples of Spanish ancestry, and settlers from the eastern United States struggled to claim the land as their own. Many Native American groups tried to establish lines of communication and trade with explorers and settlers in an effort to preserve their homelands. Eventually, though, settlers made their way into the West, often forcing Native Americans off their traditional lands. Unfamiliar with the climate and terrain of this new land, settlers faced adversity and danger as they tried to find a better life in the new territories.

This unit offers students the opportunity to learn more about the American West and to further investigate the aspects of that time and place that interest them most. Investigation activities might lead students along the routes of early explorers, into the camps and villages of Native American groups, onto the homesteads of early settlers, and into the rings of Western rodeos with the early cowboys.

Teacher's Edition page numbers correspond to page numbers in the *Student Anthology.*

Investigation and Inquiry Goals

The conceptual goals of investigation for this unit are

- to understand the motivation of the various cultural groups who struggled to claim the land of the American West.
- to extend knowledge of the cultures and ways of life of the settlers of the American West.
- to get a sense of the impact settlers had on the land and animals in the American West.
- to realize that the beautiful, sweeping plains and mountain ranges of the American West presented unfamiliar and dangerous challenges to early explorers and settlers of the region.
- to understand that Native Americans struggled to retain their traditional lands as they were forced westward by European settlers of North America.

Learning Goals

Within each of the general investigation goals, a number of more specific learning goals are pursued. Students will

- **form and revise questions for investigations** of the American West.
- **use text organizers to locate and organize information** about the American West.
- **interpret and use graphic sources of information** to address research questions about the American West.
- **use a variety of reference materials** to locate information relevant to research questions about the American West.
- **summarize and organize information from multiple sources** by outlining ideas and making charts.
- **take notes** about the American West from relevant and authoritative sources.
- **organize prior knowledge** about the American West.
- **evaluate their research** and **raise new questions** for further investigation of the American West.
- **use technology** to create visual aids for presentations.

Teacher Tip Study of the American West raises a broad range of questions. In order to prepare students for this unit, you might model asking yourself questions such as the following.

- ✔ To whom does the land in the West "really" belong?
- ✔ Would Native Americans and Spanish Americans be better or worse off today if the settlers from the rest of the United States had remained east of the Mississippi?
- ✔ What difference did railroads make to the history of the American West?

Exploring the Theme

Supporting Student Investigations

Students are encouraged throughout ***Open Court Reading*** to deepen their knowledge of each of the themes presented. In learning more about the American West, students will need to talk to people about the American West as well as read selections and articles that revolve around the theme of Going West.

Encourage students to use their prior knowledge and experiences to interpret the literature they read on the topic of the American West. Because it is also important for students to extend their thinking and for their views to be challenged and developed, encourage them to use this literature to reinterpret their prior knowledge and experiences.

Explain to students that they will gain a better understanding of the American West. Remind them of the investigations they have conducted for each of the previous units. For this unit, students may choose from these project options:

- A retelling of a Native American legend.
- An illustrated time line of events in western expansion from the early to late 1800s.
- An original monologue from the perspective of a frontier person that tells about a day in his or her life.
- An Internet search for information about the Hispanic influence on the culture of the American West.
- An original tall tale based on research of the American West.
- A photo essay about immigrants from different cultures who went to the American West to make their fortunes.
- A library search for books about early Native American communities of the Northwest, Southwest, and Plains regions.

Unit Investigations

Unit activities are student-driven and should emerge from students' interests, encouraged or ignited by reading and class discussions. Unit activities should involve reading beyond program material and address the conceptual aims of the unit.

Suggested Activities

The suggested activities below are intended to support the unit investigation. Students may want to research the life of one of the mountain men or create a model of a Native American community. Activities that may help provide input for this project include

- discussions of the American West.
- library searches of print sources and other media about the American West.
- discussions and map study of the Lewis and Clark expedition.
- conjecture sessions and idea exchanges on research problems related to the American West.
- time line of major events in westward expansion.

	OVERVIEW OF SELECTION	LINK TO THE THEME	UNIT ACTIVITIES	SUPPORTING STUDENT INVESTIGATIONS
Lesson 1 ***Sacagawea's Journey***	■ This biography traces the journey of a young Shoshone guide who saved Lewis and Clark's expedition from disaster.	■ Early explorers like Lewis and Clark faced many perils on their journeys through the unknown territory of the West. ■ Many Native Americans cooperated with newcomers to their lands.	■ Generate ideas to investigate	■ Investigation Activities ■ Using maps
Lesson 2 ***Buffalo Hunt***	■ This nonfiction piece illustrates how the Plains Indians' way of life changed forever with the depletion of the buffalo population, from which they obtained food, clothing, and shelter.	■ When pioneers began settling the West, the Plains Indians' lives were greatly affected. ■ Native Americans and eastern settlers valued the buffalo for different reasons.	■ Formulate questions and conjectures	■ Investigation Activities ■ Listening and taking notes
Lesson 3 ***The Journal of Wong Ming-Chung***	■ This historical fiction piece traces the trials and tribulations of two early Chinese settlers in their quest for finding gold in the American West.	■ The Western gold rush was a competitive and often dangerous undertaking for early settlers. ■ People from all over the world were drawn to the American West as the word of endless opportunities there spread.	■ Make conjectures	■ Investigation Activities ■ Conducting a library search
Lesson 4 ***The Coming of the Long Knives***	■ This historical fiction piece depicts the trials of a Navaho village when white soldiers, the Long Knives, command that they leave their home in the Canyon de Chelly.	■ As the land in the American West became more valuable to the U.S. government, soldiers were sent to remove Native Americans from strategic locations. ■ The lives of these Native American groups were forever changed as they were forced from their traditional lands.	■ Establish investigation needs	■ Investigation Activities ■ Verifying facts
Lesson 5 ***Old Yeller and the Bear***	■ This piece of historical fiction illustrates the lives of early cattle ranch families who were left to fend for themselves for months while men drove cattle to "cow towns."	■ In the early days of the American West, wives and children of cattle ranchers had to learn to survive the harsh new conditions of the West while the men were away. ■ These people battled challenges presented by climate, terrain, and wild animals.	■ Establish investigation plans	■ Investigation Activities ■ Time lines
Lesson 6 ***Bill Pickett: Rodeo-Ridin' Cowboy***	■ This biographical selection tells the life story of the first African American inducted into the National Cowboy Hall of Fame.	■ Freed from slavery as a result of the Civil War, many African Americans partook in the settling of the West. ■ Rodeos offered cowboys a chance to show off their skills.	■ Continue investigation and get feedback	■ Investigation Activities ■ Technology in Presentations
Lesson 7 ***McBroom the Rainmaker***	■ This tall tale illustrates the hardships of pioneer families living in a rugged, unpredictable land.	■ Pioneers struggled with severe weather conditions and harsh terrain in the American West. ■ Tall tales include specific elements that identify them as part of a genre. Many tall tales, such "McBroom the Rainmaker" and "Pecos Bill" were inspired by life in the American West.	■ Present investigation findings	■ Investigation Activities ■ Reading and using graphic sources of information

Student Materials

Student Anthology
Pages 388–507

Inquiry Journal
Pages 112–140

Writer's Workbook
Pages 78–105

Comprehension and Language Arts Skills
Pages 142–175

Spelling and Vocabulary Skills
Pages 106–133

Language Arts Handbook

Additional Materials

- Listening Library Audiocassettes/CDs
- Unit 5 Assessment
- Program Assessment
- Writing Folder
- Research Assistant CD-ROM
- Science/Social Studies Connection Center
- Ultimate Writing and Creativity Center CD-ROM
- OCR Spelling CD-ROM

Differentiating Instruction

- English Learner Support Activities
- Intervention Workbook
- Reteach
- Challenge
- Leveled Classroom Library

Teacher Materials

Teacher's Edition
Pages 388–507P

Home Connection
Pages 61–76

Read Aloud “Connecting the Country”
Pages 389L–389N

Comprehension and Language Arts Skills Teacher's Edition
Pages 142–175

Spelling and Vocabulary Skills Teacher's Edition
Pages 106–133

Writer's Workbook Teacher's Edition
Pages 78–105

Additional Materials

- Overhead Transparencies
- Teacher's Professional Guides
- Teacher Read Aloud Anthology
- Online Professional Development
- Teacher Resource Library
- Online Assessment

Differentiating Instruction

- English Learner Support Guide
- Intervention Guide
- Intervention Annotated Bibliography
- Reteach Teacher's Edition
- Challenge Teacher's Edition
- Differentiating Instruction Support Activities

Leveled Classroom Library*

Easy

Average

Advanced

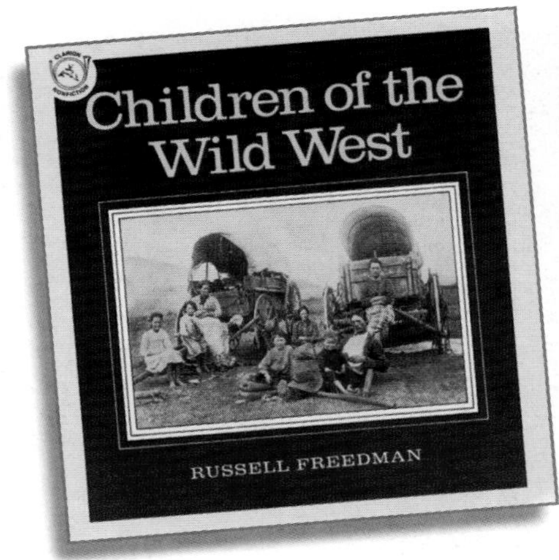

Bibliography**

The True Adventures of Grizzly Adams **by Robert McClung**

Dear Levi: Letters from the Overland Trail **by Elvira Woodruff**

Black Cowboy Wild Horses **by Julius Lester and Jerry Pinkney**

Call Me Francis Tucket **by Gary Paulsen**

Note: Teachers should preview any trade books and videos for appropriateness in their classrooms before recommending them to students.

* These books, which all support the unit theme Going West, are part of a 36-book ***Leveled Classroom Library*** available for purchase from SRA/McGraw-Hill.

** Check libraries or bookstores for availability.

TECHNOLOGY

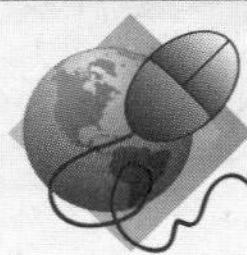

Web Connections

Going West Web site

Information about Going West and links to sites concerning Going West can be found at www.sra4kids.com.

Online Assessment offers automated delivery and scoring of End of Unit and Program Assessments. Data is analyzed and compiled into reports that help teachers make classroom instructional decisions and guide individualized instruction. Available at www.SRAonline.com.

Online Professional Development

Online Professional Development delivers twenty courses with full-motion video teaching examples for Grades K–6. In addition, teachers can participate in Learning Communities and Discussion Boards available exclusively through the site. Available at www.SRAonline.com.

CD-ROMs

U.S. Geography Series: The West

CLEARVIEW/EAV

Explore the land, people, and industry on this multimedia tour of the west.

* Research Assistant

SRA/McGRAW-HILL, 2002

As students continue their investigation, encourage them to use the ***Research Assistant*** CD-ROM program to help them organize and share their findings.

* Ultimate Writing and Creativity Center

THE LEARNING COMPANY

Students can use this word processing software to get ideas, research, draft, revise, edit, and publish their Writing Process Strategies activities in this unit.

*OCR Spelling

SRA/McGRAW-HILL, 2002

Use this software for extra Spelling review in this unit.

* Teacher Resource Library

SRA/McGRAW-HILL, 2004

Teacher Resource Library covers subjects such as classroom management, English Learners, assessment, and more. Included are videos of real teachers and students in their classrooms and a wealth of text-based resources for teachers of Grades K–6.

Audiocassettes/CDs

*Listening Library: Going West

SRA/McGRAW-HILL, 2002

Students will enjoy listening to the selections they have read. Encourage them to listen during Workshop.

Computer Skills

*TechKnowledge

The word processing unit of the ***TechKnowledge*** program can be used to help students develop computer skills within the context of the unit theme.

Videocassettes

Native Americans: People of the Plains

RAINBOW EDUCATIONAL MEDIA

Learn about the daily life of Native American groups who made the plains of the American West their home. 24 min.

The Oregon Trail

100% EDUCATIONAL VIDEOS

Find out about the pioneers who left the east in wagon trains to create a new life on the western frontier. 16 min.

Titles preceded by an asterisk (*) are available through SRA/McGraw-Hill. Other titles can be obtained by contacting the publisher listed with the title.

UNIT 5 OVERVIEW

UNIT SKILLS OVERVIEW

Lesson	Word Knowledge	Comprehension	Literary Elements
Lesson 1 *Sacagawea's Journey* **Genre: Biography**	■ Derivatives of *explore* ■ /k/ sound spelled *c* ■ Closed compound words ■ Homophones	**Strategies** ■ Summarizing ■ Asking Questions ■ Visualizing **Skill** ■ Drawing Conclusions	■ Author's Perspective
Lesson 2 *Buffalo Hunt* **Genre: Expository Text**	■ Homophones ■ Irregular plural nouns ■ /ch/ sound spelled *tch* ■ Words with *mis-* or *dis-*	**Strategies** ■ Summarizing ■ Asking Questions ■ Monitoring and Clarifying ■ Monitoring and Adjusting Reading Speed **Skill** ■ Main Idea and Details	■ Expository Text
Lesson 3 *The Journal of Wong Ming-Chung* **Genre: Historical Fiction**	■ Words ending in *-ing* ■ Contractions ■ Long e spelled *ee* ■ Words with *-ent* or *-ant*	**Strategies** ■ Making Connections ■ Predicting ■ Monitoring and Clarifying **Skill** ■ Sequence	■ Character Analysis
Lesson 4 *The Coming of the Long Knives* **Genre: Historical Fiction**	■ Antonyms ■ Levels of Specificity ■ Plural forms of words ending in *f* or *fe* ■ Words with *-tion*, *-sion*, or *-sure*	**Strategies** ■ Predicting ■ Summarizing ■ Asking Questions **Skills** ■ Compare and Contrast ■ Drawing Conclusions	■ Genre: Historical Fiction
Lesson 5 *Old Yeller and the Bear* **Genre: Historical Fiction**	■ Synonyms ■ /j/ sound spelled *dge* or *g* ■ /er/ sound spelled *er*, *ir*, and *ur* ■ Words with *-ed* and *-ing*	**Strategies** ■ Predicting ■ Summarizing ■ Monitoring and Clarifying **Skills** ■ Making Inferences ■ Author's Point of View	■ Plot
Lesson 6 *Bill Pickett: Rodeo-Ridin' Cowboy* **Genre: Biography**	■ Hyphenated compound words ■ Long a spelled *ai* ■ Inflectional ending *-ed* ■ Words with *-er* and *-est*	**Strategies** ■ Predicting ■ Summarizing ■ Visualizing **Skill** ■ Fact and Opinion	■ Genre: Biography
Lesson 7 *McBroom the Rainmaker* **Genre: Tall Tale**	■ Short u sound ■ /z/ sound spelled *s* or *z* ■ /k/ sound spelled *k*, *c*, or *ck* ■ Words with *-tion*, *-ed*, *-ing*, and *-est*	**Strategies** ■ Making Connections ■ Summarizing ■ Visualizing ■ Monitoring and Adjusting Reading Speed **Skill** ■ Cause and Effect	■ Genre: Tall Tale

INQUIRY	WORD ANALYSIS	WRITING PROCESS STRATEGIES	ENGLISH LANGUAGE CONVENTIONS
■ Using Maps	**Spelling** ■ Homophones **Vocabulary** ■ Concept Words	**Personal Writing** ■ Journal Entry ■ Learning Log ■ Literature Response	**Grammar and Usage** ■ Sentence Fragments **Listening, Speaking, Viewing** ■ Listening: Drawing Conclusions and Making Inferences **Penmanship** ■ Joining with *A* and *d*
■ Listening and Taking Notes	**Spelling** ■ Words with *dis-* or *mis-* **Vocabulary** ■ Synonyms	**Personal Writing** ■ Invitation ■ Thank-You Note ■ E-Mail Message/Literature Response	**Mechanics** ■ Commas **Listening, Speaking, Viewing** ■ Speaking: Proper Grammar **Penmanship** ■ Joining with *E* and *f*
■ Conducting a Library Search	**Spelling** ■ Words with *-ent* or *-ant* **Vocabulary** ■ Words with Multiple Meanings	**Personal Writing** ■ Friendly Letter **Writer's Craft** ■ Structure of a Personal Letter	**Mechanics** ■ Punctuation and Capitalization **Listening, Speaking, Viewing** ■ Language: Literary Devices **Penmanship** ■ Joining with *U* and *q*
■ Verifying Facts	**Spelling** ■ Words with *-tion*, *-sion*, or *-sure* **Vocabulary** ■ Foreign Words	**Personal Writing** ■ Letter of Concern **Writer's Craft** ■ Structure of a Business Letter	**Mechanics** ■ Punctuation and Capitalization **Listening, Speaking, Viewing** ■ Viewing: Exaggeration **Penmanship** ■ Joining with *Z* and *o*
■ Time Lines	**Spelling** ■ Words with *-ed* or *-ing* **Vocabulary** ■ Simile	**Personal Writing** ■ Friendly Letter **Writer's Craft** ■ Tone of a Personal Letter	**Mechanics** ■ Commas **Listening, Speaking, Viewing** ■ Interacting: Group Discussions **Penmanship** ■ Joining with *Y* and *w*
■ Technology in Presentations	**Spelling** ■ Words with *-er* and *-est* **Vocabulary** ■ Compound Words	**Personal Writing** ■ Letter of Request	**Mechanics** ■ Commas and Quotations **Listening, Speaking, Viewing** ■ Interacting: Group Presentations **Penmanship** ■ Joining with *N* and *t*
■ Reading and Using Graphic Sources of Information	**Spelling** ■ Review **Vocabulary** ■ Review	**Personal Writing** ■ Memo **Writer's Craft** ■ Structure of a Memo	**Grammar, Usage, and Mechanics** ■ Review **Listening, Speaking, Viewing** ■ Presenting: Oral Presentations **Penmanship** ■ Joining with *R* and *s*

DIFFERENTIATING INSTRUCTION

DIFFERENTIATING INSTRUCTION

	Reteach	English Learner	Challenge	Intervention
Lesson 1 *Sacagawea's Journey*	**Reading and Responding** ■ **Comprehension:** Drawing Conclusions **Language Arts** ■ **Spelling:** Homophones ■ **Vocabulary:** Concept Words ■ **Grammar and Usage:** Sentence Fragments	**Reading and Responding** ■ Vocabulary ■ Reading the Selection ■ Word Meaning Tip ■ Comprehension: Drawing Conclusions ■ Clarifying Tip	**Reading and Responding** ■ **Comprehension:** Drawing Conclusions **Language Arts** ■ **Spelling:** Homophones ■ **Vocabulary:** Concept Words ■ **Grammar and Usage:** Sentence Fragments	**Preparing to Read** ■ Word Knowledge ■ Fluency **Reading and Responding** ■ Clarifying and Asking Questions ■ Reading the Selection ■ Repeated Readings **Language Arts** ■ Sentence Fragments ■ Writing
Lesson 2 *Buffalo Hunt*	**Reading and Responding** ■ **Comprehension:** Main Idea and Details **Language Arts** ■ **Spelling:** Words with *dis-* or *mis-* ■ **Vocabulary:** Synonyms ■ **Mechanics:** Commas	**Reading and Responding** ■ Vocabulary ■ Reading the Selection ■ Comprehension: Main Idea and Details	**Reading and Responding** ■ **Comprehension:** Main Idea and Details **Language Arts** ■ **Spelling:** Words with *dis-* or *mis-* ■ **Vocabulary:** Synonyms ■ **Mechanics:** Commas	**Preparing to Read** ■ Word Knowledge ■ Fluency **Reading and Responding** ■ Clarifying and Summarizing ■ Reading the Selection ■ Repeated Readings **Language Arts** ■ Commas in a Series ■ Writing
Lesson 3 *The Journal of Wong Ming-Chung*	**Reading and Responding** ■ **Comprehension:** Sequence **Language Arts** ■ **Spelling:** Words with *-ent* or *-ant* ■ **Vocabulary:** Words with Multiple Meanings ■ **Mechanics:** Punctuation and Capitalization ■ **Writer's Craft:** Structure of a Personal Letter	**Reading and Responding** ■ Vocabulary ■ Reading the Selection ■ Comprehension: Sequence	**Reading and Responding** ■ **Comprehension:** Sequence **Language Arts** ■ **Spelling:** Words with *-ent* or *-ant* ■ **Vocabulary:** Words with Multiple Meanings ■ **Mechanics:** Punctuation and Capitalization ■ **Writer's Craft:** Structure of a Personal Letter	**Preparing to Read** ■ Word Knowledge Fluency **Reading and Responding** ■ Making Connections and Visualizing ■ Reading the Selection ■ Repeated Readings **Language Arts** ■ Commas ■ Writing
Lesson 4 *The Coming of the Long Knives*	**Language Arts** ■ **Spelling:** Words with *-tion*, *-sion*, or *-sure* ■ **Vocabulary:** Foreign Words ■ **Mechanics:** Punctuation and Capitalization ■ **Writer's Craft:** Structure of a Business Letter	**Reading and Responding** ■ Vocabulary ■ Reading the Selection ■ Comprehension: Drawing Conclusions ■ Understanding Character Tip	**Language Arts** ■ **Spelling:** Words with *-tion*, *-sion*, or *-sure* ■ **Vocabulary:** Foreign Words ■ **Mechanics:** Punctuation and Capitalization ■ **Writer's Craft:** Structure of a Business Letter	**Preparing to Read** ■ Word Knowledge Fluency **Reading and Responding** ■ Summarizing and Asking Questions ■ Reading the Selection ■ Repeated Readings **Language Arts** ■ Capitalization and Punctuation ■ Writing
Lesson 5 *Old Yeller and the Bear*	**Reading and Responding** ■ **Comprehension:** Making Inferences **Language Arts** ■ **Spelling:** Words with *-ed* or *-ing* ■ **Vocabulary:** Simile ■ **Mechanics:** Commas ■ **Writer's Craft:** Tone of a Personal Letter	**Reading and Responding** ■ Vocabulary ■ Reading the Selection ■ Comprehension: Making Inferences ■ Character Study Tip	**Reading and Responding** ■ **Comprehension:** Making Inferences **Language Arts** ■ **Spelling:** Words with *-ed* or *-ing* ■ **Vocabulary:** Simile ■ **Mechanics:** Commas ■ **Writer's Craft:** Tone of a Personal Letter	**Preparing to Read** ■ Word Knowledge ■ Fluency **Reading and Responding** ■ Asking Questions and Clarifying ■ Reading the Selection ■ Repeated Readings **Language Arts** ■ Coordinating Conjunctions ■ Writing
Lesson 6 *Bill Pickett: Rodeo-Ridin' Cowboy*	**Reading and Responding** ■ **Comprehension:** Fact and Opinion **Language Arts** ■ **Spelling:** Words with *-er* and *-est* ■ **Vocabulary:** Compound Words ■ **Mechanics:** Commas and Quotations	**Reading and Responding** ■ Vocabulary ■ Reading the Selection ■ Comprehension: Fact and Opinion ■ Sharing Knowledge Tip	**Reading and Responding** ■ **Comprehension:** Fact and Opinion **Language Arts** ■ **Spelling:** Words with *-er* and *-est* ■ **Vocabulary:** Compound Words ■ **Mechanics:** Commas and Quotations	**Preparing to Read** ■ Word Knowledge Fluency **Reading and Responding** ■ Making Connections and Visualizing ■ Reading the Selection ■ Repeated Readings **Language Arts** ■ Commas with Appositives ■ Writing
Lesson 7 *McBroom the Rainmaker*	**Reading and Responding** ■ **Comprehension:** Cause and Effect **Language Arts** ■ **Spelling:** Review ■ **Vocabulary:** Review ■ **Grammar, Usage, and Mechanics:** Review ■ **Writer's Craft:** Structure of a Memo	**Reading and Responding** ■ Vocabulary ■ Reading the Selection ■ Comprehension: Cause and Effect ■ Reviewing the Plot Tip	**Reading and Responding** ■ **Comprehension:** Cause and Effect **Language Arts** ■ **Spelling:** Review ■ **Vocabulary:** Review ■ **Grammar, Usage, and Mechanics:** Review ■ **Writer's Craft:** Structure of a Memo	**Preparing to Read** ■ Word Knowledge ■ Fluency **Reading and Responding** ■ Summarizing and Visualizing ■ Reading the Selection ■ Repeated Readings **Language Arts** ■ Review ■ Writing

Above are suggestions for adapting instruction to meet the individual needs of students. These are the same skills shown on Unit Skills Overview; however, these pages provide extra practice opportunities or enriching activities to meet the varied needs of students.

ASSESSMENT

Informal Assessment	Progress Assessment	Formal Assessment
*Comprehension Strategies, pp. 390J, 390 *Concept Connections, p. 404 *Grammar and Usage, p. 405H *Listening, Speaking, Viewing, p. 405I *Vocabulary, p. 405J *Penmanship, p. 405J	Comprehension and Language Arts Skills, pp. 142–145 Reteach, pp. 140–144 Challenge, pp. 124–127 Writer's Workbook, pp. 78–81 Spelling and Vocabulary Skills, pp. 106–109 Inquiry Journal, pp. 112–113, 116–121	**Lesson 1** Unit 5 Assessment ■ Lesson Assessment, pp. 2–5 ■ Spelling Pretest, p. 30 ■ Spelling Final Test, p. 31 * Writing Process Strategies Rubrics, p. 405J * Research Rubrics, p. 390J
*Comprehension Strategies, pp. 406J, 406 *Concept Connections, p. 426 *Mechanics, p. 427H *Listening, Speaking, Viewing, p. 427I *Vocabulary, p. 427J *Penmanship, p. 427J	Comprehension and Language Arts Skills, pp. 146–149 Reteach, pp. 145–149 Challenge, pp. 128–131 Writer's Workbook, pp. 82–85 Spelling and Vocabulary Skills, pp. 110–113 Inquiry Journal, pp. 113, 122–125	**Lesson 2** Unit 5 Assessment ■ Lesson Assessment, pp. 6–9 ■ Spelling Pretest, p. 32 ■ Spelling Final Test, p. 33 * Writing Process Strategies Rubrics, p. 427J * Research Rubrics, p. 406J
*Comprehension Strategies, pp. 430J, 430 *Concept Connections, p. 442 *Mechanics, p. 443H *Listening, Speaking, Viewing, p. 443I *Vocabulary, p. 443J *Penmanship, p. 443J	Comprehension and Language Arts Skills, pp. 150–155 Reteach, pp. 150–155 Challenge, pp. 132–136 Writer's Workbook, pp. 86–89 Spelling and Vocabulary Skills, pp. 114–117 Inquiry Journal, pp. 113, 126	**Lesson 3** Unit 5 Assessment ■ Lesson Assessment, pp. 10–13 ■ Spelling Pretest, p. 34 ■ Spelling Final Test, p. 35 * Writing Process Strategies Rubrics, p. 443J * Research Rubrics, p. 430J
*Comprehension Strategies, pp. 446J, 446 *Concept Connections, p. 460 *Mechanics, p. 461H *Listening, Speaking, Viewing, p. 461I *Vocabulary, p. 461J *Penmanship, p. 461J	Comprehension and Language Arts Skills, pp. 156–159 Reteach, pp. 156–159 Challenge, pp. 137–140 Writer's Workbook, pp. 90–93 Spelling and Vocabulary Skills, pp. 118–121 Inquiry Journal, pp. 114, 127–131	**Lesson 4** Unit 5 Assessment ■ Lesson Assessment, pp. 14–17 ■ Spelling Pretest, p. 36 ■ Spelling Final Test, p. 37 * Writing Process Strategies Rubrics, p. 461J * Research Rubrics, p. 446J
*Comprehension Strategies, pp. 462J, 462 *Concept Connections, p. 472 *Mechanics, p. 473H *Listening, Speaking, Viewing, p. 473I *Vocabulary, p. 473J *Penmanship, p. 473J	Comprehension and Language Arts Skills, pp. 160–165 Reteach, pp. 160–165 Challenge, pp. 141–145 Writer's Workbook, pp. 94–97 Spelling and Vocabulary Skills, pp. 122–125 Inquiry Journal, pp. 114, 132–134	**Lesson 5** Unit 5 Assessment ■ Lesson Assessment, pp. 18–21 ■ Spelling Pretest, p. 38 ■ Spelling Final Test, p. 39 * Writing Process Strategies Rubrics, p. 473J * Research Rubrics, p. 462J
*Comprehension Strategies, pp. 474J, 474 *Concept Connections, p. 494 *Mechanics, p. 495H *Listening, Speaking, Viewing, p. 495I *Vocabulary, p. 495J *Penmanship, p. 495J	Comprehension and Language Arts Skills, pp. 166–169 Reteach, pp. 166–170 Challenge, pp. 146–149 Writer's Workbook, pp. 98–101 Spelling and Vocabulary Skills, pp. 126–129 Inquiry Journal, pp. 115, 135–136	**Lesson 6** Unit 5 Assessment ■ Lesson Assessment, pp. 22–25 ■ Spelling Pretest, p. 40 ■ Spelling Final Test, p. 41 * Writing Process Strategies Rubrics, p. 495J * Research Rubrics, p. 474J
*Comprehension Strategies, pp. 496J, 496 *Concept Connections, p. 506 *Grammar and Usage, p. 507H *Listening, Speaking, Viewing, p. 507I *Vocabulary, p. 507J *Penmanship, p. 507J	Comprehension and Language Arts Skills, pp. 170–175 Reteach, pp. 171–176 Challenge, pp. 150–154 Writer's Workbook, pp. 102–105 Spelling and Vocabulary Skills, pp. 130–133 Inquiry Journal, pp. 115, 137–138	**Lesson 7** Unit 5 Assessment ■ Lesson Assessment, pp. 26–29 ■ Spelling Pretest, p. 42 ■ Spelling Final Test, p. 43 * Writing Process Strategies Rubrics, p. 507J * Research Rubrics, p. 496J End of Unit 5 Assessment, pp. 44–63

*****_Teacher's Edition_ page references

Activating Prior Knowledge

Good readers relate what they know to what they are reading. As you are reading these selections, make certain you relate what you already know about going west to what you are reading.

- What do you know about the American West before we read these pieces?
- Why do people study western expansion in the United States?
- Have you already read books about the American West?

As students read the selections, they will encounter some of these ideas and new ideas as well. When they read something they already know, encourage them to make a note about this information. When they learn something new, have them be sure to notice that too. This will help students learn about going west as they read the selections.

- Have students recall the genres an author could choose from to write about an historical topic such as the American West, including biography and historical fiction. Ask students to tell the features of each genre type.
- Encourage students to share any stories they have read about an American West related topic.
- Students should get into the habit of thinking about an upcoming theme or selection and activating relevant background knowledge.
- For English Learners and others with limited language experiences, exploring the American West on the Internet may be helpful.

Read Aloud

Read aloud to students the selection "Connecting the Country" by Angela M. Herb. Prior to reading, provide students with the following background information.

- Although, in 1800, few Americans had traveled west of the Mississippi, the land was not empty. Many Native American tribes lived there, along with a plentitude of animals and plants.
- England wasn't the only European country to have land holdings in America at the end of the eighteenth century. Holland, France, Spain, and Russia all claimed American territory, and often this land figured in disputes between the European powers.

As students listen to the Read Aloud, have them think about what drew Americans to explore the West.

Ask them to listen for qualities that the westward journey required the explorers to have.

It is important for you as the teacher to let your students know that you use the comprehension strategies being taught in the program when you read. Thus, as you read "Connecting the Country," make some predictions aloud as to what it might be about. As you are reading, let students know what questions are occurring to you, what images pop up in your mind as you are reading, and how points made in the reading relate to ideas you already know.

Toward the end of the reading, sum up for students. If you cannot sum up the selection well, let students see you go back and reread to fill in the gaps in your summary. One of the most powerful ways to get students to use comprehension strategies is for them to see you using them.

About the Author

Angela M. Herb lives in Seattle, Washington. She has written other books about the Civil War and about Alaska. In addition to writing, she works as an editor.

Focus Questions Why was President Jefferson interested in exploring the western territory? Who were the explorers he assigned to this task?

Focus Questions Why was President Jefferson interested in exploring the western territory? Who were the explorers he assigned to this task?

Connecting the Country

from *Beyond the Mississippi: Early Westward Expansion of the United States*
by Angela M. Herb

On August 12, 1805, Meriwether Lewis knelt and took a drink from the icy waters of the Missouri River near its source in the Rocky Mountains. It was the most satisfying drink he had ever taken. In six days, the army captain and Virginia native would be thirty-one years old, and he was in the middle of the most exciting adventure of his life.

With a small troop of soldiers, backwoodsmen, interpreters, and boatmen, Lewis and his trusted friend, William Clark, had traveled overland farther west than any other Americans. The group had instructions from President Thomas Jefferson to find "the most direct and practicable water [route]" across the North American continent to the Pacific Ocean. President Jefferson hoped the route—if it existed—could be used to transport cargo from the East Coast to the West Coast, thus providing access to the sea otter fur trade in the Pacific and the growing trade with China. If Lewis and Clark were successful, the United States would gain power over its rivals—Great Britain, France, Russia, and Spain.

32

Connecting the Country

From *Beyond the Mississippi: Early Westward Expansion of the United States*

by Angela M. Herb

On August 12, 1805, Meriwether Lewis knelt and took a drink from the icy waters of the Missouri River near its source in the Rocky Mountains. It was the most satisfying drink he had ever taken. In six days, the army captain and Virginia native would be thirty-one years old, and he was in the middle of the most exciting adventure of his life.

With a small troop of soldiers, backwoodsmen, interpreters, and boatmen, Lewis and his trusted friend, William Clark, had traveled overland farther west than any other Americans. The group had instructions from the President Thomas Jefferson to find "the most direct and practicable water [route]" across the North American continent to the Pacific Ocean. President Jefferson hoped the route—if it existed—could be used to transport cargo from the East Coast to the West Coast, thus providing access to the sea otter fur trade in the Pacific and the growing trade with China. If Lewis and Clark were successful, the United States would gain power over its rivals—Great Britain, France, Russia, and Spain.

In a way, the journey had begun almost twenty years earlier—as a nagging idea in Jefferson's mind. He was curious about the vast, unknown region that stretched west from the Mississippi River to the Rocky Mountains and on to the Pacific Ocean. What little was known to the outside world about this area had come from such explorers as David Thompson and Alexander Mackenzie, who in the 1790s had ventured westward across upper Canada scouting fur-trading opportunities for their employer, the North West Company of Montreal. Several Spanish exploring parties had attempted to reach the Pacific Ocean from New Orleans; but the most successful traveled only sixteen hundred miles up the Missouri River (halfway across the continent) before turning back. Jefferson dreamed of sending a large U.S. expedition through the heart of the continent to be the first to reach the Pacific. The main obstacle was that Spain claimed Louisiana Territory, the huge wilderness area between the Mississippi River and the Rocky Mountains.

PREVIEWING THE UNIT

READ ALOUD

In October 1800, under pressure from the powerful French leader Napoleon Bonaparte, King Charles IV of Spain ceded the great expanse of land to France, which in turn sold it to the United States in 1803. Jefferson, who had become U.S. president in 1801, saw his opportunity. He had already chosen Meriwether Lewis, a young, trustworthy, and adventurous army captain, to lead the expedition.

Lewis had left active military duty to serve as Jefferson's private secretary in 1801. With the expedition in mind, the president encouraged Lewis to learn about the subjects that would make him a competent explorer: mapmaking, botany, natural history, and anthropology. He also sent Lewis to meet with some of the country's leading scientists. In a letter to Dr. Benjamin Rush, a famous Philadelphia physician, Jefferson asked the doctor to "prepare some notes on such particulars as may occur in [Lewis's] journey & which you think should draw his attention and inquiry." Rush complied and later helped Lewis choose medical supplies to take on the journey.

In June 1803, Lewis wrote to his long-time friend, William Clark, and asked him to help lead the expedition. A red-haired army lieutenant, Clark had once been Lewis's commanding officer. He was an intelligent, even-tempered man, who had wilderness experience from living on the Kentucky frontier and serving in military campaigns against the Ohio Valley Indians.

While Lewis waited for Clark's reply, he spent the summer preparing. He stocked up on food, clothing, and medical supplies; a stash of presents to gain the friendship of the Indian tribes they would meet; guns and ammunition to hunt and protect themselves from wild animals or hostile Indians; and scientific instruments, journals, and logs in which to record details on the geography, climate, plants, and animals. Lewis also recruited men who were strong, disciplined, and able to be away from home for a year or more. He wanted men who would not abandon the expedition, despite the isolation, exhaustion, and dangers they were sure to encounter. For transportation, Lewis chose two pirogues (large, flat-bottomed canoes) and a fifty-five-foot-long keelboat with a canvas sail. And finally he spent twenty dollars on a special companion—a large Newfoundland dog.

In late October, the expedition sailed down the Ohio River to its confluence with the Mississippi. On December 12, they stopped near St. Louis for their first winter away from home. The men constructed four sturdy log cabins directly across from the mouth of the Missouri River and called the site Camp Wood. While they waited five long months for spring to melt the ice on the river, they checked and repacked supplies, began keeping scientific records, talked to fur traders who had traveled part way up the Missouri, and visited with the Sauk and Fox Indians.

Lewis was glad to have Clark share the command. While Lewis coordinated their final preparations, the more outgoing Clark trained the men. After the final recruits had been selected, the Corps of Discovery, as the expedition was formally called, consisted of fourteen enlisted soldiers, nine volunteers from Kentucky, two French rivermen, one interpreter, and Clark's slave, York. An additional nine rivermen and seven soldiers would accompany them until the following autumn and then return to St. Louis.

On May 14 at four o'clock in the afternoon, the forty-three-man expedition departed. Two weeks later, they passed the small village of La Charette, the last white settlement on the Missouri River. They had entered the wilderness.

Discussing the Read Aloud

After finishing the Read Aloud, ask students these questions:

- Why did President Jefferson want to send an expedition to the West? *(Possible answer: Jefferson wanted to study the unexplored area to learn about it, and he wanted to find a water trade route to the Pacific Ocean.)*
- What made Captain Lewis and Captain Clark particularly well suited to lead the Corps of Discovery? *(Possible answer: Captain Lewis was knowledgeable about many things the group might need to know about, like mapmaking and botany, while Captain Clark was a good leader the members of the Corps trusted and felt confident obeying.)*
- Why might the explorers have taken journals and logs with them? *(Possible answer: They wanted to keep a record of all the new things they saw to take back east with them.)*
- Why might Lewis's drink from the Rocky Mountain source of the Missouri be "the most satisfying drink of his life?" *(Possible answer: Lewis had led a team of Americans to accomplish something no other Americans had ever done.)*
- How do you think this read aloud selection connects to the theme Going West? *(Possible answer: Answers will vary. Students might note that Lewis and Clark's expedition paved the way for further exploration of the West by white explorers and settlers.)*

Remind students of what you asked them to think about before you read the story:

- What drew Americans to explore the west?
- What qualities were important for explorers who journeyed west to have?

Also revisit the Focus Questions asked at the beginning of the Read Aloud. Discuss these questions in relation to the story. Have students think about how they might have felt being a member of Lewis and Clark's Corps of Discovery, venturing past the last white settlement into the unknown wilderness. Ask students to share their thoughts with the class.

Concept/Question Board

The Concept/Question Board is a place for students to ask questions and find answers in order to have a better understanding of the unit theme. It is also a place to publish the results of their investigations.

This Board could be a standard bulletin board or a large 3-sided board placed in the front or to the side of the classroom. The Board will be a permanent place for students to ask questions, post articles or objects, add comments, and so on throughout the study of each unit theme. Students should have easy access to the Concept/Question Board, as they will need to be able to attach items to it on their own and also read what is attached.

Have a large supply of self-stick notepads or index cards and thumbtacks available. Paper cut in various shapes that represent each story could be made available for students to use. For example, you could cut brown construction paper in the shape of a buffalo to represent the selection "Buffalo Hunt." Students could write their questions, comments, or theme words on these cutout shapes, which would easily identify the story in the unit.

To begin using your Concept/Question Board, ask the students to formulate statements about what they know about the unit theme or what they believe to be important about the theme after listening to the Read Aloud. Write these statements and attach them to the Concept side of the Board. Then, write any preliminary questions they have about the unit theme and attach those to the Question side of the Board.

As the students progress through the unit, they can refer to the Board to learn which of their classmates have interests similar to their own. This information can be used to form groups to investigate questions and ideas about the unit theme.

Throughout the unit, have the students reread and reflect on the contributions listed on the Concept/Question Board. Have them note, in their ***Writer's Workbooks,*** the contributions that mean the most to them. Suggest that they expand on the original contributions by adding their own thoughts, articles, pictures, and so on. Discuss whether the selection has provided information that might be added or that might revise existing postings.

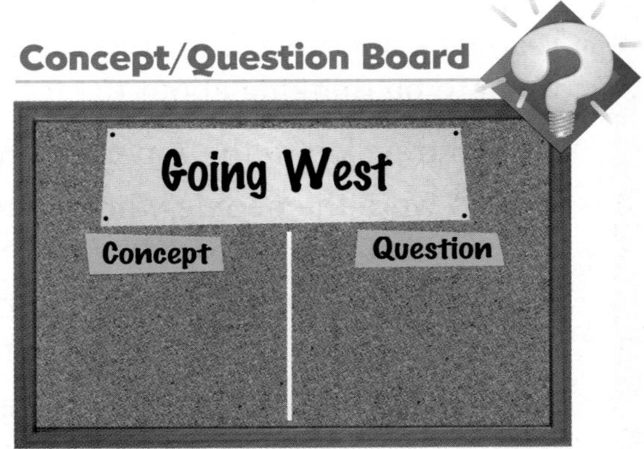

PREVIEWING THE UNIT

Setting Reading Goals

Have students examine and share their thoughts on the unit opener on ***Student Anthology*** pages 388–389. Remind them that good readers are always thinking when they read. Ask students what they were thinking about as they read the unit opener. Remind them that good readers browse what they are going to read before reading. Invite them to browse the selections in the unit at this time.

Tell students that good readers make predictions about what might be in the selections they are about to read. Ask them if they are making predictions about the selections or if they are asking themselves questions about the selections they are about to read. Model asking questions with any that might have occurred to you as you browsed the selections.

Explain that they will be given ample opportunity to think, read, and write about the American West. Remind students that good readers regularly set goals when they are reading. Also, make certain they know that they should get into the habit of setting reading goals for themselves, because they should know why they are reading something. Tell students that you would like them to be thinking about the following questions:

- Who traveled to the American West during the 1800s?
- Who were the people who already lived in the American West before the settlers arrived?
- Do you already know some stories about the American West? What did they teach you?

Model for students some questions that came to you while browsing the unit. Invite students to share some of their questions with you.

Inquiry Journal

- After the students have discussed what they think this unit might be about, have them complete page 112 in their ***Inquiry Journals.***
- Have students share ideas about the American West that they would like to learn more about.

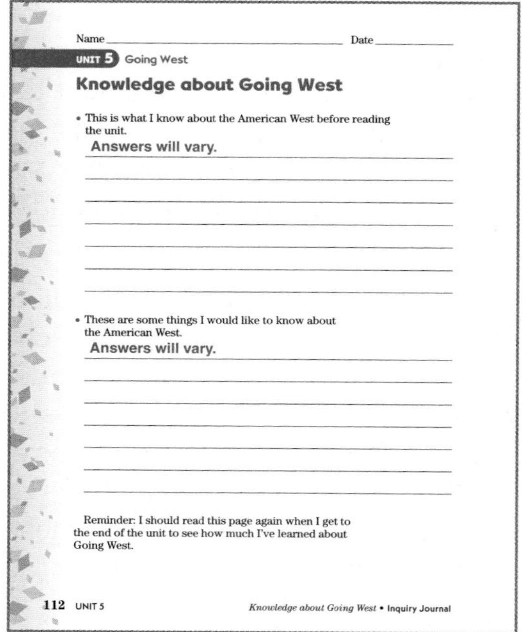

Name ______ Date ______

UNIT 5 Going West

Knowledge about Going West

- This is what I know about the American West before reading the unit.
  Answers will vary.

- These are some things I would like to know about the American West.
  Answers will vary.

Reminder: I should read this page again when I get to the end of the unit to see how much I've learned about Going West.

112 UNIT 5 *Knowledge about Going West* • Inquiry Journal

Inquiry Journal p. 112

Professional Resources

Brown, Dee. *Wondrous Times on the Frontier.* Little Rock: August House Publishers, 1991. Over fifty years of research resulted in this humorous and informative collection of anecdotes about pioneers, western women, cowboys, schoolteachers, Native Americans, and others in the region.

White, Richard. *"It's Your Misfortune and None of My Own": A New History of the American West.* University of Oklahoma Press, 1993. This book examines the new residents of the historical West, their disregard for the existing inhabitants, and the effects their presence has had on the emerging culture of the region.

Schlissel, Lillian; Gibbens, Byrd; and Hampsten, Elizabeth. *Far from Home: Families of the Westward Journey.* Schlocken Books, 1990. Letters, diaries, and informative text piece together the trials of families living on the frontier and the effects that mobility and individualism had on a growing nation.

Home Connection

Distribute page 61 of ***Home Connection.*** Students can read books and articles about the American West with their families. This ***Home Connection*** is also available in Spanish on page 62.

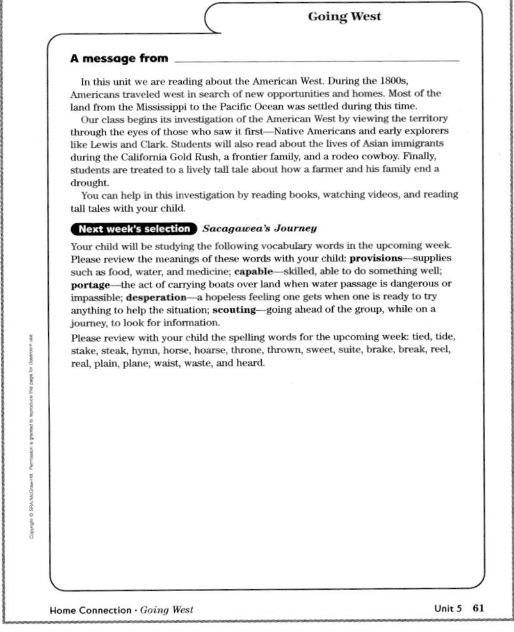

Going West

A message from ____________

In this unit we are reading about the American West. During the 1800s, Americans traveled west in search of new opportunities and homes. Most of the land from the Mississippi to the Pacific Ocean was settled during this time.

Our class begins its investigation of the American West by viewing the territory through the eyes of those who saw it first—Native Americans and early explorers like Lewis and Clark. Students will also read about the lives of Asian immigrants during the California Gold Rush, a frontier family, and a rodeo cowboy. Finally, students are treated to a lively tall tale about how a farmer and his family end a drought.

You can help in this investigation by reading books, watching videos, and reading tall tales with your child.

Next week's selection ***Sacagawea's Journey***

Your child will be studying the following vocabulary words in the upcoming week. Please review the meanings of these words with your child: **provisions**—supplies such as food, water, and medicine; **capable**—skilled, able to do something well; **portage**—the act of carrying boats over land when water passage is dangerous or impassible; **desperation**—a hopeless feeling one gets when one is ready to try anything to help the situation; **scouting**—going ahead of the group, while on a journey, to look for information.

Please review with your child the spelling words for the upcoming week: tied, tide, stake, steak, hymn, horse, hoarse, throne, thrown, sweet, suite, brake, break, reel, real, plain, plane, waist, waste, and heard.

Home Connection • *Going West* Unit 5 61

Home Connection p. 61

Joe Campione on Discussion

Students come to understand written language from and through oral language. Discussions that require students, either as part of the class or in a small-group setting, to reflect on their experiences and to communicate their ideas stimulate the cognitive processes that are necessary for knowledge building. Discussions that are tied to reading selections in which students are encouraged to raise questions, offer interpretations, wonder, and challenge, lead to joint construction of meaning and greater comprehension of a selection for all group members.

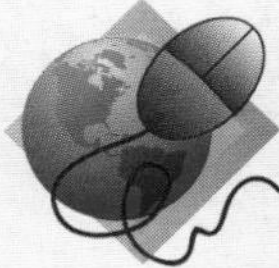

www.sra4kids.com
Web Connection
Check the Reading link of the SRA Web page for more information on Research in Reading.

Focus Questions Why did Lewis and Clark explore the West? How was Sacagawea important to the expedition? What were her reasons for making the trip?

Sacagawea's Journey

from *Sacagawea*
by Betty Westrom Skold
illustrated by Craig Spearing

In 1803, President Thomas Jefferson purchased the Louisiana Territory, an area that extended from the Mississippi River to the Rocky Mountains and that doubled the size of the United States. In 1804, he sent an expedition headed by Meriwether Lewis and William Clark to explore this region and to find a route through it to the Pacific Ocean. About forty-five men set off from St. Louis and traveled up the Missouri River to the territory of the Mandan Indians. There they met a French fur trader, Toussaint Charbonneau, and his wife, Sacagawea. Sacagawea was not a Mandan. She was a Shoshone, a member of a group living in the Rocky Mountains. Sacagawea had been captured as a young girl and brought east. At the time she met Lewis and Clark she was sixteen or seventeen years old and had recently given birth to a son that the men nicknamed Pompy. She and her husband were hired to go with the expedition as interpreters and guides.

Sacagawea stuffed a little more soft, dry grass into Pompy's cradleboard, put the child into it, and tied the rawhide thongs. Her eyes swept the room that had sheltered her through the winter, now stripped of the buffalo robes and the hunting and cooking gear. The last fire was dying on the hearth as she stepped outside.

390

SELECTION INTRODUCTION

Selection Summary

Genre: Biography

The epic journey of Lewis and Clark was full of excitement and danger. This journey was recorded by the explorers. Their journals provide readers with glimpses of the day-to-day details of this famous expedition, guided up the Missouri River by the Shoshone woman Sacagawea.

Some of the elements of biography are listed below. A biography may have one or more of these elements.

- It is written about a real person's life by someone else.
- It contains important information about a person's life and includes details about how a person talks, feels, and thinks about things.
- It may span the person's life, or may tell about only part of the person's life. If spanning the person's life, it is almost always told in chronological order.
- It often focuses on the most important events in a person's life and usually describes the person's achievements or talents.

About the Author

Betty Westrom Skold has worked as a writer and editor for several small town and big city newspapers. Skold won the Woman of Achievement Award from the West Suburban Chamber of Commerce. She has written books for both children and adults.

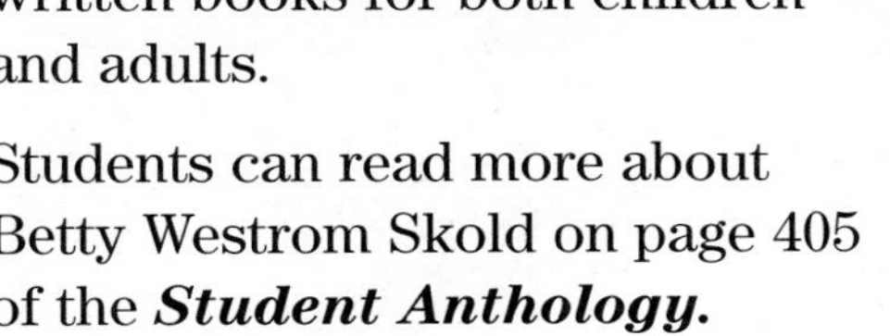

Students can read more about Betty Westrom Skold on page 405 of the ***Student Anthology.***

About the Illustrator

Craig Spearing graduated from the Rhode Island School of Design with a degree in Illustration/Printmaking. He has illustrated numerous children's educational books and magazines. Time period pieces and Western themes are two of his favorite subjects.

Students can read more about Craig Spearing on page 405 of the ***Student Anthology.***

Also Illustrated by Craig Spearing:

- *Prairie Dog Pioneers*

Inquiry Connections

A major aim of ***Open Court Reading*** is knowledge building. Because inquiry is at the root of knowledge building, students are encouraged to investigate topics and questions within each selection that relate to the unit theme.

"Sacagawea's Journey" tells how more than once, the young Shoshone guide Sacagawea saved the expedition from disaster. This selection reminds us that Sacagawea had her own reasons for wanting to make the journey.

Key concepts to be explored are:

- The Lewis and Clark expedition was key in opening up the West for explorers and settlers.
- Sacagawea's was not a journey into new land, but a return to her homeland.
- Sacagawea helped the expedition's members survive many hardships.

Before reading the selection:

- Point out that students may post a question, concept, word, illustration, or object on the Concept/Question Board at any time during the course of their unit investigation. Be sure that students include their names or initials on the items they post so that others will know whom to go to if they have an answer or if they wish to collaborate on a related activity.
- Students should feel free to write an answer or a note on someone else's question or to consult the Board for ideas for their own investigations throughout the unit.
- Encourage students to read about the American West at home and to bring in articles or pictures that are good examples to post on the Board.

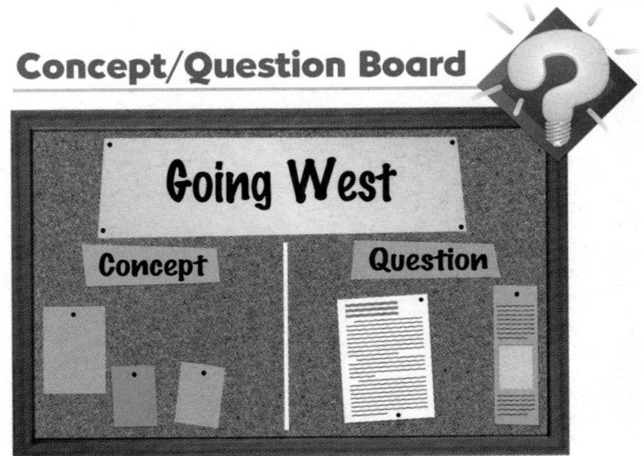

PROGRAM RESOURCES

Leveled Practice

Reteach
Pages 140–144

Challenge
Pages 124–127

English Learner Support Activities

Intervention Workbook

Leveled Classroom Library*

Have students read at least 30 minutes daily outside of class. Have them read books from the ***Leveled Classroom Library,*** which supports the unit theme and helps students develop their vocabulary by reading independently.

Striking It Rich: The Story of the California Gold Rush

BY STEPHEN KRENSKY. ALADDIN, 1996.

A concise history of the Gold Rush, simply told, including how the miners came West, how they panned for gold, how some got rich without finding gold, and the Rush's effect on the growth of California. **(Easy)**

By the Great Horn Spoon!

BY SID FLEISCHMAN. LITTLE, BROWN AND COMPANY, 1963.

Narrated with flair, these are the adventures of young Jack Flagg and his unflappable butler Praiseworthy as they hop a gold ship bound from Boston to California to save Jack's aunt's fortune by striking gold. **(Average)**

Children of the Wild West

BY RUSSELL FREEDMAN. CLARION, 1983.

Historic and fascinating photographs accompany Freedman's details about the experiences of pioneer and Native American children in the West, including the journey west, schools, work and play. **(Advanced)**

* These books, which all support the unit theme Going West, are part of a 36-book ***Leveled Classroom Library*** available for purchase from SRA/McGraw-Hill. Note: Teachers should preview any trade books for appropriateness in their classrooms before recommending them to students.

SRA TECHNOLOGY

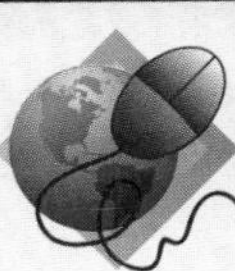

Web Connections

- Going West Web site
- Online Professional Development
- Online Assessment

CD-ROMs

- Research Assistant
- Ultimate Writing and Creativity Center
- Teacher Resource Library

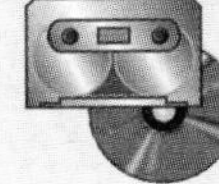

Audiocassettes/CDs

- Listening Library: Going West

Computer Skills

- TechKnowledge

Materials are available through SRA/McGraw-Hill.

LESSON PLANNER

Suggested Pacing: 3–5 days

	DAY 1	DAY 2
	DAY 1	DAY 2
1 Preparing to Read **Materials** ■ Inquiry Journal, p. 112 ■ Home Connection, p. 61 ■ Routine Card 1	**Unit Overview** ■ Previewing the Unit, p. 389K ■ Read Aloud, pp. 389L–389O **Word Knowledge,** p. 390K ■ Root word *explore* ■ /k/ Sound Spelled *c* ■ Closed Compounds ■ Homophones **About the Words and Sentences,** p. 390K	**Developing Oral Language,** p. 390L
2 Reading & Responding **Materials** ■ Student Anthology, pp. 390–405 ■ Reading Transparencies 39, 54, 67 ■ Routine Card 1 ■ Comprehension and Language Arts Skills, pp. 142–143 ■ Reteach, pp. 140–141 ■ Challenge, p. 124 ■ Program Assessment ■ Science/Social Studies Connection Center Cards 64–66 ■ Home Connection, pp. 63–64 ■ Inquiry Journal, p. 113 ■ Unit 5 Assessment, pp. 2–5	**Build Background,** p. 390M **Preview and Prepare,** pp. 390M–390N **Selection Vocabulary,** p. 390N **Reading Recommendations,** pp. 390O–390P **Student Anthology,** pp. 390–403 First Read ✓ **Comprehension Strategies** ■ Asking Questions, pp. 390, 396, 398, 402 ■ Visualizing, pp. 392, 394, 396, 400 ■ Summarizing, pp. 394, 400 **Discussing Strategy Use,** p. 402 **Discussing the Selection,** p. 403A	**Student Anthology,** pp. 390–403 Second Read **Comprehension Skills** ■ Drawing Conclusions, pp. 391, 393, 395, 397, 399, 401, 403 **Supporting the Reading,** ■ Drawing Conclusions, pp. 403C–403D ✓ **Checking Comprehension,** p. 403
Inquiry **Materials** ■ Student Anthology, pp. 390–405 ■ Reading Transparency 40 ■ Inquiry Journal, pp. 116–121 ■ Research Assistant	**Investigation** ■ Investigating Concepts Beyond the Text, p. 405A	**Investigation** ■ Concept/Question Board, p. 405B
3 Language Arts **Materials** ■ Comprehension and Language Arts Skills, pp. 144–145 ■ Language Arts Handbook ■ Spelling and Vocabulary Skills, pp. 106–109 ■ Unit 5 Assessment, pp. 30–31 ■ Reteach, pp. 142–144 ■ Challenge, pp. 125–127 ■ Student Anthology ■ Student Writing and Research Center ■ Writer's Workbook, pp. 78–81	**Word Analysis** ✓■ Spelling: Homophones Pretest, p. 405F **Writing Process Strategies** ■ Personal Writing: Dialogue Journal, p. 405F **English Language Conventions** ■ Grammar and Usage: Sentence Fragments, p. 405F	**Word Analysis** ■ Spelling: Homophones, p. 405G ■ Vocabulary: Concept Words, p. 405G **Writing Process Strategies** ✓■ Personal Writing: Dialogue Journal, p. 405G **English Language Conventions** ■ Grammar and Usage: Sentence Fragments, p. 405G

✓ Informal Assessment Available ✓ Formal Assessment Available

DAY 2 continued	DAY 3	
DAY 3	**DAY 4**	**DAY 5**
General Review	**General Review**	**Review Word Knowledge**
Student Anthology, pp. 404–405 ✓■ Concept Connections ■ Meet the Author/Illustrator	**Review Selection Vocabulary,** p. 403B **Literary Elements,** p. 403E ■ Author's Perspective	✓ **Lesson Assessment** ■ *Unit 5 Assessment:* Lesson Assessment, pp. 2–5 **Home Connection,** p. 403B **Social Studies Connection,** p. 403F ■ Mapping the Frontier
Investigation ✓■ Generating Ideas to Investigate, p. 405C	**Supporting the Investigation** ■ Using Maps, p. 405D	**Investigation** ■ Unit Investigation Continued ■ Update Concept/Question Board
Word Analysis ■ Spelling: Homophones, p. 405H ■ Vocabulary: Concept Words, p. 405H **Writing Process Strategies** ■ Personal Writing: Learning Log, p. 405H **English Language Conventions** ✓■ Grammar and Usage: Sentence Fragments, p. 405H	**Word Analysis** ■ Spelling: Homophones, p. 405I ■ Vocabulary: Concept Words, p. 405I **Writing Process Strategies** ✓■ Personal Writing: Learning Log Question Box, p. 405I **English Language Conventions** ✓■ Listening, Speaking, Viewing: Listening: ✓ Drawing Conclusions and Making Inferences, p. 405I	**Word Analysis** ✓■ Spelling: Homophones Final Test, p. 405J ✓■ Vocabulary: Concept Words, p. 405J **Writing Process Strategies** ✓■ Personal Writing: Literature Response, p. 405J **English Language Conventions** ✓■ Penmanship: Joining with *A* and *d*, p. 405J

Below are suggestions for differentiating instruction. These are the same skills shown on the Lesson Planner; however, these pages provide extra practice opportunities or enriching activities to meet the varied needs of students.

WORKSHOP

Differentiating

Teacher: Individual and Small-Group Instruction

Spend time each day with individuals and small groups to individualize instruction. Each day:

- preteach students who need help with the next lesson.
- reteach students who need to solidify their understanding of content previously taught.
- listen to students read to check their fluency.
- hold writing and inquiry conferences.

Use the following program components to support instruction:

- ***Reteach*** with students who need a bit more practice.
- ***Intervention*** with students who exhibit a lack of understanding of the lesson concepts.
- ***English Learner Support*** with students who need language help.

Student: Independent Activities

Students can work alone, with a partner, or in small groups on such activities as:

- Review sound/spellings
- Partner Reading
- Practice fluency
- Independent Reading
- Reading Roundtable
- Concept vocabulary
- Selection vocabulary
- Writing in progress
- Conference
- Language Arts
- ***Challenge*** Activities
- Inquiry and Investigation Activities
- Listening Library

Professional Development

Teacher Resource Library CD-ROMs or ***Online Professional Development*** provides courses that help you better understand the Workshop/Intervention instruction in ***Open Court Reading.*** For more information on this program, visit SRAonline.com.

	DAY 1
Word Knowledge	**Teacher Directed** ■ Teach meanings of blended words ■ Reading Words and About the Words, ***Intervention Guide,*** p. 233
Fluency	**Independent Activities** ■ Self-test fluency rate
Comprehension	**Teacher Directed** ■ Preteach "Sacagawea's Journey," ***Intervention Guide,*** pp. 234–235 ■ Intervention Selection 1, ***Intervention Guide,*** pp. 235–236 ■ ***English Learner Support Guide,*** pp. 364–367 **Independent Activities** ■ Record reaction to Read Aloud in Writer's Notebook ■ Browse ***Leveled Classroom Library*** ■ ***Listening Library Audiocassette/CD*** ■ Add vocabulary in Writer's Notebook ■ Record response to selection in Writer's Notebook ■ Knowledge about Going West, ***Inquiry Journal,*** p. 112
Inquiry	**Independent Activities** ■ Concept/Question Board ■ Explore OCR Web site for theme connections ■ Changes in the American West, ***Inquiry Journal,*** pp. 116–117
Language Arts	**Teacher Directed** ■ Seminar: Plan and Draft a Dialogue Journal Entry, p. 405F ■ Sentence Fragments, ***Intervention Guide,*** p. 238 **Independent Activities** ■ Fragments, ***Comprehension and Language Arts Skills,*** pp. 144–145

	DAY 2	DAY 3	DAY 4	DAY 5
	Teacher Directed ▪ Developing Oral Language, ***Intervention Guide,*** p. 233	**Teacher Directed** ▪ Dictation and Spelling, ***Intervention Guide,*** pp. 233–234	**Independent Activities** ▪ Add words to Word Bank	**Teacher Directed** ▪ General review as necessary
	Independent Activities ▪ Oral reading of "Sacagawea's Journey"	**Independent Activities** ▪ Partner read "Sacagawea's Journey"	**Independent Activities** ▪ Fluency rate check ▪ Reread "Sacagawea's Journey"	**Teacher Directed** ▪ Repeated Readings, ***Intervention Guide,*** p. 238 **Independent Activities** ▪ Fluency rate check
	Teacher Directed ▪ Preteach "Sacagawea's Journey," ***Intervention Guide,*** pp. 234–235 ▪ Reread Intervention Selection 1 ▪ Teach Comprehension Strategies, ***Intervention Guide,*** p. 236 ▪ ***English Learner Support Guide,*** pp. 367–370 ▪ Review Drawing Conclusions ▪ Drawing Conclusions, ***Reteach,*** pp. 140–141 **Independent Activities** ▪ Choose ***Leveled Classroom Library*** book ▪ Drawing Conclusions • ***Comprehension and Language Arts Skills,*** pp. 142–143 • ***Challenge,*** p. 124 • Challenge Tip, p. 393 ▪ ***Listening Library Audiocassette/CD***	**Teacher Directed** ▪ Teach Intervention Selection 2, ***Intervention Guide,*** pp. 236–237 ▪ ***English Learner Support Guide,*** pp. 370–373 ▪ Discuss Concept Connections, p. 404 **Independent Activities** ▪ ***English Learner Support Activities,*** p. 54 ▪ Read ***Leveled Classroom Library*** book ▪ ***Listening Library Audiocassette/CD*** ▪ Supporting the Reading: Link to Writing, p. 403D ▪ Recording Concept Information, ***Inquiry Journal,*** p. 113	**Teacher Directed** ▪ Teach Comprehension Strategies, ***Intervention Guide,*** p. 237 ▪ Reread Intervention Selection 2 ▪ ***English Learner Support Guide,*** pp. 373–375 **Independent Activities** ▪ Read ***Leveled Classroom Library*** book ▪ Literary Elements: Independent Practice, p. 403E	**Teacher Directed** ▪ Reading Roundtable ▪ ***English Learner Support Guide,*** pp. 376–377 **Independent Activities** ▪ Read ***Leveled Classroom Library*** book ▪ Social Studies Connection, p. 403F ▪ ***English Learner Support Activities,*** p. 55
	Independent Activities ▪ Concept/Question Board ▪ Explore OCR Web site for theme connections ▪ The Geography of the American West, ***Inquiry Journal,*** pp. 118–119	**Independent Activities** ▪ Concept/Question Board ▪ Use ***Research Assistant*** to begin investigation	**Independent Activities** ▪ Concept/Question Board ▪ Ideas about Going West, ***Inquiry Journal,*** p. 120	**Independent Activities** ▪ Concept/Question Board ▪ Telling Stories with Maps, ***Inquiry Journal,*** p. 121 ▪ Continue research
	Teacher Directed ▪ Sentence Fragments, ***Intervention Guide,*** p. 238 ▪ Spelling: Word Sort, p. 405G ▪ Seminar: Plan and Draft a Dialogue Journal Entry, p. 405G ▪ Fragments, ***Reteach,*** p. 144 **Independent Activities** ▪ Vocabulary: Concept Words, ***Spelling and Vocabulary Skills,*** pp. 106–107 ▪ Fragments, ***Challenge,*** p. 127	**Teacher Directed** ▪ Seminar: Plan and Draft a Learning Log Entry, p. 405H ▪ Writing Activity, ***Intervention Guide,*** p. 239 ▪ Vocabulary: Concept Words, ***Reteach,*** p. 143 **Independent Activities** ▪ Spelling: Homophones, ***Spelling and Vocabulary Skills,*** p. 108 ▪ Vocabulary: Concept Words, ***Challenge,*** p. 126	**Teacher Directed** ▪ Seminar: Plan and Draft a Learning Log Question Box, p. 405I ▪ Writing Activity, ***Intervention Guide,*** p. 239 ▪ Spelling: Homophones, ***Reteach,*** p. 142 **Independent Activities** ▪ Spelling: Homophones • ***Spelling and Vocabulary Skills,*** p. 109 • Challenge, p. 125	**Teacher Directed** ▪ Seminar: Plan and Draft a Literature Response Journal Entry, p. 405J **Independent Activities** ▪ Penmanship: Cursive Letters *A* and *d,* p. 405J

ASSESSMENT

Formal Assessment Options

Use these summative assessments along with your informal observations to assess student progress.

Name ______________ Date ________ Score ____

UNIT 5 Going West • Lesson 1

LESSON ASSESSMENT

Sacagawea's Journey

Read the following questions carefully. Then completely fill in the bubble of each correct answer. You may look back at the story to find the answer to each of the questions.

1. Why was it so hard to travel on the Missouri River?
   - ● The expedition was traveling upstream, against the current.
   - Ⓑ The river was frozen most of the year.
   - Ⓒ The wind was blowing against them so they couldn't use sails.
2. Captain Lewis charted their trip by studying
   - Ⓐ mathematics
   - ● the stars
   - Ⓒ business

Read the following questions carefully. Use complete sentences to answer the questions.

3. Why is the journey special to Sacagawea?
   She is returning to her homeland where she was captured years ago.
4. Why does Sacagawea examine the ball and the moccasin at the abandoned camp?
   She examines them to see if they belong to the Shoshones.
5. How did the Missouri River pose a challenge to the explorers?
   The river was a challenge because it branched off in different directions, and the explorers were not sure which branch to follow.

2 Unit 5 • Lesson 1 *Sacagawea's Journey* • Unit 5 Assessment

Unit 5 Assessment p. 2

Sacagawea's Journey *(continued)*

LESSON ASSESSMENT

6. How was Sacagawea useful to the expedition?
   Sacagawea knew the territory and was a good guide. She often helped the expedition find food and landmarks.
7. Why did the expedition decide to leave the red pirogue at Maria's River camp?
   They needed to lighten their load a little bit.
8. How does Captain Lewis treat Sacagawea's illness?
   He treats Sacagawea's illness by giving her fresh mineral water.

Read the following questions carefully. Then completely fill in the bubble of each correct answer.

9. Sacagawea was taken from the Shoshone by
   - Ⓐ a Mandan chief
   - Ⓑ Lewis and Clark
   - ● a Hidatsa warrior
10. The Shoshone call their territory the Land of
   - Ⓐ Many Great Rivers
   - ● Shining Mountains
   - Ⓒ Silver Lakes

Unit 5 Assessment • *Sacagawea's Journey* Unit 5 • Lesson 1 3

Unit 5 Assessment p. 3

Sacagawea's Journey *(continued)*

LESSON ASSESSMENT

Read the questions below. Use complete sentences in your answers.

Linking to the Concepts Why did Sacagawea agree to go with Lewis and Clark?

Answers will vary. Accept all reasonable answers.

Personal Response Do you think Lewis and Clark trusted and valued Sacagawea? Explain your answer.

Answers will vary. Accept all reasonable answers.

4 Unit 5 • Lesson 1 *Sacagawea's Journey* • Unit 5 Assessment

Unit 5 Assessment p. 4

Sacagawea's Journey *(continued)*

LESSON ASSESSMENT

Vocabulary

Read the following questions carefully. Then completely fill in the bubble of each correct answer.

1. Lewis and Clark took many provisions with them. **Provisions** are
   - Ⓐ warnings
   - ● supplies
   - Ⓒ workers
2. Sergeant Ordway was a capable commander. Being **capable** means
   - Ⓐ being happy to have work
   - ● being able to do something well
   - Ⓒ being willing to take dangerous risks
3. The explorers organized a portage around the falls. A **portage** is the act of
   - ● carrying boats over land
   - Ⓑ building a temporary bridge
   - Ⓒ learning how to cross a waterfall
4. In desperation, Captain Lewis poured mineral water down Sacagawea's throat. When you are in **desperation**
   - Ⓐ you give up completely and refuse to try anything
   - ● you feel hopeless and are willing to try anything
   - Ⓒ you know there are plenty of solutions available
5. Captain Clark and a few others scouted for signs of the Shoshones. In this sentence, **scouting** means
   - Ⓐ practicing survival
   - Ⓑ looking for friends
   - ● going ahead of the group

Unit 5 Assessment • *Sacagawea's Journey* Unit 5 • Lesson 1 5

Unit 5 Assessment p. 5

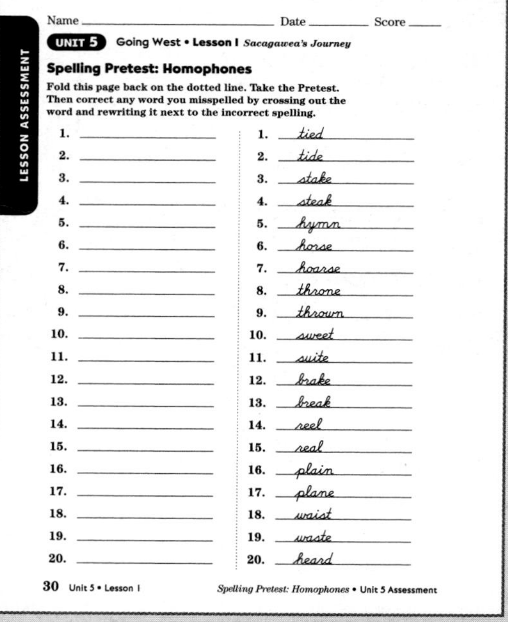

Name ______________ Date ________ Score ____

UNIT 5 Going West • Lesson 1 *Sacagawea's Journey*

LESSON ASSESSMENT

Spelling Pretest: Homophones

Fold this page back on the dotted line. Take the Pretest. Then correct any word you misspelled by crossing out the word and rewriting it next to the incorrect spelling.

1.	______	1.	tied
2.	______	2.	tide
3.	______	3.	stake
4.	______	4.	steak
5.	______	5.	hymn
6.	______	6.	horse
7.	______	7.	hoarse
8.	______	8.	throne
9.	______	9.	thrown
10.	______	10.	sweet
11.	______	11.	suite
12.	______	12.	brake
13.	______	13.	break
14.	______	14.	reel
15.	______	15.	real
16.	______	16.	plain
17.	______	17.	plane
18.	______	18.	waist
19.	______	19.	waste
20.	______	20.	heard

30 Unit 5 • Lesson 1 *Spelling Pretest: Homophones* • Unit 5 Assessment

Unit 5 Assessment p. 30

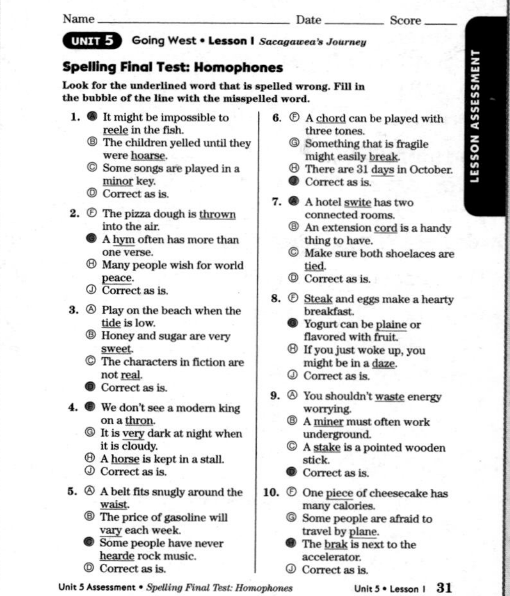

Name ______________ Date ________ Score ____

UNIT 5 Going West • Lesson 1 *Sacagawea's Journey*

LESSON ASSESSMENT

Spelling Final Test: Homophones

Look for the underlined word that is spelled wrong. Fill in the bubble of the line with the misspelled word.

1. ● It might be impossible to reele in the fish.
   - Ⓑ The children yelled until they were hoarse.
   - Ⓒ Some songs are played in a minor key.
   - Ⓓ Correct as is.
2. Ⓕ The pizza dough is thrown into the air.
   - ● A hym often has more than one verse.
   - Ⓗ Many people wish for world peace.
   - Ⓙ Correct as is.
3. Ⓐ Play on the beach when the tide is low.
   - Ⓑ Honey and sugar are very sweet.
   - Ⓒ The characters in fiction are not real.
   - ● Correct as is.
4. ● We don't see a modern king on a thron.
   - Ⓖ It is very dark at night when it is cloudy.
   - Ⓗ A horse is kept in a stall.
   - Ⓙ Correct as is.
5. Ⓐ A belt fits snugly around the waist.
   - Ⓑ The price of gasoline will vary each week.
   - ● Some people have never hearde rock music.
   - Ⓓ Correct as is.
6. Ⓕ A chord can be played with three tones.
   - Ⓖ Something that is fragile might easily break.
   - Ⓗ There are 31 days in October.
   - ● Correct as is.
7. ● A hotel swite has two connected rooms.
   - Ⓑ An extension cord is a handy thing to have.
   - Ⓒ Make sure both shoelaces are tied.
   - Ⓓ Correct as is.
8. Ⓕ Steak and eggs make a hearty breakfast.
   - ● Yogurt can be plaine or flavored with fruit.
   - Ⓗ If you just woke up, you might be in a daze.
   - Ⓙ Correct as is.
9. Ⓐ You shouldn't waste energy worrying.
   - Ⓑ A miner must often work underground.
   - Ⓒ A stake is a pointed wooden stick.
   - ● Correct as is.
10. Ⓕ One piece of cheesecake has many calories.
   - Ⓖ Some people are afraid to travel by plane.
   - ● The brak is next to the accelerator.
   - Ⓙ Correct as is.

Unit 5 Assessment • *Spelling Final Test: Homophones* Unit 5 • Lesson 1 31

Unit 5 Assessment p. 31

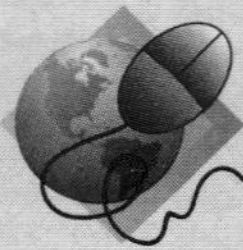

Online Assessment for ***Open Court Reading*** helps teachers differentiate classroom instruction based on students' scores from the weekly and end-of-unit assessments. It provides exercises best suited to meet the needs of each student. For more information visit SRAonline.com.

Informal Comprehension Strategies Rubrics

Summarizing

- The student paraphrases text, reporting main ideas and a summary of what is in text.
- The student decides which parts of the text are important in his or her summary.
- The student draws conclusions from the text.
- The student makes global interpretations of the text, such as recognizing the genre.

Asking Questions

- The student asks questions about ideas or facts presented in the text and attempts to answer these questions by reading the text.

Visualizing

- The student visualizes ideas or scenes described in the text.

Research Rubrics

During Workshop, assess students using the rubrics below. The rubrics range from 1–4 in most categories, with 1 being the lowest score. Record each student's score on the inside back cover of his or her ***Inquiry Journal.***

Formulating Research Questions and Problems

1 With help, identifies things she or he wonders about in relation to a topic.

2 Expresses curiosity about topics; with help, translates this into specific questions.

3 Poses an interesting problem or question for research; with help, refines it into a researchable question.

4 Identifies something she or he genuinely wonders about and translates it into a researchable question.

Objectives

- Students use word origins and prefixes and suffixes to determine meaning.
- Students identify and decode words beginning with the /k/ sound spelled *c.*
- Students identify closed compound words.
- Students recognize and spell homophones.

Materials

- Routine Card 1

Routine Card Refer to Routine 1 for the Reading the Words and Sentences procedure.

Teacher Tip SYLLABICATION To help students blend words and build fluency, demonstrate syllabication using decodable multisyllabic words in the word lines.

ex • plore	con • tact
ex • plor • ers	com • mand
ex • plor • ing	af • ter • noon
ex • plor • a • tion	out • side
cur • tain	hail • stones
camp • fire	rain • storm

Differentiating Instruction

If...	Then...
Students need extra help with closed compound words	Use ***Intervention Guide,*** pages 233–234

Teacher Tip PRONUNCIATION Have students note that knowing the pronunciation of the word *explore* gives them a clue as to how the words *explorers* and *exploring* are pronounced. In these words, the second syllable is accented, and the first two vowels make the same sounds. Have students note that the pronunciation of the word *exploration* is similar, differing only in that the accent moves from the root word to the *a* in the suffix *-ation.* Tell students that it is typical for the *a* in *-ation* to take the accent in words (for example, *communication, restoration,* and so on).

WORD KNOWLEDGE

Word Knowledge

Reading the Words and Sentences

Use direct teaching to teach the Word Knowledge lesson. Write each word and sentence on the board. Have students read each word together. After all the words have been read, have students read each sentence in natural phrases or chunks. Use the suggestions in About the Words and Sentences to discuss the different features of the listed words.

Line 1:	explore explorers exploring exploration
Line 2:	curtain campfire crime contact command
Line 3:	afternoon homecoming hailstones rainstorm
Line 4:	plain plane waist waste herd heard
Sentence 1:	The exploration party buried a cache of food near the campfire.
Sentence 2:	The explorers made contact with the captain.
Sentence 3:	This afternoon there was a shower of hailstones outside.
Sentence 4:	From the window of the plane, we could see the river winding through the plains.

About the Words and Sentences

- **Line 1:** These words build on the word *explore,* which comes from the combination of the Latin prefix *ex-* meaning "out" and the Latin word *plorare,* meaning "to cry." Ask students to offer other words containing the prefix *ex- (exhale, exhaust, exit).* Then, to help students increase their vocabulary of related words, point out to students that the addition of suffixes and endings to the word change the meaning slightly. For example, *explore* means to travel over new territory for discovery; *explorer* means one who travels in search of information; and *exploration* means the act of exploring.
- **Line 2:** These words begin with the /k/ sound spelled *c. C* is pronounced /k/ at the beginning of a word when it is followed by *a, o, u,* and any consonant except *h.* Ask students to offer other words beginning with the /k/ sound spelled *c. (could, copper, cabin, canoe)*
- **Line 3:** These words are closed compounds. Explain that closed compounds are two words placed together as one word without a hyphen or a space. Have students identify the single words in the compounds *(after, noon, home, coming, hail, stones, rain, storm)*
- **Line 4:** The words in the last line review homophones. Homophones are words that are pronounced the same but have different meanings.

- **Sentences 1–2:** Have students read the sentences aloud. Then, have students point out the words derived from *explore. (exploration, explorers)* Then have students read aloud the words beginning with the /k/ sound spelled *c. (cache, campfire, contact, captain)*
- **Sentence 3:** Have students read the sentence aloud. Then, have students identify the closed compound words in the sentence. *(afternoon, hailstones, outside)*
- **Sentence 4:** Have students identify the words in the last sentence that are homophones. *(plane, plain)*

Developing Oral Language

Use direct teaching to review the words. Choose from the following activities.

- Remind students that the Latin prefix *ex-*, meaning "out," is often combined with other Latin roots to make words. Provide students with the following complex words and their origins, and ask volunteers to use their knowledge of the Latin prefix and roots to analyze the meanings of the words and offer definitions for them aloud. Then have volunteers use the word in an appropriate sentence.

exhibit	from *ex-* + *habere*, meaning "to have" or "to hold"
exit	from *ex-* + *ire*, meaning "to go"
exhale	from *ex-* + *halare*, meaning "to breathe"
exclaim	from *ex-* + *clamare*, meaning "to cry out"
exclude	from *ex-* + *claudere*, meaning "to close"
excuse	from *ex-* + *causa*, meaning "cause" or "explanation"
expect	from *ex-* + *specere*, meaning "to look"
except	from *ex-* + *capere*, meaning "to take"

- Write several of the words on the board. Have a student choose two words and use them in a sentence; for example, "The *explorers* waited out the *rainstorm* inside of a cave." Then tell another student to create a new sentence using the original words, plus a new word from the list; for example, "The *explorers* built a *campfire* and waited out the *rainstorm* inside of a cave." Continue the activity to see how many words from the list the students can use to create sentences. Be sure sentences still make sense.
- Have a student use a word from line four in a sentence. Have a volunteer determine which word of the homophone pair was used. Have the volunteer explain what context clues from the sentence helped them determine the word.

WORD KNOWLEDGE

Teacher Tip BUILDING FLUENCY By this time in grade 5 students should be reading approximately 151 words per minute with fluency and expression. Gaining a better understanding of the spellings of sounds and structure of words will help students as they encounter unfamiliar words in their reading. As students read, you may notice that some need work in building fluency. During Workshop, have these students choose a section of the text (a minimum of 160 words) to read several times in order to build fluency.

Differentiating Instruction

If...	Then...
Students need extra fluency practice	Use the Intervention Selections activities, ***Intervention Guide,*** pages 235–237

English Learner Tip

WORD MEANING Make sure that English Learners understand the meaning of the words on the wordlines before you do the exercises with them. Use pictures, photos, and bilingual dictionaries.

Spelling
See pages 405F–405J for the corresponding spelling lesson for homophones.

Objectives

- Students will understand the selection vocabulary before reading.
- Students will identify and decode words beginning with the /k/ sound spelled *c,* closed compound words, and derivatives of *explore.*
- Students will use the comprehension strategies Asking and Answering Questions, Visualizing, and Summarizing as they read the story the first time.
- Students will use the comprehension skill Drawing Conclusions as they read the story the second time.

Materials

- Student Anthology, pp. 390–405
- Reading Transparencies 39, 40, 54, 67
- Comprehension and Language Arts Skills, pp. 142–143
- Inquiry Journal, p. 113
- Routine Card 1
- Listening Library
- Program Assessment
- Unit 5 Assessment, pp. 2–5
- Home Connection, pp. 63–64
- Science/Social Studies Connection Center Cards 64–66

Differentiating Instruction

If...	Then...
Students need extra help with the selection vocabulary	Use ***Intervention Guide***, page 234

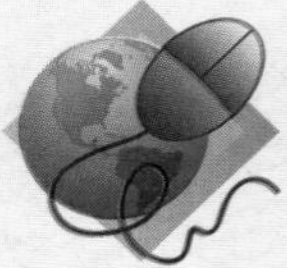

www.sra4kids.com
Web Connection
Students can use the connections to Going West in the Reading link of the SRA Web page for more background information about the American West.

Build Background

Activate Prior Knowledge

Discuss the following with students to find out what they may already know about the selection and have already learned about the theme of Going West.

- Preteach "Sacagawea's Journey" by first determining students' prior knowledge of who Sacagawea was.
- Have students discuss what they remember about the Lewis and Clark expedition from the Read Aloud for this unit.

Background Information

The following information may help students understand the selection they are about to read.

- Some students may have difficulty with the geographical references in the story. You might want to post a large map of the United States that shows the route of the Lewis and Clark expedition to help the students "see" the journey.
- The expedition began in 1804, and the Corp reached the Pacific Ocean on September 23, 1806. Lewis noted this date in his journal, which was published posthumously by Clark in 1814.
- The importance of the role Sacagawea played in the expedition was recently commemorated by the United States. Her face appears on the one-dollar coin.
- Have the students discuss what they know about the genre of this selection. Refer to page 390A of the ***Teacher's Edition*** for elements of this selecion's genre.

Preview and Prepare

Browse

- Have a student read aloud the title and the names of the author and illustrator. Demonstrate how to browse. Then, since this is a nonfiction piece, have the students preview the selection by browsing the illustrations and text in the entire piece. This helps them to establish what they want to learn from the selection and activate prior knowledge in a way that is relevant to the selection. Then discuss what they think this story might have to do with westward expansion.

- Have the students search for clues that tell them something about the story. Also, have them look for any problems, such as unfamiliar words or long sentences, that they notice while reading. Use ***Reading Transparency 54*** to record their observations as they browse. For example, the fact that this is a biography might be a clue that the events will be factual. For the Problems column, students might say they don't know the meaning of the word *cradleboard.* They might wonder why the trip was so important to Sacagawea. To save time and model note taking, write students' observations as brief notes rather than complete sentences.
- As students prepare to read the selection, have them browse the Focus Questions on the first page of the selection. Tell them to keep these questions in mind as they read.

Set Purposes

Before they read, have students set their own purposes. As they read, have students think about journeys into the unknown, like Lewis and Clark's, and journeys home, like Sacagawea's. Remind students that good readers have a purpose when they read. Let them know that they should make sure they know the purpose for reading whenever they read.

Selection Vocabulary

As students study vocabulary, they will use a variety of skills to determine the meaning of a word. These include context clues, word structure, and apposition. Students will apply these same skills while reading to clarify unfamiliar words.

Display ***Reading Transparency 39*** before reading the selection to introduce and discuss the following words and their meanings.

provisions: supplies such as food, water, and medicine (page 391)
capable: skilled or able to do something well (page 393)
portage: the act of carrying boats over land when water passage is dangerous or impossible (page 398)
desperation: a hopeless feeling, when you are ready to try anything to help the situation (page 399)
scouting: When someone on a journey is going ahead to look for information (page 402)

Have students read the words in the Word Box, stopping to blend any words that they have trouble reading. Demonstrate how to decode multisyllabic words by breaking the words into syllables and blending the syllables. Then have students try. If the word is not decodable, give the students the pronunciation.

Have students read the sentences on ***Reading Transparency 39*** and use the skills of context, word structure (structural analysis), or apposition to figure out the meanings of the words. Be sure students explain which skill(s) they are using and how they figured out the meanings of the words.

Clues	Problems	Wonderings
Lewis and Clark Sacagawea Biography	The word *cradleboard*	Why was the trip so important to Sacagawea?

OPEN COURT READING — Reading Transparency 54

Reading Transparency 54

Teacher Tip SELECTION VOCABULARY To help students decode words, divide them into the syllables shown below. The information following each word tells how students can figure out the meaning of each transparency word.

pro • vi • sions	context clues
ca • pa • ble	context clues
por • tage	context clues
des • per • a • tion	context clues, word structure
scout • ing	context clues, word structure

Routine Card
Refer to Routine 2 for the Selection Vocabulary procedure. Refer to Routine 3 for the Clues, Problems, and Wonderings procedure.

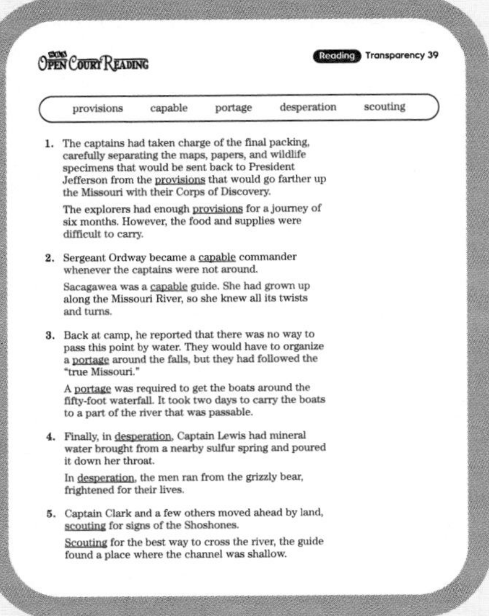

OPEN COURT READING — Reading Transparency 39

provisions capable portage desperation scouting

1. The captains had taken charge of the final packing, carefully separating the maps, papers, and wildlife specimens that would be sent back to President Jefferson from the provisions that would go farther up the Missouri with their Corps of Discovery.
   The explorers had enough provisions for a journey of six months. However, the food and supplies were difficult to carry.
2. Sergeant Ordway became a capable commander whenever the captains were not around.
   Sacagawea was a capable guide. She had grown up along the Missouri River, so she knew all its twists and turns.
3. Back at camp, he reported that there was no way to pass this point by water. They would have to organize a portage around the falls, but they had followed the "true Missouri."
   A portage was required to get the boats around the fifty-foot waterfall. It took two days to carry the boats to a part of the river that was passable.
4. Finally, in desperation, Captain Lewis had mineral water brought from a nearby sulfur spring and poured it down her throat.
   In desperation, the men ran from the grizzly bear, frightened for their lives.
5. Captain Clark and a few others moved ahead by land, scouting for signs of the Shoshones.
   Scouting for the best way to cross the river, the guide found a place where the channel was shallow.

Reading Transparency 39

Students will enjoy using the ***Listening Library Audiocassette/CD*** and listening to the selection they are about to read. Encourage them to listen to the selection during Workshop. Have students discuss with each other and with you their personal listening preferences (for example, nonfiction, poetry, drama, and so on).

Routine Card

Refer to Routine 4 for the Reading the Selection procedure.

Differentiating Instruction

If...	Then...
Students need extra help with the comprehension strategy Asking Questions	Use ***Intervention Guide,*** page 237

Reading Recommendations

Oral Reading

Reading this selection aloud will give students the opportunity to pause and ask questions about more difficult information and vocabulary. Have students help each other with unfamiliar words and difficult ideas. As students read aloud, have them read expressively, at an appropriate pace, in natural phrases. Remind students to keep their audience in mind as they read aloud, adjusting volume as necessary, enunciating, and using proper intonation. Reading the selection with fluency and accuracy will help students comprehend the text. If students have trouble reading decodable words, have them break the words into sounds or syllables and then blend them together to read the word.

Have students make use of the comprehension strategies below to help them understand the selection. Have them stop reading periodically or wait until they have completed the selection to discuss the reading strategies. After the students have finished reading the selection, use the "Discussing the Selection" questions on page 403A to see if they understand what they have read.

Using Comprehension Strategies 

Comprehension strategy instruction allows students to become aware of how good readers read. Good readers constantly check their understanding as they are reading and ask themselves questions. In addition, skilled readers recognize when they are having problems and stop to use various comprehension strategies to help them make sense of what they are reading.

During the first reading of "Sacagawea's Journey," teacher model and prompt the use of the following comprehension strategies. Take turns reading the selection aloud with the students.

- **Summarizing** prompts readers to keep track of what they are reading and to focus their minds on important information.
- **Asking Questions** prepares readers for what they want to learn.
- **Visualizing** helps readers to understand descriptions of settings, characters, and events in a story.

As students read, they should be using a variety of strategies to help them understand the selection. Encourage students to use the strategies listed on the previous page as the class reads the story aloud. Do this by stopping at the points indicated by the numbers in magenta circles on the reduced student page and using a particular strategy. Students can also stop reading periodically to discuss what they have learned and what problems they may be having.

In Unit 5, students should be assuming more responsibility for the use of comprehension strategies. Continue Teacher Modeling and Prompting as needed. Prompting provides a springboard for students from which to respond using the strategy mentioned in the prompt. The Student Sample is written in the language that students might use in their actual responses.

The Student Sample may be one of many possible student responses. Accept other responses that are reasonable and appropriate. If student responses indicate that the students do not understand the strategy, be ready to discuss their responses and to provide additional instruction. As students proceed through the lessons, teacher modeling and prompting of strategy use should become less and less necessary as students assume more responsibility for using strategies.

Building Comprehension Skills 

Revisiting or rereading a selection allows students to apply skills that give them a more complete understanding of the text. Some follow-up comprehension skills help students organize information. Others lead to deeper understanding—to "reading between the lines," as mature readers do. An extended lesson on the comprehension skill Drawing Conclusions can be found in the Supporting the Reading section of pages 403C–403D. This lesson is intended to give students extra practice with Drawing Conclusions. However, the Teach portion of the lesson may be used at this time to introduce the comprehension skill to students.

- **Drawing Conclusions (Review):** Readers draw conclusions when they take from the text small pieces of information and use this information to make a statement about that character or event.

Reading with a Purpose

Have students think about explorations and journeys home as they read. Have them record their thoughts in the Response Journal section of their Writer's Notebooks.

Teacher Tip GENRE Remind students that since this is a biography, it was written about the life of a real person by someone else, and may include details about how that person speaks, thinks, and feels.

Differentiating Instruction

If...	Then...
Students need extra help with reading "Sacagawea's Journey"	• Preread the selection during Workshop; use the ***Listening Library*** to give students a good reading model • Use ***English Learner Support Guide,*** pages 362–379 • Use ***Intervention Guide,*** pages 234–235

Teacher Tip ORAL READING FLUENCY AND RETELL FLUENCY For extra practice in oral fluency, have individual students read aloud to you a selection they have previously read, either from a Decodable Book or a passage from the Student Anthology. Time each student for one minute. If the student reads more than 151 words correctly, have the student retell the selection he or she has just read. Use one prompt if the student seems to be stuck, and allow a maximum of one minute for the student to retell the story. If the student does not read more than 151 words correctly, have the student try reading from an easier selection, such as a Decodable Book from a prior grade level, to help you determine where the problem lies.

COMPREHENSION

Read pages 390–403.

Comprehension Strategies

Read the story aloud, taking turns with the students. Model and prompt the use of strategies for the students.

Prompting

1 Asking Questions *Who can tell me why asking questions is a good strategy to use at this point in the selection, and then model for the class how it is done?*

Student Sample

Asking Questions *Asking questions is a good strategy to use right now because it is the beginning of the story, and it will help me know what things I need to figure out by the end. I wonder why the introduction mentions that Sacagawea was not Mandan, but Shoshone. I'll bet it's important later in the story. I'm going to remember that she's Shoshone.*

Word Knowledge

SCAFFOLDING The skills students are reviewing in Word Knowledge should help them in reading the story. This lesson focuses on words beginning with the /k/ sound spelled *c*. These words will be found in boxes similar to this one throughout the selection.

/k/ sound spelled *c*:

Sacagawea **captured**

Teacher Tip PRONUNCIATION This selection contains many unfamiliar words. Help students pronounce these. Sacagawea is pronounced **sa kə jə wē′ yə.** Toussaint Charbonneau is pronounced **tōō sän shär bôn ō.** Mandan is pronounced **man′ dan.** Shoshone is pronounced **shō shō′ nē.**

First Reading Recommendation

ORAL • CHORAL • SILENT

Focus Questions Why did Lewis and Clark explore the West? How was Sacagawea important to the expedition? What were her reasons for making the trip?

Sacagawea's Journey

from ***Sacagawea***
by Betty Westrom Skold
illustrated by Craig Spearing

In 1803, President Thomas Jefferson purchased the Louisiana Territory, an area that extended from the Mississippi River to the Rocky Mountains and that doubled the size of the United States. In 1804, he sent an expedition headed by Meriwether Lewis and William Clark to explore this region and to find a route through it to the Pacific Ocean. About forty-five men set off from St. Louis and traveled up the Missouri River to the territory of the Mandan Indians. There they met a French fur trader, Toussaint Charbonneau, and his wife, Sacagawea.
1 *Sacagawea was not a Mandan. She was a Shoshone, a member of a group living in the Rocky Mountains. Sacagawea had been captured as a young girl and brought east. At the time she met Lewis and Clark she was sixteen or seventeen years old and had recently given birth to a son that the men nicknamed Pompy. She and her husband were hired to go with the expedition as interpreters and guides.*

Sacagawea stuffed a little more soft, dry grass into Pompy's cradleboard, put the child into it, and tied the rawhide thongs. Her eyes swept the room that had sheltered her through the winter, now stripped of the buffalo robes and the hunting and cooking gear. The last fire was dying on the hearth as she stepped outside.

390

Informal Assessment

Observe individual students as they read and use the Teacher Observation Log found in the ***Program Assessment Teacher's Edition*** to record anecdotal information about each student's strengths and weaknesses.

Differentiating Instruction

If...	Then...
English Learners need extra support with reading "Sacagawea's Journey" and using the skill Drawing Conclusions	Preteach ***Student Anthology*** pages 390–394 using Day 1 of the "Sacagawea's Journey" lesson, found on ***English Learner Support Guide,*** pages 364–367

The ground under her moccasins was spongy and damp from the melting snow. Tender new buds dotted the cottonwoods. For several days Lewis and Clark had seen swans and wild geese flying northeastward in the evening. The Hidatsas had been leaping across the ice cakes to catch the buffalo floating downstream. Soon the river would be ice-free and ready. The captains had taken charge of the final packing, carefully separating the maps, papers, and wildlife specimens that would be sent back to President Jefferson from the provisions that would go farther up the Missouri with their Corps of Discovery.

Now it was April 7, 1805. Today they would say good-bye to the Mandans and Hidatsas, who watched from the banks of the river. It would also be a day of parting for six American soldiers and two French traders, who would return to St. Louis with the keelboat and two canoes. The main part of the Corps of Discovery——Captains Lewis and Clark, Sacagawea, Pompy, Charbonneau and another interpreter, three sergeants, twenty-three privates, and a black slave named York——would follow the Missouri westward in the two long pirogues and six dugout canoes.

391

Teacher Tip PRONUNCIATION
Hidatsa is pronounced **hē dä´ sä.** Corps is pronounced **kōr.** Pirogue is pronounced **pē´ rōg.**

COMPREHENSION

Comprehension Skills

Drawing Conclusions

Explain to students that authors do not always provide complete descriptions or information about a topic, character, thing, or event. They do provide clues that readers can use to draw conclusions about the subject of the writing. Tell students that drawing conclusions will help them understand what the author is implying. Point out the following clues from page 390 to students, and help them conclude that this selection will be about Sacagawea's return home.

- The title of the excerpt is "Sacagawea's Journey."
- " . . . an area that extended from the Mississippi River to the Rocky Mountains . . . an expedition . . . to explore this region . . ."
- "She was a Shoshone, a member of a group living in the Rocky Mountains."
- "Sacagawea had been captured as a young girl and brought east."

Word Knowledge

/k/ sound spelled *c*:

cottonwoods **cakes** **catch**
carefully **captains** **canoes**

Drawing Conclusions

Introduced in Grade 1.
Scaffolded throughout Grades 2–5.

REINTRODUCED: Unit 1, Lesson 1
REINFORCED: Unit 2, Lesson 1
Unit 3, Lesson 3
Unit 3, Lesson 5
Unit 4, Lesson 5
TESTED: Unit 5 Assessment

Second Reading Recommendation

ORAL • **SILENT**

COMPREHENSION

Comprehension Strategies

Prompting

2 Visualizing *Good readers form mental pictures of what they are reading to help them understand. How do you visualize Sacagawea as she embarks on the trip?*

Student Sample

Visualizing *I imagine a lot of commotion. Everyone is waving and yelling good-bye. In the middle of all of this, Sacagawea sits quietly with a far-away look in her eyes, thinking about the last time she saw her family and her village and wondering what it will be like to see her people again.*

Word Knowledge

/k/ sound spelled *c*:
canoes calm

Shadows were lengthening into late afternoon when the big keelboat and two canoes began to move back down the Missouri toward St. Louis. Almost at the same time, the six dugout canoes and two pirogues of the westbound party pushed away from the shoreline and started up the river.

The men were in good spirits—talking, laughing, waving at the Indians along the banks. Sacagawea began the journey more quietly. No sign of excitement showed on her face, and her voice was calm. Only months later would the others
2 realize the depth of her feeling as she started the journey.

Sacagawea took her turn with the others, sometimes paddling in one of the boats, often walking along the shore. The world of the plains seemed to flow by. Flocks of geese fed in the young grass, while sparrow hawks wheeled across the sky. Patches of juniper spread along the sides of the hills. Maple trees were budding and plum bushes were in bloom, but winter was not quite over. Once in a while snow would sift down briefly on a land that had already felt the touch of spring.

392

Informal Assessment

Use the Informal Comprehension Strategies Rubrics on page 390J to determine whether a student is using the strategies being taught.

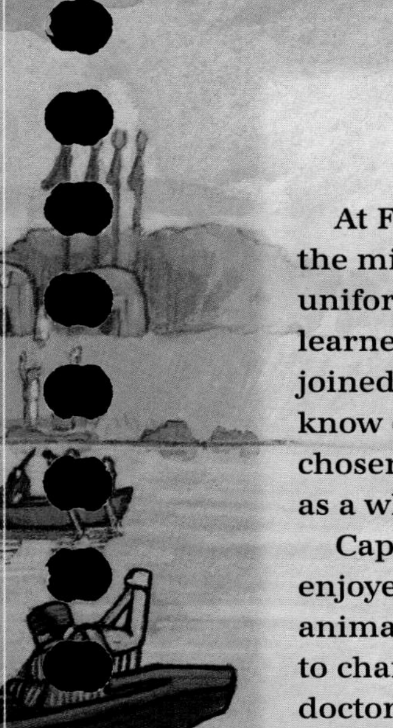

At Fort Mandan Sacagawea had become acquainted with the military life of the Americans. She had grown used to the uniforms, the salutes, the sentinels, the commands, and had learned the names of the thirty men whom her family had joined. As the real work of the expedition began, she came to know each person as an individual. Each one had been chosen for the skills that would help the Corps of Discovery as a whole.

Captain Lewis was a brave and thoughtful leader who enjoyed walking alone out on the prairie, studying the animals or gathering bits of plant life. It was he who learned to chart their route by the stars. Captain Lewis also served as doctor for the expedition, giving out medicines from his small leather bag. Sacagawea learned that Captain Clark's talents as mapmaker and peacemaker were equaled by his leadership skills.

Private Cruzatte, whose violin music had delighted her at Fort Mandan parties, was experienced in river travel. Sergeant Gass was a carpenter, and Private Shields was an expert gunsmith. Drewyer served as an interpreter, but he was also an able hunter. The black man, York, worked as Captain Clark's personal servant, and he provided entertainment for the whole Corps with his story-telling. Sergeant Ordway became a capable commander whenever the captains were not around. John Colter, from the Kentucky woods, had been chosen for hunting skills, and in a single day he bagged an elk, three deer, a wolf, and five turkeys. Charbonneau proved to be a surprisingly good trail cook.

393

Comprehension Skills

Drawing Conclusions

Prompt students to tell you that when drawing conclusions, one puts together clues from the text to form a more complete idea of something described in the text. Ask students what conclusion they can draw from the following clue from the second paragraph on page 392:

- "The men were in good spirits—talking, laughing, waving at the Indians along the bank." *(The men were excited about beginning the expedition.)*

COMPREHENSION

Word Knowledge

SCAFFOLDING The skills students are reviewing in Word Knowledge should help them in reading the story. This lesson focuses on closed compound words. The words will be found in boxes similar to this one throughout the selection.

Closed compound words:

mapmaker **peacemaker** **gunsmith**

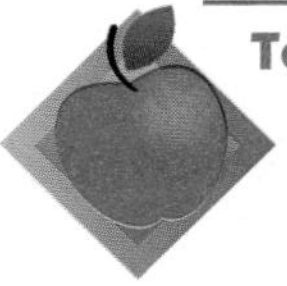

Teacher Tip **CONTEXT** Encourage students to think of the time frame of events as they read this selection. Ask them to consider how the author created an adventurous story that encompasses only a small segment of the expedition's journey.

Teacher Tip **PRONUNCIATION** Cruzatte is pronounced kroo zet′.

Differentiating Instruction

Challenge Tip

MAIN IDEA AND DETAILS Have the students reread the selection and break it into sections. Have them give each section a title or heading that reflects the main idea. Have them list several details under each heading.

COMPREHENSION

Comprehension Strategies

Prompting

3 Summarizing *We know that good readers sum up often to check their understanding. Who would like to model a summary of what we've read so far?*

Student Sample

Summarizing *Sacagawea and the Corps of Discovery started up the Missouri River. The Corps included Captain Lewis and Captain Clark. Everyone in the group had a set job to do.*

Teacher Modeling

4 Summarizing *This is a good spot to stop and summarize. The journey was pleasant and Sacagawea seemed cheerful. They passed through prairie country. By April, they reached the Yellowstone River. Some men almost got killed by a grizzly bear and one pirogue almost sank. Sacagawea stayed calm and managed to save some valuable things.*

Teacher Modeling

5 Visualizing *I can just imagine the scene. The river is high and moving quickly because of the melted snow. Suddenly a strong wind blows and a pirogue tips over. Everyone is panicking. Sacajewea calmly reaches over and grabs valuable things out of the water. I'm sure the rest of the people were amazed by her. Good readers are always getting images in their heads about what they read. If you get a good one, tell the class about it.*

Word Knowledge

Closed compound words:

watchdog	cradleboard	homecoming
campfire	sometimes	buckskins

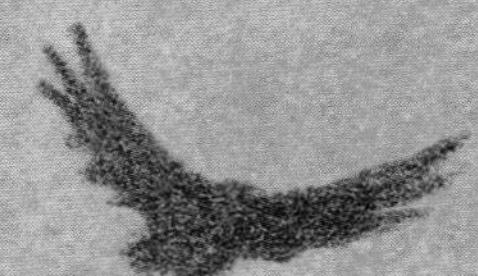

Even Scannon, Captain Clark's big, black, Newfoundland dog, had his chores. An alert watchdog, he frightened away animals who wandered into camp during the night. He also helped with Pompy, lying like a faithful guardian beside the baby's cradleboard. 3

Sacagawea cheerfully kept pace along the trail, moving with a light, firm step. Food-gathering skills from her Shoshone childhood proved useful again and again. Just two days from Fort Mandan, when they had halted for dinner, she sharpened a digger stick and began to poke around in small piles of driftwood. She uncovered a good supply of wild artichokes, buried there by mice.

Day after day Sacagawea walked along the shore or rode in a canoe with the others, but in a sense she made the journey alone. Not even the child on her shoulders shared her experience. No one else could share her dream of homecoming.

Evenings around the campfire were a pleasant time. After supper the men would often throw quoits, a game in which they tossed rope rings at stakes. Sometimes they danced to the music of violin and mouth harp. The captains and several of the others faithfully wrote down each day's events in their journals by the dim light of the fire. Sacagawea sat cross-legged on the ground, mending buckskins and watching over Pompy.

For several days they passed through prairie country like one large grassy pasture. Gentle herds of buffalo, elk, and antelope gazed at them curiously, sometimes following the men who walked on shore. Deer peered shyly from the brush.

394

Teacher Tip PRONUNCIATION Quoits is pronounced **kwoits.**

By late April they had reached the woodlands at the mouth of the Yellowstone River. Happy to have arrived at this first important landmark, they celebrated with music, dancing, and a small ration of spirits.

May 14 brought troubles to the expedition. Six of the hunters wounded a brown grizzly. Crazed by pain, the bear charged and chased them along the bank. The men plunged into the river, and others in the party were able to kill the bear with eight shots.

After sunset that evening the white pirogue was almost destroyed. The sail had been raised to take advantage of a brisk wind. Steering was Charbonneau, a timid and clumsy river pilot. A sudden squall struck the boat at an angle, ripping the brace of the sail from the man who held it, and the boat tipped over on its side. Charbonneau had never learned to swim. He cried out to God in terror and dropped the rudder. Cruzatte, in the bow, threatened to shoot him if he did not take hold of the rudder and do his duty. A trembling Charbonneau obeyed.

Meanwhile Sacagawea, balancing the baby on her back, calmly reached far out over the side and grabbed the
4 5 valuable cargo that had fallen overboard. After the pirogue had been dragged to shore and bailed out with kettles, the rescued articles were spread out on the ground to dry. By her quick thinking Sacagawea had saved many things of value to the expedition. She had rescued instruments for navigation, scientific books needed by the captains for their work, and trading goods needed to make peaceful contact with Indians they would meet along the way.

395

DIFFERENTIATING INSTRUCTION

If...	Then...
English Learners need extra support with reading "Sacagawea's Journey" and using the skill Drawing Conclusions	Preteach ***Student Anthology*** pages 395–397 using Day 2 of the "Sacagawea's Journey" lesson, found on ***English Learner Support Guide,*** pages 367–370

Comprehension Skills

COMPREHENSION

Drawing Conclusions

Tell students that as they read, they should be aware of the clues the author gives them. For example, point out the following:

- "Sacagawea cheerfully kept pace along the trail, moving with a light, firm step." (p. 394)
- "Food-gathering skills from her Shoshone childhood proved useful again and again." (p. 394)
- "By her quick thinking Sacagawea had saved many things of value to the expedition." (p. 395)

Help students understand that these clues lead readers to draw the conclusion that Sacagawea, despite being the only woman on the trip, was able to keep up with the rest of the corps and be useful.

Word Knowledge

Closed compound words:

Woodlands **landmark** **overboard**

COMPREHENSION

Comprehension Strategies

Teacher Modeling

6 Asking Questions *I wonder why this says that the branching of the river gave the party a problem. Let's read on to see if we can figure this out.*

Teacher Modeling

7 Visualizing *I can see how everyone would be very confused here. I can just picture the party standing there, trying to decide which way to go.*

Teacher Modeling

8 Answering Questions *Now I see why choosing the wrong river would have been a big mistake. They needed to find the part of the river that led into the mountains to get there before winter. Otherwise, with the cold and the snow, they would be trapped until spring and lose valuable time.*

Word Knowledge

/k/ sound spelled *c*:
could confident captain cooking carefully

Teacher Tip ASKING QUESTIONS Inform students that they should keep asking questions and trying to answer them as they read.

Almost every day the travelers reached some new tributary of the Missouri. They remembered maps drawn on skins or in the earth by Hidatsa warriors back at Fort Mandan. As each river was identified by its Hidatsa name, they could feel confident that they were on the right track. When they came to a river with water the tan color of milky tea, they named it the Milk River. This was the river known to the Hidatsas as "The River Which Scolds At All Others." Small, unnamed streams were given new names by Lewis and Clark. When a lively, clear-running river was named for Sacagawea, she accepted the honor with shy pleasure. Another stream was called Blowing Fly Creek for the hordes of flies that swarmed over their meat. Judith's River was named for a friend of Captain Clark's from Virginia.

In the high country near the mouth of Judith's River, they found the remains of a large Indian camp that had been deserted a short time before. All over the hills were the scattered ashes of cooking fires where tipis had stood. A child's ball and a moccasin found on the site were brought to Sacagawea. She looked at them carefully, then shook her head. They were not Shoshones.

396

Differentiating Instruction

English Learner Tip

CLARIFYING This selection contains many difficult words. Be sure that English Learners receive whatever clarification is needed.

Intervention Tip

ASKING QUESTIONS Remind students that asking questions is a natural response by good readers to their reading. Impress upon them that no question is too odd. Have students share with the class anything they wonder about the text.

In early June the party came to a branching of the river that gave them a problem. Which of the branches was the "true Missouri"? Was it the one that seemed to come from the north, or was it the branch that flowed from the southwest? Most of the Corps were sure that the northern branch was the Missouri. It looked like the river they had followed all the way from the Mississippi, broad and thick with mud. The captains, on the other hand, wanted to follow the southern branch, a clear, swift-running stream with a rock and gravel bed. They reasoned that the Missouri had its source in the mountains and that a mountain stream would be swift and clear. 6 7

A wrong decision could be a costly mistake. Already they could see snow-topped mountains in the distance. Even if they should find the "Northwest Passage," crossing the
8 mountains in winter would be a risky business. If they should turn up the wrong river, it could waste precious weeks of summer travel time. The captains decided that a camp should be set up for a few days at the fork of the rivers. Small exploring parties would go up each of the branches and decide which fork led to the Great Falls described by the Hidatsas, and from there to Shoshone country.

397

Comprehension Skills

Drawing Conclusions

Invite students to ask questions about the characters and the events in the text. Then, help them use clues to draw conclusions and answer their questions. Point out the following clue, and ask students to draw a conclusion from it:

- "They remembered maps drawn on skins or in the earth by Hidatsa warriors back at Fort Mandan." (p. 396)

Students should understand that the Corps of Discovery does not have a map to follow, just their memories of the maps.

Word Knowledge

/k/ sound spelled *c*:

Corps costly could camp country

Teacher Tip GEOGRAPHICAL CONTEXT The part of the journey described in this selection began in what is now North Dakota and ended in what is now Montana, just east of the Rocky Mountains.

COMPREHENSION

COMPREHENSION

Comprehension Strategies

Prompting

9 **Asking Questions** *Good readers ask themselves questions about things they don't understand and find answers to those questions as they read. Who would like to tell the group what questions have been raised or answered for you by the text we just read?*

Student Sample

Asking Questions *Why is "true Missouri" in quotes? I've seen it that way twice now. I know that quotation marks are used to show when someone's exact words have appeared in a piece of writing. Maybe "true Missouri" is in quotes because that is what the people on the expedition were calling the river. That would make sense because until Lewis explored the southern branch of the river no one knew whether the southern or northern branch of the river was the real Missouri.*

Research in Action

Strategy Use

Modeling cannot be totally effective if it remains solely in the hands of the teacher. Just as students can become dependent on teachers for answers, they can become dependent on a teacher for thinking. For students to fully understand and utilize thinking processes, it is crucial that they become responsible for thinking for themselves. Such independence cannot occur without careful teaching. In addition to modeling thinking, you must be willing and able to turn over the responsibility of thinking to the students. *(Jan Hirshberg)*

Clearly it was a good time to pause. Those not in the exploring parties could spend their time dressing skins for clothing. Uniforms had fallen to shreds, and buckskin clothing had to be made to replace them. Moccasins had been so cut by the rocky trails that they had been thrown away, and the men could barely walk on their bruised feet. Many of them were exhausted from towing the boats free from sandbars or sloshing through cold water up to their armpits. Poor diet and muddy water caused diarrhea and nausea, while chilling rains brought raging fever.

Lewis was so sure that the muddy northern branch could not be the Missouri that he named it Maria's River, after his cousin, Maria Wood. Nevertheless, he agreed to take a party up this river while Captain Clark explored the southern branch. The Lewis party found out that the northern branch flowed through a picture book country of beautiful birds, wild roses, and herds of game animals, but both he and Clark were still convinced that the southern branch was the Missouri. To find out for sure, they decided that Lewis would take four men and follow the southern branch on foot in search of the Great Falls.

Lewis and a small land party pushed up into the rolling hills and across a level plain. Suddenly he heard the distant sound of falling water and saw spray rising above the horizon. He followed the sound of roaring water until he stood on a pile of rocks and looked in wonder at the water cascading over huge bluffs, nine hundred feet wide and eighty feet high. In some places the water fell in great sheets, while at other points it was broken by rocks into glittering spray. He had reached the Great Falls of the Missouri River. Back at camp, he reported that there was no way to pass this point by water. They would have to organize a portage around the falls, but they had followed the "true Missouri." 9

398

Teacher Tip VISUALIZING It might help students visualize the journey if they track it on a map. Photocopy a map of the Lewis and Clark route so that all the students can mark the location of important events as they read this story.

Differentiating Instruction

If...	Then...
English Learners need extra linguistic support with reading "Sacagawea's Journey" and using the skill Drawing Conclusions	Preteach ***Student Anthology*** pages 398–399 using Day 3 of the "Sacagawea's Journey" lesson, found on ***English Learner Support Guide,*** pages 370–373

Captain Lewis learned that Sacagawea had become ill during his absence. The young woman who had met all the hardships of the journey now lay sick in the covered part of the white pirogue, shaded from the July heat. She was gripped by many pains, weak, and exhausted. Her pulse was irregular, and her fingers twitched. Captain Clark had tried medicines and had bled her, but she was no better.

The white explorers were worried. They had grown fond of this brave Shoshone woman, and she had been useful to them in finding roots, sewing buckskin, and pointing out the landmarks along the way. Now, just when they needed her most, on the very edge of Shoshone country, she lay close to death.

Finally, in desperation, Captain Lewis had mineral water brought from a nearby sulfur spring and poured it down her throat. Within minutes Sacagawea began to perspire, and her pulse grew stronger. The crisis had passed.

The captains decided that the Maria's River camp would be a good place to leave the large red pirogue and some of the provisions to lighten the load for the portage around the falls and for travel through the mountains. The men dug deep, bottle-shaped holes called caches in the ground and filled them with salt, tools, powder, and lead. Signs of the digging were removed. They dragged the pirogue up on an island, tied it to trees, and covered it with brush.

399

Teacher Tip **CONTEXT** The text mentions that one of the things the Corps of Discovery hoped to find was the Northwest Passage. An idea rather than an actual route, the Northwest Passage was thought to be an easily navigable water route between the Atlantic and the Pacific. Such a route was never found.

Comprehension Skills

COMPREHENSION

Drawing Conclusions

Ask students to explain what the skill of drawing conclusions requires. Then ask them how drawing conclusions helps them as they read. *(Drawing conclusions helps readers read between the lines to understand what the author is implying. It helps readers form a more complete idea of the events being described.)* Point out the following clues from page 398 for students:

- "Uniforms had fallen to shreds, and buckskin clothing had to be made to replace them."
- "Moccasins had been so cut by the rocky trails that they had been thrown away, and the men could barely walk on their bruised feet."
- "Poor diet and muddy water caused diarrhea and nausea, while chilling rains brought raging fever."

Ask students to draw conclusions about the morale of the group based on these clues. Students should conclude that the morale was likely quite low. Students should also consider that the Corps were at a point in the expedition where the wrong turn could be quite costly.

Word Knowledge

/k/ sound spelled *c*:
camp **caches**

COMPREHENSION

Comprehension Strategies

Prompting

10 Summarizing *Let's stop and summarize. After Sacagawea saved the things from the pirogue, the party continued moving up the river. In June, they reached a split in the river. They had to pick the right part of the river, so they sent scouts up each branch to see where they went. Who would like to continue the summary?*

Student Sample

Summarizing *When Captain Lewis got back from exploring the river, Sacagawea was very ill, but he managed to make her better. They decided to carry their boats around the falls on wagons. It was hard and dangerous, and it took a long time. They found signs of the Shoshones, but not the people themselves. Sacagawea started recognizing places.*

Prompting

11 Visualizing *How do you visualize the portage, when the expedition members had to carry the pirogues around the falls?*

Student Sample

Visualizing *I visualize them trying to find their way through a lot of trees and brush, going down steep, rocky hills. There are maybe four or five men supporting the weight of each pirogue over their heads, while trying to keep their footing on the uneven ground. Other people are carrying supplies and belongings and may be trying to cut a trail for the others. I can see the falls in the background and the spray from the water.*

Word Knowledge

/k/ sound spelled *c*:

cut	cottonwood	cactus
carry	completed	called

To move the six dugouts around the falls, they built makeshift wagons. The mast of the white pirogue was cut up for axles and rounds were sliced from a huge cottonwood tree to form wheels.

The eighteen-mile portage around the Great Falls was an eleven-day struggle. The explorers limped in thin moccasins over needle-sharp ground covered with buffalo tracks and prickly pear cactus, shoving the two heavy, clumsy carts. Axles cracked and wagon tongues broke, so new ones had to be made from willow trees. In a stiff breeze the men hoisted a sail on one of the canoes and the wind helped carry it along on the wagon wheels.

One day a sudden storm pelted the party with huge, bouncing hailstones. Water filled runoff channels, almost sweeping Captain Clark, Sacagawea, and Pompy away in a flash flood. They found shelter under a rock shelf and watched a wall of water moving down the creek. Pushing the mother and baby ahead of him, Captain Clark scrambled up
10 the hill to safety just before they would have been swept away.

After they had completed the exhausting portage, they built two canoes and moved up the river, which was narrow and crowded with islands. At a place where the Missouri loops like a rattlesnake, huge rocks hung out over the

400

Differentiating Instruction

Intervention Tip

SUMMARIZING If students are having difficulty summing up this section, it may be because there are terms or ideas that need to be clarified first. Reread this section with students to make sure that they understand it, and have them jot down main points as they read, to add to their summaries.

banks and pressed the river into a narrow channel. Captain Lewis marveled at the scene and called it the "Gates of the Rocky Mountains."

Time had been lost in the portage, and the explorers were impatient to find the Shoshones. Each day they found new signs that the Shoshones were near, including many small, deserted camps among the hills. Sacagawea pointed out remains of willow shelters and trees that had been stripped of bark, explaining that the Shoshones used the soft underpart of the wood for food. One morning they saw smoke rising in the distance. They guessed that the Shoshones might have seen their party and set the prairie afire to warn other families that Blackfeet or Hidatsa warriors might be near.

In a green valley Sacagawea identified White Earth Creek, where her people used to gather earth for their paint.
11 The Three Forks of the Missouri were near. For Sacagawea and for the Corps of Discovery, it was a time of hope. Soon they would set foot in the land of her people, the Land of the Shining Mountains.

401

Comprehension Skills

Second Read

Drawing Conclusions

Challenge students to draw conclusions about Captain Clark based on the following clues:

- "Sacagawea learned that Captain Clark's talents as mapmaker and peacemaker were equaled by his leadership skills." (page 393, second paragraph)
- "Pushing the mother and baby ahead of him, Captain Clark scrambled up the hill to safety just before they would have been swept away." (page 400)

Lead students to understand that Clark was a brave man who put Sacagawea's and Pompy's safety before his own. Students may draw other conclusions based on his role as peacemaker.

Word Knowledge

/k/ sound spelled *c*:

camps **Corps**

Teacher Tip **CONTEXT** Tell the students that this selection is an excerpt from Betty Westrom Skold's book, *Sacagawea: The Story of an American Indian.*

Teacher Tip **FLUENCY** By this time in grade 5 good readers should be reading approximately 151 words per minute with fluency and expression. The only way to gain this fluency is through practice. Have students reread the selection to you and to one another during Workshop to help build fluency.

COMPREHENSION

Differentiating Instruction

If...	Then...
English Learners need extra linguistic support with reading "Sacagawea's Journey" and using the skill Drawing Conclusions	Preteach ***Student Anthology*** pages 400–403 using Day 4 of the "Sacagawea's Journey" lesson, found on ***English Learner Support Guide,*** pages 373–375

COMPREHENSION

Comprehension Strategies

Prompting

⑫ **Answering Questions** *Has anyone kept track of the questions from the beginning of the selection? Does anyone have an example of a question that has been answered?*

Student Sample

Answering Questions *This is the answer to the question I asked at the beginning. Sacagawea's Shoshone heritage was important to remember because it explained her interest in the expedition.*

Discussing Strategy Use

While students are reading the selection, encourage them to share any problems they encountered and tell what strategies they used.

- What questions did they ask as they read?
- How did they summarize the text?
- What did they visualize as they were reading?

Remind students that good readers use all of the strategies listed above and that they should be using them whenever they read. Make sure that students explain how using the strategies helped them to better understand the selection. For example, "Visualizing images of the scenes in the story helped me understand everything that was going on."

Word Knowledge

/k/ sound spelled *c*:

contact could cactus

Every day brought fresh signs that the Shoshones were near, creating new hope that contact could be made. Sacagawea rode in the river party with Lewis, while Captain Clark and a few others moved ahead by land, scouting for signs of the Shoshones. The Rocky Mountains crowded in close to the river like tall, rugged giants, and Captain Lewis was worried. They might be headed toward savage rapids or waterfalls. Could the river possibly run through these mountains without suddenly tossing their canoes into some wild, unexpected danger? Sacagawea assured him that the river would not suddenly change. There would be a strong and rapid flow, but no waterfalls that could wreck the canoes.

Misery followed them up the river. Shoulders ached from poling canoes between rocks. Cactus needles pierced their feet, and barbed seeds poked through their leggings. Each evening Sacagawea huddled close to the fire, protecting

402

Teacher Tip BUILDING FLUENCY As students read, you may notice that some need work in building fluency. During Workshop, have these students choose a section of text (a minimum of 160 words) to read several times in order to build fluency.

Pompy from the mosquitoes and gnats that swarmed around his head. They slept under mosquito biers, gauzy netting stretched over wooden frames.

On the morning of July 27, the river route opened suddenly on a beautiful stretch of plains and meadows surrounded by distant high mountains. Sacagawea grew silent and her body became tense. Her eyes moved quickly from water to shore, and then off to the forest that covered the mountain slopes. Quietly she identified this as the place of the Hidatsa raid five summers before. She pointed to the rocky shoals in the middle of the river where she had been pulled up on the horse of the Hidatsa warrior. No word from her could possibly explain the mixture of feelings that almost overwhelmed her. No word from these white men could take away the painful memory of violence. No word
12 from them could possibly add to the joy of her return.

COMPREHENSION

Comprehension Skills

Drawing Conclusions

Point students to the last paragraph of the excerpt. Ask them to draw conclusions about the way that Sacagawea felt at her return. Help them understand that despite the painful memories ignited by the scene, Sacagawea embraced her homeland. Her horrible memories were not enough to make her want to stay away.

Checking Comprehension

Ask students the following questions to check their comprehension of the selection.

- Why do you think it was necessary to have people with such varied talents in the Corps? *(The party could only rely on themselves for everything they would need for several years.)*
- Why do you suppose the Shoshones were trying to hide from the expedition? *(They were afraid because they had never seen people like the members of the expedition.)*
- Why was this journey so special to Sacagawea? *(She was heading to the home of her people after being kidnapped years earlier.)*
- How has this selection connected with your knowledge of the unit theme? *(Answers will vary—students should compare/contrast examples of American West from this selection with their own experiences or past reading and use these connections to make a general statement about the unit theme.)*

Differentiating Instruction

If...	Then...
English Learners have been participating in the "Sacagawea's Journey" ***English Learner Support Guide*** activities	Review the selection and the skill Drawing Conclusions using Day 5 of the lesson, found on ***English Learner Support Guide,*** pages 376–377

Formal Assessment

See pages 2–5 in ***Unit 5 Assessment*** to test students' comprehension of "Sacagawea's Journey."

Routine Card
Refer to Routine 5 for the *handing-off process.*

Clues	Problems	Wonderings
Lewis and Clark Sacagawea Biography	The word *cradleboard*	Why was the trip so important to Sacagawea?

Reading Transparency 54

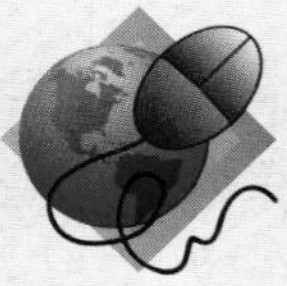

www.sra4kids.com
Web Connection
Some students may choose to conduct a computer search for additional books or information about the American West. Invite them to make a list of these books and sources of information to share with classmates and the school librarian. Check the Reading link of the SRA Web page for additional links to theme-related Web sites.

Discussing the Selection

After the first read, the whole group discusses the selection and any personal thoughts, reactions, problems, or questions that it raises. To stimulate discussion, students can ask one another the kinds of questions that good readers ask themselves about a text: *How does it connect to going west? What have I learned that is new? What did I find interesting? What is important here? What was difficult to understand? Why would someone want to read this?* It is important for students to see you as a contributing member of the group.

Routine 5 To emphasize that you are part of the group, actively participate in the *handing-off process:* Raise your hand to be called on by the last speaker when you have a contribution to make. Point out unusual and interesting insights verbalized by students so that these insights are recognized and discussed. As the year progresses, students will take more and more responsibility for the discussion of selections.

Engage students in a discussion to determine whether they have discerned the following concepts:

- throughout history, explorers have taken great risks to understand new lands
- courage, cooperation, and determination are necessary for a team to accomplish goals

In discussing the above ideas, students should identify and assess evidence from the text that supports them.

During this time, have students return to the clues, problems, and wonderings that they noted during browsing to determine whether the clues were borne out by the selection, whether and how their problems were solved, and whether their wonderings were answered or deserve further discussion and exploration. Let the students decide which items deserve further discussion. Also have students return to the Focus Questions on the first page of the selection. Select a student to read the questions aloud, and have volunteers answer the questions. If students do not know the answers to the questions, have them return to the text to find the answers.

You may also want to review the elements of biography with the students. Discuss with them how they can tell that "Sacagawea" is a biography.

Have students break into small groups to discuss how this story reflects the theme. Groups can then share their ideas with the rest of the class.

Students may wish to record their thoughts about and reactions to this selection. Encourage students to discuss how Sacagawea must have felt upon returning home.

Review Selection Vocabulary

Have students review the definitions of the selection vocabulary words that they wrote in the vocabulary section of their Writer's Notebooks. Remind them that they discussed the meanings of these words before reading the selection. Students can use these definitions to study for the vocabulary portion of their Lesson Assessment. Have them add to the personal dictionary section of their Writer's Notebook any other interesting words that they clarified while reading. Encourage students to refer to the selection vocabulary words throughout the unit. The words from the selection are:

provisions **capable** **desperation** **portage** **scouting**

Create a Word Bank for the students to help them organize the vocabulary words throughout the year. Rather than organizing the words in alphabetical order, create a Word Bank that divides root words from word endings. Headings for words to be organized in this fashion should include Root Word, *-ing* ending, *-ed* ending, *-ly* ending, *-tion* ending, and so on. Write the vocabulary words in large black letters on colored index cards. Have students place the words under the appropriate endings in the Word Bank. Encourage the students to find other words related to the unit theme and add them to the Word Bank.

Home Connection

Distribute ***Home Connection,*** page 63. Encourage students to discuss "Sacagawea's Journey" with their families. Students can list and discuss the contributions Sacagawea made to the Lewis and Clark expedition. ***Home Connection*** is also available in Spanish, page 64.

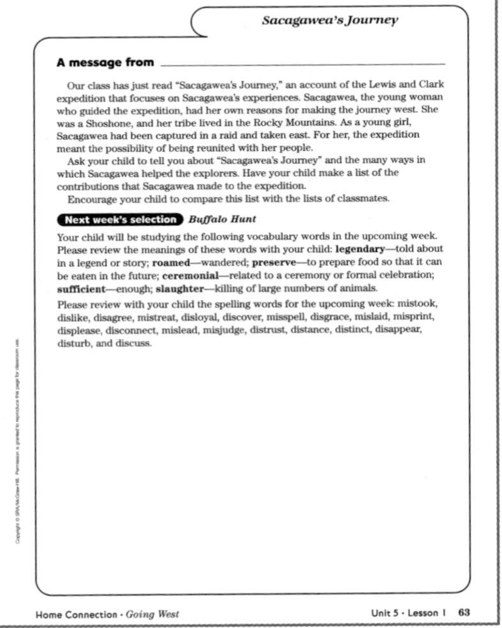

Sacagawea's Journey

A message from ______________________

Our class has just read "Sacagawea's Journey," an account of the Lewis and Clark expedition that focuses on Sacagawea's experiences. Sacagawea, the young woman who guided the expedition, had her own reasons for making the journey west. She was a Shoshone, and her tribe lived in the Rocky Mountains. As a young girl, Sacagawea had been captured in a raid and taken east. For her, the expedition meant the possibility of being reunited with her people.

Ask your child to tell you about "Sacagawea's Journey" and the many ways in which Sacagawea helped the explorers. Have your child make a list of the contributions that Sacagawea made to the expedition.

Encourage your child to compare this list with the lists of classmates.

Next week's selection ***Buffalo Hunt***

Your child will be studying the following vocabulary words in the upcoming week. Please review the meanings of these words with your child: **legendary**—told about in a legend or story; **roamed**—wandered; **preserve**—to prepare food so that it can be eaten in the future; **ceremonial**—related to a ceremony or formal celebration; **sufficient**—enough; **slaughter**—killing of large numbers of animals.

Please review with your child the spelling words for the upcoming week: mistook, dislike, disagree, mistreat, disloyal, discover, misspell, disgrace, mislaid, misprint, displease, disconnect, mislead, misjudge, distrust, distance, distinct, disappear, disturb, and discuss.

Home Connection · *Going West* Unit 5 · Lesson 1 63

***Home Connection* p. 63**

Teacher Tip VOCABULARY Encourage students to use the vocabulary words in their own sentences. You might also have students offer synonyms and antonyms for appropriate words.

Differentiating Instruction

If...	Then...
Students would benefit from repeated readings of "Sacagawea's Journey" or the Intervention Selections	Use ***Intervention Guide,*** page 238

Teacher Tip DRAWING CONCLUSIONS You might also consult the Clues, Problems, and Wonderings Transparency to come up with additional topics for drawing conclusions.

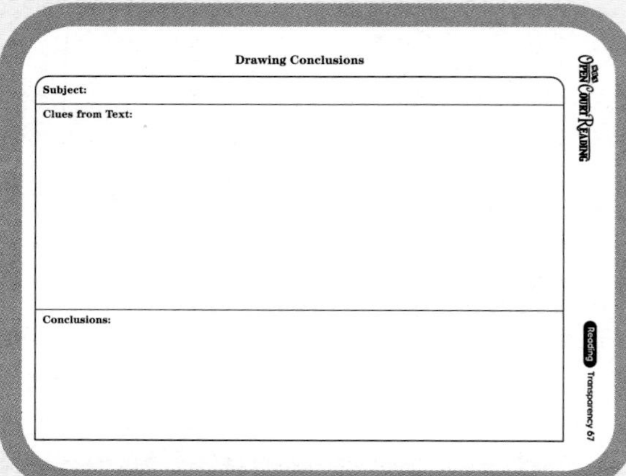

Reading Transparency 67

Supporting the Reading

Comprehension Skills: Drawing Conclusions

Teach Explain to students that as they read, they should gather information about how characters act, what they say, and when and where the story takes place, and what happens. They can put this information together to draw conclusions or make statements, about characters, events, and settings. Explain that conclusions are not directly stated in a text, but they are supported by details from the text. Emphasize that drawing conclusions allows readers to better understand characters and their motivations, as well as events and circumstances, in a text.

Guided Practice Use the graphic organizer on ***Reading Transparency 67*** to help students organize the information needed to draw conclusions. Invite students to list several characters, events, and topics from the text. *(Students might suggest things like Sacagawea, Captain Clark or Captain Lewis, exploring the American West, the flash flood, or arriving in Shoshone country.)* Choose one or two suggestions to draw conclusions about. Write the character, event, or topic in the first row of the chart. Then, ask students to provide clues from the text about the subject. List these in the second row of the transparency. *(Students might list clues about Sacagawea, for example, such as "Sacagawea stuffed a little more soft, dry grass into Pompey's cradleboard, put the child into it, and tied the rawhide thongs,"* from page 390, *and "Each evening Sacagawea huddled close to the fire, protecting Pompey from the mosquitoes and gnats that swarmed around his head,"* from pages 402–403.) Finally, discuss as a class the conclusions that can be drawn based on the clues listed. *(For example, a conclusion that could be drawn from the clues listed above is that despite her other duties as a member of the Corps of Discovery, one of Sacagawea's main concerns was the safety and comfort of her son. Students might conclude that Sacagawea was a good parent.)* Have students support their conclusions by identifying the clues from the text they used to draw them. List students' conclusions in the third row of the transparency. You may want to link the conclusions to the clues that support them by connecting them with lines or arrows on the transparency, or by giving each clue a number that can be listed after each conclusion it supports.

Independent Practice Read the **Focus** and **Identify** sections of the ***Comprehension and Language Arts Skills,*** page 142 with students. Guide students through the **Identify** portion, and help them come up with support from the story. Then have students complete the **Practice** and **Apply** portions of the ***Comprehension and Language Arts Skills,*** page 143 as homework.

Link to Writing Explain to students that when responding to literature in an essay, they will need to draw conclusions and make a statement about the literature or a character, event, or setting from it. In order to write a good essay, they will need to support their conclusions with clues from the text. Have students choose a selection to write about. They should draw a specific conclusion, state it, and support it with clues from the text.

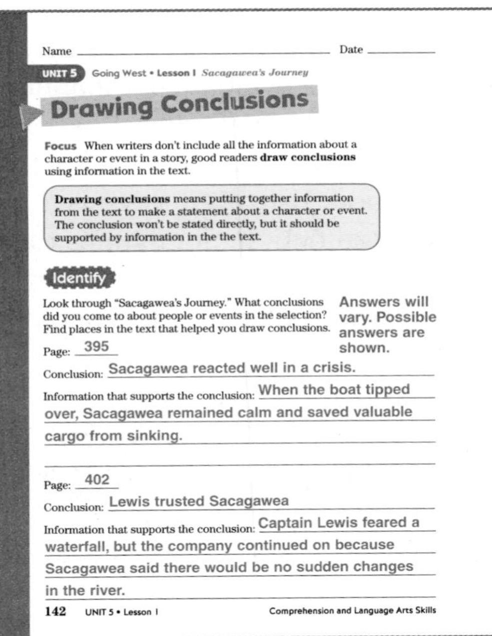

Name ________________________ Date ____________

UNIT 5 Going West • **Lesson 1** *Sacagawea's Journey*

Drawing Conclusions

Focus When writers don't include all the information about a character or event in a story, good readers **draw conclusions** using information in the text.

Drawing conclusions means putting together information from the text to make a statement about a character or event. The conclusion won't be stated directly, but it should be supported by information in the the text.

Identify

Look through "Sacagawea's Journey." What conclusions did you come to about people or events in the selection? Find places in the text that helped you draw conclusions. Answers will vary. Possible answers are shown.

Page: 395

Conclusion: Sacagawea reacted well in a crisis.

Information that supports the conclusion: When the boat tipped over, Sacagawea remained calm and saved valuable cargo from sinking.

Page: 402

Conclusion: Lewis trusted Sacagawea

Information that supports the conclusion: Captain Lewis feared a waterfall, but the company continued on because Sacagawea said there would be no sudden changes in the river.

142 UNIT 5 • Lesson 1 Comprehension and Language Arts Skills

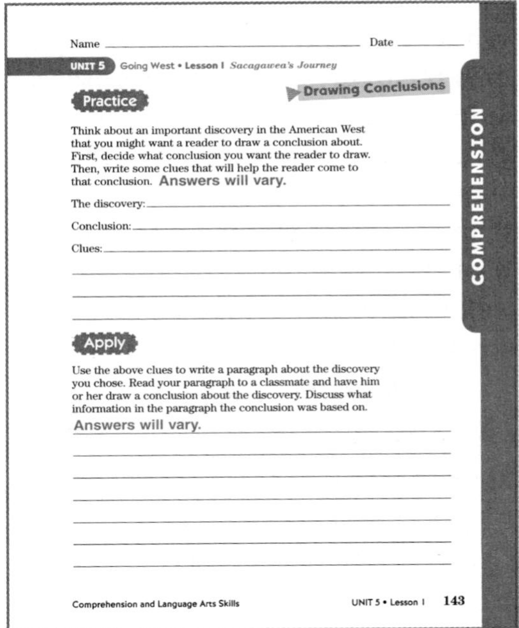

Name ________________________ Date ____________

UNIT 5 Going West • **Lesson 1** *Sacagawea's Journey*

Drawing Conclusions

Practice

Think about an important discovery in the American West that you might want a reader to draw a conclusion about. First, decide what conclusion you want the reader to draw. Then, write some clues that will help the reader come to that conclusion. Answers will vary.

The discovery: ____________

Conclusion: ____________

Clues: ____________

Apply

Use the above clues to write a paragraph about the discovery you chose. Read your paragraph to a classmate and have him or her draw a conclusion about the discovery. Discuss what information in the paragraph the conclusion was based on.

Answers will vary.

Comprehension and Language Arts Skills UNIT 5 • Lesson 1 143

COMPREHENSION

Comprehension and Language Arts Skills pp. 142–143

Differentiating Instruction

If...	Then...
Students need extra help with Drawing Conclusions	• Use ***Reteach,*** pages 140–141 • Use ***English Learner Support Guide,*** pages 362–377
Students would enjoy a challenge with Drawing Conclusions	Use ***Challenge,*** page 124

Drawing Conclusions

Introduced in Grade 1.
Scaffolded throughout Grades 2–5.

REINTRODUCED: Unit 1, Lesson 1
REINFORCED: Unit 2, Lesson 1
Unit 3, Lesson 3
Unit 3, Lesson 5
Unit 4, Lesson 5
TESTED: Unit 5 Assessment

Professional Development

Teacher Resource Library CD-ROMs or ***Online Professional Development*** provides courses that help you better understand the Comprehension/Knowledge Building instruction in ***Open Court Reading.*** For more information about this program, visit SRAonline.com.

Teacher Tip AUTHOR'S PERSPECTIVE Have students think of ways that they incorporate their own viewpoints into their writing, even when they are writing about a factual subject.

Literary Elements

Author's Perspective

Teach Remind students that "Sacagawea's Journey" is a biographical account of Sacagawea's experiences with the Lewis and Clark Expedition. Point out that biographies are based on facts, and the characters in the story were real people. Sacagawea's shared journey with Lewis and Clark was an actual historical event that helped expand the geographical boundaries of our country's early westward movement.

Explain that authors sometimes allow their own opinions about the people or events they are writing about to slip into their writings. This is true even for authors of nonfiction. For example, if the author thinks highly of the person he or she is writing about, the author will be more likely to include facts that put the person in a positive light or to interpret negative events in a sympathetic manner. Often authors make inferences about how their subjects felt or thought. It is possible that the author guessed correctly, if these inferences are based on fact and considered within the context of the historical period. However, there is a fine line between making inferences and turning fact into fiction. Sometimes the author assigns feelings or thoughts that probably did not occur to the character for the sake of making a story seem more exciting or interesting. Readers should take steps to evaluate whether or not the information they read is factual.

Guided Practice Have students recall the Unit 4 selection "The Midnight Ride of Paul Revere." Have students tell how Henry Wadsworth Longfellow included facts, opinions, inferences, and fiction in his famous poem about the historical event. Discuss with them how cross-referencing the story with the Historical Note helped them to know what in the story was fact and what was fiction.

Independent Practice Have students skim "Sacagawea's Journey." First have them state what they think the author's perspective on Sacagawea is *(she thinks Sacagawea is heroic)*. Have students cite information from the text that supports this conclusion. Then have them cite statements of fact, opinion, inference, and fiction from the text. If students have difficulty, refer them to the last paragraph of the selection. They should see that the author has no way of knowing what emotions Sacagawea felt at this moment. Encourage students to cross-reference this selection with other pieces about Sacagawea to help them determine whether this characterization of Sacagawea is mostly fiction or inference supported by fact.

Social Studies Connection: Mapping the Frontier

Explain to students that maps of early 1800s America are very different from contemporary maps of the United States. Divide students into groups, and distribute a blank map to each group. Tell students that they will be making maps of what the United States looked like at the time of the Lewis and Clark expedition. Explain that students will need to map both the states and the territories. Then students will need to map the expedition of Lewis and Clark, highlighting the geographical features they encountered, such as mountains, rivers, plains, and so on. Students should search the library and the Internet if they need information on which to base their maps. When students have completed the project, display the maps in the classroom. They might refer to these maps later to compare and contrast the country at different times in history.

Teacher Tip **MATERIALS** To complete this activity, students will need the following materials: blank maps of the United States, posterboard, markers, pencils, and library sources.

Science/Social Studies Connection Center

Refer to the ***Science/Social Studies Connection Center Cards*** 64–66 for social studies activities that students can investigate.

Concept Connections

Linking the Selection

- She gathered food, sewed buckskins, and guided the team by identifying landmarks.
- They used their memories of rivers from maps drawn by Hidatsa warriors.
- She was saddened by painful memories but joyful about seeing her homeland.

Exploring Concept Vocabulary

The concept word for this lesson is ***expedition.*** Write the word on the board. Work with the students to develop a definition that clearly links to the unit theme. Have students copy the words and definitions into the Vocabulary section of their Writer's Notebooks.

Expedition: a journey made for a specific purpose, such as exploration. For example, Meriwether Lewis and William Clark led the expedition to explore the new Louisiana Territory.

- Expeditions involve a variety of tasks, such as leading, navigating, translating, hunting, cooking, and entertaining.
- Timing was important because weather changes affected the ability to travel.

The students' sentences should show an understanding of both vocabulary words.

Expanding the Concept

Have students carry on dialogues in small groups. After the small-group discussions, bring students together to share their ideas with the whole class.

As students complete their discussion, have them record their ideas about the selection on page 113 of their ***Inquiry Journal.***

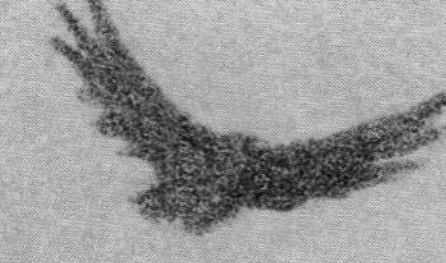

Sacagawea's Journey

Concept Connections

Linking the Selection

Think about the following questions, and then record your responses in the Response Journal section of your Writer's Notebook.

- In what ways was Sacagawea an important member of the Corps of Discovery?
- How did Lewis and Clark make sure they were staying on the right track?
- What emotions did Sacagawea feel upon returning to the land of the Shoshone?

Exploring Concept Vocabulary

The concept word for this lesson is ***expedition.*** If you do not know what this word means, look it up in a dictionary. Answer these questions.

- Why is it important for members of an ***expedition*** to have different skills?
- Why was timing critical to the success of Lewis and Clark's ***expedition?***

Make up an oral sentence that includes the word ***expedition*** and a word from the selection vocabulary.

Expanding the Concept

Discuss whether Sacagawea wanted to take the journey with Lewis and Clark. Consider her age, her background, and the fact that she had a baby when deciding. Try to use the word ***expedition*** in your discussion. Add new ideas about the American West to the Concept/Question Board.

404

Teacher Tip **INQUIRY AND INVESTIGATION** Have groups report and discuss their ideas with the class. As these ideas are stated, have students add them to the Concept/Question Board. As students complete their discussions, have them sum up what they have learned and tell how they might use this information in further investigations.

Informal Assessment

This may be a good time to observe students working in small groups and to mark your observations in the Teacher Observation Log found in the ***Program Assessment Teacher's Edition.***

Meet the Author

Betty Westrom Skold's four-and-a-half year battle with tuberculosis made her childhood dream of becoming a teacher impossible. During her sickness, however, she spent a lot of time reading and writing. So, she became a writer on a small town newspaper instead.

Skold met an educational publisher who asked her to write a children's biography of Sacagawea. It became her first book as a professional writer. Today, Skold writes for a variety of age groups and tries new kinds of writing all the time. She has been a journalist, a poet, an essayist, a biographer, and a fiction writer.

Meet the Illustrator

Craig Spearing has a degree in illustration and printmaking. The first trade book he illustrated was *Prairie Dog Pioneers* by Jo and Josephine Harper. Since, he has created many illustrations for children's educational books and magazines.

His father was a geologist and his mother was a historian. He admires that his father was an eternal "Boy Scout" and his mother always valued careful research. He says that both his parents played an important part in shaping the way he does illustrations.

405

Meet the Author

After the students read the information about Betty Westrom Skold, discuss the following questions with them.

- Betty Westrom Skold has been a journalist, a poet, an essayist, a biographer, and a fiction writer. What qualities might a person need to have to be able to write in so many different genres? *(Possible answer: One would have to be a very good communicator, and also be very imaginative.)*
- *Sacagawea: The Story of an American Indian* was Betty Westrom Skold's first story as a professional writer. Why do you think she and her publisher thought this was an important story for her to tell? *(Possible answer: This might have been because many people may have heard about the Lewis and Clark Expedition, and never known the important role Sacagawea played in making that expedition successful.)*

Meet the Illustrator

After students read the information about Craig Spearing, discuss the following question with them.

- Craig Spearing says that his illustrations reflect his father's and mother's influence. How do you think this has benefited his work? *(Possible answer: It has given him the ability to reflect the positive side of life and to pay attention to details.)*

Teacher Tip REALISTIC EXPERIENCES Invite students to think of ways to incorporate realistic experiences into their diary entries.

Objectives

- Students gain a deeper understanding of the American West.
- Students come up with questions that they would like to investigate about the American West.
- Students participate in investigation activities.
- Students read maps and use them to represent information.

Materials

- Student Anthology, pp. 390–405
- Inquiry Journal, pp. 116–121
- Research Assistant
- Reading Transparency 40

Differentiating Instruction

If...	Then...
Students are having difficulty with their Inquiry activities	Encourage them to consider using unanswered questions that came up while reading this lesson's ***Student Anthology*** selection to inspire investigation topics

INVESTIGATION

Investigating Concepts Beyond the Text

To facilitate students' investigation of the American West, you might have them participate in the following activities. Tell students that if they have activity ideas of their own that they would like to pursue, they are free to do so as an alternative to these activity suggestions. Tell students that they may work on these activities alone, in pairs, or in small groups, with an option to write about them or to present them to the group upon completion.

The activity suggestions for this lesson are:

- Many changes occurred as the American West was being settled. Tell the students that as they read the selections in the unit and begin their investigation they will record these changes in their ***Inquiry Journals,*** pages 116–117. Encourage students to think about and list reasons for these changes and the effects each had on the lives of the inhabitants of the region. Provide time for students to share their findings with their classmates.
- If possible, obtain and display a relief map of the United States to help students better understand the geography of the American West. Then, have students collaboratively work on ***Inquiry Journal,*** pages 118–119, to record the geography of the American West. Encourage students to use outside resources when completing this activity. Provide time for students to share the results of their work.

Upon completion of their activities, have students share with the group anything new they learned about the American West through discussion and by adding information to the Concept/Question Board.

Name ______________________ Date __________

UNIT 5 Going West

Changes in the American West

Many changes occurred as the American West was being settled. Throughout your reading and investigation for this unit, record these changes on the chart. For each change, list the causes, the groups involved, and the effects on the people of the region. Answers will vary.

Change	Causes

116 UNIT 5 *Changes in the American West* • Inquiry Journal

Inquiry Journal p. 116

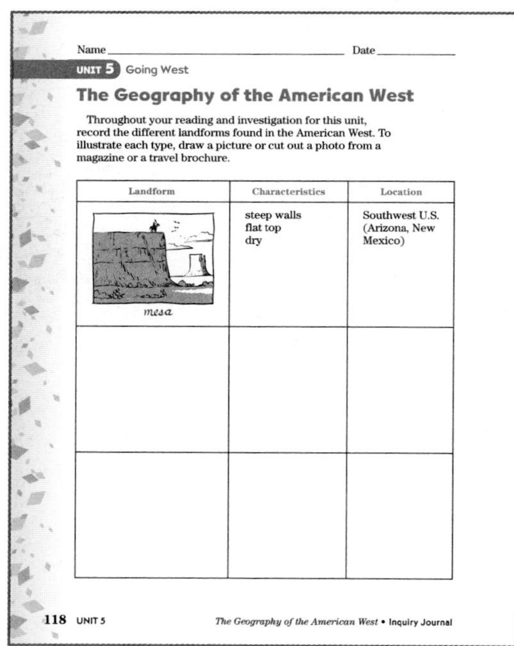

Name ______________________ Date __________

UNIT 5 Going West

The Geography of the American West

Throughout your reading and investigation for this unit, record the different landforms found in the American West. To illustrate each type, draw a picture or cut out a photo from a magazine or a travel brochure.

Landform	Characteristics	Location
mesa	steep walls flat top dry	Southwest U.S. (Arizona, New Mexico)

118 UNIT 5 *The Geography of the American West* • Inquiry Journal

Inquiry Journal p. 118

Concept/Question Board

After reading each selection, students should use the Concept/Question Board to

- post any questions they asked about a selection before reading that have not yet been answered.
- refer to as they formulate statements about concepts that apply to their investigations.
- post general statements formulated by each collaborative group.
- continue to post news articles, or other items that they find during the unit investigation.
- read and think about posted questions, articles, or concepts that interest them and provide answers to the questions.

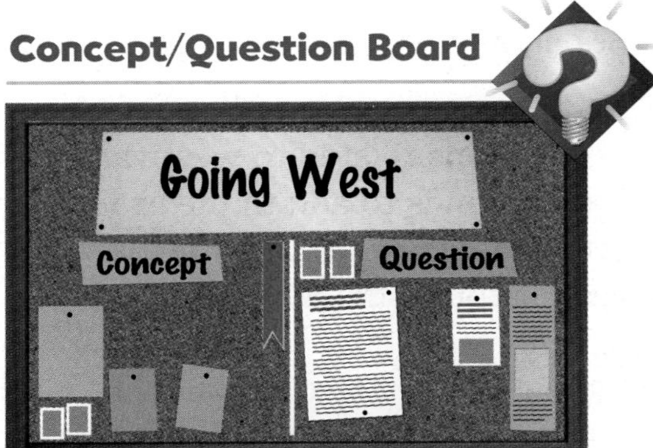

Unit 5 Research Management

Lesson 1	Collaborative Investigation **Students generate questions and ideas for investigation.** Supplementary Activities **Students participate in investigation activities and learn to use maps.**
Lesson 2	Students formulate questions and problems for investigation.
Lesson 3	Students make conjectures.
Lesson 4	Students establish investigation needs.
Lesson 5	Students establish investigation plans.
Lesson 6	Students continue investigation and get feedback from other groups.
Lesson 7	Students present their investigation findings to the class.

INVESTIGATION

www.sra4kids.com
Web Connection
Students can use the connections to Going West in the Reading link of the SRA Web page for more background information about Going West.

Research Assistant

The Research Assistant helps students in their investigations.

Teacher Tip ULTIMATE WRITING AND CREATIVITY CENTER Have students use the ***Ultimate Writing and Creativity Center CD-ROM*** as they work on their investigation activities.

OPEN COURT READING Reading Transparency 40

Unit 5 Investigation Possibilities

- **A retelling** of a Native American legend.
- **An illustrated time line** of events in western expansion from the early to late 1800s.
- **An original monologue** from the perspective of a frontier person that tells about a day in his or her life. The monologue should contain facts about frontier life.
- **An Internet search** for information about the Hispanic influence on the culture of the American West. Findings could be illustrated and posted in a scrapbook.
- **An original tall tale** based on research of the American West.
- **A photo essay** about immigrants from different cultures who went to the American West to make their fortunes.
- **A library search** for books about Native American communities of the Northwest, Southwest, and Plains regions.

Reading Transparency 40

Teacher Tip INVESTIGATION ACTIVITIES Continue to guide students' ideas toward explorable questions rather than general topics. You might model this concept to help students understand. For example, *"The American Frontier" is a topic. "How did expansion of the settlements affect Native Americans?" is an explorable question.*

Formal Assessment

Use the Research Rubrics on page 390J to assess students' ability to formulate research questions and problems.

Name ______ Date ______

UNIT 5 Going West

Ideas about Going West

Of the ideas discussed in class about the American West, these are the ones I found most interesting.

Answers will vary.

120 UNIT 5 *Ideas about Going West* • Inquiry Journal

Inquiry Journal p. 120

INVESTIGATION

Generating Ideas to Investigate

During the course of this unit, students will be investigating westward expansion. You will be guiding them through the investigation process by having them

- generate ideas to investigate.
- formulate questions and problems from their ideas.
- make conjectures as to how they might solve their problems or answer their questions.
- establish their investigation needs.
- establish their investigation plans.
- present their findings visually and/or orally to the group.

As students progress through this investigation process, emphasize that they can use the steps of this process to investigate anything they want to know more about, whether it is related to school or to personal interests.

Tell students that they will be performing an investigation of problems and questions related to westward expansion and that the purpose of their investigation is to add to the group's knowledge of the unit theme. They will frame questions about an important idea, issue, or event to direct the investigation, establish a controlling idea or topic, and develop the topic with simple facts, details, examples, and explanations. Explain to the students that the type of investigation they will conduct will take several weeks and will require them to make important decisions about managing their time. They are free to decide what it is about westward expansion they want to investigate and with whom they want to work. At the end of the time allotted to this unit, they will present their investigation findings to the group. Display the menu of Investigation Possibilities on ***Reading Transparency 40.*** Tell students that these are all ideas for how they might publish their investigation findings. Tell students that these ideas are options; students are also encouraged to come up with their own ideas for publishing their findings.

Have students begin the investigation process by brainstorming problems or questions related to the concepts of westward expansion. Have students examine the questions they raised during discussion of the anthology selection, their ideas about westward expansion posted on the Concept/Question Board, and anything they learned from the activities in Investigating the Concepts Beyond the Text. Conduct a free-floating discussion of aspects of westward expansion that interest the students. Then have students list the ideas they found most interesting on ***Inquiry Journal,*** page 120.

Professional Development

Teacher Resource Library CD-ROMs or ***Online Professional Development*** provides courses that help you better understand the Inquiry and Investigation instruction in ***Open Court Reading.*** For more information about this program, visit SRAonline.com.

SUPPORTING THE INVESTIGATION

Using Maps

Teach Ask students what they already know about using maps. Review the following features of maps, explaining them to students as necessary: *legend; scale; directions* (compass); *place names; physical features* (bodies of water, mountains, and so on); *historic information;* and *borders.*

Guided Practice Have students define and point out examples of each feature mentioned above on several different kinds of maps. Have students share how maps have made information more accessible and usable for them.

Independent Practice Have encyclopedias, nonfiction books, a social studies textbook, or the information in "Sacagawea's Journey" available to find information on the Lewis and Clark Expedition's route west. Then have students complete ***Inquiry Journal,*** page 121.

Teacher Tip USING MAPS
Encourage students to use maps to help clarify and illustrate their unit activities.

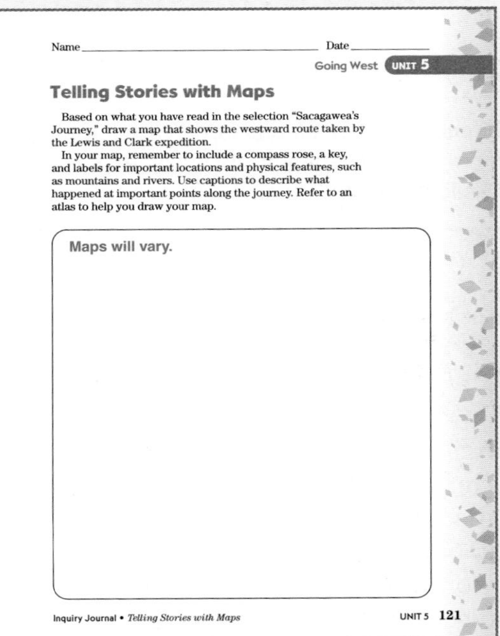

Name____________________ Date__________

Going West UNIT 5

Telling Stories with Maps

Based on what you have read in the selection "Sacagawea's Journey," draw a map that shows the westward route taken by the Lewis and Clark expedition.

In your map, remember to include a compass rose, a key, and labels for important locations and physical features, such as mountains and rivers. Use captions to describe what happened at important points along the journey. Refer to an atlas to help you draw your map.

Maps will vary.

Inquiry Journal • *Telling Stories with Maps* UNIT 5 121

Inquiry Journal p. 121

Objectives

Word Analysis

Spelling

- **Spelling Patterns for Homophones.** Develop understanding of spelling patterns for homophones introduced in Word Knowledge in Part 1.

Vocabulary

- Using words from "Sacagawea's Journey," reinforce the idea of concept words.

Writing Process Strategies

- **Personal Writing.** Students learn a variety of personal writing techniques including those needed for a dialogue journal, a learning log, and a literature response.

English Language Conventions

Grammar and Usage

- **Usage.** Understand proper sentence structure and identify it in "Sacagawea's Journey."

Listening, Speaking, Viewing

- **Listening: Drawing Conclusions and Making Inferences.** Draw conclusions and make inferences from oral reports.

Penmanship

- **Joining With *A* and *d*.** Review handwriting skills by practicing joining letters with *A* and *d*.

Materials

- Spelling and Vocabulary Skills, pp. 106–109
- Language Arts Handbook
- Comprehension and Language Arts Skills, pp. 144–145
- Writer's Workbook, pp. 78–81
- Student Anthology
- Unit 5 Assessment, pp. 30–31

Differentiating Instruction

Reteach, Challenge, and ***Intervention*** lessons are available to support the language arts instruction in this lesson.

Research in Action

A speller without a fully functional visual coding mechanism can learn the correct spelling of an unfamiliar word . . . then not think about or have occasion to write the word for three or four weeks, and discover that he or she has forgotten how to spell it. (*J. Richard Gentry and Jean Wallace Gillet,* Teaching Kids to Spell)

OVERVIEW

Language Arts Overview

Word Analysis

Spelling The spelling activities on the following pages support the Word Knowledge introduction of homophones by developing understanding of the spellings for homophones.

Selection Spelling Words

These words from "Sacagawea's Journey" are homophones.

plain **plane** **waist** **waste** **heard**

Vocabulary The vocabulary activities once again challenge students to discover the meanings of concept words found in the reading selection.

Vocabulary Skill Words

keelboat **pirogues** **portage*** **rudder** **shoals**

**Also Selection Vocabulary.*

Additional Materials On Day 3, students will need dictionaries.

Writing Process Strategies

This lesson involves instruction in personal writing techniques that do not require the use of all five steps in the writing process.

To help students identify the Internet as a source of information for writing, have students review Web basics, search the World Wide Web, and compare various Web search engines. You might want to help students research ideas for their writing assignment by using different search engines to find different Web pages. ***TechKnowledge*** Level 5 Lessons 85–87 teach these Internet reference skills.

Professional Development

Teacher Resource Library CD-ROMs or ***Online Professional Development*** provides courses that help you better understand the Writing instruction in ***Open Court Reading.*** For more information about this program, visit SRAonline.com.

English Language Conventions

Grammar and Usage **Sentence Fragments.** This lesson develops understanding of proper sentence structure.

Listening, Speaking, Viewing **Listening: Drawing Conclusions and Making Inferences.** The Listening, Speaking, Viewing lessons are divided into six categories: Listening, Speaking, Language, Viewing, Interacting, and Presenting. In this Listening lesson, students draw conclusions and make inferences from oral reports.

Penmanship **Joining with *A* and *d*.** This lesson continues the development of handwriting skills. Students join letters with *A* and *d* and then write paragraphs from the literature, focusing on joining letters.

DAY 1

Word Analysis

Spelling

Assessment: Pretest

Spelling Patterns for Homophones

Give students the Pretest on page 30 of ***Unit 5 Assessment.*** Have them proofread and correct any misspellings.

Pretest Sentences

1. **tied** Gifts are sometimes **tied** with fancy ribbon.
2. **tide** It is dangerous to swim in the ocean when the **tide** is going out.
3. **stake** To grow a tomato plant, you must place a **stake** next to the vine.
4. **steak** Most of the **steak** you eat probably comes from a steer.
5. **hymn** *The Battle **Hymn** of the Republic* is a popular song.
6. **horse** A **horse** can weigh more than one thousand pounds.
7. **hoarse** A cup of tea might help if you become **hoarse.**
8. **throne** Kings and queens were often painted sitting on a **throne.**
9. **thrown** Has the first pitch been **thrown** at the baseball game?
10. **sweet** Certain taste buds taste **sweet** flavors.
11. **suite** A hotel **suite** has rooms connected by inner doors.
12. **brake** A car has a **brake** on every wheel.
13. **break** If a satellite falls into the atmosphere, it may **break** apart.
14. **reel** A deep-sea fisherman needs an especially large **reel.**
15. **real** An illusion is something that is not **real.**
16. **plain** You can have a sesame bagel or a **plain** bagel for breakfast.
17. **plane** Chuck Yeager flew a **plane** faster than the speed of sound.
18. **waist** She tied a scarf around her **waist.**
19. **waste** You shouldn't **waste** time.
20. **heard** Have you **heard** the story of Little Red Riding Hood?

Writing Process Strategies

Teach

Introduce the Writing Form

- Read ***Language Arts Handbook*** pages 68–69 for the unit introduction to personal writing and pages 70–75 on journals.
- Tell students that there are some times when they will not use every step in the writing process. Much of the personal writing that students do will be for their eyes only and will not require formal drafting, revising, and editing/proofreading stages.
- Explain to students that a dialogue journal is simply two people writing back and forth as if they were having a conversation, or dialogue.
- **Teacher Model** writing a journal entry response to "Sacagawea's Journey." Choose an aspect of the story that interests you. An example might be to explore what it might have been like to be a young mother leading an expedition.

Independent Practice

- Have students choose a topic or focus for their responses to your entry about "Sacagawea's Journey." This focus should stem directly from the journal entry that you wrote.
- Have students complete a journal entry to submit to you.

Language Arts Handbook p. 70

English Language Conventions

Grammar and Usage

Fragments

Teach

- Use ***Language Arts Handbook*** page 360 for examples of fragments and complete sentences.
- Remind students that a fragment is a group of words that is only a piece, or a fragment, of a complete sentence.
- Sometimes, students will punctuate a fragment as if it were a complete sentence. Three common ways this error occurs are as follows:
  - a group of words without a subject. *drove 300 miles.*
  - a group of words without a complete predicate, especially a group that contains a verb or verb phrase. *my youngest sister* or *my youngest sister running in the race.*
  - a subordinate clause. *if my cat gets the yarn.*

Independent Practice

Use ***Comprehension and Language Arts Skills*** pages 144–145 to practice identification and capitalization of complete sentences.

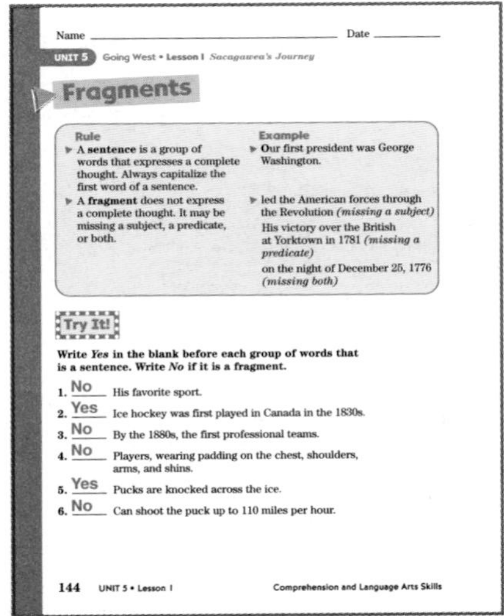

Name ______________________ Date __________

UNIT 5 Going West • Lesson 1 *Sacagawea's Journey*

Fragments

Rule	Example
A **sentence** is a group of words that expresses a complete thought. Always capitalize the first word of a sentence.	Our first president was George Washington.
A **fragment** does not express a complete thought. It may be missing a subject, a predicate, or both.	led the American forces through the Revolution *(missing a subject)* His victory over the British at Yorktown in 1781 *(missing a predicate)* on the night of December 25, 1776 *(missing both)*

Try It!

Write *Yes* in the blank before each group of words that is a sentence. Write *No* if it is a fragment.

1. No His favorite sport.
2. Yes Ice hockey was first played in Canada in the 1830s.
3. No By the 1880s, the first professional teams.
4. No Players, wearing padding on the chest, shoulders, arms, and shins.
5. Yes Pucks are knocked across the ice.
6. No Can shoot the puck up to 110 miles per hour.

144 UNIT 5 • Lesson 1 Comprehension and Language Arts Skills

Comprehension and Language Arts Skills p. 144

DAY 2

Word Analysis

Spelling

Homophones

As a class or in groups, have students examine the homophone pairs among the spelling words. Students should note the differences in spelling and recite the definitions for each word.

Vocabulary

Concept Words

Teach

- Tell students that the reading selection in this lesson will contain specific words related to the American frontier.
- As a class or in groups, have students come up with their own lists of concept words related to the Unit 5 theme of Going West. Students may want to use word mapping to arrange their words. Possible words include *cowboy*, *Native American*, *stagecoach*, *Gold Rush*, *miner*, *railroad*, *settlers*, *claims*, *California*, *rancher*, *covered wagon*, and *rodeo*.

Guided Practice

Assign page 106 of ***Spelling and Vocabulary Skills.*** Students can complete page 107 of ***Spelling and Vocabulary Skills*** for homework.

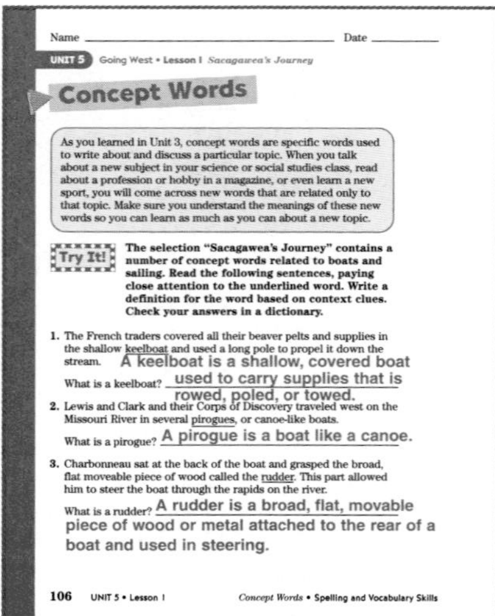

Name ______________________ Date __________

UNIT 5 Going West • Lesson 1 *Sacagawea's Journey*

Concept Words

As you learned in Unit 3, concept words are specific words used to write about and discuss a particular topic. When you talk about a new subject in your science or social studies class, read about a profession or hobby in a magazine, or even learn a new sport, you will come across new words that are related only to that topic. Make sure you understand the meanings of these new words so you can learn as much as you can about a new topic.

Try It! **The selection "Sacagawea's Journey" contains a number of concept words related to boats and sailing. Read the following sentences, paying close attention to the underlined word. Write a definition for the word based on context clues. Check your answers in a dictionary.**

1. The French traders covered all their beaver pelts and supplies in the shallow keelboat and used a long pole to propel it down the stream.
   What is a keelboat? A keelboat is a shallow, covered boat used to carry supplies that is rowed, poled, or towed.
2. Lewis and Clark and their Corps of Discovery traveled west on the Missouri River in several pirogues, or canoe-like boats.
   What is a pirogue? A pirogue is a boat like a canoe.
3. Charbonneau sat at the back of the boat and grasped the broad, flat moveable piece of wood called the rudder. This part allowed him to steer the boat through the rapids on the river.
   What is a rudder? A rudder is a broad, flat, movable piece of wood or metal attached to the rear of a boat and used in steering.

106 UNIT 5 • Lesson 1 *Concept Words* • Spelling and Vocabulary Skills

***Spelling and Vocabulary Skills* p. 106**

Writing Process Strategies

Teach

Tell students that a dialogue journal can continue for any length of time; it might be a week, a semester, or a year. The journal you are sharing will require them to respond once more to your last entry.

Independent Practice

Return students' journal entries from Day 1 along with your response to their entries. Have them complete a second journal entry in response to yours. Have them use ***Writer's Workbook,*** page 78, for guidance. Have students refer to their dialogue journals for writing project ideas.

Formal Assessment

Total Point Value: 10

1. The content of the dialogue entry is suitable for the reader/audience. (2 points)
2. The purpose of the entry is clearly stated. (2 points)
3. The sentences are complete. There are no fragments. (2 points)
4. Students responded to your entries in a thoughtful manner. (1 point)
5. The handwriting is legible. (1 point)
6. The entry relates to "Sacagawea's Journey." (1 point)
7. The entry submitted to you looks edited. (1 point)

Name ______________________ Date __________

UNIT 5 Going West • Lesson 1 *Sacagawea's Journey*

Writing a Dialogue Journal Response

Objective: Students plan to write a dialogue journal entry.

Write a dialogue journal entry to record your response to your teacher's journal entry.

Write some ideas you can use in your dialogue journal response. You might want to tell about
- **how you agree or disagree with specific points**
- **how you feel about your teacher's response**
- **meanings you understood from the original literature selection**

Have students write ideas. These do not need to be in complete sentences.

Did your teacher's dialogue journal entry make you think of any questions for him or her? If so, write them below.

Write any other ideas about the original reading selection that you want to talk about.

- **Using your ideas from above, write your response to your teacher's journal entry on a separate sheet of paper.**
- **When you have finished, check your entry. Make sure there are no mistakes. Make sure your entry tells all your ideas.**

78 UNIT 5 • Lesson 1 *Writing a Dialogue Journal Response* • Writer's Workbook

***Writer's Workbook* p. 78**

English Language Conventions

Grammar and Usage

Fragments

Teach

- Review fragments and the capitalization of the first word of a complete sentence.
- Explain that fragments appear in stories, novels, and plays because they reflect normal conversation or are included intentionally for effect. In works such as essays and reports, however, care should be taken to use only complete sentences.
- Write these words on the board. Have students tell whether the word groups are complete sentences.
  - Occur in several places. (fragment)
  - A meeting is scheduled for today. (complete)
  - The doctor was late. (complete)
  - Two related statements. (fragment)
  - When you are finished with the test. (fragment)
  - Please pass the potatoes. (complete)

Guided Practice in Reading

Have students look for fragments in a previously read selection (there are none in "Sacagawea's Journey.") Choose a selection that has dialogue, because there are often fragments in conversation.

DAY 3

Word Analysis

Spelling

Spelling Patterns for Homophones

Teach

Introduce the concept of homophones, or words that sound the same but are spelled differently and have different meanings. Tell students that they must memorize which spelling goes with which meaning. Challenge students to think of other homophones, spell them, and attach a different meaning to each one. For example, students might think of the words *weigh* and *way*. Ask them to spell and define each homophone.

Guided Practice

Have students complete page 108 from ***Spelling and Vocabulary Skills*** to practice identifying homophone pairs.

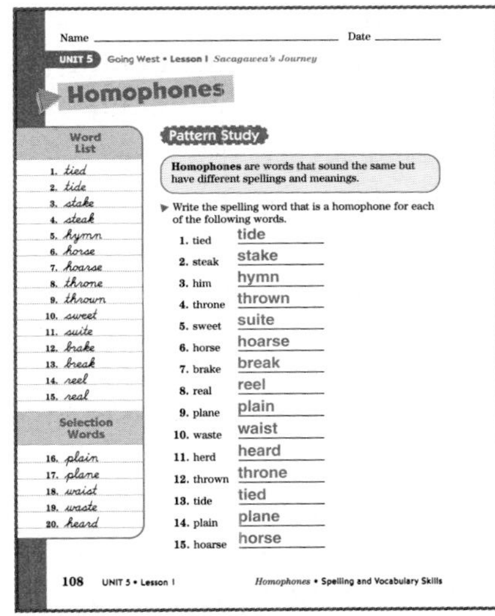
Name ______________ Date ________

UNIT 5 Going West • Lesson 1 *Sacagawea's Journey*

Homophones

Word List
1. tied
2. tide
3. stake
4. steak
5. hymn
6. horse
7. hoarse
8. throne
9. thrown
10. sweet
11. suite
12. brake
13. break
14. reel
15. real

Selection Words
16. plain
17. plane
18. waist
19. waste
20. heard

Pattern Study

Homophones are words that sound the same but have different spellings and meanings.

▶ Write the spelling word that is a homophone for each of the following words.

1. tied tide
2. steak stake
3. him hymn
4. throne thrown
5. sweet suite
6. horse hoarse
7. brake break
8. real reel
9. plane plain
10. waste waist
11. herd heard
12. thrown throne
13. tide tied
14. plain plane
15. hoarse horse

108 UNIT 5 • Lesson 1 *Homophones* • Spelling and Vocabulary Skills

Spelling and Vocabulary Skills p. 108

Vocabulary (continued)

Concept Words

Write several of the words about the American West generated on Day 2 on the board. As a class, discuss the meanings of some of these words. Students might want to clarify some meanings with a dictionary. Then have students use two of these words in a sentence.

Writing Process Strategies

Teach

Learning Log

- Explain that a learning log is where students can take notes. Let them know that they can write questions about what they have read, make a list of unfamiliar words, and record what they know and what they don't know about a subject. This is a good place for students to write summaries so they don't forget information. Learning logs also can be a good source for writing project ideas.

Brainstorming

Using the theme Going West as a springboard for ideas, encourage students to suggest ideas or details that they might use in a learning-log entry about "Sacagawea's Journey" or other literature selection. Students may also wish to write a learning-log entry about another school subject.

Independent Practice

Have students complete ***Writer's Workbook,*** page 79, on learning logs.

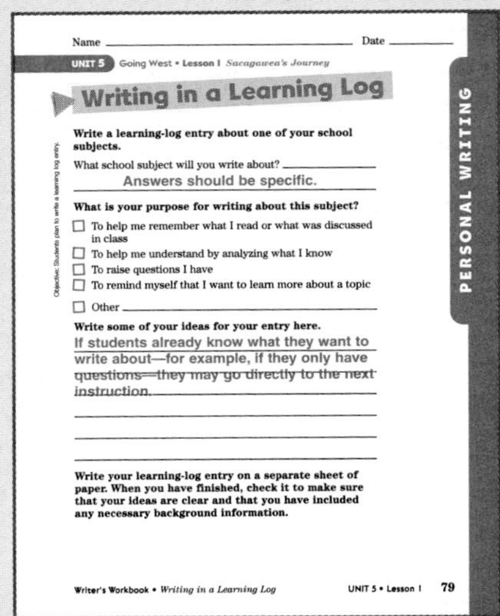
Name ______________ Date ________

UNIT 5 Going West • Lesson 1 *Sacagawea's Journey*

Writing in a Learning Log

PERSONAL WRITING

Objective: Students plan to write a learning log entry.

Write a learning-log entry about one of your school subjects.

What school subject will you write about? Answers should be specific.

What is your purpose for writing about this subject?

☐ To help me remember what I read or what was discussed in class
☐ To help me understand by analyzing what I know
☐ To raise questions I have
☐ To remind myself that I want to learn more about a topic
☐ Other ______________

Write some of your ideas for your entry here.

If students already know what they want to write about—for example, if they only have questions—they may go directly to the next instruction.

Write your learning-log entry on a separate sheet of paper. When you have finished, check it to make sure that your ideas are clear and that you have included any necessary background information.

Writer's Workbook • *Writing in a Learning Log* UNIT 5 • Lesson 1 79

Writer's Workbook p. 79

English Language Conventions

Grammar and Usage

Fragments

Teach

- Capitalize the first word of a complete sentence in personal writing.
- Explain that in writing dialogue, such expressions as *Hello* and *Good-bye*, although they do not contain a subject and a predicate, make clear statements and are acceptable.

Guided Practice in Writing

Have students choose several fragments they have found in a selection. Then, have them add words (a subject, a predicate, or both) to make them complete sentences. Remind students that checking for correct capitalization and complete sentence structure is an important part of proofreading their personal writing.

Informal Assessment

Make certain that the students are using only complete sentences in their writing. This is often a difficult concept for students to grasp, so be prepared for some possible conferencing on the topic to help students progress.

DAY 4

Word Analysis

Spelling

Spelling Patterns for Homophones

Teach

Remind students to keep working on memorizing the definitions of homophones. Model the meaning strategy exercise by writing this sentence on the board: *The baseball was ____ to home plate.* Ask students to fill in the blank with the correct homophone, *thrown.*

Guided Practice

Have students complete the Spelling Strategies exercises on page 109 of ***Spelling and Vocabulary Skills.***

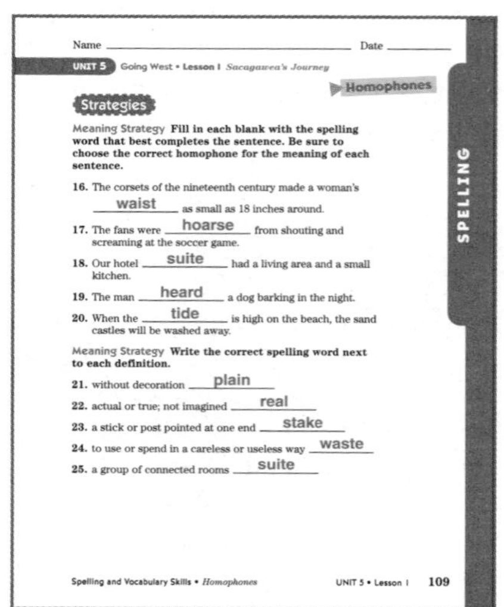
Name ______________ Date ________

UNIT 5 Going West • Lesson I *Sacagawea's Journey*

Homophones

Strategies

Meaning Strategy **Fill in each blank with the spelling word that best completes the sentence. Be sure to choose the correct homophone for the meaning of each sentence.**

16. The corsets of the nineteenth century made a woman's __waist__ as small as 18 inches around.
17. The fans were __hoarse__ from shouting and screaming at the soccer game.
18. Our hotel __suite__ had a living area and a small kitchen.
19. The man __heard__ a dog barking in the night.
20. When the __tide__ is high on the beach, the sand castles will be washed away.

Meaning Strategy **Write the correct spelling word next to each definition.**

21. without decoration __plain__
22. actual or true; not imagined __real__
23. a stick or post pointed at one end __stake__
24. to use or spend in a careless or useless way __waste__
25. a group of connected rooms __suite__

SPELLING

Spelling and Vocabulary Skills • *Homophones* UNIT 5 • Lesson I 109

***Spelling and Vocabulary Skills* p. 109**

Vocabulary (continued)

Concept Words

Divide students into groups of three or more and have them create a word map with *Native Americans* as the central word. Students may generate terms like *tipi, buffalo, squaw, chief, arrow, headdress, beads, moccasins,* and *totem poles.*

Writing Process Strategies

Teach

Learning Log

- Explain that when writing to learn, students should not try to show how well they write or how much they already know. The purpose is to write to learn more.
- A question box is one way students can learn about a subject. Let students know that they date each entry and then write the questions they have about the subject. Suggest that students give you their questions before or after class so you can respond to them at an appropriate time.

Independent Practice

Have students write question-box entries for their learning logs about any selection from the Going West unit on ***Writer's Workbook,*** page 80.

Formal Assessment

Total Point Value: 10

1. The questions in the journal relate to the selection. (3 points)
2. The sentences are complete. There are no fragments. (2 points)
3. The questions required thinking and learning on the part of the student. (3 points)
4. The entry is dated. (2 points)

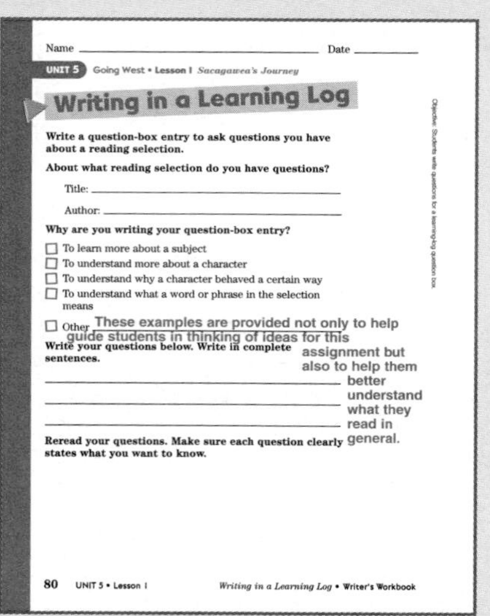
Name ______________ Date ________

UNIT 5 Going West • Lesson I *Sacagawea's Journey*

Writing in a Learning Log

Write a question-box entry to ask questions you have about a reading selection.

About what reading selection do you have questions?

Title: ______________

Author: ______________

Why are you writing your question-box entry?

- ☐ To learn more about a subject
- ☐ To understand more about a character
- ☐ To understand why a character behaved a certain way
- ☐ To understand what a word or phrase in the selection means
- ☐ Other ______________

These examples are provided not only to help guide students in thinking of ideas for this assignment but also to help them better understand what they read in general.

Write your questions below. Write in complete sentences.

____

____

____

Reread your questions. Make sure each question clearly states what you want to know.

Objective: Students write questions for a learning-log question box.

80 UNIT 5 • Lesson I *Writing in a Learning Log* • Writer's Workbook

***Writer's Workbook* p. 80**

English Language Conventions

Listening, Speaking, Viewing

Listening: Drawing Conclusions and Making Inferences

Teach

- Tell students that when listening to an oral presentation they should ask themselves these questions: *What is the main point or idea? How can I relate this information to my experiences or to what I know?*
- Remind students that they can help to understand the main points of any oral presentation by asking questions or by paraphrasing what is said in order to confirm their understanding.
- Emphasize to students that, in order to be able to draw conclusions and make inferences, it is essential that they pay careful attention to the speaker's message. It will help them to pay attention if they first establish their purpose for listening, or decide what it is they want to learn by listening.

Guided Practice

- Allow student volunteers to retell particular sections of "Sacagawea's Journey." Ask the class to share their conclusions about each retelling and to draw inferences relating the importance of this famous Shoshone woman to the expedition.
- Remind students to listen attentively for main ideas within each retelling, assessing how these ideas relate to what they know or what they have experienced. Have students share their purposes for listening and tell whether or not their inferences or conclusions related to what they wanted to learn.

Informal Assessment

Observe whether students can draw conclusions and make inferences from oral reports.

DAY 5

Word Analysis

Spelling

Assessment: Final Test

Spelling Patterns for Homophones

Teach

Repeat the Pretest for this lesson or use the Final Test on page 31 of ***Unit 5 Assessment.***

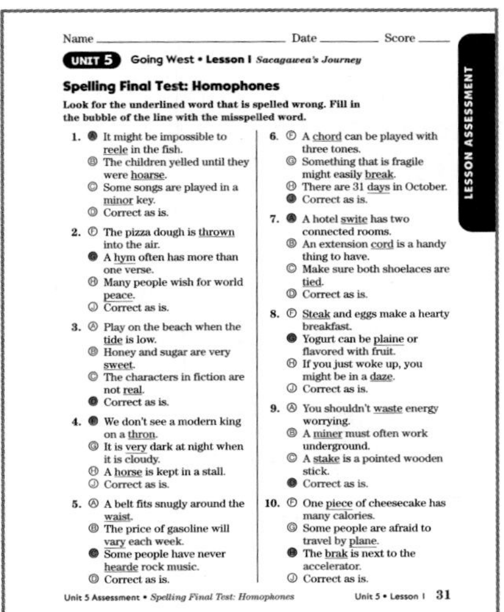

Name ______ Date ______ Score ______

UNIT 5 Going West • Lesson 1 *Sacagawea's Journey*

LESSON ASSESSMENT

Spelling Final Test: Homophones

Look for the underlined word that is spelled wrong. Fill in the bubble of the line with the misspelled word.

1. Ⓐ It might be impossible to reele in the fish.
   Ⓑ The children yelled until they were hoarse.
   Ⓒ Some songs are played in a minor key.
   Ⓓ Correct as is.
2. Ⓕ The pizza dough is thrown into the air.
   Ⓖ A hym often has more than one verse.
   Ⓗ Many people wish for world peace.
   Ⓙ Correct as is.
3. Ⓐ Play on the beach when the tide is low.
   Ⓑ Honey and sugar are very sweet.
   Ⓒ The characters in fiction are not real.
   Ⓓ Correct as is.
4. Ⓕ We don't see a modern king on a thron.
   Ⓖ It is very dark at night when it is cloudy.
   Ⓗ A horse is kept in a stall.
   Ⓙ Correct as is.
5. Ⓐ A belt fits snugly around the waist.
   Ⓑ The price of gasoline will vary each week.
   Ⓒ Some people have never hearde rock music.
   Ⓓ Correct as is.
6. Ⓕ A chord can be played with three tones.
   Ⓖ Something that is fragile might easily break.
   Ⓗ There are 31 days in October.
   Ⓙ Correct as is.
7. Ⓐ A hotel swite has two connected rooms.
   Ⓑ An extension cord is a handy thing to have.
   Ⓒ Make sure both shoelaces are tied.
   Ⓓ Correct as is.
8. Ⓕ Steak and eggs make a hearty breakfast.
   Ⓖ Yogurt can be plaine or flavored with fruit.
   Ⓗ If you just woke up, you might be in a daze.
   Ⓙ Correct as is.
9. Ⓐ You shouldn't waste energy worrying.
   Ⓑ A miner must often work underground.
   Ⓒ A stake is a pointed wooden stick.
   Ⓓ Correct as is.
10. Ⓕ One piece of cheesecake has many calories.
    Ⓖ Some people are afraid to travel by plane.
    Ⓗ The brak is next to the accelerator.
    Ⓙ Correct as is.

Unit 5 Assessment • *Spelling Final Test: Homophones* Unit 5 • Lesson 1 31

Unit 5 Assessment p. 31

Guided Practice

Have students categorize any mistakes they made on the Final Test.

Are they careless errors?
Are they lesson pattern problems?

Vocabulary

Concept Words

Informal Assessment

- Periodically check to see if students remember concept words related to astronomy, the American Revolution, and the American West. Encourage students to discover the meanings of concept words when they find them in other texts.
- Remind students to continue adding concept words to their Writer's Notebooks.

Writing Process Strategies

Teach

Literature Response

- Writing a response to literature helps students make the most of their reading experience.
- Tell students that a literature response can take many forms, ranging from a journal entry to a poem to a letter to an author. Any of these is appropriate as long as the student is exploring the connection between the literature and the feelings it elicits in them.

Guided Practice

Have students write a literature response to "Sacagawea's Journey." Remind students that they are free to choose what form their responses will take. Have students complete ***Writer's Workbook,*** page 81, for practice.

Formal Assessment

Total Point Value: 10

1. The focus is on ideas. (1 point)
2. Each entry is dated. (2 points)
3. The comments relate to the selection. (3 points)
4. The sentences are complete. There are no fragments. (2 points)
5. The response shows an understanding of the selection. (2 points)

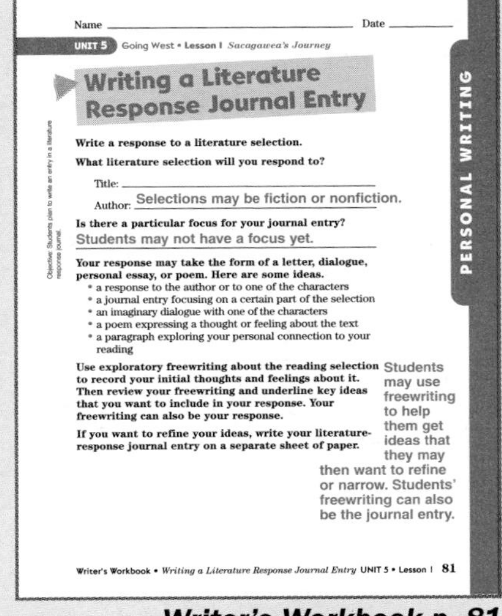

Name ______ Date ______

UNIT 5 Going West • Lesson 1 *Sacagawea's Journey*

PERSONAL WRITING

Writing a Literature Response Journal Entry

Objective: Students plan to write an entry in a literature response journal.

Write a response to a literature selection.

What literature selection will you respond to?

Title: ______

Author: Selections may be fiction or nonfiction.

Is there a particular focus for your journal entry?

Students may not have a focus yet.

Your response may take the form of a letter, dialogue, personal essay, or poem. Here are some ideas.

- a response to the author or to one of the characters
- a journal entry focusing on a certain part of the selection
- an imaginary dialogue with one of the characters
- a poem expressing a thought or feeling about the text
- a paragraph exploring your personal connection to your reading

Use exploratory freewriting about the reading selection to record your initial thoughts and feelings about it. Then review your freewriting and underline key ideas that you want to include in your response. Your freewriting can also be your response.

If you want to refine your ideas, write your literature-response journal entry on a separate sheet of paper.

Students may use freewriting to help them get ideas that they may then want to refine or narrow. Students' freewriting can also be the journal entry.

Writer's Workbook • *Writing a Literature Response Journal Entry* UNIT 5 • Lesson 1 81

Writer's Workbook p. 81

English Language Conventions

Penmanship

Joining with *A* and *d*

Teach

- Tell students they are going to review joining letters, an important component of cursive writing.
- **Teacher Model:** Review formation of uppercase *A* and lowercase *d* on the board.

A Starting point, downcurve
Undercurve to starting point
Slant down, undercurve: capital *A*

d Starting point, downcurve
Undercurve past starting point
Slant down, undercurve: small *d*

- Tell students that only *A, C, E, K, U, M, Z, H, Y, R, N,* and *J* can be joined to other letters.

Guided Practice

- In the Writer's Notebook, have students join *A* with the letters *n, t, s,* and *i* and join *d* with *o, a, e,* and *u*.
- From "Sacagawea's Journey," ask students to write two paragraphs to practice joining letters.

Informal Assessment

Check students' handwriting for legibility and properly joined letters.

Reading and Language Arts Skills Traces

Language Arts

WORD ANALYSIS

Skills Trace

Spelling: Homophones

Introduced in Grade 2.
Scaffolded throughout Grades 3–5.

REINTRODUCED: **Unit 5, Lesson 1**, p. 405F
PRACTICED: **Unit 5, Lesson 1**, pp. 405G–405I
Spelling and Vocabulary Skills, pp. 108–109
TESTED: **Unit 5, Lesson 1**, p. 405J
Unit 5 Assessment

Skills Trace

Vocabulary: Concept Words

Introduced in Grade 1.
Scaffolded throughout Grades 2–5.

REINTRODUCED: **Unit 5, Lesson 1**, p. 405G
PRACTICED: **Unit 5, Lesson 1**, pp. 405H–405I
Spelling and Vocabulary Skills, pp. 106–107
TESTED: **Informal Assessment**, p. 405J
Unit 5 Assessment

Reading

COMPREHENSION

Drawing Conclusions

Introduced in Grade 1.
Scaffolded throughout Grades 2–5.

REINTRODUCED: **Unit 1, Lesson 1**
REINFORCED: **Unit 2, Lesson 1**
Unit 3, Lesson 3
Unit 3, Lesson 5
Unit 4, Lesson 5
TESTED: **Unit 5 Assessment**

WRITING PROCESS STRATEGIES

Skills Trace

Personal Writing

Introduced in Grade K.
Scaffolded throughout Grades K–5.

REINTRODUCED: **Unit 5, Lesson 1**, p. 405F
PRACTICED: **Unit 5, Lessons 1 and 2**, pp. 405F–405J and 427F–427J
Writer's Workbook, pp. 78–85
TESTED: **Formal Assessment**
Unit 5, Lesson 1, pp. 405G, 405I, 405J
Unit 5, Lesson 2, pp. 427G, 427H, 427J
Unit 5 Assessment

ENGLISH LANGUAGE CONVENTIONS

Skills Trace

Grammar and Usage: Sentence Fragments

Introduced in Grade 2.
Scaffolded throughout Grades 2–5.

REINTRODUCED: **Unit 5, Lesson 1**, p. 405F
PRACTICED: **Unit 5, Lesson 1**, pp. 405F–405H
Comprehension and Language Arts Skills, pp. 144–145
TESTED: **Unit 5 Assessment**

Skills Trace

Listening, Speaking, Viewing
Listening: Drawing Conclusions and Making Inferences

Introduced in Grade 5.
Scaffolded throughout Grade 5.

INTRODUCED: **Unit 5, Lesson 1**, p. 405I
PRACTICED: **Unit 5, Lesson 1**, p. 405I
TESTED: **Informal Assessment**, p. 405I

Skills Trace

Penmanship: Joining with A and d

Introduced in Grade 3 (*A*) and Grade 2 (*d*).
Scaffolded throughout Grades 4–5 and Grades 3–5.

INTRODUCED: **Unit 5, Lesson 1**, p. 405J
PRACTICED: **Unit 5, Lesson 1**, p. 405J
TESTED: **Informal Assessment**, p. 405J

Professional Development: Comprehension

Teaching Techniques

Deciding how you and your students will interact most effectively, how you will best help all of your students learn, how your students can interact with each other to optimize their learning—these are the decisions and considerations all teachers take into account when they decide which teaching techniques will work best. The different techniques include:

- **Whole-Class Instruction** The understanding that all students in a classroom—the stars as well as those who are faltering—will benefit from the presentation, discussion, and review of all of the subject matter covered is the basis for whole-class instruction. By making whole-class presentations, the student who is struggling gets the benefit of the initial instruction and the discussion and then benefits from the reteaching and reinforcement. He or she is not left out and expected to do and learn less than his or her classmates. Rather than breaking the class into "ability groups," present the initial instruction to all students. Some will understand it right away, some will understand it as a result of the discussions that take place about the subject, and some won't understand at all. It is only after students have been presented with the material that those who don't understand are singled out for extra help and encouragement.
- **Collaborative Learning** Collaborative learning can take place in whole-class or small-group situations. Collaboration is the process of working with others on classroom instruction as well as on projects and occurs in discussion, in research, and in presenting and reviewing another's work. In whole-class or small-group situations, students learn to express their opinions, defend their positions, and explain their thoughts during discussion. They discover that by working together, they all learn much more than they would have learned individually. Discussion also offers English Language Learners the nonthreatening environment needed for expressing opinions and verifying understandings.
- **Small-Group Instruction** Small-group instruction is useful for collaborative research and study, and it is also appropriate for reteaching. Students can strengthen their knowledge and skills and can work with the teacher or their peers to gain the skills and knowledge that they need. In addition, small groups and individuals who are excelling can benefit from the extra encouragement and affirmation that working in small groups or meeting individually with the teacher can afford. Workshop, built into every day's lesson plan, is the opportune time to administer this extra help.
- **Individual Instruction** Individual instruction provides an opportunity to address the specific needs of a student. It may be listening to him or her read aloud, discussing a piece of writing, answering and asking questions, or providing specific, focused instruction or help with the particular needs of one student. Again, Workshop is an excellent time for the teacher to meet individually with students.

Professional Development

Teacher Resource Library CD-ROMs or ***Online Professional Development*** provides courses that help you better understand the Comprehension/Knowledge Building instruction in ***Open Court Reading.*** For more information about this program, visit SRAonline.com.

Additional information about comprehension, as well as resource references, can be found in the ***Professional Development Guide: Comprehension.***

Focus Questions In what ways were the buffalo important to the Native Americans of the Great Plains? How did the building of the Transcontinental Railroad affect the buffalo?

Buffalo Hunt

from the book by Russell Freedman

A Gift from the Great Spirit

Over blazing campfires on winter nights, Indian storytellers spoke of the buffalo. They told tales of buffalo giants and buffalo ghosts, of buffalo that changed magically into men, of children who were raised by buffalo and understood their language.

In olden times, it was said, buffalo used to eat Indians. They ate so many Indians that a legendary figure called Old Man had to put a stop to it. He organized a race between the buffalo and the Indians to decide who should eat whom. The Indians won.

On the Great Plains of North America, every Indian tribe had a rich and ready store of buffalo tales and legends. According to the Comanche, buffalo came from gigantic caves somewhere on the windswept ranges of the Texas Panhandle. Each spring, the Great Spirit sent throngs of buffalo from those hidden caves onto the open plains, as a gift to the Indian people.

Up North, the Blackfoot said that a lake in Canada was the place where the buffalo began. They were born beneath the water, in the darkest depths of the lake. If you could visit that sacred spot on the right night, at exactly the right time, you would hear an eerie rumbling coming from the middle of the lake. Then you would see the buffalo rise out of the water and crowd onto the shore, their shaggy fur wet and dripping, their curved horns gleaming in the moonlight.

To the Plains Indians, the buffalo, or American bison, was the most important animal on Earth. This snorting, lumbering beast provided almost everything the Indians needed to stay alive. The buffalo kept their bellies full and

407

SELECTION INTRODUCTION

Selection Summary

Genre: Expository Text

Russell Freedman takes us on a buffalo hunt with a group of Plains Indians, then back to their camp, where the women find a use for virtually every part of the slain animals. The Plains Indians expected their mighty prey to be around forever. The coming of the settlers was about to change everything. Striking historic illustrations by George Catlin and Charles Russell complement Freedman's thorough research.

Some of the elements of nonfiction are listed below. Nonfiction may have one or more of these elements.

- Its purpose is to share information with the reader.
- It includes facts about real people or events.
- Information is often presented in a straightforward way. It could be in narrative form.
- It may be organized by topics.
- Diagrams, photographs, maps, or other illustrations may be included to help the reader understand the subject better.
- The factual information can often be checked by referring to other sources.

About the Author

RUSSELL FREEDMAN believes that nonfiction books should be pleasurable to read as well as informative. He states, "If I'm excited enough about a subject to spend months researching and writing about it, I want my reader to be excited, too." *Buffalo Hunt* was selected as an American Library Association Notable Book and a School Library Journal Best Book.

Students can read more about Russell Freedman on page 427 of the ***Student Anthology.***

Other Books by Russell Freedman:

- *The Wright Brothers: How They Invented the Airplane*
- *Franklin Delano Roosevelt*
- *Cowboys of the Wild West*
- *Children of the Wild West*
- *Lincoln: A Photobiography*

About the Illustrators

GEORGE CATLIN and **CHARLES RUSSELL** painted numerous scenes of the American West. Many of the illustrations in this selection are photographs of paintings by Catlin and Russell. Other illustrations are taken from period paintings, one of which is by Albert Bierstadt.

Students can read more about George Catlin and Charles Russell on page 427 of the ***Student Anthology.***

Inquiry Connections

A major aim of ***Open Court Reading*** is knowledge building. Because inquiry is at the root of knowledge building, students are encouraged to investigate topics and questions within each selection that relate to the unit theme.

In the days when herds of buffalo thundered across the vast expanse of the West, the Plains Indians planned their lives around the movement of the herds.

In "Buffalo Hunt," Freedman includes many vivid details to tell how the buffalo became nearly extinct and how this tragic loss forever changed the lives of the Plains Indians and the landscape of the American West.

Key concepts explored are:

- The Plains Indians relied on the buffalo for food, material, and other uses vital to their survival.
- As settlers moved into the area, they hunted the buffalo for food and for sport.
- The dwindling buffalo populations forced the Plains Indians to change their way of life.

Before reading the selection:

- Point out that students may post a question, concept, word, illustration, or object on the Concept/Question Board at any time during the course of their unit investigation. Be sure that students include their names or initials on the items they post so that others will know whom to go to if they have an answer or if they wish to collaborate on a related activity.
- Students should feel free to write an answer or a note on someone else's question or to consult the Board for ideas for their own investigations throughout the unit.
- Encourage students to read about the American West at home and to bring in articles or pictures that are good examples to post on the Board.

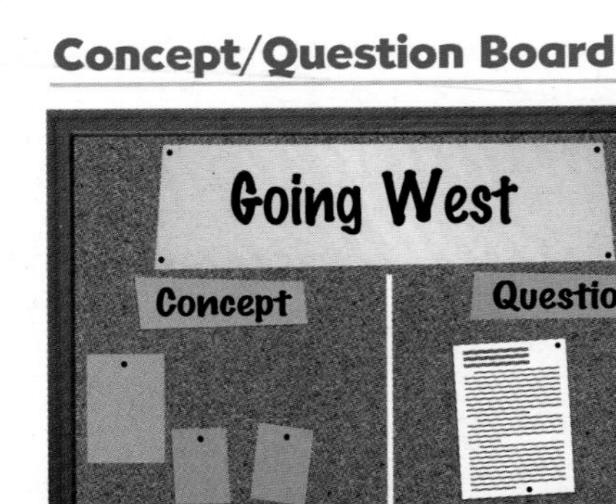

Leveled Practice

Reteach
Pages 145–149

Challenge
Pages 128–131

English Learner Support Activities

Intervention Workbook

Leveled Classroom Library*

Have students read at least 30 minutes daily outside of class. Have them read books from the ***Leveled Classroom Library,*** which supports the unit theme and helps students develop their vocabulary by reading independently.

Striking It Rich: The Story of the California Gold Rush

BY STEPHEN KRENSKY. ALADDIN, 1996.

A concise history of the Gold Rush, simply told, including how the miners came West, how they panned for gold, how some got rich without finding gold, and the Rush's effect on the growth of California. **(Easy)**

Black-Eyed Susan

BY JENNIFER ARMSTRONG. KNOPF, 1995.

While her father builds their homestead, Susie's efforts to cure her mother's prairie loneliness are helped by the arrival of some visitors to the isolated sod house. **(Average)**

Children of the Wild West

BY RUSSELL FREEDMAN. CLARION, 1983.

Historic and fascinating photographs accompany Freedman's details about the experiences of pioneer and Native American children in the West, including the journey west, schools, work and play. **(Advanced)**

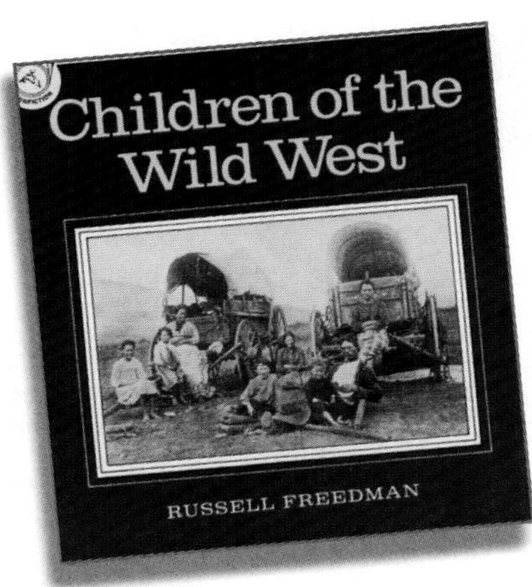

* These books, which all support the unit theme Going West, are part of a 36-book ***Leveled Classroom Library*** available for purchase from SRA/McGraw-Hill. Note: Teachers should preview any trade books for appropriateness in their classrooms before recommending them to students.

SRA TECHNOLOGY

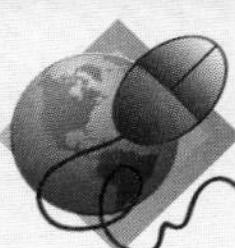

Web Connections

- Going West Web site
- Online Professional Development
- Online Assessment

CD-ROMs

- Research Assistant
- Ultimate Writing and Creativity Center
- Teacher Resource Library

Audiocassettes/CDs

- Listening Library: Going West

Computer Skills

- TechKnowledge

Materials are available through SRA/McGraw-Hill.

LESSON PLANNER

Suggested Pacing: 3–5 days

	DAY 1	DAY 2
1 Preparing to Read **Materials** ■ Routine Card 1	**Word Knowledge,** p. 406K ■ Homophones ■ Irregular Plural Nouns ■ /ch/ Spelled *tch* ■ Prefix *dis-* **About the Words and Sentences,** p. 406K	**Developing Oral Language,** p. 406L
2 Reading & Responding **Materials** ■ Student Anthology, pp. 406–427 ■ Routine Card 1 ■ Reading Transparencies 41, 54, 69 ■ Comprehension and Language Arts Skills, pp. 146–147 ■ Reteach, pp. 145–146 ■ Challenge, p. 128 ■ Program Assessment ■ Science/Social Studies Connection Center Cards 67–70 ■ Home Connection, pp. 65–66 ■ Inquiry Journal, p. 113 ■ Unit 5 Assessment, pp. 6–9	**Build Background,** p. 406M **Preview and Prepare,** pp. 406M–406N **Selection Vocabulary,** p. 406N **Reading Recommendations,** pp. 406O–406P **Student Anthology,** pp. 406–425 First Read ✓ **Comprehension Strategies** ■ Monitoring and Adjusting Reading Speed, p. 406 ■ Summarizing, pp. 406, 408, 416, 420, 422, 424 ■ Monitoring and Clarifying, pp. 410, 412, 418 ■ Visualizing, pp. 414, 418, 422 **Discussing Strategy Use,** p. 424 **Discussing the Selection,** p. 425A	**Student Anthology,** pp. 406–425 Second Read **Comprehension Skills** ■ Main Idea and Details, pp. 407, 409, 411, 413, 415, 417, 419, 421, 423, 425 **Supporting the Reading,** pp. 425C–425D ■ Main Idea and Details ✓ **Checking Comprehension,** p. 425
Inquiry **Materials** ■ Student Anthology, pp. 406–427 ■ Inquiry Journal, pp. 122–125 ■ Research Assistant	**Investigation** ■ Investigating Concepts Beyond the Text, p. 427A	**Investigation** ■ Concept/Question Board, p. 427B
3 Language Arts **Materials** ■ Comprehension and Language Arts Skills, pp. 148–149 ■ Language Arts Handbook ■ Spelling and Vocabulary Skills, pp. 110–113 ■ Unit 5 Assessment, pp. 32–33 ■ Reteach, pp. 147–149 ■ Challenge, pp. 129–131 ■ Student Anthology ■ Student Writing and Research Center ■ Writer's Workbook, pp. 82–85	**Word Analysis** ✓■ Spelling: Words with *dis-* or *mis-* Pretest, p. 427F **Writing Process Strategies** ■ Personal Writing: Invitation, p. 427F **English Language Conventions** ■ Mechanics: Commas, p. 427F	**Word Analysis** ■ Spelling: Words with *dis-* or *mis-*, p. 427G ■ Vocabulary: Synonyms, p. 427G **Writing Process Strategies** ✓■ Personal Writing: Invitation, p. 427G **English Language Conventions** ■ Mechanics: Commas, p. 427G

✓ Informal Assessment Available ✓ Formal Assessment Available

DAY 2 continued	DAY 3	
DAY 3	**DAY 4**	**DAY 5**
General Review	**General Review**	**Review Word Knowledge**
Student Anthology, pp. 426–427 ✓■ Concept Connections ■ Meet the Author/Illustrators	**Review Selection Vocabulary,** p. 425B **Literary Elements** ■ Expository Text, p. 425E **Poetry,** pp. 428–429B ■ "The Whole World is Coming" ■ "The Flower-Fed Buffaloes"	✓ **Lesson Assessment** ■ *Unit 5 Assessment:* Lesson Assessment, pp. 6–9 **Home Connection,** p. 425B **Social Studies Connection,** p. 425F ■ Citizenship
Investigation ✓■ Formulating Questions and Problems, p. 427C	**Supporting the Investigation** ■ Listening and Taking Notes, p. 427D	**Investigation** ■ Unit Investigation Continued ■ Update Concept/Question Board
Word Analysis ■ Spelling: Words with *dis-* or *mis-*, p. 427H ■ Vocabulary: Synonyms, p. 427H **Writing Process Strategies** ✓■ Personal Writing: Thank-You Note, p. 427H **English Language Conventions** ✓■ Mechanics: Commas, p. 427H	**Word Analysis** ■ Spelling: Words with *dis-* or *mis-*, p. 427I ■ Vocabulary: Synonyms, p. 427I **Writing Process Strategies** ■ Personal Writing: E-Mail Message/ Literature Response, p. 427I **English Language Conventions** ✓■ Listening, Speaking, Viewing Speaking: Proper Grammar, p. 427I	**Word Analysis** ✓■ Spelling: Words with *dis-* or *mis-* Final Test, p. 427J ✓■ Vocabulary: Synonyms, p. 427J **Writing Process Strategies** ✓■ Personal Writing: E-Mail Message/ Literature Response, p. 427J **English Language Conventions** ✓■ Penmanship: Joining with *E* and *f*, p. 427J

Below are suggestions for differentiating instruction. These are the same skills shown on the Lesson Planner; however, these pages provide extra practice opportunities or enriching activities to meet the varied needs of students.

WORKSHOP

Differentiating Instruction

Teacher: Individual and Small-Group Instruction

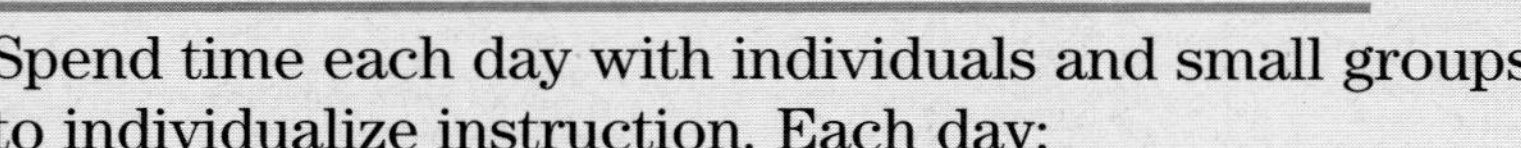

Spend time each day with individuals and small groups to individualize instruction. Each day:

- preteach students who need help with the next lesson.
- reteach students who need to solidify their understanding of content previously taught.
- listen to students read to check their fluency.
- hold writing and inquiry conferences.

Use the following program components to support instruction:

- ***Reteach*** with students who need a bit more practice.
- ***Intervention*** with students who exhibit a lack of understanding of the lesson concepts.
- ***English Learner Support*** with students who need language help.

Student: Independent Activities

Students can work alone, with a partner, or in small groups on such activities as:

- Review sound/spellings
- Partner Reading
- Practice fluency
- Independent Reading
- Reading Roundtable
- Concept vocabulary
- Selection vocabulary
- Writing in progress
- Conference
- Language Arts
- ***Challenge*** Activities
- Inquiry and Investigation Activities
- Listening Library

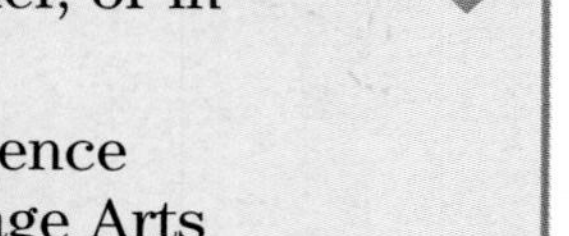

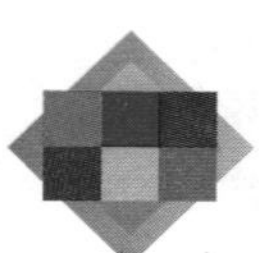

Professional Development

Teacher Resource Library CD-ROMs or ***Online Professional Development*** provides courses that help you better understand the Workshop/Intervention instruction in ***Open Court Reading.*** For more information about this program, visit SRAonline.com.

	DAY I
Word Knowledge	**Teacher Directed** ■ Teach meanings of blended words ■ Reading Words and About the Words, ***Intervention Guide,*** p. 241
Fluency	**Independent Activities** ■ Self-test fluency rate
Comprehension	**Teacher Directed** ■ Preteach "Buffalo Hunt," ***Intervention Guide,*** pp. 242–243 ■ Intervention Selection 1, ***Intervention Guide,*** pp. 243–244 ■ ***English Learner Support Guide,*** pp. 380–383 **Independent Activities** ■ Record response to selection in Writer's Notebook ■ ***Listening Library Audiocassette/CD*** ■ Add vocabulary in Writer's Notebook
Inquiry	**Independent Activities** ■ Concept/Question Board ■ Explore OCR Web site for theme connections
Language Arts	**Teacher Directed** ■ Seminar: Plan and Draft an Invitation, p. 427F ■ Commas in a Series, ***Intervention Guide,*** p. 246 **Independent Activities** ■ Commas with Introductory Phrases, ***Comprehension and Language Arts Skills,*** pp. 148–149

DAY 2	DAY 3	DAY 4	DAY 5
Teacher Directed ▪ Developing Oral Language, ***Intervention Guide,*** p. 241	**Teacher Directed** ▪ Dictation and Spelling, ***Intervention Guide,*** pp. 241–242	**Independent Activities** ▪ Add words to Word Bank	**Teacher Directed** ▪ General review as necessary
Independent Activities ▪ Oral reading of "Buffalo Hunt"	**Independent Activities** ▪ Partner read "Buffalo Hunt"	**Independent Activities** ▪ Fluency rate check ▪ Reread "Buffalo Hunt"	**Teacher Directed** ▪ Repeated Readings, ***Intervention Guide,*** p. 245 **Independent Activities** ▪ Fluency rate check
Teacher Directed ▪ Preteach "Buffalo Hunt," ***Intervention Guide,*** pp. 242–243 ▪ Reread Intervention Selection 1 ▪ Teach Comprehension Strategies, ***Intervention Guide,*** p. 244 ▪ ***English Learner Support Guide,*** pp. 383–385 ▪ Review Main Idea and Details ▪ Main Idea and Details, ***Reteach,*** pp. 145–146 **Independent Activities** ▪ Main Idea and Details • ***Comprehension and Language Arts Skills,*** pp. 146–147 • ***Challenge,*** p. 128 ▪ Challenge Tip: Main Idea and Details, p. 421	**Teacher Directed** ▪ Teach Intervention Selection 2, ***Intervention Guide,*** pp. 244–245 ▪ ***English Learner Support Guide,*** pp. 386–388 ▪ Discuss Concept Connections, p. 426 **Independent Activities** ▪ ***English Learner Support Activities,*** p. 56 ▪ ***Listening Library Audiocassette/CD*** ▪ Independent reading ▪ Supporting the Reading: Link to Writing, p. 425D ▪ Recording Concept Information, ***Inquiry Journal,*** p. 113	**Teacher Directed** ▪ Teach Comprehension Strategies, ***Intervention Guide,*** p. 245 ▪ Reread Intervention Selection 2 ▪ ***English Learner Support Guide,*** pp. 389–391 **Independent Activities** ▪ Literary Elements: Independent Practice, p. 425E ▪ Elements of Poetry: Writing, p. 429A ▪ ***Listening Library Audiocassette/CD*** ▪ Record response to Poetry selections in Writer's Notebook	**Teacher Directed** ▪ Reading Roundtable ▪ ***English Learner Support Guide,*** pp. 391–393 **Independent Activities** ▪ Social Studies Connection, p. 425F ▪ ***English Learner Support Activities,*** p. 57
Independent Activities ▪ Concept/Question Board ▪ Explore OCR Web site for theme connections	**Independent Activities** ▪ Concept/Question Board ▪ Use ***Research Assistant*** to continue investigation ▪ Formulating Questions and Problems, ***Inquiry Journal,*** pp. 122–123	**Independent Activities** ▪ Concept/Question Board ▪ Audio Resources, ***Inquiry Journal,*** pp. 124–125	**Independent Activities** ▪ Concept/Question Board ▪ Supporting the Investigation: Independent Practice, p. 427D ▪ Continue research
Teacher Directed ▪ Commas in a Series, ***Intervention Guide,*** p. 246 ▪ Spelling: Word Sort, p. 427G ▪ Seminar: Edit and Publish an Invitation, p. 427G ▪ Commas with Introductory Phrases, ***Reteach,*** p. 149 **Independent Activities** ▪ Vocabulary: Synonyms, ***Spelling and Vocabulary Skills,*** pp. 110–111 ▪ Commas with Introductory Phrases, ***Challenge,*** p. 131	**Teacher Directed** ▪ Seminar: Plan and Draft a Thank-You Note, p. 427H ▪ Writing Activity, ***Intervention Guide,*** p. 247 ▪ Vocabulary: Synonyms, ***Reteach,*** p. 148 **Independent Activities** ▪ Spelling: Words with *dis-* and *mis-*, ***Spelling and Vocabulary Skills,*** p. 112 ▪ Vocabulary: Synonyms, ***Challenge,*** p. 130	**Teacher Directed** ▪ Seminar: Plan, Draft, and Publish an E-Mail Literature Response, p. 427I ▪ Writing Activity, ***Intervention Guide,*** p. 247 ▪ Spelling: Words with *dis-* and *mis-*, ***Reteach,*** p. 147 **Independent Activities** ▪ Spelling: Words with *dis-* and *mis-* • ***Spelling and Vocabulary Skills,*** p. 113 • ***Challenge,*** p. 129	**Teacher Directed** ▪ Seminar: Plan, Draft, and Publish an E-Mail Literature Response, p. 427J **Independent Activities** ▪ Penmanship: Cursive Letters *E* and *f*, p. 427J

ASSESSMENT

Formal Assessment Options

Use these summative assessments along with your informal observations to assess student progress.

Name ______ Date ______ Score ______

UNIT 5 Going West • Lesson 2

LESSON ASSESSMENT

Buffalo Hunt

Read the following questions carefully. Then completely fill in the bubble of each correct answer. You may look back at the story to find the answer to each of the questions.

1. Buffalo have extremely sharp senses of
   - Ⓐ sight and hearing
   - Ⓑ hearing and touch
   - ● hearing and smell
2. In winter, a buffalo hunter would sometimes
   - ● disguise himself with a buffalo robe
   - Ⓑ hide under a mound of snow
   - Ⓒ train a wolf to track the buffalo

Read the following questions carefully. Use complete sentences to answer the questions.

3. How does the Blackfoot legend say that the buffalo began?
   The Blackfoot legend says that the buffalo were born beneath a lake and rose out of the water to crowd onto the shore.
4. How did early Native Americans hunt buffalo?
   They hunted buffalo on foot, using arrows and spears.
5. How did horses come to North America?
   Horses were brought to North America by Spanish explorers in the 1500s.

6 Unit 5 • Lesson 2 *Buffalo Hunt* • Unit 5 Assessment

Unit 5 Assessment p. 6

Buffalo Hunt *(continued)*

6. Why did the Plains Indians give up on farming and fishing?
   They wanted to follow and hunt the buffalo herds instead.
7. What did the Plains Indians do once or twice a year?
   Once or twice a year, all the different bands of Plains Indians gathered for a big religious ceremony, a tribal council, or a communal hunt.
8. What were the women's responsibilities once the buffalo had been killed?
   The women's responsibilities were to skin and butcher the buffalo, to preserve the meat, and to tan the hides.

Read the following questions carefully. Then completely fill in the bubble of each correct answer.

9. One good-sized buffalo cow could feed
   - Ⓐ ten people
   - Ⓑ fifty people
   - ● one hundred people
10. What is the main idea of this story?
   - Ⓐ Horses made it easier for Plains Indians to hunt buffalo.
   - Ⓑ The female buffalo is called a cow.
   - ● Plains Indians depended on the buffalo for many things.

LESSON ASSESSMENT

Unit 5 Assessment • *Buffalo Hunt* Unit 5 • Lesson 2 7

Unit 5 Assessment p. 7

Buffalo Hunt *(continued)*

LESSON ASSESSMENT

Read the questions below. Use complete sentences in your answers.

Linking to the Concepts How did the advance of white settlers affect the Plains Indians?
Answers will vary. Accept all reasonable answers.

Personal Response Can you think of anything that you depend on as much as the Plains Indians depended on the buffalo? How would you react if someone took this from you?
Answers will vary. Accept all reasonable answers.

8 Unit 5 • Lesson 2 *Buffalo Hunt* • Unit 5 Assessment

Unit 5 Assessment p. 8

Buffalo Hunt *(continued)*

Vocabulary

Read the following questions carefully. Then completely fill in the bubble of each correct answer.

1. Indian storytellers speak of a legendary figure called Old Man. If something is **legendary**, it is
   - Ⓐ told only by older men
   - Ⓑ about far-away places
   - ● told of for generations
2. As recently as 150 years ago, countless buffalo roamed the prairies and plains. Another word for **roamed** is
   - ● wandered
   - Ⓑ chased
   - Ⓒ protected
3. It was a woman's job to preserve the meat and tan the hides. To **preserve** something means to
   - Ⓐ share it with people who are in your own family
   - Ⓑ make it look fancy enough to wear as clothing
   - ● prepare it so that it can be eaten in the future
4. A typical tipi had sufficient living space for the family. If something is **sufficient**, it is
   - Ⓐ lacking
   - ● enough
   - Ⓒ wonderful
5. A scout was given a ceremonial pipe to smoke after a herd had been found. **Ceremonial** means
   - ● related to a ceremony
   - Ⓑ from another country
   - Ⓒ dealing with buffalo

LESSON ASSESSMENT

Unit 5 Assessment • *Buffalo Hunt* Unit 5 • Lesson 2 9

Unit 5 Assessment p. 9

Name ______ Date ______ Score ______

UNIT 5 Going West • Lesson 2 *Buffalo Hunt*

LESSON ASSESSMENT

Spelling Pretest: Words with *dis-* and *mis-*

Fold this page back on the dotted line. Take the Pretest. Then correct any word you misspelled by crossing out the word and rewriting it next to the incorrect spelling.

1. mistook
2. dislike
3. disagree
4. mistreat
5. disloyal
6. discover
7. misspell
8. disgrace
9. mislaid
10. misprint
11. displease
12. disconnect
13. mislead
14. misjudge
15. distrust
16. distance
17. distinct
18. disappear
19. disturb
20. discuss

32 Unit 5 • Lesson 2 *Spelling Pretest: Words with dis- and mis-* • Unit 5 Assessment

Unit 5 Assessment p. 32

Name ______ Date ______ Score ______

UNIT 5 Going West • Lesson 2 *Buffalo Hunt*

LESSON ASSESSMENT

Spelling Final Test: Words with *dis-* and *mis-*

Look for the underlined word that is spelled wrong. Fill in the bubble of the line with the misspelled word.

1. Ⓐ Losing will disappoint an athlete.
   Ⓑ I mistook a cricket for a grasshopper.
   ● Try not to mispell a single word.
   Ⓓ Correct as is.
2. Ⓕ Don't wear mismatched socks to school.
   ● I mislade my glasses.
   Ⓗ The country suffered under misrule.
   Ⓙ Correct as is.
3. ● You must disconect the stereo to remove it.
   Ⓑ A hurricane is a natural disaster.
   Ⓒ Parents sometimes disagree.
   Ⓓ Correct as is.
4. Ⓕ This equation will disprove the theory.
   Ⓖ The leopard has distinct markings.
   Ⓗ Do not disturb the rattlesnake.
   ● Correct as is.
5. Ⓐ The talk show host has a sunny disposition.
   Ⓑ You may be fined if you mistreat an animal.
   ● A flat tire will dissable a bicycle.
   Ⓓ Correct as is.
6. Ⓕ Don't misjudge her.
   Ⓖ The mountains can be seen in the distance.
   ● A low grade will dissplease your parents.
   Ⓙ Correct as is.
7. Ⓐ The witness was misquoted.
   Ⓑ We will discuss the Civil War.
   Ⓒ It is a disadvantage not to have a computer.
   ● Correct as is.
8. Ⓕ The general surrendered in disgrace.
   ● The mist will disapear when the sun rises.
   Ⓗ Don't take a gift from someone you distrust.
   Ⓙ Correct as is.
9. Ⓐ Miners hoped to discover gold.
   Ⓑ An editor hopes there won't be a misprint.
   ● The candle melted and became mishapen.
   Ⓓ Correct as is.
10. ● Many colonists were dissloyal to England.
   Ⓖ How can you dislike chocolate?
   Ⓗ A false statement will mislead the detective.
   Ⓙ Correct as is.

Unit 5 Assessment • *Spelling Final Test: Words with dis- and mis-* Unit 5 • Lesson 2 33

Unit 5 Assessment p. 33

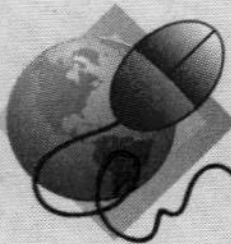

Online Assessment for ***Open Court Reading*** helps teachers differentiate classroom instruction based on students' scores from the weekly and end-of-unit assessments. It provides exercises best suited to meet the needs of each student. For more information visit SRAonline.com.

ASSESSMENT

Informal Comprehension Strategies Rubrics

Summarizing

- The student paraphrases text, reporting main ideas and a summary of what is in text.
- The student decides which parts of the text are important in his or her summary.
- The student draws conclusions from the text.
- The student makes global interpretations of the text, such as recognizing the genre.

Visualizing

- The student visualizes ideas or scenes described in the text.

Monitoring and Clarifying

- The student notes characteristics of the text, such as whether it is difficult to read or whether some sections are more challenging or more important than others.
- The student shows awareness of whether he or she understands the text and takes appropriate action, such as rereading, in order to understand the text better.
- The student rereads to reconsider something presented earlier in the text.
- The student recognizes problems during reading, such as a loss of concentration, unfamiliar vocabulary, or lack of sufficient background knowledge to comprehend the text.

Monitoring and Adjusting Reading Speed

The student changes reading speed in reaction to text, exhibiting such behavior as

- Skimming parts of the text that are not important or relevant.
- Purposely reading more slowly because of difficulty in comprehending the text.

Research Rubrics

During Workshop, assess students using the rubrics below. The rubrics range from 1–4 in most categories, with 1 being the lowest score. Record each student's score on the inside back cover of his or her ***Inquiry Journal.***

Formulating Research Questions and Problems

1 With help, identifies things she or he wonders about in relation to a topic.

2 Expresses curiosity about topics; with help, translates this into specific questions.

3 Poses an interesting problem or question for research; with help, refines it into a researchable question.

4 Identifies something she or he genuinely wonders about and translates it into a researchable question.

Objectives

- Students recognize homophones to help them determine meaning and increase vocabulary.
- Students recognize and read irregular forms of nouns.
- Students recognize and read words with the /ch/ sound spelled *tch*.
- Students recognize and spell words with the prefixes *dis-* and *mis-*.

Materials

- Routine Card

Routine Card
Refer to Routine 1 for the Reading the Words and Sentences procedure.

Teacher Tip SYLLABICATION To help students blend words and build fluency, demonstrate syllabication using decodable multisyllabic words in the word lines.

cor•ral	dis•a•gree
chor•ale	mis•took
buf•fa•lo	dis•ap•pear
bi•son	mis•treat
dis•please	

Differentiating Instruction

If...	Then...
Students need extra help with words containing the prefix *dis-*	Use *Intervention Guide,* pages 241–242

WORD KNOWLEDGE

Word Knowledge

Reading the Words and Sentences

Use direct teaching to teach the Word Knowledge lesson. Write each word and sentence on the board. Have students read each word together. After all the words have been read, have students read each sentence in natural phrases or chunks. Use the suggestions in About the Words and Sentences to discuss the different features of the listed words.

Line 1:	corral chorale		wade weighed		tale tail
Line 2:	buffalo	deer	bison	elk	fish
Line 3:	stretch	watch	stitch	notch	match
Line 4:	disappear	disagree	displease	mistreat	mistook

Sentence 1: He had to wade across the wide river carrying a pack on his back that weighed fifty pounds.

Sentence 2: The Plains Indians depended on the buffalo for most of their needs.

Sentence 3: The women would stretch and stitch the skins of bison to make clothing.

Sentence 4: It would displease our parents if they thought we would mistreat our little sister.

About the Words and Sentences

- **Line 1:** These words are homophones. A homophone is a word that sounds the same as another word but has a different meaning and, sometimes, a different spelling. Have students pronounce the word pairs aloud. Discuss the meaning of each word with students. Encourage students to illustrate the words' different meanings by using each one in a sentence and saying it aloud.
- **Line 2:** Each of these words illustrates the irregular plural form of nouns. The spelling of these words is the same in both their singular and plural forms. Encourage students to consult a dictionary if they are ever unsure about the plural form of a word. Ask volunteers to use these words—both singular and plural forms—in sentences and say them aloud.
- **Line 3:** These words illustrate the /ch/ sound spelled *tch.* The *tch* spelling occurs only at the end of words or syllables. Point out that suffixes or other word endings might follow the *tch,* as in *stretched* or *watching.* Encourage students to think of other words with the /ch/ sound spelled *tch.* You might write them on the board and have students pronounce them with you.
- **Line 4:** The words in the last line review the prefixes *dis-* and *-mis.*

WORD KNOWLEDGE

- **Sentence 1:** Have students read the sentence aloud. Ask them to identify the two words in the sentence that sound alike *(wade, weighed)*. Have students give the name for words that sound the same but have different meanings and often different spellings. Have them explain the definition of each of these words.
- **Sentence 2:** Read the sentence aloud for students and point out the plural words *Plains*, *Indians*, *buffalo*, and *needs*. Have students say these words aloud. Then, ask them: *What is different about the plural word* buffalo *compared to the other plural words?* Point out that *buffalo* does not have an *s*.
- **Sentence 3:** Have students read the sentence aloud. Ask them to identify the words in the sentence that have the /ch/ sound spelled *tch*. Have students think of suffixes or other endings that they could add to *stretch* and *stitch* to form new words, such as *stretching*, *stitched*, *stretcher*, or *stitches*. Point out that the words still have the /ch/ sound even after adding different endings.
- **Sentence 4:** Have students notice the words in the last sentence that contain the prefixes *dis-* and *mis-*.

Developing Oral Language

Use direct teaching to review the words. Have students do one or both of the following activities.

- Have a volunteer write a homophone pair on the board and use the two words in one sentence *(e.g. "The plane landed on the plain.")*. Have a second student determine which word goes with which meaning. To increase students' vocabularies of homophones, continue the activity using new homophone pairs that the students come up with, perhaps with the help of a dictionary.
- Have a student point to one word in the lines above and select a classmate to read the word aloud and use it in a sentence. Then have another student add a word from the list to the sentence. See how many words they can fit into the sentence logically. Encourage students to extend sentences at the beginning as well as at the end of sentences.

Teacher Tip **BUILDING FLUENCY** By this time in grade 5, students should be reading approximately 151 words per minute with fluency and expression. Gaining a better understanding of the spellings of sounds and the structure of words will help students as they encounter unfamiliar words in their reading. As students read, you may notice that some need work in building fluency. During Workshop, have these students choose a section of the text (a minimum of 160 words) to read several times in order to build fluency.

Differentiating Instruction

If...	Then...
Students need extra fluency practice	Use the Intervention Selection activities, ***Intervention Guide,*** pages 243–245

Spelling
See pages 427F–427J for the corresponding spelling lesson for the prefixes *dis-* and *mis-*.

Objectives

- Students will understand the selection vocabulary before reading.
- Students will recognize homophones to help them determine meaning and increase vocabulary.
- Students will recognize and read nouns with irregular plural forms.
- Students will recognize and read words with the /ch/ sound spelled *tch.*
- Students will use the comprehension strategies Monitoring and Clarifying, Monitoring and Adjusting Reading Speed, Summarizing, and Visualizing as they read the story the first time.
- Students will use the comprehension skill Main Idea and Details as they read the story the second time.

Materials

- Student Anthology, pp. 406–427
- Reading Transparencies 41, 54, 69
- Comprehension and Language Arts Skills, pp. 146–147
- Inquiry Journal, p. 113
- Listening Library
- Routine Card 1
- Program Assessment
- Unit 5 Assessment, pp. 6–9
- Home Connection, pp. 65–66
- Science/Social Studies Connection Center Cards 67–70

Differentiating Instruction

If...	Then...
Students need extra help with the selection vocabulary	Use ***Intervention Guide,*** page 242

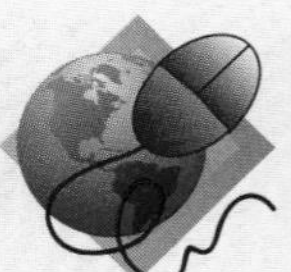

www.sra4kids.com
Web Connection
Students can use the connections to Going West in the Reading link of the SRA Web page for more background information about the American West.

Build Background

Activate Prior Knowledge

Discuss the following with students to find out what they may already know about the selection and have already learned about the theme of Going West.

- Preteach "Buffalo Hunt" by first determining students' prior knowledge about buffalo. Ask them, "What were some ways that Native Americans used parts of the buffalo?"
- Have students tell where the Great Plains are located.

Background Information

The following information may help students understand the selection they are about to read.

- Different Native American groups had different ways of life. Some who lived near rivers and lakes relied on fishing for survival; others who lived on fertile land relied on farming. The Plains Indians, who lived where the buffalo were plentiful, relied on hunting buffalo to fulfill their needs.
- The life that Native Americans had established in North America changed drastically as European settlers began to explore and colonize the continent. Some tribes were pushed westward by settlers and forced to leave traditional lands. Other tribes were influenced by European culture as they traded and communicated with settlers.
- Explain that the Native Americans did not consider land as property owned by an individual or one particular group; everyone used what they needed.
- As colonists pushed westward, they encountered many tribes unwilling to give up their traditional lands without a fight. Tensions between European settlers and Native Americans escalated to battles over lands and rights. Eventually, most Native Americans were relocated to reservations set up by the U.S. government.
- Have the students discuss what they know about the genre of this selection. Refer to page 406A of the ***Teacher's Edition*** for elements of this selection's genre.

Preview and Prepare

Browse

- Have a student read aloud the title and the names of the author and illustrator. Demonstrate how to browse. Then, since this is a nonfiction piece, have the students preview the selection by browsing the illustrations and text in the entire piece. This helps them to establish what they want to learn from the selection and activate prior knowledge in a way that is relevant to the selection. Then discuss what they think this story might have to do with going west.

- Have the students search for clues that tell them something about the selection. Also, have them look for any problems, such as unfamiliar words or long sentences, that they notice while reading. Use ***Reading Transparency 54*** to record their observations as they browse. For example, the heading "The Hunt" may be a clue that though nonfiction, there may be some adventure in this selection. For the Problems column, students might say they don't know the meaning of the word *encampment.* They might wonder why the buffalo were so important to the Native Americans. To save time and model note taking, write students' observations as brief notes rather than complete sentences.
- As students prepare to read the selection, have them browse the Focus Questions on the first page of the selection. Tell them to keep these questions in mind as they read.

Set Purposes

Have students set their own purposes for reading this selection. You might suggest that they look for information about the Native American way of life before and after the demise of the buffalo. Remind students that good readers have a purpose when they read. Let them know that they should make sure they know the purpose for reading whenever they read.

Selection Vocabulary

As students study vocabulary, they will use a variety of skills to determine the meaning of a word. These include context clues, word structure, and apposition. Students will apply these same skills while reading to clarify unfamiliar words.

Display ***Reading Transparency 41*** before reading the selection to introduce the following words and their meanings.

legendary: told about in a legend or story (page 407)
roamed: wandered (page 408)
preserve: to prepare food so that it can be eaten in the future (page 411)
ceremonial: describes something related to a ceremony or formal celebration (page 414)
sufficient: enough (page 421)
slaughter: killing of large numbers of animals (page 424)

Have students read the words in the Word Box, stopping to blend any words that they have trouble reading. Demonstrate how to decode multisyllabic words by breaking the words into syllables and blending the syllables. Then have students try. If the word is not decodable, give the students the pronunciation.

Have students read the sentences on ***Reading Transparency 41*** and use the skills of context, word structure (structural analysis), or apposition to figure out the meanings of the words. Be sure students explain which skill(s) they are using and how they figured out the meanings of the words.

Clues	Problems	Wonderings
Campfires "The Hunt" Captions Headings Nonfiction Comanche	The word *encampment*	Why were the buffalo so important to the Native Americans? What happened to the buffalo?

Open Court Reading — Reading Transparency 54

Reading Transparency 54

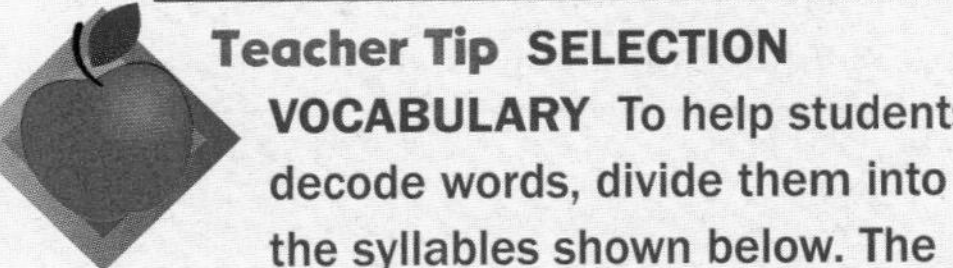

Teacher Tip SELECTION VOCABULARY To help students decode words, divide them into the syllables shown below. The information following each word tells how to figure out the meaning of each word on the transparency.

leg•end•ar•y	context clues, word structure
roamed	context clues
pre•serve	context clues
cer•e•mo•ni•al	context clues, word structure
suf•fi•cient	context clues
slaugh•ter	context clues

Routine Card
Refer to Routine 2 for the Selection Vocabulary procedure. Refer to Routine 3 for the Clues, Problems, and Wonderings procedure.

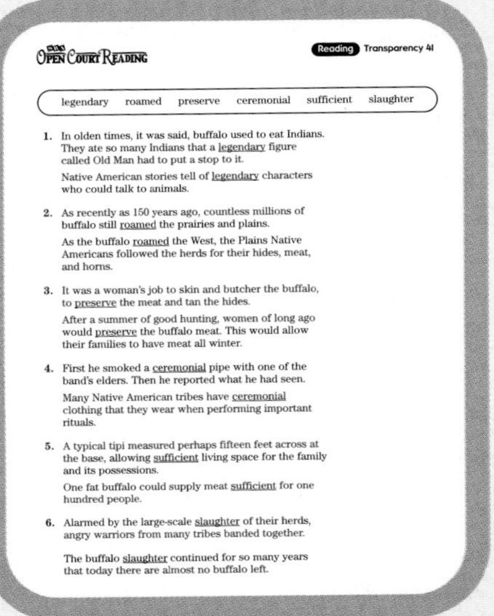

Open Court Reading — Reading Transparency 41

legendary roamed preserve ceremonial sufficient slaughter

1. In olden times, it was said, buffalo used to eat Indians. They ate so many Indians that a legendary figure called Old Man had to put a stop to it.
   Native American stories tell of legendary characters who could talk to animals.
2. As recently as 150 years ago, countless millions of buffalo still roamed the prairies and plains.
   As the buffalo roamed the West, the Plains Native Americans followed the herds for their hides, meat, and horns.
3. It was a woman's job to skin and butcher the buffalo, to preserve the meat and tan the hides.
   After a summer of good hunting, women of long ago would preserve the buffalo meat. This would allow their families to have meat all winter.
4. First he smoked a ceremonial pipe with one of the band's elders. Then he reported what he had seen.
   Many Native American tribes have ceremonial clothing that they wear when performing important rituals.
5. A typical tipi measured perhaps fifteen feet across at the base, allowing sufficient living space for the family and its possessions.
   One fat buffalo could supply meat sufficient for one hundred people.
6. Alarmed by the large-scale slaughter of their herds, angry warriors from many tribes banded together.
   The buffalo slaughter continued for so many years that today there are almost no buffalo left.

Reading Transparency 41

Students will enjoy using the ***Listening Library Audiocassette/CD*** and listening to the selection they are about to read. Encourage them to listen to the selection during Workshop. Have students discuss with each other and with you their personal listening preferences (for example, nonfiction, poetry, drama, and so on).

Teacher Tip COMPREHENSION STRATEGIES Create a poster with the comprehension strategies listed. Refer to the Comprehension Strategies poster as the class reads the selection. As students are reading, ask them which of the strategies listed on the poster might be good to use at this point in the selection?

Routine Card
Refer to Routine 4 for the Reading the Selection procedure.

Differentiating Instruction

If...	Then...
Students need extra help with the comprehension strategies Monitoring and Clarifying and Summarizing	Use ***Intervention Guide***, pages 244–245

Reading Recommendations

Oral Reading ■ Silent Reading

Because this expository text is lengthy, you may want to divide it into two parts. Have students read the first half orally and continue silently once they feel they can handle the content and vocabulary. When reading orally, have students read expressively, at an appropriate pace, in natural phrases and chunks. Remind students to keep their audience in mind as they read aloud, adjusting volume as necessary and enunciating words clearly. Reading the selection with fluency and accuracy will help students comprehend the text. If students have trouble reading decodable words, have them break the words into sounds or syllables and then blend them together to read the word.

Page 418 is a good place to have students begin to read silently for at least 15 minutes at a time. As they become better readers, students will read silently with increasing ease, over longer periods of time. Have them make use of the comprehension strategies listed below by recording in their Writer's Notebooks the strategies they used while reading silently. You may want to stop periodically to discuss the selection and strategies used. You may prefer to talk about strategies after the students have read the selection.

After the students have finished reading the selection, use the "Discussing the Selection" questions to see if they understood what they have read. If they have not, refer to the ***Intervention Guide*** for further strategies.

Using Comprehension Strategies 

Comprehension strategy instruction allows students to become aware of how good readers read. Good readers constantly check their understanding as they are reading and ask themselves questions. In addition, skilled readers recognize when they are having problems and stop to use various comprehension strategies, to help them make sense of what they are reading.

During the first reading of "Buffalo Hunt," model and prompt the use of the following comprehension strategies. Take turns reading the story aloud with the students.

- **Summarizing** prompts readers to keep track of what they are reading and to focus their minds on important information.
- **Visualizing** helps readers to understand descriptions of settings, characters, and events in a story.
- **Monitoring and Clarifying** prompts readers to track and immediately clear up unfamiliar words and ideas by using context, word structure, apposition, and outside resources. Stop and check that students understand when something is unclear.
- **Monitoring and Adjusting Reading Speed** prompts readers to assess the difficulty level of a text and adapt their reading pace accordingly.

As students read, they should be using a variety of strategies to help them understand the selection. Encourage students to use the strategies listed on the previous page as the class reads the story aloud. Do this by stopping at the points indicated by the numbers in magenta circles on the reduced student page and using a particular strategy. Students can also stop reading periodically to discuss what they have learned and what problems they may be having.

In Unit 5, students should be assuming more responsibility for the use of comprehension strategies. Continue Modeling and Prompting as needed. Prompting provides a springboard for students to respond using the strategy mentioned in the prompt. The Student Sample is written in the language that students might use in their actual responses.

The Student Sample may be one of many possible student responses. Accept other responses that are reasonable and appropriate. If student responses indicate that the students do not understand the strategy, be ready to discuss their responses and to provide additional instruction. As students proceed through the lessons, teacher modeling and prompting of strategy use should become less and less necessary as students assume more responsibility for using strategies.

Building Comprehension Skills 

Revisiting or rereading a selection allows students to apply skills that give them a more complete understanding of the text. Some follow-up comprehension skills help students organize information. Others lead to deeper understanding—to "reading between the lines," as mature readers do. An extended lesson on the comprehension skill Main Idea and Details can be found in the Supporting the Reading section on pages 425C–425D. This lesson is intended to give students extra practice with Main Idea and Details. However, the Teach portion of the lesson may be used at this time to introduce the comprehension skill to students.

- **Main Idea and Details (Review):** Readers distinguish the main points in a piece of writing from the information that supports them.

Reading with a Purpose

As they read have students look for ways the buffalo sustained the Plains Indians and how the demise of the buffalo changed their way of life and list them in the Response Journal section of their Writer's Notebooks.

Teacher Tip READING RATE As this is a nonfiction selection and students are reading to be informed, allow students more time for reading. Have students adjust their reading rate by reading more slowly or by rereading certain sections of the selection in order to comprehend the information presented.

Differentiating Instruction

If...	Then...
Students need extra help with reading "Buffalo Hunt"	• Preread the selection during Workshop; use the ***Listening Library*** to give students a good reading model • Use ***English Learner Support Guide,*** pages 378–393 • Use ***Intervention Guide,*** pages 242–243

COMPREHENSION

Read pages 406–425.

Comprehension Strategies

Student Sample

1 Monitoring and Adjusting Reading Speed *I think I may have been reading too fast—I'm not sure I understand who this "Old Man" is. I'll go back and reread this part. Then I'll make sure that I read the rest of the selection more slowly so that I catch all of the new information.*

Teacher Modeling

2 Summarizing *Let's summarize the information we've learned here to check our understanding, before we move on to the rest of the selection. There are many Native American legends about buffalo. One was that buffalo used to eat Native Americans. According to the Commanche, the buffalo came from hidden caves, as a gift from the Great Spirit. The Blackfoot thought buffalo came from deep inside a lake in Canada. Let's continue reading, and as we do, remember to summarize what we are reading. Make sure you understand what you have just read. Let me know if you would like to share your summary with the group.*

Word Knowledge

SCAFFOLDING The skills students are reviewing in Word Knowledge should help them in reading the story. This lesson focuses on homophones. Homophones will be found in boxes similar to this one throughout the selection.

Homophones:

nights	**knights**	**tales**	**tails**
won	**one**	**right**	**write**

First Reading Recommendation

ORAL • CHORAL • SILENT

Buffalo Hunter. c.1844. **Artist Unknown.**
Oil on canvas. Santa Barbara Museum of Art.

406

Informal Assessment

Observe individual students as they read and use the Teacher Observation Log found in the ***Program Assessment Teacher's Edition*** to record anecdotal information about each student's strengths and weaknesses.

Teacher Tip COMPREHENSION STRATEGIES Refer to the Comprehension Strategies poster as the class reads the selection. As students are reading, ask them, which of the strategies listed on the poster might be good to use at this point in the selection?

Focus Questions In what ways were the buffalo important to the Native Americans of the Great Plains? How did the building of the Transcontinental Railroad affect the buffalo?

Buffalo Hunt

from the book by Russell Freedman

A Gift from the Great Spirit

Over blazing campfires on winter nights, Indian storytellers spoke of the buffalo. They told tales of buffalo giants and buffalo ghosts, of buffalo that changed magically into men, of children who were raised by buffalo and understood their language.

In olden times, it was said, buffalo used to eat Indians.
1 They ate so many Indians that a legendary figure called
Old Man had to put a stop to it. He organized a race
between the buffalo and the Indians to decide who should
eat whom. The Indians won.

On the Great Plains of North America, every Indian tribe had a rich and ready store of buffalo tales and legends. According to the Comanche, buffalo came from gigantic caves somewhere on the windswept ranges of the Texas Panhandle. Each spring, the Great Spirit sent throngs of buffalo from those hidden caves onto the open plains, as a gift to the Indian people.

Up North, the Blackfoot said that a lake in Canada was
the place where the buffalo began. They were born beneath
the water, in the darkest depths of the lake. If you could
visit that sacred spot on the right night, at exactly the right
time, you would hear an eerie rumbling coming from the
middle of the lake. Then you would see the buffalo rise out
of the water and crowd onto the shore, their shaggy fur wet
2 and dripping, their curved horns gleaming in the moonlight.

To the Plains Indians, the buffalo, or American bison, was the most important animal on Earth. This snorting, lumbering beast provided almost everything the Indians needed to stay alive. The buffalo kept their bellies full and

407

Comprehension Skills

COMPREHENSION

Main Idea and Details

Remind students that the main idea is what a paragraph or passage is mostly about. Details support the main idea by further explaining or giving more information about it. Explain to students that good readers look for main ideas in writing. This helps them focus on the most important parts of what they are reading.

Point out the heading "A Gift from the Great Spirit" on page 407. Explain that students will see several more of these headings as they read on. Suggest that these headings are clues to the main idea of each section. Ask students: *What might the main idea of this section be, based on the heading?* Lead students to understand that the section deals with traditional Native American beliefs about the buffalo. Ask students to identify details on this page that support this main idea.

Main Idea and Details

Introduced in Grade 1.
Scaffolded throughout Grades 2–5.

REINTRODUCED:	Unit 2, Lesson 2
REINFORCED:	Unit 2, Lesson 4
	Unit 2, Lesson 7
	Unit 3, Lesson 2
	Unit 3, Lesson 6
TESTED:	Unit 5 Assessment

Second Reading Recommendation

ORAL • **SILENT**

Differentiating Instruction

If...	Then...
English Learners need extra support with reading "Buffalo Hunt" and using the skill Main Idea and Details	Preteach ***Student Anthology*** pages 406–412 using Day 1 of the "Buffalo Hunt" lesson, found on ***English Learner Support Guide,*** pages 380–383

Teacher Tip **PRONUNCIATION** Help the students pronounce any unfamiliar words. Comanche is pronounced **kə man´ chē**.

COMPREHENSION

Comprehension Strategies

Prompting

3 Summarizing *This seems like a good spot to stop and summarize what we've read because many new facts have been presented. The Plains Indians relied on the buffalo for food and materials to make weapons and tools. Before horses arrived, the Indians hunted the buffalo on foot. Who will volunteer to continue the summary up to the point where we left off?*

Student Sample

Summarizing *When horses came to North America, the Indians were able to travel longer distances and hunt the best buffalo. They became experts at hunting and fighting on horseback.*

Word Knowledge

Homophones:

their there they're herd heard
knew new

Teacher Tip CLARIFYING Encourage students to collaborate with each other in their effort to clarify concept words. Tell students to feel free to consult outside resources, such as a dictionary or encyclopedia, to clarify confusing words and ideas.

Teacher Tip SUMMARIZING If students try to summarize the story but have difficulty, you might ask, "When you have trouble summarizing, what should you do?" Suggestions might include rereading the selection, jotting down notes and then using these notes to make a selection summary, or writing paragraph summaries and using them later as the basis for a summary of the entire selection.

their bodies warm. It supplied raw materials for their weapons, tools, ornaments, and toys. The rhythm of their daily lives was ruled by the comings and goings of the great buffalo herds.

It is little wonder that the Indians worshipped the buffalo as a sacred animal. Before and after every hunt, they praised the spirit of the buffalo and thanked him for giving his meat. Men, women, and children carried buffalo-shaped rocks and fossils for good luck. They believed in the powerful magic of buffalo dreams. When they died, they hoped to go to a happy hunting ground in the sky where buffalo flourished. Looking into the night sky, the Pawnee believed that the Milky Way was formed by dust left behind by the spirit-buffalo.

As recently as 150 years ago, countless millions of buffalo still roamed the prairies and plains. They ranged from the Mississippi River westward to the Rockies, and from Canada down to the Rio Grande. Native American hunters had been stalking the animals for many thousands of years. During most of that time, the Indians had neither horses nor guns. They hunted on foot, and they killed their prey with stone-tipped arrows and spears. They knew how to creep up on a grazing herd, how to surround the buffalo, and how to drive them into corrals or stampede them over cliffs.

Without horses, the Indians had to travel on foot whenever they moved their encampments. Back then, they used big shaggy dogs as pack animals to help carry their tipis and other belongings. Sometimes on a long journey the dogs would grow tired and begin to droop and lag and hang their tongues. Then someone would cry, "Buffalo ahead! Fresh meat in plenty!" And the dogs

408

Informal Assessment

Use the Informal Comprehension Strategies Rubrics on page 406J to determine whether a student is using the strategies being taught.

would bound forward as though they had just set out. Later, the Indians would remember that era as their
3 Dog Days.

The first horses were brought to North America by Spanish explorers in the 1500s. Within a century or so, runaway horses had drifted northward from Spanish settlements in Mexico and were roaming the plains in wild herds. The Indians learned to capture and tame those wild horses, and the horses changed their lives.

Now they could travel long distances to find the buffalo. They could chase the herds and kill the choicest animals. And with pack horses, they could

Catching the Wild Horse. **George Catlin.** The Thomas Gilcrease Institute of American History and Art, Tulsa, Oklahoma.

409

Comprehension Skills

COMPREHENSION

Main Idea and Details

Have students explain what a *main idea* is and why *details* are important to a main idea. *(The main idea is what a paragraph or section is mostly about. Details support main ideas by providing evidence or examples, explaining further, or giving more information.)* Explain to students that the main idea of a paragraph is usually stated in one sentence, called a topic sentence, that appears at the very beginning or very end of the paragraph. Point out that sometimes a few paragraphs will contain details that support one topic sentence. Direct students' attention to the paragraph on page 409 that begins "The first horses. . . ." Ask them to try to find the topic sentence, or the sentence that states the main idea. Lead students to understand that the last sentence of the paragraph, particularly "the horses changed their lives," is the topic sentence. Then have students review that paragraph and the following one to identify details that support the topic sentence.

Word Knowledge

Homophones:

would	**wood**	
so	**sew**	
by	**buy**	**bye**

COMPREHENSION

Comprehension Strategies

Prompting

4 Monitoring and Clarifying *Who sees any terms or ideas that should be clarified before we read on?*

Student Sample

Monitoring and Clarifying *I don't understand the way* tan *is used in this sentence. I know a* tan *is something you get by sitting in the sun. I think* tan *must have a meaning I don't know about.*

Maybe the author will explain more about it later in the selection.

Prompting

5 Monitoring and Clarifying *What other unusual terms should we find definitions for so we can better understand the text?*

Student Sample

Monitoring and Clarifying *This is an odd figure of speech:* dim-sighted. *The rest of the sentence contrasts* dim-sighted *with amazing hearing and ability to smell. I think that* dim-sighted *is the author's way of saying that the buffalo couldn't see very well.*

Word Knowledge

SCAFFOLDING The skills students are reviewing in Word Knowledge should help them in reading the story. This lesson focuses on irregular plural forms of nouns. Irregular plural forms of nouns will be found in boxes similar to this one throughout the selection.

Irregular plural forms of nouns:

deer antelope elk

carry bigger tipis and more possessions with them as they traveled across the plains. In time, the Indians became some of the world's finest horsemen, experts at hunting and fighting on horseback.

When white trappers and traders began to visit the Great Plains in the early 1800s, about 250,000 Indians were living in the region. They belonged to some two dozen distinct tribes, each with its own language and customs. Many of these tribes had migrated from the woodlands of the East, but only a few, like the Pawnee of Kansas and Nebraska, still practiced the old arts of farming and fishing.

Most of the Plains Indians had given up the settled life of farmers and fishermen to follow the buffalo herds. They spent the winter in sheltered camps. But in spring they folded their tipis and roamed the plains. They hunted other animals besides the buffalo, of course—deer, antelope, elk, and an occasional bear. But buffalo meat was their staple food, buffalo hunting their main occupation.

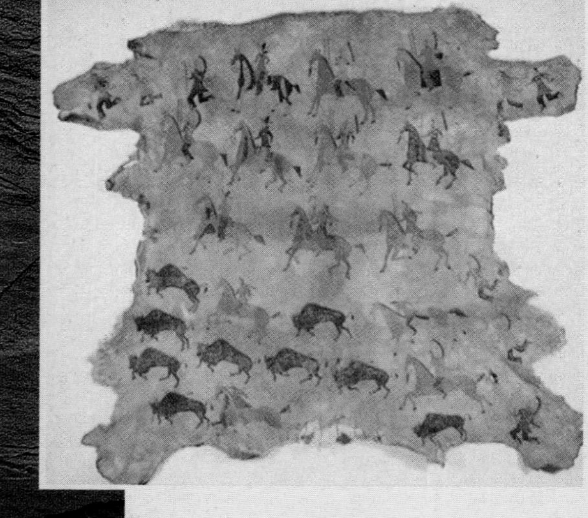

Painted elkskin robe. Late 19th Century. Crow. The National Museum of the American Indian, Smithsonian Institution.

410

A Plains tribe was made up of many small, independent bands. Once or twice a year, all the bands belonging to a tribe would assemble for a great religious ceremony, a tribal council, or a communal hunt. But mostly, the bands moved about on their own. Each band had its own encampments, or villages. And each band hunted in a different part of the tribal territory.

Hunting was a man's responsibility. Every able-bodied boy was taught that he should become a fearless hunter and warrior. Small boys ran about yip-yapping in play hunts, dreaming of the day when they would be big enough to ride after a herd of stampeding buffalo. A successful hunter could provide for many people. He became a man of influence, entitled to honors and privileges.

Women were responsible for putting the buffalo and other game to good use. It was a woman's job to skin and butcher the buffalo, to preserve the meat and tan the hides. As Indian girls grew up, they learned 4 from their mothers and grandmothers the art of transforming a dead buffalo into a thousand practical and useful objects.

The buffalo was the biggest animal on the plains. A full-grown bull stood six feet tall at the humped shoulders and weighed a ton or more. An angry bull could stab a bear to death. He could toss a wolf so high into the air that the wolf would be killed by the fall. 5

While buffalo were somewhat dim-sighted, they could hear the faintest sounds and smell enemies from three miles away. And when they sensed danger, they moved fast. A bull or cow could wheel about on its slim hind legs and run as fast as a horse. When a whole herd stampeded, the earth trembled.

411

Comprehension Skills

COMPREHENSION

Main Idea and Details

Review with the students that each paragraph usually contains one *main idea.* If there is a clearly stated main idea, it can usually be found in either the first or last sentence of the paragraph. *Details* give more information about the main idea.

Point out the following topic sentences to the students:

- "Hunting was a man's responsibility." (paragraph 2, page 411)
- "The buffalo was the biggest animal on the plains." (paragraph 4, page 411)

Have the students tell which sentences in each of these paragraphs add supporting details to the main idea. Then have students focus their attention on the third paragraph on page 411. Ask them to identify the main idea of that paragraph on their own. *(Women were responsible for putting the buffalo and other game to good use.)* Then ask students to list three details in the paragraph that support the main idea. You might have them use a graphic organizer like the one mentioned in the Teacher Tip below.

Word Knowledge

SCAFFOLDING The skills students are reviewing in Word Knowledge should help them in reading the story. This lesson focuses on the /ch/ sound spelled *tch.* Words with the /ch/ sound spelled *tch* will be found in boxes similar to this one throughout the selection.

Word with the /ch/ sound spelled *tch:*
butcher

Teacher Tip GRAPHIC ORGANIZER The students may find it helpful to graphically represent the relationship between the main idea and details. For example:

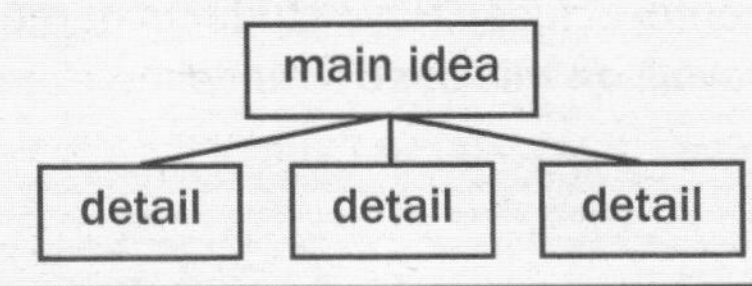

COMPREHENSION

Comprehension Strategies

Teacher Modeling

6 Monitoring and Clarifying

What is a travois? I think I need to reread.

Okay, now I understand. It's a platform that is pulled along the ground by horses. It's used for hauling things or carrying people. I'm glad the author explained it and also told how to pronounce it. But it's even better to have a picture of one. I think there are some travois in the painting by George Catlin.

Word Knowledge

Word with the /ch/ sound spelled *tch:*
stretched

Teacher Tip **PRONUNCIATION** Tipi is pronounced tē′ pē.

White explorers were astonished at the size of the herds they saw as they crossed the Great Plains. There were times when buffalo stretched endlessly across the countryside as far as the eye could see. Artist George Catlin described these herds when he traveled west during the 1830s to study and paint the Indians. "Buffalo graze in immense herds and almost incredible numbers," he wrote. "And they roam over vast tracts of country."

No one really knows how many buffalo roamed the prairies and plains before the white man came. The Indians thought there were enough buffalo to last forever. It seemed impossible that they could ever disappear.

The Hunt

On the day set for starting a hunt, everyone was up at sunrise. The women went right to work, packing their household belongings and getting everything ready for the move. Youngsters rounded up the horses and dogs. The men gathered in small groups to discuss the day's plans.

After a quick morning meal, the leaders of the hunt, the marshals, assembled. They took their feathered banners in their hands, mounted their horses, and gave the signal to break camp.

With that, the Indian village disappeared almost like a puff of smoke. Tipis dropped to the ground as the women removed the buffalo-skin walls and took down the long poles that held the tipis erect.

The poles were now put to a different use. Lashed to the sides of a horse so they trailed behind on the ground, the poles supported a sturdy rawhide platform
6 called a travois (tra-VOY). This platform held the folded tipi walls and the family's household goods. Sometimes

412

Differentiating Instruction

Intervention Tip

MONITORING AND CLARIFYING Prompt students to tell you the four methods one can use to clarify a word (using prior knowledge, discussing with peers, referring to outside resources, and using context clues). Have students name which clarifying method can be used to clarify the term *travois* on this page's modeling exercise. (context clues: apposition)

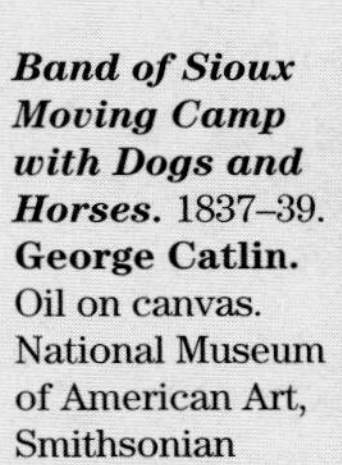

Band of Sioux Moving Camp with Dogs and Horses. 1837–39. **George Catlin.** Oil on canvas. National Museum of American Art, Smithsonian Institution.

small children or sick people sat on top of the pile to be hauled along by a strong packhorse. Dogs also worked as pack animals, pulling travois designed to fit their size and strength.

When the horses and dogs were harnessed and loaded and ready to go, the people and their animals moved out across the plains. The warriors, mounted on the best hunting horses, rode along in front. They were followed by boys and girls driving the herd of extra horses. Behind them came the women leading the packhorses, along with the small children and the old folks, some riding, some walking, and some being carried on the travois. Every woman had a heavy pack on her back. The men never carried packs. They kept their arms free to use their weapons in case of a surprise attack.

Scouts rode far ahead of the marching people, and far to either side, watching for signs of buffalo or lurking enemies. Other warriors acted as a rear guard. They followed the group at a distance, seeing that no one lagged behind.

413

Comprehension Skills

Second Read

COMPREHENSION

Main Idea and Details

Have volunteers provide definitions of *main idea* and *supporting details.* Then have students practice their skills.

- Ask the students to read paragraphs 3 and 4 on page 412. Tell them to identify the main idea in each paragraph. *(In both cases, the main idea is stated in the first sentence.)*
- Have the students identify the supporting details in each paragraph. *(All the other sentences in each paragraph contain supporting details.)*

Remind the students that, especially in selections with a lot of information and facts, identifying main ideas can help them remember important information.

Word Knowledge

Word with the /ch/ sound spelled *tch:*
watching

Differentiating Instruction

If...	Then...
English Learners need extra support with reading "Buffalo Hunt" and using the skill Main Idea and Details	Preteach ***Student Anthology*** pages 412–417 using Day 2 of the "Buffalo Hunt" lesson, found on ***English Learner Support Guide,*** pages 383–385

COMPREHENSION

Comprehension Strategies

First Read

Prompting

7 Visualizing *Forming a mental image of what we are reading about will help us to recall and make sense of it. Can you visualize the "signs" Native Americans looked for from different animals?*

Student Sample

Visualizing *Yes, I can picture a raven circling like a dark spot in the big sky, and then cawing as it moves out toward the buffalo. I can also imagine the Cheyenne hunter, still kneeling, after catching the cricket in his hands, and watching to see in what direction its antennae point.*

Prompting

8 Visualizing *Can you imagine one of the Cheyenne warriors approaching a buffalo with only a spear? What do you see?*

Student Sample

Visualizing *I see the warrior moving silently toward the buffalo, through knee-high prairie grass, with his spear held over his shoulder, ready to be launched from his hand at a moment's notice.*

Word Knowledge

Words with the /ch/ sound spelled *tch*:
pitch catch watched

Teacher Tip SELF-EVALUATING COMPREHENSION Good readers constantly evaluate their understanding of what they read. Stop often to make sure students are doing this.

Strung out across the prairie, the Indians formed a grand procession. People sang as they marched along, dogs barked, horses whinnied, bells jingled. They moved forward each day by easy stages, so their horses would be in good condition when they found the buffalo.

At the end of a day's march, the marshals picked the spot where they would pitch camp. The women quickly put up the tipis and prepared the evening meal as the men gathered to chat and smoke. On the open plains, the Indians usually camped in a circle, with the doorway of each tipi facing east to catch the morning sun.

When they reached the territory where they expected to hunt, the scouts fanned out across the countryside, looking for buffalo. Everyone else waited in the hushed camp. Marshals moved quietly from one tipi to the next. They reminded people in low tones not to sing or shout or make any loud noise that might scare off the buffalo, which could hear weak and distant sounds.

The scouts, meanwhile, searched for buffalo signs.
7 Sometimes they relied on animal helpers. The Comanche watched for ravens. They thought that if a raven circled four times overhead and cawed, it would then fly off toward the buffalo. A Cheyenne hunter would find a cricket, hold it in his hand, and wait to see which way its antennae pointed. The buffalo, he believed, would be found in that direction.

When a herd was sighted, the successful scout rushed back to camp. As he arrived, people crowded around, greeting him with congratulations and thanks. First he smoked a ceremonial pipe with one of the band's elders. Then he reported what he had seen.

The chase usually started the next morning. As soon as it was light enough to see, the hunters mounted their horses. Riding close together, they stayed downwind from the herd, so the buffalo would not catch their scent.

414

When they were as close as they could get without disturbing the buffalo, they paused and waited. The marshals looked over the area and selected the best spot to launch the attack. Silently, they led the hunters forward and spaced them evenly, so that each would have a fair start. Then one of the marshals rode out in view of both hunters and buffalo. He waved his hand
8 above his head, and the chase began.

Bending low over their horses, the Indians galloped toward the grazing herd. At first the buffalo paid little attention. Often the hunters would almost reach the herd before the buffalo became alarmed and started to run.

Each man acted on his own now. Holding his bow in his left hand, urging his horse on with the whip strapped to his right wrist, a hunter picked his target and went after it at full speed. His horse was trained to approach the buffalo from the right, so the rider could shoot his arrow to the left, toward the animal. As he closed in, he aimed for a spot just behind the buffalo's last rib, where the arrow would pierce the animal's lungs. A single well-aimed arrow could kill the biggest buffalo.

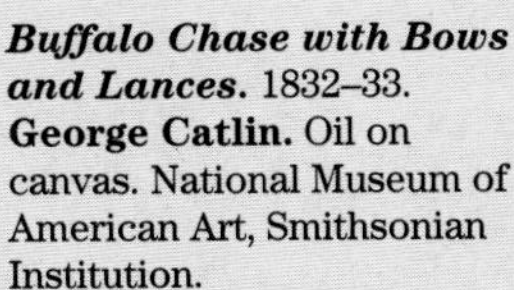

Buffalo Chase with Bows and Lances. 1832–33. **George Catlin.** Oil on canvas. National Museum of American Art, Smithsonian Institution.

415

Comprehension Skills

Second Read

COMPREHENSION

Main Idea and Details

Remind the students to look at both the first and last sentences of paragraphs when trying to identify the main idea. Have them skim the first few paragraphs on page 414 and determine whether the topic sentence is at the beginning or end of each paragraph. For example, in the first paragraph on page 414, the first sentence tells the main idea of the paragraph.

Explain to students that these pages include many descriptive details. These details describe the scenes of preparing for and engaging in the buffalo hunt. Help students understand that some main ideas are not stated directly in a text. Work with students to review pages 414–415, concentrating on why the author might have included so many descriptive details. Lead students to uncover an implied main idea about the buffalo hunt. For example, your class may conclude that the buffalo hunt was a complicated, but well-planned, event for the Plains Indians.

Word Knowledge

Homophones:

led lead fair fare

Teacher Tip GRAPHIC ORGANIZERS Keep a chart of the most important facts contained in this selection. Point out that the students can use main ideas to help them summarize the selection.

Teacher Tip PRONUNCIATIONS Cheyenne is pronounced **shī yan′**.

COMPREHENSION

Comprehension Strategies

Prompting

9 Summarizing *We have just read about what takes place during an actual hunt, so now would be a good time to sum up what we've learned. Who will volunteer to summarize this section on the hunt?*

Student Sample

Summarizing *After the scouts found a herd of buffalo, the hunters would space themselves evenly. Then they would rush toward the herd. Each warrior would try to shoot the buffalo just behind the last rib. It was dangerous. Horses could stumble, and the buffalo could kill you. The chase wasn't the best way to kill buffalo, but it was exciting.*

Prompting

10 Summarizing *We have learned that Native Americans were not always on horseback while hunting buffalo; sometimes they were on foot. Who can paraphrase how they hunted buffalo on foot?*

Student Sample

Summarizing *They would creep up on the buffalo, hiding in the grass. They could kill many before the buffalo even knew they were there. In winter, they might hide under buffalo robes or white wolfskin. Sometimes they would surround small herds. They would kill the animals on the outside of the circle, trapping the others inside.*

Word Knowledge

Irregular plural forms of nouns:
buffalo men

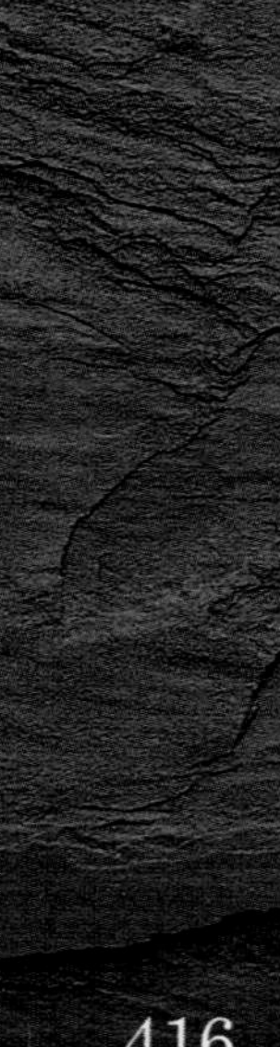

Sometimes an arrow would strike with such force that it would be completely buried. It might pass all the way through the animal, come out the other side, and drop to the ground. If an arrow failed to go deep enough, the hunter might reach over, pull it out of the buffalo, and use it again.

Once an arrow hit its mark, the hunter instantly took off after another buffalo. His horse understood exactly what to do. Running free, guided only by words or knee pressure, a trained hunting pony would leap away from a buffalo's horns as soon as it heard the twang of the bowstring.

Some men found the bow and arrow too tame. They preferred to use spears, for it took more strength and courage to spear a buffalo. To carry only a spear on the hunt was a mark of daring and pride.

With any weapon, the chase was risky. Horses stumbled in prairie-dog holes. Wounded buffalo lashed out with their horns. Sometimes an enraged bull crashed headlong into a horse and rider. The buffalo claimed many victims as hunters were trampled in the
9 dust or died of broken bones.

While the chase was thrilling, it wasn't always the best way to hunt. During a typical chase on horseback, each hunter might bring down two or three buffalo. Under the right conditions, the Indians could get better results with less danger by hunting in the old way—on foot.

In that case, they would stake their horses and creep up on the buffalo, crawling on hands and knees through tall grass. As long as the Indians were hidden, the buffalo would go right on grazing, even as arrows flew silently around them. Each man might shoot several buffalo in quick succession before the others became frightened and ran off.

416

In winter, when the grass offered little cover, a hunter might sneak up on a herd disguised in a buffalo robe. Or he could drape himself in the skin of a white wolf. Healthy buffalo in herds did not fear wolves and didn't run when they saw one.

If a herd was small enough, the Indians sometimes surrounded the buffalo on foot. Approaching downwind, they fanned out, moved in from all sides, and formed a tight ring. Then they ran in circles around the herd, whooping and yelling and waving their arms as the terrified animals milled about in confusion. Slowly the Indians closed the circle until they were close enough to let go with their arrows and spears.

The first buffalo to be hit would fall near the outside of the circle, blocking the path of those inside the ring. As more buffalo fell, their bodies trapped the others.
10 Sometimes not a single animal escaped alive.

On horseback, the Indians could surround bigger herds, galloping around them in a circle. One afternoon in 1832, the artist George Catlin, armed with his pencil and sketchbook, watched from a distance as 500 Sioux horseman surrounded a herd near the present site of Pierre, South Dakota. By sundown, the hunters had killed 1,400 buffalo.

The Buffalo Hunt No. 39. 1919. **Charles M. Russell.** Oil on canvas. Amon Carter Museum, Fort Worth, Texas.

417

Comprehension Skills

Main Idea and Details

Because these pages end the section *The Hunt*, it is a good time to have students write down the main idea and details for this section.

Encourage students to use the title *The Hunt* as the main idea for the section. Then have them review pages 412–417 and make a list of some of the most important details that explain the buffalo hunt. Challenge students to assess the importance of each detail on their lists. Ask them to rank the details in order of importance, with the most important details listed first. Have volunteers share their lists with the class and explain why they think some details are more important than others in understanding the nature of the buffalo hunt.

Word Knowledge

Homophones:

not knot **site sight**

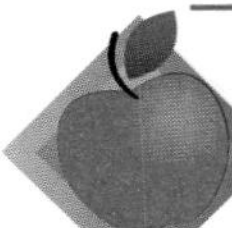

Teacher Tip PRONUNCIATION Pierre is pronounced **pē yer′**.

Teacher Tip CHECKING COMPREHENSION To test students' comprehension of the first half of this selection, have them answer the following true-and-false questions.

- According to Native American legend, buffalo used to eat people until the Old Man put a stop to it. *(true)*
- Horses are native to North America. *(false)*
- Scouts were responsible for planning and leading the buffalo chase. *(false)*
- Hunting on foot could bring better results and less danger than hunting on horseback. *(true)*

COMPREHENSION

Comprehension Strategies

Prompting

11 Visualizing *This heading is strange—"From the Brains to the Tail." What do you picture as you read this? What do you think this section will be about?*

Student Sample

Visualizing *I picture a brain, like those shown in science textbooks, and a long, skinny, brown tail. I assume that this section will be about different parts of the buffalo.*

Prompting

12 Monitoring and Clarifying *One of the terms we were looking for clarification on earlier has come up again. Who can tell me what the term is and what new information has been given to clarify it?*

Student Sample

Monitoring and Clarifying *The author gave an explanation of* tanning. *It's a way of working with the buffalo hides to make them soft! This explanation helps me to better picture what tanning is.*

Word Knowledge

Homophones:

meat meet see sea

Teacher Tip SILENT READING This is a good place for students to begin reading silently. If the students read the first part of the selection during another class period, have volunteers summarize what has happened so far before they begin reading the second part.

The Silk Robe. c. 1890. **Charles M. Russell.** Oil on canvas. Amon Carter Museum, Fort Worth, Texas.

11 From the Brains to the Tail

A successful hunt called for a feast. Beside the campfire that evening, a medicine man offered prayers of thanksgiving. He thanked the spirits for their aid during the chase, and he thanked the buffalo for giving his meat to the people. Choice bits of meat were sliced off, held up for the spirits to see, then buried as an offering.

There was plenty for everyone to eat. A single fat buffalo cow supplied enough meat to feed a hundred hungry people. They gorged themselves on fresh tongue roasted over the open fire, on tasty morsels cut from the buffalo's hump. They ate hot, dripping ribs and steaks. And they feasted on yards of roasted gut, turned inside out, stuffed with chunks of meat, and seared over glowing coals. The sweet, nutritious bone marrow was saved for the old folks. It was the only meat their toothless gums could chew.

Most of the meat taken during a big hunt was preserved for the future. The women cut the meat into strips and hung it over high poles to dry. After several days, this sun-dried meat, called jerky, was so well preserved that it would last for months. It could be carried anywhere and would not spoil, even during the hottest months.

418

Differentiating Instruction

If...	Then...
English Learners need extra linguistic support with reading "Buffalo Hunt" and using the skill Main Idea and Details	Preteach ***Student Anthology*** pages 418–422 using Day 3 of the "Buffalo Hunt" lesson, found on ***English Learner Support Guide,*** pages 386–388

Some of the dried meat was pounded to a pulp, mixed with buffalo fat, and flavored with crushed nuts, berries, and fruit. This was called pemmican. Packed in buffalo-skin bags, pemmican would last for years without spoiling. Sliced and dipped in wild honey, it was nourishing and delicious, a favorite food among the Indians, and later the white fur traders as well.

Every part of the buffalo that could be chewed, swallowed, and digested was used for food. And every other part was put to some use.

Indian women spent a great deal of time and effort
12 tanning buffalo hides. After a hunt, the fresh hides were spread out on the ground, hairy side down, and pegged in place. Using scrapers made of buffalo bone, the women scraped all the flesh, fat, and blood from the hides. They cured and bleached the hides in the sun, and soaked them in a tanning fluid of buffalo brains, liver, and fat mixed with water. Then they worked the hides for several days—rubbing, kneading, squeezing, stretching—to make them soft and supple. A good hunter might have several wives working on hides taken from the animals he had killed.

If the hides were to be used as winter robes, the hair was left in place. Thick-furred buffalo robes made warm and comfortable cloaks and bedding. They could be cut and stitched into caps, earmuffs, leggings, and mittens. The finest robes came from buffalo killed during the winter, when nature gave the animal a full coat to protect it from snow and cold.

With the hair scraped off, the hides were smoked over fires to make them waterproof. They could then be fashioned into dozens of useful articles. They were used for the walls of tipis, for clothing and moccasins, for pouches, purses, and saddlebags. Babies were carried in

419

Teacher Tip HIGHLIGHTING DETAILS Emphasize the importance of the Plains Indians not hunting merely for sport. They stopped hunting after they had enough food and hides for the winter.

COMPREHENSION

Comprehension Skills

Main Idea and Details

Direct the students' attention to the heading at the top of page 418. Prompt students to tell you that headings refer to the main idea in a particular selection.

Have the students write down the heading. Explain that they will be developing an outline that will contain the main ideas in this section. The main ideas will become the supporting details for the overall main idea of this particular selection.

Once the students have finished writing down the heading, have them write down the topic sentence of each paragraph following the heading.

After they have written a few sentences, discuss how each sentence gives the main idea of the paragraph and adds to the understanding of the main idea of the section.

Help the students comment on the meaning of the section heading *From the Brains to the Tail.* What does this title imply? What other title could they give the section?

Word Knowledge

Words with the /ch/ sound spelled *tch:*
stretching stitched

Teacher Tip PRONUNCIATION Pemmican is pronounced **pe´ mə kən.**

COMPREHENSION

Comprehension Strategies

Prompting

13 **Summarizing** *We have just read about all the uses Native Americans found for parts of the buffalo. Now is a good time to sum up all these uses to make sure that we understand them. Who will volunteer to do this for the class?*

Student Sample

Summarizing *The Native Americans preserved the meat in jerky or pemmican. They used the hides for robes and other kinds of clothing. They used the horns, the hooves, and the bones. Even the droppings were burned.*

Word Knowledge

Word with the /ch/ sound spelled *tch:*
stretched

Comanche Village in Texas, Women Dressing Robes and Drying Meat. 1834–35. **George Catlin.** Oil on canvas. National Museum of Art, Smithsonian Institution.

cradleboards lined with the softest buffalo calfskin. The dead were laid to rest wrapped in buffalo-hide winding sheets.

Thick rawhide from the necks of old bulls was stretched to make tough war shields and the soles of winter moccasins. Strong sinews from the neck and back of the buffalo provided bowstrings and thread. The buffalo's hair was twisted into ropes and bridles, woven into ornaments, stuffed into leather balls. Its stomach became a water jug, its tail a flyswatter.

Buffalo horns were used for cups, ladles, and spoons, and to carry hot coals to the next campground. The hooves produced glue; the fat, soap. The bones were shaped into knives, spears, and tools of many kinds. On the northern plains, the backbone with ribs attached made a toboggan for children in winter.

420

Even the buffalo's droppings were valuable. On the treeless plains, firewood was scarce. But there was an endless supply of sundried buffalo dung left behind by the grazing herds. These prized "buffalo chips" burned slowly, produced a hot fire, and were ideal for cooking. They were used for that purpose by the Indians, and

13 later by white settlers too.

A fall buffalo hunt would continue until the band had all the hides and meat it needed for the winter. Then the Indians would settle down in their winter camps. Every band had its favorite winter camping sites near woods, in a sheltered canyon, or along a river bottom. Instead of camping in a circle, as they did on the open plains, the Indians pitched their winter tipis in a line that sometimes stretched for miles along the canyon floor or the river's banks.

A tipi provided a warm and cozy winter home. Because it was shaped like a cone, it could withstand the most violent winds and blizzards. Its walls were waterproof. An open fire in the center of the tipi furnished heat, light, and a stove for indoor cooking. The smoke spiraled up through an adjustable smoke hole at the top of the tipi. At night, firelight would shine through the translucent buffalo-skin walls, and from the outside, the tipi glowed like a lantern.

Tipis were usually owned by the women who made them. A typical tipi measured perhaps fifteen feet across at the base, allowing sufficient living space for the family and its possessions. It could be put up in fifteen minutes by the women of the household. It could be taken down in five minutes. And it could be packed on a horse travois and carried anywhere.

When the hunting was good, the Indians went into winter camp with tons of sun-dried buffalo meat. They

421

Differentiating Instruction

Challenge Tip

MAIN IDEA AND DETAILS Have the students outline other sections in this selection the same way they outlined "From the Brains to the Tail."

Comprehension Skills

COMPREHENSION

Main Idea and Details

Encourage students to continue writing down the topic sentence of each paragraph as they compile an outline for this section. In this way, they can learn to consider the "big picture" of how various details in a text work to support a larger main idea.

It is a good time to once again have students practice their skills on a single paragraph. Have students focus on the third paragraph on page 421. Ask them to identify the topic sentence of the paragraph. *(The topic sentence is the first sentence.)*

Work with students to assess the importance of the details in the paragraph that support the main idea. Point out that the details seem to be listed in the order of their importance. For example, it seems logical that the safety of a tipi was more important than the fact that it produced a warm glow like a lantern.

Word Knowledge

Homophones:

too to two **hole whole**

Teacher Tip BEYOND THE TEXT Some students may be interested in the efforts to preserve buffalo that are being carried out today. Suggest that they start by looking in the library or on the Internet for information about buffalo conservation efforts.

COMPREHENSION

Comprehension Strategies

Prompting

14 **Summarizing** *Who can sum up what the Native Americans did after fall hunting was over?*

Student Sample

Summarizing *After the fall hunting was done, the Native Americans would go to their winter homes. They stayed in tipis in the winter. In the winter, the Indians didn't have to hunt. They were free to do whatever they wanted.*

Teacher Modeling

15 **Visualizing** *It says here the number of buffalo started to dwindle once the white people came to the West. I can visualize how that must've looked before and after. Before the coming of the white settlers, I see more buffalo than I can count, spread out over the prairies, moving in great herds. After the settlers came, I picture small groups of buffalo crossing the prairie, looking very vulnerable. Good readers are always getting images in their heads about what they read. If you get a good one, tell the class about it.*

Word Knowledge

Homophones:

do dew great grate

didn't have to hunt day after day, all winter long, for fear of starving. Between hunts, they were free to do as they wished. "It was a great life," said Tom Le Forge, a white man who lived several years with the Crows. "At all times I had ample leisure for lazy loafing and
14 dreaming and visiting."

With the Buffalo Gone

Year after year without fail, the buffalo drifted back and forth across the plains in tune with the seasons. Usually they traveled in small bands. But during the late summer rutting season, they gathered in enormous herds that numbered hundreds of thousands of animals. A truly great herd might be fifty miles long and take days to pass by.

Buffalo Chase, A Single Death. 1832-33. **George Catlin.** National Museum of American Art, Smithsonian Institution, Washington, DC.

422

Differentiating Instruction

If...	Then...
English Learners need extra linguistic support with reading "Buffalo Hunt" and using the skill Main Idea and Details	Preteach ***Student Anthology*** pages 422–425 using Day 4 of the "Buffalo Hunt" lesson, found on ***English Learner Support Guide,*** pages 389–391

Indians had hunted the buffalo for thousands of years without making much of a dent in the herds. Sometimes they killed more animals than they could use. When they drove a herd over a cliff, they could not always carry away all the meat. But for the most part, the Indians were not wasteful. They hunted when they needed meat and hides.

As white people came to the plains, the buffalo herds began to dwindle. By the early 1800s, trading posts were springing up all over the West. White traders wanted buffalo robes and tongues for profitable markets in the East. In exchange, they offered guns, tools, tobacco, whiskey, and trinkets. The Indians had always hunted for their own needs. Now, by killing a few more buffalo, they could obtain the white man's goods.

Soon the Indians were killing buffalo for their hides and tongues alone. Tongues packed in salt were shipped in barges down the Missouri River, to be sent to the cities of the East, where they were sold as an expensive delicacy. Buffalo robes became fashionable as lap robes and blankets. White people had them made into fur coats. During the 1830s and 1840s, hundreds of thousands of robes were shipped east.

By then, white hunters were beginning to kill more buffalo than the Indians. Pioneers traveling westward in covered wagons shot the animals for food along the
15 way, scaring off entire herds. Before long, few buffalo could be found along the great trails leading west. Then the United States Army hired professional hunters to supply buffalo meat to western military posts. And as railroads were built across the prairies and plains, white hunters furnished buffalo meat for the railroad construction crews.

423

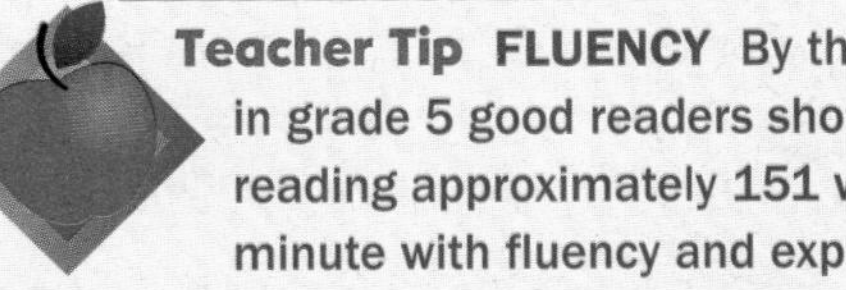

Teacher Tip FLUENCY By this time in grade 5 good readers should be reading approximately 151 words per minute with fluency and expression. The only way to gain this fluency is through practice. Have students reread the selection to you and to one another during Workshop to help build fluency.

Comprehension Skills

COMPREHENSION

Main Idea and Details

Have the students continue to write down the topic sentence of each paragraph in this section.

Point out to students that the details they are recording should now come under a new heading, or main idea, *With the Buffalo Gone.* Have students draw some conclusions about what that heading might mean. Ask students to write one sentence based on this heading that predicts the main idea of this section. Lead them to understand that this section describes how the buffalo herds were affected by Native Americans' and white settlers' hunting patterns.

Explain to the students that by breaking down this section this way, they can easily summarize the main ideas in the section.

Word Knowledge

Irregular plural forms of nouns:
buffalo **people**

Teacher Tip DIGGING DEEPER Knowing the importance of the buffalo, students may find it odd that some Plains Indians would kill the sacred animals for their hides and tongues alone. It is important for students to understand that outside influences were beginning to affect the lifestyle of the Plains Indians in dramatic ways. If students wonder about the Plains Indians' actions, you may want to suggest that a volunteer model *asking questions* and finding the answers in the text that explain the reasons for the Plains Indians' behavior. Encourage students to post unanswered questions on the Concept/Question Board.

COMPREHENSION

Comprehension Strategies

Prompting

16 **Summarizing** *Who can sum up why buffalo herds started to dwindle?*

Student Sample

Summarizing *Native Americans started killing buffalo to trade with white people. Then, white people started killing buffalo for sport. Finally, a new tanning process was invented, and hunters killed millions of buffalo. By the 1880s, there were only a few hundred left.*

Discussing Strategy Use

While they are reading the selection, have students share any problems they encountered and tell what strategies they used.

- How did they clarify confusing passages?
- How did they summarize the text?
- What did they visualize as they were reading?

Remind students that good readers use all of the strategies listed above and that they should be using them whenever they read. Make sure that students explain how using the strategies helped them to better understand the selection. For example, "This selection has a lot of details. Summarizing helped me focus on the most important ones so I could understand the main ideas I was reading about."

Word Knowledge

Homophones:

die dye eight ate

The Herd on the Move. 1862. **William J. Hays.** Toned lithograph. Amon Carter Museum, Fort Worth, Texas.

Buffalo hunting became a popular sport. Many travelers felt that a trip west wasn't complete unless they had shot themselves a buffalo. American millionaires and European noblemen toured the West in style, with servants to hand them their guns and champagne to drink after the hunt. Railroads began to feature special excursion trains through buffalo country. As the trains chugged along, passengers could poke their guns through the open windows and fire away at the grazing herds.

By the 1860s, Indian tribes found that the buffalo were disappearing from their traditional hunting grounds. When they went elsewhere to hunt, they were followed almost immediately by white hunters, soldiers, and settlers. "Wherever the whites are established, the buffalo is gone," complained the Sioux Chief White Cloud, "and the red hunters must die of hunger."

Indians who once had been friendly to white people vowed to go on the warpath. Alarmed by the large-scale slaughter of their herds, angry warriors from many tribes banded together. They began to attack wagon trains, ranch houses, and railroad construction crews.

There were still about eight million buffalo left on the plains in 1870, when a newly invented tanning process sealed the fate of the remaining herds. For the first time, commercial tanneries in the East could turn buffalo hides into expensive leather. A single hide now brought

424

Teacher Tip EXTRA HELP Reread the selection with students who had difficulty understanding it. Continue modeling and prompting the use of strategies and skills as you reread.

Teacher Tip BUILDING FLUENCY As students read, you may notice that some need work in building fluency. During Workshop, have these students choose a section of text (a minimum of 160 words) to read several times in order to build fluency.

as much as $3—more than a factory worker earned in a week in those days. A professional hide hunter could bag as many as two hundred buffalo in one day.

Organized bands of hide hunters shot their way south from Kansas to Texas. Armed with powerful long-range rifles with telescopic sights, they began to slaughter buffalo at the rate of a million a year. As the animals fell, gangs of skinners stripped them of their valuable hides and left the carcasses to rot on the prairie.

Indian war parties attacked the hide hunters wherever they found them, but the hunters could not be stopped. Within a few years, the Indians saw their main source of food, clothing, and shelter vanish.

At one time, perhaps sixty or seventy million buffalo had roamed the plains. By the early 1880s, the endless herds had been wiped out. Only a few hundred wild
16 buffalo were still hiding out in remote mountain valleys.

With the buffalo gone, the proud and independent Plains Indians became a conquered people. Their way of life was destroyed, their hunting grounds taken over by white ranchers and settlers. Swept by starvation and disease, the great hunting tribes were confined to reservations, where they depended on government food rations. Their children were sent to boarding schools to learn the language and customs of the white man.

The days of the buffalo hunters had faded like a dream. But Indian storytellers still gather on winter nights to keep the old tales alive. They speak of a time when buffalo ruled the plains, and Indian warriors rode out to meet them.

I go to kill the buffalo.
The Great Spirit sent the buffalo.
On hills, in plains and woods.
So give me my bow; give me my bow;
I go to kill the buffalo.

—SIOUX SONG

425

Comprehension Skills

Main Idea and Details

Have students review the section outlines they made as they read. Ask them to explain in their own words the main idea of each section. (Remind them to use the section titles as clues.) Then ask students to summarize the main idea of the entire selection in a sentence or two. Have volunteers share and discuss their ideas with the class.

Checking Comprehension

Ask students the following questions to check their comprehension of the selection.

- Why were the Plains Indians able to kill buffalo for thousands of years without making the herds smaller? *(They only killed as many as they needed to live through the winter, leaving most of the buffalo alive.)*
- What parts of the buffalo did the Plains Indians use? *(They used all the parts of the buffalo from the horns to the buffalo droppings.)*
- How did the white people change the way of life for the Plains Indians? *(They killed almost all the buffalo, they put the Indians on reservations, and made the children attend schools where they learned English and new customs.)*
- How has this selection connected with your knowledge of the unit theme? *(Answers will vary—students should compare/contrast examples of life in the American West from this selection with their own experiences or past reading and use these connections to make a general statement about the unit theme.)*

COMPREHENSION

Differentiating Instruction

If...	Then...
English Learners have been participating in the "Buffalo Hunt" ***English Learner Support Guide*** activities	Review the selection and the skill Main Idea and Details using Day 5 of the "Buffalo Hunt" lesson, found on ***English Learner Support Guide,*** pages 391–393

Formal Assessment

See pages 6–9 in ***Unit 5 Assessment*** to test students' comprehension of "Buffalo Hunt."

Teacher Tip HANDING-OFF PROCESS To facilitate the *handing-off process,* use a seating arrangement that allows students to see and hear one another easily. A circle or semicircle is effective. This will also create a relaxed atmosphere, making students more likely to contribute to the discussion.

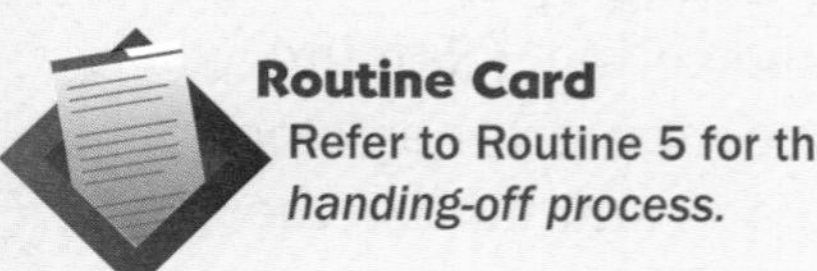

Routine Card Refer to Routine 5 for the *handing-off process.*

Clues	Problems	Wonderings
Campfires "The Hunt" Captions Headings Nonfiction Comanche	The word *encampment*	Why were the buffalo so important to the Native Americans? What happened to the buffalo?

Reading Transparency 54

www.sra4kids.com Web Connection Some students may choose to conduct a computer search for additional books or information about the American West. Invite them to make a list of these books and sources of information to share with classmates and the school librarian. Check the Reading link of the SRA Web page for additional links to theme-related Web sites.

Teacher Tip LOCATING AND RECALLING INFORMATION Have students scan the selection for text that supports ideas being discussed. Have them use what they know about text structure to help them locate information. For example, ask them under what heading they can find a description of how the Plains Indians hunted buffalo. (*The Hunt*) Have them also use the illustrations to help them recall what they read and where they read it.

Discussing the Selection

After the first read, the whole group discusses the selection and any personal thoughts, reactions, problems, or questions that it raises. To stimulate discussion, students can ask one another the kinds of questions that good readers ask themselves about a text: *How does it connect to going west? What have I learned that is new? What did I find interesting? What is important here? What was difficult to understand? Why would someone want to read this?* It is important for students to see you as a contributing member of the group.

Routine 5 To emphasize that you are part of the group, actively participate in the *handing-off process:* Raise your hand to be called on by the last speaker when you have a contribution to make. Point out unusual and interesting insights verbalized by students so that these insights are recognized and discussed. As the year progresses, students will take more and more responsibility for the discussion of selections.

Engage students in a discussion to determine whether they have discerned the following concepts:

- The buffalo was vital to the Plains Indians' way of life.
- The arrival of white settlers greatly contributed to the demise of the buffalo.
- Without the buffalo, the plains were no longer equipped to support the needs of Native Americans who lived there.

In discussing the above ideas, students should identify and assess evidence from the text that supports them.

During this time, have students return to the clues, problems, and wonderings that they noted during browsing to determine whether the clues were borne out by the selection, whether and how their problems were solved, and whether their wonderings were answered or deserve further discussion and exploration. Let the students decide which items deserve further discussion. Also have students return to the Focus Questions on the first page of the selection. Select a student to read the questions aloud, and have volunteers answer the questions. If students do not know the answers to the questions, have them return to the text to find the answers.

You may also want to review the elements of expository text with the students. Discuss with them how they can tell that "Buffalo Hunt" is expository text.

Have students break into small groups to discuss how the story reflects the theme. Groups can then share their ideas with the rest of the class.

Students may wish to record their personal responses to the selection. If they have learned something new about the American West or Native Americans, encourage them to record this information.

Review Selection Vocabulary

Have students review the definitions of the selection vocabulary words that they wrote in the vocabulary section of their Writer's Notebooks. Remind them that they discussed the meanings of these words before reading the selection. Students can use these definitions to study for the vocabulary portion of their Lesson Assessment. Have them add to the personal dictionary section of their Writer's Notebook any other interesting words that they clarified while reading. Encourage students to refer to the selection vocabulary words throughout the unit. The words from the selection are:

ceremonial legendary roamed preserve slaughter sufficient

Have students place the words under the appropriate endings in the Word Bank. Encourage the students to find other words related to the unit theme and add them to the Word Bank. Have students also use other strategies for determining the meaning and increasing their vocabulary of theme-related words. For example, when appropriate, have students write both synonyms and antonyms for words related to the American West in their Writer's Notebooks. For each synonym and antonym, have them also write a sentence in which the word could be used. Have them also write explanations of any subtle differences in meaning between synonyms.

Home Connection

Distribute ***Home Connection,*** page 65. Encourage students to discuss "Buffalo Hunt" with their families. Students can work with their families to list the different uses Native Americans had for buffalo, the reasons the settlers killed them, and their opinions on which group had more of a "right" to the buffalo. ***Home Connection*** is also available in Spanish, page 66.

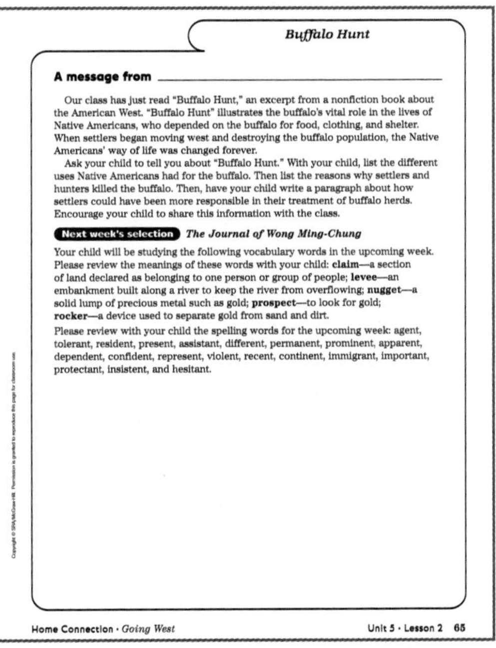

Buffalo Hunt

A message from ______________________

Our class has just read "Buffalo Hunt," an excerpt from a nonfiction book about the American West. "Buffalo Hunt" illustrates the buffalo's vital role in the lives of Native Americans, who depended on the buffalo for food, clothing, and shelter. When settlers began moving west and destroying the buffalo population, the Native Americans' way of life was changed forever.

Ask your child to tell you about "Buffalo Hunt." With your child, list the different uses Native Americans had for the buffalo. Then list the reasons why settlers and hunters killed the buffalo. Then, have your child write a paragraph about how settlers could have been more responsible in their treatment of buffalo herds. Encourage your child to share this information with the class.

Next week's selection *The Journal of Wong Ming-Chung*

Your child will be studying the following vocabulary words in the upcoming week. Please review the meanings of these words with your child: **claim**—a section of land declared as belonging to one person or group of people; **levee**—an embankment built along a river to keep the river from overflowing; **nugget**—a solid lump of precious metal such as gold; **prospect**—to look for gold; **rocker**—a device used to separate gold from sand and dirt.

Please review with your child the spelling words for the upcoming week: agent, tolerant, resident, present, assistant, different, permanent, prominent, apparent, dependent, confident, represent, violent, recent, continent, immigrant, important, protectant, insistent, and hesitant.

Home Connection • *Going West* Unit 5 • Lesson 2 65

***Home Connection* p. 65**

Teacher Tip SELECTION VOCABULARY Have students write sentences using the selection vocabulary words.

Differentiating Instruction

If...	Then...
Students would benefit from repeated readings of "Buffalo Hunt" or the Intervention Selections	Use ***Intervention Guide,*** page 245

Teacher Tip CONTENT AREA VOCABULARY Tell students that as they read and discuss text for the unit theme Going West, they will encounter terminology used to speak about the lives and experiences of people native to and living in the American West during the 1800s. Have students record in their Writer's Notebooks any vocabulary they find useful or relevant and use resources during Workshop to help them write definitions for the words. Have students refer to their Writer's Notebooks when choosing words for their writing, discussions, and presentations.

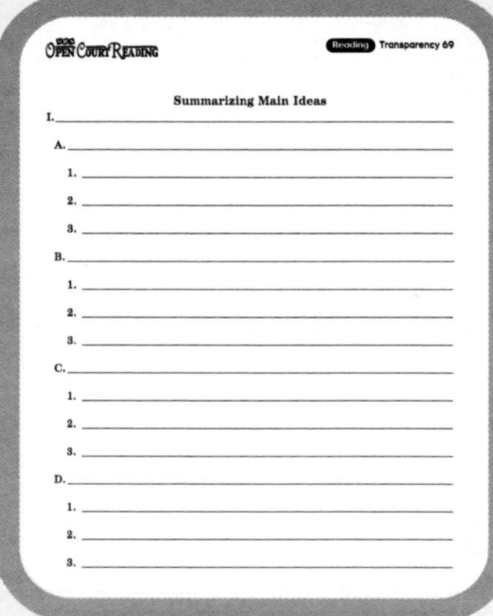

Open Court Reading — Reading Transparency 69

Summarizing Main Ideas

I. ______

A. ______
1. ______
2. ______
3. ______

B. ______
1. ______
2. ______
3. ______

C. ______
1. ______
2. ______
3. ______

D. ______
1. ______
2. ______
3. ______

Reading Transparency 69

Teacher Tip MAIN IDEA AND DETAILS It might be helpful to have students summarize or paraphrase the selection's main ideas and the three most important details in order to fit them easily on to the transparency.

Supporting the Reading

Comprehension Skills: Main Idea and Details

Teach Remind students that a *main idea* is the most important idea in a paragraph, a passage, or a selection. Tell them that *details* prove or further explain a main idea. Point out that writers usually state the main idea of a paragraph in a topic sentence, which is often found at the beginning or the end of the paragraph.

Guided Practice Remind students that the selection "Buffalo Hunt" is separated into four sections by subtitles. Use the outline on ***Reading Transparency 69*** to record the main idea and supporting details for each of these sections. Have students write them in their own words. Work with students to identify and assess the details that support the main idea of each section. Have students decide on and include only the three most important details from each section. Have students discuss why the details they included are the most important, and why other details may have been less important. Have them discuss also how each detail supports its main idea (for example, by providing evidence or proof of a statement, by further explaining an idea or principle, or by listing examples of something.)

Independent Practice Read the **Focus** and **Identify** sections of the ***Comprehension and Language Arts Skills,*** page 146, with students. Guide students through the **Identify** portion, and help them come up with examples found in the story. Then have students complete the **Practice** and **Apply** portions of the ***Comprehension and Language Arts Skills,*** page 147 as homework.

Link to Writing Have students choose one of their previous writing assignments and review it for main ideas and supporting details. Ask them to analyze each paragraph and identify the main idea, note whether it is clearly stated in a topic sentence, and evaluate the details they include to support it. Encourage students to revise any paragraphs that do not state the main idea in a topic sentence. Also, have them reorganize details, listing the strongest ones first and omitting those that are unimportant or unrelated, so that they better support the main idea of each paragraph.

Name ______ Date ______

UNIT 5 Going West • Lesson 2 *Buffalo Hunt*

Main Idea and Details

Focus Writers usually include a **main idea** in every paragraph of their writing. These main ideas are supported by **details** that make up the rest of the paragraph.

A **main idea** is the most important idea in a paragraph, a passage, or an entire work.
- In paragraphs, the main idea is usually stated in a topic sentence.
- The main idea of a larger section of text or an entire work sometimes must be inferred.
- The other sentences in the paragraph include details that support the main idea.

Identify

Read the fourth paragraph on page 425 in "Buffalo Hunt." Identify the topic sentence of the paragraph and the details that support this main idea.

Topic Sentence: At one time, perhaps sixty or seventy million buffalo had roamed the plains.

Supporting Details: By the early 1800s, the endless herds had been wiped out. Only a few hundred wild buffalo were still hiding out in remote mountain valleys.

146 UNIT 5 • Lesson 2 Comprehension and Language Arts Skills

Name ______ Date ______

UNIT 5 Going West • Lesson 2 *Buffalo Hunt*

Main Idea and Details

COMPREHENSION

Practice

Think about some of the things you just learned about buffalo and the Native Americans. Choose one thing you want to say about what you learned. Write that as your main idea. Then write three details that support your main idea. Answers will vary.

Main Idea: ______

Detail 1: ______

Detail 2: ______

Detail 3: ______

Apply

Use the above main idea and details to write a paragraph about the Native Americans and buffalo. Make sure your paragraph states your main idea in a topic sentence. When you are finished, read your paragraph to a classmate and see if he or she can identify the main idea of the paragraph.

Answers will vary.

Comprehension and Language Arts Skills UNIT 5 • Lesson 2 147

Comprehension and Language Arts Skills pp. 146–147

Differentiating Instruction

If...	Then...
Students need extra help with Main Idea and Details	• Use ***Reteach,*** pages 145–146 • Use ***English Learner Support Guide,*** pages 378–393
Students would enjoy a challenge with Main Idea and Details	Use ***Challenge,*** page 128

Main Idea and Details

Introduced in Grade 1.

Scaffolded throughout Grades 2–5.

REINTRODUCED:	Unit 2, Lesson 2
REINFORCED:	Unit 2, Lesson 4
	Unit 2, Lesson 7
	Unit 3, Lesson 2
	Unit 3, Lesson 6
TESTED:	Unit 5 Assessment

Professional Development

Teacher Resource Library CD-ROMs or ***Online Professional Development*** provides courses that help you better understand the Comprehension/Knowledge Building instruction in ***Open Court Reading.*** For more information about this program, visit SRAonline.com.

Teacher Tip EXPOSITORY TEXT Have students share examples of expository text they have read that informs, explains, persuades, and entertains. Encourage students to find expository texts that serve each of these purposes to use in their investigations of the American West.

Literary Elements

Genre: Expository Text

Teach Have students tell you what they know about expository text. If necessary, tell them that the main purpose of expository text is to share information with the reader. Write on the board these elements of expository text and discuss them with students.

- The purpose of expository text is to share information with the reader.
- Facts about real events or real people are often included.
- Information is presented in a straightforward way.
- Events are presented in the order in which they happened, or steps are written in the order in which they should be done.
- The writing may be organized by topics.
- Diagrams, photographs, maps, or other illustrations are often included to help the reader understand the subject better.
- The factual information can often be checked by referring to other sources. For example, reference books can be used to check facts in science or history articles, while newspapers might provide information for checking details or recent events.

Point out to students that some expository text might share facts with the primary goal of simply informing readers. However, other informational text might share facts in order to put forth a message or an opinion. Explain to students that they should always be on the lookout for bias, or the author putting forth his or her own stance on an issue, when they read expository text.

Guided Practice Have students analyze "Buffalo Hunt" and note which of the elements of expository text are present in the selection. You might also have them explain how this selection differs from fiction or other genres of nonfiction, such as biography and autobiography. Then have students discuss whether Freedman's main goal is to simply inform readers or to encourage readers to share his opinion about the subject.

Independent Practice Ask students to locate a factual article in a magazine or newspaper. Have them identify the elements of expository text in the article. You might also challenge them to analyze the article to decide whether the author is trying to put forth his or her own stance on the subject.

Social Studies Connection: Citizenship

Have students work with partners or in small groups for this activity. Place this list of Native American groups on the board: Cheyenne, Comanche, Pawnee, Sioux, Iroquois, Osage, Hopi, Navajo, Nez Percé and Blackfoot. Ask students to choose one of these groups to investigate or to choose a group on their own. Have students learn more about their group, particularly which region they are associated with and how the climate and geography of that region influenced their way of life. Encourage students to also learn about folklore and cultural traditions. Have students record and organize the information they find on posterboard. Suggest that students include photographs or maps to enhance their posters. You might hold a Native American festival in which groups share their posters and explain their findings. Display posters in the classroom for students to reference as they continue studying this unit.

Teacher Tip **MATERIALS** To complete this activity, students will need the following materials: posterboard, markers, and library and Internet sources.

Science/Social Studies Connection Center

Refer to the ***Science/Social Studies Connection Center Cards*** 67–70 for social studies activities that students can investigate.

Concept Connections

Linking the Selection

- The Plains Indians depended on buffalo for food, clothing, shelter, and tools.
- Buffalo were hunted to feed railroad construction crews, and railroads offered hunting excursions during which passengers shot at buffalo without even leaving the train.
- Hide hunters killed large quantities of buffalo in a very short time and left the carcasses to spoil.

Exploring Concept Vocabulary

The concept word for this lesson is ***devastation.*** Write the word on the board. Work with the students to develop a definition that clearly links to the unit theme. Have students copy the word and definition into the Vocabulary section of their Writer's Notebooks.

Devastation: total destruction. For example, a new tanning process helped bring about the final stage of the buffalo's devastation.

- With the buffalo gone, the Plains Indians lost their food source, and therefore their independence. Their hunting grounds were taken over, and they were sent to live on reservations.
- People in the East were paying a high price for buffalo hides and tongues, so the animals were hunted for only these parts.

The students' sentences should show an understanding of both vocabulary words.

Expanding the Concept

Have students carry on dialogues in small groups. After the small-group discussions, bring students together to share their ideas with the whole class.

Have students record their ideas about the selection on page 113 of their ***Inquiry Journal.***

Buffalo Hunt

Concept Connections

Linking the Selection

Think about the following questions, and then record your responses in the Response Journal section of your Writer's Notebook.

- Why were the lives of Plains Indians so closely linked to the buffalo?
- How did railroads contribute to the destruction of the buffalo?
- Why were hide hunters especially hated by Native Americans?

Exploring Concept Vocabulary

The concept word for this lesson is ***devastation.*** If you do not know what this word means, look it up in a dictionary. Answer these questions.

- How did the disappearance of buffalo contribute to the ***devastation*** of the Plains Indians' way of life?
- What did people living in the East have to do with the ***devastation*** of the buffalo?

Make up an oral sentence that includes the word ***devastation*** as well as one of the selection vocabulary words.

Expanding the Concept

Compare the description of the relationship between Native Americans and white people in "Sacagawea's Journey" to the description in this selection. Consider the goals and lifestyles of the people in the two selections. Try to use the word ***devastation*** in your discussion. Add new ideas about the American West to the Concept/Question Board.

426

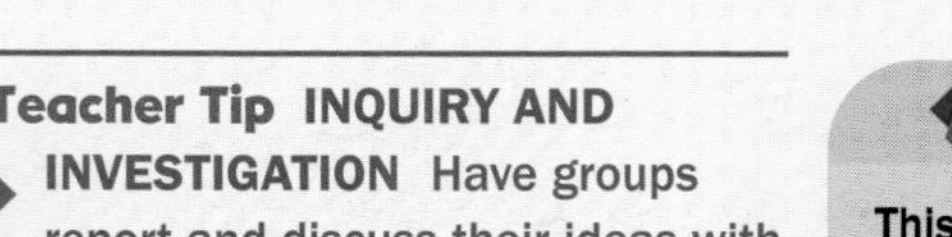

Teacher Tip INQUIRY AND INVESTIGATION Have groups report and discuss their ideas with the class. As these ideas are stated, have students add them to the Concept/Question Board. As students complete their discussions, have them sum up what they have learned and tell how they might use this information in further investigations.

Informal Assessment

This may be a good time to observe students working in small groups and to mark your observations in the Teacher Observation Log found in the ***Program Assessment Teacher's Edition.***

Meet the Author

Russell Freedman seemed destined to be a writer. He grew up in a home frequently visited by authors. He later became a reporter and stumbled across a story about a sixteen-year-old boy who invented the braille typewriter. The story inspired his first book, *Teenagers Who Made History.*

Mr. Freedman travels widely to do the research for his books. When he is not writing, he enjoys attending films, concerts, and plays.

Meet the Illustrators

George Catlin made a series of journeys into unmapped Native American territory, visiting most of the major tribes from the Upper Missouri River to the Mexican Territory in the far Southwest. He wandered alone from tribe to tribe, fearlessly entering their villages, where he was greeted with courtesy and friendship. From these visits, he created hundreds of paintings and drawings, giving most of the outside world its first glimpse at Native American life.

Charles M. Russell visited the Montana Territory when he was sixteen and soon made that part of the country his home. He worked as a hunter and as a cowboy, while painting and sculpting in his spare time. He later became a full-time artist, famous for his paintings and sculptures of cowboy life.

427

Meet the Author

After the students read the information about Russell Freedman, discuss the following questions with them.

- There are two selections in this book that are written by Russell Freedman, "The Night the Revolution Began" and "Buffalo Hunt." How are these selections similar? How are they different? *(Possible answer: They are similar in that they are both about historic events. They are different in that "The Night the Revolution Began" is written more like a story, whereas "Buffalo Hunt" reads more like expository text because it has headings.)*
- Why do you think attending films, concerts, and plays might be especially enjoyable to a writer? *(Possible answer: Each of these activities tells a story in a different way. Authors like to listen to other people's stories, and use them as ideas for different ways they can tell their own stories.)*

Meet the Illustrators

After the students read the information about George Catlin and Charles M. Russell, discuss the following question with them.

- George Catlin and Charles M. Russell became famous for their paintings of the American West and the lives of Native Americans. Why do you think they were able to create such true-to-life pictures of these people and this territory? *(Possible answer: Both artists actually spent time getting to know the people and living on the land. Because of this, they were able to paint pictures that not only showed the American West as it looked, but communicated how the people who lived there may have felt.)*

Objectives

- Students gain a deeper understanding of the American West.
- Students formulate questions and problems about the American West.
- Students participate in investigation activities.
- Students learn to listen and take notes.

Materials

- Student Anthology, pp. 406–427
- Inquiry Journal, pp. 122–125
- Research Assistant

INVESTIGATION

Investigating Concepts Beyond the Text

To facilitate students' investigation of the American West, you might have them participate in the following activity. Tell students that if they have activity ideas of their own that they would like to pursue, they are free to do so as an alternative to this activity suggestion. Tell students that they may work on these activities alone, in pairs, or in small groups, with an option to write about them or to present them to the group upon completion.

The activity suggestion for this lesson is:

- Have students discuss how the materials and resources used by the Plains Indians of the Old West compare to those used today in the students' community. Interested students may want to make a chart of items, such as a house, furniture, pants/shirts, shoes, bowls, and forks or spoons, which were used both in the Old West and today. Have them include information in the chart about how these items were made then as compared to now.

Upon completion of their activities, have students share with the group anything new they learned about the American West through discussion and by adding information to the Concept/Question Board.

Concept/Question Board

After reading each selection, students should use the Concept/Question Board to

- post any questions they asked about a selection before reading that have not yet been answered.
- refer to as they formulate statements about concepts that apply to their investigations.
- post general statements formulated by each collaborative group.
- continue to post news articles, or other items that they find during the unit investigation.
- read and think about posted questions, articles, or concepts that interest them and provide answers to the questions.

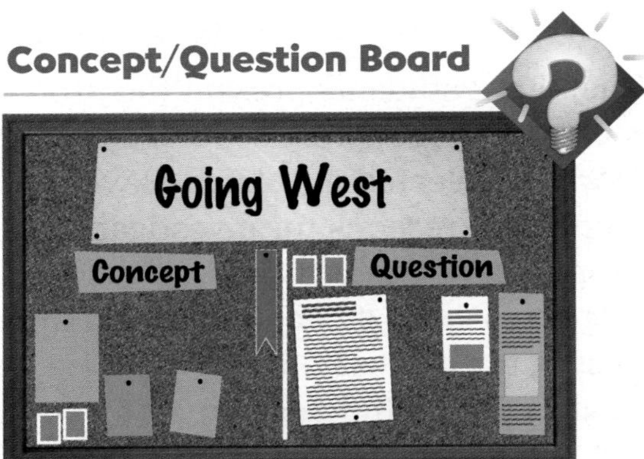

Unit 5 Investigation Management

Lesson 1	Students generate questions and ideas for investigation.
Lesson 2	Collaborative Investigation **Students formulate questions and problems for investigation.** Supplementary Activities **Students participate in investigation activities and learn to listen and take notes.**
Lesson 3	Students make conjectures.
Lesson 4	Students establish investigation needs.
Lesson 5	Students establish investigation plans.
Lesson 6	Students continue investigation and get feedback from other groups.
Lesson 7	Students present their investigation findings to the class.

INVESTIGATION

www.sra4kids.com
Web Connection
Students can use the connections to Going West to the Reading link of the SRA Web page for more background information about Going West.

Teacher Tip **NATIVE AMERICAN ARTWORK** Some students might be interested in learning more about Native American artwork. Encourage them to research the subject and post their findings on the Concept/Question Board.

Research Assistant

The Research Assistant helps students in their investigations.

Teacher Tip **ULTIMATE WRITING AND CREATIVITY CENTER** Have students use the ***Ultimate Writing and Creativity Center CD-ROM*** as they work on their investigation activities.

Teacher Tip GROUP KNOWLEDGE Students should be ever mindful that the purpose of their investigations is to contribute to the whole class's knowledge of their chosen topics.

Formal Assessment

Use the Research Rubrics on page 406J to assess students' ability to formulate research questions and problems.

Name ______ Date ______

UNIT 5 Going West

Formulating Questions and Problems

A good question or problem to investigate:
Answers will vary.

Why this is an interesting question or problem:
Answers will vary.

Some other things I wonder about this question or problem:
Answers will vary.

122 UNIT 5 *Formulating Questions and Problems* • Inquiry Journal

My investigation group's question or problem:
Answers will vary.

What our investigation will contribute to the rest of the class:
Answers will vary.

Some other things I wonder about this question or problem:
Answers will vary.

Inquiry Journal • *Formulating Questions and Problems* UNIT 5 123

***Inquiry Journal* pp. 122 and 123**

INVESTIGATION

Formulating Questions and Problems

Tell students that to continue the investigation process, they must narrow the ideas about the American West that interest them into investigation problems or questions. Model for them how to do this. For example, have them consider the difference between the idea to investigate pioneers and the problem, How did pioneers travel west? Explain to them that if they choose to investigate the topic of pioneers, it will be very difficult to choose what about pioneers to investigate and that this will make it hard for them to organize their findings. Choosing a specific question or problem that interests them will help them focus their investigation and advance their understanding. Explain to the students that a good investigation problem or question will not only require them to consult multiple sources, but will add to the group's knowledge of the unit theme, be engaging, and generate further questions. As a group, have students generate a list of potential investigation problems and questions. When they have completed, assign ***Inquiry Journal,*** page 122.

Then have students present the problems or questions that interest them the most to the group. This will lead to the creation of investigation groups to work on selected problems. Have students present their proposed problems, along with reasons for investigating them, allowing open discussion of how promising and interesting various proposed problems are. To aid the formation of groups, have students record and initial their problems on the board. During the discussion, draw arrows between problems to link ones that are related. Have students take notes on who has similar interests to their own. When all of the students have had a chance to propose questions and problems, have them form investigation groups based on shared interests.

During Workshop, have each group meet to agree on an investigation problem. Tell them that they will be required to state the problem that they will be working on and tell how working on that problem will contribute to the class's knowledge. Have them record this in their ***Inquiry Journals,*** page 123.

Professional Development

Teacher Resource Library CD-ROMs or ***Online Professional Development*** provides courses that help you better understand the Inquiry and Investigation instruction in ***Open Court Reading.*** For more information about this program, visit SRAonline.com.

Listening and Taking Notes

Teach Tell students that note-taking is a helpful method for collecting and organizing information from research sources. Tell students that it is especially helpful to take notes when listening to audio resources. Have students brainstorm some audio resources from which they could derive information for their investigation activities. *(Students may mention, for example, live and recorded informational speeches, editorials, radio shows, news broadcasts, drama, and audio tapes.)* Then tell students that note taking before, during, and after they listen to an audio resource is a good strategy for comprehending and organizing information from the resource. Review the following suggestions with them.

- Before listening, note what questions you expect to have answered in the audio resource. Leave several lines between each question so that there is plenty of room to jot down notes as you listen.
- While listening, take brief notes, using abbreviations whenever possible, to help you remember answers to the questions you listed, interesting information to investigate further, and unfamiliar words and ideas to clarify later. At points when you are not writing, exhibit the body language of an effective listener by focusing your eyes on the speaker or audiovisual recording. If there is no visual information accompanying the audio message, try to focus all of your attention on what you are hearing and how it relates to your purpose for listening. Consider closing your eyes if it would help you to keep from being distracted.
- After listening, read over your notes while what you learned from the audio resource is fresh in your mind. There may be notes that you left incomplete or ideas you did not have time enough to note while you were listening. Fill those in now.

Guided Practice Have students listen to one of the audio resources listed for the theme Going West. (Audiocassettes/CDs and videocassettes are listed under Technology on Unit 5 Overview page 389F.) Have them take notes before, during, and after listening to aid their comprehension.

Independent Practice Have students complete ***Inquiry Journal*** page 124 to identify their listening preferences. Then have them complete ***Inquiry Journal,*** page 125, to help them organize their notes prior to listening to an audio resource of their choice.

SUPPORTING THE INVESTIGATION

Differentiating Instruction

If...	Then...
Students are having difficulty with their Inquiry activities	Have them take notes during group discussions of investigation questions and problems

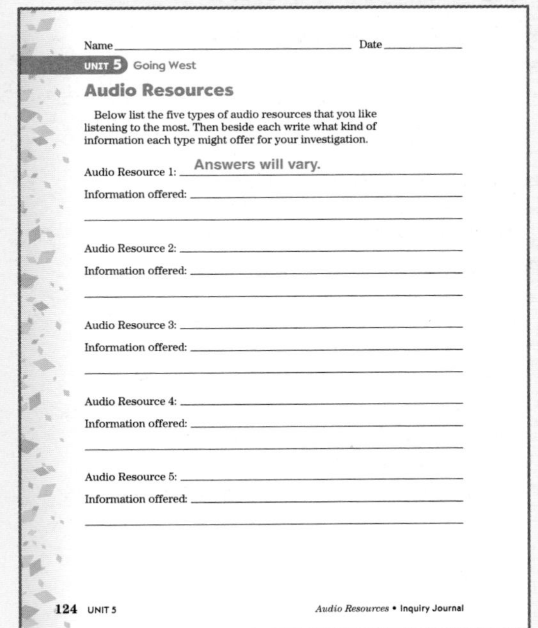

Name ______ Date ______

UNIT 5 Going West

Audio Resources

Below list the five types of audio resources that you like listening to the most. Then beside each write what kind of information each type might offer for your investigation.

Audio Resource 1: Answers will vary.
Information offered: ______

Audio Resource 2: ______
Information offered: ______

Audio Resource 3: ______
Information offered: ______

Audio Resource 4: ______
Information offered: ______

Audio Resource 5: ______
Information offered: ______

124 UNIT 5 *Audio Resources* • Inquiry Journal

From the list you created, choose the audio resource that you think is most likely to provide information valuable to your investigation. On the following lines, write places you might find this type of resource. Then write three questions you would like to answer using this resource.

Audio Resource: Answers will vary.

Where I might find it:
- ______
- ______
- ______

What I want to learn:

Question 1: ______

Question 2: ______

Question 3: ______

Inquiry Journal • *Audio Resources* UNIT 5 125

Inquiry Journal pp. 124–125

Objectives

Word Analysis

Spelling

- **Spelling Patterns for words with *dis-* or *mis-*.** Develop understanding of spelling patterns for words with *dis-* or *mis-* introduced in Word Knowledge in Part 1.

Vocabulary

- Using words from "Buffalo Hunt," give students further practice recognizing and defining synonyms.

Writing Process Strategies

- **Personal Writing.** Students continue to learn personal writing techniques. During this week, the focus will be on invitations, thank-you notes, and e-mail messages.

English Language Conventions

Mechanics

- **Commas.** Understand correct use of commas with phrases in personal writing and identify them in "Buffalo Hunt."

Listening, Speaking, Viewing

- **Speaking: Proper Grammar.** Use proper elements of grammar in speech.

Penmanship

- **Joining with *E* and *f*.** Review handwriting skills by practicing joining letters with *E* and *f*.

Materials

- Spelling and Vocabulary Skills, pp. 110–113
- Language Arts Handbook
- Comprehension and Language Arts Skills, pp. 148–149
- Writer's Workbook, pp. 82–85
- Student Anthology
- Unit 5 Assessment, pp. 32–33

Differentiating Instruction

Reteach, Challenge, and ***Intervention*** lessons are available to support the language arts instruction in this lesson.

Research in Action

People with only the rudiments of literacy can, if sufficiently motivated, redirect their oral language abilities into producing a written text. (*Carl Bereiter and Marlene Scardamalia,* The Psychology of Written Composition)

OVERVIEW

Language Arts Overview

Word Analysis

Spelling The spelling activities on the following pages support the Word Knowledge introduction of words with *dis-* or *mis-* by developing understanding of the spelling patterns for these prefixes.

Selection Spelling Words

These words from "Buffalo Hunt" contain *dis-*.

distance distinct disappear disturb discuss

Vocabulary The vocabulary activities reinforce the concept of synonyms and the importance of context clues when choosing a particular synonym for a word in a sentence.

Vocabulary Skill Words

procession gorged seared dwindle sufficient*

**Also Selection Vocabulary.*

Additional Materials On Day 3, students will need thesauri.

Writing Process Strategies

This Writing Process Strategies lesson involves instruction in a variety of personal writing techniques.

To help students identify the Internet as a source of information for writing, have students use punctuation signs in a search engine and use electronic bookmarks. You might want to help students bookmark Web pages that they often visit. ***TechKnowledge*** Level 5 Lessons 88–89 teach these Internet reference skills.

Professional Development

Teacher Resource Library CD-ROMs or ***Online Professional Development*** provides courses that help you better understand the Writing instruction in ***Open Court Reading.*** For more information about this program, visit SRAonline.com.

English Language Conventions

Mechanics **Commas.** This lesson develops understanding of correct comma usage with introductory and participial phrases.

Listening, Speaking, Viewing **Speaking: Proper Grammar.** In this Speaking lesson, students use proper grammar in speech.

Penmanship **Joining with *E* and *f*.** This lesson continues the development of handwriting skills. Students join letters with *E* and *f* and then write paragraphs from the literature, focusing on joining letters.

DAY 1

Word Analysis

Spelling

Assessment: Pretest

Spelling Patterns for Words with *dis-* or *mis-*

Give students the Pretest on page 32 of ***Unit 5 Assessment.*** Have them proofread and correct any misspellings.

Pretest Sentences

1. **mistook** We **mistook** the park ranger for a policeman.
2. **dislike** Most residents of the Caribbean **dislike** snow.
3. **disagree** Judges on the Supreme Court frequently **disagree.**
4. **mistreat** Don't **mistreat** animals.
5. **disloyal** Benedict Arnold was **disloyal** to the Continental Army.
6. **discover** Columbus wanted to **discover** a short route to India.
7. **misspell** It is easy to **misspell** foreign words.
8. **disgrace** The losing general surrendered in **disgrace.**
9. **mislaid** Those old letters in the attic were **mislaid** years ago.
10. **misprint** Newspaper editors are embarrassed by a **misprint.**
11. **displease** It will **displease** a musician if her oboe is not tuned.
12. **disconnect** The phone company might **disconnect** your phone.
13. **mislead** Hunters use decoys to **mislead** ducks.
14. **misjudge** Be careful not to **misjudge** another person.
15. **distrust** A babysitter should not be someone you **distrust.**
16. **distance** The **distance** to New York City is about 3,000 miles.
17. **distinct** Sulfur has a **distinct** odor that resembles rotten eggs.
18. **disappear** The streams in west Texas **disappear** every summer.
19. **disturb** At night, the bears might **disturb** the campers.
20. **discuss** At a summit, world leaders **discuss** global issues.

Writing Process Strategies

Teach

Invitation

- Have students read ***Language Arts Handbook*** pages 76–81 on notes and cards.
- The purpose for writing an invitation determines how it is written. Tell students that this invitation, unlike those for parties and celebrations, is to invite a speaker to the class. Discuss with them the format the invitation should take. Allow students to come to a consensus as to the format.
- Whatever format and graphics students use, let them know that the content of the invitation should answer the five *W's: what, where, when, who,* and *why.*

Inspiration

Teacher Model: *I want to write an invitation to Russell Freedman to come to speak to the class about "Buffalo Hunt." I enjoyed reading "Buffalo Hunt" so much that I really would like to learn more about Mr. Freedman's research of the topic.*

Guided Practice

- Have the class develop a draft from the ideas they gathered earlier. Write students' suggestions about the draft on the board.

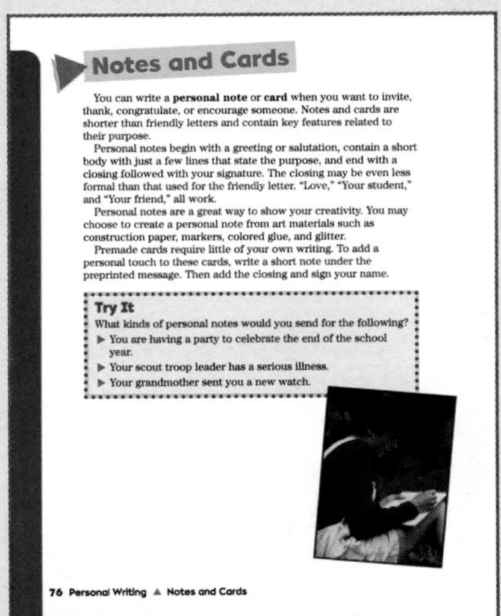

Notes and Cards

You can write a **personal note** or **card** when you want to invite, thank, congratulate, or encourage someone. Notes and cards are shorter than friendly letters and contain key features related to their purpose.

Personal notes begin with a greeting or salutation, contain a short body with just a few lines that state the purpose, and end with a closing followed with your signature. The closing may be even less formal than that used for the friendly letter. "Love," "Your student," and "Your friend," all work.

Personal notes are a great way to show your creativity. You may choose to create a personal note from art materials such as construction paper, markers, colored glue, and glitter.

Premade cards require little of your own writing. To add a personal touch to these cards, write a short note under the preprinted message. Then add the closing and sign your name.

Try It

What kinds of personal notes would you send for the following?

- You are having a party to celebrate the end of the school year.
- Your scout troop leader has a serious illness.
- Your grandmother sent you a new watch.

76 Personal Writing ▲ Notes and Cards

Language Arts Handbook p. 76

English Language Conventions

Mechanics

Commas

Teach

- Use ***Language Arts Handbook*** pages 355 and 384 for examples of commas with phrases.
- Explain that a comma is used after a long introductory phrase or participial phrase to separate it from the main sentence: *Eagerly staking out their claims, the settlers began a new life.*
- A short introductory clause does not need a comma unless confusion results: *At noon we ate lunch* but *The day after, the student became ill.*

Independent Practice

Use ***Comprehension and Language Arts Skills*** pages 148–149 to practice using commas with introductory and participial phrases.

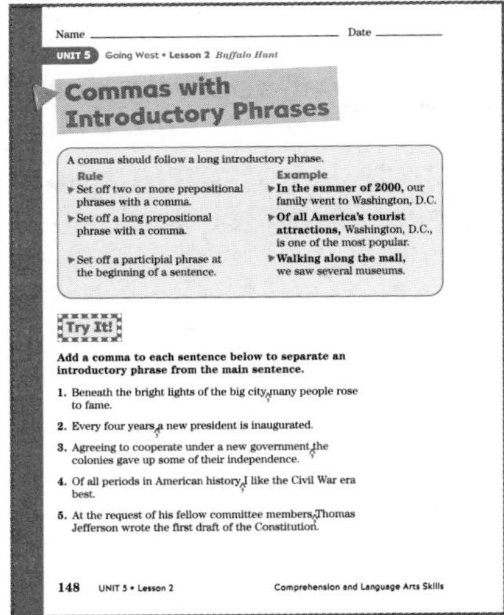

Name ______________ Date ________

UNIT 5 Going West • Lesson 2 *Buffalo Hunt*

Commas with Introductory Phrases

A comma should follow a long introductory phrase.

Rule	Example
Set off two or more prepositional phrases with a comma.	**In the summer of 2000,** our family went to Washington, D.C.
Set off a long prepositional phrase with a comma.	**Of all America's tourist attractions,** Washington, D.C., is one of the most popular.
Set off a participial phrase at the beginning of a sentence.	**Walking along the mall,** we saw several museums.

Try It!

Add a comma to each sentence below to separate an introductory phrase from the main sentence.

1. Beneath the bright lights of the big city many people rose to fame.
2. Every four years a new president is inaugurated.
3. Agreeing to cooperate under a new government the colonies gave up some of their independence.
4. Of all periods in American history I like the Civil War era best.
5. At the request of his fellow committee members Thomas Jefferson wrote the first draft of the Constitution.

148 UNIT 5 • Lesson 2 Comprehension and Language Arts Skills

Comprehension and Language Arts Skills p. 148

DAY 2

Word Analysis

Spelling

Word Sorting

Open Word Sort Have students sort the spelling words according to the prefixes. Have students explain their answers.

Vocabulary

Synonyms

Teach

- Remind students that synonyms are words with similar meanings and antonyms are opposites.
- Write the **Vocabulary Skill Words** *procession*, *gorged*, *seared*, *dwindle*, and *sufficient* on the board. Have students find these words in the selection "Buffalo Hunt" and discuss possible definitions for these words. Tell students that they will be dealing with synonyms for these words on page 110 of ***Spelling and Vocabulary Skills.***

Guided Practice

Assign page 110 of ***Spelling and Vocabulary Skills.*** Students can complete page 111 of ***Spelling and Vocabulary Skills*** for homework.

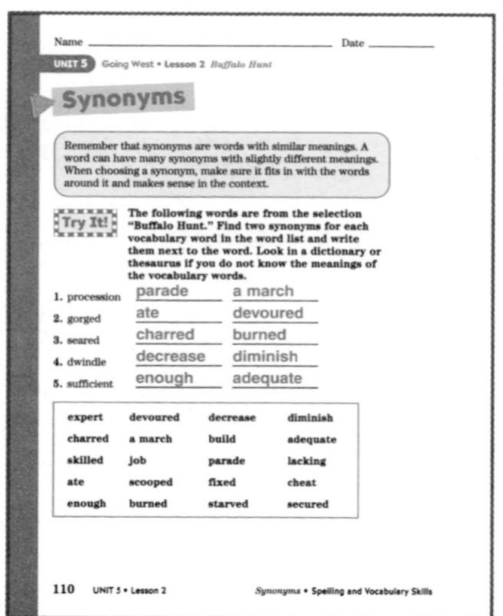

Name ____________ Date ______

UNIT 5 Going West • Lesson 2 *Buffalo Hunt*

Synonyms

Remember that synonyms are words with similar meanings. A word can have many synonyms with slightly different meanings. When choosing a synonym, make sure it fits in with the words around it and makes sense in the context.

Try It! The following words are from the selection "Buffalo Hunt." Find two synonyms for each vocabulary word in the word list and write them next to the word. Look in a dictionary or thesaurus if you do not know the meanings of the vocabulary words.

1. procession parade a march
2. gorged ate devoured
3. seared charred burned
4. dwindle decrease diminish
5. sufficient enough adequate

expert	devoured	decrease	diminish
charred	a march	build	adequate
skilled	job	parade	lacking
ate	scooped	fixed	cheat
enough	burned	starved	secured

110 UNIT 5 • Lesson 2 *Synonyms* • Spelling and Vocabulary Skills

***Spelling and Vocabulary Skills* p. 110**

Writing Process Strategies

Teach

Invitation

Focus on presentation and making the invitation look appealing.

- Discuss with students the importance of a final copy that is easy to process and is visually appealing. Discuss visual appeal. Tell the students that it means that the invitation will be pleasing to the recipient's eye. Some ways to incorporate visual appeal are to make certain the text is free from errors and erasures and to include graphics.

Guided Practice

- Have students complete ***Writer's Workbook,*** page 82.

Formal Assessment

Total Point Value: 10

1. The content of the invitation answers the five W's. (2 points)
2. Graphics are used effectively. (2 points)
3. It is clear why the request is being made. (2 points)
4. The final copy is visually appealing. (2 points)
5. The conventions are followed, and there are no obvious errors. (2 points)

Name ____________ Date ______

UNIT 5 Going West • Lesson 2 *Buffalo Hunt*

Writing an Invitation

Work with your classmates to create an invitation asking an author of one of the literature selections in your book to come to speak to your class.

Prewriting

1. **Who is the audience? Choose an author whose work everyone enjoyed and wanted to know more about. Include the title of the selection along with the author's name.**

Author: Responses should be the result of a democratic vote.

Title: ____________

2. **What is the purpose for writing the invitation?** Students' answers may include that they wanted to know about the research behind the work or they wanted to learn more about the author.
3. **What will the format for the invitation be?** Answers may include a letter, a standard invitation, a drawing, or any acceptable creative format.
4. **Develop the body of the invitation with your classmates by answering the five Ws. You should have answered *who?* and *why?* above.**

What? ____________

When? ____________

Where? ____________

Drafting

Write your invitation on a separate sheet of paper. Include the answers to the questions above.

82 UNIT 5 • Lesson 2 *Writing an Invitation* • Writer's Workbook

Objective: Students plan for an invitation.

***Writer's Workbook* p. 82**

English Language Conventions

Mechanics

Commas

Teach

- Review commas with introductory and participial phrases.
- Write the following sentences on the board and have students suggest the insertion or moving of commas to set apart introductory and participial phrases:
  - Panning for gold the miner, waded into the stream. *(Panning for gold, the miner waded into the stream.)*
  - At the end of the long, winding trail settlers stopped their wagons. *(At the end of the long, winding trail, settlers stopped their wagons.)*
  - Before he can, play baseball he needs to finish the dishes. *(Before he can play baseball, he needs to finish the dishes.)*

Guided Practice in Reading

Have students search for commas with phrases in "Buffalo Hunt."

DAY 3

Word Analysis

Spelling

Spelling Patterns for Words with *dis-* or *mis-*

Teach

Introduce the prefixes *dis-* and *mis-* and their meanings. Explain that *dis-* means "not" or "apart" and *mis-* means "bad," and that adding these prefixes changes the meaning of a base word. Have students locate words in "Buffalo Hunt" with the prefixes *dis-* and *mis-*.

Guided Practice

Have students complete page 112 from ***Spelling and Vocabulary Skills.***

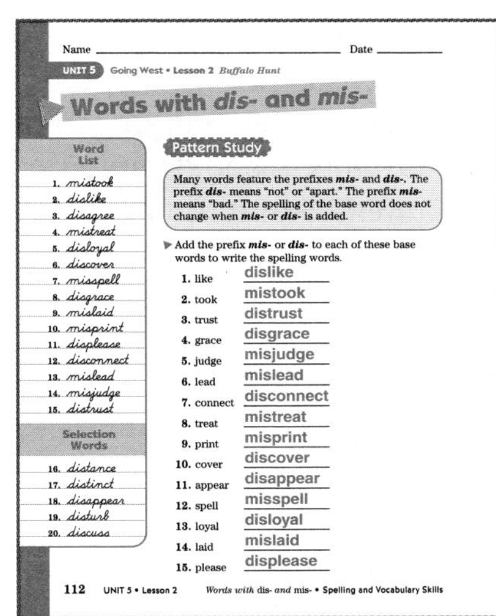

Name ______________________ Date ________

UNIT 5 Going West • Lesson 2 *Buffalo Hunt*

Words with *dis-* and *mis-*

Word List

1. mistook
2. dislike
3. disagree
4. mistreat
5. disloyal
6. discover
7. misspell
8. disgrace
9. mislaid
10. misprint
11. displease
12. disconnect
13. mislead
14. misjudge
15. distrust

Selection Words

16. distance
17. distinct
18. disappear
19. disturb
20. discuss

Pattern Study

Many words feature the prefixes ***mis-*** and ***dis-***. The prefix ***dis-*** means "not" or "apart." The prefix ***mis-*** means "bad." The spelling of the base word does not change when ***mis-*** or ***dis-*** is added.

▶ Add the prefix ***mis-*** or ***dis-*** to each of these base words to write the spelling words.

1. like dislike
2. took mistook
3. trust distrust
4. grace disgrace
5. judge misjudge
6. lead mislead
7. connect disconnect
8. treat mistreat
9. print misprint
10. cover discover
11. appear disappear
12. spell misspell
13. loyal disloyal
14. laid mislaid
15. please displease

112 UNIT 5 • Lesson 2 *Words with* dis- *and* mis- • Spelling and Vocabulary Skills

***Spelling and Vocabulary Skills* p. 112**

Vocabulary (continued)

Synonyms

As a class or in groups of two or three, have students find two different synonyms in a thesaurus for all or some of the following words from "Buffalo Hunt": *blazing*, *crowd*, *hunted*, *drive*, *sense*, *trapped*, and *hides*. Students should then choose two of the words and write a sentence for each synonym, noting the differences in meaning.

Writing Process Strategies

Teach

Thank-You Note

Remind students to consider the following when writing a thank-you note.

- Write the date in the upper right corner, skip two lines, and write the salutation.
- State the reason for the note in the first sentence.
- Conclude the note by summing up your reason for writing.
- Skip two lines, write a closing with the first letter capitalized, as in *Yours truly,* at the right margin, and end the line with a comma.
- Sign below the closing.

Independent Practice

- Have students complete ***Writer's Workbook,*** pages 83–84.

Formal Assessment

Total Point Value: 10

1. The format of the note is according to acceptable standards. (3 points)
2. The first sentence states the reason for the note. (2 points)
3. Commas are used correctly. (2 points)
4. The final copy is visually appealing. (3 points)

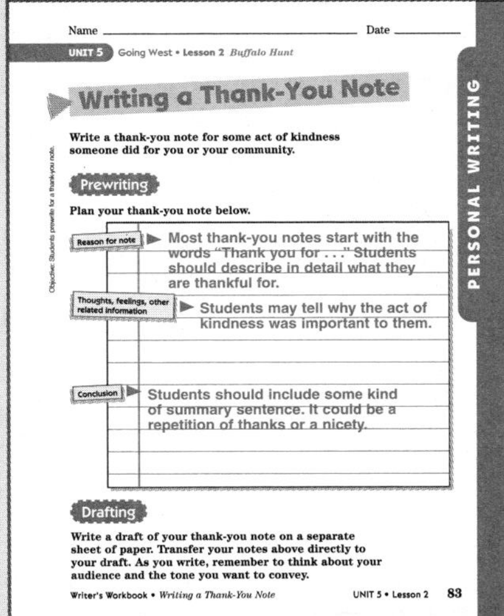

Name ______________________ Date ________

UNIT 5 Going West • Lesson 2 *Buffalo Hunt*

PERSONAL WRITING

Writing a Thank-You Note

Write a thank-you note for some act of kindness someone did for you or your community.

Objective: Students prewrite for a thank-you note.

Prewriting

Plan your thank-you note below.

Reason for note ▶ Most thank-you notes start with the words "Thank you for . . ." Students should describe in detail what they are thankful for.

Thoughts, feelings, other related information ▶ Students may tell why the act of kindness was important to them.

Conclusion ▶ Students should include some kind of summary sentence. It could be a repetition of thanks or a nicety.

Drafting

Write a draft of your thank-you note on a separate sheet of paper. Transfer your notes above directly to your draft. As you write, remember to think about your audience and the tone you want to convey.

Writer's Workbook • *Writing a Thank-You Note* UNIT 5 • Lesson 2 83

***Writer's Workbook* p. 83**

English Language Conventions

Mechanics

Commas

Teach

- For students having problems identifying introductory and participial phrases, explain that a phrase is a part of a sentence that can be easily moved to the end of the sentence. *Around the warm, roaring campfire, the family cooked their meal.* → *The family cooked their meal around the warm, roaring campfire.*

Guided Practice in Writing

Remind students that checking for correct usage of commas with participial and introductory phrases is an essential part of editing their personal writing.

Informal Assessment

Check to see that students are progressing in their understanding and usage of the skills covered in this lesson.

DAY 4

Word Analysis

Spelling

Spelling Patterns for Words with *dis-* or *mis-*

Teach

Remind students of the meanings for *dis-* and *mis-* and that they are simply added to the beginnings of words and roots. Model the visualization strategy exercise by writing *_i_took* on the board and asking students to fill in the missing consonants to write the word *mistook.*

Guided Practice

Have students complete the Spelling Strategies exercises on page 113 of ***Spelling and Vocabulary Skills.***

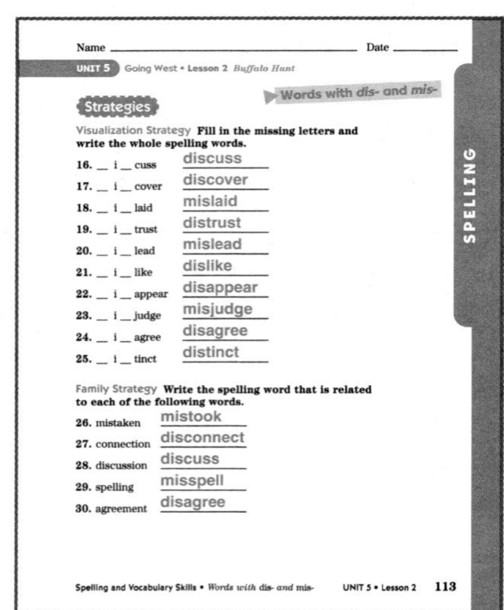

Name ______ Date ______

UNIT 5 Going West • Lesson 2 *Buffalo Hunt*

Words with *dis-* and *mis-*

Strategies

Visualization Strategy **Fill in the missing letters and write the whole spelling words.**

16. __ i __ cuss discuss
17. __ i __ cover discover
18. __ i __ laid mislaid
19. __ i __ trust distrust
20. __ i __ lead mislead
21. __ i __ like dislike
22. __ i __ appear disappear
23. __ i __ judge misjudge
24. __ i __ agree disagree
25. __ i __ tinct distinct

Family Strategy **Write the spelling word that is related to each of the following words.**

26. mistaken mistook
27. connection disconnect
28. discussion discuss
29. spelling misspell
30. agreement disagree

SPELLING

Spelling and Vocabulary Skills • *Words with* dis- *and* mis- UNIT 5 • Lesson 2 113

***Spelling and Vocabulary Skills* p. 113**

Vocabulary (continued)

Synonyms

Write these **analogies** on the board and have students complete them with words from Day 3. Discuss possible synonyms for the words.

(Blazing) is to *fire* as *twinkling* is to *star.*
(Crowd) is to *people* as *herd* is to *cattle.*
(Trapped) is to *set free* as *closed* is to *opened.*
(Hides) is to *covers up* as *leaps* is to *jumps.*

Writing Process Strategies

Teach

E-Mail Message/Literature Response

- Explain to students that e-mail is electronic mail.
- Stress that correct conventions, tone, and language are still important.
- Stress to students that the most important point to consider with an e-mail message is that it is instantaneous. Tell them they should pause before hitting the "send" button to make sure the tone and content of their message is what they intend.

Inspiration

Teacher Model: *I want to send a literature response to my class via e-mail about how I felt after reading "The Whole World Is Coming."*

Independent Practice

- Have students write their e-mail messages to you. If there are no computers available in the classroom or media center, have students each write an e-mail message mock-up.

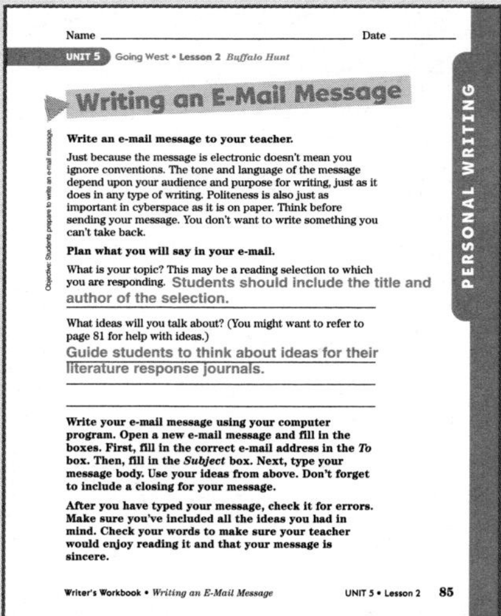

Name ______ Date ______

UNIT 5 Going West • Lesson 2 *Buffalo Hunt*

Writing an E-Mail Message

Objective: Students prepare to write an e-mail message.

Write an e-mail message to your teacher.

Just because the message is electronic doesn't mean you ignore conventions. The tone and language of the message depend upon your audience and purpose for writing, just as it does in any type of writing. Politeness is also just as important in cyberspace as it is on paper. Think before sending your message. You don't want to write something you can't take back.

Plan what you will say in your e-mail.

What is your topic? This may be a reading selection to which you are responding. Students should include the title and author of the selection.

What ideas will you talk about? (You might want to refer to page 81 for help with ideas.)
Guide students to think about ideas for their literature response journals.

Write your e-mail message using your computer program. Open a new e-mail message and fill in the boxes. First, fill in the correct e-mail address in the *To* box. Then, fill in the *Subject* box. Next, type your message body. Use your ideas from above. Don't forget to include a closing for your message.

After you have typed your message, check it for errors. Make sure you've included all the ideas you had in mind. Check your words to make sure your teacher would enjoy reading it and that your message is sincere.

PERSONAL WRITING

Writer's Workbook • *Writing an E-Mail Message* UNIT 5 • Lesson 2 85

***Writer's Workbook* p. 85**

English Language Conventions

Listening, Speaking, Viewing

Speaking: Proper Grammar

Teach

- Stress the importance of using sentence variety and proper elements of grammar in speech. Discuss the primary areas of grammar that are usually problematic, such as subject/verb agreement, consistent verb tense (past, present, future, and progressive) word order, and proper pronoun usage.
- Point out to students that proper use of these grammatical elements is vital, especially when making oral presentations in front of others.
- To dramatize this point, you may wish to present a short speech in which you demonstrate incorrect grammatical usage in an exaggerated manner. Encourage students to voice their feelings about the effect your grammar had on them as they listened to your talk. Elicit that the grammatical problems interfered with the message.

Guided Practice

- You may wish to give students a copy of the short speech that you gave to the class, directing them to find and correct the grammatical errors.
- Then allow students to work in pairs and peer edit a recent paper for each other, focusing specifically on grammar errors. Have them present their edited papers to a partner.

Informal Assessment

Observe whether students can use correct grammar in speech.

DAY 5

Word Analysis

Spelling

Assessment: Final Test

Spelling Patterns for Words with *dis-* or *mis-*

Teach

Repeat the Pretest for this lesson or use the Final Test on page 33 of ***Unit 5 Assessment.***

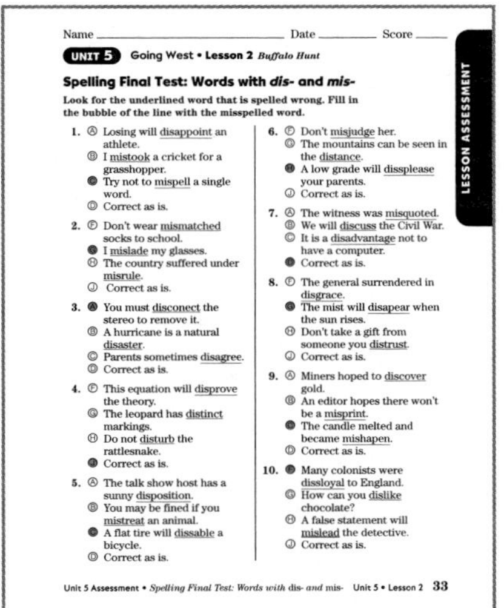

Name ______ Date ______ Score ______

UNIT 5 Going West • Lesson 2 *Buffalo Hunt*

Spelling Final Test: Words with *dis-* and *mis-*

Look for the underlined word that is spelled wrong. Fill in the bubble of the line with the misspelled word.

1. Ⓐ Losing will disappoint an athlete.
   Ⓑ I mistook a cricket for a grasshopper.
   Ⓒ Try not to mispell a single word.
   Ⓓ Correct as is.
2. Ⓕ Don't wear mismatched socks to school.
   Ⓖ I mislade my glasses.
   Ⓗ The country suffered under misrule.
   Ⓙ Correct as is.
3. Ⓐ You must disconect the stereo to remove it.
   Ⓑ A hurricane is a natural disaster.
   Ⓒ Parents sometimes disagree.
   Ⓓ Correct as is.
4. Ⓕ This equation will disprove the theory.
   Ⓖ The leopard has distinct markings.
   Ⓗ Do not disturb the rattlesnake.
   Ⓙ Correct as is.
5. Ⓐ The talk show host has a sunny disposition.
   Ⓑ You may be fined if you mistreat an animal.
   Ⓒ A flat tire will dissable a bicycle.
   Ⓓ Correct as is.
6. Ⓕ Don't misjudge her.
   Ⓖ The mountains can be seen in the distance.
   Ⓗ A low grade will dissplease your parents.
   Ⓙ Correct as is.
7. Ⓐ The witness was misquoted.
   Ⓑ We will discuss the Civil War.
   Ⓒ It is a disadvantage not to have a computer.
   Ⓓ Correct as is.
8. Ⓕ The general surrendered in disgrace.
   Ⓖ The mist will disapear when the sun rises.
   Ⓗ Don't take a gift from someone you distrust.
   Ⓙ Correct as is.
9. Ⓐ Miners hoped to discover gold.
   Ⓑ An editor hopes there won't be a misprint.
   Ⓒ The candle melted and became mishapen.
   Ⓓ Correct as is.
10. Ⓕ Many colonists were dissloyal to England.
    Ⓖ How can you dislike chocolate?
    Ⓗ A false statement will mislead the detective.
    Ⓙ Correct as is.

LESSON ASSESSMENT

Unit 5 Assessment • *Spelling Final Test: Words with* dis- *and* mis- Unit 5 • Lesson 2 33

Unit 5 Assessment p. 33

Guided Practice

Have students categorize any mistakes they made on the Final Test.

Are they careless errors?
Are they lesson pattern problems?

Vocabulary

Synonyms

Informal Assessment

- Make sure that students examine context clues when finding synonyms or using them in their writing. Also, encourage students to think carefully about the specific meanings they want to convey when using a thesaurus.
- Remind students to continue adding synonyms to their Writer's Notebooks.

Writing Process Strategies

Teach

E-Mail Message/Literature Response

Inspiration

Teacher Model: *I want to send a literature response to my class via e-mail about how "The Flower-Fed Buffaloes" made me feel.*

Brainstorming

Using the theme Going West and "The Flower-Fed Buffaloes" as a springboard, encourage students to suggest ideas, thoughts, or details that they might include in their e-mail literature responses to you.

Guided Practice

- Have students draft their responses from their brainstorming ideas.
- Have students write their e-mail messages to you.

Formal Assessment

Share this rubric with students before they begin the assignment to give them a foundation from which to work.

Total Point Value: 10

1. Lowercase is used appropriately. (2 points)
2. Sentences and paragraphs are short. (2 points)
3. The language and tone are appropriate for the audience. (3 points)
4. The conventions are followed, and there are no obvious errors. (3 points)

English Language Conventions

Penmanship

Joining with *E* and *f*

Teach

- **Teacher Model:** Review formation of uppercase *E* and lowercase *f* on the board.

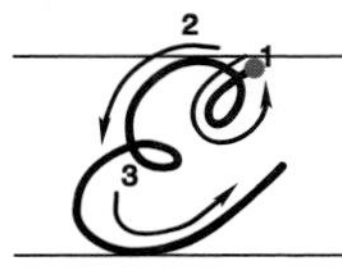

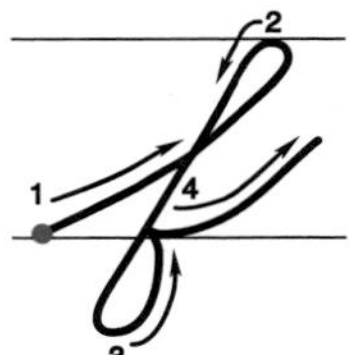

E Starting point, loop around left
Downcurve
Loop back, downcurve
Undercurve: capital *E*

f Starting point, undercurve
Loop back, slant down
Loop forward, undercurve: small *f*

- Remind students to not join letters that should not be joined. Tell students that these uppercase letters are not joined: *G, F, O, S, T, X, B, Q, L, D, P, I, V,* and *W.*

Guided Practice

- In the Writer's Notebook, have students join *E* with the letters *r, l, p,* and *i* and join *f* with *i, o, e,* and *a.*
- From "Buffalo Hunt," "The Whole World is Coming," and "The Flower-Fed Buffaloes," ask students to write a paragraph from each to practice joining letters.

Informal Assessment

Check students' handwriting for proper letter formation and legible joinings.

LESSON WRAP-UP

Reading and Language Arts Skills Traces

Language Arts

WORD ANALYSIS

Skills Trace

Spelling: Words with dis- or mis-

Introduced in Grade 5.
Scaffolded throughout Grade 5.

INTRODUCED: **Unit 5, Lesson 2,** p. 427F
PRACTICED: **Unit 5, Lesson 2,** pp. 427G–427I; ***Spelling and Vocabulary Skills,*** pp. 112–113
TESTED: **Unit 5, Lesson 2,** p. 427J; **Unit 5 Assessment**

Vocabulary: Synonyms

Introduced in Grade 1.
Scaffolded throughout Grades 2–5.

REINTRODUCED: **Unit 5, Lesson 2,** p. 427G
PRACTICED: **Unit 5, Lesson 2,** pp. 427H–427I; ***Spelling and Vocabulary Skills,*** pp. 110–111
TESTED: **Informal Assessment,** p. 427J; **Unit 5 Assessment**

WRITING PROCESS STRATEGIES

Skills Trace

Personal Writing

Introduced in Grade K.
Scaffolded throughout Grades K–5.

REINTRODUCED: **Unit 5, Lesson 1,** p. 405F
PRACTICED: **Unit 5, Lessons 1 and 2,** pp. 405F–405J and 427F–427J; ***Writer's Workbook,*** pp. 78–85
TESTED: **Formal Assessment**; **Unit 5, Lesson 1,** pp. 405G, 405I, 405J; **Unit 5, Lesson 2,** p. 427G, 427H, 427J; **Unit 5 Assessment**

ENGLISH LANGUAGE CONVENTIONS

Skills Trace

Grammar and Usage: Commas

Introduced in Grade 4.
Scaffolded throughout Grades 4–5.

REINTRODUCED: **Unit 5, Lesson 2,** p. 427F
PRACTICED: **Unit 5, Lesson 2,** pp. 427F–427H; ***Comprehension and Language Arts Skills,*** pp. 148–149
TESTED: **Unit 5 Assessment**

Listening, Speaking, Viewing: Speaking: Proper Grammar

Introduced in Grade 4.
Scaffolded throughout Grade 5.

INTRODUCED: **Unit 5, Lesson 2,** p. 427I
PRACTICED: **Unit 5, Lesson 2,** p. 427I
TESTED: **Informal Assessment,** p. 427I

Skills Trace

Penmanship: Joining with E and f

Introduced in Grade 3 (*E*) and Grade 2 (*f*).
Scaffolded throughout Grades 4–5 and Grades 3–5.

REINTRODUCED: **Unit 5, Lesson 2,** p. 427J
PRACTICED: **Unit 5, Lesson 2** p. 427J
TESTED: **Informal Assessment,** p. 427J

Reading

COMPREHENSION

Main Idea and Details

Introduced in Grade 1.
Scaffolded throughout Grades 2–5.

REINTRODUCED: **Unit 2, Lesson 2**
REINFORCED: **Unit 2, Lesson 4**; **Unit 2, Lesson 7**; **Unit 3, Lesson 2**; **Unit 3, Lesson 6**
TESTED: **Unit 5 Assessment**

Professional Development: Comprehension

Reading Aloud

Research has shown that students who are read to by teachers, parents, or other adults are more likely than those who do not have this experience to develop the skills they need to read successfully on their own. Reading aloud serves multiple purposes for both readers and nonreaders as it

- provokes students' curiosity about text.
- conveys an awareness that text has meaning.
- offers both teachers and students the opportunity to model critical reading strategies such as clarifying, predicting, and summarizing—the strategies that students will need in order to become successful readers.
- demonstrates the various reasons for reading text (for example, to find out about the world around them, to learn useful new information and new skills, or simply for pleasure).
- exposes students to the "language of literature" which is more complex than the language they ordinarily use and hear.
- enables good readers to model their own interest in and enjoyment of reading.
- provides an opportunity to teach the problem-solving strategies that good readers employ.
- introduces students to a variety of literature.
- develops vocabulary.
- builds knowledge.
- fosters important reading behaviors.
- provides a natural avenue for discussion.

The importance of reading aloud to students cannot be overemphasized. Reading aloud provides an opportunity to communicate the active nature of reading. As students observe you interacting with the text, expressing your own enthusiasm, and modeling your thinking aloud, they perceive these as valid responses and begin to respond to text in similar ways. They become active listeners and later, when they begin reading on their own, they will begin engaging in the same behaviors.

Teachers introduce students to the unit theme at all grade levels with the Read Aloud selections in the ***Teacher's Editions,*** which are directly related to the theme. Suggestions in the ***Teacher's Edition*** for stopping to think aloud and to stimulate discussion are included to help teachers focus ***Read Aloud*** sessions.

Professional Development

Teacher Resource Library CD-ROMs or ***Online Professional Development*** provides courses that help you better understand the Comprehension/Knowledge Building instruction in ***Open Court Reading.*** For more information about this program, visit SRAonline.com.

Additional information about comprehension, as well as resource references, can be found in the ***Professional Development Guide: Comprehension.***

Objectives

- Students will read and comprehend the poems.
- Students will demonstrate an understanding of the poetry element of Repetition.
- Students will demonstrate an understanding of the presentation skill Oral Interpretation.

Materials

- Student Anthology, pp. 428–429
- Listening Library

Activating Prior Knowledge

- Preteach the poems by having students tell what they have learned in this unit about Native Americans and the buffalo.
- Direct the students' attention to the titles and the illustrations of these poems and have them discuss their feelings about the near-extinction of the buffalo.

Reading the Poem

- These poems are meant to be chanted. Read each one aloud once to students, then have the students chant the poems along with you. Finally, have students read the poems aloud while you listen for appropriate reading rate, intonation, and expression. Repeat each poem aloud for students if they are still having difficulty reading with fluency.
- In the time you designate for Workshop, encourage students to listen to the recordings of the poems on the ***Listening Library Audiocassette/CD.***

Teacher Tip REPETITION Point out to students that both of these poems have several repeated words and phrases. Explain that repetition adds rhythm to poetry. It also helps to stress important words or ideas.

Focus Questions How did the Sioux feel about the coming of the buffalo? Why do you think they referred to buffalo as "the whole world?"

The Whole World Is Coming

a Sioux Indian poem
illustrated by Stella Ormai

The whole world is coming,
A nation is coming, a nation is coming,
the eagle has brought the message to the tribe.
Over the whole earth they are coming;
the buffalo are coming, the buffalo are coming,
the crow has brought the message to the tribe.

428

Focus Questions How has the prairie in this poem changed? How do you think this poem's author feels about those changes?

The Flower-Fed Buffaloes

Vachel Lindsay
illustrated by Stella Ormai

The flower-fed buffaloes of the spring
In the days of long ago,
Ranged where the locomotives sing
And the prairie flowers lie low:
The tossing, blooming, perfumed grass
Is swept away by the wheat,
Wheels and wheels and wheels spin by
In the spring that still is sweet.
But the flower-fed buffaloes of the spring
Left us, long ago.
They gore no more, they bellow no more,
They trundle around the hills no more:
With the Blackfeet, lying low,
With the Pawnees, lying low,
Lying low.

429

Writer's Notebook

Have the students write the following question in their Writer's Notebooks:

- Do these poems have any themes that are similar to those in the selections you have read so far in this unit?

Then have students write their answers to this question in the response section of their Writer's Notebooks.

Meet the Poet

"The Whole World Is Coming" appears in *Songs of the Dream People*, a collection of Native American songs, chants, and poems compiled by James Houston.

Vachel Lindsay's "The Flower-Fed Buffaloes" appears in *Going to the Stars.* Lindsay began writing poetry during his wanderings through the American West, following his failure as an artist and his inability to find suitable work in the Midwest. He recited his poems in return for food and shelter. Following each recitation, he distributed a leaflet of his poems called *Rhymes to Be Traded for Bread.* The subjects of these poems included Native Americans, African-Americans, the Salvation Army, and the American West. Most of his poetry was meant to be chanted and many of his best-known poems represented the optimism of a growing nation.

In his lifetime, he earned many honors, including the Helen H. Levinson Prize, from *Poetry Magazine*, for the poem "The Chinese Nightingale"; the Award of Honor from *Poetry*, and honorary degrees from Baylor and Hiram Colleges. He was the first American poet ever invited to recite his poetry at Oxford University.

Teacher Tip REVIEWING ELEMENTS OF POETRY Review with students the function and effects of literary terms such as theme, simile, metaphor, personification, alliteration, imagery, and symbolism that are often used when discussing and writing poetry. Have students identify examples of these terms in "The Flower Fed Buffalos" and "The Whole World is Coming." Encourage students to include these elements of poetry along with the element repetition in their own poems.

ELEMENTS OF POETRY

Elements of Poetry

As students study poetry, they will learn that there are many elements that make up a poem. Have students look at "The Whole World Is Coming" and "The Flower-Fed Buffaloes" and discuss the following element with them.

Repetition

Remind students that *repetition* is the use of a word or a group of words over and over in a literary work. Explain that writers might use repetition to call attention to important words or ideas in their writing. Other times, a writer might use repetition to add rhythm, or a musical quality, to the work. Repetition can also help a writer fit a poem into a particular pattern of rhyme.

Have students look at the poems on the previous pages. Ask volunteers to identify some words and phrases that are repeated in each poem. Discuss with students why each poet might have chosen to repeat certain words and phrases. Challenge them to describe how repetition affects the mood of each poem.

Writing

Have them think about the two poems they have just read. Then ask them to think about the things they learned in this unit about Native Americans, the buffalo, or the American West. You might encourage them to review the writing topics in their Writer's Notebooks. Ask them to choose one thing that they found really interesting, exciting, or sad and write a poem about it. Challenge them to use repetition in their poems to enhance the musical quality of their writing or to stress the words and ideas that they think are most important. Students may want to free-write about their topic of choice as a prewriting activity. Remind students that *free-writing* is "writing thoughts as they come into one's head, without worrying about using correct grammar and spelling." Students may also want to brainstorm words and phrases they associate with the American West that could be repeated within the poem.

Presentation

Oral Interpretation

Explain to students that poetry is a special kind of writing in which ideas are expressed through a careful combination of words and sounds. Point out that poets choose words carefully and organize them in a particular way in order to create rhythm and emphasize ideas. Explain that, when reading a poem, a reader should think about why the poet chose certain words instead of others and how the organization of those words contributes to the poem's message.

Have students work in groups of three or four. Ask them to choose one of the poems on the previous pages to read aloud for the class. Have students read the poem several times and discuss how it makes them feel, what message they think it sends to readers, and why it is written the way it is.

Have students also identify examples of imagery in the poems. (If necessary, remind students that *imagery* is language, such as metaphor and simile, used in literature to create vivid images.) Have them describe how each example of imagery functions in their chosen poem and its effects on the poem's message. *(For example, if students have chosen the poem "The Whole World Is Coming," they may note that "the whole world" is used as a metaphor for the buffalo. They may say that the function of this imagery may be to communicate how important the buffalo were to the Sioux or to create a visual of the buffalo's numbers. They may say that this imagery of the whole world coming effects the poem's message by creating a sense of anticipation and excitement.)*

Tell students that, when they present the poem aloud, each group member should contribute orally. They might want to read the poem together or they might want to assign certain lines to certain group members. Encourage students to write the poem out on paper and prepare it for reading aloud. Students might mark pauses, words they want to emphasize, and places where they will speed up their reading or slow it down. Have them base their decisions about what words to emphasize on their discussions about the poem's meaning and how it is communicated.

Before students read the poems aloud, remind them that a reader can emphasize words by changing his or her volume, pitch, or speed. Point out that by reading more slowly, they can be more in control of the emphasis they put on words. As students read the poem aloud to their classmates, have the audience take notes on the reading. Encourage students to provide their classmates with compliments, as well as constructive comments. You might have the audience explain how each group's interpretation of the poem made them feel and have the group members tell whether or not that was their goal.

LISTENING/SPEAKING/VIEWING

Teacher Tip READING ALOUD Remind students that they should look up at their audience while they read aloud and use gestures and facial expressions to make their reading more meaningful. Encourage audience members to listen attentively and to feel free to ask the reader questions about why he or she chose to emphasize certain words or phrases.

Differentiating Instruction

If...	Then...
Students are having difficulty identifying uses of imagery in the poems	Discuss with students additional examples of imagery, such as "the locomotive sings," in "The Flower-Fed Buffaloes"

Focus Questions Why does Wong Ming-Chung emigrate from China to the western United States? How does he accomplish what he came to do?

The Journal of Wong Ming-Chung

Laurence Yep
illustrated by Karen Jerome

Wong Ming-Chung's family has sent him to America to help his uncle strike it rich on the "Golden Mountain." In 1852 he joins his uncle on a gold claim outside of San Francisco. He works there with a company of Chinese immigrants led by the Fox. He also befriends an American boy named Hiram and comes to love the beauty of northern California. However, his company must constantly endure the raids of American "bullies." The company is able to keep its claim because the Fox comes up with clever ways to disguise their gold from the raiders. He hides it in a chamber pot and molds it into chopsticks. However, a mob finally runs the company off their claim. The Fox does not lose hope. He decides to take his company to the Sacramento delta to build levees. Wong Ming-Chung and his uncle agree to join them. However, his uncle, who is known back home for his big ideas and bad luck, is beginning to lose heart.

April 23

We followed the river all day without seeing anyone else. It's like the end of the world. The only signs that humans had been here were the rotting rockers and ruined shacks.

We've camped for the night on an abandoned claim. The shack's roof is gone. A broken rocker sits beside the bank. Holes dot the banks. It looks like a battlefield.

430

SELECTION INTRODUCTION

Selection Summary

Genre: Historical Fiction

This historical fiction selection is presented through the journal entries of a young Chinese man who joins his uncle on a gold claim outside San Francisco. Wong Ming-Chung explains that the group of Chinese men was run off their claim and decide to go build levees instead of search for gold. The main character's uncle knows that he needs to make more money than can be made building levees, so he stays behind to search for gold. Even though he tries to convince Wong Ming-Chung to stay with the group, the young man accompanies his uncle. Through a stroke of luck and a lot of hard work, they succeed in finding enough gold to send money home to their family in China.

Some of the elements of historical fiction are listed below. Historical fiction may have one or more of these elements.

- The story is set in the past.
- The plot includes events or problems from that time.
- Characters act the way people of that time would have acted.
- Details relating to clothing, homes, speech, modes of transportation, or tools are correct for that time and place and help make the story more realistic.
- Though the story is made up, the characters may include real people, and the plot may include actual events.

About the Author

LAURENCE YEP has written many historical fiction, science fiction, fantasy, and realistic fiction books. Many of the books reveal his own experiences of "otherness" as a Chinese adolescent in American culture. All of his books have similar themes of family, the past, and imagination. Yep has done doctoral work in literature and psychology at State University in New York.

Yep's book *Child of the Owl* won an American Library Association notable Children's Book Award and the Boston Globe-Horn Book Award for Fiction. Yep's *Dragonwings* won the Newbery Honor Book and the Phoenix Award for being a book of lasting importance.

Students can read more about Laurence Yep on page 443 of the ***Student Anthology.***

Other Books by Laurence Yep:

- *Dragon of the Lost Sea*
- *Liar, Liar*
- *The Star Fisher*
- *Later, Gator*

About the Illustrator

KAREN JEROME has illustrated numerous books for children. Five illustrations were accepted into the International Children's Book Fair in Bologna, Italy (one of seven American illustrators), which later traveled to four museums in Japan. When Karen Jerome is not illustrating books, she is teaching drawing and painting to children.

Students can read more about Karen Jerome on page 443 of the ***Student Anthology.***

Other Books by Illustrated by Karen Jerome:

- *Dragonfly Secret*
- *If Nathan Were Here*
- *The Littlest Tree*

Inquiry Connections

A major aim of ***Open Court Reading*** is knowledge building. Because inquiry is at the root of knowledge building, students are encouraged to investigate topics and questions within each selection that relate to the unit theme.

"The Journal of Wong Ming-Chung" chronicles the hardships faced by the many who rushed to California in search of gold in the middle of the nineteenth century. The journal also reveals the particular hardships encountered by Chinese and other non-whites in the Gold Rush. Key concepts explored are

- gold miners' lives were filled with uncertainty and danger.
- surviving in the American West required hard work, skill, and intelligence.
- some people who participated in the Gold Rush hoped to take advantage of the opportunity to help their families.

Before reading the selection:

- Point out that students may post a question, concept, word, illustration, or object on the Concept/Question Board at any time during the course of their unit investigation. Be sure that students include their names or initials on the items they post so that others will know whom to go to if they have an answer or if they wish to collaborate on a related activity.
- Students should feel free to write an answer or a note on someone else's question or to consult the Board for ideas for their own investigations throughout the unit.
- Encourage students to read about the American West at home and to bring in articles or pictures that are good examples to post on the Board.

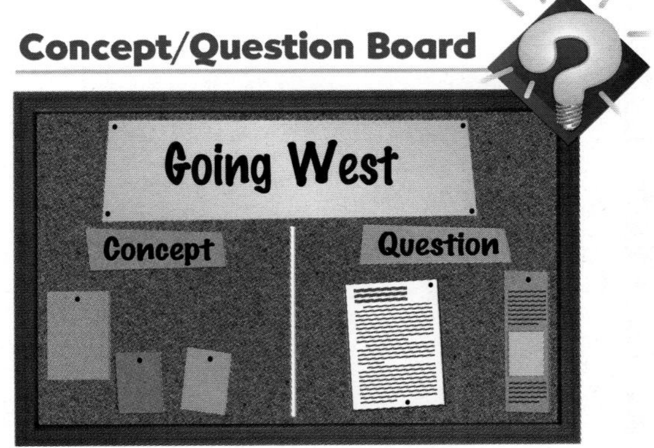

PROGRAM RESOURCES

Leveled Practice

Reteach
Pages 150–155

Challenge
Pages 132–136

English Learner Support Activities

Intervention Workbook

Leveled Classroom Library*

Have students read at least 30 minutes daily outside of class. Have them read books from the ***Leveled Classroom Library,*** which supports the unit theme and helps students develop their vocabulary by reading independently.

Boom Town

BY SONIA LEVITIN. ORCHARD BOOKS, 1998.

Dedicated to a real-life girl who baked $11,000 worth of pies in a small iron skillet, this tale describes how a town grows up around a young girl's bakery, while her father vainly pans for gold. **(Easy)**

By the Great Horn Spoon!

BY SID FLEISCHMAN. LITTLE, BROWN AND COMPANY, 1963.

Narrated with flair, these are the adventures of young Jack Flagg and his unflappable butler Praiseworthy as they hop a gold ship bound from Boston to California to save Jack's aunt's fortune by striking gold. **(Average)**

Children of the Wild West

BY RUSSELL FREEDMAN. CLARION, 1983.

Historic and fascinating photographs accompany Freedman's details about the experiences of pioneer and Native American children in the west, including the journey west, schools, work and play. **(Advanced)**

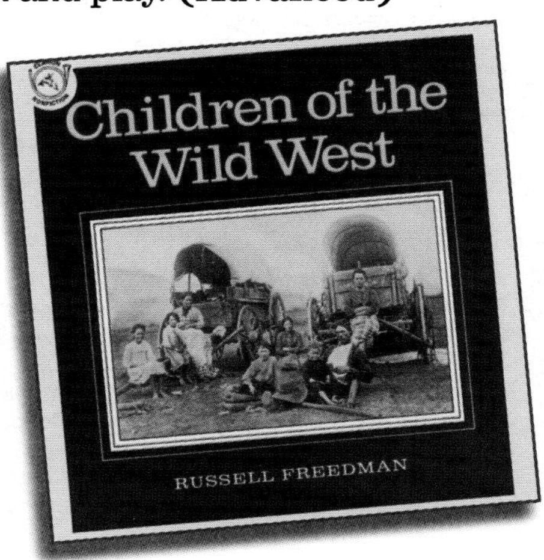

* These books, which all support the unit theme Going West, are part of a 36-book ***Leveled Classroom Library*** available for purchase from SRA/McGraw-Hill. Note: Teachers should preview any trade books for appropriateness in their classrooms before recommending them to students.

SRA TECHNOLOGY

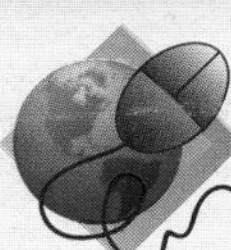

Web Connections

- Going West Web site
- Online Professional Development
- Online Assessment

CD-ROMs

- Research Assistant
- Ultimate Writing and Creativity Center
- Teacher Resource Library

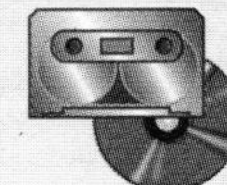

Audiocassettes/CDs

- Listening Library: Going West

Computer Skills

- TechKnowledge

Materials are available through SRA/McGraw-Hill.

LESSON PLANNER

Suggested Pacing: 3–5 days

	DAY 1	DAY 2
1 Preparing to Read **Materials** ■ Routine Card 1	**Word Knowledge,** p. 430K ■ Ending *-ing* ■ Root Word *mount* ■ /əl/ Spelled *-le* ■ Suffixes *-ent* and *-ant* **About the Words and Sentences,** p. 430K	**Developing Oral Language,** p. 430L
2 Reading & Responding **Materials** ■ Student Anthology, pp. 430–445 ■ Routine Card 1 ■ Reading Transparencies 42, 54, 70 ■ Comprehension and Language Arts Skills, pp. 150–151 ■ Reteach, pp. 150–151 ■ Challenge, p. 132 ■ Unit 5 Assessment, pp. 10–13 ■ Program Assessment ■ Home Connection, pp. 67–68 ■ Inquiry Journal, p. 113	**Build Background,** p. 430M **Preview and Prepare,** pp. 430M–430N **Selection Vocabulary,** p. 430N **Reading Recommendations,** pp. 430O–430P **Student Anthology,** pp. 430–441 First Read ✓ **Comprehension Strategies** ■ Predicting, pp. 430, 432, 436, 440 ■ Monitoring and Clarifying, pp. 432, 436, 438 ■ Making Connections, p. 434 **Discussing Strategy Use,** p. 440 **Discussing the Selection,** p. 441A	**Student Anthology,** pp. 430–441 Second Read **Comprehension Skills** ■ Sequence, pp. 431, 433, 435, 437, 439, 441 **Supporting the Reading** ■ Sequence, pp. 441C–441D ✓ **Checking Comprehension,** p. 441
Inquiry **Materials** ■ Student Anthology, pp. 430–443 ■ Inquiry Journal, p. 126 ■ Research Assistant	**Investigation** ■ Investigating Concepts Beyond the Text, p. 443A	**Investigation** ■ Concept/Question Board, p. 443B
3 Language Arts **Materials** ■ Comprehension and Language Arts Skills, pp. 152–155 ■ Language Arts Handbook ■ Language Arts Transparency 11 ■ Spelling and Vocabulary Skills, pp. 114–117 ■ Student Anthology ■ Student Writing and Research Center ■ Writer's Workbook, pp. 86–89 ■ Unit 5 Assessment, pp. 34–35 ■ Reteach, pp. 152–155 ■ Challenge, pp. 133–136	**Word Analysis** ✓■ Spelling: Words with *-ent* or *-ant* Pretest, p. 443F **Writing Process Strategies** ■ Personal Writing: Friendly Letter, Getting Ideas, p. 443F **English Language Conventions** ■ Mechanics: Punctuation and Capitalization, p. 443F	**Word Analysis** ■ Spelling: Words with *-ent* or *-ant,* p. 443G ■ Vocabulary: Words with Multiple Meanings, p. 443G **Writing Process Strategies** ■ Personal Writing: Friendly Letter, Prewriting, p. 443G **English Language Conventions** ■ Mechanics: Punctuation and Capitalization, p. 443G

✓ Informal Assessment Available ✓ Formal Assessment Available

DAY 2 continued	DAY 3	
DAY 3	**DAY 4**	**DAY 5**
General Review	**General Review**	**Review Word Knowledge**
Student Anthology, pp. 442–443 ✓ ■ Concept Connections ■ Meet the Author/Illustrator	**Review Selection Vocabulary,** p. 441B **Literary Elements,** p. 441E ■ Character Analysis	✓ **Lesson Assessment** ■ *Unit 5 Assessment:* Lesson Assessment, pp. 10–13 **Home Connection,** p. 441B **Social Studies Connection,** p. 441F ■ The Journal of Wong Ming-Chung
Investigation ✓ ■ Making Conjectures, p. 443C	**Supporting the Investigation** ■ Conducting a Library Search, p. 443D	**Investigation** ■ Unit Investigation Continued ■ Update Concept/Question Board
Word Analysis ■ Spelling: Words with *-ent* or *-ant,* p. 443H ■ Vocabulary: Words with Multiple Meanings, p. 443H **Writing Process Strategies** ■ Personal Writing: Friendly Letter, Drafting, p. 443H ■ Writer's Craft: Structure of a Personal Letter, p. 443H **English Language Conventions** ✓ ■ Mechanics: Punctuation and Capitalization, p. 443H	**Word Analysis** ■ Spelling: Words with *-ent* or *-ant,* p. 443I ■ Vocabulary: Words with Multiple Meanings, p. 443I **Writing Process Strategies** ■ Personal Writing: Friendly Letter, Revising, p. 443I **English Language Conventions** ✓ ■ Listening, Speaking, Viewing Language: Literary Devices, p. 443I	**Word Analysis** ✓ ■ Spelling: Words with *-ent* or *-ant* Final Test, p. 443J ✓ ■ Vocabulary: Words with Multiple Meanings, p. 443J **Writing Process Strategies** ✓ ■ Personal Writing: Friendly Letter, Editing/Proofreading and Publishing, p. 443J **English Language Conventions** ✓ ■ Penmanship: Joining *U* and *q,* p. 443J

Below are suggestions for differentiating instruction. These are the same skills shown on the Lesson Planner; however, these pages provide extra practice opportunities or enriching activities to meet the varied needs of students.

WORKSHOP

Differentiating Instruction

Teacher: Individual and Small-Group Instruction

Spend time each day with individuals and small groups to individualize instruction. Each day:

- preteach students who need help with the next lesson.
- reteach students who need to solidify their understanding of content previously taught.
- listen to students read to check their fluency.
- hold writing and inquiry conferences.

Use the following program components to support instruction:

- ***Reteach*** with students who need a bit more practice.
- ***Intervention*** for students who exhibit a lack of understanding of the lesson concepts.
- ***English Learner Support*** with students who need language help.

Student: Independent Activities

Students can work alone, with a partner, or in small groups on such activities as:

- Review sound/spellings
- Partner Reading
- Practice fluency
- Independent Reading
- Reading Roundtable
- Concept vocabulary
- Selection vocabulary
- Writing in progress
- Conference
- Language Arts
- *Challenge* Activities
- Inquiry and Investigation Activities
- Listening Library

Professional Development

Teacher Resource Library CD-ROMs or ***Online Professional Development*** provides courses that help you better understand the Workshop/Intervention instruction in ***Open Court Reading.*** For more information on this program, visit SRAonline.com.

	DAY I
Word Knowledge	**Teacher Directed** ▪ Teach meanings of blended words ▪ Reading Words and About the Words, ***Intervention Guide,*** p. 249
Fluency	**Independent Activities** ▪ Self-test fluency rate
Comprehension	**Teacher Directed** ▪ Preteach "The Journal of Wong Ming-Chung," ***Intervention Guide,*** pp. 250–251 ▪ Intervention Selection 1, ***Intervention Guide,*** pp. 251–252 ▪ ***English Learner Support Guide,*** pp. 396–398 **Independent Activities** ▪ Record response to selection in Writer's Notebook ▪ Browse ***Leveled Classroom Library*** ▪ ***Listening Library Audiocassette/CD*** ▪ Add vocabulary in Writer's Notebook
Inquiry	**Independent Activities** ▪ Concept/Question Board ▪ Explore OCR Web site for theme connections
Language Arts	**Teacher Directed** ▪ Seminar: Select a Topic for a Friendly Letter, p. 443F ▪ Commas in Dates, Addresses, and Letters, ***Intervention Guide,*** pp. 152–153 **Independent Activities** ▪ Punctuation and Capitalization in Friendly Letters, ***Comprehension and Language Arts Skills,*** pp. 152–153

	DAY 2	DAY 3	DAY 4	DAY 5
	Teacher Directed ■ Developing Oral Language, ***Intervention Guide***, p. 249	**Teacher Directed** ■ Dictation and Spelling, ***Intervention Guide,*** pp. 249–250	**Independent Activities** ■ Add words to Word Bank	**Teacher Directed** ■ General review as necessary
	Independent Activities ■ Oral reading of "The Journal of Wong Ming-Chung"	**Independent Activities** ■ Partner read "The Journal of Wong Ming-Chung"	**Independent Activities** ■ Fluency rate check ■ Reread "The Journal of Wong Ming-Chung"	**Teacher Directed** ■ Repeated Readings, ***Intervention Guide,*** p. 254 **Independent Activities** ■ Fluency rate check
	Teacher Directed ■ Preteach "The Journal of Wong Ming-Chung," ***Intervention Guide***, pp. 250–251 ■ Reread Intervention Selection 1 ■ Teach Comprehension Strategies, ***Intervention Guide***, p. 252 ■ ***English Learner Support Guide***, pp. 399–401 ■ Review Sequence ■ Sequence, ***Reteach***, pp. 150–151 **Independent Activities** ■ Sequence • ***Comprehension and Language Arts Skills***, pp. 150–151 • ***Challenge***, p. 132 ■ Choose ***Leveled Classroom Library*** book ■ ***Listening Library Audiocassette/CD***	**Teacher Directed** ■ Teach Intervention Selection 2, ***Intervention Guide***, pp. 252–253 ■ ***English Learner Support Guide***, pp. 401–403 ■ Discuss Concept Connections, p. 442 **Independent Activities** ■ ***English Learner Support Activities***, p. 58 ■ Read ***Leveled Classroom Library*** book ■ ***Listening Library Audiocassette/CD*** ■ Recording Concept Information, ***Inquiry Journal***, p. 113 ■ Supporting the Reading: Link to Writing, p. 441D	**Teacher Directed** ■ Teach Comprehension Strategies, ***Intervention Guide***, p. 253 ■ Reread Intervention Selection 2 ■ ***English Learner Support Guide***, pp. 404–406 **Independent Activities** ■ Read ***Leveled Classroom Library*** book ■ Literary Elements: Independent Practice, p. 441E	**Teacher Directed** ■ Reading Roundtable ■ ***English Learner Support Guide,*** pp. 406–407 **Independent Activities** ■ Read ***Leveled Classroom Library*** book ■ Social Studies Connection, p. 441F ■ ***English Learner Support Activities***, p. 59
	Independent Activities ■ Concept/Question Board ■ Explore OCR Web site for theme connections	**Independent Activities** ■ Concept/Question Board ■ Use ***Research Assistant*** to continue investigation	**Independent Activities** ■ Concept/Question Board ■ Making Conjectures, ***Inquiry Journal,*** p. 126	**Independent Activities** ■ Concept/Question Board ■ Supporting the Investigation: Independent Practice, p. 443D ■ Continue research
	Teacher Directed ■ Commas in Dates, Addresses, and Letters, ***Intervention Guide***, p. 254 ■ Spelling: Word Sort, p. 443G ■ Seminar: Plan a Friendly Letter, p. 443G ■ Punctuation and Capitalization in Friendly Letters, ***Reteach***, p. 154 **Independent Activities** ■ Vocabulary: Words with Multiple Meanings, ***Spelling and Vocabulary Skills***, pp. 114–115 ■ Punctuation and Capitalization in Friendly Letters, ***Challenge***, p. 134	**Teacher Directed** ■ Seminar: Draft a Friendly Letter, p. 443H ■ Writing Activity, ***Intervention Guide,*** p. 255 ■ Vocabulary: Words with Multiple Meanings, ***Reteach***, p. 153 **Independent Activities** ■ Spelling: Words with *-ent* and *-ant*, ***Spelling and Vocabulary Skills,*** p. 116 ■ Vocabulary: Words with Multiple Meanings, ***Challenge***, p. 134 ■ Writer's Craft: Structures of a Personal Letter, ***Comprehension and Language Arts Skills,*** pp. 154-155	**Teacher Directed** ■ Seminar: Revise a Friendly Letter, p. 443I ■ Writing Activity, ***Intervention Guide***, p. 255 ■ Spelling: Words with *-ent* and *-ant*, ***Reteach***, p. 152 **Independent Activities** ■ Spelling: Words with *-ent* and *-ant* • ***Spelling and Vocabulary Skills,*** p. 117 • ***Challenge***, p. 133	**Teacher Directed** ■ Seminar: Edit and Publish a Friendly Letter, p. 443J ■ Writer's Craft: Structure of a Personal Letter, ***Reteach***, p. 155 **Independent Activities** ■ Penmanship: Cursive Letters *U* and *q*, p. 443J ■ Writer's Craft: Structure of a Personal Letter, ***Challenge***, p. 136

ASSESSMENT

Formal Assessment Options

Use these summative assessments along with your informal observations to assess student progress.

Name ________________ Date ________ Score ______

UNIT 5 Going West • Lesson 3

LESSON ASSESSMENT

The Journal of Wong Ming-Chung

Read the following questions carefully. Then completely fill in the bubble of each correct answer. You may look back at the story to find the answer to each of the questions.

1. What did the Chinese men do after they were run off their claim?
   - Ⓐ They took a ship back to China.
   - Ⓑ They started a bank in San Francisco.
   - ● They went away to build levees.
2. In town, why does Uncle let Wong Ming-Chung do the talking?
   - ● Wong Ming-Chung speaks better English.
   - Ⓑ Wong Ming-Chung is more clever than Uncle.
   - Ⓒ Wong Ming-Chung knows more about gold.

Read the following questions carefully. Use complete sentences to answer the questions.

3. Why does the river look like a battlefield?
   The river banks are filled with holes.
4. Why did Uncle say such hurtful things to Wong Ming-Chung?
   Uncle said hurtful things because he thought Wong Ming-Chung would be safer with Fox.
5. Why do the Americans laugh at Wong Ming-Chung and Uncle when they register their claim?
   The Americans laugh because they think there is no gold left at the claim.

10 Unit 5 • Lesson 3 *The Journal of Wong Ming-Chung* • Unit 5 Assessment

Unit 5 Assessment p. 10

The Journal of Wong Ming-Chung *(continued)*

6. Why do Wong Ming-Chung and Uncle go from abandoned claim to abandoned claim?
   They find gold dust that others have left behind.
7. What does Wong Ming-Chung want to do with the money he and Uncle make from the gold?
   He would like to buy a store and bring some of his cousins over from China.
8. Why do Wong Ming-Chung and Uncle make themselves look dirty and shabby on their trip to Sacramento?
   They don't want anyone to suspect they have a basket filled with gold.

Read the following questions carefully. Then completely fill in the bubble of each correct answer.

9. What is new in Sacramento?
   - Ⓐ the gold rush
   - ● the buildings
   - Ⓒ the deposit slips
10. When people ask Wong Ming-Chung and Uncle questions, Wong Ming-Chung and Uncle
    - Ⓐ introduce themselves
    - ● smile and say little
    - Ⓒ answer proudly

Unit 5 Assessment • *The Journal of Wong Ming-Chung* Unit 5 • Lesson 3 11

Unit 5 Assessment p. 11

The Journal of Wong Ming-Chung *(continued)*

Read the questions below. Use complete sentences in your answers.

Linking to the Concepts How do Wong Ming-Chung and Uncle's actions throughout the story show that they are clever?

Answers will vary. Accept all reasonable answers.

Personal Response Imagine that you kept a journal like Wong Ming-Chung, and then a hundred years in the future someone finds your journal and reads it. What will they learn about by reading your journal?

Answers will vary. Accept all reasonable answers.

12 Unit 5 • Lesson 3 *The Journal of Wong Ming-Chung* • Unit 5 Assessment

Unit 5 Assessment p. 12

The Journal of Wong Ming-Chung *(continued)*

Vocabulary

Read the following questions carefully. Then completely fill in the bubble of each correct answer.

1. The only signs that humans had been to the river were the rotting rockers and ruined shacks. A **rocker** is
   - Ⓐ a river boulder that is very large and very old
   - Ⓑ a person who enjoys skipping rocks on water
   - ● a tool used to separate gold from sand or dirt
2. A line from the journal says, "We've camped for the night on an abandoned claim." What is a **claim** in this sentence?
   - Ⓐ a piece of paper that says where you are from
   - ● a section of land that belongs to someone
   - Ⓒ a city street that has been suddenly abandoned
3. What does it mean to **prospect** in this story?
   - Ⓐ defend a claim
   - Ⓑ cover your tracks
   - ● search for gold
4. Uncle says he doesn't see how they'd get rich piling up dirt for levees. A **levee** is
   - ● a dirt bank that keeps a river from overflowing
   - Ⓑ a business person who buys, trades, and sells gold
   - Ⓒ a green leafy vegetable used in Chinese cooking
5. The owner of the claim probably thought there would be nuggets just waiting to be picked upriver. A **nugget** is
   - Ⓐ a round fruit
   - Ⓑ a thick forest
   - ● a solid lump

Unit 5 Assessment • *The Journal of Wong Ming-Chung* Unit 5 • Lesson 3 13

Unit 5 Assessment p. 13

Name ________________ Date ________ Score ______

UNIT 5 Going West • Lesson 3 *The Journal of Wong Ming-Chung*

Spelling Pretest: Words with *-ent* and *-ant*

Fold this page back on the dotted line. Take the Pretest. Then correct any word you misspelled by crossing out the word and rewriting it next to the incorrect spelling.

1. ________	1. agent
2. ________	2. tolerant
3. ________	3. resident
4. ________	4. present
5. ________	5. assistant
6. ________	6. different
7. ________	7. permanent
8. ________	8. prominent
9. ________	9. apparent
10. ________	10. dependent
11. ________	11. confident
12. ________	12. represent
13. ________	13. violent
14. ________	14. recent
15. ________	15. continent
16. ________	16. immigrant
17. ________	17. important
18. ________	18. protectant
19. ________	19. insistent
20. ________	20. hesitant

34 Unit 5 • Lesson 3 *Spelling Pretest: Words with -ent and -ant* • Unit 5 Assessment

Unit 5 Assessment p. 34

Name ________________ Date ________ Score ______

UNIT 5 Going West • Lesson 3 *The Journal of Wong Ming-Chung*

Spelling Final Test: Words with *-ent* and *-ant*

Look for the underlined word that is spelled wrong. Fill in the bubble of the line with the misspelled word.

1. Ⓐ Mice and rats are rodents.
   ● A child is considered a dependent.
   Ⓒ An apartment resident must pay rent.
   ● Correct as is.
2. ● Mount Rushmore is a prominant landmark.
   Ⓖ The recent storms have caused flooding.
   Ⓗ An honest and decent person is well liked.
   Ⓙ Correct as is.
3. ● A permenant marker will not smudge.
   Ⓑ Navy and azure are different shades of blue.
   Ⓒ In the myth, the sea god has a trident.
   Ⓓ Correct as is.
4. Ⓕ A lawyer will represent you in court.
   Ⓖ A violent movie is to be seen by adults.
   ● Asia is the largest continant in the world.
   Ⓙ Correct as is.
5. Ⓐ Breakfast is the most important meal.
   ● We could not be tolerent of the bad weather.
   Ⓒ The character in the novel is a secret agent.
   Ⓓ Correct as is.
6. Ⓕ Prevent drowning by wearing a life jacket.
   Ⓖ It is evident that speed caused the accident.
   ● An immigrent might escape oppression.
   Ⓙ Correct as is.
7. ● The constent noise of a factory is annoying.
   Ⓑ Our books don't tell about recent history.
   Ⓒ A student can get a discount at the movies.
   Ⓓ Correct as is.
8. Ⓕ A cow is content to graze.
   Ⓖ All the students in the class are present.
   Ⓗ An assistant gains valuable training.
   ● Correct as is.
9. Ⓐ I wasn't going to go, but she was insistent.
   Ⓑ Car wax is a protectant for the car's finish.
   ● It was apparant that recess was over.
   Ⓓ Correct as is.
10. Ⓕ The shy boy was hesitant to speak up.
    ● A confidint athlete has an advantage.
    Ⓗ I am shocked the mob grew to this extent.
    Ⓙ Correct as is.

Unit 5 Assessment • *Spelling Final Test: Words with -ent and -ant* Unit 5 • Lesson 3 35

Unit 5 Assessment p. 35

Online Assessment for ***Open Court Reading*** helps teachers differentiate classroom instruction based on students' scores from the weekly and end-of-unit assessments. It provides exercises best suited to meet the needs of each student. For more information visit SRAonline.com.

ASSESSMENT

Informal Comprehension Strategies Rubrics

Making Connections

- The student activates prior knowledge and related knowledge.
- The student uses prior knowledge to explain something encountered in the text.
- The student connects ideas presented later in the text to ideas presented earlier in the text.
- The student notes ideas in the text that are new to him or her or conflict with what he or she thought previously.

Predicting

- The student makes predictions about what the text is about.
- The student updates predictions during reading, based on information in the text.

Monitoring and Clarifying

- The student notes characteristics of the text, such as whether it is difficult to read or whether some sections are more challenging or more important than others.
- The student shows awareness of whether he or she understands the text and takes appropriate action, such as rereading, in order to understand the text better.
- The student rereads to reconsider something presented earlier in the text.
- The student recognizes problems during reading, such as a loss of concentration, unfamiliar vocabulary, or lack of sufficient background knowledge to comprehend the text.

Research Rubrics

During Workshop, assess students using the rubrics below. The rubrics range from 1–4 in most categories, with 1 being the lowest score. Record each student's score on the inside back cover of his or her ***Inquiry Journal.***

Making Conjectures

1 Offers conjectures that are mainly expressions of fact or opinion. ("I think the Anasazi lived a long time ago." "I thing tigers should be protected.")

2 Offers conjectures that partially address the research question. ("I think germs make you sick because they get your body upset." "I think germs make you sick because they multiply really fast.")

3 Offers conjectures that address the research question with guesses. ("I think the Anasazi were wiped out by a meteor.")

4 Offers reasonable conjectures that address the question and that can be improved through further research.

Objectives

- Students expand vocabulary by using participle forms as verbs, adjectives, and nouns.
- Students identify words with the root word "mount."
- Students identify and decode words containing the /əl/ sound spelled *-le.*
- Students recognize and spell words with the suffixes *-ant* and *-ent.*

Materials

- Routine Card 1

Routine Card Refer to Routine 1 for the Reading the Words and Sentences procedure.

Teacher Tip SYLLABICATION To help students blend words and build fluency, demonstrate syllabication using decodable multisyllabic words in the word lines.

writ • ing	tram • ple
glit • ter • ing	grum • ble
spend • ing	am • ble
climb • ing	re • gret • ta • ble
par • a • mount	im • mi • grant
moun • tain	pro • tect • ant
moun • tain • eer	in • sist • ent
Un • cle	hes • i • tant

Differentiating Instruction

If...	Then...
Students need extra help with words containing the suffixes *-ent* and *-ant*	Use ***Intervention Guide,*** pages 249–250

Teacher Tip INFLECTIONAL ENDINGS Check that students' reading and writing reflect an understanding of how the inflectional ending *-ing* is used to change a verb's tense or its part of speech. Remind students to use context clues to determine the meaning of words with this ending. Also remind them to edit their writing for standard use of inflections.

WORD KNOWLEDGE

Word Knowledge

Reading the Words and Sentences

Use direct teaching to teach the Word Knowledge lesson. Write each word and sentence on the board. Have students read each word together. After all the words have been read, have students read each sentence in natural phrases or chunks. Use the suggestions in About the Words and Sentences to discuss the different features of the listed words.

Line 1:	writing	glittering	spending	climbing	
Line 2:	mount	paramount	mountain	mountaineer	
Line 3:	Uncle	trample	amble	grumble	regrettable
Line 4:	immigrant	protectant	insistent	hesitant	

Sentence 1: He was writing about spending the glittering gold.
Sentence 2: It is paramount that the climber make it to the mountain peak before the sun sets.
Sentence 3: With a chuckle, Uncle copied me.
Sentence 4: The Statue of Liberty was a welcome sight for an immigrant arriving in the United States.

About the Words and Sentences

- **Line 1:** These words all end in *-ing.* Explain to students that words ending in *-ing* are the participle forms of verbs. They can function in sentences as parts of verbs or as adjectives. They can also be used as nouns. When they are used as nouns, they are called gerunds. Ask volunteers to come up with three sentences for each word, using it as a verb, an adjective, and a noun. You might give the following examples: *I was* spending *money (verb). I went on a* spending *spree (adjective).* Spending *money frivolously is dangerous (gerund).*
- **Line 2:** These words build on the root word *mount,* which comes from the Latin word *montmons,* meaning "to project or threaten." Have students use the Latin root to help come up with a working definition for the word *mount.* Ask students to think of other words that contain the word *mount* as either a noun or a verb *(dismount, mountable).* Then point out that the prefixes and endings to the root word change the meaning. For example, mount means "a hill or rising of land," and the prefix *para-* means "closely related to." Therefore, *paramount* means "something of high status" or "very important."
- **Line 3:** These words all contain /əl/ spelled *-le.* Have students notice that a consonant precedes this spelling. Ask for volunteers to think of other words that have this spelling *(fable, table, uncomfortable).* Ask them to identify a suffix that contains this spelling pattern of the /əl/ sound *(-able).*
- **Line 4:** The words in the last line review the suffixes *-ent* and *-ant.*

- **Sentence 1:** Have students identify the *-ing* words in the sentence. Point out that *writing* is used as a verb, and tell students that when *-ing* words are used as verbs they always have a helping verb (in this case, *was*). Helping verbs are forms of the verb "to be." Have students discuss how *spending* functions as a noun, and ask how they can determine this. *(It is the object of a preposition.)* Finally, ask students how *glittering* functions in this sentence *(as an adjective)*. Have students read the sentence aloud.
- **Sentence 2:** Have students read this sentence aloud. Then, have students identify the words in the sentence that share root words *(paramount, mountain)*. Next, students should use these words in a related sentence.
- **Sentence 3:** This sentence is from the selection. Have the students read the sentence aloud. Then, have students identify the words in the sentence with /əl/ spelled *-le (chuckle, uncle)*.
- **Sentence 4:** Have students notice the word in the last sentence that contains the suffix *-ant.*

Developing Oral Language

Use direct teaching to review the words. Have students do one or more of the following activities.

- Have students give clues about different words on the board. As students guess the correct word, have them use it in a sentence. Then, have another student extend the sentence by adding vivid details onto the original sentence.
- Have students find synonyms, antonyms, or related words for the words on the board. Write these words above the corresponding word and have students make sentences using the new words. Then, if the new word is a synonym, have students switch out the new word for the old to see if it still makes sense. If the word is a related word, have the students extend the sentence by using both the original word and new word in the same sentence. If the word is an antonym, have the students make up a second sentence meaning the opposite of the first.
- Have a student find a classroom-appropriate word in the dictionary that has an abstract, derived root or affix from the Greek or Latin language. Have him or her read it aloud to the class along with the word origin and original meaning for each of its word parts. Have a volunteer use this information to determine the meaning of the word. Then have the student who chose the word read aloud its present-day definition. Have students offer their analyses of how the present-day word meaning relates to the original meanings of its word parts. Then have the dictionary passed to the volunteer to choose the next word. To help increase their vocabulary, students may wish to record each word from this exercise, along with its definition and word-origin information, in the personal dictionary section of their Writer's Notebook.

WORD KNOWLEDGE

Teacher Tip BUILDING FLUENCY By this time in grade 5 students should be reading approximately 151 words per minute with fluency and expression. Gaining a better understanding of the spellings of sounds and structure of words will help students as they encounter unfamiliar words in their reading. As students read, you may notice that some need work in building fluency. During Workshop, have these students choose a section of the text (a minimum of 160 words) to read several times in order to build fluency.

Differentiating Instruction

If...	Then...
Students need extra fluency practice	Use the Intervention Selections activities, ***Intervention Guide,*** pages 251–253

Spelling
See pages 443F–443J for the corresponding spelling lesson for the suffixes *-ent* and *-ant*.

Objectives

- Students will understand the selection vocabulary before reading.
- Students will identify the suffixes *-ent* and *-ant* and words with the *-ing* ending.
- Students will use the comprehension strategies Predicting, Making Connections, and Monitoring and Clarifying as they read the story the first time.
- Students will use the comprehension skill Sequence as they read the story the second time.

Materials

- Student Anthology, pp. 430–443
- Reading Transparencies 42, 54, 70
- Comprehension and Language Arts Skills, pp. 150–151
- Inquiry Journal, p. 113
- Listening Library
- Program Assessment
- Unit 5 Assessment, pp 10–13
- Home Connection, pp. 67–68
- Routine Card 1

www.sra4kids.com
Web Connection
Students can use the connections to Going West in the Reading link of the SRA Web page for more background information about the American West.

Differentiating Instruction

If...	Then...
Students need extra help with the selection vocabulary	Use ***Intervention Guide,*** page 250

Build Background

Activate Prior Knowledge

Discuss the following with students to find out what they may already know about the selection and have already learned about the theme of Going West.

- Preteach "The Journal of Wong Ming-Chung" by first determining their prior knowledge of the Gold Rush. Ask them, "What was the Gold Rush?" *(It happened in 1848; fortune hunters from around the world went to California to find gold.)*

Background Information

The following information may help students understand the selection they are about to read.

- By 1852, the year in which this story takes place, approximately 25,000 Chinese had immigrated to California to find gold. Because of starvation in China, many people were willing to risk taking the trip to California simply to survive.
- The gold mining did irreversible damage to the land. Because of the mining, the land in some places will not support the growth of any plant.
- Many Chinese immigrants did not strike it rich with gold, but they were able to survive on the money from other work, usually manual labor. With this money, they were able to support their families at home in China.
- Chinese miners often established their own camps as a form of protection against other prejudiced miners.
- Have the students discuss what they know about the genre of this selection. Refer to page 430A of the ***Teacher's Edition*** for elements of this selection's genre.

Preview and Prepare

Browse

- Have a student read aloud the title and the names of the author and illustrator. Demonstrate how to browse. Since this is a fiction piece, have the students browse only its first couple of pages, so that the ending will not be spoiled. This helps them to activate prior knowledge in a way that is relevant to the selection. Then discuss what they think this story might have to do with the American West.

- Have the students search for clues that tell them something about the story. Also, have them look for any problems, such as unfamiliar words or long sentences, that they notice while reading. Use ***Reading Transparency 54*** to record their observations as they browse. For example, the phrase "strike it rich" may be a clue that someone is going to come into some money in the selection. For the Problems column, students might say they don't know the meaning of the word *rockers*. They might wonder if the characters will get rich. To save time and model note taking, write students' observations as brief notes rather than complete sentences.
- As students prepare to read the selection, have them browse the Focus Questions on the first page of the selection. Tell them to keep these questions in mind as they read.

Set Purposes

Have students set their own purposes before they read. Also, have them consider how difficult life was in the American West as they read. Remind students that good readers have a purpose when they read. Let them know that they should make sure they know the purpose for reading whenever they read.

Selection Vocabulary

As students study vocabulary, they will use a variety of skills to determine the meaning of a word. These include context clues, word structure, and apposition. Students will apply these same skills while reading to clarify unfamiliar words.

Display ***Transparency 42*** before reading the selection to introduce and discuss the following words and their meanings.

claim: a section of land declared as belonging to one person or group of people (p. 430)
levee: an embankment built along a river to keep the river from overflowing (p. 430)
rocker: a device used to separate gold from sand and dirt (p. 430)
prospect: to look for gold (p. 432)
nugget: a solid lump (p. 437)

Have students read the words in the Word Box, stopping to blend any words that they have trouble reading. Demonstrate how to decode multisyllabic words by breaking them into syllables and blending the syllables. Then have students try. If the word is not decodable, give the students the pronunciation.

Have students read the sentences on ***Reading Transparency 42*** and use the skills of context, word structure (structural analysis), or apposition to figure out the meaning of the words. Be sure students explain which skill(s) they are using and how they figured out the meanings of the words.

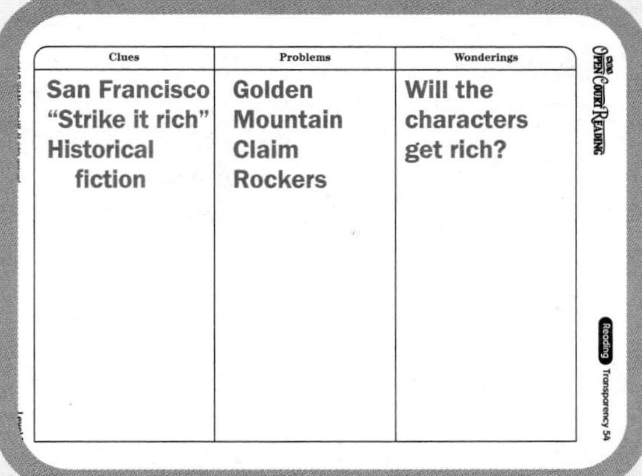

Clues	Problems	Wonderings
San Francisco "Strike it rich" Historical fiction	Golden Mountain Claim Rockers	Will the characters get rich?

Reading Transparency 54

Teacher Tip SELECTION VOCABULARY To help students decode words, divide them into the syllables shown below. The information following each word tells how students can figure out the meaning of each word from the sentences on the transparency.

claim	context clues
lev • ee	context clues
rock • er	context clues, word structure
pros • pect	context clues, word structure
nug • get	context clues

Routine Card
Refer to Routine 2 for the Selection Vocabulary procedure. Refer to Routine 3 for the Clues, Problems, and Wonderings procedure.

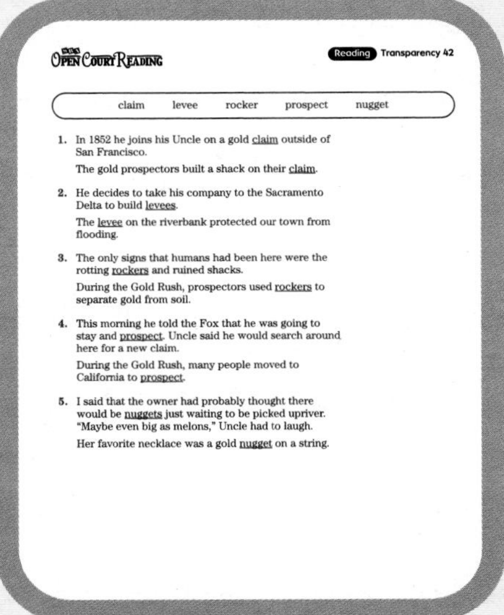

Open Court Reading — Reading Transparency 42

claim levee rocker prospect nugget

1. In 1852 he joins his Uncle on a gold claim outside of San Francisco.
   The gold prospectors built a shack on their claim.
2. He decides to take his company to the Sacramento Delta to build levees.
   The levee on the riverbank protected our town from flooding.
3. The only signs that humans had been here were the rotting rockers and ruined shacks.
   During the Gold Rush, prospectors used rockers to separate gold from soil.
4. This morning he told the Fox that he was going to stay and prospect. Uncle said he would search around here for a new claim.
   During the Gold Rush, many people moved to California to prospect.
5. I said that the owner had probably thought there would be nuggets just waiting to be picked upriver. "Maybe even big as melons," Uncle had to laugh.
   Her favorite necklace was a gold nugget on a string.

Reading Transparency 42

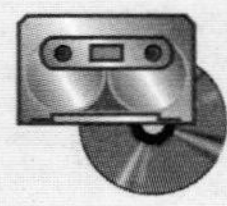

Students will enjoy using the ***Listening Library Audiocassette/CD*** and listening to the selection they are about to read. Encourage them to listen to the selection during Workshop. Have students discuss with each other and with you their personal listening preferences (for example, nonfiction, poetry, drama, and so on).

Routine Card

Refer to Routine 4 for the Reading the Selection procedure.

Differentiating Instruction

If...	Then...
Students need extra help with the comprehension strategies Visualizing and Making Connections	Use ***Intervention Guide,*** pages 252–253

Reading Recommendations

Silent Reading

Because this is a very personal story with a central character to whom the students can easily relate, this is a good selection to have students read silently. Have students read silently for at least fifteen minutes at a time. As they become better readers, students will read silently with increasing ease over longer periods of time. Have them make use of the strategies listed below by recording in their Writer's Notebooks the strategies they used while reading silently. You may want to stop periodically to discuss the selection and strategies used. You may prefer to talk about strategies after the students have completed the selection. After the students have finished reading the selection, use the "Discussing the Selection" questions on page 441A to see if they understand what they have read.

Using Comprehension Strategies 

Comprehension strategy instruction allows students to become aware of how good readers read. Good readers constantly check their understanding as they are reading and ask themselves questions. In addition, skilled readers recognize when they are having problems and stop to use various comprehension strategies, to help them make sense of what they are reading.

During the first reading of "The Journal of Wong Ming-Chung," model and prompt the use of the following comprehension strategies. Take turns reading the story aloud with the students.

- **Making Connections** deepens students' understanding of what they read by linking it to their own past experiences and previous reading.
- **Predicting** causes readers to analyze information given about story events and characters in the context of how it may logically connect to the story's conclusion.
- **Monitoring and Clarifying** prompts readers to track and immediately clear up unfamiliar words and ideas by using context, word structure, apposition, and outside resources. Stop and check that students understand when something is unclear.

As students read, they should be using a variety of strategies to help them understand the selection. Encourage students to use the strategies listed on the previous page as the class reads the story aloud. Do this by stopping at the points indicated by the numbers in magenta circles on the reduced student page and using a particular strategy. Students can also stop reading periodically to discuss what they have learned and what problems they may be having.

In Unit 5, students should be assuming more responsibility for the use of comprehension strategies. Continue Modeling and Prompting as needed. Prompting provides a springboard for students to respond using the strategy mentioned in the prompt. The Student Sample is written in the language that students might use in their actual responses.

The Student Sample may be one of many possible student responses. Accept other responses that are reasonable and appropriate. If student responses indicate that the students do not understand the strategy, be ready to discuss their responses and to provide additional instruction. As students proceed through the lessons, teacher modeling and prompting of strategy use should become less and less necessary as students assume more responsibility for using strategies.

Building Comprehension Skills 

Revisiting or rereading a selection allows students to apply skills that give them a more complete understanding of the text. Some follow-up comprehension skills help students organize information. Others lead to deeper understanding—to "reading between the lines," as mature readers do. An extended lesson on the comprehension skill Sequence can be found in the Supporting the Reading section on pages 441C–441D. This lesson is intended to give students extra practice with Sequence. However, the Teach portion of the lesson may be used at this time to introduce the comprehension skill to students.

- **Sequence (Review):** Readers use time words and order words in the text in order to follow the author's line of thought.

Reading with a Purpose

Have students consider the hardships immigrants underwent in the hope of finding gold and record their thoughts in the Response Journal section of their Writer's Notebooks.

Differentiating Instruction

If...	Then...
Students need extra help with reading "The Journal of Wong Ming-Chung"	• Preread the selection during Workshop; use the ***Listening Library*** to give students a good reading model • Use ***English Learner Support Guide,*** pages 394–407 • Use ***Intervention Guide,*** pages 250–251

Teacher Tip SEQUENCE The comprehension skill Sequence will help students identify the structure of the plot as well as the events of the story.

Teacher Tip ORAL READING FLUENCY AND RETELL FLUENCY For extra practice in oral fluency, have individual students read aloud to you a selection they have previously read, either from a Decodable Book or a passage from the Student Anthology. Time each student for one minute. If the student reads more than 151 words correctly, have the student retell the selection he or she has just read. Use one prompt if the student seems to be stuck, and allow a maximum of one minute for the student to retell the story. If the student does not read more than 151 words correctly, have the student try reading from an easier selection, such as a Decodable Book from a prior grade level, to help you determine where the problem lies.

COMPREHENSION

Read pages 430–441.

Comprehension Strategies

Prompting

1 Predicting *Writers often provide clues in a text about what will happen next. Who wants to make a prediction about what will happen and tell what clue or clues you based the prediction on?*

Student Sample

Predicting *Based on the fact that Wong Ming-Chung's uncle is beginning to lose heart and that he is known for his big ideas, I think he will go off on his own. When I am sad, sometimes I like to be alone, too.*

Word Knowledge

SCAFFOLDING The skills students are reviewing in Word Knowledge should help them in reading the story. This lesson focuses on words ending in *-ent* and *-ant*. These words will be found in boxes similar to this one throughout the selection.

-ant:

immigrant **constant**

First Reading Recommendation

ORAL • CHORAL • **SILENT**

Focus Questions Why does Wong Ming-Chung emigrate from China to the western United States? How does he accomplish what he came to do?

The Journal of Wong Ming-Chung

Laurence Yep

illustrated by Karen Jerome

Wong Ming-Chung's family has sent him to America to help his uncle strike it rich on the "Golden Mountain." In 1852 he joins his uncle on a gold claim outside of San Francisco. He works there with a company of Chinese immigrants led by the Fox. He also befriends an American boy named Hiram and comes to love the beauty of northern California. However, his company must constantly endure the raids of American "bullies." The company is able to keep its claim because the Fox comes up with clever ways to disguise their gold from the raiders. He hides it in a chamber pot and molds it into chopsticks. However, a mob finally runs the company off their claim. The Fox does not lose hope. He decides to take his company to the Sacramento delta to build levees. Wong Ming-Chung and his uncle agree to join them. However, his uncle, who is known back home for his big ideas and bad luck, is beginning to lose heart. 1

April 23

We followed the river all day without seeing anyone else.

It's like the end of the world. The only signs that humans had been here were the rotting rockers and ruined shacks.

We've camped for the night on an abandoned claim. The shack's roof is gone. A broken rocker sits beside the bank. Holes dot the banks. It looks like a battlefield.

430

Informal Assessment

Observe individual students as they read and use the Teacher Observation Log found in the ***Program Assessment Teacher's Edition*** to record anecdotal information about each student's strengths and weaknesses.

Differentiating Instruction

If...	Then...
English Learners need extra support with reading "The Journal of Wong Ming-Chung" and using the skill Sequence	Preteach ***Student Anthology*** pages 430–434 using Day 1 of the "The Journal of Wong Ming-Chung" lesson, found on ***English Learner Support Guide,*** pages 396–398

The bank juts out like a finger, forming a breakwater. The river forms a lazy eddy behind it, which the Fox said would be a good spot for gold to drop out.

It's a good thing we've stopped, too. My feet are so sore that I soaked them in the river. For once, I'm grateful the water is icy cold.

Uncle sat like a lump beside me. He said he didn't see how we'd ever get really rich piling up dirt for levees. It's like we're in prison and every day we have to do hard work.

I reminded him of what the Fox said—that we'll still be sending home something. It might be less but it will still be a lot by Chinese standards. But Uncle just kept staring at the river.

The cook fixed a quick meal. Since we can eat only what we could carry away, everything's rationed. The meals are small—about what they'd be back in China.

But we're alive. That's the important thing.

431

Teacher Tip SEQUENCE Ask students whether any of them keep a journal. Then, have a volunteer describe how he or she orders journal entries. Tell students that this selection is written like a journal. Point out to students the head "April 23." Explain that this is the date of the narrator's first entry in his journal.

Comprehension Skills

COMPREHENSION

Sequence

Explain to students that the sequence of events means the order in which events occur. Students should be aware of words that indicate order, such as *first*, *second*, *last*, *earlier*, *later*, *now*, *then*, *following*, *next*, *after*, *during*, and *finally.* They should also be aware of time words such as *morning*, *afternoon*, *evening*, and *night.* Point out the following passages to students:

- "However, a mob *finally* runs the company off of their claim." (page 430)
- "We followed the river all *day* without seeing anyone else." (page 430)
- "We've camped for the *night*." (page 430)

Explain that sometimes writers do not describe each event in the order it occurred, but they give readers the sequence information by using time or order words.

Sequence

Introduced in Grade 1.

Scaffolded throughout Grades 2–5.

REINTRODUCED: Unit 1, Lesson 4

REINFORCED: Unit 4, Lesson 2
Unit 5, Lesson 3
Unit 6, Lesson 1

TESTED: Unit 5 Assessment

Second Reading Recommendation

ORAL • **SILENT**

COMPREHENSION

Comprehension Strategies

Prompting

2 Confirming Predictions *How do the events in the text compare to the predictions you made earlier?*

Student Sample

Confirming Predictions *My prediction was confirmed. His uncle did leave to continue his search for gold by himself.*

Teacher Modeling

3 Monitoring and Clarifying *I don't understand why Uncle is being so mean to Wong Ming-Chung. Wait; I think both of them realize how dangerous it will be to prospect alone. I think that Uncle does not want his nephew to accompany him because it will be dangerous. The only way he knows to convince his nephew is to say mean things to him to get him to go with the Fox.*

Research in Action

Strategy Use

It is important for students to recognize that they may understand all the words in a sentence without understanding the sentences. Just as important, they may understand what the sentence as a whole means even if they are unclear about a certain word. These ideas are best conveyed using modeling—that is, thinking aloud using strategies for clarifying. *(Jan Hirshberg)*

April 24

I can hardly write these words. Uncle's left me.

2 This morning he told the Fox that he was going to stay and prospect. He bought his own ticket here, so he was free to leave like any employee. The Fox didn't need a carpenter anymore.

The Fox thought he'd lost his senses. After all, we'd just gotten chased off our claim by a mob. Uncle might not survive the next mob.

Uncle said he would search around here for a new claim. The Fox had said it was safe enough.

The Fox tapped his nose and said, "That's because there's no gold, or this would have told me."

Uncle has plans for home. He can't carry them out piling up dirt.

The Fox shook his head but suggested that I go with him.

I was scared at the idea of staying in the gold country. However, I thought of Uncle left alone in the mountains with his bad luck. He wouldn't last a week.

So I said I was going to help Uncle.

432

Teacher Tip CONFIRMING PREDICTIONS Remind students that good readers continuously make predictions as they read. They also confirm their predictions or revise them as they acquire more information.

Informal Assessment

Use the Informal Comprehension Strategies Rubrics on page 430J to determine whether a student is using the strategies being taught.

Uncle tried to use his authority as the head of the family and tell me to go with the Fox.

I refused.

Uncle said I was useless to him. He didn't want me hanging around his neck anymore like a stone.

I started to cry. Even if Father and Mother didn't need me, I had been sure Uncle did.

Uncle kept saying a lot of hurtful things. I tried to remind him that he had been glad when I came. 3

He insisted that had been a lie and said I was nothing but a burden on him.

The Fox came over and put his hands on my shoulders. As we walked away, he told the cook to leave some supplies and a few tools with Uncle.

The others made their farewells to Uncle, but I stood by the path ready to go. When we left Uncle, I didn't even look back.

We've made camp for our noon meal. However, I've had no appetite. I have to talk to someone, even if it's only my diary.

How could Uncle say those things? How?

433

Comprehension Skills

Sequence

Remind students that sometimes in texts events are not presented in the order they occur, but writers provide their sequence by using time and order words. Help students understand the following sequence of events:

- Uncle says he is going to leave.
- Wong says he will go with him.
- Uncle says mean things to Wong and tells him to stay with the Fox.
- They leave Uncle.
- They make camp for the noon meal, and Wong relays the morning's events in the journal.

COMPREHENSION

Word Knowledge

SCAFFOLDING The skills students are reviewing in Word Knowledge should help them in reading the selection. This lesson focuses on the *-ing* ending. These words will be found in boxes similar to this one throughout the selection.

***-ing* ending:**

hanging **saying**

Teacher Tip COMPREHENSION Help students understand that Uncle thinks saying those hurtful things to Wong is for Wong's own good. He does not want the young man to risk his life to accompany him.

COMPREHENSION

Comprehension Strategies

Prompting

4 Making Connections *Good readers make connections to the emotions of the characters to help them better understand the characters. Has anyone ever had a disagreement with someone that was cheerfully resolved? What did that feel like? Who would like to share your thoughts with the class?*

Student Sample

Making Connections *I have. Once I had an argument with my best friend, and when we finally made up, it was such a relief. I bet Wong Ming-Chung feels relieved, too.*

Word Knowledge

-ing ending:

writing sitting

Teacher Tip MAKING CONNECTIONS Have students consider the content of Wong's journal or diary and have them compare it to the content of their own diaries. Students might note that it is common to write about personal fears and feelings in a diary because it is private.

Evening

I am writing this quickly by moonlight. I tossed and turned for hours. I can't let Uncle die in the mountains. Even if he doesn't love me, he is still family.

Everyone is asleep. I'm going to leave a note for the Fox and then sneak away and find Uncle.

April 25

About an hour after midnight last night, I reached the shack where we had left Uncle.

Uncle was sitting by the river. His shoulders were silvery in the moonlight.

I hesitated, expecting him to say more hurtful things. However, I'd had time to rehearse a speech. So I told him I'd try my best not to be a burden.

4 Uncle came rushing toward me before I could finish. He gave me a big hug. He told me he hadn't meant what he said.

I asked him why he had said it then.

Uncle thought I would be safer with the Fox. Those hurtful words were maybe the hardest things he'd ever had to say.

I'm not ashamed to say that we both wept. When we finished, we decided to look for gold in the morning.

434

Differentiating Instruction

If...	Then...
English Learners need extra support with reading "The Journal of Wong Ming-Chung" and using the skill Sequence	Preteach ***Student Anthology*** pages 434–437 using Day 2 of the "The Journal of Wong Ming-Chung" lesson, found on ***English Learner Support Guide,*** pages 399–401

To change our luck, I spun on my heel and recited, "Spin around, turn around, luck changes."

With a chuckle, Uncle copied me.

When we entered the shack to go to sleep, I had to laugh. There isn't any roof. We might just as well sleep outside.

However, the shack does have a fireplace. After we had gathered branches, I got a good fire roaring in the fireplace. Then we lay down in our blankets.

As I stared at the flickering flames, I thought of Mother. I used to squat by the front of the stove feeding the fire while she cooked. She used to like to hum, and the flames seemed to dance to her tune.

When will I see her again?

Later

Just had the worst nightmare. The mob was chasing me. I tried to run, but there was mud all around. I kept slipping and sliding and the mob kept gaining.

I must not have slept for very long, though, because the fire is just now dying. There are little dots of light all over the dirt floor of the cabin. They look like the torches the mob carried.

We're safe. We're safe. For now.

435

Comprehension Skills

COMPREHENSION

Sequence

Ask students to define sequence and describe how it aids readers. Then, point them to the following headings:

- Evening
- April 25
- Later

Ask students to give you a time frame for the headings. For example, the *Evening* heading refers to the evening of April 24, the *April 25* heading refers to just after midnight, and *Later* refers to early morning hours of April 25.

Word Knowledge

***-ing* ending:**

flickering	**feeding**
sliding	**gaining**

COMPREHENSION

Comprehension Strategies

Prompting

5 **Monitoring and Clarifying** *It seems like a lot has happened so far during this entry. Would someone please clarify the time of day that "Still Later" refers to?*

Student Sample

Monitoring and Clarifying *Is it late at night? Oh, I see. The April 25 entry begins just after midnight. His encounter with his uncle probably took a couple of hours. So, the "Later" entry was probably about 2 A.M. I think that the "Still Later" entry must be at about 3 A.M.*

Prompting

6 **Predicting** *Now is a good time to stop and predict what Wong and his uncle will do about the gold on the floor. Who would like to make a prediction?*

Student Sample

Predicting *I think that they will be able to get a little bit of gold from the floor. But, if the gold is in small flakes that couldn't be seen in the daylight, I bet it won't be very much.*

Word Knowledge

***-ing* ending:**

trembling **touching**

Teacher Tip CHECKING COMPREHENSION Ask students one or more of the following questions to make sure they understand what they are reading: "Is anyone confused? Do you need clarification? Can you summarize what you have read so far? Does what you are reading make sense to you?"

5 *Still later*

I'm trembling so badly I can barely write these words.

As I stared at the glittering floor, my curiosity got the better of my fear. What was reflecting the light?

So I crawled out of my blanket and crept across the floor with my nose almost touching the dirt.

I smelled gold. After spending all that time drying it and weighing it with the Fox, I know its smell by now.

That's it. Drying it!

The owner of the claim probably got the gold from the river. That means he had to dry it at night just as the Fox did with his gold.

6 There is gold dust scattered all around us.

I've got to wake Uncle and tell him.

Night

When I first told Uncle my theory, he didn't get excited.

Instead, he said it was an interesting idea, but why didn't the owner pick up the gold?

I said that maybe the light had to be just right from the fireplace.

Uncle looked thoughtful. He admitted that he hadn't noticed it when he first came in here. And it had still been day then.

I tried another explanation. The Fox had said this area had been worked in the early months of the gold rush. There was still plenty of easy gold then.

Uncle eagerly agreed. He said that maybe the owner thought the floor wasn't worth the time.

436

I said that the owner had probably thought there would be nuggets just waiting to be picked upriver.

"Maybe even big as melons," Uncle had to laugh.

His boast in the village seems so long ago now.

We'll wait until sunrise. One of the walls should give us the lumber to build a rocker. Then we'll know.

I don't know how much sleep I'll get, though.

April 26

It took half the day to build the rocker. Then Uncle dug up a shovelful of soil by the fireplace. Carefully he carried it over to the rocker. I used my hat to pour water in.

Gently we began to make the rocker sway. Water ran through the holes at the bottom.

Then we held our breaths as the water poured out.

Uncle got discouraged right away when he didn't see anything.

I leaned my head this way and that, studying the wooden cleats from all angles. "Wait," I said. There was a faint gleam of light.

I ran my fingertips along the edge and held it up. Bits of gold clung to it.

437

Comprehension Skills

Sequence

Explain to students that the journal entry headed "Still Later" happened before sunrise on April 25. The "Night" entry happened the evening of April 25. Ask students to organize the events that took place in the order that they occurred (pp. 436–437).

- Wong Ming-Chung sees the gold on the floor.
- Wong Ming-Chung tells his uncle.
- They discuss the possible reasons the gold would be there and decide to build the rocker the next day.
- They build the rocker.
- They find gold.

Word Knowledge

***-ing* ending:**

studying

Teacher Tip CONTEXT To help students understand how a rocker works, you might provide them with photographs and an explanation of the device.

COMPREHENSION

Differentiating Instruction

If...	Then...
English Learners need extra linguistic support with reading "The Journal of Wong Ming-Chung" and using the skill Sequence	Preteach ***Student Anthology*** pages 437–439 using Day 3 of the "The Journal of Wong Ming-Chung" lesson, found on ***English Learner Support Guide,*** pages 401–403

COMPREHENSION

Comprehension Strategies

Prompting

7 Monitoring and Clarifying

Let's stop and clarify why they did not want to bring too much gold into town with them. Who has ideas?

Student Sample

Monitoring and Clarifying *I think that they don't want anyone else to know how much gold they have found because they are likely to be robbed. The "bullies" ran them off their first claim, and Wong was afraid that his uncle wouldn't make it alone because of the "bullies." So I think it is best for them to keep their gold a secret until they can put it in a bank.*

Word Knowledge

***-ing* ending:** **talking** **mining**

Teacher Tip PREJUDICE Point out the sentence "We're just the crazy Chinese to them." Explain to students that at the time there was such a great influx of immigrants, many Americans were extremely prejudiced. Some Americans thought that the gold should only go to the Americans. In fact, the government instituted a gold tax that in the end applied to only Chinese immigrants.

Teacher Tip BUILDING FLUENCY As students read, you may notice that some need work in building fluency. During Workshop, have these students choose a section of text (a minimum of 160 words) to read several times in order to build fluency.

April 27
Evening

We're rich!

It took only one and a half days to get a small pouch of gold! Uncle says we'll make our melon-sized nuggets the hard way, one flake at a time.

April 29

We went into town to buy supplies and tools like pails and things, but we were careful not to bring too much gold with us. Uncle let me do the talking since I've learned more American than he has. 7

The Americans laughed at us when we registered our claim. Then they told us there is no gold up there.

Uncle was curious when I insisted on buying a big chamber pot but he gave in.

Later, when I told him what the Fox used his chamber pot for, Uncle had a good chuckle.

May 4

We've cleaned out the cabin floor.

Uncle says our method of mining is worth more than the gold itself. We have to protect it.

I agree, so we've filled in the holes and smoothed over the dirt floor with branches. When we were finished, it looked just as we had first seen it.

Now it's on to the next abandoned claim.

438

May 24

We stop only at abandoned claims where there was likely to have been gold at one time. Uncle and I have picked up a lot from the Fox and his nose for gold. We look for spots where the river widens and the water slows, or behind breakwaters like our first claim. Sometimes we look inside the bends of the river or in the pool of slow water that forms just before the rapids.

So far we've tried ten more abandoned claims on this side of the river. Not every miner was careless, but two more have paid off. One of them was the richest of all.

Every time we file a new claim in town, they laugh at us some more. We're just the crazy Chinese to them.

We just smile.

While we work, I tell Uncle about some of the investment schemes I heard from my friends and some of the miners' letters. Uncle agrees with me that a store might be a good idea sometime in the future.

Uncle says that maybe once we have the store, we'll bring some of our cousins over from China.

439

Comprehension Skills

Sequence

Point out to students that in the beginning of the story Wong Ming-Chung was recording journal entries every day. Have them look at the headings now:

- April 27
- April 29
- May 4
- May 24

Ask students what events happened between May 4 and May 24.

- They have stopped at ten abandoned claims.
- They have filed claims in town.
- They have discussed investment schemes.

Word Knowledge

-ent **ending:**

investment

Teacher Tip FLUENCY By this time in grade 5 good readers should be reading approximately 151 words per minute with fluency and expression. The only way to gain this fluency is through practice. Have students reread the selection to you and to one another during Workshop to help build fluency.

COMPREHENSION

COMPREHENSION

Comprehension Strategies

Prompting

8 Predicting *Who wants to predict how the story will end?*

Student Sample

Predicting *I think that they will make it to Sacramento safely and put their money in the bank. I also think they will be sure to send some money home to China. They are here to help their families after all. Maybe they will open up a store with the money they have left.*

Discussing Strategy Use

While students are reading the selection, encourage them to share any problems they encountered and tell what strategies they used.

- How did they clarify confusing passages?
- What connections did they make between the reading and what they already know?
- On what basis did they make and confirm predictions?

Remind students that good readers use all of the strategies listed above and that they should be using them whenever they read. Make sure that students explain how using the strategies helped them to better understand the selection. For example, "Predicting helped me think ahead, using what I had already read. I wanted to keep reading to see if my predictions were confirmed."

Word Knowledge

***-ing* ending:**

riding **bringing**

May 26

8 We're going to take our gold into Sacramento. It's time to bank it.

May 27
En route to Sacramento

It's so strange to be riding a wagon back to Sacramento. The wagon's going directly there, so the trip is much shorter than when I first went into the gold fields.

Our gold is in a basket that I'm sitting on. No one looks twice at two dirty, raggedy guests. And we muddied up our basket to look just as run-down as us.

The hills are green from the winter rains. In the dells where the water gathers, flowers are blooming. I think you could grow anything here.

Hiram's right. It's the soil here that's the real gold in America. Once the metal's gone, it's gone. The earth will keep bringing up new crops each year.

I wonder what happened to Hiram and his dream of a farm?

440

Teacher Tip CONFIRMING PREDICTIONS Good readers check to see if their predictions are confirmed as they read. The prediction made in the Student Sample on this page can be confirmed on page 441.

Differentiating Instruction

If...	Then...
English Learners need extra linguistic support with reading "The Journal of Wong Ming-Chung" and using the skill Sequence	Preteach ***Student Anthology*** pages 440–441 using Day 4 of the "The Journal of Wong Ming-Chung" lesson, found on ***English Learner Support Guide,*** pages 404–406

May 31
Sacramento

I am writing this while the clerk in the American bank finishes weighing and recording our deposits.

When we arrived on the wagon in Sacramento, I saw that it was all new. About a month after I came through here, a terrible fire burned down everything.

When we opened our basket in the American bank, the bank clerk was very curious. He kept wanting to know if we had made a big strike. On the way down here, though, Uncle and I had already decided to just smile and say as little as possible.

Once we get our bank draft, we'll go over to Chinatown to the headquarters of our district back in China.

Then we can send some of the money in the American bank back to China. I wish I could hear the clan when our money gets there. They'll say Uncle must have luck as big as a mountain.

441

Comprehension Skills

Second Read

COMPREHENSION

Sequence

Have students explain what sequence is. Then, challenge them to identify the sequence of the main events in the story. Students should use the headings and time and order words to help them identify sequence.

Checking Comprehension

Ask students the following questions to check their comprehension of the selection.

- Why did Wong Ming-Chung and his uncle come to California? *(They hoped to strike it rich in order to help their families back home in China.)*
- Why did the group led by the Fox decide to work on the levees instead of prospect? *(Their claim was stolen by bullies and they were tired of dealing with the threats and finding little gold. They knew that they would be able to make some money building levees to help their families at home.)*
- How did Wong Ming-Chung and his uncle "strike it rich?" *(They prospected abandoned claims for the gold the other prospectors might have left behind.)*
- How has this selection connected with your knowledge of the unit theme? *(Answers will vary. Students should compare/contrast examples of the American West from this selection with their own experiences or past reading and use these connections to make a general statement about the unit theme.)*

Word Knowledge

-ing ending:
writing **weighing**

Differentiating Instruction

If...	Then...
English Learners have been participating in the "The Journal of Wong Ming-Chung" ***English Learner Support Guide*** activities	Review the selection and the skill Sequence using Day 5 of the "The Journal of Wong Ming-Chung" lesson, found on ***English Learner Support Guide,*** pages 406–407

Formal Assessment

See pages 10–13 in ***Unit 5 Assessment*** to test students' comprehension of "The Journal of Wong Ming-Chung."

Routine Card
Refer to Routine 5 for the *handing-off process.*

Clues	Problems	Wonderings
San Francisco "Strike it rich" Historical fiction	Golden Mountain Claim Rockers	Will the characters get rich?

Reading Transparency 54

www.sra4kids.com
Web Connection
Some students may choose to conduct a computer search for additional books or information about the American West. Invite them to make a list of these books and sources of information to share with classmates and the school librarian. Check the Reading link of the SRA Web page for additional links to theme-related Web sites.

Discussing the Selection

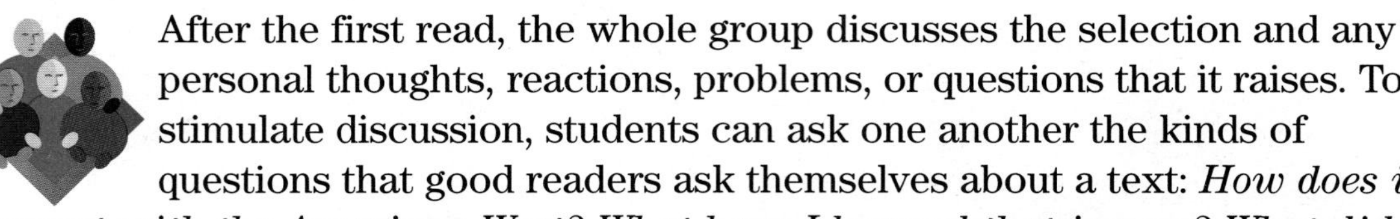

After the first read, the whole group discusses the selection and any personal thoughts, reactions, problems, or questions that it raises. To stimulate discussion, students can ask one another the kinds of questions that good readers ask themselves about a text: *How does it connect with the American West? What have I learned that is new? What did I find interesting? What is important here? What was difficult to understand? Why would someone want to read this?* It is important for students to see you as a contributing member of the group.

Routine 5 To emphasize that you are part of the group, actively participate in the *handing-off process:* Raise your hand to be called on by the last speaker when you have a contribution to make. Point out unusual and interesting insights verbalized by students so that these insights are recognized and discussed. As the year progresses, students will take more and more responsibility for the discussion of selections.

Engage students in a discussion to determine whether they have discerned the following main ideas:

- prospectors' lives were filled with uncertainty and danger
- surviving in the American West took courage, skill, and ingenuity

In discussing the above ideas, students should identify and assess evidence from the text that supports them.

During this time, have students return to the clues, problems, and wonderings that they noted during browsing to determine whether the clues were borne out by the selection, whether and how their problems were solved, and whether their wonderings were answered or deserve further discussion and exploration. Let the students decide which items deserve further discussion. Also have students return to the Focus Questions on the first page of the selection. Select a student to read the questions aloud, and have volunteers answer the questions. If students do not know the answers to the questions, have them return to the text to find the answers.

You may also want to review the elements of historical fiction with the students. Discuss with them how they can tell that "The Journal of Wong Ming-Chung" is historical fiction.

Have students break into small groups to discuss how the story reflects the theme. Groups can then share their ideas with the rest of the class.

Students may wish to record their thoughts about and reactions to this selection. Encourage students to discuss the relationship between Wong Ming-Chung, his uncle, and their family in China. Have them also consider how this story relates to what they know about the Gold Rush and immigrants to the United States.

Review Selection Vocabulary

Have students review the definitions of the selection vocabulary words that they wrote in the vocabulary section of their Writer's Notebooks. Remind them that they discussed the meanings of these words before reading the selection. Students can use these definitions to study for the vocabulary portion of their Lesson Assessment. Have them add to the personal dictionary section of their Writer's Notebooks any other interesting words that they clarified while reading. Encourage students to refer to the selection vocabulary words throughout the unit. The words from the selection are:

claim **levee** **nugget** **prospect** **rocker**

Have students place the words under the appropriate endings in the Word Bank. Encourage the students to find other words related to the unit theme and add them to the Word Bank.

Home Connection

Distribute ***Home Connection,*** page 67. Encourage students to discuss "The Journal of Wong Ming-Chung" with their families. Students can search for information about the process of prospecting during the gold rush and write a paragraph about what they learned. ***Home Connection*** is also available in Spanish, page 68.

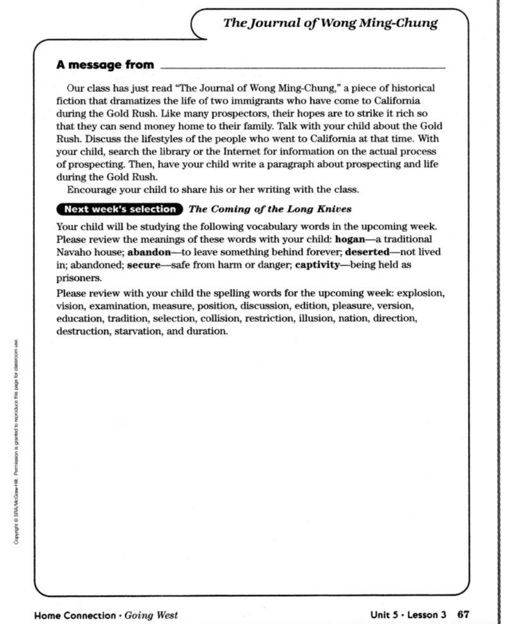

The Journal of Wong Ming-Chung

A message from ______________

Our class has just read "The Journal of Wong Ming-Chung," a piece of historical fiction that dramatizes the life of two immigrants who have come to California during the Gold Rush. Like many prospectors, their hopes are to strike it rich so that they can send money home to their family. Talk with your child about the Gold Rush. Discuss the lifestyles of the people who went to California at that time. With your child, search the library or the Internet for information on the actual process of prospecting. Then, have your child write a paragraph about prospecting and life during the Gold Rush.

Encourage your child to share his or her writing with the class.

Next week's selection ***The Coming of the Long Knives***

Your child will be studying the following vocabulary words in the upcoming week. Please review the meanings of these words with your child: **hogan**—a traditional Navaho house; **abandon**—to leave something behind forever; **deserted**—not lived in; abandoned; **secure**—safe from harm or danger; **captivity**—being held as prisoners.

Please review with your child the spelling words for the upcoming week: explosion, vision, examination, measure, position, discussion, edition, pleasure, version, education, tradition, selection, collision, restriction, illusion, nation, direction, destruction, starvation, and duration.

Home Connection • *Going West* Unit 5 • Lesson 3 67

***Home Connection* p. 67**

Teacher Tip **SELECTION VOCABULARY** Have students write sentences using the selection vocabulary words.

Differentiating Instruction

If...	Then...
Students would benefit from repeated readings of "The Journal of Wong Ming-Chung" or the Intervention Selections	Use ***Intervention Guide,*** page 254

Teacher Tip SEQUENCE As you fill in *Reading Transparency 70* with students, remind them that they need to only include main events.

Teacher Tip SEQUENTIAL ORDER Point out to students that unless an author has a specific reason for not doing so, narratives are usually less confusing and more accessible to readers when presented in sequential order.

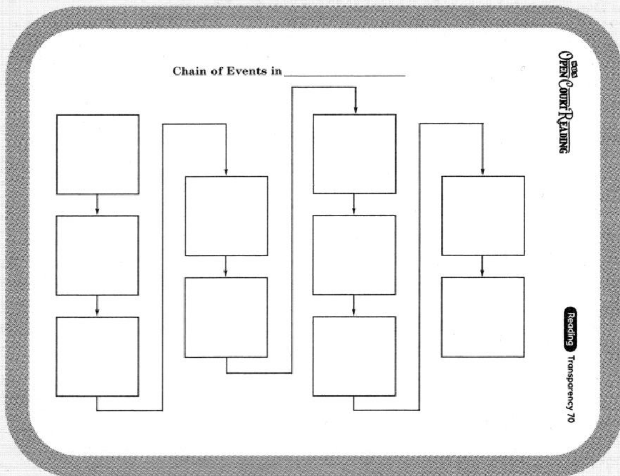

Reading Transparency 70

Supporting the Reading

Comprehension Skills: Sequence

Teach Explain to students that sequence is the order in which events occur. Tell students that they must identify the sequence of events in a text in order to understand the text. Explain that events are not always in the same sequence as the words they hear. For instance, in the sentence "Before dinner, I walked the dog." Students should recognize that first the dog was walked and then dinner was eaten. Ask students how they identified that order. *(The word before indicates order.)* Explain that students must be aware of time and order words to identify sequence. Such words include *first, second, last, earlier, later, now, then, following, next, after, during, finally, morning, day, evening, night,* and so on.

Guided Practice Use ***Reading Transparency 70*** to map the sequence of events in "The Journal of Wong Ming-Chung." Tell students that the dated entries will help them identify sequence, but they should be careful because some entries refer to previous days.

Once the transparency has been completed, ask students to look at the sequence of events in the story. Have students discuss how placing the information in the story in sequential order makes it more usable and more accessible to readers. *(Students might suggest that the author's choice to put the events in sequential order makes it easy for readers to understand and remember everything that happened.)* Challenge students to define the relationship each event on the transparency has to the ones before and after it. *(Students should notice the cause and effect relationships between events.)* Point out that this is another way sequence helps readers use information in a story.

Tell students that sometimes, authors might choose to present events to readers out of sequential order. Ask students to think of and name reasons authors might choose to do this. *(Students might suggest that authors may want to keep something hidden from the readers and surprise them with it later, or may want to get the story started before they provide readers with what happened before the story's beginning.)*

Ask students to tell what they know about *foreshadowing.* Explain that sometimes authors will hint at, or foreshadow, events that will happen later in order to build suspense or curiosity in readers.

Have students list examples they have read in which the author has presented events out of sequential order. *(Students may cite mystery stories they have read, or "The Night Journey," from Unit 3 as examples.)* Have students evaluate their examples and decide why the author may have presented the information as he or she did. Have them also evaluate whether or not the story's non-sequential format made it better, and why.

Independent Practice Read the **Focus** and **Identify** sections of the ***Comprehension and Language Arts Skills,*** page 150 with students. Guide students through the **Identify** portion, and help them come up with support from the story. Then have students complete the **Practice and Apply** portion of the ***Comprehension and Language Arts Skills,*** page 151 as homework.

Link to Writing Point out to students that describing sequence clearly is important in writing. If sequence is unclear, readers will become confused. Have students write a short story that spans a day. Tell students to include time words to indicate the sequence of events, time of day, and passage of time.

Name ______ Date ______

UNIT 5 Going West • Lesson 3 *The Journal of Wong Ming-Chung*

Sequence

Focus When writers tell a story or explain a process, they must express the **sequence** in which events occur.

Sequence is indicated by time words and order words.
- Words such as *earlier, later, now, then, morning, day, evening,* and *night* indicate **time.**
- Words such as *first, second, last, following, next, after, during,* and *finally* indicate **order.**

Identify

Look through "The Journal of Wong Ming-Chung." Choose one of the diary entries and summarize the sequence of events on the lines provided. Be sure to include time words and order words.

Answers will vary. Possible answers are shown.

Page: 432–434

Entry date: April 24

Events in sequence: First, Uncle announced his plans to prospect. Then Wong said he would stay with Uncle, but Uncle told Wong that he had to stay with Fox. After that, Uncle left without Wong. Late that night Wong decided to go find his uncle.

150 UNIT 5 • Lesson 3 Comprehension and Language Arts Skills

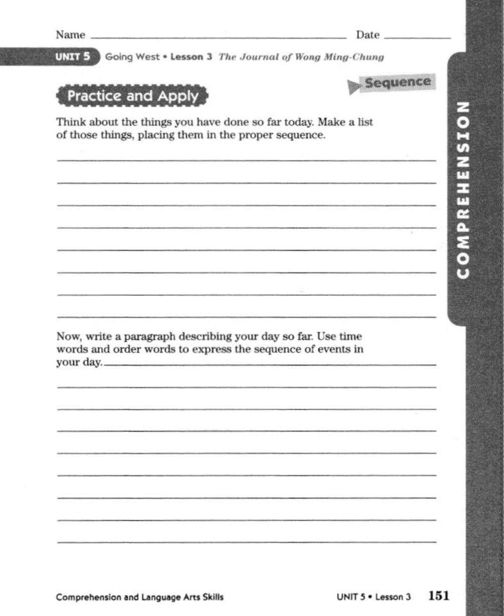

Name ______ Date ______

UNIT 5 Going West • Lesson 3 *The Journal of Wong Ming-Chung*

Practice and Apply

Sequence

COMPREHENSION

Think about the things you have done so far today. Make a list of those things, placing them in the proper sequence.

Now, write a paragraph describing your day so far. Use time words and order words to express the sequence of events in your day.

Comprehension and Language Arts Skills UNIT 5 • Lesson 3 151

Comprehension and Language Arts Skills pp. 150–151

Differentiating Instruction

If...	Then...
Students need extra help with Sequence	• Use ***Reteach,*** pages 150–151 • Use ***English Learner Support Guide,*** pages 394–407
Students would enjoy a challenge with Sequence	Use ***Challenge,*** page 132

Sequence

Introduced in Grade 1.

Scaffolded throughout Grades 2–5.

REINTRODUCED: Unit 1, Lesson 4

REINFORCED: Unit 4, Lesson 2

Unit 5, Lesson 3

Unit 6, Lesson 1

TESTED: Unit 5 Assessment

Professional Development

Teacher Resource Library CD-ROMs or ***Online Professional Development*** provides courses that help you better understand the Comprehension/Knowledge Building instruction in ***Open Court Reading.*** For more information about this program, visit SRAonline.com.

Teacher Tip CHARACTER ANALYSIS As students analyze characters, have them consider how they would react in the same situation in which the character finds him or herself. This will help students make inferences about characters' motivations.

Literary Elements

Character Analysis

Teach Have students discuss how the characters in a story are important to the story's plot and theme. *(If necessary, point out that it is usually through the characters' experiences that changes in the plot occur. Also, theme is communicated when characters make meaningful discoveries about themselves or things around them.)* Point out to students that many stories contain two contrasting characters, and it is through their interaction that the plot progresses and thematic messages are communicated.

Guided Practice Have students turn to the selection "The Journal of Wong Ming-Chung." Write the names *Uncle* and *Wong Ming-Chung* on the board. Then have students look for text that gives clues about the motives, appearances, and actions of these characters. As students cite information from the text, list it under the appropriate name on the board. Then have students discuss how this information shapes their perception of each character.

Next have students discuss how Wong Ming-Chung's motives, appearance, and actions might be compared and contrasted with Uncle's. For example, Uncle appears not to care about Wong Ming-Chung, while Wong Ming-Chung very clearly cares about Uncle. Uncle tries to help his nephew by pushing him away; Wong Ming-Chung tries to help Uncle by going to him even though he thinks he will be rejected. Have students discuss the importance of these contrasts to the plot and theme of the story. Students may mention that much of the plot centers on a misunderstanding between Wong Ming-Chung and Uncle that would not exist if Uncle was as open with his nephew as his nephew was with him. The resolution to this misunderstanding contributes to the story's message, or theme, about the importance of family.

Independent Practice Have students find contrasting characters in other stories they have read and tell how the characters' differences affected the plot and theme of each story.

Social Studies Connection: The Journal of Wong Ming-Chung

Explain to students that at the time of the gold rush, not only were people immigrating to California and the West from other countries, they were also coming from the east coast. Have students work in groups to identify the routes these settlers took; the purposes of their journeys; and the influences terrain, rivers, and climate had on the travelers. You might have each group focus on one group of settlers or on one specific migration route. When students have completed their investigation, have each group map the routes taken and illustrate the geographical features encountered on the trip. Students should also describe how these geographical features affected travel. Finally, students should give brief summaries of what life was like once the settlers reached their final destinations.

Teacher Tip MATERIALS To complete this activity students will need the following materials: posterboard, markers, and library sources.

Concept Connections

Linking the Selection

- No one thought there was any gold there, so raiders left the area alone.
- The soil can produce an endless amount of crops, but there was a limited amount of gold.

Exploring Concept Vocabulary

The concept word for this lesson is ***aspiration.*** Write the word on the board. Work with the students to develop a definition that clearly links to the unit theme. Have students copy the word and definition into the Vocabulary section of their Writer's Notebooks.

Aspiration: a strong desire to attain something good or grand. For example, the aspiration for wealth brought many people to California searching for gold in the mid-1800s.

- Uncle knew that he wouldn't make much money working on levees. He needed to make money to support relatives back in China, so he decided to continue prospecting.
- They talked about having a store and bringing some relatives from China to America.

The students' sentences should show an understanding of both vocabulary words and make a reasonable statement about miners' aspirations.

Expanding the Concept

Have students carry on dialogues in small groups. After the small-group discussions, bring students together to share their ideas with the whole class.

As students complete their discussion, have them record their ideas about the selection on page 113 of their ***Inquiry Journal.***

The Journal of Wong Ming-Chung

Concept Connections

Linking the Selection

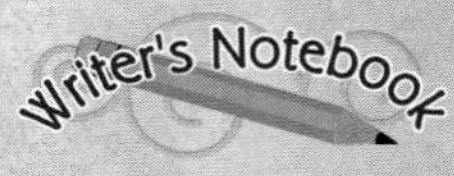

Think about the following questions, and then record your responses in the Response Journal section of your Writer's Notebook.

- Why was the area where Uncle decided to stay considered to be safe?
- Why did Hiram feel that soil was more valuable than gold?

Exploring Concept Vocabulary

The concept word for this lesson is ***aspiration.*** If you do not know what this word means, look it up in a dictionary. Answer these questions.

- How did a commitment to family help Uncle realize his ***aspiration*** of finding gold?
- What ***aspiration*** did Wong Ming-Chung and Uncle discuss as they built their supply of gold?

In the Vocabulary section of your Writer's Notebook, write the sentence beginning shown below. Then make up your own ending, and write it to complete the sentence. Include a selection vocabulary word in your sentence ending.

The ***aspiration*** shared by many gold miners ____.

Expanding the Concept

Compare the gold miners' view of the land with white traders' view of the buffalo in "Buffalo Hunt." Consider what was gained and what was lost in each situation. Try to use the word ***aspiration*** in your discussion of the selections. Add new ideas about the American West to the Concept/Question Board.

442

Teacher Tip INQUIRY AND INVESTIGATION Have groups report and discuss their ideas with the class. As these ideas are stated, have students add them to the Concept/Question Board. As students complete their discussions, have them sum up what they have learned and tell how they might use this information in further investigations.

Informal Assessment

This may be a good time to observe students working in small groups and to make your observations in the Teacher Observation Log found in the ***Program Assessment Teacher's Edition.***

Meet the Author

Laurence Yep was born in San Francisco, California. His Chinese-American family lived in an African-American section of the city, so he had to commute to a bilingual school in Chinatown. Yep says he never encountered white culture in America until high school, and always felt like an outsider. Growing up, he found few books that dealt with being a Chinese-American. Because of this, he uses his own writing to fight racial stereotypes. He likes to write about this feeling of being an outsider and believes this is the reason he is so popular with young adult readers.

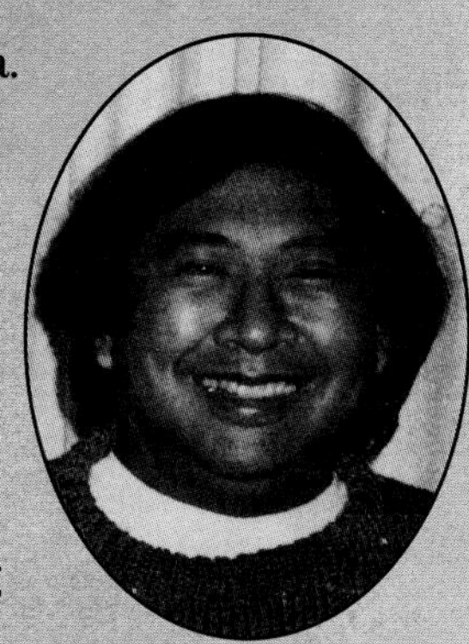

Meet the Illustrator

Karen Jerome teaches drawing and painting to children when she is not illustrating books. *"We draw from photographs, famous painters' artwork, stuffed animals, horse statues, mirrors and much more. That's how I learned to improve my skills as an artist, and that's how my students are improving theirs."* Karen also likes to fish, ski, play tennis, take photographs, paint landscapes, and write children's stories.

443

Meet the Author

After the students read the information about Laurence Yep, discuss the following questions with them.

- Laurence Yep likes writing about being an outsider. Why do you think this makes his writing popular with young readers? *(Possible answer: Everyone feels like an outsider from time to time, especially young people.)*
- Why do you think it is important to Laurence Yep to break down racial stereotypes? *(Possible answer: He knows firsthand that people can get wrong ideas about unfamiliar cultures because they don't have all the facts. Therefore, he wants to make sure that correct information is available to readers.)*

Meet the Illustrator

After the students read the information about Karen Jerome, discuss the following question with them.

- How might it improve an artist's skills to draw from another artist's work? *(Possible answer: One can try to tell what techniques the original artist used and use the same techniques in his or her own work.)*

Objectives

- Students acquire a deeper understanding of the American West.
- Students make conjectures about their questions.
- Students participate in investigation activities.
- Students conduct a library search.

Materials

- Student Anthology, pp. 430–443
- Inquiry Journal, p. 126
- Research Assistant

Teacher Tip USING TECHNOLOGY Encourage students to use the Internet to find out more about the Gold Rush. You may want to preview some Web sites so that you may recommend ones to the students that are age-appropriate.

INVESTIGATION

Investigating Concepts Beyond the Text

To facilitate students' investigation of the American West, you might have them participate in the following activities. Tell students that if they have activity ideas of their own that they would like to pursue, they are free to do so as an alternative to these activity suggestions. For example, students may want to pursue activities of their own choosing that relate more directly to the problems and questions they are investigating with their groups. Tell students that they may work on these activities alone, in pairs, or in small groups, with an option to write about them or to present them to the group upon completion.

The activity suggestions for this lesson are:

- Have students go to the library to find out more about the history of the California Gold Rush. Have them search letters on volumes, historical accounts, and fiction about this time period. Have students compare and contrast the ways this time period is portrayed in different books of different genres. Students should choose their reading based on a variety of criteria, including author's style, themes, knowledge of genres, text difficulty, and recommendations of others.
- Encourage students to find out more about the Chinese pioneers who immigrated to the United States at the time of the Gold Rush. Students might also be interested in investigating other groups of people who immigrated to California and other states in the Pacific Northwest during this time period.

Upon completion of their activities, have students share with the group anything new they learned about the American West through discussion and by adding information to the Concept/Question Board.

Concept/Question Board

After reading each selection, students should use the Concept/Question Board to

- post any questions they asked about a selection before reading that have not yet been answered.
- refer to as they formulate statements about concepts that apply to their investigations.
- post general statements formulated by each collaborative group.
- continue to post news articles, or other items that they find during the unit investigation.
- read and think about posted questions, articles, or concepts that interest them and provide answers to the questions.

Unit 5 Research Management

Lesson 1	Students generate questions and ideas for investigation.
Lesson 2	Students formulate questions and problems for investigation.
Lesson 3	Collaborative Investigation **Students make conjectures.** Supplementary Activities **Students participate in investigation activities and learn to conduct a library search.**
Lesson 4	Students establish investigation needs.
Lesson 5	Students establish investigation plans.
Lesson 6	Students continue investigation and get feedback from other groups.
Lesson 7	Students present their investigation findings to the class.

INVESTIGATION

www.sra4kids.com
Web Connection
Students can use the connections to Going West in the Reading link of the SRA Web page for more background information about Going West.

Research Assistant

The Research Assistant helps students in their investigations.

Teacher Tip ULTIMATE WRITING AND CREATIVITY CENTER Have students use the ***Ultimate Writing and Creativity Center CD-ROM*** as they work on their investigation activities.

Formal Assessment

Use the Research Rubrics on page 430J to assess students' ability to make conjectures.

Name ______ Date ______

UNIT 5 Going West

Making Conjectures

Our question or problem:
Answers will vary.

Conjecture (my first theory or explanation):
Answers will vary.

As you collect information, your conjecture will change. Return to this page to record your new theories or explanations about your question or problem.

126 UNIT 5 *Making Conjectures* • Inquiry Journal

Inquiry Journal p. 126

Differentiating Instruction

If...	Then...
Students are having difficulty with their Inquiry activities	Conference with investigation groups during Workshop, and help them make conjectures based on the questions and problems they've chosen to pursue

Professional Development

Teacher Resource Library CD-ROMs or ***Online Professional Development*** provides courses that help you better understand the Inquiry and Investigation instruction in ***Open Court Reading.*** For more information about this program, visit SRAonline.com.

INVESTIGATION

Making Conjectures

Tell students that the investigations of their stated problems and questions will be more productive if they first form conjectures as to how their problems might be solved or their questions answered. Explain to the students that a *conjecture* is a kind of educated guess, an explanation that we suggest for something before we have a great deal of evidence. Conjectures may be proved right, proved wrong, or modified in some way by evidence uncovered in the investigation process.

If students are unsure of how to make conjectures, it will be helpful to have group discussion featuring modeling of conjectures. For this, you might choose a problem that has already been suggested for investigation but has not been chosen by any group. (Using such a problem, the whole class can engage in conjecturing without taking anything away from an individual groups' project.) For example, you might present the problem, How did pioneers travel west? Then model conjectures such as, They traveled west on horses.

Have students get into their investigation groups to discuss conjectures they have for the solution to their investigation problem. Have group members write their conjectures on ***Inquiry Journal,*** page 126.

Tell students that as they begin to read and organize information for their investigations, they will revisit their conjectures and revise them based on new information, if necessary. Explain to the students that they will continuously return to the previous phases of investigation to assess how their problems and the conjectures have changed and what new information they need.

Conducting a Library Search

Teach Tell students that whenever they conduct an investigation they should use multiple sources of information. This will help them to ensure their information is correct and complete. Tell students that as they are searching they should use the following organizational features of print resources to assess what information is available to them and to get ideas for other resources that they might use. Review with students the following organizational features. Have on hand examples of these features to show to the students.

- **Table of Contents:** This is a list that usually appears within the first few pages of a print resource. It shows what topics or chapters are contained in the resource.
- **Index:** This is an alphabetical list at the end of a book. It tells on what page or pages a particular subject or name can be found.
- **Citation:** This is a piece of quoted material that has been excerpted from a larger work. Citations are usually followed by information about the name of the work, its author, and the page number(s) on which the quoted material can be found.
- **End Note:** This is a comment that explains a part of a book and it appears at the book's end.
- **Bibliography:** This is a list of books referred to in a text or used by the author to create a text, and it appears at the end of a book.
- **Footnote:** A note of explanation at the bottom of a page. These notes usually appear in small print. They may give extra information about a reference in the text, whether that information helps to define the reference or gives its bibliographic source.
- **Glossary:** A list of difficult words and their meanings. The words in a glossary are in alphabetical order. A glossary is usually found at the end of a book, and it only contains words that can be found within the book.

Discuss with students how each of these features might be helpful in their search for information and resources to use in their research.

Guided Practice Take students to the library and have them do a search of books related to their investigation topics containing the organizational features listed above. Challenge them to find and record a different title and author for each of the organizational features listed.

Independent Practice Have students incorporate one or all of the organizational features listed above into their investigation activities. All activities should be accompanied by at least a bibliography of resources.

Teacher Tip ORGANIZATIONAL FEATURES Have students use organizational features such as the ones mentioned in this lesson for ideas on other resources to use for their investigations. Tell them that even if an actual title is not given in the feature, they might find key words that could be cross-referenced in other sources.

Teacher Tip CHOOSING WHAT TO READ Have students use a variety of criteria to choose their own reading, including knowledge of author's style and text difficulty, knowledge of genres and themes, and the recommendations of others.

Encourage students to use *TechKnowledge* to help them learn how to use a computer to conduct a library search.

Teacher Tip ACCESSING INFORMATION Also check that students are able to use these reference and text features on their own to access information for their investigations.

Objectives

Word Analysis

Spelling

- **Spelling Patterns for Words with *-ent* or *-ant*.** Develop understanding of spelling patterns for words with *-ent* or *-ant* introduced in Word Knowledge in Part 1.

Vocabulary

- Using words from "The Journal of Wong Ming-Chung" reinforce the concept of words with multiple meanings.

Writing Process Strategies

- **Personal Writing: Friendly Letter.** Building on the Going West theme and "The Journal of Wong Ming-Chung," students will learn to write a friendly letter.

English Language Conventions

Mechanics

- **Punctuation and Capitalization.** Understand correct use of punctuation and capitalization in friendly letters.

Listening, Speaking, Viewing

- **Language: Literary Devices.** Use literary devices, such as similes, metaphors, analogies, and alliteration.

Penmanship

- **Joining with *U* and *q*.** Review handwriting skills by practicing joining letters with *U* and *q*.

Materials

- Spelling and Vocabulary Skills, pp. 114–117
- Language Arts Handbook
- Comprehension and Language Arts Skills, pp. 152–155
- Writer's Workbook, pp. 86–89
- Language Arts Transparency 11
- Student Anthology
- Unit 5 Assessment, pp. 34–35

Differentiating Instruction

Reteach, Challenge, and ***Intervention*** lessons are available to support the language arts instruction in this lesson.

Research in Action

Numerous factors contribute to successful writing assignments, but developing a sequence that allows students to incorporate skills they have practiced in previous work with new skills they are trying to master is absolutely crucial. (*James D. Williams*, Preparing to Teach Writing: Research, Theory, and Practice)

OVERVIEW

Language Arts Overview

Word Analysis

Spelling The spelling activities on the following pages support the Word Knowledge introduction of words with *-ent* or *-ant* by developing understanding of the spelling patterns for these suffixes.

Selection Spelling Words

These words from "The Journal of Wong Ming-Chung" contain the *-ent* or *-ant* spelling patterns.

immigrant important protectant insistent hesitant

Vocabulary The vocabulary activities introduce students to multiple meanings of words from the selection "The Journal of Wong Ming-Chung" and other more common words.

Vocabulary Skill Words

rockers* prospect* lumber registered deposits

**Also Selection Vocabulary.*

Writing Process Strategies

This Writing Process Strategies lesson involves instruction in writing a friendly letter. Friendly letters reveal the author's thoughts and observations. They can also reflect values, concerns, and hopes.

To help students identify the Internet as a source of information for writing, show students how to open a new browser window while another is open and how to evaluate Web search results and Web sites. ***TechKnowledge*** Level 5, Lessons 90–92 teach these Internet reference skills.

Professional Development

Teacher Resource Library CD-ROMs or ***Online Professional Development*** provides courses that help you better understand the Writing instruction in ***Open Court Reading.*** For more information about this program, visit SRAonline.com.

English Language Conventions

Mechanics **Punctuation and Capitalization.** This lesson develops understanding of punctuation and capitalization in friendly letters.

Listening, Speaking, Viewing **Language: Literary Devices.** In this Language lesson, students identify and use literary devices, such as similes, metaphors, analogies, and alliteration.

Penmanship **Joining with *U* and *q*.** This lesson continues the development of handwriting skills. Students join letters with *U* and *q* and then write paragraphs from the literature, focusing on joining letters.

DAY 1

Word Analysis

Spelling

Assessment: Pretest

Spelling Patterns for Words with *-ent* or *-ant*

Give students the Pretest on page 34 of ***Unit 5 Assessment.*** Have them proofread and correct any misspellings.

Pretest Sentences

1. **agent** An insurance **agent** might visit the scene of an accident.
2. **tolerant** A scientist must be **tolerant** of working long hours.
3. **resident** To run for president, one must be a U.S. **resident.**
4. **present** Her parents were **present** at her graduation.
5. **assistant** Frank Lloyd Wright was Louis Sullivan's **assistant.**
6. **different** London and Paris are in **different** time zones.
7. **permanent** Write a label with a **permanent** marker.
8. **prominent** Red Square is a **prominent** attraction in Moscow.
9. **apparent** It is **apparent** that autumn is coming.
10. **dependent** Islanders are **dependent** on ships.
11. **confident** Muhammad Ali was always **confident** that he would win.
12. **represent** A senator is elected to **represent** his or her voters.
13. **violent** The American Civil War was a very **violent** conflict.
14. **recent** The Internet and electric cars are **recent** developments.
15. **continent** Asia is a **continent.**
16. **immigrant** An **immigrant** is a person who comes to a new country.
17. **important** An **important** job of teachers is helping students learn.
18. **protectant** A coat of varnish is a **protectant** for wood.
19. **insistent** Elizabeth Cady Stanton was **insistent** that women vote.
20. **hesitant** She is **hesitant** to climb a ladder.

Writing Process Strategies

Getting Ideas

Friendly Letter

Teach

Have students read ***Language Arts Handbook*** pages 82–85 on friendly letters.

Inspiration

Teacher Model: *I will imagine that I am Wong Ming-Chung and I will write a friendly letter to my family in China. I want to describe to them some of the exciting things that have happened while I have been searching for gold.*

Brainstorming

Ask students to suggest ideas, thoughts, or details that they might use in their friendly letters. Encourage students to list some of the topics about which Wong Ming-Chung might write. Then help them see how some of their suggestions might relate to letters they might write to their own families or friends. For example, Wong Ming-Chung might tell his family about the new place he is experiencing or the people he is meeting. He might also ask his family about life at home.

Independent Practice

Selecting a Topic

Have each student select an audience and choose a focus for his or her letter.

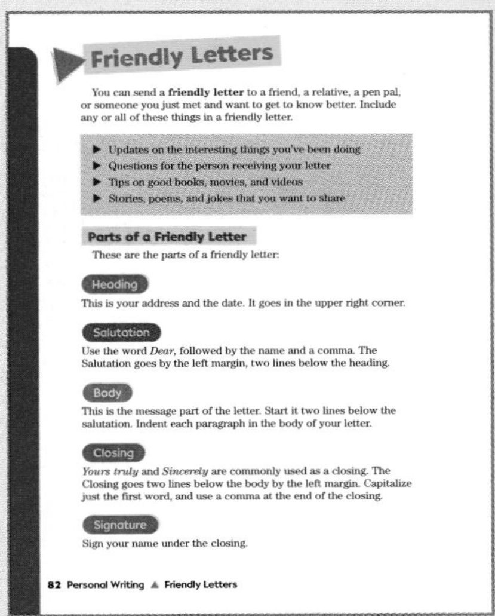

Friendly Letters

You can send a **friendly letter** to a friend, a relative, a pen pal, or someone you just met and want to get to know better. Include any or all of these things in a friendly letter.

- Updates on the interesting things you've been doing
- Questions for the person receiving your letter
- Tips on good books, movies, and videos
- Stories, poems, and jokes that you want to share

Parts of a Friendly Letter

These are the parts of a friendly letter:

Heading

This is your address and the date. It goes in the upper right corner.

Salutation

Use the word *Dear*, followed by the name and a comma. The Salutation goes by the left margin, two lines below the heading.

Body

This is the message part of the letter. Start it two lines below the salutation. Indent each paragraph in the body of your letter.

Closing

Yours truly and *Sincerely* are commonly used as a closing. The Closing goes two lines below the body by the left margin. Capitalize just the first word, and use a comma at the end of the closing.

Signature

Sign your name under the closing.

82 Personal Writing ▲ Friendly Letters

Language Arts Handbook p. 82

English Language Conventions

Mechanics

Punctuation and Capitalization

Teach

- Use ***Language Arts Handbook,*** pages 82–83, for examples of punctuation and capitalization in friendly letters.
- Remind students that a friendly letter has a heading, a salutation, a body, a closing, and a signature.
- The greeting begins with a capitalized word and ends with a comma: *Dear Penny,*
- The closing also begins with a capitalized word and ends with a comma: *Yours truly,*
- Remind students that street names, names of months, and place names should be capitalized: *Main Street, September, Tampa Bay.*
- If available, show students several examples of friendly letters, pointing out the parts covered in this lesson.

Independent Practice

Use ***Comprehension and Language Arts Skills,*** pages 152–153, to practice punctuation and capitalization in friendly letters.

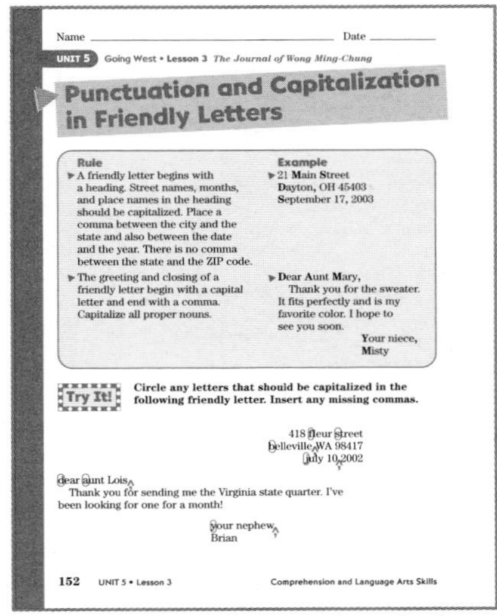

Name ____________ Date ______

UNIT 5 Going West • **Lesson 3** *The Journal of Wong Ming-Chung*

Punctuation and Capitalization in Friendly Letters

Rule	Example
A friendly letter begins with a heading. Street names, months, and place names in the heading should be capitalized. Place a comma between the city and the state and also between the date and the year. There is no comma between the state and the ZIP code.	21 **M**ain **S**treet **D**ayton, OH 45403 **S**eptember 17, 2003
The greeting and closing of a friendly letter begin with a capital letter and end with a comma. Capitalize all proper nouns.	**D**ear **A**unt **M**ary, Thank you for the sweater. It fits perfectly and is my favorite color. I hope to see you soon. Your niece, Misty

Try It! **Circle any letters that should be capitalized in the following friendly letter. Insert any missing commas.**

418 fleur street
belleville WA 98417
july 10 2002

dear aunt Lois

Thank you for sending me the Virginia state quarter. I've been looking for one for a month!

your nephew
Brian

152 UNIT 5 • Lesson 3 Comprehension and Language Arts Skills

Comprehension and Language Arts Skills p. 152

DAY 2

Word Analysis

Spelling

Word Sorting

Open Word Sort Have students sort the spelling words according to their suffixes. Have students explain their answers.

Vocabulary

Words with Multiple Meanings

Teach

- Remind students that many words in our language have multiple meanings. Students must use context clues to determine which meaning is being used in a particular text.
- Write several of the following words on the board and, as a class, discuss their multiple meanings: *mouth, movement, perform, grease,* and *feature.*

Guided Practice

Assign page 114 of ***Spelling and Vocabulary Skills*** to give students practice identifying multiple meanings. Students can complete page 115 of ***Spelling and Vocabulary Skills*** for homework.

Name _______ Date _______

UNIT 5 Going West • Lesson 3 *The Journal of Wong Ming-Chung: A Chinese Miner*

Words with Multiple Meanings

As you read, you will come across many words that have more than one meaning. You will also notice that in the dictionary there are a number of entries with more than one definition. Words with multiple meanings can be confusing, but you can discover which meaning is being used by looking at context clues.

Try It! The following words from "The Journal of Wong Ming-Chung: A Chinese Miner" have multiple meanings. One definition is provided for you. Use context clues or the dictionary to write a different definition for each word.

1. rockers: Rocking chairs. Another definition of *rockers* is Answers will vary.
2. prospect: Something looked forward to or expected. Another definition of *prospect* is Answers will vary.
3. lumber: To move about in a clumsy, noisy way. Another definition of *lumber* is Answers will vary.
4. registered: Showed or expressed. Another definition of *registered* is Answers will vary.
5. deposits: Large amounts of a mineral in rock or in the ground. Another definition of *deposits* is Answers will vary.

114 UNIT 5 • Lesson 3 *Multiple Meanings* • Spelling and Vocabulary Skills

***Spelling and Vocabulary Skills* p. 114**

Writing Process Strategies

Prewriting

Friendly Letter

Teach

- Review ideas for writing a friendly letter that students wrote on Day 1.
- Remind students to consider their audience. The audience helps them decide on the tone, mood, theme, and focus of what they will write.
- **Teacher Model** deciding on a purpose and audience for a friendly letter: I will imagine I am Wong Ming-Chung. *I want to send my family money and describe to them some of the exciting things that happened while I was searching for gold.*

Guided Practice

Have students complete the prewriting pages for writing a friendly letter on ***Writer's Workbook,*** page 86.

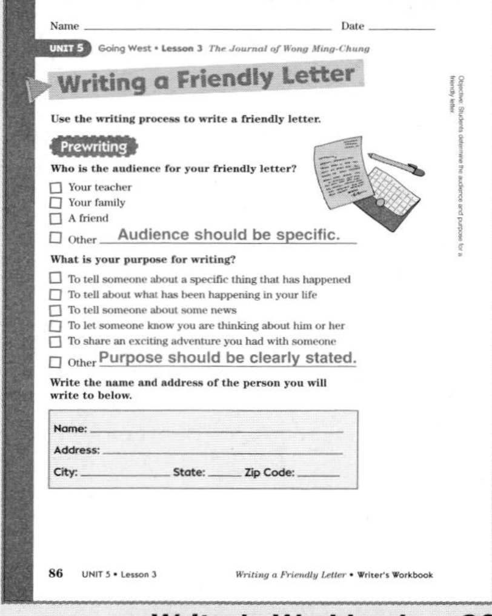

Name _______ Date _______

UNIT 5 Going West • Lesson 3 *The Journal of Wong Ming-Chung*

Writing a Friendly Letter

Use the writing process to write a friendly letter.

Prewriting

Who is the audience for your friendly letter?

- ☐ Your teacher
- ☐ Your family
- ☐ A friend
- ☐ Other Audience should be specific.

What is your purpose for writing?

- ☐ To tell someone about a specific thing that has happened
- ☐ To tell about what has been happening in your life
- ☐ To tell someone about some news
- ☐ To let someone know you are thinking about him or her
- ☐ To share an exciting adventure you had with someone
- ☐ Other Purpose should be clearly stated.

Write the name and address of the person you will write to below.

Name: _______
Address: _______
City: _______ State: _______ Zip Code: _______

86 UNIT 5 • Lesson 3 *Writing a Friendly Letter* • Writer's Workbook

***Writer's Workbook* p. 86**

English Language Conventions

Mechanics

Punctuation and Capitalization

Teach

- **Review** punctuation and capitalization in friendly letters.
- Remind students that a comma should separate the day from the year in a date: July 21, 2003.
- Use a comma between the name of a city and the abbreviation of a state: Tallahassee, FL.
- Write the following friendly letter on the board and have students identify the punctuation and capital letters that need to be added.

  120 elm street
  woodward NY 07870
  march 4 2002

  dear nicki

  I'm so excited to hear you're going to camp. We're going to have a great time.

  your cousin
  Sam

Guided Practice in Reading

Have students search for punctuation and capitalization in friendly letters of previously read selections or letters you have collected and brought to class. Have students identify the headings, salutations, and closings.

DAY 3

Word Analysis

Spelling

Spelling Patterns for Words with *-ent* or *-ant*

Teach

Introduce the spelling patterns for words with *-ent* and *-ant*, and the meanings of these word parts when used as suffixes. When added to verbs to make nouns, they mean "one who performs," as in *assistant.* When added to verbs to make adjectives, they mean "inclined to," "performing," or "being." Have students skim an earlier reading selection for words with the suffixes *-ent* or *-ant.* (Not all words with *-ent* and *-ant* use these spellings as suffixes.)

Guided Practice

Have students complete page 116 from ***Spelling and Vocabulary Skills.***

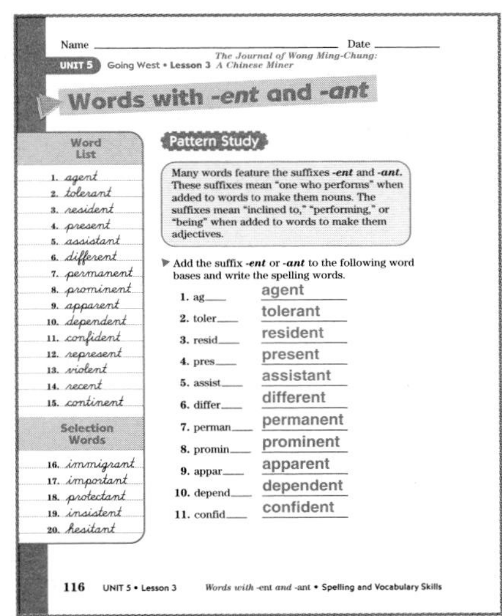
Name ______ Date ______

UNIT 5 Going West • Lesson 3 *The Journal of Wong Ming-Chung: A Chinese Miner*

Words with -ent and -ant

Word List
1. agent
2. tolerant
3. resident
4. present
5. assistant
6. different
7. permanent
8. prominent
9. apparent
10. dependent
11. confident
12. represent
13. violent
14. recent
15. continent

Selection Words
16. immigrant
17. important
18. protectant
19. insistent
20. hesitant

Pattern Study

Many words feature the suffixes ***-ent*** and ***-ant.*** These suffixes mean "one who performs" when added to words to make them nouns. The suffixes mean "inclined to," "performing," or "being" when added to words to make them adjectives.

Add the suffix ***-ent*** or ***-ant*** to the following word bases and write the spelling words.

1. ag___ agent
2. toler___ tolerant
3. resid___ resident
4. pres___ present
5. assist___ assistant
6. differ___ different
7. perman___ permanent
8. promin___ prominent
9. appar___ apparent
10. depend___ dependent
11. confid___ confident

116 UNIT 5 • Lesson 3 *Words with -ent and -ant* • Spelling and Vocabulary Skills

***Spelling and Vocabulary Skills* p. 116**

Vocabulary (continued)

Words with Multiple Meanings

Have students choose two of the words discussed on Day 2 and use each in two sentences, each sentence conveying a different meaning for the word.

For additional information regarding words with multiple meanings, see page 322 in the ***Language Arts Handbook.***

Writing Process Strategies

Drafting

Writing a Friendly Letter

Teach

Writer's Craft

Structure of a Personal Letter

Remind students of the parts of a friendly letter.

- The **heading** includes the writer's address and the date.
- The **salutation** is the part in which the writer addresses the reader with words such as *Dear* or *Hi* followed by the first name of the receiver such as in *Dear Martha.*
- The **body** follows the salutation. Tell students that the body includes everything the writer wants to say. It starts two lines below the salutation, and it is broken into paragraphs and indented as needed.
- The **closing** is placed two lines under the body. The closing might say *Yours truly,* or *Sincerely.*
- The **signature** of the writer follows the closing.

Have students complete ***Comprehension and Language Arts Skills*** pages 154–155.

Independent Practice

Have students complete ***Writer's Workbook,*** page 87.

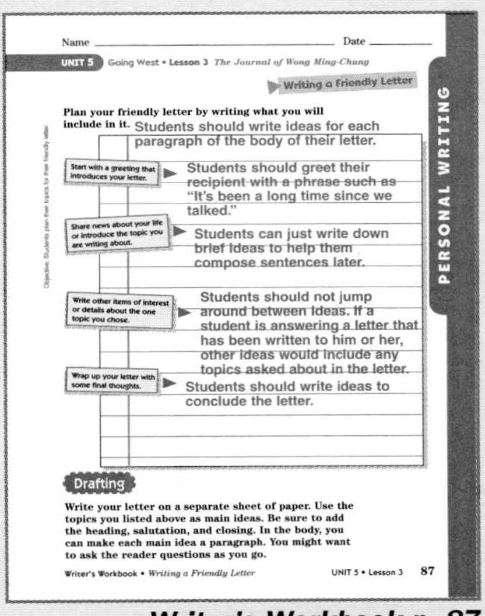
Name ______ Date ______

UNIT 5 Going West • Lesson 3 *The Journal of Wong Ming-Chung*

Writing a Friendly Letter

PERSONAL WRITING

Plan your friendly letter by writing what you will include in it. Students should write ideas for each paragraph of the body of their letter.

Start with a greeting that introduces your letter. ▶ Students should greet their recipient with a phrase such as "It's been a long time since we talked."

Share news about your life or introduce the topic you are writing about. ▶ Students can just write down brief ideas to help them compose sentences later.

Write other items of interest or details about the one topic you chose. ▶ Students should not jump around between ideas. If a student is answering a letter that has been written to him or her, other ideas would include any topics asked about in the letter.

Wrap up your letter with some final thoughts. ▶ Students should write ideas to conclude the letter.

Objective: Students plan their topics for their friendly letter.

Drafting

Write your letter on a separate sheet of paper. Use the topics you listed above as main ideas. Be sure to add the heading, salutation, and closing. In the body, you can make each main idea a paragraph. You might want to ask the reader questions as you go.

Writer's Workbook • *Writing a Friendly Letter* UNIT 5 • Lesson 3 87

***Writer's Workbook* p. 87**

English Language Conventions

Mechanics

Punctuation and Capitalization

Teach

- Place a comma after the greeting and the closing.
- Place a comma between the date and the year in the heading.
- Place a comma between the city and the state in the heading.

Guided Practice in Writing

Have students select a short paragraph from one of the diary entries in "The Journal of Wong Ming-Chung" and use it as the body of a letter. Then have them invent a heading, a salutation, a closing, and a signature. Remind students that checking for correct use of punctuation and capitalization in friendly letters is an important part of proofreading their personal writing.

Informal Assessment

Check to make certain that students understand and are incorporating the rules of punctuation and capitalization in their letters.

DAY 4

Word Analysis

Spelling

Spelling Patterns for Words with *-ent* or *-ant*

Teach

Remind students of the meanings for the suffixes *-ent* and *-ant.* Model the proofreading strategy by writing the following sentence on the board: *Africa is a large continant.* Have students identify the misspelled word, *continant*, and spell it correctly.

Guided Practice

Have students complete the Spelling Strategies exercises on page 117 of ***Spelling and Vocabulary Skills.***

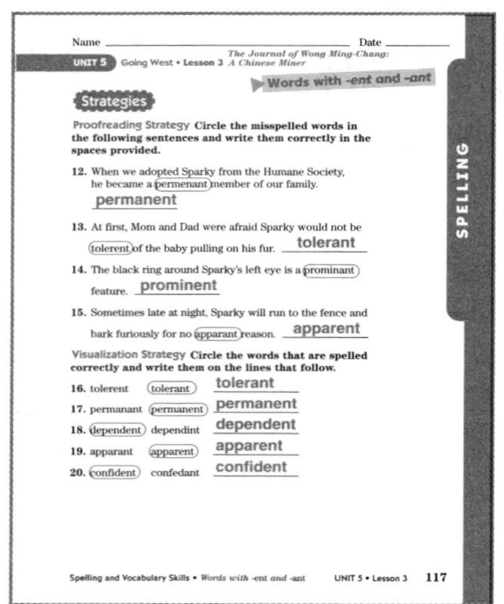

Name ______ Date ______

UNIT 5 Going West • Lesson 3 *The Journal of Wong Ming-Chung: A Chinese Miner*

Words with -ent and -ant

Strategies

Proofreading Strategy **Circle the misspelled words in the following sentences and write them correctly in the spaces provided.**

12. When we adopted Sparky from the Humane Society, he became a (permenant) member of our family. permanent
13. At first, Mom and Dad were afraid Sparky would not be (tolerent) of the baby pulling on his fur. tolerant
14. The black ring around Sparky's left eye is a (prominant) feature. prominent
15. Sometimes late at night, Sparky will run to the fence and bark furiously for no (apparant) reason. apparent

Visualization Strategy **Circle the words that are spelled correctly and write them on the lines that follow.**

16. tolerent (tolerant) tolerant
17. permanant (permanent) permanent
18. (dependent) dependint dependent
19. apparant (apparent) apparent
20. (confident) confedant confident

SPELLING

Spelling and Vocabulary Skills • *Words with* -ent *and* -ant UNIT 5 • Lesson 3 117

Spelling and Vocabulary Skills p. 117

Vocabulary (continued)

Words with Multiple Meanings

Collect students' sentences from Day 3. Read each sentence aloud to the class and ask students to identify each multiple-meaning word and its use in the sentence.

Writing Process Strategies

Revising

Friendly Letter

Teach

- **Teacher Model** revising by using ***Language Arts Transparency 11,*** Revising for Additions. Show students that adding information can make their letters clearer and more interesting. For example, instead of saying, *We won the baseball game*, a student might say, *I hit a triple that scored the winning run in the baseball game.*
- **Troubleshooting**
  - Students often think that they don't have to put their own address and the date at the top of the letter. When the letter is answered, however, this information needs to be readily available.
  - Students often fail to write legibly. It is annoying to have to struggle to read careless writing.
  - Sometimes students write that they are enclosing something and they forget it. They may want to get the enclosure and put it in the envelope as soon as they mention it.

Independent Practice

Have students use the checklist in the ***Writer's Workbook*** on page 88 to revise their letters.

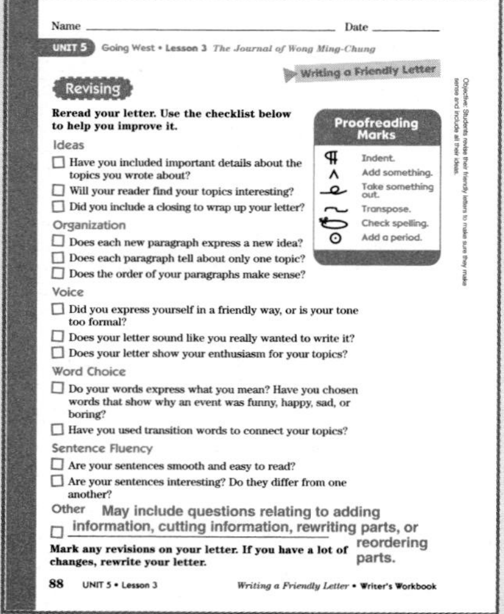

Name ______ Date ______

UNIT 5 Going West • Lesson 3 *The Journal of Wong Ming-Chung*

Writing a Friendly Letter

Revising

Reread your letter. Use the checklist below to help you improve it.

Ideas
- ☐ Have you included important details about the topics you wrote about?
- ☐ Will your reader find your topics interesting?
- ☐ Did you include a closing to wrap up your letter?

Organization
- ☐ Does each new paragraph express a new idea?
- ☐ Does each paragraph tell about only one topic?
- ☐ Does the order of your paragraphs make sense?

Voice
- ☐ Did you express yourself in a friendly way, or is your tone too formal?
- ☐ Does your letter sound like you really wanted to write it?
- ☐ Does your letter show your enthusiasm for your topics?

Word Choice
- ☐ Do your words express what you mean? Have you chosen words that show why an event was funny, happy, sad, or boring?
- ☐ Have you used transition words to connect your topics?

Sentence Fluency
- ☐ Are your sentences smooth and easy to read?
- ☐ Are your sentences interesting? Do they differ from one another?

Other
- ☐ May include questions relating to adding information, cutting information, rewriting parts, or reordering parts.

Mark any revisions on your letter. If you have a lot of changes, rewrite your letter.

Proofreading Marks
- Indent.
- Add something.
- Take something out.
- Transpose.
- Check spelling.
- Add a period.

Objective: Students revise their friendly letters to make sure they make sense and include all their ideas.

88 UNIT 5 • Lesson 3 *Writing a Friendly Letter* • Writer's Workbook

Writer's Workbook p. 88

English Language Conventions

Listening, Speaking, Viewing

Language: Literary Devices

Teach

- Explain and provide examples of the following literary devices: **metaphor** *(directly compares two unlike things);* **simile** *(directly compares two unlike things using the words* like *or* as*);* **alliteration** *(repetition of initial sounds);* **analogy** *(comparing two things to reinforce meanings or ideas);* **symbol** *(one thing that stands for or represents something else.)*
- Discuss with students how these literary devices help to clarify meaning and add more interest and rhythm to language.

Guided Practice

- Have students write the literary devices listed above as headings on paper. Then challenge them to find as many of these techniques in "The Journal of Wong Ming-Chung" as they can. Allow students to share their findings with the class.
- As a follow-up to the above activity, have students create their own examples of each of the literary devices. Have volunteers share examples of each type.

Informal Assessment

Observe students' ability to identify and use literary devices such as similes, metaphors, analogies, and alliteration.

DAY 5

Word Analysis

Spelling

Assessment: Final Test

Spelling Patterns for Words with *-ent* or *-ant*

Teach

Repeat the Pretest for this lesson or use the Final Test on page 35 of ***Unit 5 Assessment.***

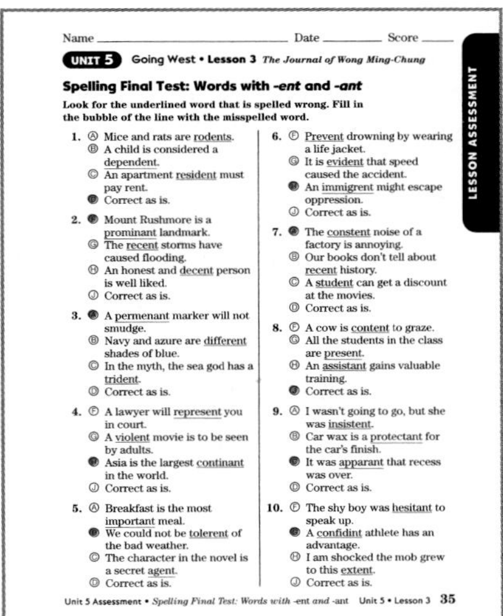

Name ______ Date ______ Score ______

UNIT 5 Going West • Lesson 3 *The Journal of Wong Ming-Chung*

Spelling Final Test: Words with *-ent* and *-ant*

Look for the underlined word that is spelled wrong. Fill in the bubble of the line with the misspelled word.

1. (A) Mice and rats are rodents.
   (B) A child is considered a dependent.
   (C) An apartment resident must pay rent.
   (D) Correct as is.
2. (F) Mount Rushmore is a prominant landmark.
   (G) The recent storms have caused flooding.
   (H) An honest and decent person is well liked.
   (J) Correct as is.
3. (A) A permenant marker will not smudge.
   (B) Navy and azure are different shades of blue.
   (C) In the myth, the sea god has a trident.
   (D) Correct as is.
4. (F) A lawyer will represent you in court.
   (G) A violent movie is to be seen by adults.
   (H) Asia is the largest continant in the world.
   (J) Correct as is.
5. (A) Breakfast is the most important meal.
   (B) We could not be tolerent of the bad weather.
   (C) The character in the novel is a secret agent.
   (D) Correct as is.
6. (F) Prevent drowning by wearing a life jacket.
   (G) It is evident that speed caused the accident.
   (H) An immigrent might escape oppression.
   (J) Correct as is.
7. (A) The constent noise of a factory is annoying.
   (B) Our books don't tell about recent history.
   (C) A student can get a discount at the movies.
   (D) Correct as is.
8. (F) A cow is content to graze.
   (G) All the students in the class are present.
   (H) An assistant gains valuable training.
   (J) Correct as is.
9. (A) I wasn't going to go, but she was insistent.
   (B) Car wax is a protectant for the car's finish.
   (C) It was apparant that recess was over.
   (D) Correct as is.
10. (F) The shy boy was hesitant to speak up.
    (G) A confidint athlete has an advantage.
    (H) I am shocked the mob grew to this extent.
    (J) Correct as is.

LESSON ASSESSMENT

Unit 5 Assessment • *Spelling Final Test: Words with -ent and -ant* Unit 5 • Lesson 3 35

Unit 5 Assessment p. 35

Guided Practice

Have students categorize any mistakes they made on the Final Test.

Are they careless errors?
Are they lesson pattern problems?

Vocabulary

Words with Multiple Meanings

Informal Assessment

- Periodically remind students that words can have multiple meanings. When new words are encountered in class readings, occasionally ask students for alternate meanings.
- Remind students that they can add more meanings to the words in their Writer's Notebooks.

Writing Process Strategies

Editing/Proofreading and Publishing

Friendly Letter

Teach

Teacher Model using editing marks by addressing each of the editing checklist items on ***Writer's Workbook*** page 89.

Guided Practice

Have students use the checklist on page 89 of their ***Writer's Workbooks*** to proofread and edit their letters.

Formal Assessment

Share this rubric with students before they begin the assignment to give them a foundation from which to work.

Total Point Value: 10

1. The address and date are at the top of the letter. (2 points)
2. The penmanship is legible. (2 points)
3. The details of the letter support the topic. (1 point)
4. The enclosure was remembered. (1 point)
5. The format or structure follows the guidelines. (2 points)
6. The mechanics are correct. (1 point)
7. The reader can easily understand the language. (1 point)

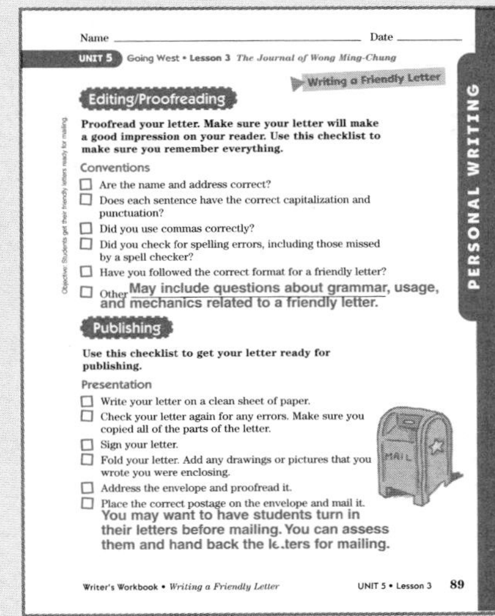

Name ______ Date ______

UNIT 5 Going West • Lesson 3 *The Journal of Wong Ming-Chung*

Writing a Friendly Letter

Editing/Proofreading

Proofread your letter. Make sure your letter will make a good impression on your reader. Use this checklist to make sure you remember everything.

Conventions

- ☐ Are the name and address correct?
- ☐ Does each sentence have the correct capitalization and punctuation?
- ☐ Did you use commas correctly?
- ☐ Did you check for spelling errors, including those missed by a spell checker?
- ☐ Have you followed the correct format for a friendly letter?
- ☐ Other May include questions about grammar, usage, and mechanics related to a friendly letter.

Publishing

Use this checklist to get your letter ready for publishing.

Presentation

- ☐ Write your letter on a clean sheet of paper.
- ☐ Check your letter again for any errors. Make sure you copied all of the parts of the letter.
- ☐ Sign your letter.
- ☐ Fold your letter. Add any drawings or pictures that you wrote you were enclosing.
- ☐ Address the envelope and proofread it.
- ☐ Place the correct postage on the envelope and mail it.

You may want to have students turn in their letters before mailing. You can assess them and hand back the le.ters for mailing.

Objective: Students get their friendly letters ready for mailing.

PERSONAL WRITING

Writer's Workbook • *Writing a Friendly Letter* UNIT 5 • Lesson 3 89

Writer's Workbook p. 89

English Language Conventions

Penmanship

Joining with *U* and *q*

Teach

- **Teacher Model:** Review formation of uppercase *U* and lowercase *q* on the board.

U Starting point, loop
Curve forward, slant down
Undercurve
Slant down, undercurve: capital *U*

q Starting point, downcurve
Undercurve to starting point
Slant down, and loop back
Undercurve: small *q*

- Write the following sentence to model proper joining of letters: *Ultimately, the decision should be quick.*

Guided Practice

- In the Writer's Notebook, have students join *U* with the letters *n*, *l*, *p*, and *r*. Then have students write a row of *U*-*q* joinings.
- From "The Journal of Wong Ming-Chung," have students write two paragraphs to practice joining letters.

Informal Assessment

Check students' handwriting for equal height of tall and small letters.

Reading and Language Arts Skills Traces

Language Arts

WORD ANALYSIS

Skills Trace

Spelling: Words with -ent and -ant

Introduced in Grade 5.
Scaffolded throughout Grade 5.

INTRODUCED: Unit 5, Lesson 3, p. 443F
PRACTICED: Unit 5, Lesson 3, pp. 443G–443I
Spelling and Vocabulary Skills, pp. 116–117
TESTED: Unit 5, Lesson 3, p. 443J
Unit 5 Assessment

Skills Trace

Vocabulary: Words with Multiple Meanings

Introduced in Grade 2.
Scaffolded throughout Grades 3–5.

REINTRODUCED: Unit 5, Lesson 3, p. 443G
PRACTICED: Unit 5, Lesson 3, pp. 443H–443I
Spelling and Vocabulary Skills, pp. 114–115
TESTED: Informal Assessment, p. 443J
Unit 5 Assessment

Reading

COMPREHENSION

Sequence

Introduced in Grade 1.
Scaffolded throughout Grades 2–5.

REINTRODUCED: Unit 1, Lesson 4
REINFORCED: Unit 4, Lesson 2
Unit 5, Lesson 3
Unit 6, Lesson 1
TESTED: Unit 5 Assessment

WRITING PROCESS STRATEGIES

Skills Trace

Personal Writing: Friendly Letter

Introduced in Grade 1.
Scaffolded throughout Grades 1–5.

REINTRODUCED: Unit 5, Lesson 3, p. 443F
PRACTICED: Unit 5, Lessons 3 and 5, pp. 443F–443J and 473F–473J
Writer's Workbook, pp. 86–89 and 94–97
TESTED: Formal Assessment
Unit 5, Lesson 3, p. 443J
Unit 5, Lesson 5, p. 473J
Unit 5 Assessment

Skills Trace

Writer's Craft: Structure of a Personal Letter

Introduced in Grade 1.
Scaffolded throughout Grades 1–5.

REINTRODUCED: Unit 5, Lesson 3, p. 443H
PRACTICED: Unit 5, Lesson 3, p. 443H
Comprehension and Language Arts Skills, pp. 154–155
TESTED: Unit 5 Assessment

ENGLISH LANGUAGE CONVENTIONS

Skills Trace

Grammar and Usage: Punctuation and Capitalization

Introduced in Grade 1.
Scaffolded throughout Grades 1–5.

REINTRODUCED: Unit 5, Lesson 3, p. 443F
PRACTICED: Unit 5, Lesson 3, pp. 443F–443H
Comprehension and Language Arts Skills, pp. 152–153
TESTED: Unit 5 Assessment

Skills Trace

Listening, Speaking, Viewing Language: Literary Devices

Introduced in Grade 3.
Scaffolded throughout Grades 4–5.

REINTRODUCED: Unit 5, Lesson 3, p. 443I
PRACTICED: Unit 5, Lesson 3, p. 443I
TESTED: Informal Assessment, p. 443I

Skills Trace

Penmanship: Joining with U and q

Introduced in Grade 3 (*U*) and Grade 2 (*q*).
Scaffolded throughout Grades 4–5 and Grades 3–5.

REINTRODUCED: Unit 5, Lesson 3, p. 443J
PRACTICED: Unit 5, Lesson 3, p. 443J
TESTED: Informal Assessment, p. 443J

Professional Development: Comprehension

Literature

Literature is defined as "writing that is regarded as having permanent worth through the very nature of its excellence." Whether the piece of literature is a finely turned short story, a riveting mystery, a moving essay, or a masterful drama, literature is defined by its excellence.

Literature is often organized by *genre*, a term used to designate the type or categories of forms of literature. Traditional genres include kinds of literature such as tragedy, comedy, or poetry. Today genre would include novel, short story, essay, drama, mystery, realistic fiction, fantasy, fable, or even television play and informational article.

Literature in *Open Court Reading*

The literature selections in ***Open Court Reading*** as well as the approach to teaching the selections represent a long-standing commitment to teachers who are, in turn, committed to teaching children to be competent, independent learners through reading, writing, speaking, and listening. What better way for children to learn to read and grow as readers than through reading and listening to literature that has the stamp of approval of generations of readers?

One of the founding principles of ***Open Court Reading*** is that children need to read fine literature. Through fine literature of every genre they would and could learn from the best thinkers of every age. They would learn the beauty of the language and the beauty of an idea. They would and could learn the importance of clarity of thought and word.

Through each level of ***Open Court Reading,*** students have a sampling of fine traditional literature that has withstood the test of time along with contemporary pieces that will someday join the ranks of the classics. Since the literature pieces form the core of the instructions, abundant care is taken to present the students with fine, thought-provoking models that they can follow in their own writing and that they can use as springboards for their thinking, researching, and knowledge building. Students learn from classic and contemporary children's fiction authors such as Arnold Lobel, Don Freeman, Eve Bunting, Patricia MacLachlan, John Steptoe, Myra Cohn Livingston, Hans Christian Andersen, and Patricia Polacco as well as a growing number of fine writers of nonfiction for children—Milton Meltzer, Russell Freedman, and Barbara Bash.

Each selection in ***Open Court Reading*** from Levels K–6 was chosen specifically because it added a new dimension to unit concept and because it was the best possible example of how different forms of literature can all express a particular theme. These two criteria—deepening of the concept and quality of the literature—formed the basis for all selections found in the program.

Through fine writing, fine minds can be developed.

Professional Development

Teacher Resource Library CD-ROMs or ***Online Professional Development*** provides courses that help you better understand the Comprehension/Knowledge Building instruction in ***Open Court Reading.*** For more information about this program, visit SRAonline.com.

Additional information about comprehension, as well as resource references, can be found in the ***Professional Development Guide: Comprehension.***

Viewing the Theme Through Fine Art

Have students use the artworks on these pages to explore the unit theme Going West in images rather than words. Have them talk about their impressions of the artworks and how each one might relate to the unit theme.

Below is some background information about each of the artworks. Share with students whatever you feel is appropriate. You might also encourage students to find out more about artists and artistic styles that interest them.

Buckskin Ghost Dance Arapaho Dress

The Arapaho were forced by the white settlers to leave their agricultural villages in northern Minnesota during the eighteenth century. They fought their way westward across Indian territory towards the plains. In the 1830s they split into two groups and moved to Wyoming and Colorado.

Buckskin Ghost Dance Arapaho Dress shows the special clothing that was worn only for the ceremonial Ghost Dance. The Dance lasted several days. The dancers joined hands forming a circle, chanting, praying, and dancing themselves into a trance, sometimes falling from fatigue. They believed this dance had the power to create a world free of white men.

Among the Sierra Nevada in California

Albert Bierstadt (1830–1910) made his first westward journey as part of a railroad surveying team. The many sketches of his journey were the basis for his famous grand landscapes.

Fine Art

Going West

Buckskin Ghost Dance Arapaho Dress. Buckskin. Courtesy of the National Museum of the American Indian. Smithsonian Institution.

Among the Sierra Nevada in California. 1868. **Albert Bierstadt.** Oil on canvas. 183 × 305 cm. National Museum of American Art, Smithsonian Institution, Washington, DC.

444

Advice on the Prairie. **William T. Ranney.** Oil on canvas. 14 × 20 in. From the Collection of Gilcrease Museum, Tulsa.

Vaqueros in a Horse Corral. 1877. **James Walker.** Oil on canvas. 24 × 40 in. From the Collection of Gilcrease Museum, Tulsa.

445

Among the Sierra Nevada in California portrays the spectacular vista Bierstadt encountered on his trips to the West. By contrasting sharp small-scaled details such as the animals near the water against a huge canvas, he was better able to heighten the illusion of grandness in his paintings.

Advice on the Prairie

WILLIAM T. RANNEY (1813–1857) is best known for his intimate portrayals of the West. In 1836 he enlisted in the Texas Army to avenge the Alamo, where he created several sketches which were later used in his western paintings.

Advice on the Prairie was painted after Ranney had traveled out West. The man sitting and giving advice to the pioneers is believed to be Jim Bridger, known to many as the "Daniel Boone of the Rocky Mountains." This piece is typical of Ranney's work; a feeling of optimism and charm portrayed within a frontier setting.

Vaqueros in a Horse Corral

JAMES WALKER (1819–1889) was born in England and settled near Albany, New York, in 1824. When Mexico City was sieged during the Mexican War, Walker was the only active American painter depicting portrayals of the Spanish horsemen and military scenes.

Vaqueros in a Horse Corral portrays a typical horse ranch in the Southwest. The Spanish horsemen, or vaqueros, are busy rounding up the horses using long ropes called *reatas*.

Focus Questions What are the characteristics of the Navaho settlement in this story? How do the soldiers force the Navaho to leave the canyon?

The Coming of the Long Knives

from *Sing Down the Moon*
by Scott O'Dell
illustrated by Den Schofield

The year is 1864. Bright Morning, a fourteen-year-old Navaho girl, lives with her family in what is now Arizona. Bright Morning, her family, and her friend Tall Boy, who was crippled saving Bright Morning from Spanish slave traders, have no idea that an encounter with the United States soldiers they call the Long Knives will change their lives forever.

The pinto beans pushed up through the earth and the peaches began to swell. Wool from the shearing was stored away for the winter weaving. My father and brother went into the mountains and brought back deer meat which we cut into strips and dried. It was a good summer and a good autumn.

Then early one winter morning three Long Knives came. They were from the white man's fort and they brought a message from their chief. When all of our people were gathered in the meadow one of the soldiers read the message, using Navaho words. He read fast and did not speak clearly, but this is what I remember.

People of the Navaho Tribe are commanded to take their goods and leave Canyon de Chelly.

The Long Knife read more from the paper which I do not remember. Then he fastened the paper to a tree where all in the village could see it and the three soldiers rode away.

There was silence after the soldiers left. Everyone was too stunned to speak or move. We had been threatened before by the Long Knives, but we lived at peace in our canyon, so why should they wish to harm us?

446

SELECTION INTRODUCTION

Selection Summary

Genre: Historical Fiction

Following a fruitful summer and autumn, fourteen-year-old Bright Morning and the people of her village are rudely surprised one winter morning by the arrival of three Long Knives—U.S. soldiers—who have come to evict them from their peaceful home in the beautiful Canyon de Chelly. Thus begins the physically and spiritually devastating three-hundred-mile journey of the bewildered Navahos into captivity at Fort Sumner, New Mexico.

Some of the elements of historical fiction are listed below. Historical fiction may have one or more of these elements.

- The story is set in the past.
- The plot includes events or problems from that time.
- Characters act the way people of that time would have acted.
- Details relating to clothing, homes, speech, modes of transportation, or tools are correct for that time and place and help make the story more realistic.
- Though the story is made up, the characters may include real people, and the plot may include actual events.

About the Author

Scott O'Dell was a prolific writer. His books include more than 25 written for young people. In honor of his contribution to children's literature, the annual Scott O'Dell award for Historical Fiction was established. *Sing Down the Moon*, the book from which "The Coming of the Long Knives" is excerpted, was selected as a Newbery Honor Book and an American Library Association Notable Book.

Students can read more about Scott O'Dell on page 461 of the ***Student Anthology.***

Other Books by Scott O'Dell:

- *Island of the Blue Dolphins*
- *Black Pearl*
- *Child of Fire*
- *The Hawk That Dare Not Hunt by Day*

About the Illustrator

Den Schofield graduated from college with a degree in illustration. According to Schofield, it was the artwork in the books that he read as a child that captured his attention and directed him toward illustrating and publishing. Upon graduation, he enlisted in the military. He began his career in illustration upon completion of his active duty. He credits his parents for encouraging and supporting him in his interests in art and history. Schofield's favorite subjects to illustrate are history, the outdoors, and western or adventure themes.

Students can read more about Den Schofield on page 461 of the ***Student Anthology.***

Also Illustrated by Den Schofield:

- *Danger at Sand Cave*

Inquiry Connections

A major aim of ***Open Court Reading*** is knowledge building. Because inquiry is at the root of knowledge building, students are encouraged to investigate topics and questions within each selection that relate to the unit theme.

In this historical fiction piece, movingly narrated by a young Navaho girl, author Scott O'Dell brings to life an unfortunate event in United States and Navaho history.

Key concepts explored are:

- The United States claimed ownership of desirable lands occupied by Native Americans and forced them to move to remote locations.
- As lands were made available for settlers to start new lives, Native Americans saw their familiar way of life come to an end.

Before reading the selection:

- Point out that students may post a question, concept, word, illustration, or object on the Concept/Question Board at any time during the course of their unit investigation. Be sure that students include their names or initials on the items they post so that others will know whom to go to if they have an answer or if they wish to collaborate on a related activity.
- Students should feel free to write an answer or a note on someone else's question or to consult the Board for ideas for their own investigations throughout the unit.
- Encourage students to read about the American West at home and to bring in articles or pictures that are good examples to post on the Board.

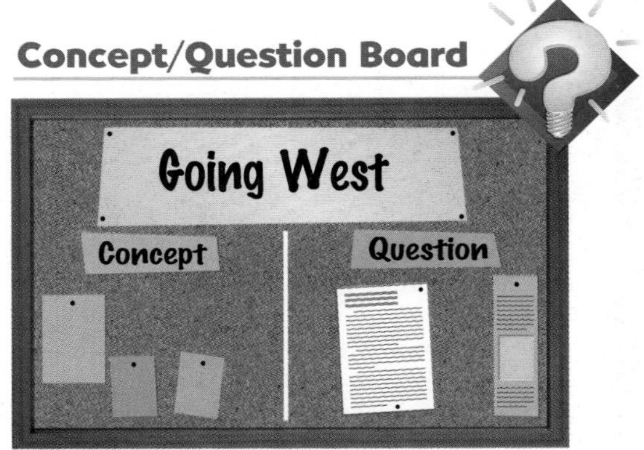

Leveled Practice

Reteach
Pages 156–159

Challenge
Pages 137–140

English Learner Support Activities

Intervention Workbook

Leveled Classroom Library*

Encourage students to read at least 30 minutes daily outside of class. Have them read books from the ***Leveled Classroom Library,*** which supports the unit theme and helps students develop their vocabulary by reading independently.

Black-Eyed Susan

BY JENNIFER ARMSTRONG. KNOPF, 1995.

While her father builds their homestead, Susie's efforts to cure her mother's prairie loneliness are helped by the arrival of some visitors to the isolated sod house. **(Average)**

Caddie Woodlawn

BY CAROL RYRIE BRINK. ALADDIN, 1990.

Based on the author's grandmother, the real Caddie Woodlawn, this is the story of a misunderstood prairie girl who is friends with the Indians and loves to play outside. (Newbery Medal Winner) **(Advanced)**

Children of the Wild West

BY RUSSELL FREEDMAN. CLARION, 1983.

Historic and fascinating photographs accompany Freedman's details about the experiences of pioneer and Native American children in the West, including the journey west, schools, work, and play. **(Advanced)**

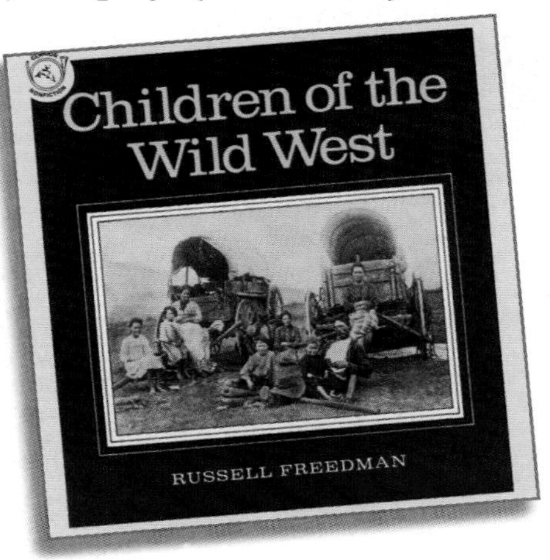

* These books, which all support the unit theme Going West, are part of a 36-book ***Leveled Classroom Library*** available for purchase from SRA/McGraw-Hill. Note: Teachers should preview any trade books for appropriateness in their classrooms before recommending them to students.

SRA TECHNOLOGY

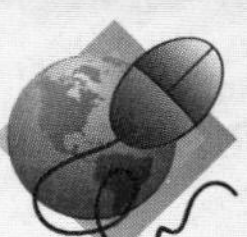

Web Connections

- Going West Web site
- Online Professional Development
- Online Assessment

CD-ROMs

- Research Assistant
- Ultimate Writing and Creativity Center
- Teacher Resource Library

Audiocassettes/CDs

- Listening Library: Going West

Computer Skills

- TechKnowledge

Materials are available through SRA/McGraw-Hill.

LESSON PLANNER

Suggested Pacing: 3–5 days

	DAY 1	DAY 2
1 Preparing to Read Materials ■ Routine Card 1	**Word Knowledge,** p. 446K ■ Antonyms ■ Levels of Specificity ■ Changing *f* or *fe* to *v* in Plurals ■ Suffix *-tion* **About the Words and Sentences,** p. 446K	**Developing Oral Language,** p. 446L
2 Reading & Responding Materials ■ Student Anthology, pp. 446–461 ■ Routine Card 1 ■ Reading Transparencies 43, 54, 58, 71 ■ Unit 5 Assessment, pp. 14–17 ■ Science/Social Studies Connection Center Card 71 ■ Program Assessment ■ Home Connection, pp. 69–70 ■ Inquiry Journal, p. 114	**Build Background,** p. 446M **Preview and Prepare,** pp. 446M–446N **Selection Vocabulary,** p. 446N **Reading Recommendations,** pp. 446O–446P **Student Anthology,** pp. 446–459 First Read ✓ **Comprehension Strategies** ■ Asking Questions, pp. 446, 448, 450, 454 ■ Predicting, pp. 446, 450, 452, 454, 456, 458 ■ Summarizing, pp. 452, 454, 456, 458 ✓ **Supporting the Reading** ■ Predicting, p. 459C **Discussing Strategy Use,** p. 458 **Discussing the Selection,** p. 459A	**Student Anthology,** pp. 446–459 Second Read **Comprehension Skills** ■ Drawing Conclusions, pp. 447, 449, 451 ■ Compare and Contrast, pp. 453, 455, 457, 459 ✓ **Checking Comprehension,** p. 459
Inquiry Materials ■ Student Anthology, pp. 446–461 ■ Inquiry Journal, pp. 127–131 ■ Research Assistant	**Investigation** ■ Investigating Concepts Beyond the Text, p. 461A	**Investigation** ■ Concept/Question Board, p. 461B
3 Language Arts Materials ■ Comprehension and Language Arts Skills, pp. 156–159 ■ Language Arts Handbook ■ Language Arts Transparencies 6, 13 ■ Spelling and Vocabulary Skills, pp. 118–121 ■ Student Anthology ■ Student Writing and Research Center ■ Writer's Workbook, pp. 90–93 ■ Unit 5 Assessment, pp. 36–37 ■ Reteach, pp. 156–159 ■ Challenge, pp. 137–140	**Word Analysis** ✓■ Spelling: Words with *-tion, -sion,* or *-sure* Pretest, p. 461F **Writing Process Strategies** ■ Personal Writing: Letter of Concern, Getting Ideas, p. 461F **English Language Conventions** ■ Mechanics: Punctuation and Capitalization, p. 461F	**Word Analysis** ■ Spelling: Words with *-tion, -sion,* or *-sure,* p. 461G ■ Vocabulary: Foreign Words, p. 461G **Writing Process Strategies** ■ Personal Writing: Letter of Concern, Prewriting, p. 461G **English Language Conventions** ■ Mechanics: Punctuation and Capitalization, p. 461G

✓Informal Assessment Available ✓Formal Assessment Available

DAY 2 continued	DAY 3	
DAY 3	**DAY 4**	**DAY 5**
General Review	**General Review**	**Review Word Knowledge**
Student Anthology, pp. 460–461 ✓■ Concept Connections ■ Meet the Author/Illustrator	**Review Selection Vocabulary,** p. 459B **Literary Elements** ■ Historical Fiction, p. 459D	✓ **Lesson Assessment** ■ *Unit 5 Assessment:* Lesson Assessment, "The Coming of the Long Knives," pp. 14–17 **Home Connection,** p. 459B **Social Studies Connection** ■ Native Americans and the New Settlers, p. 459E ■ Significant Leaders, p. 459F
Investigation ✓■ Establishing Investigation Needs, p. 461C	**Supporting the Investigation** ■ Verifying Facts, p. 461D	**Investigation** ■ Unit Investigation Continued ■ Update Concept/Question Board
Word Analysis ■ Spelling: Words with *-tion, -sion,* or *-sure,* p. 461H ■ Vocabulary: Foreign Words, p. 461H **Writing Process Strategies** ■ Personal Writing: Letter of Concern, Drafting, p. 461H ■ Writer's Craft: Structure of a Business Letter, p. 461H **English Language Conventions** ✓■ Mechanics: Punctuation and Capitalization, p. 461H	**Word Analysis** ■ Spelling: Words with *-tion, -sion,* or *-sure,* p. 461I ■ Vocabulary: Foreign Words, p. 461I **Writing Process Strategies** ■ Personal Writing: Letter of Concern, Revising, p. 461I **English Language Conventions** ✓■ Listening, Speaking, Viewing Viewing: Exaggeration, p. 461I	**Word Analysis** ✓■ Spelling: Words with *-tion, -sion,* or *-sure* Final Test, p. 461J ✓■ Vocabulary: Foreign Words, p. 461J **Writing Process Strategies** ✓■ Personal Writing: Letter of Concern, Editing/Proofreading and Publishing, p. 461J **English Language Conventions** ✓■ Penmanship: Joining with *Z* and *o*, p. 461J

Below are suggestions for differentiating instruction. These are the same skills shown on the Lesson Planner; however, these pages provide extra practice opportunities or enriching activities to meet the varied needs of students.

WORKSHOP

Differentiating Instruction

Teacher: Individual and Small-Group Instruction

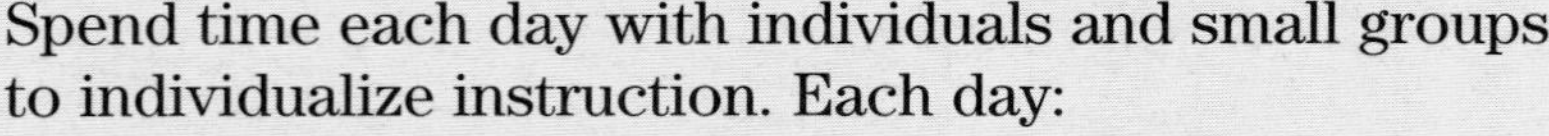

Spend time each day with individuals and small groups to individualize instruction. Each day:

- preteach students who need help with the next lesson.
- reteach students who need to solidify their understanding of content previously taught.
- listen to students read to check their fluency.
- hold writing and inquiry conferences.

Use the following program components to support instruction:

- ***Reteach*** with students who need a bit more practice.
- ***Intervention*** with students who exhibit a lack of understanding of the lesson concepts.
- ***English Learner Support*** with students who need language help.

Student: Independent Activities

Students can work alone, with a partner, or in small groups on such activities as:

- Review sound/spellings
- Partner Reading
- Practice fluency
- Independent Reading
- Reading Roundtable
- Concept vocabulary
- Selection vocabulary
- Writing in progress
- Conference
- Language Arts
- ***Challenge*** Activities
- Inquiry and Investigation Activities
- Listening Library

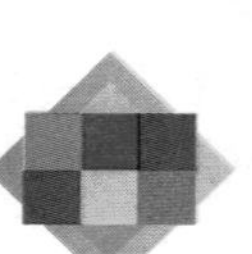

Professional Development

Teacher Resource Library CD-ROMs or ***Online Professional Development*** provides courses that help you better understand the Workshop/Intervention instruction in ***Open Court Reading.*** For more information about this program, visit SRAonline.com.

	DAY I
Word Knowledge	**Teacher Directed** ■ Teach meanings of blended words ■ Reading Words and About the Words, ***Intervention Guide,*** p. 257
Fluency	**Independent Activities** ■ Self-test fluency rate
Comprehension	**Teacher Directed** ■ Preteach "The Coming of the Long Knives," ***Intervention Guide,*** pp. 258–259 ■ Intervention Selection 1, ***Intervention Guide,*** pp. 259–260 ■ ***English Learner Support Guide,*** pp. 410–412 **Independent Activities** ■ Record response to selection in Writer's Notebook ■ ***Listening Library Audiocassette/CD*** ■ Add vocabulary in Writer's Notebook ■ Supporting the Reading: Independent Practice, p. 459C
Inquiry	**Independent Activities** ■ Concept/Question Board ■ Explore OCR Web site for theme connections
Language Arts	**Teacher Directed** ■ Seminar: Select a Topic for a Letter of Concern, p. 461F ■ Capitalization and Punctuation of Names, ***Intervention Guide,*** p. 262 **Independent Activities** ■ Capitalization and Punctuation in Business Letters, ***Comprehension and Language Arts Skills,*** pp. 118–119

DAY 2	DAY 3	DAY 4	DAY 5
Teacher Directed ■ Developing Oral Language, ***Intervention Guide,*** p. 257	**Teacher Directed** ■ Dictation and Spelling, ***Intervention Guide,*** pp. 257–258	**Independent Activities** ■ Add words to Word Bank	**Teacher Directed** ■ General review as necessary
Independent Activities ■ Oral reading of "The Coming of the Long Knives"	**Independent Activities** ■ Partner read "The Coming of the Long Knives"	**Independent Activities** ■ Fluency rate check ■ Reread "The Coming of the Long Knives"	**Teacher Directed** ■ Repeated Readings, ***Intervention Guide,*** p. 261 **Independent Activities** ■ Fluency rate check
Teacher Directed ■ Preteach "The Coming of the Long Knives," ***Intervention Guide,*** pp. 258–259 ■ Reread Intervention Selection 1 ■ Teach Comprehension Strategies, ***Intervention Guide,*** p. 260 ■ ***English Learner Support Guide,*** pp. 413–415 **Independent Activities** ■ Supporting the Reading: Link to Writing, p. 459C ■ ***Listening Library Audiocassette/CD*** ■ Challenge Tip: Drawing Conclusions, p. 451 ■ Challenge Tip: Compare and Contrast, p. 455	**Teacher Directed** ■ Teach Intervention Selection 2, ***Intervention Guide,*** pp. 260–261 ■ ***English Learner Support Guide,*** pp. 416–418 ■ Discuss Concept Connections, p. 460 **Independent Activities** ■ ***Listening Library Audiocassette/CD*** ■ Independent reading ■ Recording Concept Information, ***Inquiry Journal,*** p. 114	**Teacher Directed** ■ Teach Comprehension Strategies, ***Intervention Guide,*** p. 261 ■ Reread Intervention Selection 2 ■ ***English Learner Support Guide,*** pp. 418–421 **Independent Activities** ■ Literary Elements: Independent Practice, p. 459D ■ ***English Learner Support Activities,*** p. 60	**Teacher Directed** ■ Reading Roundtable ■ ***English Learner Support Guide,*** p. 421 **Independent Activities** ■ Social Studies Connection, pp. 459E–459F ■ ***English Learner Support Activities,*** p. 61
Independent Activities ■ Concept/Question Board ■ Explore OCR Web site for theme connections	**Independent Activities** ■ Concept/Question Board ■ Use ***Research Assistant*** to continue investigation ■ Establishing Investigation Needs, ***Inquiry Journal,*** p. 127	**Independent Activities** ■ Concept/Question Board ■ Project Planning, ***Inquiry Journal,*** p. 127	**Independent Activities** ■ Concept/Question Board ■ Verifying Facts and Comparing Sources, ***Inquiry Journal,*** pp. 130–131 ■ Continue research
Teacher Directed ■ Capitalization and Punctuation of Names, ***Intervention Guide,*** p. 262 ■ Spelling: Word Sort, p. 461G ■ Seminar: Plan a Letter of Concern, p. 461G ■ Punctuation and Capitalization in Business Letters, ***Reteach,*** p. 158 **Independent Activities** ■ Vocabulary: Foreign Words, ***Spelling and Vocabulary Skills,*** pp. 118–119 ■ Punctuation and Capitalization in Business Letters, ***Challenge,*** p. 139	**Teacher Directed** ■ Seminar: Draft a Letter of Concern, p. 461H ■ Writing Activity, ***Intervention Guide,*** p. 263 ■ Vocabulary: Foreign Words, ***Reteach,*** p. 157 **Independent Activities** ■ Spelling: Words with *-tion, -sion,* or *-sure,* ***Spelling and Vocabulary Skills,*** p. 120 ■ Vocabulary: Foreign Words, ***Challenge,*** p. 138 ■ Writer's Craft: Structure of a Business Letter, ***Comprehension and Language Arts Skills,*** pp. 158–159	**Teacher Directed** ■ Seminar: Revise a Letter of Concern, p. 461I ■ Writing Activity, ***Intervention Guide,*** p. 263 ■ Spelling: Words with *-tion, -sion,* or *-sure,* ***Reteach,*** p. 156 **Independent Activities** ■ Spelling: Words with *-tion, -sion,* or *-sure* • ***Spelling and Vocabulary Skills,*** p. 121 • ***Challenge,*** p. 137	**Teacher Directed** ■ Seminar: Edit and Publish a Letter of Concern, p. 461J ■ Writer's Craft: Structure of a Business Letter, ***Reteach,*** p. 159 **Independent Activities** ■ Penmanship: Cursive Letters *Z* and *o*, p. 461J ■ Writer's Craft: Structure of a Business Letter, ***Challenge,*** p. 140

ASSESSMENT

Formal Assessment Options

Use these summative assessments along with your informal observations to assess student progress.

Name ____________ Date ______ Score ______

UNIT 5 Going West • Lesson 4

LESSON ASSESSMENT

The Coming of the Long Knives

Read the following questions carefully. Then completely fill in the bubble of each correct answer. You may look back at the story to find the answer to each of the questions.

1. The warriors leave Tall Boy behind because
   - Ⓐ they want him to protect the village
   - ● they don't think he will be of any use
   - Ⓒ they want him to attack the soldiers from behind
2. The Navahos expect the soldiers to be gone
   - ● in a week
   - Ⓑ before winter
   - Ⓒ in a month

Read the following questions carefully. Use complete sentences to answer the questions.

3. Why do the Navahos call the soldiers "the Long Knives"?
   The Navahos call the soldiers "Long Knives" because they carry cavalry swords.
4. What do the Navaho elders plan to do?
   They plan to leave the area instead of fight the white men.
5. Why does Bright Morning's father want Tall Boy and the other warriors to come with the rest of the tribe?
   Bright Morning's father needs strong young men to help everyone get to the high country safely and quickly.

14 Unit 5 • Lesson 4 *The Coming of the Long Knives* • Unit 5 Assessment

Unit 5 Assessment p. 14

The Coming of the Long Knives *(continued)*

LESSON ASSESSMENT

6. What do the Navahos do with their sheep and goats?
   The Navahos drive their sheep and goats into a secret canyon where they can graze.
7. What do the Long Knives do when they find the peach trees?
   They chop off the branches and strip away the bark.
8. Why does Tall Boy miss when he throws his lance at the leader of the Long Knives?
   He cannot use his right hand.

Read the following questions carefully. Then completely fill in the bubble of each correct answer.

9. Bright Morning's father realizes that the Long Knives intend to
   - Ⓐ build a village of their own
   - ● starve the Navahos out
   - Ⓒ start a war with the Navahos
10. Which of these comparisons would help you understand this story best?
    - Ⓐ what life is like in the winter and the summer
    - Ⓑ where the Long Knives came from and where they would return to
    - ● what life would be like before and after the coming of the Long Knives

Unit 5 Assessment • *The Coming of the Long Knives* Unit 5 • Lesson 4 15

Unit 5 Assessment p. 15

The Coming of the Long Knives *(continued)*

LESSON ASSESSMENT

Read the questions below. Use complete sentences in your answers.

Linking to the Concepts Why are the Long Knives taking the Navahos away from their homes?

Answers will vary. Accept all reasonable answers.

Personal Response What would you have done if you were with the Navahos when this happened? Would you have tried to fight the soldiers, hide, or obey the soldiers right away? Why?

Answers will vary. Accept all reasonable answers.

16 Unit 5 • Lesson 4 *The Coming of the Long Knives* • Unit 5 Assessment

Unit 5 Assessment p. 16

The Coming of the Long Knives *(continued)*

LESSON ASSESSMENT

Vocabulary

Read the following questions carefully. Then completely fill in the bubble of each correct answer.

1. Little Beaver fell in front of a hogan. What is a **hogan**?
   - ● a traditional Navaho house
   - Ⓑ a steep canyon wall
   - Ⓒ a winding riverbed
2. Bright Morning would never have abandoned her flock of thirty sheep. **Abandon** means
   - Ⓐ hide away
   - Ⓑ bring along
   - ● leave behind
3. At the end, the Navahos were marching into captivity. To be in **captivity** means you
   - ● are no longer free
   - Ⓑ do not have to hide
   - Ⓒ are welcome to leave
4. When the soldiers came back to the village, it was deserted. If a place is **deserted**, it
   - Ⓐ is full of life
   - ● is empty
   - Ⓒ is hard to find
5. Bright Morning and her tribe felt secure on the rim of the mesa. To feel **secure** means to feel
   - Ⓐ tired from work
   - Ⓑ thankful for a gift
   - ● safe from harm

Unit 5 Assessment • *The Coming of the Long Knives* Unit 5 • Lesson 4 17

Unit 5 Assessment p. 17

Name ____________ Date ______ Score ______

UNIT 5 Going West • Lesson 4 *The Coming of the Long Knives*

LESSON ASSESSMENT

Spelling Pretest: Words with *-tion*, *-sion*, or *-sure*

Fold this page back on the dotted line. Take the Pretest. Then correct any word you misspelled by crossing out the word and rewriting it next to the incorrect spelling.

1. explosion
2. vision
3. examination
4. measure
5. position
6. discussion
7. edition
8. pleasure
9. version
10. education
11. tradition
12. selection
13. collision
14. restriction
15. illusion
16. nation
17. direction
18. destruction
19. starvation
20. duration

36 Unit 5 • Lesson 4 *Spelling Pretest: Words with -tion, -sion, or -sure* • Unit 5 Assessment

Unit 5 Assessment p. 36

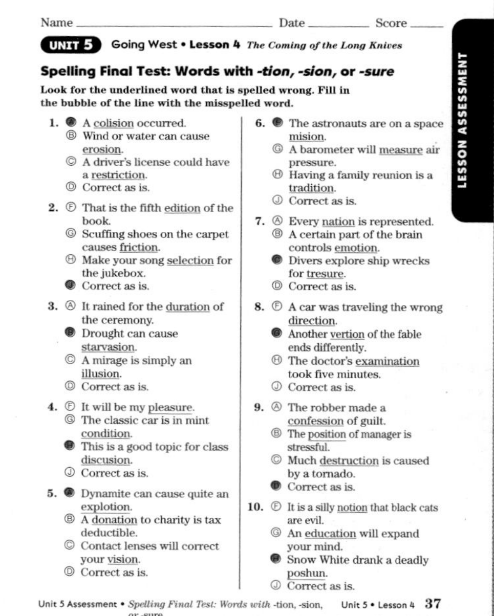

Name ____________ Date ______ Score ______

UNIT 5 Going West • Lesson 4 *The Coming of the Long Knives*

LESSON ASSESSMENT

Spelling Final Test: Words with *-tion*, *-sion*, or *-sure*

Look for the underlined word that is spelled wrong. Fill in the bubble of the line with the misspelled word.

1. ● A colision occurred.
   Ⓑ Wind or water can cause erosion.
   Ⓒ A driver's license could have a restriction.
   Ⓓ Correct as is.
2. Ⓔ That is the fifth edition of the book.
   Ⓖ Scuffing shoes on the carpet causes friction.
   Ⓗ Make your song selection for the jukebox.
   ● Correct as is.
3. Ⓐ It rained for the duration of the ceremony.
   ● Drought can cause starvasion.
   Ⓒ A mirage is simply an illusion.
   Ⓓ Correct as is.
4. Ⓔ It will be my pleasure.
   Ⓖ The classic car is in mint condition.
   ● This is a good topic for class discusion.
   Ⓙ Correct as is.
5. ● Dynamite can cause quite an explotion.
   Ⓑ A donation to charity is tax deductible.
   Ⓒ Contact lenses will correct your vision.
   Ⓓ Correct as is.
6. ● The astronauts are on a space mision.
   Ⓖ A barometer will measure air pressure.
   Ⓗ Having a family reunion is a tradition.
   Ⓙ Correct as is.
7. Ⓐ Every nation is represented.
   Ⓑ A certain part of the brain controls emotion.
   ● Divers explore ship wrecks for tresure.
   Ⓓ Correct as is.
8. Ⓔ A car was traveling the wrong direction.
   ● Another vertion of the fable ends differently.
   Ⓗ The doctor's examination took five minutes.
   Ⓙ Correct as is.
9. Ⓐ The robber made a confession of guilt.
   Ⓑ The position of manager is stressful.
   Ⓒ Much destruction is caused by a tornado.
   ● Correct as is.
10. Ⓔ It is a silly notion that black cats are evil.
    Ⓖ An education will expand your mind.
    ● Snow White drank a deadly poshun.
    Ⓙ Correct as is.

Unit 5 Assessment • *Spelling Final Test: Words with -tion, -sion, or -sure* Unit 5 • Lesson 4 37

Unit 5 Assessment p. 37

Online Assessment for ***Open Court Reading*** helps teachers differentiate classroom instruction based on students' scores from the weekly and end-of-unit assessments. It provides exercises best suited to meet the needs of each student. For more information visit SRAonline.com.

ASSESSMENT

Informal Comprehension Strategies Rubrics

Predicting

- The student makes predictions about what the text is about.
- The student updates predictions during reading, based on information in the text.

Summarizing

- The student paraphrases text, reporting main ideas and a summary of what is in text.
- The student decides which parts of the text are important in his or her summary.
- The student draws conclusions from the text.
- The student makes global interpretations of the text, such as recognizing the genre.

Asking Questions

- The student asks questions about ideas or facts presented in the text and attempts to answer these questions by reading the text.

Research Rubrics

During Workshop, assess students using the rubrics below. The rubrics range from 1–4 in most categories, with 1 being the lowest score. Record each student's score on the inside back cover of his or her ***Inquiry Journal.***

Recognizing Information Needs

1 Identifies topics about which more needs to be learned. ("I need to learn more about the brain.")

2 Identifies information needs that are relevant though not essential to the research question. ("To understand how Leeuwenhoek invented the microscope, I need to know what size germs are.")

3 Identifies questions that are deeper than the one originally asked. (Original question: "How does the heart work?" Deeper question: "Why does blood need to circulate?")

Objectives

- Students recognize antonyms to help them determine meaning and increase vocabulary.
- Students recognize and read words, demonstrating knowledge of levels of specificity among words from a variety of categories.
- Students recognize and read words that change *f* or *fe* to *v* in their plural forms.
- Students recognize and spell words with the ending *-tion.*

Materials

- Routine Card 1

Routine Card Refer to Routine 1 for the Reading the Words and Sentences procedure.

Teacher Tip SYLLABICATION To help students blend words and build fluency, demonstrate syllabication using decodable multisyllabic words in the word lines.

weak • ness	be • yond
peo • ple	di • rec • tion
A • mer • i • cans	de • struc • tion
Nav • a • ho	star • va • tion
veg • e • tab • le	du • ra • tion

Differentiating Instruction

If...	Then...
Students need extra help with words containing the suffix *-tion*	Use ***Intervention Guide,*** pages 257–258

WORD KNOWLEDGE

Word Knowledge

Reading the Words and Sentences

Use direct teaching to teach this Word Knowledge lesson. Write each word and sentence on the board. Have students read each word together. After all the words have been read, have students read each sentence in natural phrases or chunks. Use the suggestions in About the Words and Sentences to discuss the different features of the listed words.

Line 1:	harm help strength weakness fast slow
Line 2:	people Americans Navaho vegetable plants corn
Line 3:	knife knives life lives leaf leaves
Line 4:	direction destruction starvation duration
Sentence 1:	I worked to help homeless animals.
Sentence 2:	Bright Morning, a fourteen-year-old Navaho girl, lives with her family in what is now Arizona.
Sentence 3:	The leaves are gone from the trees.
Sentence 4:	I lost my sense of direction while in the woods.

About the Words and Sentences

- **Line 1:** These words are antonym pairs. An *antonym* is a word whose meaning is the opposite or nearly the opposite of another word. Encourage students to think of other word pairs that are antonyms. Have students create a sentence using one of the words. Have them then substitute the antonym in the sentence and explain how the meaning of the sentence changes.
- **Line 2:** Explain that the first three words demonstrate levels of specificity among related words. *People* is the general term and *Navaho* is the most specific type of people. Ask the students to explain the relationship in terms of specificity for the last three words. Ask students if they can get any more specific with these words; for example, *kernel* could be placed after corn. Ask students to give category titles for these two sets of words.
- **Line 3:** These words end in *f* or *fe* in their singular forms and are made plural by changing the *f* or *fe* to *v* and adding *-es.* Point out to students that not all words ending in *f* or *fe* change their spellings, as in *roofs.* Have students pronounce these words aloud.
- **Line 4:** The words in the last line review the suffix *-tion.*

WORD KNOWLEDGE

- **Sentence 1:** Have students read the sentence aloud. Erase the word *help* and write its antonym, *harm*, in its place. Have students read the new sentence aloud. Discuss with students how the antonym changes the meaning of the sentence.
- **Sentence 2:** This sentence is from the beginning of the selection. Have students read the sentence aloud. Remind the students about how to demonstrate knowledge of levels of specificity by classifying. Have the students select one of the nouns from the sentence, for example, *Arizona.* Then have them choose other words that are more or less specific than their chosen word *(United States, Southwest, Phoenix).* Finally, have the students place the words in order from general to specific.
- **Sentence 3:** Have students read the sentence aloud. Ask students what the singular form of *leaves* is *(leaf).* Have students explain how plurals for words that end in *f* or *fe* are formed (change the final *f* or *fe* to *v* and add *-es*). Encourage students to think of other words that follow this rule and say both the singular and plural forms of the words aloud *(half/halves, shelf/shelves).*
- **Sentence 4:** Have students identify the word in the last sentence that contains the suffix *-tion (direction).*

Developing Oral Language

Use direct teaching to review the words. Have students do one or both of the following activities.

- Have a student use a word in a sentence and point to another student to give an antonym of the word. That student provides the antonym, explaining what context clues in the sentence helped her or him deduce the antonym. The second student continues the activity using a new word.
- Have different students choose words from the board for other students to use in a sentence. The first student should then extend the original sentence by answering *who, what, why, where, when* or *how.*
- Have a student offer a broad word, such as "places." Have other students offer related words that become increasingly specific, such as "countries, states, cities, streets, buildings, rooms." Continue the activity using words from a variety of categories.

Teacher Tip BUILDING FLUENCY By this time in grade 5 students should be reading approximately 151 words per minute with fluency and expression. Gaining a better understanding of the spellings of sounds and structure of words will help students as they encounter unfamiliar words in their reading. As students read, you may notice that some need work in building fluency. During Workshop, have these students choose a section of the text (a minimum of 160 words) to read several times in order to build fluency.

Differentiating Instruction

If...	Then...
Students need extra fluency practice	Use the Intervention Selections activities, ***Intervention Guide,*** pages 259–261

Spelling
See pages 461F–461J for the corresponding spelling lesson for the endings *-tion, -sion,* and *-sure.*

Objectives

- Students will understand the selection vocabulary before reading.
- Students will recognize antonyms to help them determine meaning and increase vocabulary.
- Students will recognize and read words with the short o sound.
- Students will recognize and read words that change *f* or *fe* to *v* in the plural form.
- Students will use the comprehension strategies Asking Questions, Predicting, and Summarizing as they read the story the first time.
- Students will use the comprehension skills Compare and Contrast and Drawing Conclusions as they read the story the second time.

Materials

- Student Anthology, pp. 446–461
- Inquiry Journal, p. 114
- Listening Library
- Science/Social Studies Connection Center Card 71
- Program Assessment
- Unit 5 Assessment, pp 14–17
- Home Connection, pp. 69–70
- Routine Card 1

Differentiating Instruction

English Learner Tip

INTRODUCING THE NAVAHO English Learners may not know that the Southwest was populated by tribes different from the Plains Indians. The Navaho, one of these tribes, lived in more established villages, and depended on agriculture and sheep-herding. Help English Learners make a list of the ways the Navaho lifestyle differed from that of the Plains Indians.

If...	Then...
Students need extra help with the selection vocabulary	Use ***Intervention Guide,*** page 258

www.sra4kids.com
Web Connection
Students can use the connections to Going West in the Reading link of the SRA Web page for more background information about the American West.

Build Background

Activate Prior Knowledge

Discuss the following with students to find out what they may already know about the selection and have already learned about the theme Going West.

- Preteach "The Coming of the Long Knives" by first determining students' prior knowledge of the Navaho peoples. Ask them "Who are the Navaho?" *(They are a Native American people who originated in Canada but who came to be centralized in Arizona, New Mexico, and Utah.)*

Background Information

The following information may help students understand the selection they are about to read.

- Explain that "The Coming of the Long Knives" recounts the forced migration of the Navaho from Arizona to Fort Sumner, New Mexico. In 1863 Colonel Kit Carson and his troops were sent to Arizona to destroy the Navaho's crops and livestock in order to drive them to Fort Sumner. This 300-mile journey is referred to as the Long Walk by the Navaho. Thousands died during the trip. The Navaho remained as prisoners at Fort Sumner until 1868, when they agreed to settle on a reservation.
- Have the students discuss what they know about the genre of this selection. Refer to page 446A of the ***Teacher's Edition*** for elements of this selection's genre.

Preview and Prepare

Browse

- Have a student read aloud the title and the names of the author and illustrator. Demonstrate how to browse. Since this is a fiction piece, have the students browse only its first couple of pages so that the ending will not be spoiled. This helps them to activate prior knowledge in a way that is relevant to the selection. Then discuss what they think this story might have to do with going west.

- Have the students search for clues that tell them something about the story. Also, have them look for any problems, such as unfamiliar words or long sentences, that they notice while reading. Use ***Reading Transparency 54*** to record their observations as they browse. For example, the soldiers might be a clue that there will be a conflict in this selection. For the Problems column, students might say they don't know the meaning of the word *shearing.* They might wonder what will happen to the Navaho. To save time and model note taking, write students' observations as brief notes rather than complete sentences.
- As students prepare to read the selection, have them browse the Focus Questions on the first page of the selection. Tell them to keep these questions in mind as they read.

Set Purposes

Have students set their own purpose for reading this selection. You might suggest that they think about the changes in the West that are described in this story. Remind students that good readers have a purpose when they read. Let them know that they should make sure they know the purpose for reading whenever they read.

Selection Vocabulary

As students study vocabulary, they will use a variety of skills to determine the meaning of a word. These include context clues, word structure, and apposition. Students will apply these same skills while reading to clarify additional unfamiliar words.

Display ***Transparency 43*** before reading the selection to introduce and discuss the following words and their meanings.

hogan:	a traditional Navaho house (page 447)
abandon:	to leave something behind forever (page 449)
deserted:	not lived in, abandoned (page 450)
secure:	safe from harm or danger (page 452)
captivity:	held as prisoners (page 459)

Have students read the words in the Word Box, stopping to blend any words that they have trouble reading. Demonstrate how to decode multisyllabic words by breaking them into syllables and blending the syllables. Then have students try. If the word is not decodable, give the students the pronunciation.

Have students read the sentences on ***Reading Transparency 43*** and use the skills of context, word structure (structural analysis), or apposition to figure out the meaning of the words. Be sure students explain which skill(s) they are using and how they figured out the meanings of the words.

Clues	Problems	Wonderings
Soldiers White man's fort Historical fiction	Shearing The word *lean-to*	What will happen to the Navaho? What is a hogan?

Reading Transparency 54

Teacher Tip SELECTION VOCABULARY To help students decode words, divide them into the syllables shown below. The information following each word tells how students can figure out the meaning of each word from the sentences on the transparency.

ho•gan	context clues
a•ban•don	context clues
de•sert•ed	context clues, word structure
se•cure	context clues
cap•tiv•i•ty	context clues, word structure

Routine Card
Refer to Routine 2 for the Selection Vocabulary procedure. Refer to Routine 3 for the Clues, Problems, and Wonderings procedure.

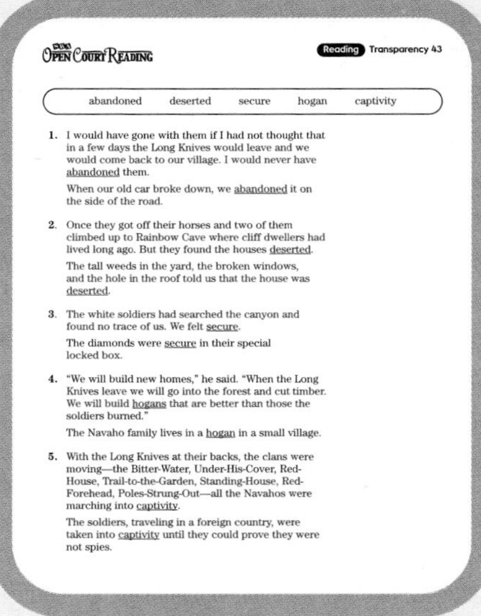

Open Court Reading — Reading Transparency 43

abandoned deserted secure hogan captivity

1. I would have gone with them if I had not thought that in a few days the Long Knives would leave and we would come back to our village. I would never have abandoned them.
   When our old car broke down, we abandoned it on the side of the road.
2. Once they got off their horses and two of them climbed up to Rainbow Cave where cliff dwellers had lived long ago. But they found the houses deserted.
   The tall weeds in the yard, the broken windows, and the hole in the roof told us that the house was deserted.
3. The white soldiers had searched the canyon and found no trace of us. We felt secure.
   The diamonds were secure in their special locked box.
4. "We will build new homes," he said. "When the Long Knives leave we will go into the forest and cut timber. We will build hogans that are better than those the soldiers burned."
   The Navaho family lives in a hogan in a small village.
5. With the Long Knives at their backs, the clans were moving—the Bitter-Water, Under-His-Cover, Red-House, Trail-to-the-Garden, Standing-House, Red-Forehead, Poles-Strung-Out—all the Navahos were marching into captivity.
   The soldiers, traveling in a foreign country, were taken into captivity until they could prove they were not spies.

Reading Transparency 43

DIFFERENTIATING INSTRUCTION

If...	Then...
Students need extra help with the comprehension strategies Summarizing and Asking Questions	Use ***Intervention Guide,*** pages 260–261

Students will enjoy using the ***Listening Library Audiocassette/CD*** and listening to the selection they are about to read. Encourage them to listen to the selection during Workshop. Have students discuss with each other and with you their personal listening preferences (for example, nonfiction, poetry, drama, and so on).

Routine Card
Refer to Routine 4 for the Reading the Selection procedure.

Reading Recommendations

Oral Reading

Because the plot of this classic story is rather complicated and much incidental information is presented, the students may need assistance; have them take turns reading this story aloud as classmates listen. Have students help each other with unfamiliar words and difficult ideas. As students read aloud, have them read expressively, at an appropriate pace, in natural phrases and chunks. Remind students to keep their audience in mind as they read aloud, adjusting volume as necessary and enunciating words clearly. Reading the selection with fluency and accuracy will help students comprehend the text. If students have trouble reading decodable words, have them break the words into sounds or syllables and then blend them together to read the word.

Have students make use of the reading strategies below to help them understand the selection. Have them stop reading periodically or wait until they have completed the selection to discuss the reading strategies. After the students have finished reading the selection, use the "Discussing the Selection" questions on page 459A to see if they understand what they have read.

Using Comprehension Strategies 

Comprehension strategy instruction allows students to become aware of how good readers read. Good readers constantly check their understanding as they are reading and ask themselves questions. In addition, skilled readers recognize when they are having problems and stop to use various comprehension strategies to help them make sense of what they are reading.

During the first reading of "The Coming of the Long Knives," model and prompt the use of the following comprehension strategies. Take turns reading the story aloud with the students. An extended lesson on the comprehension strategy Predicting can be found in the Supporting the Reading section on page 459C. This lesson is intended to give students extra practice with Predicting. However, it may be used at this time to introduce the comprehension strategy to students.

- **Predicting** causes readers to analyze information given about story events and characters in the context of how it may logically connect to the story's conclusion.
- **Summarizing** prompts readers to keep track of what they are reading and to focus their minds on important information.
- **Asking Questions** prepares readers for what they want to learn.

As students read, they should be using a variety of strategies to help them understand the selection. Encourage students to use the strategies listed on the previous page as the class reads the story aloud. Do this by stopping at the points indicated by the numbers in magenta circles on the reduced student page and using a particular strategy. Students can also stop reading periodically to discuss what they have learned and what problems they may be having.

In Unit 5, students should be assuming more responsibility for the use of comprehension strategies. Continue Teacher Modeling and Prompting as needed. Prompting provides a springboard for students to respond using the strategy mentioned in the prompt. The Student Sample is written in the language that students might use in their actual responses.

The Student Sample may be one of many possible student responses. Accept other responses that are reasonable and appropriate. If student responses indicate that the students do not understand the strategy, be ready to discuss their responses and to provide additional instruction. As students proceed through the lessons, teacher modeling and prompting of strategy use should become less and less necessary as students assume more responsibility for using strategies.

Building Comprehension Skills 

Revisiting or rereading a selection allows students to apply skills that give them a more complete understanding of the text. Some follow-up comprehension skills help students organize information. Others lead to deeper understanding—to "reading between the lines," as mature readers do.

- **Compare and Contrast (Review):** Comparing and contrasting unfamiliar thoughts, ideas, or things with familiar thoughts, ideas, and things gives readers something within their own experience base to use in understanding the selection.
- **Drawing Conclusions (Review):** Readers draw conclusions when they take from the text small pieces of information they pull from the selection and use this information to make a statement about that character or event.

Reading with a Purpose

Have students list ways that the coming of the Long Knives to the West forever changed the lives of Native Americans in the Response Journal section of their Writer's Notebooks.

Teacher Tip **HISTORICAL FICTION** Before students begin reading, remind them that "The Coming of the Long Knives" is historical fiction. Explain that it is based on real events, but some of the details were made up by the author.

Differentiating Instruction

If...	Then...
Students need extra help with reading "The Coming of the Long Knives"	• Preread the selection during Workshop; use the ***Listening Library*** to give students a good reading model • Use ***English Learner Support Guide,*** pages 408–423 • Use ***Intervention Guide,*** pages 258–259

COMPREHENSION

Read pages 446–459.

Comprehension Strategies

Read the story aloud, taking turns with the students. Model and prompt the use of strategies for the students.

Teacher Modeling

1 Asking Questions *Good readers think about what they want to find out from their reading. I wonder why the Navaho called the soldiers Long Knives. Many of them carried swords, which are, basically, "long knives." That might explain why the Navaho came up with that name.*

Teacher Modeling

2 Asking Questions *I wonder what the Navaho will do now that they've been told they have to leave. I guess I'll have to keep reading to find out.*

Prompting

3 Predicting *Who wants to predict the story's outcome, to help focus our reading?*

Student Sample

Predicting *Based on what I remember from history class, I don't think it'll have a happy ending. Many Native Americans were forced to leave their land during this time.*

Word Knowledge

SCAFFOLDING The skills students are reviewing in Word Knowledge should help them in reading the story. This lesson focuses on words that change *f* or *fe* to *v* in the plural form. These words will be found in boxes similar to this one throughout the selection.

Words that change *fe* to *v* in the plural form:

knives lives

First Reading Recommendation

ORAL • CHORAL • SILENT

Focus Questions What are the characteristics of the Navaho settlement in this story? How do the soldiers force the Navaho to leave the canyon?

The Coming of the Long Knives

from ***Sing Down the Moon***
by Scott O'Dell
illustrated by Den Schofield

The year is 1864. Bright Morning, a fourteen-year-old Navaho girl, lives with her family in what is now Arizona. Bright Morning, her family, and her friend Tall Boy, who was crippled saving Bright Morning from Spanish slave traders, have no idea that an encounter with the United States soldiers they call the Long
1 *Knives will change their lives forever.*

The pinto beans pushed up through the earth and the peaches began to swell. Wool from the shearing was stored away for the winter weaving. My father and brother went into the mountains and brought back deer meat which we cut into strips and dried. It was a good summer and a good autumn.

Then early one winter morning three Long Knives came. They were from the white man's fort and they brought a message from their chief. When all of our people were gathered in the meadow one of the soldiers read the message, using Navaho words. He read fast and did not speak clearly, but this is what I remember.

> People of the Navaho Tribe are commanded to take their goods and leave Canyon de Chelly.

The Long Knife read more from the paper which I do not remember. Then he fastened the paper to a tree where all in the
2 village could see it and the three soldiers rode away.

There was silence after the soldiers left. Everyone was too stunned to speak or move. We had been threatened before by the Long Knives, but we lived at peace in our canyon, so why should they wish to harm us?

446

Informal Assessment

Observe individual students as they read and use the Teacher Observation Log found in the ***Program Assessment Teacher's Edition*** to record anecdotal information about each student's strengths and weaknesses.

Differentiating Instruction

If...	Then...
English Learners need extra support with reading "The Coming of the Long Knives" and using the skill Drawing Conclusions	Preteach ***Student Anthology*** pages 446–449 using Day 1 of the "The Coming of the Long Knives" lesson, found on ***English Learner Support Guide,*** pages 410–412

3 Everyone stared at the yellow paper fastened to the cottonwood tree, as if it were alive and had some evil power. Then, after a long time, Tall Boy walked to the tree. Grasping the paper, he tore it into many pieces and threw them into the river. We watched the pieces float away, thinking as they disappeared that so had the threat of the white men. But we were wrong. At night, in the dark of the moon, the Long Knives came.

The morning of that day we knew they were coming. Little Beaver, who was tending his mother's sheep, saw them from the high mesa. He left his flock and ran across the mesa and down the trail, never stopping.

He fell in front of his mother's hogan and lay there like a stone until someone threw a gourd of water in his face. By that time all the people in the village stood waiting for him to speak. He jumped to his feet and pointed into the south.

"The white men come," he cried. "The sun glints on their knives. They are near."

447

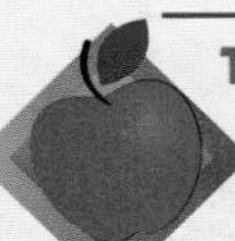

Teacher Tip PREFERRED SPELLING Tell students that in this selection the preferred spelling of *Navajo* is not used—they will find it spelled *Navaho.*

Comprehension Skills

COMPREHENSION

Drawing Conclusions

Have students tell what they know about drawing conclusions. If necessary, remind students that *drawing conclusions* means using clues from the text to make a statement about a character or a story event.

Ask students to reread the soldiers' note on page 446. Ask them what they know about the word *commanded.* Point out that a command is usually a forceful statement. Encourage students to draw some conclusions about why the Navaho were worried about the soldiers returning to their village. Lead them to understand that they were afraid that the soldiers would use force to make them leave their land.

Word Knowledge

The skills students are reviewing in Word Knowledge should help them in reading the story. This lesson focuses on antonyms. Antonyms will be found in boxes similar to this one throughout the selection.

Antonyms

wrong right long short

Drawing Conclusions

Introduced in Grade 1.
Scaffolded throughout Grades 2–5.

REINTRODUCED: Unit 1, Lesson 1
REINFORCED: Unit 2, Lesson 1
Unit 3, Lesson 3
Unit 3, Lesson 5
Unit 4, Lesson 5
TESTED: Unit 5 Assessment

Second Reading Recommendation

ORAL • **SILENT**

COMPREHENSION

Comprehension Strategies

Prompting

4 Asking Questions *Why is Tall Boy being so stubborn?*

I think this might answer my question. He does get upset when Bright Morning's father points out his injured arm. Maybe Tall Boy is upset because he feels useless. Maybe he needs to fight the soldiers to feel strong and brave. What questions do you have? Share them as we read on.

Student Sample

5 Asking Questions *I wonder why Bright Morning talks about abandoning her sheep. I hope she and her family don't have to run away without getting the sheep back. I'll keep reading to find out for sure.*

Word Knowledge

Antonyms:

high low	**stay leave**
young old	**strength weakness**

Teacher Tip BEYOND THE TEXT Bright Morning raised sheep and probably used the wool to make rugs and blankets. Some students might enjoy researching Navaho blankets and other art forms such as sand painting and pottery.

Teacher Tip ANSWERING QUESTIONS The answer to the question asked in the Student Sample on this page can be inferred from the conclusion of the story.

"How many?" Tall Boy said.

"Many," cried Little Beaver, "too many."

My father said, "We will take our goods and go into the high country. We will return when they are gone."

"We will go," said the other men.

But Tall Boy held up his hand and shouted, facing the elder Indians, "If we flee they will follow. If we flee, our goods will remain to be captured. It is better to stay and fight the Long Knives."

"It is not wise to fight," my father said.

"No, it is not," my uncle said, and all the older men repeated what he said.

It was decided then that we should go. But Tall Boy still would not yield. He called to five of the young men to join him in the fight. They went and stood by him.

"We will need you," my father said to the six young men. "We will have to go into high country. Your strength will help us there."

4 Tall Boy was unbending. My father looked at him, at his arm held helplessly at his side.

"How is it, Tall Boy, that you will fight?" he said. "You cannot string a bow or send a lance. Tell me, I am listening."

I watched Tall Boy's face darken.

"If you stay and cannot fight, what will happen?" my father asked him. "You will be killed. Others will be killed."

Tall Boy said nothing. It hurt me to watch his face as he listened to words that he knew were true. I left them talking and went down to the river. When I came back Tall Boy had gathered his band of warriors and gone.

448

Informal Assessment

Use the Informal Comprehension Strategies Rubrics on page 446J to determine whether a student is using the strategies being taught.

We began to pack at once. Each family took what it could carry. There were five horses in the village and they were driven up the mesa trail and left there. The sheep and goats were driven a league away into a secret canyon where they could graze. My flock, my thirty sheep, went too, with the rest. I would have gone with them if I had not thought that in a few days the Long Knives would leave and we could come back to
5 our village. I would never have abandoned them.

When the sun was high we filed out of the village and followed the river north, walking through the shallow water. At dusk we reached the trail that led upward to the south mesa. Before we went up the trail the jars were filled with water. We took enough to last us for a week and five sheep to slaughter. The cornmeal we carried would last that long. By that time the soldiers would be gone.

The soldiers could not follow our path from the village because the flowing water covered our footsteps as fast as they were made. But when we moved out of the river our steps showed clear in the sand. After we were all on the trail some of the men broke branches from a tree and went back and swept away the marks we had left. There was no sign for the soldiers to see. They could not tell whether we had gone up the river or down.

The trail was narrow and steep. It was mostly slabs of stone which we scrambled over, lifting ourselves from one to the other. We crawled as much as we walked. In places the sheep had to be carried and two of them slipped and fell into a ravine. The trail upward was less than half a mile long, but night was falling before we reached the end.

We made camp on the rim of the mesa, among rocks and stunted piñon trees. We did not think that the soldiers would come until morning, but we lighted no fires and ate a cold supper of corncakes. The moon rose and in a short time shone down into the canyon. It showed the river winding toward the south, past our peach orchards and corrals and hogans. Where the tall cliffs ended, where the river wound out of the canyon into the flatlands, the moon shone on white tents and tethered horses.

449

Comprehension Skills

Drawing Conclusions

Remind the students that writers don't always include all the information in a story. Writers depend on readers to *draw conclusions* about characters and story events. This keeps the readers actively involved.

- Point out the exchange between Tall Boy and Bright Morning's father on page 448. Tell the students to draw a conclusion about how Tall Boy felt about what Bright Morning's father said. *(He knew it was true but didn't like it or want to hear it.)*
- What can they conclude about Tall Boy's character? *(He is stubborn and has a lot of pride.)*

Be sure to have students "back up" their conclusions with evidence from the text.

Word Knowledge

Antonyms:

flowing stiff stunted thriving

COMPREHENSION

Differentiating Instruction

Intervention Tip

DRAWING CONCLUSIONS Remind students that good readers draw conclusions about what they have read, based on the facts presented in the text. Point out that conclusions about a character can be based on what the character says, the character's actions, what others say about the character, how others react to the character, and the character's history. Have students draw conclusions about Tall Boy.

COMPREHENSION

Comprehension Strategies

Prompting

6 Predicting *The Navaho have come up with a plan for waiting out the Long Knives. How well do you predict it will work?*

Student Sample

Predicting *The soldiers didn't find out where the Navaho are hiding. I think maybe they will just stay for a time and then go away again.*

Prompting

7 Asking Questions *I wonder what happened to Tall Boy. It sounds as if he hurt himself, but it doesn't say how. Let's read on carefully. Let me know where you find the answer to my question.*

Student Sample

8 Answering Questions *I've found the answer to your question. I guess Tall Boy's warriors didn't do too well against the soldiers. They didn't need Tall Boy anymore, so the warriors went off to find a new place to live. Then Tall Boy had to climb up the canyon by himself.*

Word Knowledge

Antonyms:

narrow wide   far near   larger smaller

Teacher Tip UNDERSTANDING CHARACTER Reread with students all the references to Tall Boy. Ask, "What can you know about Tall Boy from what the author tells us? How did he lose the use of his arm? What does that tell you about him? What does he do to the notice posted by the Long Knives? Who gets the young warriors to decide to fight the Long Knives? Do you think Tall Boy is a wise leader?

"The soldiers have come," my uncle said. "They will not look for us until morning. Lie down and sleep."

We made our beds among the rocks but few of us slept. At dawn we did not light fires, for fear the soldiers would see the rising smoke, and ate a cold breakfast. My father ordered everyone to gather stones and pile them where the trail entered the mesa. He posted a guard of young men at the trail head to use the stones if the soldiers came to attack us. He then sent three of the fastest runners to keep watch on the army below.

I was one of the three sent. We crawled south along the rim of the mesa and hid among the rocks, within sight of each other. From where I crouched behind a piñon tree, I had a clear view of the soldiers' camp.

As the sun rose and shone down into the narrow canyon I could see the Long Knives watering their horses. They were so far below me that the horses seemed no larger than dogs. Soon afterward six of the soldiers rode northward. They were riding along the banks of the river in search of our tracks. Once they got off their horses and two of them climbed up to Rainbow Cave where cliff dwellers had lived long ago. But they found the houses deserted.

The soldiers went up the river, past the trail that led to the place where we were hidden. They did not return until the sun was low. As they rode slowly along, they scanned the cliff that soared above them, their eyes sweeping the rocks and trees, but they did not halt. They rode down the river to their tents and unsaddled the horses. We watched until they lighted their
6 supper fires, then we went back to our camp.

450

Differentiating Instruction

If...	Then...
English Learners need extra support with reading "The Coming of the Long Knives" and using the skill Drawing Conclusions	Preteach ***Student Anthology*** pages 450–453 using Day 2 of the "The Coming of the Long Knives" lesson, found on ***English Learner Support Guide,*** pages 413–415

Tall Boy was sitting on a rock near the top of the trail, at work on a lance. He held the shaft between his knees, using his teeth and a hand to wrap it with a split reed.

I was surprised to see him sitting there, for he and the other young warriors had ridden out of the canyon on the morning the Long Knives came. No one had heard from them since that day. Even his mother and father and sisters, who were hiding with us on the mesa, did not know where he was. At first I thought that he had changed his mind and come back to help protect them. But this was not the reason for his return.

Mumbling something that I could not understand, he went on with his work. I stood above him and as I looked down I noticed a deep scratch across his forehead and that a loop of his braided hair had pulled loose.

"Did you hurt yourself climbing the trail?" I said.

He knotted the reed around the shaft and bit the ends off
7 with his teeth. His right arm hung useless at his side.

"The climb is not difficult," he said.

It was a very difficult climb, but I did not say so, since he wanted me to think otherwise. "Where are the warriors?" I asked him. "Are they coming to help us?"

"They have left the canyon," he said.

"But you did not go," I said, noticing now that he had lost one of his moccasins.

For an instant he glanced up at me. In his eyes I saw a look of shame, or was it anger? I saw that the young warriors had left him behind with the women and old men and children.
8 He was no longer of any use to them.

451

Comprehension Skills

Drawing Conclusions

Encourage students to continue drawing conclusions about story characters and events.

- Have students reread the last two paragraphs on page 450 about the Long Knives. Encourage students to draw a conclusion about the Long Knives' plans. Ask students: *Do you think the Long Knives plan to leave soon, or might they be staying for a while?* Have students support their conclusions with evidence from the text. *(The last two sentences on the page seem to indicate that the Long Knives will be staying at least one night.)*
- Have students draw a conclusion about why Tall Boy returned to the tribe. Remind students to identify evidence from the text. Ask volunteers to explain their conclusions.

Word Knowledge

Antonyms:

top bottom **knotted disentangled**

Teacher Tip ILLUSTRATIONS Remind students to look at the illustrations at the top of the pages. Encourage them to identify which story events are being depicted in each illustration.

COMPREHENSION

Differentiating Instruction

Challenge Tip

DRAWING CONCLUSIONS Have the students keep lists of conclusions they can draw about the characters in the story. Have them compare their lists and discuss how they can support their conclusions with clues from the text.

COMPREHENSION

Comprehension Strategies

Prompting

9 Summarizing *A break in the action is always a good place to stop and summarize what we've learned so far. This will help us remember what we have read. First, the soldiers came and told everyone to leave the village. Who can continue the summary?*

Student Sample

Summarizing *Tall Boy wanted to stay and fight, but the older men decided it was better to move into the mountains until the soldiers left the area. Bright Morning went up the mesa with her family. The soldiers came, but they didn't find the secret trail.*

Prompting

10 Confirming Predictions *We have made predictions about whether or not the Navahos' plan to wait out the Long Knives will work. Does anyone need to revise his or her prediction?*

Student Sample

Confirming Predictions *The plan seems to be working. I think that the soldiers have been fooled and they'll leave after a few days.*

Word Knowledge

Antonyms:

cold hot **good bad**
quiet loud **same different**

Teacher Tip SELF-EVALUATING COMPREHENSION Good readers constantly evaluate their understanding of what they read. Stop often to make sure students are doing this.

He held up the lance and sighted along the shaft. "It has an iron point," he said. "I found it in the west country."

"It will be a mighty weapon against the Long Knives," I said.

"It is a weapon that does not require two hands."

"One hand or the other," I said, "it does not matter."

That night we ate another cold supper, yet everyone was in good spirits. The white soldiers had searched the canyon and found no trace of us. We felt secure. We felt that in the morning
9 they would ride away, leaving us in peace.

10 In the morning guards were set again at the head of the trail. Running Bird and I crawled to our places near the piñon tree and crouched there as the sun rose and shone down on the camp of the Long Knives. Other lookouts hid themselves along the rim of the mesa, among the rocks and brush.

Nothing had changed in the night. There were the same number of tents among the trees and the same number of horses tethered on the riverbank. Our hogans were deserted. No smoke rose from the ovens or the fire pits. There was no sound of sheep bells.

The camp of the Long Knives was quiet until the sun was halfway up the morning sky. Men strolled about as if they had nothing to do. Two were even fishing in the river with long willow poles. Then—while Running Bird and I watched a squirrel in the piñon tree, trying to coax him down with a nut—I saw from the corner of an eye a puff of smoke rise slowly from our village. It seemed no larger than my hand. A second puff rose in the windless air and a third.

452

Differentiating Instruction

Intervention Tip

PREDICTING Remind students that their predictions should be based on the text. If students are having problems making predictions, reread sections of the text with them. At points where the action changes, stop and ask students what they think will happen next. Have students write down their predictions.

"Our homes are burning!"

The word came from the lookout who was far out on the mesa rim, closest to the village. It was passed from one lookout to the other, at last to me, and I ran with it back to our camp and told the news to my father.

"We will build new homes," he said. "When the Long Knives leave we will go into the forest and cut timber. We will build hogans that are better than those the soldiers burned."

"Yes," people said when they heard the news, "we will build a new village."

Tall Boy said nothing. He sat working on his lance, using his teeth and one hand, and did not look up.

I went back to the piñon and my father went with me. All our homes had burned to the ground. Only gray ashes and a mound of earth marked the place where each had stood. The Long Knives were sitting under a tree eating, and their horses cropped the meadow grass.

My father said, "They will ride away now that they have destroyed our village."

But they did not ride away. While we watched, ten soldiers with hatchets went into our peach orchard, which still held its summer leaves. Their blades glinted in the sunlight. Their voices drifted up to us where we were huddled among the rocks.

Swinging the hatchets as they sang, the soldiers began to cut the limbs from the peach trees. The blows echoed through the canyon. They did not stop until every branch lay on the ground and only bare stumps, which looked like a line of scarecrows, were left.

453

Comprehension Skills

Compare and Contrast

Explain to the students that good readers *compare and contrast* different elements in a story to better understand each element.

Have the students discuss the differences and similarities between the Navaho in this story and the Plains Indians in "Buffalo Hunt." Some points for discussion are: What the Navaho/Plains Indians eat; hunting vs. agriculture; moving vs. living in one place all year; and the different attitudes toward white people.

Word Knowledge

Word that changes *f* to *v* in the plural form:
leaves

Compare and Contrast

Introduced in Grade 1.
Scaffolded throughout Grades 2–5.

REINTRODUCED:	Unit 1, Lesson 5
REINFORCED:	Unit 2, Lesson 5
	Unit 2, Lesson 6
	Unit 3, Lesson 2
	Unit 4, Lesson 3
TESTED:	Unit 5 Assessment

COMPREHENSION

COMPREHENSION

Comprehension Strategies

First Read

Prompting

Asking Questions *What are some questions that you have?*

Student Sample

11 **Asking Questions** *I wonder why the soldiers are stripping the bark from the trees. Without their bark they'll die, and won't be of any use to anyone. I guess they really want the Navaho to move out of the area.*

Prompting

12 **Summarizing** *So much has happened to the Navaho that we should stop and sum up again. The Navaho thought the soldiers were going to go away, but they didn't. First they burned all the houses in the village. Who can pick up where I've left off?*

Student Sample

Summarizing *They cut down all the peach trees and stripped the bark from the stumps. Then they trampled all the crops to the ground. Finally the Navaho realized that the soldiers weren't going to leave.*

Student Sample

13 **Confirming Predictions** *This is terrible. I thought the soldiers would go away, but I was wrong. They destroyed the village and all the food. Now the Navaho are trapped on the mesa. I hope they can get away somehow.*

Word Knowledge

Antonyms:
last first   large small

11 Then, at the last, the Long Knives stripped all the bark from the stumps, so that we would not have this to eat when we were starving.

"Now they will go," my father said, "and leave us in peace."

But the soldiers laid their axes aside. They spurred their horses into a gallop and rode through the cornfield, trampling the green corn. Then they rode through the field of ripening beans and the melon patch, until the fields were no longer green but the color of the red earth.

"We will plant more melons and corn and beans," my father said.

"There are no seeds left," I said. "And if we had seeds and planted them they would not bear before next summer."

We watched while the soldiers rode back to their camp. We waited for them to fold their tents and leave. All that day and the next we watched from the rim of the mesa. On the third day the soldiers cut alder poles and made a large lean-to, which they roofed over with the branches. They also dug a fire pit and started to build an oven of mud and stones.

It was then we knew that the Long Knives did not plan to
12 leave the canyon.

"They have learned that we are camped here," my father said. "They do not want to climb the cliff and attack us. It is
13 easier to wait there by the river until we starve."

454

Teacher Tip VISUALIZING Students might benefit from visualizing the village in this story. Encourage them to draw a picture of the village as they imagine it looking either before or after the soldiers arrived.

Differentiating Instruction

If...	Then...
English Learners need extra linguistic support with reading "The Coming of the Long Knives" and using the skill Drawing Conclusions	Preteach ***Student Anthology*** pages 454–456 using Day 3 of the "The Coming of the Long Knives" lesson, found on ***English Learner Support Guide,*** pages 416–418

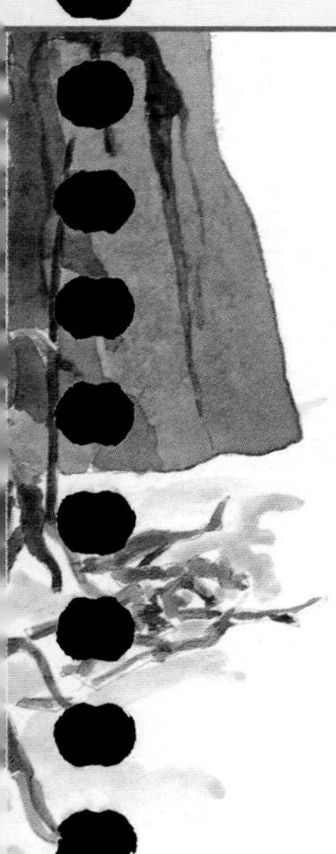

Clouds blew up next morning and it began to rain. We cut brush and limbs from the piñon pines and made shelters. That night, after the rain stopped, we went to the far side of the mesa where our fires could not be seen by the soldiers and cooked supper. Though there was little danger that the soldiers would attack us, my father set guards to watch the trail.

We were very careful with our jars of water, but on the sixth day the jars were empty. That night my father sent three of us down the trail to fill the jars at the river. We left soon after dark. There was no moon to see by so we were a long time getting to the river. When we started back up the trail we covered our tracks as carefully as we could. But the next day the soldiers found that we had been there. After that there were always two soldiers at the bottom of the trail, at night and during the day.

The water we carried back lasted longer than the first. When the jars were nearly empty it rained hard for two days and we caught water in our blankets and stored it. We also discovered a deep stone crevice filled with rainwater, enough for the rest of the summer. But the food we had brought with us, though we ate only half as much as we did when we were home in the village, ran low. We ate all of the corn and slaughtered the sheep we had brought. Then we ground up the sheep bones and made a broth, which was hard to swallow. We lived on this for two days and when it was gone we had nothing to eat.

Old Bear, who had been sick since we came to the mesa, died on the third day. And that night the baby of Shining Tree died. The next night was the first night of the full moon. It was then that my father said that we must leave.

Dawn was breaking high over the mesa when we reached the bottom of the trail. There was no sign of the soldiers.

My father led us northward through the trees, away from our old village and the soldiers' camp. It would have been wiser if we had traveled in the riverbed, but there were many who were so weak they could not walk against the current.

455

Comprehension Skills

COMPREHENSION

Compare and Contrast

Have students compare what happened after the Long Knives arrived with what the Navaho thought would happen by asking:

- What did the Navaho think would happen when the Long Knives arrived? *(They thought the soldiers would come, see that everyone was gone, and leave.)*
- What really happened? *(The soldiers came, looked for the Navaho, burned the houses and destroyed the crops and the orchard, then prevented the Navaho from getting any water.)*

Now work with students to identify comparisons made in the text. As an example, point out to students the last sentence of paragraph 3 on page 454. Explain that the narrator compares and contrasts the color of the fields.

Have students look for other examples of places in the text where the narrator compares things. *(In paragraph 3 on page 455, the narrator describes how long their second batch of water lasted compared with the first.)*

Differentiating Instruction

Challenge Tip

COMPARE AND CONTRAST Point out to students that good readers can draw conclusions about what they've read, based on information they have compared and contrasted. Have students write a paragraph about what conclusions they can draw about the Navaho, based on the information they compared and contrasted in the Comprehension exercise.

COMPREHENSION

Comprehension Strategies

Prompting

14 Summarizing *We've come to the end of another section. Who will volunteer to summarize this section we have just finished reading?*

Student Sample

Summarizing *After the soldiers destroyed the village and the crops, Bright Morning's father realized he was wrong. The soldiers were going to stay until the Navaho starved to death. So the whole group moved northward, away from the soldiers. They were able to find some food and rest in a cave. In the morning, they decided to stay and camp in the canyon.*

Prompting

15 Predicting *It says here that the Navaho can hear hooves approaching. Who do you predict is on the horses, and what does this mean for the Navaho?*

Student Sample

Predicting *Those hooves must be the soldiers coming. I hope the Navaho don't get caught or hurt, but every time I think it won't get worse in this story, it does.*

Word Knowledge

Antonyms:

light dark **sweet sour** **day night**

Teacher Tip BUILDING FLUENCY As students read, you may notice that some need work in building fluency. During Workshop, have these students choose a section of text (a minimum of 160 words) to read several times in order to build fluency.

As soon as it grew light we found patches of wild berries among the trees and ate them while we walked. The berries were ripe and sweet and gave us strength. We walked until the sun was overhead. Then, because four of the women could go no farther, we stopped and rested in a cave.

We gathered more berries and some roots and stayed there until the moon came up. Then we started off again, following the river northward, traveling by the moon's white glow. When it swung westward and left the canyon in darkness we lay down among the trees. We had gone no more than two leagues in a day and part of a night, but we were hopeful that the soldiers would not follow us.

456

Differentiating Instruction

Intervention Tip

SUMMARIZING Remind students that it is important to sum up what they have read in their own words. Select a paragraph from this section to reread with students. After reading the paragraph, help them put it into their words. Tell them to clarify any terms that are making it difficult to break down the text into their own way of saying things.

In the morning we built a small fire and roasted a basket of roots. Afterward the men held council to decide whether to go on or to stay where we were camped.

"They have burned our homes," my father said. "They have cut down the trees of our orchard. They have trampled our gardens into the earth. What else can the soldiers do to us that they have not already done?"

"The Long Knives can drive us out of the canyon," my uncle said, "and leave us to walk the wilderness."

At last it was decided that we stay. 14

We set about the cutting of brush and poles to make shelters. About mid-morning, while we were still working on the lean-tos, the sound of hoofs striking stone came from the direction of the river. 15

Taking up his lance, Tall Boy stepped behind a tree. The rest of us stood in silence. Even the children were silent. We were like animals who hear the hunter approach but from terror cannot flee.

The Long Knives came out of the trees in single file. They were joking among themselves and at first did not see us. The leader was a young man with a red cloth knotted around his neck. He was looking back, talking to someone, as he came near the place where Tall Boy stood hidden.

Tall Boy stepped from behind the tree, squarely in his path. Still the leader did not see him.

Raising the lance, Tall Boy quickly took aim and drew back, ready to send it toward the leader of the Long Knives. He had

457

Differentiating Instruction

If...	Then...
English Learners need extra linguistic support with reading "The Coming of the Long Knives" and using the skill Drawing Conclusions	Preteach ***Student Anthology*** pages 457–459 using Day 4 of the "The Coming of the Long Knives" lesson, found on ***English Learner Support Guide***, pages 418–420

Teacher Tip FLUENCY By this time in grade 5 good readers should be reading approximately 151 words per minute with fluency and expression. The only way to gain this fluency is through practice. Have students reread the selection to you and to one another during Workshop to help build fluency.

COMPREHENSION

Comprehension Skills

Compare and Contrast

Ask students to look for a place where the narrator uses a simile, or a comparison using *like* or *as*, on this page. *(We were like animals who hear the hunter approach but from terror cannot flee.)* Point out that a simile is a figure of speech in which two things are compared in a creative way.

Then have the students discuss how the lives of the Navaho changed after the Long Knives arrived. Remind the students that before the soldiers came, the Navaho had houses, fields of vegetables, and orchards filled with fruit. Bright Morning alone had thirty sheep, and most of the people were healthy. Have the students contrast those conditions with the condition of the group now.

Use ***Reading Transparency 58*** to help students connect, compare, and contrast ideas, themes, and issues from the selections they have been reading. Have students compare the issues of settling the West as described in several selections in this unit.

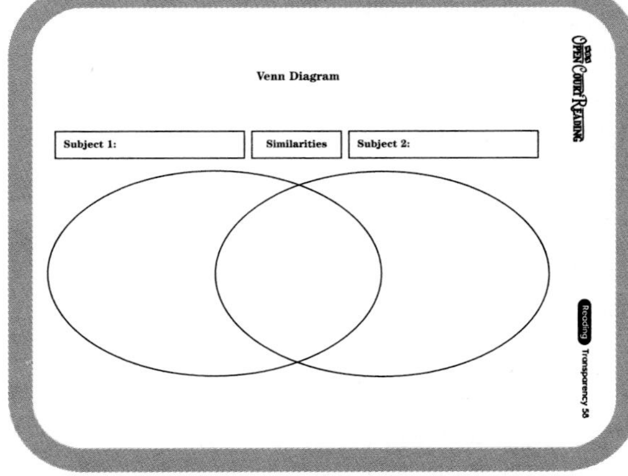

Reading Transparency 58

COMPREHENSION

Comprehension Strategies

Prompting

16 Confirming Predictions *Let's make a final check to see if our predictions were confirmed.*

Student Sample

Confirming Predictions *I was right. Things did get worse for the Navaho. The Navaho were captured after all they had been through.*

Teacher Modeling

17 Summarizing *Let's summarize the last part of the story. Tall Boy tried to fight, but the soldiers surrounded the Navaho and forced them to march into captivity.*

Discussing Stategy Use

While they are reading the selection, have students share any problems they encountered and tell what strategies they used.

- On what basis did they make and confirm predictions?
- What questions did they ask as they read?
- How did they summarize the text?

Remind students that good readers use all of the strategies listed above and that they should be using them whenever they read. Make sure that students explain how using the strategies helped them to better understand the selection. For example, "Summarizing helped me remember and understand what I read because I had to think hard about the story so I could put the events in my own words."

Word Knowledge

Antonyms:
beyond within dodged bumped

practiced with the lance before we came down the mesa, time after time during all of one day, trying to get used to throwing it with his left hand. With his right hand he had been the best of all the warriors. It was with a lance that he had killed the brown bear beyond Rainbow Mountain, a feat of great skill.

But now, as the iron-tipped weapon sped from his grasp, it did not fly straight. It wobbled and then curved upward, struck the branch of a tree, and fell broken at the feet of the soldier's horse.

The horse suddenly stopped, tossing its head. Only then did the soldier turn to see the broken lance lying in front of him. He looked around, searching for the enemy who had thrown it. He looked at my father, at my uncle, at me. His eyes swept the small open space where we stood, the women, the children, the old people, all of us still too frightened to move or speak.

Tall Boy, as soon as he had thrown the lance, dodged behind the tree where he had hidden before, backed away into the brush and quietly disappeared. I saw his face as he went past me. He no longer looked like a warrior. He looked like a boy, crushed and beaten, who flees for his life.

The rest of the Long Knives rode up and surrounded us. They searched us one by one, making certain that no one carried a weapon, then they headed us down the canyon.

458

Teacher Tip EXTRA HELP Reread the selection with students who had difficulty understanding it. Continue modeling and prompting the use of strategies and skills as you reread.

Teacher Tip SHARING OPINIONS Encourage students to express their opinions about the actions of both the Navaho people and the soldiers.

We passed the ruined fields of beans and corn and melons, the peach trees stripped of their bark and branches, our burned-out homes. We turned our eyes away from them and set our faces. Our tears were unshed.

Soon we were to learn that others bore the same fate, that the whole nation of the Navahos was on the march. With the Long Knives at their backs, the clans were moving—the Bitter-Water, Under-His-Cover, Red-House, Trail-to-the-Garden, Standing-House, Red-Forehead, Poles-Strung-Out—all the

 16 17 Navahos were marching into captivity.

459

DIFFERENTIATING INSTRUCTION

If...	Then...
English Learners have been participating in the "The Coming of the Long Knives" ***English Learner Support Guide*** activities	Review the selection and the skill Drawing Conclusions using Day 5 of the lesson, found on ***English Learner Support Guide***, pages 421–423

Formal Assessment

See pages 14–17 in ***Unit 5 Assessment*** to test students' comprehension of "The Coming of the Long Knives."

COMPREHENSION

Comprehension Skills

Second Read

Compare and Contrast

Ask students to look closely at the last paragraph on page 459. Ask them to identify the things being compared here *(different Navaho tribes)*. Then ask students to explain how the similarities are discussed. *(Different Navaho tribes suffered the same fate: captivity.)*

You might have students reflect on the fate of the Plains Indians as described at the end of "Buffalo Hunt." Ask students to compare and contrast the cause of each group's fate.

Checking Comprehension

Ask students the following questions to check their comprehension of the story.

- Did you learn anything new about how the Navaho lived in the old West? *(Answers may vary. Some students may not have known how settled the Navaho were in their homes.)*
- Why did Bright Morning's father decide to leave the canyon? *(because there was nothing left to eat, no way to get fresh water, and people were beginning to die)*
- Why do you suppose the soldiers were moving the Navaho out of the West? *(Answers will vary. Students should base their answers on what they know of this period in American history.)*
- How has this selection connected with your knowledge of the unit theme? *(Answers will vary—students should compare/contrast examples of life in the American West from this selection with their own experiences or past reading and use these connections to make a general statement about the unit theme.)*

Teacher Tip **CONNECTING IDEAS** Encourage students to connect ideas from this selection to those in the selections they have already studied. For example, point out that *freedom* is a theme that has come up in many of the selections students have read over the past four units. Have students take turns naming a selection and telling how the theme *freedom* played a part in it (for example: "SOR Losers"—Ed and his friends wanted the *freedom* to pursue their own interests; "The Coming of the Long Knives"—the Navaho wanted the *freedom* to continue their way of life; etc.). Then, have students discuss why they think *freedom* is so important to people. When they make connections among selections, suggest that students immediately post their insights on the Concept/Question Board. Their classmates might be interested in the ideas, too.

Routine Card
Refer to Routine 5 for the *handing-off process.*

Clues	Problems	Wonderings
Soldiers White man's fort Historical fiction	Shearing The word *lean-to*	What will happen to the Navaho? What is a hogan?

Reading Transparency 54

Discussing the Selection

After the first read, the whole group discusses the selection and any personal thoughts, reactions, problems, or questions that it raises. To stimulate discussion, students can ask one another the kinds of questions that good readers ask themselves about a text: *How does it connect to going west? What have I learned that is new? What did I find interesting? What is important here? What was difficult to understand? Why would someone want to read this?* It is important for students to see you as a contributing member of the group.

Routine 5 To emphasize that you are part of the group, actively participate in the *handing-off process:* Raise your hand to be called on by the last speaker when you have a contribution to make. Point out unusual and interesting insights verbalized by students so that these insights are recognized and discussed. As the year progresses, students will take more and more responsibility for the discussion of selections.

Engage students in a discussion to determine whether they have grasped the following ideas:

- the soldiers commanded the Navaho to leave the canyon and came back to enforce that command
- the Navaho tried to hold on to the belief that they would soon get their home back
- the Navaho were eventually taken into captivity

During this time, have students return to the clues, problems, and wonderings that they noted during browsing to determine whether the clues were borne out by the selection, whether and how their problems were solved, and whether their wonderings were answered or deserve further discussion and exploration. Let the students decide which items deserve further discussion. Also have students return to the Focus Questions on the first page of the selection. Select a student to read the questions aloud, and have volunteers answer the questions. If students do not know the answers to the questions, have them return to the text to find the answers.

You may also want to review the elements of historical fiction with the students. Discuss with them how they can tell that "The Coming of the Long Knives" is historical fiction.

Have students break into small groups to discuss how the story reflects the theme. Groups can then share their ideas with the rest of the class.

Students may wish to record their personal responses to the selection. If they have learned something new about the American West or Native Americans, encourage them to record this information.

Review Selection Vocabulary

Have students review the definitions of the selection vocabulary words that they wrote in the vocabulary section of their Writer's Notebooks. Remind them that they discussed the meanings of these words before reading the selection. Students can use these definitions to study for the vocabulary portion of their Lesson Assessment. Have them add to the Personal Dictionary section of their Writer's Notebook any other interesting words that they clarified while reading. Encourage students to refer to the selection vocabulary words throughout the unit. The words from the selection are:

abandoned **captivity** **deserted** **hogan** **secure**

Have students place the words under the appropriate endings in the Word Bank. Encourage the students to find other words related to the unit theme and add them to the Word Bank.

View Fine Art

The ***Buckskin Ghost Dance Arapaho Dress*** can be found on page 444 of the ***Student Anthology.*** Tell students that the Arapaho wore this type of clothing for a special ceremony that they hoped would give them the power to create a world in which they would not have to contend with white settlers. Have students discuss why the Arapaho might have held this type of ceremony, based on what they have just read in the selection, "The Coming of the Long Knives."

Fine Art Going West

Buckskin Ghost Dance Arapaho Dress. Buckskin. Courtesy of the National Museum of the American Indian. Smithsonian Institution.

Among the Sierra Nevada in California. 1868. **Albert Bierstadt.** Oil on canvas. 183 × 305 cm. National Museum of American Art, Smithsonian Institution, Washington, DC.

444

Student Anthology p. 444

Home Connection

Distribute ***Home Connection,*** page 69. Encourage students to discuss "The Coming of the Long Knives" with their families. Students can work with their families to learn more about a particular Native American group. ***Home Connection*** is also available in Spanish, page 70.

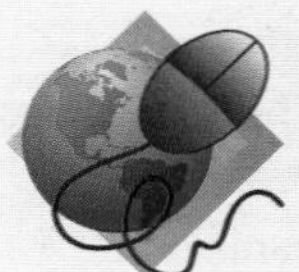

www.sra4kids.com
Web Connection
Some students may choose to conduct a computer search for additional books or information about the American West. Invite them to make a list of these books and sources of information to share with classmates and the school librarian. Check the Reading link of the SRA Web page for additional links to theme-related Web sites.

Differentiating Instruction

If...	Then...
Students would benefit from repeated readings of "The Coming of the Long Knives" or the Intervention Selections	Use ***Intervention Guide,*** page 261

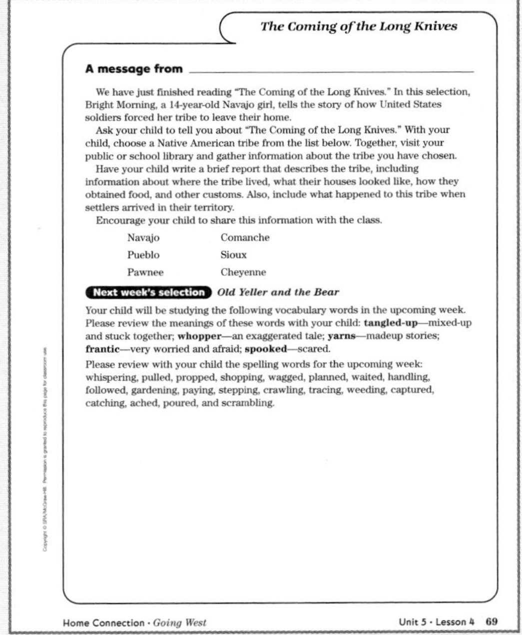
The Coming of the Long Knives

A message from ______________

We have just finished reading "The Coming of the Long Knives." In this selection, Bright Morning, a 14-year-old Navajo girl, tells the story of how United States soldiers forced her tribe to leave their home.

Ask your child to tell you about "The Coming of the Long Knives." With your child, choose a Native American tribe from the list below. Together, visit your public or school library and gather information about the tribe you have chosen.

Have your child write a brief report that describes the tribe, including information about where the tribe lived, what their houses looked like, how they obtained food, and other customs. Also, include what happened to this tribe when settlers arrived in their territory.

Encourage your child to share this information with the class.

Navajo Comanche
Pueblo Sioux
Pawnee Cheyenne

Next week's selection ***Old Yeller and the Bear***

Your child will be studying the following vocabulary words in the upcoming week. Please review the meanings of these words with your child: **tangled-up**—mixed-up and stuck together; **whopper**—an exaggerated tale; **yarns**—madeup stories; **frantic**—very worried and afraid; **spooked**—scared.

Please review with your child the spelling words for the upcoming week: whispering, pulled, propped, shopping, wagged, planned, waited, handling, followed, gardening, paying, stepping, crawling, tracing, weeding, captured, catching, ached, poured, and scrambling.

Home Connection • *Going West* Unit 5 • Lesson 4 69

Home Connection p. 69

Teacher Tip PREDICTING Emphasize to students that predicting does not simply mean making guesses about a story. Explain that it is more like being a detective: they should look for clues in the story, connect the clues to what they already know, and then make a prediction.

Open Court Reading — Reading Transparency 71

Predicting Chart II

My Prediction	Can My Prediction Come True?	Revised Prediction	Can My Prediction Come True?

Reading Transparency 71

Professional Development

Teacher Resource Library CD-ROMs or ***Online Professional Development*** provides courses that help you better understand the Comprehension/Knowledge Building instruction in ***Open Court Reading.*** For more information about this program, visit SRAonline.com.

Supporting the Reading

Comprehension Strategies: Predicting

Teach Tell students that good readers use their prior knowledge and information in a text to predict what might happen next in a story. Point out to students that predicting is a process. Once they make predictions, they should confirm or revise the predictions as new story information presents itself. Explain to students that they can use the predicting strategy in combination with other comprehension strategies to get the most out of a selection.

Guided Practice Have students use a chart like the one on ***Reading Transparency 71*** to keep track of their predictions while they read. You might revisit "The Coming of the Long Knives" and have students recall the predictions they made as they read. Encourage students to write down page numbers for every item they include in the chart.

Independent Practice Have students look at the selection in the ***Student Anthology*** that they will be reading next, "Old Yeller and the Bear." Encourage them to look at the title, author's name, and illustrations. Invite them to take a quick glance at the text to see if anything "jumps out" at them. Then have them make one or two predictions about what might happen in the selection or what it might be about. Make sure students explain how they arrived at their predictions by citing the evidence from the text and the prior knowledge they used. *(For example, students might predict that a child will be attacked by a bear, based on the title, the illustrations, and the phrase "Little Arliss's second scream . . ." on page 467.)* Remind students that they should remember to confirm or revise these predictions once they begin reading the selection.

Link to Writing Tell students that making predictions leads to suspense. When readers make a prediction about a story event, they can't wait to read ahead to see if their prediction will prove true. Ask students to keep this in mind as writers. They should feel free to build suspense in stories to keep readers excited to see what happens next. Foreshadowing, or hinting at things that will happen later without fully explaining them, is one way to accomplish this. You might also encourage them to include strange twists in their stories to keep readers on their toes. Have students review their Writer's Notebooks and identify a story or an idea that might benefit from including suspense.

Literary Elements

Genre: Historical Fiction

Teach Ask students to share what they know about historical fiction. Remind students that the story "The Coming of the Long Knives" is historical fiction. Share with students these elements of the genre.

- The story takes place in the past.
- The plot includes events or problems from that time.
- The characters act the way people of that time would have acted.
- Details about such things as clothing, homes, speech, transportation, and tools are correct for that time and place and help make the story more realistic.
- The characters may include real people, and the plot may include actual events.

Suggest that students write a definition of historical fiction, based on the elements above, in their own words.

Guided Practice Have students analyze "The Coming of the Long Knives" to identify some of the elements of historical fiction. You might encourage students to make a checklist of the elements and check them off as they find them. Ask students to provide examples or explanations for each of the elements they find. Then have students tell what distinguishes this selection's genre from the genre of the selection "Buffalo Hunt." Students should be able to tell you that "Buffalo Hunt" is expository text, which is different from historical fiction because it is nonfiction and it is not written in a narrative style.

Independent Practice Have students analyze the selections in this and other units and identify which selections are historical fiction. Students might also review their Writer's Notebooks or learning logs and dialogues written in Lesson 1 of this unit to identify writing ideas that might make good historical fiction pieces.

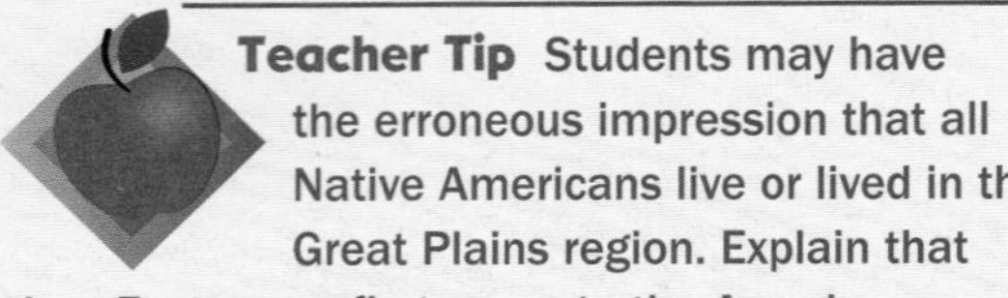

Teacher Tip Students may have the erroneous impression that all Native Americans live or lived in the Great Plains region. Explain that when Europeans first came to the Americas, a great number of differing Native American groups were living all the way from Canada to the tip of South America. Explain that even today, after many Native American nations who originally lived east of the Mississippi River were forced to move westward by the United States government, there is still a considerable number of Native American tribes living in the East. Additionally, there are large numbers of Native Americans living in assorted urban areas across the country.

Science/Social Studies Connection Center

Refer to the ***Science/Social Studies Connection Center Card 71*** for a social studies activity that students can investigate.

Social Studies Connection: Native Americans and the New Settlers

Remind students of the conflict in "The Coming of the Long Knives."

Have students tell what they know about what happened to Native Americans as more and more Europeans immigrated to America and then moved westward. Tell students that they will be making a further investigation into Native American and settler relations. Have students divide into groups and assign one of each of the following topics per group. (Feel free to modify this list according to your goals for instruction.)

- Trade between Native Americans and settlers
- The French and Indian War
- Treaties between the U.S. government and Indian nations
- Native American reservations
- Conflicts between Native American tribes, such as the Iroquois, Huron, and Lakota (Sioux)

Have each group research their topic with the goal of providing a general overview of it. Suggest that students find several important facts about their topic, as well as several unusual or interesting facts. When groups have completed their research, have them share their findings with the class.

Social Studies Connection: Significant Leaders

Have students divide into groups and use the library or the Internet to investigate leaders in the negotiations between Native Americans and settlers. Among the leaders from which students might choose are

- Chief Tecumseh
- John Marshall
- Chief Logan
- Andrew Jackson
- Chief John Ross
- Sequoyah

Students should also feel free to report on other leaders they learn of in their reading. Have the groups create posters of their chosen subjects and display their posters in the classroom for other groups to peruse.

Teacher Tip MATERIALS To complete this activity students will need the following materials: posterboard, markers, colored pencils, and library or Internet sources.

Concept Connections

Linking the Selection

- They lived peacefully in their canyon and wanted to be left alone.
- The soldiers destroyed all of the Navahos' food sources.
- Tall Boy wouldn't admit that his injury had affected his ability as a warrior. Also, as the tribe marched through the ruins of their village, they looked away and did not cry.

Exploring Concept Vocabulary

The concept word for this lesson is ***displaced.*** Write the word on the board. Work with the students to develop a definition that clearly links to the unit theme. Have students copy the term and definition into the Vocabulary section of their Writer's Notebooks.

Displaced: forced to leave one's home. For example, the elimination of buffalo herds caused Plains Indians to be displaced.

- The government took land from Native Americans to make it available to white settlers.
- When the soldiers began constructing a shelter and oven, the tribe knew the soldiers were staying until the Navaho left or starved.

The students' sentences should show an understanding of both vocabulary words and make a reasonable statement about the Navahos' displacement.

Expanding the Concept

Have students carry on dialogues in small groups. After the small-group discussions, bring students together to share their ideas with the whole class.

As students complete their discussion, have them record their ideas on page 114 of their ***Inquiry Journal.***

The Coming of the Long Knives

Concept Connections

Linking the Selection

Think about the following questions, and then record your responses in the Response Journal section of your Writer's Notebook.

- Why was it difficult for the Navaho to believe that the soldiers wanted to harm them?
- What was the soldiers' main strategy for forcing the Navaho to surrender?
- In what ways did the Navaho in this selection show they were proud people?

Exploring Concept Vocabulary

The concept word for this lesson is ***displaced.*** If you do not know what this word means, look it up in a dictionary. Answer these questions.

- Why were Native Americans ***displaced*** as the United States expanded westward?
- When did Bright Morning's tribe realize they were being ***displaced?***

In the Vocabulary section of your Writer's Notebook, write the sentence beginning shown below. Then make up your own ending, and write it to complete the sentence. Include a selection vocabulary word in your sentence ending.

After they were ***displaced,*** the Navaho ____.

Expanding the Concept

Compare the roles of Navaho tribe members with those of the members of Lewis and Clark's expedition. Discuss the jobs performed by people with various strengths and skills. Try to use the word ***displaced*** in your discussion. Add new ideas about the American West to the Concept/Question Board.

460

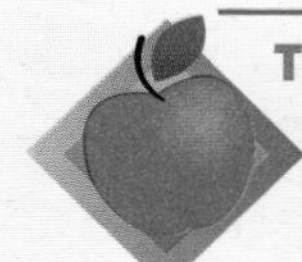

Teacher Tip INQUIRY AND INVESTIGATION As students complete their discussions, have them sum up what they have learned and tell how they might use this information in further investigations.

Informal Assessment

This may be a good time to observe students working in small groups and to mark your observations in the Teacher Observation Log found in the ***Program Assessment Teacher's Edition.***

Meet the Author

Scott O'Dell was born in Los Angeles. At that time, California was still frontier country. *"That is why,"* he told one interviewer, *"I suppose, the feel of the frontier and the sound of the sea are in my books."*

O'Dell was a cameraman on the original motion picture of *Ben Hur*, carrying the first Technicolor camera. It wasn't until after serving in the Air Force during WWII that he became involved with books. He was an editor and an author of books for adult readers before finding his true calling, writing for children. He once said, *"Writing for children is more fun than writing for adults and more rewarding."* He believed in children's special ability to live through the people they read about in stories.

Meet the Illustrator

Den Schofield was always reading as a child and the artwork in the stories captured his attention. His parents encouraged his interest in drawing and history. He pursued a degree in illustration but immediately joined the military after college. Mr. Schofield finally started working for the publishing industry after being released from active duty. He now makes an effort to obtain work relating to his favorite subjects: history, the outdoors, and western or adventure themes.

461

Meet the Author

After the students read the information about Scott O'Dell, discuss the following questions with them.

- Scott O'Dell grew up in California while it was still considered frontier country. How do you think this affected his writing? *(Possible answer: He had more of a true sense of what it was like to live in a wilderness, where people have only themselves to rely upon for survival.)*
- Scott O'Dell says that writing for children is more fun and rewarding than writing for adults. Why do you think he feels this way? *(Possible answer: Children still really use their imaginations; they put themselves into the character's life more completely than adults do.)*

Meet the Illustrator

After the students read the information about Den Schofield, discuss the following question with them.

- Den Schofield's favorite themes are history, the outdoors, and western or adventure themes. How do you think this helped him to illustrate "The Coming of the Long Knives"? *(Possible answer: All of his likes are part of the story. So he must have really enjoyed illustrating it. He probably put himself right into the story as he was illustrating.)*

Inquiry Journal p. 114

Objectives

- Students gain a deeper understanding of the American West.
- Students establish investigation needs.
- Students participate in investigation activities.
- Students learn to cross-reference information.

Materials

- Student Anthology, pp. 446–461
- Inquiry Journal, pp. 128–131
- Research Assistant

Differentiating Instruction

If...	Then...
Students are having difficulty with their Inquiry activities	Show them how to determine the accuracy of resources they are using by finding information on the resources' authors

INVESTIGATION

Investigating Concepts Beyond the Text

To facilitate students' investigation of the American West, you might have them participate in the following activity. Tell students that if they have activity ideas of their own that they would like to pursue, they are free to do so as an alternative to this activity suggestion. For example, students may want to pursue activities of their own choosing that relate more directly to the problems and questions they are investigating with their groups. Tell students that they may work on this activity alone, in pairs, or in small groups, with an option to write about it or to present it to the group upon completion.

The activity suggested for this lesson is:

- Share with the students any information you can locate that describes and depicts Navaho life today. Encourage students to learn more about life on reservations and how Native Americans have attempted to retain their culture. If possible, assign a place in your room to store and share the information you find about Native Americans of the American West today.

Upon completion of their activities, have students share with the group anything new they learned about the American West through discussion and by adding information to the Concept/Question Board.

Concept/Question Board

After reading each selection, students should use the Concept/Question Board to

- post any questions they asked about a selection before reading that have not yet been answered.
- refer to as they formulate statements about concepts that apply to their investigations.
- post general statements formulated by each collaborative group.
- continue to post news articles, or other items that they find during the unit investigation.
- read and think about posted questions, articles, or concepts that interest them and provide answers to the questions.

Unit 5 Research Management

Lesson 1	Students generate questions and ideas for investigation.
Lesson 2	Students formulate questions and problems for investigation.
Lesson 3	Students make conjectures.
Lesson 4	Collaborative Investigation **Students establish investigation needs.** Supplementary Activities **Students participate in investigation activities and learn to cross-reference information.**
Lesson 5	Students establish investigation plans.
Lesson 6	Students continue investigation and get feedback from other groups.
Lesson 7	Students present their investigation findings to the class.

INVESTIGATION

www.sra4kids.com
Web Connection
Students can use the connections to Going West in the Reading link of the SRA Web page for more background information about Going West.

Research Assistant

The Research Assistant helps students in their investigations.

Teacher Tip ULTIMATE WRITING AND CREATIVITY CENTER Have students use the ***Ultimate Writing and Creativity Center CD-ROM*** as they work on their investigation activities.

Formal Assessment

Use the Research Rubrics on page 446J to assess students' ability to recognize research needs.

Professional Development

Teacher Resource Library CD-ROMs or ***Online Professional Development*** provides courses that help you better understand the Inquiry and Investigation instruction in ***Open Court Reading.*** For more information about this program, visit SRAonline.com.

Name ______________________ Date __________

Going West UNIT 5

Establishing Investigation Needs

My group's question or problem:

Answers will vary.

Knowledge Needs—Information I need to find or figure out in order to investigate the question or problem:

A. Answers will vary.

B. ______

C. ______

D. ______

E. ______

Source	Useful?	How?
Encyclopedias		
Books		
Magazines		
Letters on Volumes		
Videotapes, filmstrips, and so on		
Television		
Interviews, observations		
Museums		
Other:		

Inquiry Journal • *Establishing Investigation Needs* UNIT 5 127

Name ______________________ Date __________

UNIT 5 Going West

Project Planning

Use the calendar to help schedule your unit investigation of the American West. Fill in the dates. Make sure that you mark any days you know you will not be able to work. Then choose the date on which you will start and the date on which you

Sunday	Monday	Tuesday	Wednesday

128 UNIT 5 *Project Planning* • Inquiry Journal

Inquiry Journal pp. 127–128

INVESTIGATION

Establishing Investigation Needs

By now, the students should have produced conjectures regarding their chosen investigation problems and discussed them in their investigation groups. A whole-class discussion of these conjectures may now be conducted, in which problems and conjectures are briefly presented and all students have a chance to contribute suggestions, constructive criticisms, and questions. These ideas should help the investigation groups establish what knowledge and resources they will need to acquire for their investigations.

To help groups get started in identifying the information they need to find or figure out in order to investigate their problems, you might focus on one of the conjectures that came out of the previous discussion. Pose questions, such as *What facts will we need to decide whether or not this conjecture is right? Where can we look for these facts? What would an expert on this problem know that we do not know?* Tell students that the manner in which they want to present their investigation findings to the group might also affect the resources they need. For example, a student who decides to make a poster might want to collect photographs and illustrations from magazines to place on the poster. Encourage students to begin thinking of interesting ways to present the information they collect. You may want to display again the Unit 1 Investigation Possibilities menu on ***Reading Transparency 40*** to get students started. Encourage them to come up with their own presentation ideas as well, and have them complete ***Inquiry Journal,*** page 127.

Then outline a schedule for students of how much time will be available until the first presentation will be due. Most projects should be completed at the time you finish the unit. Inform the students, however, that some projects take longer. Help groups set goals for their investigations on the calendar in their ***Inquiry Journals,*** pages 128–129. Tell them that their goals should include due dates for obtaining certain information and time for organizing and publishing their findings. Tell them to make note of their accomplishments each day. This will help them monitor their progress and will enable you to help them manage their time. Suggest that they record dates on the calendar in pencil, since schedules often need to be revised.

Verifying Facts

Teach Give students a variety of information sources to examine, including a dictionary, an atlas, an encyclopedia, some periodicals, and books. Also supply a primary source such as a journal or an eyewitness account. Explain that some information sources may be unreliable. Tell students why the following information sources may be unreliable.

- a book on computers written in 1976 *(outdated)*
- an article about electric cars written by an electric car company *(biased)*
- a review of a rock concert written by an orchestra conductor *(biased)*
- a book about New York City written by someone who has never been there *(not an expert)*

Students should understand that the attitudes and values that exist in a time period may affect stories and informational articles written during that time period. For example, an American article about Russia written during the height of the Cold War may contain certain biases and attitudes toward the subject matter that are unique to the time period. Students should be aware that such an article might provide useful information about the Cold War time period, but may not provide useful information about Russia.

Guided Practice Ask students what they can do to avoid getting outdated, biased, or incomplete information. If necessary, point out that when they are in doubt, they can learn a little about the author's background, and they can cross-reference facts in two or more different sources. If students fail to mention the following, add them to the discussion.

1. Find information in a variety of sources.
2. Use reliable sources. Ask yourself these questions:
   - Is the source written by an expert? Where and what has the author studied? Does the author have a reputation for knowing this field? Book jackets and notes at the beginning or the end of articles give information about authors.
   - When was the source published? Is this the most up-to-date source?
   - How detailed is the information? The more details there are in a book or article, the more complete the coverage of the subject will be.
3. When your sources do not agree on particular facts, cross-reference those facts by locating them in other sources. If two or more sources agree on the facts, the information is more likely to be accurate.
4. Use the most up-to-date sources you can find on your topic. Cross-reference information in primary sources, magazines, and newspaper articles.

Independent Practice For more practice, have students complete ***Inquiry Journal,*** pages 130–131.

SUPPORTING THE INVESTIGATION

Teacher Tip INVESTIGATION TIPS Show the students how to look up the publication date on a piece of writing, find information about the author, and determine the relevance of the information provided to the topic.

Name ______ Date ______

UNIT 5 Going West

Verifying Facts and Comparing Sources

List four facts from "The Coming of the Long Knives." List the sources you might use to verify each fact.

Atlas: a book containing many maps
Almanac: a book containing up-to-date facts, published each year
Encyclopedia: a book or set of books with information on many topics, arranged in alphabetical order
Biographical dictionary: a dictionary containing facts about famous people
Geographical dictionary: a dictionary containing facts about places

Fact: Answers will vary.

Sources: ______

Fact: ______

Sources: ______

Fact: ______

Sources: ______

Fact: ______

Sources: ______

130 UNIT 5 *Verifying Facts and Comparing Sources* • Inquiry Journal

Choose two sources that you are using for your investigation. Complete this page to evaluate the sources and the information they provide.

Answers will vary.

Source: ______

Date of publication: ______

Author's experience/qualifications: ______

Does the author's bias influence the way facts are presented?

Is detailed information provided? ______

How would you rate the usefulness of this source?

Source: ______

Date of publication: ______

Author's experience/qualifications: ______

Does the author's bias influence the way facts are presented?

Is detailed information provided? ______

How would you rate the usefulness of this source?

Inquiry Journal • *Verifying Facts and Comparing Sources* UNIT 5 131

Inquiry Journal pp. 130–131

Objectives

Word Analysis

Spelling

- **Spelling Patterns for Words with *-tion, -sion,* or *-sure.*** Develop understanding of spelling patterns for words with *-tion, -sion,* or *-sure* introduced in Word Knowledge in Part 1.

Vocabulary

- Using words from "The Coming of the Long Knives," introduce students to words from other languages that are used in English.

Writing Process Strategies

- **Personal Writing: Letter of Concern.** Building on the theme Going West and "The Coming of the Long Knives," students will learn to write a letter of concern.

English Language Conventions

Mechanics

- **Usage.** Understand punctuation and capitalization in business letters.

Listening, Speaking, Viewing

- **Viewing: Exaggeration.** Recognize the technique of exaggeration used in the media.

Penmanship

- **Joining with *Z* and *o*.** Review handwriting skills by practicing joining letters with *Z* and *o*.

Materials

- Comprehension and Language Arts Skills, pp. 156–159
- Language Arts Handbook
- Language Arts Transparencies 6, 13
- Spelling and Vocabulary Skills, pp. 118–121
- Student Anthology
- Writer's Workbook, pp. 90–93
- Unit 5 Assessment, pp. 36–37

Differentiating Instruction

Reteach, Challenge, and ***Intervention*** lessons are available to support the language arts instruction in this lesson.

Research in Action

A sonnet is built on a fourteen-line frame, each line containing five feet. . . . Most forms of composition are less clearly defined, more flexible, but all have skeletons to which the writer will bring the flesh and the blood. The more clearly he perceives the shape, the better are his chances of success. (*William Strank, Jr. and E.B. White,* The Elements of Style)

OVERVIEW

Language Arts Overview

Word Analysis

Spelling The spelling activities on the following pages support the Word Knowledge introduction of words with *-tion, -sion,* or *-sure* by developing understanding of the spelling patterns for these endings.

Selection Spelling Words

These words from "The Coming of the Long Knives" contain *-tion.*

nation **direction** **destruction** **starvation** **duration**

Vocabulary The vocabulary activities are designed to familiarize students with foreign words, especially Spanish, French, and Italian words.

Vocabulary Skill Words

pinto beans **Navaho** **mesa** **canyon** **piñon trees**

Additional Materials On Day 3, students will need dictionaries.

Writing Process Strategies

This Writing Process Strategies lesson involves instruction in writing a letter of concern. A letter of concern states the writer's concern about an issue that affects a group of people such as a school, a company, or the general public.

To help students identify the Internet as a source of information for writing, have students review e-mail procedures. You might want to have students send e-mail to a friend. ***TechKnowledge*** Level 5 Lesson 93 teaches these Internet and Electronic reference skills.

Professional Development

Teacher Resource Library CD-ROMs or ***Online Professional Development*** provides courses that help you better understand the Writing instruction in ***Open Court Reading.*** For more information about this program, visit SRAonline.com.

English Language Conventions

Mechanics **Punctuation and Capitalization.** This lesson develops understanding of the use of punctuation and capitalization in business letters.

Listening, Speaking, Viewing **Viewing: Exaggeration.** In this Viewing lesson, students recognize the technique of exaggeration used in the media to achieve a specific purpose.

Penmanship **Joining with *Z* and *o*.** This lesson continues the development of handwriting skills. Students join letters with *Z* and *o* and then write paragraphs from the literature, focusing on joining letters.

DAY 1

Word Analysis

Spelling

Assessment: Pretest

Spelling Patterns for Words with *-tion, -sion,* or *-sure*

Give students the Pretest on page 36 of ***Unit 5 Assessment.*** Have them proofread and correct any misspellings.

Pretest Sentences

1. **explosion** An **explosion** shook the windows of the house.
2. **vision** An eagle's **vision** is excellent.
3. **examination** Students must take an **examination** to get into college.
4. **measure** A seismograph will **measure** earthquake waves.
5. **position** You must **position** the chess pieces carefully on the board.
6. **discussion** A good classroom **discussion** is always enlightening.
7. **edition** The latest **edition** of the newspaper came out today.
8. **pleasure** Hopefully a trip to Hawaii will be for **pleasure** instead of business.
9. **version** She has the latest **version** of the computer software.
10. **education** It takes years to complete an **education.**
11. **tradition** It is a **tradition** to eat pork on New Year's Day.
12. **selection** A French bakery has a large **selection** of pastries.
13. **collision** The Titanic sank after a **collision** with an iceberg.
14. **restriction** A curfew is a **restriction.**
15. **illusion** A mirage is an **illusion.**
16. **nation** Canada is a **nation.**
17. **direction** A weather vane shows which **direction** the wind is blowing.
18. **destruction** A tsunami is a giant wave that causes much **destruction.**
19. **starvation** There was widespread **starvation** after the drought.
20. **duration** The naval blockade lasted for the **duration** of the war.

Writing Process Strategies

Getting Ideas

Letter of Concern

Teach

Introduce the Writing Form

Have students read ***Language Arts Handbook,*** pages 86–91, on business letters.

Inspiration

Model inspiration: *I will imagine I am a citizen living in 1864. I want to write a letter of concern to President Lincoln asking him to change the policy about moving the Navaho from their land.*

Brainstorming

Using the theme Going West and "The Coming of the Long Knives" as a springboard, encourage students to suggest ideas, thoughts, or details that might be included in a letter of concern written to President Lincoln in 1864. Write these ideas on the board. Have students include ideas that appeal to them in their ***Writing Folders.***

Independent Practice

Selecting a Topic

Have each student choose an idea for a letter of concern. It may have something to do with the Going West theme, with "The Coming of the Long Knives," or something in their own community.

Business Letters

A **business letter** is a formal letter written to a company, organization, or professional person for a specific reason. Your tone should be less personal and even more polite and direct than that normally used for a friendly letter. Below are the parts of a business letter:

Heading

The heading consists of the sender's address and the date. It goes in the upper left corner.

Inside Address

The inside address includes the name and address of the person receiving the letter. It goes two lines below the heading.
Ms. Greta Frederick, Ph.D.

Salutation

The salutation is the greeting. Put a colon after it.
Dear Ms. Samartino:
You may use salutations like these when you don't know the person's name:
To Whom It May Concern: Dear Sir or Madam:
Dear National Geographic Society:

Body

The body includes what you want to say. Be brief and polite but not overly formal or stiff. Begin the body two lines below the salutation. Leave a single line of space between each paragraph. Do not indent.

Closing

The closing goes two lines below the body, at the left margin.
Yours truly, Sincerely,

Signature

Sign your name under the closing.

86 Personal Writing ▲ Business Letters

Language Arts Handbook p. 86

English Language Conventions

Mechanics

Punctuation and Capitalization

Teach

- Remind students that a business letter has a heading, an inside address, a salutation, a body, a closing, and a signature.
- The inside address includes the name and title to whom the letter is written and the company's name.
  Mr. Jorge Alvarez
  Vice President of Customer Relations
  Bayview Surf School
  114 Bayview Circle
  San Diego, CA 94401
- The salutation is followed by a colon.
  Dear Mr. Alvarez:
- Use ***Language Arts Handbook,*** page 86, for examples of punctuation and capitalization in business letters.
- If available, show students several examples of business letters, pointing out the parts covered in this lesson.

Independent Practice

Use ***Comprehension and Language Arts Skills,*** pages 156–157, to practice the use of punctuation and capitalization in business letters.

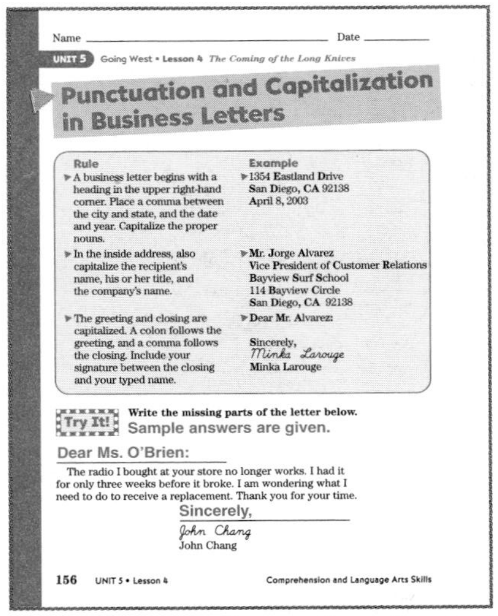

Name ______ Date ______

UNIT 5 Going West • Lesson 4 *The Coming of the Long Knives*

Punctuation and Capitalization in Business Letters

Rule	Example
A business letter begins with a heading in the upper right-hand corner. Place a comma between the city and state, and the date and year. Capitalize the proper nouns.	1354 Eastland Drive San Diego, CA 92138 April 8, 2003
In the inside address, also capitalize the recipient's name, his or her title, and the company's name.	Mr. Jorge Alvarez Vice President of Customer Relations Bayview Surf School 114 Bayview Circle San Diego, CA 92138
The greeting and closing are capitalized. A colon follows the greeting, and a comma follows the closing. Include your signature between the closing and your typed name.	Dear Mr. Alvarez: Sincerely, *Minka Larouge* Minka Larouge

Try It! **Write the missing parts of the letter below.** Sample answers are given.

Dear Ms. O'Brien:

The radio I bought at your store no longer works. I had it for only three weeks before it broke. I am wondering what I need to do to receive a replacement. Thank you for your time.

Sincerely,
John Chang
John Chang

156 UNIT 5 • Lesson 4 Comprehension and Language Arts Skills

Comprehension and Language Arts Skills p. 156

DAY 2

Word Analysis

Spelling

Word Sorting

Open Word Sort Have students sort the spelling words according to their endings. Have students explain their answers.

Vocabulary

Foreign Words

Teach

- Tell students that they will encounter words from many languages as they read. These words make writing more specific and vivid.
- Tell students that many words they use in their own conversations are actually from different languages, such as *ballet* (French), *bagel* (Yiddish), *boomerang* (Aboriginal), *safari* (Kiswahili), and *parka* (Aleut).
- Have students locate the **Vocabulary Skill Words** and any other Spanish words in the selection "The Coming of the Long Knives."

Guided Practice

Assign page 118 of ***Spelling and Vocabulary Skills.*** Students can complete page 119 of ***Spelling and Vocabulary Skills*** for homework.

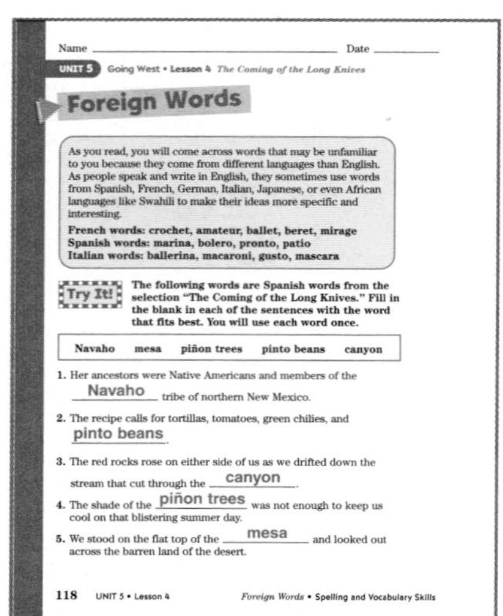

Name ______ Date ______

UNIT 5 Going West • Lesson 4 *The Coming of the Long Knives*

Foreign Words

As you read, you will come across words that may be unfamiliar to you because they come from different languages than English. As people speak and write in English, they sometimes use words from Spanish, French, German, Italian, Japanese, or even African languages like Swahili to make their ideas more specific and interesting.

French words: crochet, amateur, ballet, beret, mirage
Spanish words: marina, bolero, pronto, patio
Italian words: ballerina, macaroni, gusto, mascara

Try It! **The following words are Spanish words from the selection "The Coming of the Long Knives." Fill in the blank in each of the sentences with the word that fits best. You will use each word once.**

Navaho mesa piñon trees pinto beans canyon

1. Her ancestors were Native Americans and members of the Navaho tribe of northern New Mexico.
2. The recipe calls for tortillas, tomatoes, green chilies, and pinto beans.
3. The red rocks rose on either side of us as we drifted down the stream that cut through the canyon.
4. The shade of the piñon trees was not enough to keep us cool on that blistering summer day.
5. We stood on the flat top of the mesa and looked out across the barren land of the desert.

118 UNIT 5 • Lesson 4 *Foreign Words* • Spelling and Vocabulary Skills

***Spelling and Vocabulary Skills* p. 118**

Writing Process Strategies

Prewriting

Letter of Concern

Teach

- **Review** ideas and thoughts discussed on Day 1.
- **Teacher Model** (using ***Language Arts Transparency 6,*** Problem Resolution Chart) getting thoughts down on paper about what will be included in the body of the letter. For example, the problem could be *The Navaho are being removed from their land.* The actions to solve the problem could include *Set aside native lands to be protected from white settlers.* The resolution might be *The Navaho have protected lands and stay within those boundaries while the white settlers are free to choose other land.*
- Remind students that in a business letter, the focus should be on the reader. Students should use the reader's name instead of *Sir* or *Madam.* Also point out that the pronoun *you* (the reader) should be used more frequently than *I* (the writer).

Independent Practice

- Have students complete the prewriting for a letter of concern on ***Writer's Workbook,*** page 90.

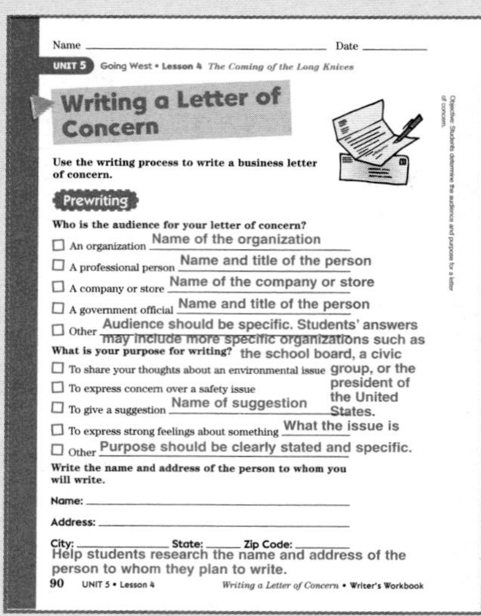

Name ______ Date ______

UNIT 5 Going West • Lesson 4 *The Coming of the Long Knives*

Writing a Letter of Concern

Use the writing process to write a business letter of concern.

Prewriting

Who is the audience for your letter of concern?

- ☐ An organization Name of the organization
- ☐ A professional person Name and title of the person
- ☐ A company or store Name of the company or store
- ☐ A government official Name and title of the person
- ☐ Other Audience should be specific. Students' answers may include more specific organizations such as the school board, a civic group, or the president of the United States.

What is your purpose for writing?

- ☐ To share your thoughts about an environmental issue
- ☐ To express concern over a safety issue
- ☐ To give a suggestion Name of suggestion
- ☐ To express strong feelings about something What the issue is
- ☐ Other Purpose should be clearly stated and specific.

Write the name and address of the person to whom you will write.

Name: ______

Address: ______

City: ______ State: ______ Zip Code: ______

Help students research the name and address of the person to whom they plan to write.

Objective: Students determine the audience and purpose for a letter of concern.

90 UNIT 5 • Lesson 4 *Writing a Letter of Concern* • Writer's Workbook

***Writer's Workbook* p. 90**

English Language Conventions

Mechanics

Punctuation and Capitalization

Teach

- Write the following business letter on the board and have students identify what punctuation and capital letters need to be added.
  - 94 summit lane
    clinton IL 47232
    june 4 2001

    Ms. joyce roy
    Newford and Company
    45 fifth avenue
    lewiston MN 04240

    Dear Ms. roy

    Thank you for coming to speak to our class. We enjoyed your talk on table tennis and the Olympics.
    sincerely
    Paula Johnston
  - *94 Summit Lane*
    Clinton, IL 47232
    June 4, 2001

    Ms. Joyce Roy
    Newford and Company
    45 Fifth Avenue
    Lewiston, MN 04240

    Dear Ms. Roy:

    Thank you for coming to speak to our class. We enjoyed your talk on table tennis and the Olympics.
    Sincerely,
    Paula Johnston
- Remind students that a comma should be placed between the date and the year and between the city and the state in the heading.

Guided Practice in Reading

Have students look for punctuation and capitalization in business letters you have collected and brought to class. Have them identify headings, inside addresses, salutations, and closings.

DAY 3

Word Analysis

Spelling

Spelling Patterns for Words with *-tion, -sion,* or *-sure*

Teach

Introduce the endings *-tion*, *-sion*, and *-sure*. Explain to students that in some, but not all, words with these endings, the endings are suffixes used to change verbs to nouns. The ending *-tion* occurs more frequently than *-sion*. The suffix *-sion* is often used to form a noun from a verb ending in double *s*, as in *discussion*, or *-mit*, as in *permission*. Have students locate words with these suffixes in "The Coming of the Long Knives" and identify the base words.

Guided Practice

Have students complete page 120 from ***Spelling and Vocabulary Skills.***

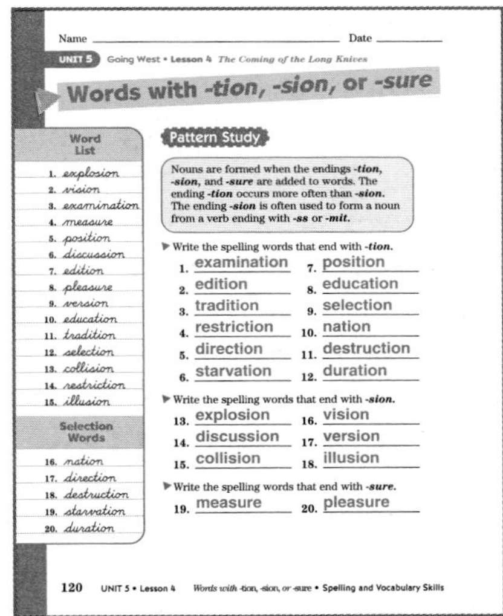

Name ______ Date ______

UNIT 5 Going West • Lesson 4 *The Coming of the Long Knives*

Words with -tion, -sion, or -sure

Word List

1. explosion
2. vision
3. examination
4. measure
5. position
6. discussion
7. edition
8. pleasure
9. version
10. education
11. tradition
12. selection
13. collision
14. restriction
15. illusion

Selection Words

16. nation
17. direction
18. destruction
19. starvation
20. duration

Pattern Study

Nouns are formed when the endings ***-tion***, ***-sion***, and ***-sure*** are added to words. The ending ***-tion*** occurs more often than ***-sion***. The ending ***-sion*** is often used to form a noun from a verb ending with ***-ss*** or ***-mit***.

▶ Write the spelling words that end with ***-tion***.

1. examination
2. edition
3. tradition
4. restriction
5. direction
6. starvation
7. position
8. education
9. selection
10. nation
11. destruction
12. duration

▶ Write the spelling words that end with ***-sion***.

13. explosion
14. discussion
15. collision
16. vision
17. version
18. illusion

▶ Write the spelling words that end with ***-sure***.

19. measure
20. pleasure

120 UNIT 5 • Lesson 4 *Words with -tion, -sion, or -sure* • Spelling and Vocabulary Skills

***Spelling and Vocabulary Skills* p. 120**

Vocabulary (continued)

Foreign Words

Write the following French, Italian, and German words on the board and have students find their definitions and origins in a dictionary.

critique **adage** **ambiance** **levee**
allegro **angst** **nuance** **polka**

Writing Process Strategies

Drafting

Writing a Letter of Concern

Teach

Writer's Craft

Structure of a Business Letter

- Draw the format of a business letter on the board and label each area.
  - The **heading** contains the sender's address and the date.
  - The **inside address** includes the name and address of the person receiving the letter.
  - A colon follows the **salutation,** or greeting.
  - The **body** of a business letter begins two lines below the salutation.
  - The **closing** contains a remark such as *Yours truly*, or *Sincerely.*
  - The writer's **signature** appears below the closing.
- Have students complete ***Comprehension and Language Arts Skills,*** pages 158–159.

Independent Practice

Have students complete ***Writer's Workbook,*** page 91. Then have students write their drafts and include them in their ***Writing Folders.***

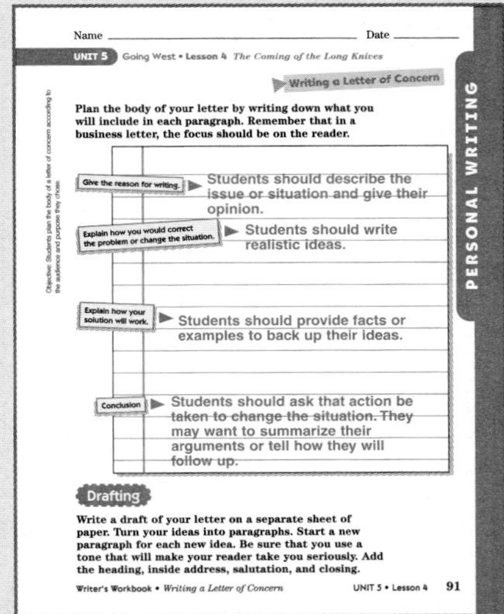

Name ______ Date ______

UNIT 5 Going West • Lesson 4 *The Coming of the Long Knives*

PERSONAL WRITING

Writing a Letter of Concern

Plan the body of your letter by writing down what you will include in each paragraph. Remember that in a business letter, the focus should be on the reader.

Objective: Students plan the body of a letter of concern according to the audience and purpose they chose.

Give the reason for writing. ▶ Students should describe the issue or situation and give their opinion.

Explain how you would correct the problem or change the situation. ▶ Students should write realistic ideas.

Explain how your solution will work. ▶ Students should provide facts or examples to back up their ideas.

Conclusion ▶ Students should ask that action be taken to change the situation. They may want to summarize their arguments or tell how they will follow up.

Drafting

Write a draft of your letter on a separate sheet of paper. Turn your ideas into paragraphs. Start a new paragraph for each new idea. Be sure that you use a tone that will make your reader take you seriously. Add the heading, inside address, salutation, and closing.

Writer's Workbook • *Writing a Letter of Concern* UNIT 5 • Lesson 4 91

***Writer's Workbook* p. 91**

English Language Conventions

Mechanics

Punctuation and Capitalization

Teach

- The inside address includes the name and title to whom the letter is written and the company's name.
- Place a colon after the greeting.

Guided Practice in Writing

Have students write a business letter to an executive of an imaginary company asking him or her to join them in writing to President Lincoln about the way the Navaho are being treated. Remind students that checking for correct punctuation and capitalization in business letters is an essential part of proofreading their personal writing.

Informal Assessment

Check to see that students are progressing in their understanding and proper usage of punctuation and capitalization in their business letters.

DAY 4

Word Analysis

Spelling

Spelling Patterns for Words with *-tion, -sion,* or *-sure*

Teach

Remind students that the endings *-tion*, *-sion*, and *-sure* are sometimes suffixes added to verbs to make them nouns. Model the visualization strategy by writing *colli___n* on the board and asking students to fill in the appropriate letters to spell the word *collision.*

Guided Practice

Have students complete the Spelling Strategies exercises on page 121 of ***Spelling and Vocabulary Skills.***

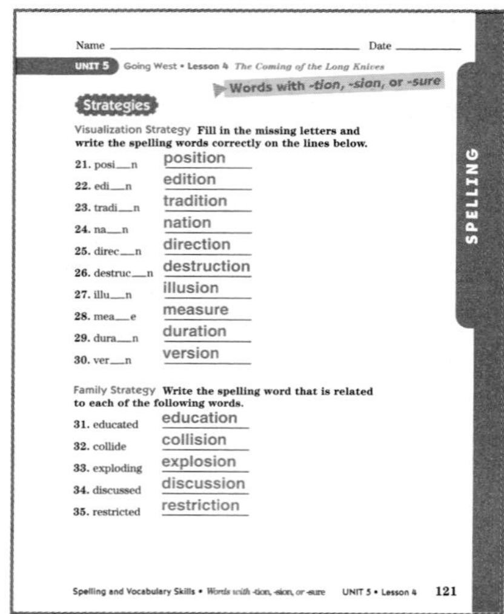

Name ______________ Date ______

UNIT 5 Going West • Lesson 4 *The Coming of the Long Knives*

Words with *-tion, -sion,* or *-sure*

Strategies

Visualization Strategy **Fill in the missing letters and write the spelling words correctly on the lines below.**

21. posi__n position
22. edi__n edition
23. tradi__n tradition
24. na__n nation
25. direc__n direction
26. destruc__n destruction
27. illu__n illusion
28. mea__e measure
29. dura__n duration
30. ver__n version

Family Strategy **Write the spelling word that is related to each of the following words.**

31. educated education
32. collide collision
33. exploding explosion
34. discussed discussion
35. restricted restriction

SPELLING

Spelling and Vocabulary Skills • *Words with -tion, -sion, or -sure* UNIT 5 • Lesson 4 121

***Spelling and Vocabulary Skills* p. 121**

Vocabulary (continued)

Foreign Words

Have students use three or four of the foreign words from Day 3 in original sentences of their own. Students can then share a sentence or two with the class.

Writing Process Strategies

Revising

Letter of Concern

Teach

- **Model** revising by using ***Language Arts Transparency 13,*** Revising for Consolidation. Tell students that the flow of their letters can be improved by consolidating sentences in which the ideas are closely related. Here is an example: *The Navaho gathered roots and berries for food. They ate deer meat, too.* These sentences can be combined in the following way. *The Navaho ate roots, berries, and deer meat.*
- **Troubleshooting**
  - Students often think they don't have to offer a solution to the area of concern they are discussing.
  - Students fail to focus on the reader. They use the pronoun *I* too often.
  - Students fail to support their purpose with facts and examples.
  - Students fail to understand that professional people expect certain conventions in a business letter.

Independent Practice

- Have students use the checklist in the ***Writer's Workbook*** on page 92 to revise their letters.

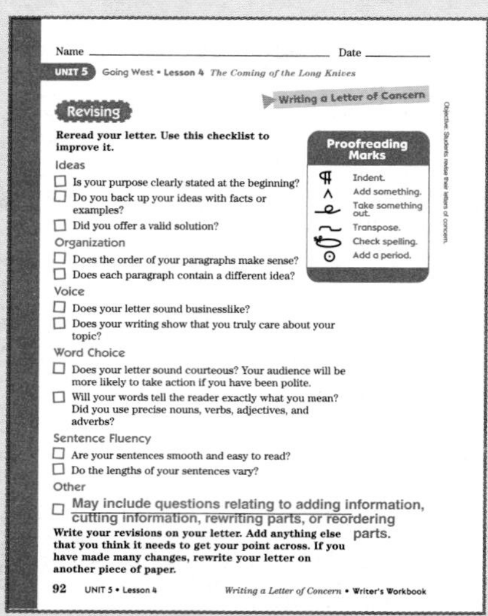

Name ______________ Date ______

UNIT 5 Going West • Lesson 4 *The Coming of the Long Knives*

Writing a Letter of Concern

Revising

Reread your letter. Use this checklist to improve it.

Ideas

- ☐ Is your purpose clearly stated at the beginning?
- ☐ Do you back up your ideas with facts or examples?
- ☐ Did you offer a valid solution?

Organization

- ☐ Does the order of your paragraphs make sense?
- ☐ Does each paragraph contain a different idea?

Voice

- ☐ Does your letter sound businesslike?
- ☐ Does your writing show that you truly care about your topic?

Word Choice

- ☐ Does your letter sound courteous? Your audience will be more likely to take action if you have been polite.
- ☐ Will your words tell the reader exactly what you mean? Did you use precise nouns, verbs, adjectives, and adverbs?

Sentence Fluency

- ☐ Are your sentences smooth and easy to read?
- ☐ Do the lengths of your sentences vary?

Other

- ☐ May include questions relating to adding information, cutting information, rewriting parts, or reordering parts.

Write your revisions on your letter. Add anything else that you think it needs to get your point across. If you have made many changes, rewrite your letter on another piece of paper.

Proofreading Marks
¶ Indent.
^ Add something.
Take something out.
Transpose.
Check spelling.
⊙ Add a period.

Objective: Students revise their letters of concern.

92 UNIT 5 • Lesson 4 *Writing a Letter of Concern* • Writer's Workbook

***Writer's Workbook* p. 92**

English Language Conventions

Listening, Speaking, Viewing

Viewing: Exaggeration

Teach

- Make students aware of the fact that the technique of exaggeration is often used in the media in order to achieve a specific purpose. Usually the purpose is to sway the audience into believing or doing something.
- Point out the fact that, when using exaggeration, the media focuses on ideas or facts that are usually true or partially true and exaggerates them, trying to change the minds of the audience members.
- Bring in editorial cartoons and/or opinion/editorial pieces from the local newspaper to illustrate this technique.
- Refer to page 288 of the ***Language Arts Handbook*** to further explore the concept of exaggeration.

Guided Practice

- Have students identify uses of exaggeration in the media. Recommend the editorial page of newspapers or editorial news shows. Another excellent source of exaggeration is advertisements. Ask students to share their examples.
- Another activity you may want to have students do is to create their own political cartoon in which they exaggerate a person or an issue in the local or national news. Display these cartoons in the classroom.

Informal Assessment

Observe whether students can recognize use of exaggeration in the media, as well as using it themselves to achieve a specific purpose.

DAY 5

Word Analysis

Spelling

Assessment: Final Test

Spelling Patterns for Words with *-tion, -sion,* or *-sure*

Teach

Repeat the Pretest for this lesson or use the Final Test on page 37 of ***Unit 5 Assessment.***

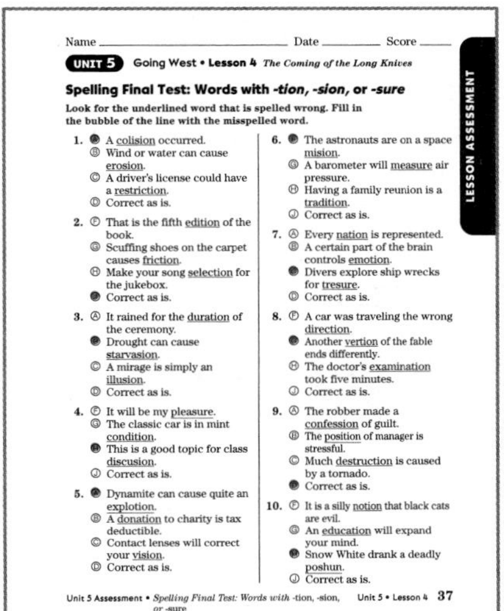

Name ______ Date ______ Score ______

UNIT 5 Going West • Lesson 4 *The Coming of the Long Knives*

LESSON ASSESSMENT

Spelling Final Test: Words with *-tion, -sion,* or *-sure*

Look for the underlined word that is spelled wrong. Fill in the bubble of the line with the misspelled word.

1. Ⓐ A colision occurred.
   Ⓑ Wind or water can cause erosion.
   Ⓒ A driver's license could have a restriction.
   Ⓓ Correct as is.
2. Ⓕ That is the fifth edition of the book.
   Ⓖ Scuffing shoes on the carpet causes friction.
   Ⓗ Make your song selection for the jukebox.
   Ⓙ Correct as is.
3. Ⓐ It rained for the duration of the ceremony.
   Ⓑ Drought can cause starvasion.
   Ⓒ A mirage is simply an illusion.
   Ⓓ Correct as is.
4. Ⓕ It will be my pleasure.
   Ⓖ The classic car is in mint condition.
   Ⓗ This is a good topic for class discusion.
   Ⓙ Correct as is.
5. Ⓐ Dynamite can cause quite an explotion.
   Ⓑ A donation to charity is tax deductible.
   Ⓒ Contact lenses will correct your vision.
   Ⓓ Correct as is.
6. Ⓕ The astronauts are on a space mision.
   Ⓖ A barometer will measure air pressure.
   Ⓗ Having a family reunion is a tradition.
   Ⓙ Correct as is.
7. Ⓐ Every nation is represented.
   Ⓑ A certain part of the brain controls emotion.
   Ⓒ Divers explore ship wrecks for tresure.
   Ⓓ Correct as is.
8. Ⓕ A car was traveling the wrong direction.
   Ⓖ Another vertion of the fable ends differently.
   Ⓗ The doctor's examination took five minutes.
   Ⓙ Correct as is.
9. Ⓐ The robber made a confession of guilt.
   Ⓑ The position of manager is stressful.
   Ⓒ Much destruction is caused by a tornado.
   Ⓓ Correct as is.
10. Ⓕ It is a silly notion that black cats are evil.
    Ⓖ An education will expand your mind.
    Ⓗ Snow White drank a deadly poshun.
    Ⓙ Correct as is.

Unit 5 Assessment • *Spelling Final Test: Words with -tion, -sion, or -sure* Unit 5 • Lesson 4 37

Unit 5 Assessment p. 37

Guided Practice

Have students categorize any mistakes they made on the Final Test.

- Are they careless errors?
- Are they lesson pattern problems?

Vocabulary

Foreign Words

Informal Assessment

- Point out foreign words when they are encountered in reading texts. Encourage students to find and remember definitions for foreign words and recognize foreign words in their reading.
- Remind students to continue adding foreign words to their Writer's Notebooks.

Writing Process Strategies

Editing/Proofreading and Publishing

Letter of Concern

Teach

Teacher Model using editing marks by addressing each of the editing checklist items on ***Writer's Workbook,*** page 93.

Guided Practice

- Have students use the checklist on page 93 of the ***Writer's Workbook*** to proofread and edit their letters.
- Finally, have students publish their letters.

Formal Assessment

Share this rubric with students before they begin the assignment to give them a foundation from which to work.

Total Point Value: 10

1. The letter focuses on the reader. (1 point)
2. The penmanship is legible. (1 point)
3. A reasonable solution is offered for the concern expressed. (2 points)
4. The purpose is supported with facts and examples. (2 points)
5. The format of the letter follows the guidelines. (2 points)
6. Standard conventions for a business letter are followed. (1 point)
7. The last paragraph indicates the next step to be taken. (1 point)

Name ______ Date ______

UNIT 5 Going West • Lesson 4 *The Coming of the Long Knives*

Writing a Letter of Concern

PERSONAL WRITING

Objective: Students edit and prepare their letters of concern for mailing.

Editing/Proofreading

Proofread your letter. If you want your reader to act, you want to make a good impression. Use this checklist to make sure you remember everything.

Conventions

- ☐ Did you use the correct spacing between the different parts of the letter?
- ☐ Did you capitalize names of streets, cities, months, and people?
- ☐ Did you capitalize the title of the recipient and the organization or company in the inside address?
- ☐ Did you capitalize the word *Dear,* all nouns in the salutation, and the first word of the closing?
- ☐ Did you use commas correctly in the address and closing?
- ☐ Did you check for spelling errors?
- ☐ Other May include questions about grammar, usage, and mechanics related to a business letter.

Publishing

Use this checklist to get your letter ready for publishing.

Presentation You may want to discuss conventions for signing business letters.

- ☐ Write your letter on a clean sheet of paper. Use only one side of the page. You may want to type and print your letter. Leave space between your closing and your name so that you can sign the letter.
- ☐ Reread your letter and correct any final errors.
- ☐ Sign your letter.
- ☐ Address and proofread the envelope. Put the person's name and title on the envelope.
- ☐ Fold the letter and place it in the envelope.
- ☐ Other You may want to read students' letters before they mail them.

Writer's Workbook • *Writing a Letter of Concern* UNIT 5 • Lesson 4 93

Writer's Workbook p. 93

English Language Conventions

Penmanship

Joining with *Z* and *o*

Teach

- **Teacher Model:** Review formation of uppercase *Z* and lowercase *o* on the board.

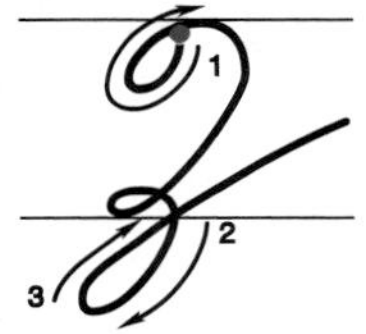

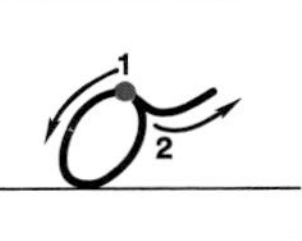

Z Starting point, loop
Curve forward, slant down
Overcurve, curve down
Loop into overcurve: capital *Z*

o Starting point, downcurve
Undercurve
Small curve to right: small *o*

- **Teacher Model:** Write the following sentences to model proper joining of letters: *Zebras or giraffes will be the next zoo exhibit to open.*

Guided Practice

- In the Writer's Notebook, have students join *Z* with the letters *i, e, o,* and *a* and join *o* with *r, p, f,* and *n.*
- From "The Coming of the Long Knives," have students write two paragraphs to practice joining letters.

Informal Assessment

Check students' handwriting for proper letter formation and legible joinings.

Reading and Language Arts Skills Traces

Language Arts

WORD ANALYSIS

Skills Trace

Spelling: Words with -tion, -sion, or -sure

Introduced in Grade 4.
Scaffolded throughout Grade 5.

REINTRODUCED: **Unit 5, Lesson 4**, p. 461F
PRACTICED: **Unit 5, Lesson 4**, pp. 461G–461I
Spelling and Vocabulary Skills, pp. 120–121
TESTED: **Unit 5, Lesson 4**, p. 461J
Unit 5 Assessment

Skills Trace

Vocabulary: Foreign Words

Introduced in Grade 3.
Scaffolded throughout Grades 4–5.

REINTRODUCED: **Unit 5, Lesson 4**, p. 461G
PRACTICED: **Unit 5, Lesson 4**, pp. 461H–461I
Spelling and Vocabulary Skills, pp. 118–119
TESTED: **Informal Assessment**, p. 461J
Unit 5 Assessment

WRITING PROCESS STRATEGIES

Skills Trace

Personal Writing: Letter of Concern

Introduced in Grade 5.
Scaffolded throughout Grade 5.

INTRODUCED: **Unit 5, Lesson 4**, p. 461F
PRACTICED: **Unit 5, Lesson 4**, pp. 461F–461J
Writer's Workbook, pp. 90–93
TESTED: **Formal Assessment**
Unit 5, Lesson 4, p. 461J
Unit 5 Assessment

Skills Trace

Writer's Craft: Structure of a Business Letter

Introduced in Grade 3.
Scaffolded throughout Grades 4–5.

REINTRODUCED: **Unit 5, Lesson 4**, p. 461H
PRACTICED: **Unit 5, Lesson 4**, p. 461H
Comprehension and Language Arts Skills, pp. 158–159
TESTED: **Unit 5 Assessment**

ENGLISH LANGUAGE CONVENTIONS

Skills Trace

Mechanics: Punctuation and Capitalization in Business Letters

Introduced in Grade 5.
Scaffolded throughout Grade 5.

INTRODUCED: **Unit 5, Lesson 4**, p. 461F
PRACTICED: **Unit 5, Lesson 4**, pp. 461F–461H
Comprehension and Language Arts Skills, pp. 156–157
TESTED: **Unit 5 Assessment**

Skills Trace

Listening, Speaking, Viewing
Viewing: Exaggeration

Introduced in Grade 4.
Scaffolded throughout Grade 5.

REINTRODUCED: **Unit 5, Lesson 4**, p. 461I
PRACTICED: **Unit 5, Lesson 4**, p. 461I
TESTED: **Informal Assessment**, p. 461I

Penmanship: Joining with Z and o

Introduced in Grade 3.
Scaffolded throughout Grades 4–5.

REINTRODUCED: **Unit 5, Lesson 4**, p. 461J
PRACTICED: **Unit 5, Lesson 4**, p. 461J
TESTED: **Informal Assessment**, p. 461J

Reading

COMPREHENSION

Skills Trace

Drawing Conclusions

Introduced in Grade 1.
Scaffolded throughout Grades 2–5.

REINTRODUCED: **Unit 1, Lesson 1**
REINFORCED: **Unit 2, Lesson 1**
Unit 3, Lesson 3
Unit 3, Lesson 5
Unit 4, Lesson 5
TESTED: **Unit 5 Assessment**

COMPREHENSION

Skills Trace

Compare and Contrast

Introduced in Grade 1.
Scaffolded throughout Grades 2–5.

REINTRODUCED: **Unit 1, Lesson 5**
REINFORCED: **Unit 2, Lesson 5**
Unit 2, Lesson 6
Unit 3, Lesson 2
Unit 3, Lesson 6
TESTED: **Unit 5 Assessment**

Professional Development: Writing

Inquiry, Research, and Investigation

As they become more fluent readers and writers, students find out that reading and writing give them power: the power to take control of their learning. Although at times the purpose of reading is the simple pleasure of a good story or a wonderful poem, most adults and all school children spend more time reading to learn specific knowledge than they do reading for pleasure. Students need to be able to read and integrate into their knowledge system such diverse areas of study as American history and biology.

Adult readers research information on topics ranging from tax laws to lawn mower repair and maintenance. The ability to read to find out what you need or want to find out is one of the prime objectives of education. Helping students learn how to do this—how to research and explore any area in which they are interested or for some reason need to know—is an aspect of education that is often neglected until high school or even college. By that time, it is very hard for many to break away from the simple read-and-report methods of research and investigation most students devise.

True research is a never-ending, recursive cycle in which the researcher actively questions, develops ideas, or conjectures about why something is the way it is, and then pursues the answers. The answers for a researcher may never come. What does come is more questions. Developing the questions, pursuing the answers, developing conjectures, revising ideas, and setting off on new avenues of research and investigation are the stuff of which strong, deep knowledge and expertise are made.

Inquiry, Research, and Investigation in *Open Court Reading*

In order to encourage them to understand how reading can enhance their lives and help them to become mature, educated adults, students are asked in each unit to use what they are learning in the unit as the basis for further investigation and research. The unit selections are the base for their investigations.

In ***Open Court Reading,*** students model the behavior of expert learners and researchers. Opportunities for students, individually and in groups, to explore, to write about, and to discuss key concepts in a specific area lead to improved critical thinking and reading skills. Students become independent, intentional, self-directed learners.

The idea of research is introduced as early as kindergarten. Procedures for collaborative research are formalized further in first grade. Beginning in second grade and continuing through sixth grade, students are led, working individually or collaboratively, to pursue problems that interest them in the same manner that an adult would conduct research.

Students use their reading selections as a knowledge base for further investigation. They read to learn, then share what they learn with each other. Because each student contributes to the research in a unique way, all students feel the sense of purpose and accomplishment achieved through collaborative research.

Professional Development

Teacher Resource Library CD-ROMs or ***Online Professional Development*** provides courses that help you better understand the Writing instruction in ***Open Court Reading.*** For more information about this program, visit SRAonline.com.

Additional information about writing, as well as resource references, can be found in the ***Professional Development Guide: Writing.***

Focus Questions What kinds of animals does Arliss encounter on the frontier? How does he get himself into trouble with the bear? Who will rescue Arliss?

Old Yeller & the Bear

from **Old Yeller**
by Fred Gipson
illustrated by Jennifer Heyd Wharton

Fourteen-year-old Travis lives with his family in Texas during the 1860s. Travis feels responsible for his mother and brother while his father is away on a long cattle drive. Travis thinks the big yellow dog that adopts his family is a useless nuisance until a bear shows him how wrong he is.

That Little Arliss! If he wasn't a mess! From the time he'd grown up big enough to get out of the cabin, he'd made a practice of trying to catch and keep every living thing that ran, flew, jumped, or crawled.

Every night before Mama let him go to bed, she'd make Arliss empty his pockets of whatever he'd captured during the day. Generally, it would be a tangled-up mess of grasshoppers and worms and praying bugs and little rusty tree lizards. One time he brought in a horned toad that got so mad he swelled out round and flat as a Mexican tortilla and bled at the eyes. Sometimes it was stuff like a young bird that had fallen out of its nest before it could fly, or a green-speckled spring frog or a striped water snake. And once he turned out of his pocket a wadded-up baby copperhead that nearly threw Mama into spasms. We never did figure out why the snake hadn't bitten him, but Mama took no more chances on snakes. She switched Arliss hard for catching that snake. Then she made me spend better than a week, taking him out and teaching him to throw rocks and kill snakes.

462

SELECTION INTRODUCTION

Selection Summary

Genre: Historical Fiction

"Old Yeller and the Bear," an excerpt from the book *Old Yeller*, takes place in the late 1860s in Texas.

With Papa away on a cattle drive, fourteen-year-old Travis Coates is in charge of looking after the family homestead on the Texas plains, miles away from the nearest neighbors. All goes well until Little Arliss, Travis's adventuresome little brother, tries to capture a young bear cub and incurs the wrath of its ferocious mother. Who will rescue Little Arliss?

Some of the elements of historical fiction are listed below. Historical fiction may have one or more of these elements.

- The story is set in the past.
- The plot includes events or problems from that time.
- Characters act the way people of that time would have acted.
- Details relating to clothing, homes, speech, modes of transportation, or tools are correct for that time and place and help make the story more realistic.
- Though the story is made up, the characters may include real people, and the plot may include actual events.

About the Author

FRED GIPSON wrote the famous book *Old Yeller*, from which "Old Yeller and the Bear" was excerpted. Gipson was born in Texas, and the hills surrounding his home provided the setting for many of his novels. He dedicated his book *Old Yeller* to his parents, who told him countless tales of Texas frontier dogs.

Old Yeller was selected as a Newbery Honor Book and won several other awards including the Young Reader's Choice Award and the Maggie Award for Western Books. It was later made into a movie.

Students can read more about Fred Gipson on page 473 of the ***Student Anthology.***

Other Books by Fred Gipson:

- *The Trail-Driving Rooster*
- *The Home Place*
- *Recollection Creek*

About the Illustrator

JENNIFER HEYD WHARTON has earned recognition as one of the best-known artists in Maryland. She graduated with honors from Moore College of Art. Wharton's work has appeared in children's books, newspapers, magazines, and galleries. Her paintings have won numerous awards from several art societies in the United States.

Students can read more about Jennifer Heyd Wharton on page 473 of the ***Student Anthology.***

Other Books Illustrated by Jennifer Heyd Wharton:

- *Chesapeake Bay Walk*
- *Broken Wings Will Fly*
- *First Sail*

Inquiry Connections

A major aim of ***Open Court Reading*** is knowledge building. Because inquiry is at the root of knowledge building, students are encouraged to investigate topics and questions within each selection that relate to the unit theme.

In the late 1800s, men who worked on cattle ranches were required to be away from home for long periods of time as they drove cattle to key railroad transportation centers in places such as Abilene, Dodge City, and Wichita, Kansas. Frontier women and children, frequently forced to manage their homesteads alone, had to be brave and self-reliant.

Key concepts explored are:

- Pioneers of the American West relied on dogs not only as trusted pets, but also for protection against such dangers as attacks by wild animals.
- Life on the rugged and dangerous frontier was filled with challenges and excitement.

Before reading the selection

- point out that students may post a question, concept, word, illustration, or object on the Concept/Question Board at any time during the course of their unit investigation. Be sure that students include their names or initials on the items they post so that others will know whom to go to if they have an answer or if they wish to collaborate on a related activity.
- students should feel free to write an answer or a note on someone else's question or to consult the Board for ideas for their own investigations throughout the unit.
- encourage students to read about the American West at home and to bring in articles or pictures that are good examples to post on the Board.

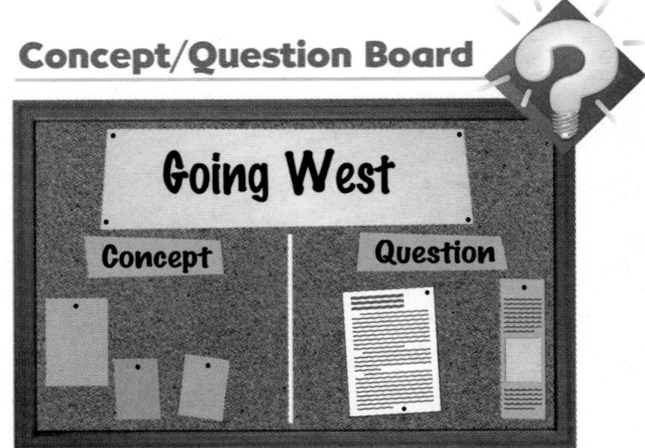

PROGRAM RESOURCES

Leveled Practice

Reteach
Pages 160–165

Challenge
Pages 141–145

English Learner Support Activities

Intervention Workbook

Leveled Classroom Library*

Encourage students to read at least 30 minutes daily outside of class. Have them read books from the ***Leveled Classroom Library,*** which supports the unit theme and helps students develop their vocabulary by reading independently.

Boom Town

BY SONIA LEVITIN. ORCHARD BOOKS, 1998.

Dedicated to a real-life girl who baked $11,000 worth of pies in a small iron skillet, this tale describes how a town grows up around a young girl's bakery, while her father vainly pans for gold. **(Easy)**

Black-Eyed Susan

BY JENNIFER ARMSTRONG. KNOPF, 1995.

While her father builds their homestead, Susie's efforts to cure her mother's prairie loneliness are helped by the arrival of some visitors to the isolated sod house. **(Average)**

Caddie Woodlawn

BY CAROL RYRIE BRINK. ALADDIN, 1990.

Based on the author's grandmother, the real Caddie Woodlawn, this is the story of a misunderstood prairie girl who is friends with the Indians and loves to play outside. (Newbery Medal Winner) **(Advanced)**

* These books, which all support the unit theme Going West, are part of a 36-book ***Leveled Classroom Library*** available for purchase from SRA/McGraw-Hill. Note: Teachers should preview any trade books for appropriateness in their classrooms before recommending them to students.

SRA TECHNOLOGY

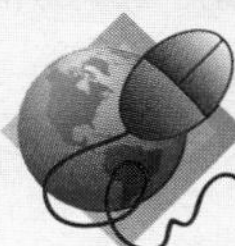

Web Connections

- Going West Web site
- Online Professional Development
- Online Assessment

CD-ROMs

- Research Assistant
- Ultimate Writing and Creativity Center
- Teacher Resource Library

Audiocassettes/CDs

- Listening Library: Going West

Computer Skills

- TechKnowledge

Materials are available through SRA/McGraw-Hill.

UNIT 5 Lesson 5

Old Yeller and the Bear

LESSON PLANNER

Suggested Pacing: 3–5 days

	DAY I	DAY 2
	DAY I	DAY 2
1 Preparing to Read **Materials** ■ Routine Card 1	**Word Knowledge,** p. 462K ■ Synonyms ■ /j/ Sound Spelled *dge* or *g* ■ /er/ Sound Spelled *er, ir,* or *ur* ■ Endings *-ed* and *-ing* **About the Words and Sentences,** p. 462K	**Developing Oral Language,** p. 462L
2 Reading & Responding **Materials** ■ Student Anthology, pp. 462–473 ■ Reading Transparencies 44, 54, 59, 63 ■ Routine Card 1 ■ Comprehension and Language Arts Skills, pp. 160–161 ■ Program Assessment ■ Home Connection, pp. 71–72 ■ Inquiry Journal, p. 114 ■ Unit 5 Assessment, pp. 18–21 ■ Reteach, pp. 160–161 ■ Challenge, p. 141	**Build Background,** p. 462M **Preview and Prepare,** pp. 462M–462N **Selection Vocabulary,** p. 462N **Reading Recommendations,** pp. 462O–462P **Student Anthology,** pp. 462–471 First Read ✓ **Comprehension Strategies** ■ Monitoring and Clarifying, pp. 462, 464 ■ Summarizing, pp. 464, 468, 470 ■ Predicting, pp. 464, 466, 468, 470 **Discussing Strategy Use,** p. 470 **Discussing the Selection,** p. 471A	**Student Anthology,** pp. 462–471 Second Read **Comprehension Skills** ■ Making Inferences, pp. 463, 465, 467 ■ Author's Point of View, pp. 469, 471 **Supporting the Reading,** pp. 471C–471D ■ Making Inferences ✓ **Checking Comprehension,** p. 471
Inquiry **Materials** ■ Student Anthology, pp. 462–473 ■ Inquiry Journal, pp. 132–134 ■ Research Assistant	**Investigation** ■ Investigating Concepts Beyond the Text, p. 473A	**Investigation** ■ Concept/Question Board, p. 473B
3 Language Arts **Materials** ■ Comprehension and Language Arts Skills, pp. 162–165 ■ Language Arts Handbook ■ Language Arts Transparency 18 ■ Spelling and Vocabulary Skills, pp. 122–125 ■ Student Anthology ■ Student Writing and Research Center ■ Writer's Workbook, pp. 94–97 ■ Unit 5 Assessment, pp. 38–39 ■ Reteach, pp. 162–165 ■ Challenge, pp. 142–145	**Word Analysis** ✓■ Spelling: Words with *-ed* or *-ing* Pretest, p. 473F **Writing Process Strategies** ■ Personal Writing: Friendly Letter, Getting Ideas, p. 473F **English Language Conventions** ■ Mechanics: Commas, p. 473F	**Word Analysis** ■ Spelling: Words with *-ed* or *-ing*, p. 473G ■ Vocabulary: Simile, p. 473G **Writing Process Strategies** ■ Personal Writing: Friendly Letter, Prewriting, p. 473G **English Language Conventions** ■ Mechanics: Commas, p. 473G

✓ Informal Assessment Available ✓ Formal Assessment Available

DAY 2 continued	DAY 3	
DAY 3	**DAY 4**	**DAY 5**
General Review	**General Review**	**Review Word Knowledge**
Student Anthology, pp. 472–473 ✓■ Concept Connections ■ Meet the Author/Illustrator	**Review Selection Vocabulary,** p. 471B **Literary Elements,** p. 471E ■ Plot	✓ **Lesson Assessment** ■ *Unit 5 Assessment:* Lesson Assessment, "Old Yeller and the Bear," pp. 18–21 **Home Connection,** p. 471B **Social Studies Connection,** p. 471F ■ Pioneer Life
Investigation ✓■ Establishing Investigation Problems, p. 473C	**Supporting the Investigation,** p. 473D ■ Time Lines	**Investigation** ■ Unit Investigation Continued ■ Update Concept/Question Board
Word Analysis ■ Spelling: Words with *-ed* or *-ing*, p. 473H ■ Vocabulary: Simile, p. 473H **Writing Process Strategies** ■ Personal Writing: Friendly Letter, Drafting, p. 473H ■ Writer's Craft: Tone of a Personal Letter, p. 473H **English Language Conventions** ✓■ Mechanics: Commas, p. 473H	**Word Analysis** ■ Spelling: Words with *-ed* or *-ing*, p. 473I ■ Vocabulary: Simile, p. 473I **Writing Process Strategies** ■ Personal Writing: Friendly Letter, Revising, p. 473I **English Language Conventions** ✓■ Listening, Speaking, Viewing Interacting: Group Discussions, p. 473I	**Word Analysis** ✓■ Spelling: Words with *-ed* or *-ing*, Final Test, p. 473J ✓■ Vocabulary: Simile, p. 473J **Writing Process Strategies** ✓■ Personal Writing: Friendly Letter, Editing/Proofreading and Publishing, p. 473J **English Language Conventions** ✓■ Penmanship: Joining with *Y* and *w*, p. 473J

Below are suggestions for differentiating instruction. These are the same skills shown on the Lesson Planner; however, these pages provide extra practice opportunities or enriching activities to meet the varied needs of students.

WORKSHOP

Differentiating Instruction

Teacher: Individual and Small Group Instruction

Spend time each day with individuals and small groups to individualize instruction. Each day:

- preteach students who need help with the next lesson.
- reteach students who need to solidify their understanding of content previously taught.
- listen to students read to check their fluency.
- hold writing and inquiry conferences.

Use the following program components to support instruction:

- ***Reteach*** with students who need a bit more practice.
- ***Intervention*** with students who exhibit a lack of understanding of the lesson concepts.
- ***English Learner Support*** with students who need language help.

Student: Independent Activities

Students can work alone, with a partner, or in small groups on such activities as:

- Review sound/spellings
- Partner Reading
- Practice fluency
- Independent Reading
- Reading Roundtable
- Concept vocabulary
- Selection vocabulary
- Writing in progress
- Conference
- Language Arts
- ***Challenge*** Activities
- Inquiry and Investigation Activities
- Listening Library

Professional Development

Teacher Resource Library CD-ROMs or ***Online Professional Development*** provides courses that help you better understand the Workshop/Intervention instruction in ***Open Court Reading.*** For more information about this program, visit SRAonline.com.

	DAY 1
Word Knowledge	**Teacher Directed** ■ Teach meanings of blended words ■ Reading Words and About the Words, ***Intervention Guide,*** p. 265
Fluency	**Independent Activities** ■ Self-test fluency rate
Comprehension	**Teacher Directed** ■ Preteach "Old Yeller and the Bear," ***Intervention Guide,*** pp. 266–267 ■ Intervention Selection 1, ***Intervention Guide,*** pp. 267–268 ■ ***English Learner Support Guide,*** pp. 424–427 **Independent Activities** ■ Record response to selection in Writer's Notebook ■ Browse ***Leveled Classroom Library*** ■ ***Listening Library Audiocassette/CD*** ■ Add vocabulary in Writer's Notebook
Inquiry	**Independent Activities** ■ Concept/Question Board ■ Explore OCR Web site for theme connections ■ Problems in the American West, ***Inquiry Journal,*** pp. 132–133
Language Arts	**Teacher Directed** ■ Seminar: Select a Topic for a Friendly Letter, p. 473F ■ Coordinating Conjunctions, ***Intervention Guide,*** p. 270 **Independent Activities** ■ Commas with Independent and Subordinate Clauses, ***Comprehension and Language Arts Skills,*** pp. 162–163

DAY 2	DAY 3	DAY 4	DAY 5
Teacher Directed ▪ Developing Oral Language, ***Intervention Guide,*** p. 265	**Teacher Directed** ▪ Dictation and Spelling, ***Intervention Guide,*** pp. 265–266	**Independent Activities** ▪ Add words to Word Bank	**Teacher Directed** ▪ General review as necessary
Independent Activities ▪ Oral reading of "Old Yeller and the Bear"	**Independent Activities** ▪ Partner read "Old Yeller and the Bear"	**Independent Activities** ▪ Fluency rate check ▪ Reread "Old Yeller and the Bear"	**Teacher Directed** ▪ Repeated Readings, ***Intervention Guide,*** p. 269 **Independent Activities** ▪ Fluency rate check
Teacher Directed ▪ Preteach "Old Yeller and the Bear," ***Intervention Guide,*** pp. 266–267 ▪ Reread Intervention Selection 1 ▪ Teach Comprehension Strategies, ***Intervention Guide,*** p. 268 ▪ ***English Learner Support Guide,*** pp. 427–429 ▪ Review Making Inferences ▪ Making Inferences, ***Reteach,*** pp. 160–161 **Independent Activities** ▪ Making Inferences • ***Comprehension and Language Arts Skills,*** pp. 160–161 • ***Challenge,*** p. 141 • Challenge Tip, p. 465 ▪ Choose ***Leveled Classroom Library*** book ▪ ***English Learner Support Activities,*** p. 62	**Teacher Directed** ▪ Teach Intervention Selection 2, ***Intervention Guide,*** pp. 268–269 ▪ ***English Learner Support Guide,*** pp. 429–431 ▪ Discuss Concept Connections, p. 470 **Independent Activities** ▪ Read ***Leveled Classroom Library*** book ▪ ***Listening Library Audiocassette/CD*** ▪ Supporting the Reading: Link to Writing, p. 471D ▪ Recording Concept Information, ***Inquiry Journal,*** p. 114	**Teacher Directed** ▪ Teach Comprehension Strategies, ***Intervention Guide,*** p. 269 ▪ Reread Intervention Selection 2 ▪ ***English Learner Support Guide,*** pp. 432–434 **Independent Activities** ▪ Read ***Leveled Classroom Library*** book ▪ Literary Elements: Independent Practice, p. 471E	**Teacher Directed** ▪ Reading Roundtable ▪ ***English Learner Support Guide,*** pp. 434–435 **Independent Activities** ▪ Read ***Leveled Classroom Library*** book ▪ Social Studies Connection, p. 471F ▪ ***English Learner Support Activities,*** p. 63
Independent Activities ▪ Concept/Question Board ▪ Explore OCR Web site for theme connections	**Independent Activities** ▪ Concept/Question Board ▪ Use ***Research Assistant*** to continue investigation	**Independent Activities** ▪ Concept/Question Board ▪ Establishing Investigation Plans, ***Inquiry Journal,*** p. 134	**Independent Activities** ▪ Concept/Question Board ▪ Supporting the Investigation: Independent Practice, p. 473D ▪ Continue research
Teacher Directed ▪ Coordinating Conjunctions, ***Intervention Guide,*** p. 270 ▪ Spelling: Word Sort, p. 473G ▪ Seminar: Plan a Friendly Letter, p. 473G ▪ Commas with Independent and Subordinate Clauses, ***Reteach,*** p. 163 **Independent Activities** ▪ Vocabulary: Similes, ***Spelling and Vocabulary Skills,*** pp. 122–123 ▪ Commas with Independent and Subordinate Clauses, ***Challenge,*** p. 143	**Teacher Directed** ▪ Seminar: Draft a Friendly Letter, p. 473H ▪ Writing Activity, ***Intervention Guide,*** pp. 270–271 ▪ Vocabulary: Similes, ***Reteach,*** p. 163 **Independent Activities** ▪ Spelling: Words with *-ed* and *-ing,* ***Spelling and Vocabulary Skills,*** p. 124 ▪ Vocabulary: Similes, ***Challenge,*** p. 143 ▪ Writer's Craft: Tone of a Personal Letter, ***Comprehension and Language Arts Skills,*** pp. 164–165	**Teacher Directed** ▪ Seminar: Revise a Friendly Letter, p. 473I ▪ Writing Activity, ***Intervention Guide,*** pp. 270–271 ▪ Spelling: Words with *-ed* and *-ing,* ***Reteach,*** p. 162 **Independent Activities** ▪ Spelling: Words with *-ed* and *-ing* • ***Spelling and Vocabulary Skills,*** p. 125 • ***Challenge,*** p. 142	**Teacher Directed** ▪ Seminar: Edit and Publish a Friendly Letter, p. 473J ▪ Writer's Craft: Tone of a Personal Letter, ***Reteach,*** p. 165 **Independent Activities** ▪ Penmanship: Cursive Letters *Y* and *w*, p. 473J ▪ Writer's Craft: Tone of a Personal Letter, ***Challenge,*** p. 145

ASSESSMENT

Formal Assessment Options

Use these summative assessments along with your informal observations to assess student progress.

Name ______ Date ______ Score ______

UNIT 5 Going West • Lesson 5

Old Yeller and the Bear

Read the following questions carefully. Then completely fill in the bubble of each correct answer. You may look back at the story to find the answer to each of the questions.

1. What is Travis doing when Arliss meets the bear?
   - ● splitting rails
   - Ⓑ chopping firewood
   - Ⓒ repairing the fence
2. This story was written
   - ● in the first-person
   - Ⓑ in the second-person
   - Ⓒ in the third-person

Read the following questions carefully. Use complete sentences to answer the questions.

3. What does Arliss do that upsets his mother?
   Arliss upsets his mother by bringing home animals of every kind.
4. How does Mama treat Arliss's hands after the fish "fins" him?
   She treats Arliss's hands by wrapping them in a poultice of mashed-up prickly-pear root to draw out the poison.
5. What does Travis say the yeller dog will do to Arliss?
   Travis says that the yeller dog will make the biggest liar in Texas out of Arliss.

LESSON ASSESSMENT

18 Unit 5 • Lesson 5 *Old Yeller and the Bear* • Unit 5 Assessment

Unit 5 Assessment p. 18

Old Yeller and the Bear *(continued)*

6. Why didn't Arliss's family worry very much when they heard Arliss scream?
   Arliss was a screamer by nature, and he screamed all the time.
7. When Travis heard Arliss scream a second time, how did Travis know Arliss was in trouble?
   Travis knew Arliss was in trouble because the scream was loud and frantic.
8. Why didn't Travis recognize the whimpering and crying as coming from Arliss?
   Travis didn't recognize it because the whimpering and crying were coming from a bear cub, not Arliss.

Read the following questions carefully. Then completely fill in the bubble of each correct answer.

9. In the story, Travis plans to
   - ● hit the bear with his axe
   - Ⓑ let the bear and Old Yeller fight
   - Ⓒ get a gun and shoot the bear
10. At the end of the story, it seems as if
    - Ⓐ the she bear wanted to be friends
    - Ⓑ Mama was annoyed at Travis
    - ● Old Yeller thought he had been playing

LESSON ASSESSMENT

Unit 5 Assessment • *Old Yeller and the Bear* Unit 5 • Lesson 5 19

Unit 5 Assessment p. 19

Old Yeller and the Bear *(continued)*

Read the questions and statements below. Use complete sentences in your answers.

Linking to the Concepts Like many pioneers, Travis's family didn't have anyone to turn to when trouble occurred. They had to take care of things themselves. Do you think you could have lived as the pioneers did? Why do you think so?

Answers will vary. Accept all reasonable answers.

Personal Response Travis says that Mama is partly responsible for Arliss's trouble with the bear. Do you agree with him? Why?

Answers will vary. Accept all reasonable answers.

LESSON ASSESSMENT

20 Unit 5 • Lesson 5 *Old Yeller and the Bear* • Unit 5 Assessment

Unit 5 Assessment p. 20

Old Yeller and the Bear *(continued)*

Vocabulary

Read the following questions carefully. Then completely fill in the bubble of each correct answer.

1. Mama reminds Travis that he used to tell some **whoppers**. What does she mean?
   - Ⓐ Travis used to talk all the time.
   - ● Travis used to tell tales.
   - Ⓒ Travis used to throw tantrums.
2. Mama found a tangled-up mess of grasshoppers. **Tangled-up** means
   - ● mixed up and stuck together
   - Ⓑ stitched together tightly
   - Ⓒ folded into a neat bundle
3. Arliss told so many big yarns. In this sentence, a **yarn** is
   - Ⓐ a woolen string
   - ● a made-up story
   - Ⓒ a long rope for trapping
4. Little Arliss's second scream was more frantic than the first. **Frantic** means
   - Ⓐ strange and unusual
   - Ⓑ full of laughing and teasing
   - ● worried and afraid
5. When Mama yells, "Hurry, son! Run!" Travis becomes spooked. Another word for **spooked** is
   - Ⓐ angry
   - ● scared
   - Ⓒ fierce

LESSON ASSESSMENT

Unit 5 Assessment • *Old Yeller and the Bear* Unit 5 • Lesson 5 21

Unit 5 Assessment p. 21

Name ______ Date ______ Score ______

UNIT 5 Going West • Lesson 5 *Old Yeller and the Bear*

Spelling Pretest: Words with *-ed* and *-ing*

Fold this page back on the dotted line. Take the Pretest. Then correct any word you misspelled by crossing out the word and rewriting it next to the incorrect spelling.

1.	______	1.	whispering
2.	______	2.	pulled
3.	______	3.	propped
4.	______	4.	shopping
5.	______	5.	wagged
6.	______	6.	planned
7.	______	7.	waited
8.	______	8.	handling
9.	______	9.	followed
10.	______	10.	gardening
11.	______	11.	paying
12.	______	12.	stepping
13.	______	13.	crawling
14.	______	14.	tracing
15.	______	15.	weeding
16.	______	16.	captured
17.	______	17.	catching
18.	______	18.	ached
19.	______	19.	poured
20.	______	20.	scrambling

LESSON ASSESSMENT

38 Unit 5 • Lesson 5 *Spelling Pretest: Words with -ed and -ing* • Unit 5 Assessment

Unit 5 Assessment p. 38

Name ______ Date ______ Score ______

UNIT 5 Going West • Lesson 5 *Old Yeller and the Bear*

Spelling Final Test: Words with *-ed* and *-ing*

Look for the underlined word that is spelled wrong. Fill in the bubble of the line with the misspelled word.

1. Ⓐ Be prepared for an emergency.
   Ⓑ The dog wagged his tail.
   ● The story of Anne Frank is inspireing.
   Ⓓ Correct as is.
2. Ⓕ The files have been erased.
   Ⓖ We planned for over 100 guests.
   Ⓗ Use transparent paper for tracing the picture.
   ● Correct as is.
3. ● We were discouraged from steping in mud.
   Ⓑ The lost dog followed us up the street.
   Ⓒ An electrician repaired the television.
   Ⓓ Correct as is.
4. Ⓕ Nothing was spared after the flood.
   ● He thinks he is ketching a cold.
   Ⓗ The truck pulled out in front of us.
   Ⓙ Correct as is.
5. Ⓐ Galileo faced persecution for his ideas.
   ● Shipping and handleing costs ten dollars.
   Ⓒ Women waited many years to get to vote.
   Ⓓ Correct as is.
6. Ⓕ Gardening is a nice, relaxing hobby.
   Ⓖ Wear gloves when you are weeding.
   ● Those scissors are meant for cuting wire.
   Ⓙ Correct as is.
7. Ⓐ The crew poured salt on the icy roads.
   ● She is paing rent and utilities.
   Ⓒ His heart ached when he said goodbye.
   Ⓓ Correct as is.
8. ● The sign was proped up against the door.
   Ⓖ The friends were caught whispering in class.
   Ⓗ In the book, Frankenstein created a monster.
   Ⓙ Correct as is.
9. Ⓐ The mayor is declaring this a holiday.
   Ⓑ Pollution is robbing us of clean air.
   ● The grocery shoping must be done soon.
   Ⓓ Correct as is.
10. Ⓕ A baby may be crawling at six months.
    Ⓖ French nobles were captured and jailed.
    Ⓗ Scrambling eggs requires a whisk.
    ● Correct as is.

LESSON ASSESSMENT

Unit 5 Assessment • *Spelling Final Test: Words with* -ed, *and* -ing Unit 5 • Lesson 5 39

Unit 5 Assessment p. 39

Online Assessment for ***Open Court Reading*** helps teachers differentiate classroom instruction based on students' scores from the weekly and end-of-unit assessments. It provides exercises best suited to meet the needs of each student. For more information visit SRAonline.com.

Informal Comprehension Strategies Rubrics

Predicting

- The student makes predictions about what the text is about.
- The student updates predictions during reading, based on information in the text.

Summarizing

- The student paraphrases text, reporting main ideas and a summary of what is in text.
- The student decides which parts of the text are important in his or her summary.
- The student draws conclusions from the text.
- The student makes global interpretations of the text, such as recognizing the genre.

Monitoring and Clarifying

- The student notes characteristics of the text, such as whether it is difficult to read or whether some sections are more challenging or more important than others.
- The student shows awareness of whether he or she understands the text and takes appropriate action, such as rereading, in order to understand the text better.
- The student rereads to reconsider something presented earlier in the text.
- The student recognizes problems during reading, such as a loss of concentration, unfamiliar vocabulary, or lack of sufficient background knowledge to comprehend the text.

Research Rubrics

During Workshop, assess students using the rubrics below. The rubrics range from 1–4 in most categories, with 1 being the lowest score. Record each student's score on the inside back cover of his or her ***Inquiry Journal.***

Finding Needed Information

1 Collects information loosely related to the topic.

2 Collects information clearly related to the topic.

3 Collects information helpful in advancing on a research problem.

4 Collects problem-relevant information from varied sources and notices inconsistencies and missing pieces.

5 Collects useful information, paying attention to the reliability of sources and reviewing information critically.

Objectives

- Students recognize synonyms to help them determine meaning and increase vocabulary.
- Students recognize and read words with the /j/ sound spelled ■*dge, ge,* and *gi_*.
- Students recognize and read words with the /er/ sound spelled *er, ir,* or *ur.*
- Students recognize and spell words with the endings *-ed* and *-ing.*

Materials

- Routine Card 1

Routine Card
Refer to Routine 1 for the Reading the Words and Sentences procedure.

Teacher Tip SYLLABICATION To help students blend words and build fluency, demonstrate syllabication using decodable multisyllabic words in the word lines.

lit • tle	loud • er
a • fraid	fur • ther
dis • lodge	cap • tured
gen • er • al	catch • ing
al • le • giance	scram • bling
cop • per • head	

Differentiating Instruction

If...	Then...
Students need extra help with words containing the /er/ sound spelled *er, ir,* or *ur*	Use ***Intervention Guide,*** pages 265–266

WORD KNOWLEDGE

Word Knowledge

Reading the Words and Sentences

Use direct teaching to teach this Word Knowledge lesson. Write each word and sentence on the board. Have students read each word together. After all the words have been read, have students read each sentence in natural phrases. Use the suggestions in About the Words and Sentences to discuss the different features of the listed words.

Line 1:	hurt harm little small slim thin scared afraid
Line 2:	wedged dislodge charge general allegiance
Line 3:	copperhead first louder further
Line 4:	captured catching ached poured scrambling
Sentence 1:	The nurse said that it will only hurt at first.
Sentence 2:	The gem was wedged between two little rocks.
Sentence 3:	I knew danger was near because the scary noise got louder.
Sentence 4:	The boat workers' arms and shoulders ached after a day of catching shrimp in nets.

About the Words and Sentences

- **Line 1:** These word pairs are synonyms. Synonyms are words that have the same, or nearly the same, meaning. Have students say these words aloud. Then ask them to think of and explain other words that mean nearly the same as these words *(injure, tiny, skinny, frightened)*. Write these new synonyms on the board. Encourage students to use one of the words in a sentence. Replace the word with a synonym and discuss with students whether the meaning of the sentence changes.
- **Line 2:** These words have the /j/ sound spelled ■*dge, ge,* and *gi_*. Have students say these words aloud. Point out that the letter *g* sometimes has a /j/ sound when placed before *e* or *i*, as in *genious* and *ginger*. The /j/ sound can also be spelled ■*dge* as in *nudge*. Ask them to think of other words that have the /j/ sound. Explain that they will be learning more words with the /j/ sound spelled with ■*dge, ge,* or *gi_* throughout this lesson.
- **Line 3:** These words have the /er/ sound spelled *er, ir,* or *ur*. Have students pronounce these words aloud. Emphasize the /er/ sound in the words and ask students to repeat it after you. Point out that various combinations of letters produce the /er/ sound. Have students think of other words with the /er/ sound spelled *er, ir,* or *ur.*
- **Line 4:** The words in the last line review the word endings *-ed* and *-ing*.

- **Sentence 1:** Have students read the sentence aloud. Ask them to identify the words in the sentence that have the /er/ sound *(nurse, hurt, first)*. Ask students to say these words aloud, emphasizing the /er/ sound. Have students underline the different spellings of /er/.
- **Sentence 2:** Read the sentence aloud for students and point out the word *wedged.* Ask students to say the word aloud. Have students underline the spellings for /j/ *(■dge)*. Have students identify another word in the sentence that has the /j/ sound *(gem)*. Now have students read the sentence aloud.
- **Sentence 3:** Have students read the sentence aloud. Ask them to identify the word in the sentence that has both the /j/ sound and the /er/ sound *(danger)*. Ask students to look closely at each word in the sentence and identify words that have synonyms. If necessary, prompt students to think of synonyms for *danger, near, scary,* and *noise (risk, close, alarming, racket)*. Rewrite the sentence several times, substituting the synonyms students propose for the appropriate words. Discuss with students if and how the meaning of the sentence changes with each new substitution.
- **Sentence 4:** Have students notice the words in the last sentence that contain the endings *-ed* and *-ing.*

Developing Oral Language

Use direct teaching to review the words. Use one or all of the following activities.

- Have the student select a word and give clues to the other students about the word. *(I'm thinking of a word that describes something that is trapped.* ***Captured.****)* Have the students continue to do this until all the words on the board have been used.
- Point to one word in the lines above and select a student to read the word and use it in a sentence. Have other students extend the sentence using more words from the board.

WORD KNOWLEDGE

Teacher Tip BUILDING FLUENCY By this time in grade 5 students should be reading approximately 151 words per minute with fluency and expression. Gaining a better understanding of the spellings of sounds and structure of words will help students as they encounter unfamiliar words in their reading. As students read, you may notice that some need work in building fluency. During Workshop, have these students choose a section of the text (a minimum of 160 words) to read several times in order to build fluency.

Differentiating Instruction

If...	Then...
Students need extra fluency practice	Use the Intervention Selections activities, ***Intervention Guide,*** pages 467–469

Spelling
See pages 473F–473J for the corresponding spelling lesson for the endings *-ed* and *-ing.*

Objectives

- Students will understand the selection vocabulary before reading.
- Students will recognize synonyms to help them determine meaning and increase vocabulary.
- Students will recognize and read words with the /er/ sound spelled *er, ir,* or *or.*
- Students will recognize and read words with the /j/ sound spelled *dge* or *g.*
- Students will use the comprehension strategies Summarizing, Monitoring and Clarifying, and Predicting as they read the story the first time.
- Students will use the comprehension skills Making Inferences and Author's Point of View as they read the story the second time.

Materials

- Student Anthology, pp. 462–473
- Comprehension and Language Arts Skills, pp. 160–161
- Inquiry Journal, p. 114
- Listening Library
- Program Assessment
- Unit 5 Assessment, pp. 18–21
- Home Connection, pp. 71–72
- Routine Card 1

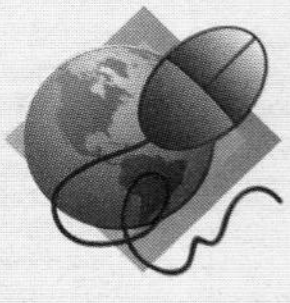

www.sra4kids.com
Web Connection
Students can use the connections to Going West in the Reading link of the SRA Web page for more background information about the American West.

Differentiating Instruction

If...	Then...
Students need extra help with the selection vocabulary	Use ***Intervention Guide,*** page 466

Build Background

Activate Prior Knowledge

Discuss the following with students to find out what they may already know about the selection and have already learned about the theme Going West.

- Preteach "Old Yeller and the Bear" by first determining students' prior knowledge of the frontier. Ask them, "What was life like for pioneers living on the frontier?"
- Have students discuss how they would feel about taking care of their families and homes for an extended period. Remind them that the settlers had to work the fields, hunt for food, and make their own clothing, candles, and soap. There was no electricity or machinery.

Background Information

The following information may help students understand the selection they are about to read.

- Explain to students that in the selection, Travis's father is absent because he is on a cattle drive. A cattle drive could take up to two months. Ranchers would herd the cattle to a "cow town" to be sold.
- Following the Civil War, Texas, which had fought for the Confederacy, was poor. Life in Texas was difficult and dangerous, and the people who populated it were characteristically rugged, hardworking, and courageous.
- Have the students discuss what they know about the genre of this selection. Refer to page 462A of the ***Teacher's Edition*** for elements of this selection's genre.

Preview and Prepare

Browse

- Have a student read aloud the title and the names of the author and illustrator. Demonstrate how to browse. Since this is a fiction piece, have the students browse only its first couple of pages, so that the ending will not be spoiled. This helps them to activate prior knowledge in a way that is relevant to the selection. Then discuss what they think this story might have to do with going west.

- Have the students search for clues that tell them something about the story. Also, have them look for any problems, such as unfamiliar words or long sentences, that they notice while reading. Use ***Reading Transparency 54*** to record their observations as they browse. For example, the word *snake* might be a clue that there is danger in the story. For the Problems column, students might say they don't know the meaning of the word *windies*. They might wonder what will happen to Old Yeller. To save time and model note taking, write students' observations as brief notes rather than complete sentences.
- As students prepare to read the selection, have them browse the Focus Questions on the first page of the selection. Tell them to keep these questions in mind as they read.

Set Purposes

Have students set their own purpose for reading this selection. You might suggest that they think about what life on the Plains must have been like for the settlers. Remind students that good readers have a purpose when they read. Let them know that they should make sure they know the purpose for reading whenever they read.

Selection Vocabulary

As students study vocabulary, they will use a variety of skills to determine the meaning of a word. These include context clues, word structure, and apposition. Students will apply these same skills while reading to clarify additional unfamiliar words.

Display ***Transparency 44*** before reading the selection to introduce and discuss the following words and their meanings.

tangled-up: mixed up and stuck together (page 462)
whopper: an exaggerated tale (page 465)
yarns: made-up stories (page 466)
frantic: very worried and afraid (page 467)
spooked: scared (page 471)

Have students read the words in the Word Box, stopping to blend any words that they have trouble reading. Demonstrate how to decode multisyllabic words by breaking them into syllables and blending the syllables. Then have students try. If the word is not decodable, give the students the pronunciation.

Have students read the sentences on ***Reading Transparency 44*** and use the skills of context, word structure (structural analysis), or apposition to figure out the meanings of the words. Be sure students explain which skill(s) they are using and how they figured out the meanings of the words.

Clues	Problems	Wonderings
Lizards Snakes Fiction	The word *finned* Splitting rails The word *windies*	What will happen to Old Yeller?

SRA Open Court Reading — Reading Transparency 54

Reading Transparency 54

Teacher Tip SELECTION VOCABULARY To help students decode words, divide them into the syllables shown below. The information following each word tells how students can figure out the meaning of each word from the sentences on the transparency.

tan • gled-up	context clues, word structure
whop • per	context clues
yarns	context clues
fran • tic	context clues
spooked	context clues, word structure

Routine Card
Refer to Routine 2 for the Selection Vocabulary procedure. Refer to Routine 3 for the Clues, Problems, and Wonderings procedure.

SRA Open Court Reading — Reading Transparency 44

tangled-up whopper yarns frantic spooked

1. Generally, it would be a tangled-up mess of grasshoppers and worms and praying bugs and little rusty tree lizards.
   The playful cat left the ball of yarn in a tangled-up pile on the floor.
2. She said that if he ever told a bigger whopper than the ones I used to tell, she had yet to hear it.
   We listened as Travis told a whopper of a tale about catching a two-foot-long catfish with his bare hands. We all laughed.
3. I think Mama had let him tell so many big yarns about his catching live game that he'd begun to believe them himself.
   My dad likes to tell yarns about his life as a small boy. We know that most of them aren't true.
4. Little Arliss's second scream, when it came, was louder and shriller and more frantic-sounding than the first.
   The woman was frantic when she could not find her purse. She raced around the store looking every place she had been.
5. That spooked me. Up till then, I'd been ready to tie into that bear myself. Now, suddenly, I was scared out of my wits again.
   Hearing that coyote howling really spooked me. I was afraid to go to sleep!

Reading Transparency 44

Students will enjoy using the ***Listening Library Audiocassette/CD*** and listening to the selection they are about to read. Encourage them to listen to the selection during Workshop. Have students discuss with each other and with you their personal listening preferences (for example, nonfiction, poetry, drama, and so on).

Routine Card
Refer to Routine 4 for the Reading the Selection procedure.

Differentiating Instruction

If...	Then...
Students need extra help with the comprehension strategy Monitoring and Clarifying	Use ***Intervention Guide,*** pages 268–269

Reading Recommendations

Oral Reading

This story's use of colorful, regional language makes it a good choice for expressive reading. Have students help each other with unfamiliar words and difficult ideas. As students read aloud, have them read expressively, at an appropriate pace, in natural phrases and chunks. Remind students to keep their audience in mind as they read aloud, adjusting volume as necessary and enunciating words clearly. Reading the selection with fluency and accuracy will help students comprehend the text. If students have trouble reading decodable words, have them break the words into sounds or syllables and then blend them together to read the word.

Have students make use of the reading strategies below to help them understand the selection. Have them stop reading periodically or wait until they have completed the selection to discuss the reading strategies. After the students have finished reading the selection, use the "Discussing the Selection" questions on page 471A to see if they understand what they have read.

Using Comprehension Strategies 

Comprehension strategy instruction allows students to become aware of how good readers read. Good readers constantly check their understanding as they are reading and ask themselves questions. In addition, skilled readers recognize when they are having problems and stop to use various comprehension strategies, to help them make sense of what they are reading.

During the first reading of "Old Yeller and the Bear," model and prompt the use of the following comprehension strategies. Take turns reading the story aloud with the students.

- **Predicting** causes readers to analyze information given about story events and characters in the context of how it may logically connect to the story's conclusion.
- **Summarizing** prompts readers to keep track of what they are reading and to focus their minds on important information.
- **Monitoring and Clarifying** prompts readers to track and immediately clear up unfamiliar words and ideas by using context, word structure, apposition, and outside resources. Stop and check that students understand when something is unclear.

As students read, they should be using a variety of strategies to help them understand the selection. Encourage students to use the strategies listed on the previous page as the class reads the story aloud. Do this by stopping at the points indicated by the numbers in magenta circles on the reduced student page and using a particular strategy. Students can also stop reading periodically to discuss what they have learned and what problems they may be having.

In Unit 5, students should be becoming more used to assuming responsibility for the use of comprehension strategies. Continue Teacher Modeling and Prompting as needed. Prompting provides a springboard for students to respond using the strategy mentioned in the prompt. The Student Sample is written in the language that students might use in their actual responses.

The Student Sample may be one of many possible student responses. Accept other responses that are reasonable and appropriate. If student responses indicate that the students do not understand the strategy, be ready to discuss their responses and to provide additional instruction. As students proceed through the lessons, teacher modeling and prompting of strategy use should become less and less necessary as students assume more responsibility for using strategies.

Building Comprehension Skills 

Revisiting or rereading a selection allows students to apply skills that give them a more complete understanding of the text. Some follow-up comprehension skills help students organize information. Others lead to deeper understanding—to "reading between the lines," as mature readers do. An extended lesson on comprehension skill Making Inferences can be found in the Supporting the Reading section on pages 471C–471D. This lesson is intended to give students extra practice with Making Inferences. However, the Teach portion of the lesson may be used at this time to introduce the comprehension skill to students.

- **Making Inferences (Review):** Readers make inferences by using information from the text along with personal knowledge or experience to gain a deeper understanding of characters and events.
- **Author's Point of View (Review):** Readers identify who is telling the story, whether it is the main character speaking from a first-person point of view or a narrator speaking from a third-person point of view.

Reading with a Purpose

Have students list ways that life on the plains challenged and endangered the new settlers in the Response Journal section of their Writer's Notebooks.

Teacher Tip COMPREHENSION SKILLS As students practice using comprehension skills to understand the text, encourage them to "think out loud" as they connect ideas. Other students might join in and offer their ideas, as well.

Differentiating Instruction

If...	Then...
Students need extra help with reading "Old Yeller and the Bear"	• Preread the selection during Workshop; use the ***Listening Library*** to give students a good reading model • Use ***English Learner Support Guide,*** pages 424–435 • Use ***Intervention Guide,*** pages 266–267

Teacher Tip ORAL READING FLUENCY AND RETELL FLUENCY SKILLS For extra practice in oral fluency, have individual students read aloud to you a selection they have previously read, either from a Decodable Book or a passage from the Student Anthology. Time each student for one minute. If the student reads more than 151 words correctly, have the student retell the selection he or she has just read. Use one prompt if the student seems to be stuck, and allow a maximum of one minute for the student to retell the story. If the student does not read more than 151 words correctly, have the student try reading from an easier selection, such as a Decodable Book from a prior grade level, to help you determine where the problem lies.

COMPREHENSION

Read pages 462–471.

Comprehension Strategies

Read the story aloud, taking turns with the students. Model and prompt the use of strategies for the students.

Teacher Modeling

1 Monitoring and Clarifying

Whenever we come across an unfamiliar word or idea, we should clarify it before reading on. Travis uses very colorful terms and words, like spasms*. By* spasms*, I think he means Mama gets angry, but the word* spasms *makes me picture her flailing around the room because she's so upset. There's probably a lot of colorful language in this story, so let's pay close attention to the words in context and see if we can figure out what they mean. Do any of you see words or phrases that need to be clarified?*

Word Knowledge

SCAFFOLDING The skills students are reviewing in Word Knowledge should help them in reading the story. This lesson focuses on synonyms. Synonyms will be found in boxes similar to this one throughout the selection.

Synonyms:

big large **little small** **mad angry**

Teacher Tip BACKGROUND Students may be interested to know that this story takes place in Texas, following the Civil War.

First Reading Recommendation

ORAL • CHORAL • SILENT

Focus Questions What kinds of animals does Arliss encounter on the frontier? How does he get himself into trouble with the bear? Who will rescue Arliss?

Old Yeller & the Bear

from ***Old Yeller***
by Fred Gipson
illustrated by Jennifer Heyd Wharton

Fourteen-year-old Travis lives with his family in Texas during the 1860s. Travis feels responsible for his mother and brother while his father is away on a long cattle drive. Travis thinks the big yellow dog that adopts his family is a useless nuisance until a bear shows him how wrong he is.

That Little Arliss! If he wasn't a mess! From the time he'd grown up big enough to get out of the cabin, he'd made a practice of trying to catch and keep every living thing that ran, flew, jumped, or crawled.

Every night before Mama let him go to bed, she'd make Arliss empty his pockets of whatever he'd captured during the day. Generally, it would be a tangled-up mess of grasshoppers and worms and praying bugs and little rusty tree lizards. One time he brought in a horned toad that got so mad he swelled out round and flat as a Mexican tortilla and bled at the eyes. Sometimes it was stuff like a young bird that had fallen out of its nest before it could fly, or a green-speckled spring frog or a striped water snake. And once he turned out of his pocket a wadded-up baby copperhead that nearly threw Mama into
1 spasms. We never did figure out why the snake hadn't bitten him, but Mama took no more chances on snakes. She switched Arliss hard for catching that snake. Then she made me spend better than a week, taking him out and teaching him to throw rocks and kill snakes.

462

Informal Assessment

Observe individual students as they read and use the Teacher Observation Log found in the ***Program Assessment Teacher's Edition*** to record anecdotal information about each student's strengths and weaknesses.

Differentiating Instruction

If...	Then...
English Learners need extra support with reading "Old Yeller and the Bear" and using the skill Making Inferences	Preteach ***Student Anthology*** pages 462–465 using Day 1 of the "Old Yeller and the Bear" lesson, found on ***English Learner Support Guide***, pages 424–427

463

Comprehension Skills

COMPREHENSION

Making Inferences

Remind the students that good readers use clues from the text and their own knowledge to better understand a character, thing, or event in a story. This is called *making inferences.*

Have the students reread page 462. Tell them to draw inferences about Arliss by asking the following questions:

- What is Arliss's relationship to Travis? *(He is Travis's little brother.)*
- How old is Arliss? *(Answers may vary. Some students might guess that Arliss is about five or six.)*

Have the students share aloud additional inferences about Arliss's character, based on the text and their own experiences with younger siblings or being his age.

Making Inferences

Introduced in Grade 2.

Scaffolded throughout Grades 3–5.

REINTRODUCED:	Unit 1, Lesson 2
REINFORCED:	Unit 2, Lesson 3
	Unit 3, Lesson 4
	Unit 5, Lesson 5
	Unit 6, Lesson 5
TESTED:	Unit 5 Assessment

Differentiating Instruction

Intervention Tip

MAKING INFERENCES Point out to students that making connections with the characters in a selection can help one make inferences about them. Ask students if any of them, like Travis, have a younger sibling. Encourage them to share with the class how they feel about their younger siblings, and use their experiences to infer what Travis's relationship with Arliss is like.

Second Reading Recommendation

ORAL • **SILENT**

COMPREHENSION

Comprehension Strategies

Prompting

2 Monitoring and Clarifying *I don't understand what Travis means by* finned *and* windy. *Who can clarify these terms?*

Student Sample

Monitoring and Clarifying *I think a "windy" is a big lie, where you tell a whole story that's made up, kind of like being "full of hot air." In the next paragraph, it says that Arliss's hands were bloody. I'll bet the fish cut him with its sharp fins, and that's why Travis said it "finned" him.*

Teacher Modeling

3 Summarizing *Let's sum up what we know about the characters, so that we'll remember who's who later on. Travis is taking care of his family while his father is on a cattle drive. Travis gets mad because Arliss boasts about catching animals, but their mother is just amused by it. What else might be important to remember as we read on?*

Prompting

4 Predicting *Making predictions will help us to focus on what we want to find out in the story. Who can predict what might happen to the characters in this selection?*

Student Sample

Predicting *In the introduction, it said that Travis would change his mind about the dog when the bear shows up. I predict that Arliss will get into trouble with the bear, and the dog will rescue him.*

That was all right with Little Arliss. If Mama wanted him to kill his snakes first, he'd kill them. But that still didn't keep him from sticking them in his pockets along with everything else he'd captured that day. The snakes might be stinking by the time Mama called on him to empty his pockets, but they'd be dead.

Then, after the yeller dog came, Little Arliss started catching even bigger game. Like cottontail rabbits and chaparral birds and a baby possum that sulled and lay like dead for the first several hours until he finally decided that Arliss wasn't going to hurt him.

Of course, it was Old Yeller that was doing the catching. He'd run the game down and turn it over to Little Arliss. Then Little Arliss could come in and tell Mama a big fib about how he caught it himself.

I watched them one day when they caught a blue catfish out of Birdsong Creek. The fish had fed out into water so shallow that his top fin was sticking out. About the time I saw it, Old Yeller and Little Arliss did, too. They made a run at it. The fish went scooting away toward deeper water, only Yeller was too fast for him. He pounced on the fish and shut his big mouth down over it and went romping to the bank, where he dropped it down on the grass and let it flop. And here came Little Arliss to fall on it like I guess he'd been doing everything else. The minute he got his hands
2 on it, the fish finned him and he went to crying.

464

DIFFERENTIATING INSTRUCTION

Intervention Tip

SUMMARIZING If students are having difficulty summing up, reread short passages within the section. At the end of each passage, have students write down important points to use in their summaries.

Informal Assessment

Use the Informal Comprehension Strategies Rubrics on page 462J to determine whether a student is using the strategies being taught.

But he wouldn't turn the fish loose. He just grabbed it up and went running and squawling toward the house, where he gave the fish to Mama. His hands were all bloody by then, where the fish had finned him. They swelled up and got mighty sore; not even a mesquite thorn hurts as bad as a sharp fish fin when it's run deep into your hand.

But as soon as Mama had wrapped his hands in a poultice of mashed-up prickly-pear root to draw out the poison, Little Arliss forgot all about his hurt. And that night when we ate the fish for supper, he told the biggest windy I ever heard about how he'd dived 'way down into a deep hole under the rocks and dragged that fish out and nearly got drowned before he could swim to the bank with it.

But when I tried to tell Mama what really happened, she wouldn't let me. "Now, this is Arliss's story," she said. "You let him tell it the way he wants to."

I told Mama then, I said: "Mama, that old yeller dog is going to make the biggest liar in Texas out of Little Arliss."

But Mama just laughed at me, like she always laughed at Little Arliss's big windies after she'd gotten off where he couldn't hear her. She said for me to let Little Arliss alone. She said that if he ever told a bigger whopper than the ones I used to tell, she had yet to hear it. 3

Well, I hushed then. If Mama wanted Little Arliss to grow up to be the biggest liar in Texas, I guessed it wasn't any of my business.

All of which, I figure, is what led up to Little Arliss's catching the bear. 4

465

Comprehension Skills

Making Inferences

Point out that there is a lot of information about the area that Travis and his family live in. Although nothing is completely described, it's possible to infer what the area is like.

- Have the students search for clues and make an inference about what the area looks like. Have students use the text to find any specific details about the setting along with any prior knowledge they might have about the state of Texas to make this inference. *(They may want to include the creek described on page 464.)*

Have them continue to make inferences as they read.

Word Knowledge

SCAFFOLDING The skills students are reviewing in Word Knowledge should help them in reading the story. This lesson focuses on words with the /er/ sound spelled *er, ir,* or *ur.* These words will be found in boxes similar to this one throughout the selection.

/er/ sound spelled;

er **her, whopper**

Teacher Tip **EXTENDING THE TEXT** Travis mentions a lot of different animals in this story. Some students might like to create a scrapbook showing the different animals mentioned. Suggest that they look in magazines for pictures and information about the animals described by Travis.

Challenge Tip

MAKING INFERENCES Have the students make up questions for each other that require making inferences to answer them.

COMPREHENSION

COMPREHENSION

Comprehension Strategies

Prompting

5 **Confirming Predictions** *Well, I see that one of our predictions about Arliss and the bear is being confirmed. Who can remember what it was?*

Student Sample

Confirming Predictions *I knew it! Arliss is in trouble. I'll bet he's stuck up a tree and that the bear is trying to grab him with his claws. I can't wait to find out.*

Word Knowledge

SCAFFOLDING The skills students are reviewing in Word Knowledge should help them in reading the story. This lesson focuses on words with the /j/ sound spelled *dge* or *g*. These words will be found in boxes similar to this one throughout the selection.

/j/ sound spelled:

dge **wedge**

Teacher Tip COMPREHENSION STRATEGIES Students should notice that comprehension strategies, once learned, come naturally and enhance the meaning and enjoyment of a selection. Encourage them to discuss with classmates the strategies they use during a lesson.

I think Mama had let him tell so many big yarns about his catching live game that he'd begun to believe them himself.

When it happened, I was down the creek a ways, splitting rails to fix up the yard fence where the bulls had torn it down. I'd been down there since dinner, working in a stand of tall slim post oaks. I'd chop down a tree, trim off the branches as far up as I wanted, then cut away the rest of the top. After that I'd start splitting the log.

I'd split the log by driving steel wedges into the wood. I'd start at the big end and hammer in a wedge with the back side of my axe. This would start a little split running lengthways of the log. Then I'd take a second wedge and drive it into this split. This would split the log further along and, at the same time, loosen the first wedge. I'd then knock the first wedge loose and move it up in front of the second one.

Driving one wedge ahead of the other like that, I could finally split a log in two halves. Then I'd go to work on the halves, splitting them apart. That way, from each log, I'd come out with four rails.

Swinging that chopping axe was sure hard work. The sweat poured off me. My back muscles ached. The axe got so heavy I could hardly swing it. My breath got harder and harder to breathe.

An hour before sundown, I was worn down to a nub. It seemed like I couldn't hit another lick. Papa could have lasted till past sundown, but I didn't see how I could. I shouldered my axe and started toward the cabin, trying to think up some excuse to tell Mama to keep her from knowing I was played clear out.

5 That's when I heard Little Arliss scream.

466

Differentiating Instruction

If...	Then...
English Learners need extra support with reading "Old Yeller and the Bear" and using the skill Making Inferences	Preteach ***Student Anthology*** pages 466–467 using Day 2 of the "Old Yeller and the Bear" lesson, found on ***English Learner Support Guide,*** pages 427–429

Well, Little Arliss was a screamer by nature. He'd scream when he was happy and scream when he was mad and a lot of times he'd scream just to hear himself make a noise. Generally, we paid no more mind to his screaming than we did to the gobble of a wild turkey.

But this time was different. The second I heard his screaming, I felt my heart flop clear over. This time I knew Little Arliss was in real trouble.

I tore out up the trail leading toward the cabin. A minute before, I'd been so tired out with my rail splitting that I couldn't have struck a trot. But now I raced through the tall trees in that creek bottom, covering ground like a scared wolf.

Little Arliss's second scream, when it came, was louder and shriller and more frantic-sounding than the first. Mixed with it was a whimpering crying sound that I knew didn't come from him. It was a sound I'd heard before and seemed like I ought to know what it was, but right then I couldn't place it.

467

Comprehension Skills

Making Inferences

Point out that sometimes characters in a story also make inferences.

- Have the students read page 467. What inference is Travis making? *(that Arliss is in real trouble)*

Ask students to identify the clues in the text that, as Travis explains, lead him to make this inference. *(Students may cite the fact that Arliss's scream was unlike any Travis had ever heard him make.)* Encourage students to put themselves in Travis's place and explain whether they would make the same inference Travis makes about Arliss's scream.

Word Knowledge

/er/ sound spelled:

er	**screamer, louder, shriller**
ir	**first**
ur	**nature**

Teacher Tip **BUILDING FLUENCY** As students read, you may notice that some need work in building fluency. During Workshop, have these students choose a section of text (a minimum of 160 words) to read several times in order to build fluency.

COMPREHENSION

Differentiating Instruction

English Learner Tip

CHARACTER STUDY Ask English Learners to write a list of words or phrases that describe Travis. Prompt by mentioning events or descriptions from the story. For example, "We know that Travis paid close attention to Arliss's safety. What words do we use to describe someone like Travis?" (*responsible, mature,* and so on)

COMPREHENSION

Comprehension Strategies

Teacher Modeling

6 Confirming Predictions *We were wrong when we predicted that Arliss would be treed by the bear. But Arliss is in trouble; he's about to drown, I think. Plus, where there's a baby bear cub, there's probably an angry mother bear somewhere. I think that Old Yeller will save Arliss somehow.*

As you read, decide whether or not you think the predictions are on target. Come up with your own prediction based on the information in the text. As you come up with predictions, let the group know what they are. Good readers are always making predictions as they read.

Prompting

7 Summarizing *Suddenly things are getting really exciting. To make sure that we remember all the important information, let's sum up what has happened since the action started to pick up. Who wants to volunteer?*

Student Sample

Summarizing *Travis was heading home after splitting rails for a fence when he heard Arliss scream. He ran as fast as he could and saw Arliss in a spring hole hanging onto the hind leg of a bear cub.*

Word Knowledge

/j/ sound spelled:

g charging, changing

Teacher Tip PREDICTING Students should sense from the increasing pace that something exciting is going to happen. Remind students that this is a cue for them to predict upcoming events.

Then, from way off to one side came a sound that I would have recognized anywhere. It was the coughing roar of a charging bear. I'd just heard it once in my life. That was the time Mama had shot and wounded a hog-killing bear and Papa had had to finish it off with a knife to keep it from getting her.

My heart went to pushing up into my throat, nearly choking off my wind. I strained for every lick of speed I could get out of my running legs. I didn't know what sort of fix Little Arliss had got himself into, but I knew that it had to do with a mad bear, which was enough.

The way the late sun slanted through the trees had the trail all cross-banded with streaks of bright light and dark shade. I ran through these bright and dark patches so fast that the changing light nearly blinded me. Then suddenly, I raced out into the open where I could see ahead. And what I saw sent a chill clear through to the marrow of my bones.

There was Little Arliss, down in that spring hole again. He was lying half in and half out of the water, holding onto the hind leg of a little black bear cub no bigger than a small coon. The bear cub was out on the bank, whimpering and crying and clawing the rocks with all three of his other feet, trying to pull away. But Little Arliss was holding on for all he was worth, scared now and screaming his head off. Too
6 scared to let go.

How the bear cub ever came to prowl close enough for Little Arliss to grab him, I don't know. And why he didn't turn on him and bite loose, I couldn't figure out, either. Unless he was like Little Arliss, too scared
7 to think.

468

Differentiating Instruction

If...	Then...
English Learners need extra linguistic support with reading "Old Yeller and the Bear" and using the skill Making Inferences	Preteach ***Student Anthology*** pages 468–469 using Day 3 of the "Old Yeller and the Bear" lesson, found on ***English Learner Support Guide,*** pages 429–431

But all of that didn't matter now. What mattered was the bear cub's mama. She'd heard the cries of her baby and was coming to save him. She was coming so fast that she had the brush popping and breaking as she crashed through and over it. I could see her black heavy figure piling off down the slant on the far side of Birdsong Creek. She was roaring mad and ready to kill.

And worst of all, I could see that I'd never get there in time!

Mama couldn't either. She'd heard Arliss, too, and here she came from the cabin, running down the slant toward the spring, screaming at Arliss, telling him to turn the bear cub loose. But Little Arliss wouldn't do it. All he'd do was hang with that hind leg and let out one shrill shriek after another as fast as he could suck in a breath.

Now the she bear was charging across the shallows in the creek. She was knocking sheets of water high in the bright sun, charging with her fur up and her long teeth bared, filling the canyon with that awful coughing roar. And no matter how fast Mama ran or how fast I ran, the she bear was going to get there first!

I think I nearly went blind then, picturing what was going to happen to Little Arliss. I know that I opened my mouth to scream and not any sound came out.

Then, just as the bear went lunging up the creek bank toward Little Arliss and her cub, a flash of yellow came streaking out of the brush.

469

Teacher Tip FLUENCY By this time in grade 5 good readers should be reading approximately 151 words per minute with fluency and expression. The only way to gain this fluency is through practice. Have students reread the selection to you and to one another during Workshop to help build fluency.

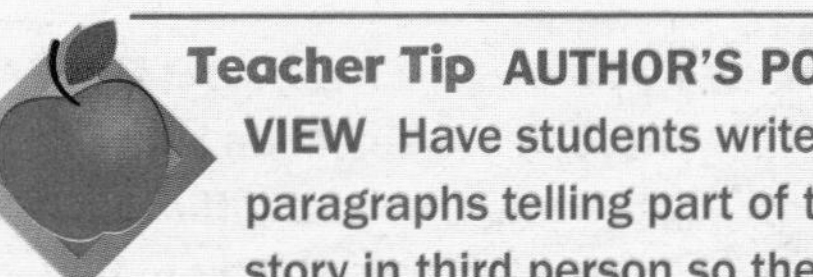

Teacher Tip AUTHOR'S POINT OF VIEW Have students write a few paragraphs telling part of the story in third person so they can observe the contrast. Have them also write several paragraphs in first person but from Arliss's perspective. Have students include things the reader might not have inferred after reading Travis' version of the story.

COMPREHENSION

Comprehension Skills

Author's Point of View

Have the students tell what they know about author's point of view. If necessary, remind them that an *author's point of view* is how the author chooses to tell a story. A *first-person narrative* is told through the eyes of a character in the story. A *third-person narrative* is told through the eyes of an outside narrator.

Ask the students what type of narrator is used in this story and how they know. *(This story is written in the first person, as if Travis were telling the story to the reader. The use of the pronouns* me, I, *and* my *are clues.)*

Have the students discuss how the story is made more interesting by having it told in Travis's words, and how it might be different if it were written in the third person. *(The students should note that we know how Travis is thinking and feeling.)*

Word Knowledge

/er/ sound spelled:

er	**over, matter**
ir	**Birdsong, first**
ur	**turn, fur**

Author's Point of View

Introduced in Grade 2.

Scaffolded throughout Grades 3–5.

REINTRODUCED:	Unit 1, Lesson 3
REINFORCED:	Unit 1, Lesson 5
	Unit 3, Lesson 1
	Unit 3, Lesson 4
	Unit 3, Lesson 5
TESTED:	Unit 5 Assessment

COMPREHENSION

Comprehension Strategies

Prompting

8 **Summarizing** *Who wants to summarize what happened while Old Yeller kept the bear away from Arliss?*

Student Sample

Summarizing *Travis pulled Arliss out of the water and threw him at Mama. Old Yeller fought the bear. Mama told Travis to run to the house. Once Travis was out of danger, Old Yeller ran to the house, too.*

Prompting

9 **Confirming Predictions** *We predicted what the outcome of this story would be. Can anyone tell me what the prediction was and whether it was confirmed?*

Student Sample

Confirming Predictions *We predicted that Old Yeller would save Arliss and our prediction was confirmed.*

Discussing Strategy Use

While they are reading the selection, have the students share any problems they encountered and tell what strategies they used.

- How did they make, confirm, and revise predictions as they read?
- How did they clarify confusing passages?
- How did they summarize the text?

Remind students that good readers use all of the strategies listed above and that they should be using them whenever they read. Make sure students explain how using the strategies helped them to better understand the selection. For example, "Predicting helped me pay close attention to what I was reading because I wanted to find out if my predictions were confirmed."

It was that big yeller dog. He was roaring like a mad bull. He wasn't one-third as big and heavy as the she bear, but when he piled into her from one side, he rolled her clear off her feet. They went down in a wild, roaring tangle of twisting bodies and scrambling feet and slashing fangs.

As I raced past them, I saw the bear lunge up to stand on her hind feet like a man while she clawed at the body of the yeller dog hanging to her throat. I didn't wait to see more. Without ever checking my stride, I ran in and jerked Little Arliss loose from the cub. I grabbed him by the wrist and yanked him up out of that water and slung him toward Mama like he was a half-empty sack of corn. I screamed at Mama. "Grab him, Mama! Grab him and run!" Then I swung my chopping axe high and wheeled, aiming to cave in the she bear's head with the first lick.

But I never did strike. I didn't need to. Old Yeller hadn't let the bear get close enough. He couldn't handle her; she was too big and strong for that. She'd stand there on her hind feet, hunched over, and take a roaring swing at him with one of those big front claws. She'd slap him head over heels. She'd knock him so far that it didn't look like he could possibly get back there before she charged again, but he always did. He'd hit the ground rolling, yelling his head off with the pain of the blow; but somehow he'd always roll to his feet. And here he'd come again, ready to tie into her for another round.

470

Teacher Tip EXTRA HELP Reread the selection with students who had difficulty understanding it. Continue modeling and prompting the use of strategies and skills as you read.

Differentiating Instruction

If...	Then...
English Learners need extra linguistic support with reading "Old Yeller and the Bear" and using the skill Making Inferences	Preteach ***Student Anthology*** pages 470–471 using Day 4 of the "Old Yeller and the Bear" lesson, found on ***English Learner Support Guide,*** pages 432–434

I stood there with my axe raised, watching them for a long moment. Then from up toward the house, I heard Mama calling: "Come away from there, Travis. Hurry, son! Run!"

That spooked me. Up till then, I'd been ready to tie into that bear myself. Now, suddenly, I was scared out of my wits again. I ran toward the cabin.

But like it was, Old Yeller nearly beat me there. I didn't see it, of course; but Mama said that the minute Old Yeller saw we were all in the clear and out of danger, he threw the fight to that she bear and lit out for the house. The bear chased him for a little piece, but at the rate Old Yeller was leaving her behind,
8 Mama said it looked like the bear was backing up.

But if the big yeller dog was scared or hurt in any way when he came dashing into the house, he didn't show it. He sure didn't show it like we all did. Little Arliss had hushed his screaming, but he was trembling all over and clinging to Mama like he'd never let her go. And Mama was sitting in the middle of the floor, holding him up close and crying like she'd never stop. And me, I was close to crying, myself.

Old Yeller, though, all he did was come bounding in to jump on us and lick us in the face and bark so loud that there, inside the cabin, the noise nearly made us deaf.

The way he acted, you might have thought that bear fight hadn't been anything more than a rowdy romp that we'd all taken part in for the fun of it. 9

471

Comprehension Skills

Author's Point of View

Remind students that this selection is told from the first-person point of view. Travis is the narrator, so readers get to hear the story the way he saw it happen. Explain to students that, in some ways, this perspective limits readers from seeing the whole picture.

Ask students to review Travis's account of the bear attack on pages 470–471 and look for places where Travis admits that he isn't sure what happened or what someone was thinking. You might ask students why they think the author chose to make Travis the narrator instead of Mama, Arliss, or an outside narrator.

Checking Comprehension

Ask students the following questions to check their comprehension of the story.

- Why was Travis's father away for so long? *(He was on a cattle drive.)*
- Why did Travis get so angry at Arliss when he told a *big windy? (Answers may vary; some students might note that Travis is trying to be very grown-up, while Arliss is childish.)*
- What did you learn about life in Texas in the 1860s? *(Answers may vary; some students might have been surprised by the wilderness and the wild animals around the house.)*
- How has this selection connected with your knowledge of the unit theme? *(Answers will vary—students should compare/contrast examples of life in the American West from this selection with their own experiences or past reading and use these connections to make a general statement about the unit theme.)*

COMPREHENSION

Differentiating Instruction

If...	Then...
English Learners have been participating in the "Old Yeller and the Bear" ***English Learner Support Guide*** activities	Review the selection and the skill Making Inferences using Day 5 of the "Old Yeller and the Bear" lesson, found on ***English Learner Support Guide,*** pages 434–435

Formal Assessment

See pages 18–21 in ***Unit 5 Assessment*** to test students' comprehension of "Old Yeller and the Bear."

Teacher Tip CONNECTING IDEAS Encourage students to tell about anything that they learned from their research that connects to this selection. You might also have them compare and contrast the descriptions of the American West in the unit selections they have read so far.

Routine Card
Refer to Routine 5 for the *handing-off process.*

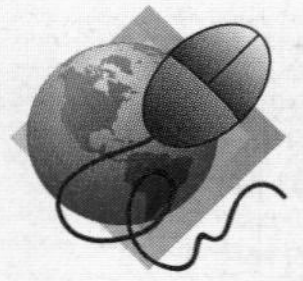

www.sra4kids.com
Web Connection
Some students may choose to conduct a computer search for additional books or information about the American West. Invite them to make a list of these books and sources of information to share with classmates and the school librarian. Check the Reading link of the SRA Web page for additional links to theme-related Web sites.

Clues	Problems	Wonderings
Lizards Snakes Fiction	The word *finned* Splitting rails The word *windies*	What will happen to Old Yeller?

Reading Transparency 54

Discussing the Selection

After the first read, the whole group discusses the selection and any personal thoughts, reactions, problems, or questions that it raises. To stimulate discussion, students can ask one another the kinds of questions that good readers ask themselves about a text: *How does it connect to going west? What have I learned that is new? What did I find interesting? What is important here? What was difficult to understand? Why would someone want to read this?* It is important for students to see you as a contributing member of the group.

Routine 5 To emphasize that you are part of the group, actively participate in the *handing-off process:* Raise your hand to be called on by the last speaker when you have a contribution to make. Point out unusual and interesting insights verbalized by students so that these insights are recognized and discussed. As the year progresses, students will take more and more responsibility for the discussion of selections.

Engage students in a discussion to determine whether they have grasped the following ideas:

- the early settlers faced a life full of danger and excitement
- families of cattle ranchers had to spend long periods of time alone while the men drove cattle to "cow towns"

During this time, have students return to the clues, problems, and wonderings that they noted during browsing to determine whether the clues were borne out by the selection, whether and how their problems were solved, and whether their wonderings were answered or deserve further discussion and exploration. Let the students decide which items deserve further discussion. Also have students return to the Focus Questions on the first page of the selection. Select a student to read the questions aloud, and have volunteers answer the questions. If students do not know the answers to the questions, have them return to the text to find the answers.

You may also want to review the elements of historical fiction with the students. Discuss with them how they can tell that "Old Yeller and the Bear" is historical fiction.

Have students break into small groups to discuss how the story reflects the theme. Groups can then share their ideas with the rest of the class.

Students may wish to record their personal responses to the selection. If they have learned something new about the American West or early settlers, encourage them to record this information.

Review Selection Vocabulary

Have students review the definitions of the selection vocabulary words that they write in the vocabulary section of their Writer's Notebook. Remind them that they discussed the meanings of these words before reading the selection. Students can use these definitions to study for the Vocabulary portion of their Lesson Assessment. Have them add to the Personal Dictionary section of their Writer's Notebook any other interesting words that they clarified while reading. Encourage students to refer to the selection vocabulary words throughout the unit. The words from the selection are:

spooked **tangled-up** **whopper** **yarns** **frantic**

Have students place the words under the appropriate endings in the Word Bank. Encourage the students to find other words related to the unit theme and add them to the Word Bank.

View Fine Art

This is ***Advice on the Prairie,*** by **William T. Ranney,** found on page 445 in the ***Student Anthology.*** In this picture, a man is giving advice to settlers on how to survive in this new frontier. Have students speculate as to what kinds of advice he is giving the settlers. Then have students think about what kinds of advice the Coates family might give to new settlers coming to live in the Texas wilderness.

Advice on the Prairie. **William T. Ranney.** Oil on canvas. 14 × 20 in. From the Collection of Gilcrease Museum, Tulsa.

Vaqueros in a Horse Corral. 1877. **James Walker.** Oil on canvas. 24 × 40 in. From the Collection of Gilcrease Museum, Tulsa.

445

Student Anthology p. 445

Home Connection

Distribute ***Home Connection,*** page 71. Encourage students to discuss "Old Yeller and the Bear" with their families. Students can work with their families to create new titles for the story based on its plot and important themes. ***Home Connection*** is also available in Spanish, page 72.

DIFFERENTIATING INSTRUCTION

If...	Then...
Students would benefit from repeated readings of "Old Yeller and the Bear" or the Intervention Selections	Use ***Intervention Guide,*** page 269

Old Yeller and the Bear

A message from ____________________

We have just finished reading "Old Yeller and the Bear," from the classic novel *Old Yeller.* In this chapter, Travis, a 14-year-old boy living with his family in Texas during the 1860s, describes how the family's big yellow dog battles a bear to save Travis's little brother, Arliss.

"Old Yeller and the Bear" is a very straightforward title for this selection. Ask your child to tell you more about the story, then have her or him use the space below to make a list of alternate titles. Together, choose the best title for this selection.

Encourage your child to share the new title with the class.

Next week's selection ***Bill Pickett: Rodeo-Ridin' Cowboy***

Your child will be studying the following vocabulary words in the upcoming week. Please review the meanings of these words with your child: **trek**—a long, slow journey; **ravage**—destroy; **brazen**—bold, fearless; **challenge**—something that may be difficult to do; **feisty**—frisky and brave; eager for excitement; **adventure**—a fun or exciting experience.

Please review with your child the spelling words for the upcoming week: happiest, wiser, slimmer, calmest, dishonest, container, scariest, daughter, easiest, saltier, cheaper, dirtiest, farthest, nearest, loser, loudest, feistiest, closer, greater, and harshest.

Home Connection • *Going West* Unit 5 • Lesson 5 71

Home Connection p. 71

Teacher Tip PRIOR KNOWLEDGE Some students might believe that prior knowledge is only what they have learned in school. Point out that using their prior knowledge includes thinking about their previous experiences and their feelings about things.

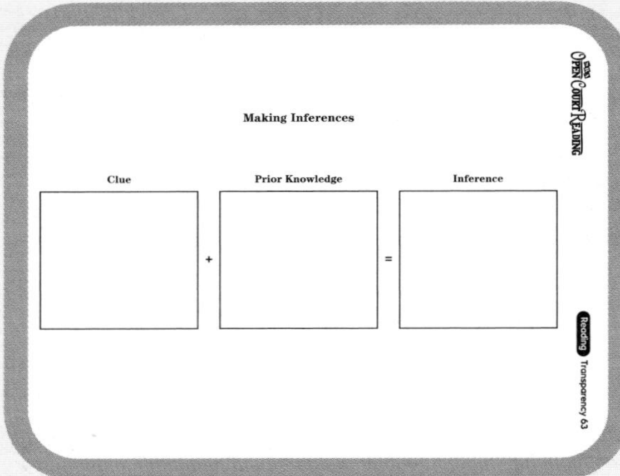

Reading Transparency 63

Supporting the Reading

Comprehension Strategies: Making Inferences

Teach Point out to students that authors do not always provide complete information about story elements. For example, an author might not always reveal how a character feels about something or why one event happened instead of another. Explain to students that authors do, however, provide clues or suggestions that readers can use to figure out these unexplained things. When readers make inferences about story elements, they use these clues in the text, along with their prior knowledge, to better understand a story element.

Guided Practice Use the chart on ***Reading Transparency 63*** to help students organize clues and their prior knowledge to make inferences about characters in "Old Yeller and the Bear." For example, under *Clue* you might list that Travis spends a long day mending a fence; under *Prior Knowledge* you might note that hard work like this is often done by adults; and under *Inference* you might say that Travis is a mature boy.

Have students suggest their own clues, describe their own prior knowledge, and then state the inferences they make based on these, and add them to the chart. Make sure students explain the thought process that led to their inferences.

Independent Practice Read through the **Focus** and **Identify** sections of the ***Comprehension and Language Arts Skills,*** page 160 with students. Guide students through the **Identify** portion, and help them come up with examples found in the selection. Then have students complete the **Practice** and **Apply** portions of the ***Comprehension and Language Arts Skills,*** pages 160–161, as homework.

Link to Writing Point out to students that it is a good idea for writers to leave some things unexplained in their works. Explain that when students write, they should remember to provide clues for readers to use to make inferences. Have students review previous writing assignments. They should identify places where readers could use clues to make inferences. If students find places in their writing where more clues would be helpful, encourage them to revise their writing to include more clues.

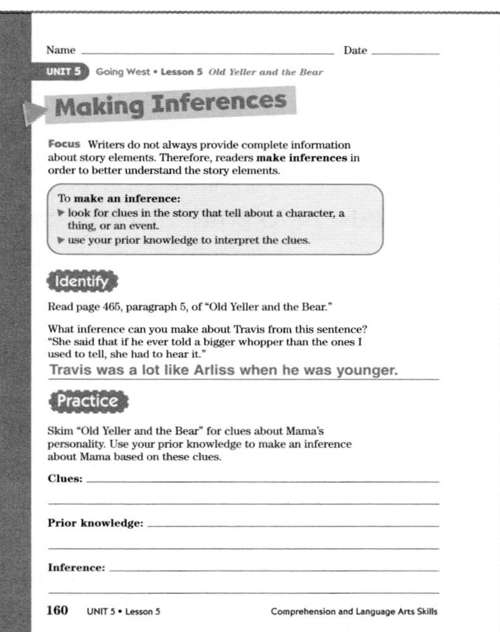

Name ______________________ Date ________

UNIT 5 Going West • Lesson 5 *Old Yeller and the Bear*

Making Inferences

Focus Writers do not always provide complete information about story elements. Therefore, readers **make inferences** in order to better understand the story elements.

To **make an inference:**
- look for clues in the story that tell about a character, a thing, or an event.
- use your prior knowledge to interpret the clues.

Identify

Read page 465, paragraph 5, of "Old Yeller and the Bear."

What inference can you make about Travis from this sentence? "She said that if he ever told a bigger whopper than the ones I used to tell, she had to hear it."

Travis was a lot like Arliss when he was younger.

Practice

Skim "Old Yeller and the Bear" for clues about Mama's personality. Use your prior knowledge to make an inference about Mama based on these clues.

Clues: ______________________

Prior knowledge: ______________________

Inference: ______________________

160 UNIT 5 • Lesson 5 Comprehension and Language Arts Skills

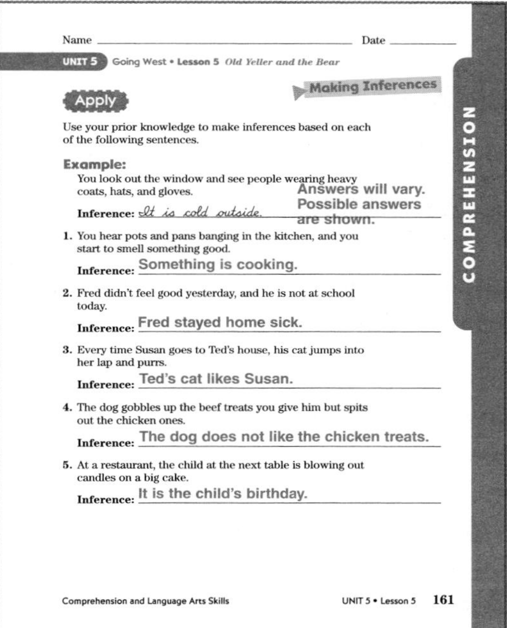

Name ______________________ Date ________

UNIT 5 Going West • Lesson 5 *Old Yeller and the Bear*

Making Inferences

Apply

Use your prior knowledge to make inferences based on each of the following sentences.

Example:
You look out the window and see people wearing heavy coats, hats, and gloves.
Inference: *It is cold outside.*

Answers will vary. Possible answers are shown.

1. You hear pots and pans banging in the kitchen, and you start to smell something good.
   Inference: Something is cooking.
2. Fred didn't feel good yesterday, and he is not at school today.
   Inference: Fred stayed home sick.
3. Every time Susan goes to Ted's house, his cat jumps into her lap and purrs.
   Inference: Ted's cat likes Susan.
4. The dog gobbles up the beef treats you give him but spits out the chicken ones.
   Inference: The dog does not like the chicken treats.
5. At a restaurant, the child at the next table is blowing out candles on a big cake.
   Inference: It is the child's birthday.

COMPREHENSION

Comprehension and Language Arts Skills UNIT 5 • Lesson 5 161

Comprehension and Language Arts Skills pp. 160–161

Differentiating Instruction

If...	Then...
Students need extra help with Making Inferences	• Use ***Reteach,*** pages 160–161 • Use ***English Learner Support Guide,*** pages 422–435
Students would enjoy a challenge with Making Inferences	Use ***Challenge,*** page 141

Making Inferences

Introduced in Grade 2.
Scaffolded throughout Grades 3–5.

REINTRODUCED: Unit 1, Lesson 2
REINFORCED: Unit 2, Lesson 3
Unit 3, Lesson 4
Unit 5, Lesson 5
Unit 6, Lesson 5
TESTED: Unit 5 Assessment

Professional Development

Teacher Resource Library CD-ROMs or ***Online Professional Development*** provides courses that help you better understand the Comprehension/Knowledge Building instruction in ***Open Court Reading.*** For more information about this program, visit SRAonline.com.

Research in Action
Intentional Learning

To prompt intentional learning, keep the students aware of what they are learning and why, rather than letting them focus on the activities. Intentional learning means turning over—gradually, of course—the responsibility for the students' learning to the students themselves. You should not forever be the one who notices misconceptions or gaps in knowledge, who decides what is learned from an activity, who monitors learning, and who thinks of remedial actions. Eventually students must learn to do these things themselves if they are to go out into the world as lifelong learners.
(Carl Bereiter)

Teacher Tip TEACHING PLOT Feel free to customize this lesson according to your students' needs. For example, if your students are advanced, add more details when discussing plot elements.

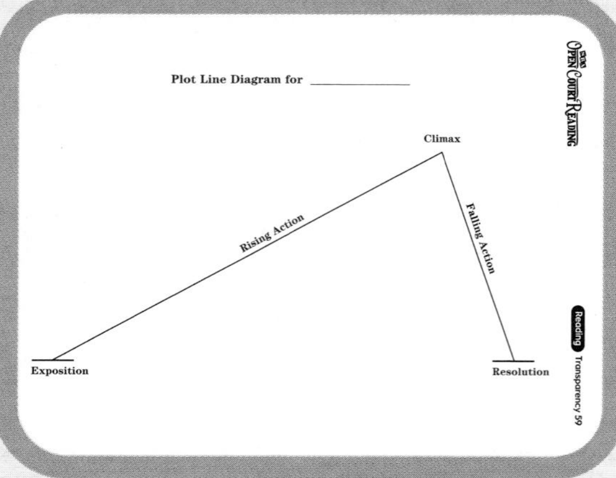

Reading Transparency 59

Literary Elements

Plot

Teach Have students tell you what they know about plot. If necessary, remind them that the *plot* of a story is the story's chain of events. Explain to students that there are several elements that make up the plot of a story. Ask students to take notes as you explain the different stages of plot development in simplified terms.

- **Exposition:** This is the beginning of the story. Story characters and setting are introduced. A problem is also introduced.
- **Rising Action:** This is the middle part of the story. The characters go through conflict as they try to solve the problem. Suspense builds over how the conflict will be resolved.
- **Climax:** Events surrounding the problem are at the highest point of interest in the story. The problem begins to be resolved.
- **Falling Action:** The problem is resolved. Details are wrapped up.
- **Resolution:** This is the end of the story.

Guided Practice Use ***Reading Transparency 59*** to help students analyze the plot of "Old Yeller and the Bear." Have students identify the main parts of the story's plot by citing pieces of text from the selection as you record them on the transparency. If necessary, lead students to understand that the climax occurs when Travis realizes that Arliss is in trouble with an angry bear.

Then have students discuss what relationships they see between the development of the plot and changes in other elements of the story, such as characters, setting, conflict, and resolution. Students should be able to tell you that as the plot progresses, characters undergo changes. For example, the character of Arliss is introduced as being carefree and full or mischief, but as the plot progresses the reader sees him frightened for the first time. The setting also changes. At the same time that Travis says he "nearly went blind then, picturing what was going to happen to Little Arliss," the sun sets behind the trees and "the changing light nearly [blinds him]." In addition, students should be able to see that the conflict is the mother bear coming after Arliss and the situation becomes increasingly intense up until the conflict is resolved by Old Yeller.

Independent Practice Encourage students to fill in another plot line for another short story in the ***Student Anthology.*** Suggest that students use the plot line to develop an original plot for a story that they want to write.

Social Studies Connection: Pioneer Life

Have students work in small groups to investigate various aspects of the lives of the early settlers. Encourage students to choose a focus for their investigation, such as the following:

- Transportation
- Customs
- Threats to survival
- Communication with the East and with other settlers
- Relations with Native American groups
- Reasons for moving to the West
- Challenges of terrain and climate

Have groups compile general information on their topics and prepare that information for an informal oral presentation. Ask students to include dates with the information they record. You might suggest that students print out pictures, draw maps, or include other visuals to complement their information. Have a "Pioneer Day" in class, during which groups share their information with each other. With each group covering a different topic, students will hear a well-rounded overview of pioneer life. Encourage students to use a variety of media to show how they came about their understanding of the topic they are presenting and to enhance the understanding of their audience. For example, students might cue up film clips from videocassettes or DVDs they have watched to portray an aspect of pioneer life. (If students choose to do this, make sure that they clear their film clip with you, to ensure its appropriateness within the classroom.)

Teacher Tip **MATERIALS** To complete this activity, students will need the following: library and computer sources, paper, pens, markers, crayons, and colored pencils.

Concept Connections

Linking the Selection

- Settlers needed to be hardworking in order to build their homes and farm the land. They also needed to be brave and clever to deal with a variety of dangers.
- Sturdy houses were needed for protection against harsh weather and wild animals.

Exploring Concept Vocabulary

The concept word for this lesson is ***peril.*** Write the word on the board. Work with the students to develop a definition that clearly links to the unit theme. Have students copy the word and definition into the Vocabulary section of their Writer's Notebooks.

Peril: the chance of injury or destruction; danger. For example, the mother bear charged when she realized her cub was in peril.

- They faced the danger of wild animal attacks and other intruders while men were away on cattle drives.
- The way Little Arliss screamed told Travis that his brother was in trouble.

The students' sentences should show an understanding of both vocabulary words.

Expanding the Concept

Have students carry on dialogues in small groups. After the small-group discussions, bring students together to share their ideas with the whole class.

As students complete their discussion, have them record their ideas about the selection on page 114 of their ***Inquiry Journal.***

Old Yeller & the Bear

Concept Connections

Linking the Selection

Think about the following questions, and then record your responses in the Response Journal section of your Writer's Notebook.

- What were some personal qualities settlers needed in order to succeed on the frontier?
- Why was it important for settlers on the frontier to have sturdy houses?

Exploring Concept Vocabulary

The concept word for this lesson is ***peril.*** If you do not know what this word means, look it up in a dictionary. Answer these questions.

- What ***perils*** did families of the Texas frontier face?
- How did Travis know that Little Arliss was in real ***peril?***

Make up an oral sentence that includes the word ***peril*** and a word from the selection vocabulary.

Expanding the Concept

Compare Travis with the boy in "The Journal of Wong Ming-Chung." Consider the boys' family responsibilities and daily activities. Try to use the word ***peril*** in your discussion of the characters. Add new ideas about the American West to the Concept/Question Board.

Teacher Tip **INQUIRY AND INVESTIGATION** Have groups report and discuss their ideas with the class. As these ideas are stated, have students add them to the Concept/Question Board. As students complete their discussions, have them sum up what they have learned and tell how they might use this information in further investigations.

Informal Assessment

This may be a good time to observe students working in small groups and to mark your observations in the Teacher Observation Log found in the ***Program Assessment Teacher's Edition.***

Meet the Author

Fred Gipson wrote adventure novels for children and adults. These stories usually featured animals. His first big success was *Hound-Dog Man*, which was later made into a film. He is best known, however, for *Old Yeller* and its sequel, *Savage Sam*, both of which were produced as movies.

A lover of animals, Mr. Gipson raised cattle and hogs on his own farm. He enjoyed fly fishing and hunting deer, wild turkey, quail, and doves. Of his work he said, *"I've always liked true adventure tales and have always felt I learned more history of my country from these tales than I ever did from history books."*

Meet the Illustrator

Jennifer Heyd Wharton's illustrations are often seen in children's books, newspapers, and magazines. She uses her skillful blending of hue and light to capture and share the joyful moments that weave the fabric of our lives. Ms. Wharton says, *"I use my art to sing what my voice cannot. And the song I strive to share is that of praise for the wonder and joy of life always present in the harmony of shapes and colors that surround us."* She currently operates her own studio in Annapolis, Maryland.

473

Meet the Author

After the students read the information about Fred Gipson, discuss the following questions with them.

- Fred Gipson's book *Old Yeller* was made into a motion picture. What elements of Fred Gipson's writing make it easily translated into a movie script? *(Possible answer: His writing is full of action, described vividly enough that one can readily picture it.)*
- Fred Gipson said he learned more history from adventure tales than from history books. Why do you think he felt this way? *(Possible answer: Many times, history books mainly list facts. Stories give you insight into how people feel and what their day-to-day lives are like.)*

Meet the Illustrator

After the students read the information about Jennifer Heyd Wharton, discuss the following question with them.

- Jennifer Heyd Wharton says that she uses her art to "sing what my voice cannot." What do you think she means by that? *(Possible answer: Art and music are similar in the way they express emotions without words. She sees her illustrations as a way to express emotions the way a musician does with music.)*

Objectives

- Students gain a deeper understanding of the American West.
- Students establish investigation plans.
- Students participate in investigation activities.
- Students learn to use time lines.

Materials

- Student Anthology, pp. 462–473
- Inquiry Journal, pp. 132–134
- Research Assistant
- Reading Transparency 65

INVESTIGATION

Investigating Concepts Beyond the Text

To facilitate students' investigation of the American West, you might have them participate in the following activity. Tell students that if they have activity ideas of their own that they would like to pursue, they are free to do so as an alternative to this activity suggestion. For example, students may want to pursue activities of their own choosing that relate more directly to the problems and questions they are investigating with their groups. Tell students that they may work on this activity alone, in pairs, or in small groups, with an option to write about it or to present it to the group upon completion.

The activity suggested for this lesson is:

- Engage the students in a discussion of the dangers faced by those who lived in the American West and the reasons for these dangers. Have the students compare these dangers with those faced in the region today. Tell students that as they read the selections in the unit and begin their investigation, they will record difficulties or problems faced by the people of this region and examine how they dealt with or solved these problems. Encourage them to consider both sides of each problem or conflict. Provide time for students to record examples in their ***Inquiry Journals*** on pages 132–133.

  Upon completion of the activity, have students share with the group anything new they learned about the American West through discussion and by adding information to the Concept/Question Board.

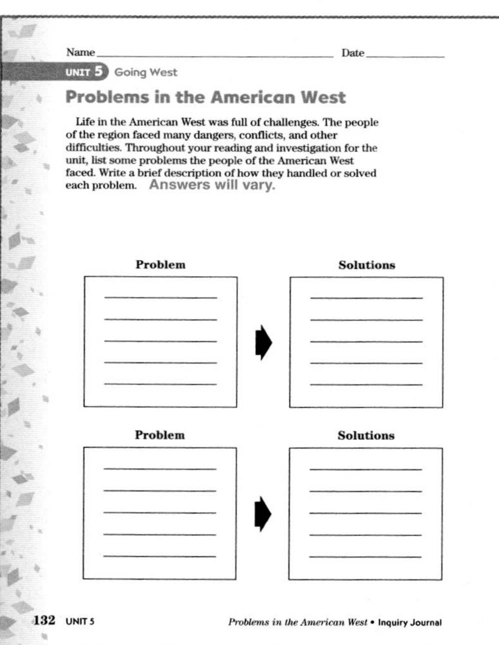

Name ______ Date ______

UNIT 5 Going West

Problems in the American West

Life in the American West was full of challenges. The people of the region faced many dangers, conflicts, and other difficulties. Throughout your reading and investigation for the unit, list some problems the people of the American West faced. Write a brief description of how they handled or solved each problem. Answers will vary.

Problem	Solutions

132 UNIT 5 *Problems in the American West* • Inquiry Journal

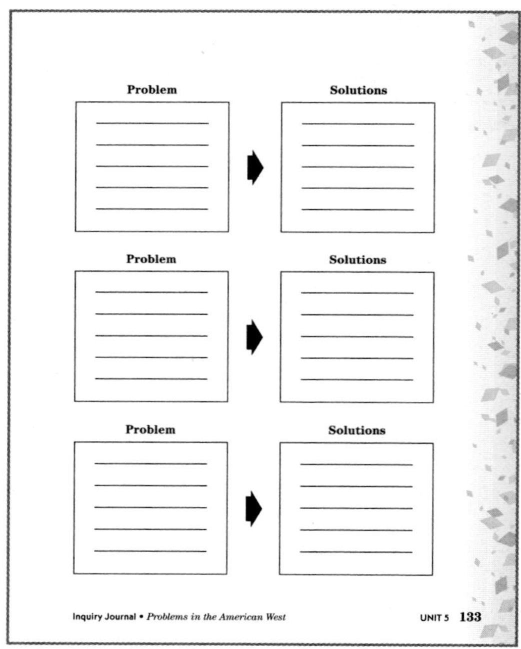

Problem	Solutions

Inquiry Journal • *Problems in the American West* UNIT 5 133

Inquiry Journal pp. 132–133

Concept/Question Board

After reading each selection, students should use the Concept/Question Board to

- post any questions they asked about a selection before reading that have not yet been answered.
- refer to as they formulate statements about concepts that apply to their investigations.
- post general statements formulated by each collaborative group.
- continue to post news articles, or other items that they find during the unit investigation.
- read and think about posted questions, articles, or concepts that interest them and provide answers to the questions.

Unit 5 Investigation Management

Lesson 1	Students generate questions and ideas for investigation.
Lesson 2	Students formulate questions and problems for investigation.
Lesson 3	Students make conjectures.
Lesson 4	Students establish investigation needs.
Lesson 5	Collaborative Investigation **Students establish investigation plans.** Supplementary Activities **Students participate in investigation activities and learn to use time lines.**
Lesson 6	Students continue investigation and get feedback from other groups.
Lesson 7	Students present their investigation findings to the class.

INVESTIGATION

www.sra4kids.com
Web Connection
Students can use the connections to Going West in the Reading link of the SRA Web page for more background information about Going West.

Research Assistant

The Research Assistant helps students in their investigations.

Teacher Tip RESEARCH TIPS Encourage students to use various resources as they research their exploration questions. Point out that only one source, such as an encyclopedia, might not offer enough information for their questions. Suggest that information from other sources, such as atlases and museums, might send their investigations in new and exciting directions. Encourage students to post titles of resources they find especially helpful on the Concept/Question Board.

Teacher Tip ULTIMATE WRITING AND CREATIVITY CENTER Have students use the ***Ultimate Writing and Creativity Center CD-ROM*** as they work on their investigation activities.

Differentiating Instruction

If...	Then...
Students are having difficulty with their Inquiry activities	Model revising conjectures based on information they have gathered from their investigations, taking care to model faulty as well as provable conjectures

Formal Assessment

Use the Research Rubrics on page 462J to assess students' ability to find needed information.

Professional Development

Teacher Resource Library CD-ROMs or ***Online Professional Development*** provides courses that help you better understand the Inquiry and Investigation instruction in ***Open Court Reading.*** For more information about this program, visit SRAonline.com.

Name ________ Date ________

UNIT 5 Going West

Establishing Investigation Plans

Our question or problem:

Answers will vary.

Knowledge Needs—Information we need to find or figure out in order to investigate the question or problem:

A. Answers will vary.

B.

C.

D.

E.

F.

Group Members	Main Jobs

Hint: To save rewriting Knowledge Needs in the Main Jobs section, put in the capital letter marking the Knowledge Needs line.

134 UNIT 5 *Establishing Investigation Plans* • Inquiry Journal

***Inquiry Journal* p. 134**

INVESTIGATION

Establishing Investigation Plans

By now, groups should have made general plans as to the time frame for carrying out the remainder of their investigations. Before groups meet to settle on definite investigation plans, whole-class discussion will be important to accomplish the following goals.

- Help students who are having difficulty identifying knowledge needs related to their conjectures.
- Remind investigation groups that they can still change the focus of their investigation problems. By this time, some groups may have discovered that their problem is not very promising. A group may choose to keep the same general problem but to formulate the problem more precisely.
- Provide any other needed discussion or guidance before students embark on formulating and carrying out their investigation plans.

Tell students that once they have established the focus of their problem and what information they need to find or figure out to solve their problem, they must come up with a plan for getting that information. Have students divide into their investigation groups to assign jobs to each group member. As you observe the groups making their job assignments, encourage the students to take on tasks that are related to their strengths and likings. For example, a student with good verbal skills might benefit from conducting interviews, while a less verbal student might primarily contribute information located in books, magazines, and other references. Whatever the job assignment, it is important that each student have a significant role in the group. Assign page 134 of the ***Inquiry Journal*** to be completed after each planning group has agreed on a final statement of its problem, its knowledge needs, and its individual job assignments. Then have students carry out their job assignments during Workshop and as homework.

SUPPORTING THE INVESTIGATION

Time Lines

Teach Have students tell you what they know about time lines and how they are used. If necessary, explain that time lines are used to show important events in chronological order. Point out that a time line may cover any chosen period of time, such as the lifetime of a person or a historical period of hundreds or even thousands of years.

Guided Practice Work with students to organize the following information about American writer Mark Twain in a time line. You might want to use ***Reading Transparency 65*** to illustrate the process step by step.

- Mark Twain published *Tom Sawyer* in 1876.
- He died on April 21, 1910.
- Twain published *Huckleberry Finn* in 1884.
- Mark Twain was born on November 30, 1835.

Then explain to students that every time line should have a focused subject. Name the subject of this time line "Events in the Life of Mark Twain." Discuss with students why each entry included on the time line is important to the subject. Then ask students how the importance of each entry changes if the time line's subject becomes "Mark Twain's Publications." The entries about Twain's life and death are not important to this new subject and, therefore, should not be included on the time line. Change the subject again, this time to "Mark Twain's Medical History." Discuss with students why a time line on this subject should include Twain's life and death but not information about his books.

Independent Practice Have students look over the information they have gathered during their investigation. Have them use a time line to organize the dates of events important to their investigation topics. Have them choose for their time line a focused subject that relates directly to the conjectures students are working to support. Then remind them to include on their time lines only those events that are most important to the subject. You may want to conference with students during Workshop to ensure that they are effectively classifying events by importance.

Teacher Tip STUDY STRATEGIES Students may find time lines are effective ways to organize information when studying for tests, such as Lesson Assessments.

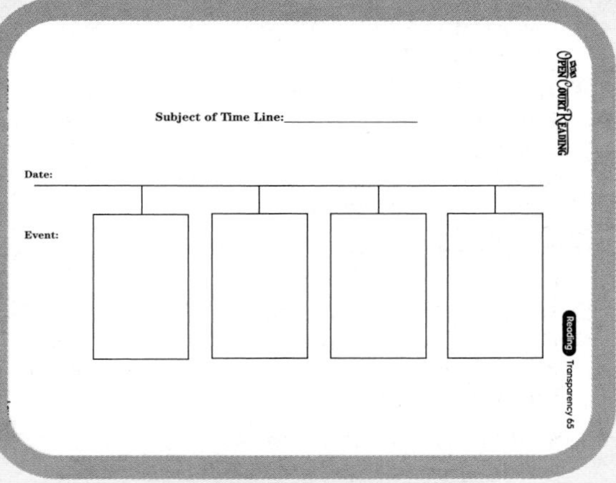

Reading Transparency 65

Objectives

Word Analysis

Spelling

- **Spelling Patterns for Words with *-ed* or *-ing*.** Develop understanding of spelling patterns for words with *-ed* or *-ing* introduced in Word Knowledge in Part 1.

Vocabulary

- Using words from "Old Yeller and the Bear," familiarize students with similes.

Writing Process Strategies

- **Personal Writing: Friendly Letter.** Students will practice the proper form of a friendly letter. Prewriting activities will be based upon "Old Yeller and the Bear."

English Language Conventions

Mechanics

- **Commas.** Understand the use of commas with coordinating conjunctions and subordinate clauses and identify them in "Old Yeller and the Bear."

Listening, Speaking, Viewing

- **Interacting: Group Discussions.** Participate in group discussions.

Penmanship

- **Joining with *Y* and *w*.** Review handwriting skills by practicing joining letters with *Y* and *w*.

Materials

- Comprehension and Language Arts Skills, pp. 162–165
- Language Arts Handbook
- Language Arts Transparency 18
- Spelling and Vocabulary Skills, pp. 122–125
- Student Anthology
- Writer's Workbook, pp. 94–97
- Unit 5 Assessment, pp. 38–39

Differentiating Instruction

Reteach, Challenge, and ***Intervention*** lessons are available to support the language arts instruction in this lesson.

Research in Action

An important goal of modern language study is to understand the conventions that govern appropriateness and public language. (*James D. Williams,* The Teacher's Grammar Book)

OVERVIEW

Language Arts Overview

Word Analysis

Spelling The spelling activities on the following pages support the Word Knowledge introduction of words ending with *-ed* or *-ing* by developing understanding of the spelling patterns for these endings.

Selection Spelling Words

These words from "Old Yeller and the Bear" contain *-ed* or *-ing.*

captured catching ached poured scrambling

Vocabulary The vocabulary activities give students practice recognizing and writing similes.

Vocabulary Skill Words

spasms lunge slung trot poultice

Writing Process Strategies

This Writing Process Strategies lesson involves practice in writing a friendly letter. The lesson includes instruction on the tone of a friendly letter.

To help students identify the Internet as a source of information for writing, show students how to send e-mail attachments. You might want to have students send an e-mail message to a friend with a file attachment. ***TechKnowledge*** Level 5 Lesson 94 teaches these Internet and electronic reference skills.

Professional Development

Teacher Resource Library CD-ROMs or ***Online Professional Development*** provides courses that help you better understand the Writing instruction in ***Open Court Reading.*** For more information about this program, visit SRAonline.com.

English Language Conventions

Mechanics **Commas.** This lesson develops understanding of the use of commas with coordinating conjunctions and subordinate clauses.

Listening, Speaking, Viewing **Interacting: Group Discussions.** In this Interacting lesson, students assume roles in participating in group discussions.

Penmanship **Joining with *Y* and *w*.** This lesson continues the development of handwriting skills. Students join letters with *Y* and *w* and then write paragraphs from the literature, focusing on joining letters.

DAY 1

Word Analysis

Spelling

Assessment: Pretest

Spelling Patterns for Words with *-ed* or *-ing*

Give students the Pretest on page 38 of ***Unit 5 Assessment.*** Have them proofread and correct any misspellings.

Pretest Sentences

1. **whispering** There is no **whispering** allowed in class.
2. **pulled** A float in a small-town parade might be **pulled** by a tractor.
3. **propped** They **propped** up their sagging shelves with blocks of wood.
4. **shopping** December is the busiest month for **shopping** in this country.
5. **wagged** The dog **wagged** its tail.
6. **planned** The Allies **planned** the D-Day invasion for months.
7. **waited** Slaves **waited** until night to make their escape.
8. **handling** A jeweler is skilled at **handling** diamonds and rubies.
9. **followed** The President's inauguration is **followed** by a ball.
10. **gardening** A popular hobby for retired people is **gardening.**
11. **paying** She is **paying** with cash.
12. **stepping** The marching band is **stepping** in time with the music.
13. **crawling** A baby will get around by **crawling** before it learns to walk.
14. **tracing** Constructing a family tree involves **tracing** your family history.
15. **weeding** If the **weeding** is not done, the plants will be overwhelmed.
16. **captured** Endangered species are often **captured** and placed in zoos.
17. **catching** If you are **catching** a cold, you should try to rest.
18. **ached** The athletes' muscles **ached** after the game.
19. **poured** The workers **poured** chocolate into molds to form candy.
20. **scrambling** You can make a good breakfast by **scrambling** eggs.

Writing Process Strategies

Getting Ideas

Friendly Letter

Teach

Introduce the Writing Form

Have students review ***Language Arts Handbook*** pages 82–85 on friendly letters.

Inspiration

Model inspiration: *I really enjoyed reading "Old Yeller and the Bear." I want to write a letter to a friend to describe some of the events in the story.*

Brainstorming

Using the theme Going West and "Old Yeller and the Bear" as a springboard, encourage students to suggest ideas, thoughts, or details that they might use if they were writing about "Old Yeller and the Bear." Write these ideas on the board. Have students write ideas that appeal to them in their Writer's Notebooks.

Guided Practice

Selecting a Topic

Have students choose a topic and audience for their letters. Suggest that students write to a friend or family member about a selection from this unit. Have students include parts of the plot or descriptions of characters that really appeal to them.

Friendly Letters

You can send a **friendly letter** to a friend, a relative, a pen pal, or someone you just met and want to get to know better. Include any or all of these things in a friendly letter.

- Updates on the interesting things you've been doing
- Questions for the person receiving your letter
- Tips on good books, movies, and videos
- Stories, poems, and jokes that you want to share

Parts of a Friendly Letter

These are the parts of a friendly letter:

Heading

This is your address and the date. It goes in the upper right corner.

Salutation

Use the word *Dear*, followed by the name and a comma. The Salutation goes by the left margin, two lines below the heading.

Body

This is the message part of the letter. Start it two lines below the salutation. Indent each paragraph in the body of your letter.

Closing

Yours truly and *Sincerely* are commonly used as a closing. The Closing goes two lines below the body by the left margin. Capitalize just the first word, and use a comma at the end of the closing.

Signature

Sign your name under the closing.

82 Personal Writing ▲ Friendly Letters

Language Arts Handbook p. 82

English Language Conventions

Mechanics

Commas

Teach

- Remind students that two related independent clauses may be connected by a comma and a conjunction. Coordinating conjunctions are *and, but, or, so, yet,* and *for. I like volleyball,* ***and*** *she likes basketball.*
- Explain that a subordinate, or dependent, clause has a subject and a predicate but does not express a complete thought, so it cannot stand alone as a sentence. A subordinate clause always relates to the independent clause. Some words that begin a subordinate clause are *as, because, before, if, unless, when, where,* and *whether.* ***When*** *you arrive, let me know.*

Independent Practice

Use ***Comprehension and Language Arts Skills*** pages 162–163 to practice the correct use of commas with coordinating conjunctions and subordinate clauses.

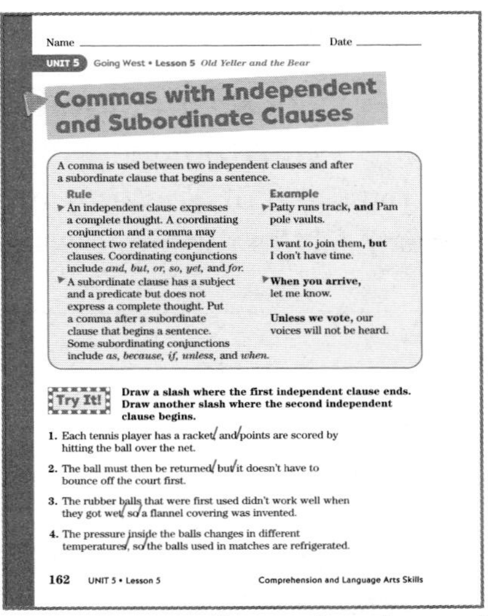

Name ______________________ Date __________

UNIT 5 Going West • Lesson 5 *Old Yeller and the Bear*

Commas with Independent and Subordinate Clauses

A comma is used between two independent clauses and after a subordinate clause that begins a sentence.

Rule	Example
An independent clause expresses a complete thought. A coordinating conjunction and a comma may connect two related independent clauses. Coordinating conjunctions include *and, but, or, so, yet,* and *for.*	Patty runs track, **and** Pam pole vaults. I want to join them, **but** I don't have time.
A subordinate clause has a subject and a predicate but does not express a complete thought. Put a comma after a subordinate clause that begins a sentence. Some subordinating conjunctions include *as, because, if, unless,* and *when.*	**When you arrive,** let me know. **Unless we vote,** our voices will not be heard.

Try It! **Draw a slash where the first independent clause ends. Draw another slash where the second independent clause begins.**

1. Each tennis player has a racket/ and/ points are scored by hitting the ball over the net.
2. The ball must then be returned/ but/ it doesn't have to bounce off the court first.
3. The rubber balls that were first used didn't work well when they got wet/ so/ a flannel covering was invented.
4. The pressure inside the balls changes in different temperatures/, so/ the balls used in matches are refrigerated.

162 UNIT 5 • Lesson 5 Comprehension and Language Arts Skills

Comprehension and Language Arts Skills p. 162

DAY 2

Word Analysis

Spelling

Word Sorting

Open Word Sort Have students sort the spelling words according to their endings. Have students explain their answers.

Vocabulary

Similes

Teach

- Remind students of previous discussions in Unit 4 about figurative language. Review the concept of similes, or original comparisons between two things using the words *like* or *as*. Remind students that similes are interesting because they compare two things that are usually not associated, as is demonstrated by the simile *I slept like a log.*
- Write the word pairs *bright* and *sun*, *deep* and *ocean*, and *dark* and *night* on the board. Ask students to create similes from these word pairs, such as *The spotlight was bright as the sun.*

Guided Practice

Assign page 122 of ***Spelling and Vocabulary Skills.*** Students can complete page 123 of ***Spelling and Vocabulary Skills*** for homework.

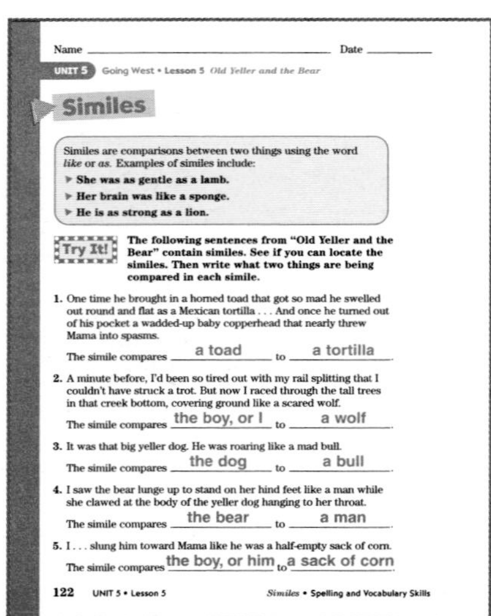
Name ______________ Date ________

UNIT 5 Going West • Lesson 5 *Old Yeller and the Bear*

Similes

Similes are comparisons between two things using the word *like* or *as*. Examples of similes include:

- **She was as gentle as a lamb.**
- **Her brain was like a sponge.**
- **He is as strong as a lion.**

Try It! **The following sentences from "Old Yeller and the Bear" contain similes. See if you can locate the similes. Then write what two things are being compared in each simile.**

1. One time he brought in a horned toad that got so mad he swelled out round and flat as a Mexican tortilla . . . And once he turned out of his pocket a wadded-up baby copperhead that nearly threw Mama into spasms.
   The simile compares a toad to a tortilla.
2. A minute before, I'd been so tired out with my rail splitting that I couldn't have struck a trot. But now I raced through the tall trees in that creek bottom, covering ground like a scared wolf.
   The simile compares the boy, or I to a wolf.
3. It was that big yeller dog. He was roaring like a mad bull.
   The simile compares the dog to a bull.
4. I saw the bear lunge up to stand on her hind feet like a man while she clawed at the body of the yeller dog hanging to her throat.
   The simile compares the bear to a man.
5. I . . . slung him toward Mama like he was a half-empty sack of corn.
   The simile compares the boy, or him to a sack of corn.

122 UNIT 5 • Lesson 5 *Similes* • Spelling and Vocabulary Skills

***Spelling and Vocabulary Skills* p. 122**

Writing Process Strategies

Prewriting

Friendly Letter

Teach

- Review ***Language Arts Handbook*** pages 82–85 on friendly letters as a class. Using the ***Language Arts Handbook*** as a guide, write down all the features of a friendly letter on the board. Tell students to follow that template when writing their letters.
- Review ideas and thoughts discussed on Day 1.
- Remind students that in a friendly letter, they should think of who they are in relationship to the reader. This will drive the tone and style of their letter.
- The students already know that the purpose of their letter will be to describe a selection from the reading that they enjoyed. The students must decide if they want to do this in an entertaining way, an informative manner, or an explanatory fashion.

Independent Practice

- Have students complete the prewriting for writing a personal letter on ***Writer's Workbook*** page 94.

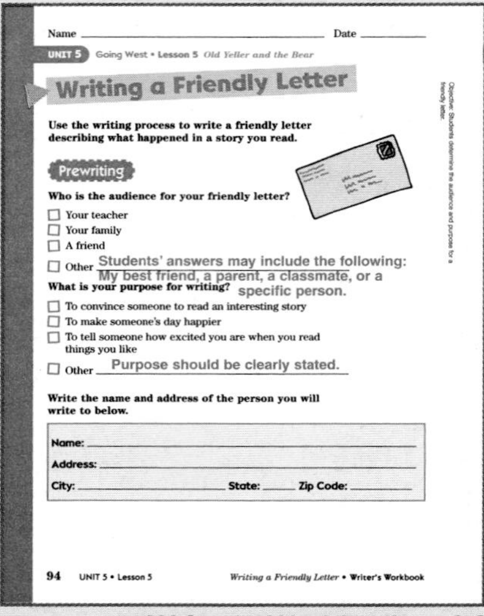
Name ______________ Date ________

UNIT 5 Going West • Lesson 5 *Old Yeller and the Bear*

Writing a Friendly Letter

Use the writing process to write a friendly letter describing what happened in a story you read.

Prewriting

Who is the audience for your friendly letter?

- ☐ Your teacher
- ☐ Your family
- ☐ A friend
- ☐ Other Students' answers may include the following: My best friend, a parent, a classmate, or a specific person.

What is your purpose for writing?

- ☐ To convince someone to read an interesting story
- ☐ To make someone's day happier
- ☐ To tell someone how excited you are when you read things you like
- ☐ Other Purpose should be clearly stated.

Write the name and address of the person you will write to below.

Name: ______________
Address: ______________
City: __________ State: _____ Zip Code: ________

Objective: Students determine the audience and purpose for a friendly letter.

94 UNIT 5 • Lesson 5 *Writing a Friendly Letter* • Writer's Workbook

***Writer's Workbook* p. 94**

English Language Conventions

Mechanics

Commas

Teach

- Review the use of commas with coordinating conjunctions and subordinate clauses.
- Write these words on the board. Have students tell whether they are sentences that contain two independent clauses or a subordinate clause and a main clause.
  - The plan seemed possible, but I wasn't sure that I had time. (two independent clauses)
  - When I heard the plan, I got excited. (subordinate clause and main clause)
  - As you get closer to the peak, you can see the snow. (subordinate clause and main clause)
  - I made cookies, and Mother made candy. (two independent clauses)
- Write these words on the board and have students write a subordinate clause for each one.
  - I am going to be a dancer. (Idea: *After I finish college, . . .*)
  - My family is going to the beach. (Idea: *Whether or not the weather is good, . . .*)

Guided Practice in Reading

Have students identify commas with coordinating conjunctions and subordinate clauses in "Old Yeller and the Bear." Point out to the students that the second sentence in the second paragraph contains a subordinate clause that might not be easily identified because of the distractor words *Every night.*

DAY 3

Word Analysis

Spelling

Spelling Patterns for Words with *-ed* or *-ing*

Teach

Introduce the spelling patterns for words with the endings *-ed* and *-ing*. Remind students of the rules they learned in Unit 4: if a word ends in *e*, drop the *e* before adding the ending, and if a word ends with a short vowel and a consonant, double that consonant before adding the ending. Have students identify the spelling words that display these rules and spell the base words.

Guided Practice

Have students complete page 124 from ***Spelling and Vocabulary Skills*** to practice identifying the *e*-drop and consonant doubling rules.

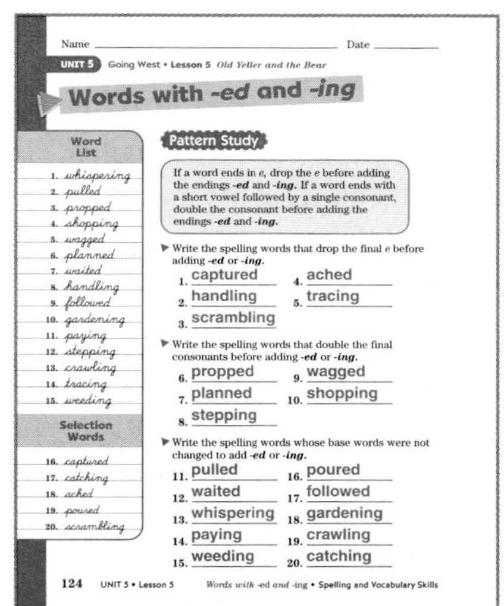

Name ____________ Date ______

UNIT 5 Going West • Lesson 5 *Old Yeller and the Bear*

Words with -ed and -ing

Word List

1. whispering
2. pulled
3. propped
4. shopping
5. wagged
6. planned
7. waited
8. handling
9. followed
10. gardening
11. paying
12. stepping
13. crawling
14. tracing
15. weeding

Selection Words

16. captured
17. catching
18. ached
19. poured
20. scrambling

Pattern Study

If a word ends in *e*, drop the *e* before adding the endings ***-ed*** and ***-ing***. If a word ends with a short vowel followed by a single consonant, double the consonant before adding the endings ***-ed*** and ***-ing***.

▶ Write the spelling words that drop the final *e* before adding ***-ed*** or ***-ing***.

1. captured
2. handling
3. scrambling
4. ached
5. tracing

▶ Write the spelling words that double the final consonants before adding ***-ed*** or ***-ing***.

6. propped
7. planned
8. stepping
9. wagged
10. shopping

▶ Write the spelling words whose base words were not changed to add ***-ed*** or ***-ing***.

11. pulled
12. waited
13. whispering
14. paying
15. weeding
16. poured
17. followed
18. gardening
19. crawling
20. catching

124 UNIT 5 • Lesson 5 *Words with -ed and -ing* • Spelling and Vocabulary Skills

Spelling and Vocabulary Skills p. 124

Vocabulary (continued)

Similes

Tell students to find the words *spasms*, *trot*, *lunge*, and *slung* in the selection "Old Yeller and the Bear." Have students come up with a definition for each word based on context clues within the selection. Then have them write sentences using each of the four words in an original simile.

Writing Process Strategies

Drafting

Friendly Letter

Teach

Writer's Craft

Tone of a Personal Letter

- *Tone* is the writer's attitude toward his or her subject. A writer's tone can be serious, sarcastic, objective, or humorous. Tone can be formal or informal.
- Ask students if they would use the same language and tone when writing to their parents that they would use when writing to a friend.
- The purpose of the letter helps determine the tone, just as the audience does. If the purpose is to tell a funny story about something that happened to the student, the tone of the letter might be humorous.
- Have students complete ***Comprehension and Language Arts Skills,*** pages 164–165, on the tone of a personal letter.

Independent Practice

- Have students complete ***Writer's Workbook,*** page 95, and then draft a letter using that page as a guide.

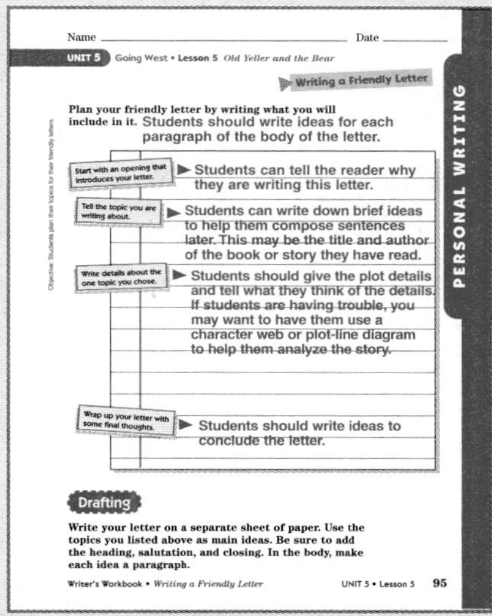

Name ____________ Date ______

UNIT 5 Going West • Lesson 5 *Old Yeller and the Bear*

Writing a Friendly Letter

PERSONAL WRITING

Plan your friendly letter by writing what you will include in it. Students should write ideas for each paragraph of the body of the letter.

Objective: Students plan their topics for their friendly letters.

Start with an opening that introduces your letter. ▶ Students can tell the reader why they are writing this letter.

Tell the topic you are writing about. ▶ Students can write down brief ideas to help them compose sentences later. This may be the title and author of the book or story they have read.

Write details about the one topic you chose. ▶ Students should give the plot details and tell what they think of the details. If students are having trouble, you may want to have them use a character web or plot-line diagram to help them analyze the story.

Wrap up your letter with some final thoughts. ▶ Students should write ideas to conclude the letter.

Drafting

Write your letter on a separate sheet of paper. Use the topics you listed above as main ideas. Be sure to add the heading, salutation, and closing. In the body, make each idea a paragraph.

Writer's Workbook • *Writing a Friendly Letter* UNIT 5 • Lesson 5 95

Writer's Workbook p. 95

English Language Conventions

Mechanics

Commas

Teach

- Remind students that short sentences combined by coordinating conjunctions make reading smoother.
- Remind students that every sentence needs to have unity—a single thought or a group of closely related thoughts. Good writers do **not** combine two independent clauses to form a sentence that lacks unity. *Betsy is a good teacher, and she has a cat named Tiger.*

Guided Practice in Writing

Have students review their friendly letters and rewrite sentences that can be combined with coordinating conjunctions or by creating a subordinate clause/main clause sentence structure. Remind students that checking sentences for the use of commas with coordinating conjunctions and subordinate clauses is an important part of proofreading their personal writing.

Informal Assessment

Check students' progress in correctly using commas in coordinating conjunctions and subordinate clauses.

DAY 4

Word Analysis

Spelling

Spelling Patterns for Words with *-ed* or *-ing*

Teach

Remind students of the *e*-drop and consonant doubling rules, and that *-ed* forms the past tense of a verb, while *-ing* forms a present tense of a verb, a noun, or adjective. Model the family strategy by writing the word *stop* on the board and asking students to spell *stopped* and *stopping.*

Guided Practice

Have students complete the Spelling Strategies exercise on page 125 of ***Spelling and Vocabulary Skills.***

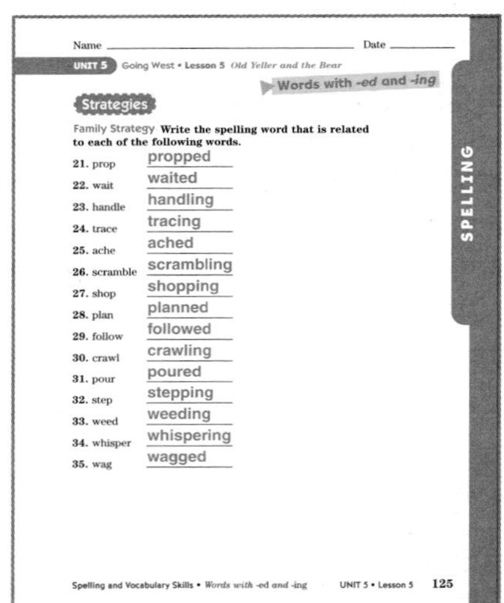

Name ______ Date ______

UNIT 5 Going West • Lesson 5 *Old Yeller and the Bear*

Words with *-ed* and *-ing*

Strategies

Family Strategy **Write the spelling word that is related to each of the following words.**

21. prop propped
22. wait waited
23. handle handling
24. trace tracing
25. ache ached
26. scramble scrambling
27. shop shopping
28. plan planned
29. follow followed
30. crawl crawling
31. pour poured
32. step stepping
33. weed weeding
34. whisper whispering
35. wag wagged

SPELLING

Spelling and Vocabulary Skills • *Words with -ed and -ing* UNIT 5 • Lesson 5 125

***Spelling and Vocabulary Skills* p. 125**

Vocabulary (continued)

Similes

Have students write a simile about each of the characters in "Old Yeller and the Bear"—the narrator, Arliss, Mama, Old Yeller, and the mama bear. An example might be *Travis ran like lightning to rescue Arliss.* Have students discuss how their similes will help describe these characters to others.

Writing Process Strategies

Revising

Friendly Letter

Teach

- **Teacher Model** using ***Language Arts Transparency 18,*** Revising for Word Choice. Write this sentence on the board. *She went through the aisles.* Then, write the following sentences on the board as well. *She strolled through the aisles. She sprinted through the aisles. She walked through the aisles.* Ask the students to tell you how one word makes a difference in the meaning of a sentence.
- Explain to students that they can improve their letters by
  - making sure that they are using the exact word that is needed.
  - making sure that sentences make sense and read smoothly.
  - checking to see that each paragraph develops a single idea.
  - including enough details to make the ideas clear, interesting, and fun to read.

Independent Practice

- Have students use the checklist on ***Writer's Workbook,*** page 96, to revise their letters.

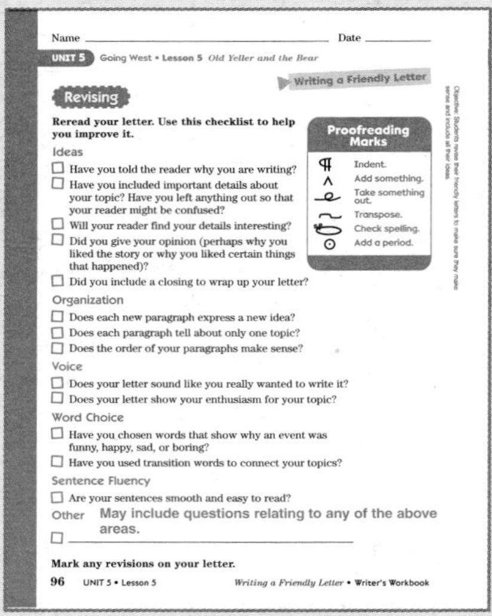

Name ______ Date ______

UNIT 5 Going West • Lesson 5 *Old Yeller and the Bear*

Writing a Friendly Letter

Revising

Reread your letter. Use this checklist to help you improve it.

Ideas

- ☐ Have you told the reader why you are writing?
- ☐ Have you included important details about your topic? Have you left anything out so that your reader might be confused?
- ☐ Will your reader find your details interesting?
- ☐ Did you give your opinion (perhaps why you liked the story or why you liked certain things that happened)?
- ☐ Did you include a closing to wrap up your letter?

Organization

- ☐ Does each new paragraph express a new idea?
- ☐ Does each paragraph tell about only one topic?
- ☐ Does the order of your paragraphs make sense?

Voice

- ☐ Does your letter sound like you really wanted to write it?
- ☐ Does your letter show your enthusiasm for your topic?

Word Choice

- ☐ Have you chosen words that show why an event was funny, happy, sad, or boring?
- ☐ Have you used transition words to connect your topics?

Sentence Fluency

- ☐ Are your sentences smooth and easy to read?

Other May include questions relating to any of the above areas.

- ☐ ______

Proofreading Marks

¶ Indent.
^ Add something.
Take something out.
Transpose.
Check spelling.
⊙ Add a period.

Objective: Students revise their friendly letters to make sure they make sense and include all their ideas.

Mark any revisions on your letter.

96 UNIT 5 • Lesson 5 *Writing a Friendly Letter* • Writer's Workbook

***Writer's Workbook* p. 96**

English Language Conventions

Listening, Speaking, Viewing

Interacting: Group Discussions

Teach

- Introduce interacting in group discussions by discussing the fact that, throughout their lives, students will find themselves working within groups. Tell students that they will need to be able to fulfill roles assigned to them within their groups. Emphasize that a necessary part of working within a group is recognizing and respecting different perspectives and opinions of others.
- Tell students that to ensure effective communication of their ideas, they should speak using Standard English, keeping in mind rules of grammar and word usage and avoiding use of slang.
- Delineate for students some of the possible roles that occur in group work: leader, recorder, active participant. Point out that when people don't fulfill their assigned roles, the whole group is let down and their effectiveness is weakened.

Guided Practice

- Break students into small groups. Give students time to get to know one another and to discuss what talents each student brings to the group. Let students within the group assign the roles in giving the presentation. Monitor the equal distribution of roles and responsibilities and the ability of students to interact within the group.
- Tell students that they will be discussing "Old Yeller and the Bear." Have students develop a time line of significant events from the selection.

Informal Assessment

Observe whether students use Standard English and effectively assume roles in participating in group discussions.

DAY 5

Word Analysis

Spelling

Assessment: Final Test

Spelling Patterns for Words with *-ed* or *-ing*

Teach

Repeat the Pretest for this lesson or use the Final Test on page 39 of ***Unit 5 Assessment.***

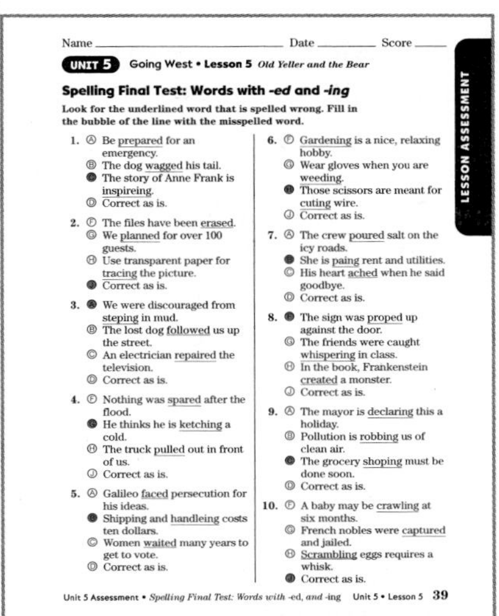

Name ______ Date ______ Score ______

UNIT 5 Going West • **Lesson 5** *Old Yeller and the Bear*

LESSON ASSESSMENT

Spelling Final Test: Words with *-ed* and *-ing*

Look for the underlined word that is spelled wrong. Fill in the bubble of the line with the misspelled word.

1. Ⓐ Be prepared for an emergency.
   Ⓑ The dog wagged his tail.
   ● The story of Anne Frank is inspireing.
   Ⓓ Correct as is.
2. Ⓕ The files have been erased.
   Ⓖ We planned for over 100 guests.
   Ⓗ Use transparent paper for tracing the picture.
   ● Correct as is.
3. ● We were discouraged from steping in mud.
   Ⓑ The lost dog followed us up the street.
   Ⓒ An electrician repaired the television.
   Ⓓ Correct as is.
4. Ⓕ Nothing was spared after the flood.
   ● He thinks he is ketching a cold.
   Ⓗ The truck pulled out in front of us.
   Ⓙ Correct as is.
5. Ⓐ Galileo faced persecution for his ideas.
   ● Shipping and handleing costs ten dollars.
   Ⓒ Women waited many years to get to vote.
   Ⓓ Correct as is.
6. Ⓕ Gardening is a nice, relaxing hobby.
   Ⓖ Wear gloves when you are weeding.
   ● Those scissors are meant for cuting wire.
   Ⓙ Correct as is.
7. Ⓐ The crew poured salt on the icy roads.
   ● She is paing rent and utilities.
   Ⓒ His heart ached when he said goodbye.
   Ⓓ Correct as is.
8. ● The sign was proped up against the door.
   Ⓖ The friends were caught whispering in class.
   Ⓗ In the book, Frankenstein created a monster.
   Ⓙ Correct as is.
9. Ⓐ The mayor is declaring this a holiday.
   Ⓑ Pollution is robbing us of clean air.
   ● The grocery shoping must be done soon.
   Ⓓ Correct as is.
10. Ⓕ A baby may be crawling at six months.
    Ⓖ French nobles were captured and jailed.
    Ⓗ Scrambling eggs requires a whisk.
    ● Correct as is.

Unit 5 Assessment • *Spelling Final Test: Words with -ed, and -ing* Unit 5 • Lesson 5 39

***Unit 5 Assessment* p. 39**

Guided Practice

Have students categorize any mistakes they made on the Final Test.

- Are they careless errors?
- Are they lesson pattern problems?

Vocabulary

Similes

Informal Assessment

- Periodically check to see if students remember how to recognize similes.
- Tell students that if they come across a simile they especially like, they can add it to their Writer's Notebooks.

Writing Process Strategies

Editing/Proofreading and Publishing

Friendly Letter

Teach

Teacher Model using editing marks by addressing each of the editing checklist items on ***Writer's Workbook*** page 97.

Independent Practice

- Have students use the checklist on page 97 of the ***Writer's Workbook*** to proofread and edit their letters.
- Have students choose a method for publishing.

Formal Assessment

Total Point Value: 10

1. The letter is easy to read and holds the reader's attention. (2 points)
2. The tone is appropriate for the audience and purpose. (2 points)
3. There are enough details to make the ideas clear, interesting, and fun to read. (2 points)
4. The sentences make sense and read smoothly. (1 point)
5. Each paragraph develops one single idea. (1 point)
6. The penmanship is legible. (1 point)
7. The reader can easily understand the language. (1 point)

Name ______ Date ______

UNIT 5 Going West • **Lesson 5** *Old Yeller and the Bear*

Writing a Friendly Letter

PERSONAL WRITING

Editing/Proofreading

Proofread your letter. Make sure you make a good impression on your reader. Use this checklist to make sure you remembered everything.

Conventions

- ☐ Are the name and address correct?
- ☐ Does each sentence have the correct capitalization and punctuation?
- ☐ Did you use commas correctly?
- ☐ Are there any spelling errors?
- ☐ Have you followed the correct format for a friendly letter?
- ☐ Other May include questions about grammar, usage, and mechanics related to a friendly letter.

Objective: Students get their friendly letters ready for mailing.

Publishing

Use this checklist to get your letter ready for publishing.

Presentation

- ☐ Write your letter on a clean sheet of paper.
- ☐ Check the letter for any errors. Make sure you copied all the parts of your letter.
- ☐ Sign your letter.
- ☐ Fold your letter.
- ☐ Address the envelope and proofread it.
- ☐ Place the correct postage on the envelope and mail it.

You may want to have students turn in their letters before mailing. You can assess them and hand back the letters for mailing.

Writer's Workbook • *Writing a Friendly Letter* UNIT 5 • Lesson 5 97

***Writer's Workbook* p. 97**

English Language Conventions

Penmanship

Joining with *Y* and *w*

Teach

- **Teacher Model:** Review formation of uppercase *Y* and lowercase *w* on the board.

Y Starting point, loop
Curve forward, slant down
Undercurve, slant down
Loop back, overcurve: capital *Y*

W Starting point, undercurve
Slant down, undercurve
Slant down, undercurve
Small curve to right: small *w*

- Write the following sentence to model proper joining of letters: *Young Yuri wanted to wave out the window.*

Guided Practice

- In their Writer's Notebook, have students join *Y* with the letters *a*, *o*, *e*, and *u* and join *w* with *u*, *a*, *e*, and *h*.
- From "Old Yeller and the Bear," have students write two paragraphs to practice joining letters.

Informal Assessment

Check students' handwriting for legibility and proper joining of letters.

LESSON WRAP-UP

Reading and Language Arts Skills Traces

Language Arts

WORD ANALYSIS

Skills Trace

Spelling: Words with -ed or -ing

Introduced in Grade 2.
Scaffolded throughout Grades 3–5.

REINTRODUCED: **Unit 5, Lesson 5**, p. 473F
PRACTICED: **Unit 5, Lesson 5**, pp. 473G–473I; ***Spelling and Vocabulary Skills,*** pp. 124–125
TESTED: **Unit 5, Lesson 5**, p. 473J; **Unit 5 Assessment**

Vocabulary: Simile

Introduced in Grade 4.
Scaffolded throughout Grade 5.

REINTRODUCED: **Unit 5, Lesson 5**, p. 473G
PRACTICED: **Unit 5, Lesson 5**, pp. 473H–473I; ***Spelling and Vocabulary Skills,*** pp. 122–123
TESTED: **Informal Assessment**, p. 473J; **Unit 5 Assessment**

WRITING PROCESS STRATEGIES

Skills Trace

Personal Writing: Friendly Letter

Introduced in Grade 1.
Scaffolded throughout Grades 1–5.

REINTRODUCED: **Unit 5, Lesson 3**, p. 443F
PRACTICED: **Unit 5, Lessons 3 and 5**, pp. 443F–443J and 473F–473J; ***Writer's Workbook,*** pp. 86–89 and 94–97
TESTED: **Formal Assessment**; **Unit 5, Lesson 5**, p. 473J; **Unit 5 Assessment**

Writer's Craft: Tone of a Personal Letter

Introduced in Grade 2.
Scaffolded throughout Grades 2–5.

REINTRODUCED: **Unit 5, Lesson 5**, p. 473H
PRACTICED: **Unit 5, Lesson 5**, p. 473H; ***Comprehension and Language Arts Skills,*** pp. 164–165
TESTED: **Unit 5 Assessment**

ENGLISH LANGUAGE CONVENTIONS

Skills Trace

Grammar and Usage: Commas

Introduced in Grade 4.
Scaffolded throughout Grades 4–5.

REINTRODUCED: **Unit 5, Lesson 5**, p. 473F
PRACTICED: **Unit 5, Lesson 5**, pp. 473F–473H; ***Comprehension and Language Arts Skills,*** pp. 162–163
TESTED: **Unit 5 Assessment**

Skills Trace

Listening, Speaking, Viewing Interacting: Group Discussions

Introduced in Grade 3.
Scaffolded throughout Grades 4–5.

REINTRODUCED: **Unit 5, Lesson 5**, p. 473I
PRACTICED: **Unit 5, Lesson 5**, p. 473I
TESTED: **Informal Assessment**, p. 473I

Skills Trace

Penmanship: Joining with Y and w

Introduced in Grade 3 (*Y*) and Grade 2 (*w*).
Scaffolded throughout Grades 4–5 and Grades 3–5.

INTRODUCED: **Unit 5, Lesson 5**, p. 473J
PRACTICED: **Unit 5, Lesson 5**, p. 473J
TESTED: **Informal Assessment**

Reading

COMPREHENSION

Making Inferences

Introduced in Grade 2.
Scaffolded throughout Grades 3–5.

REINTRODUCED: **Unit 1, Lesson 2**
REINFORCED: **Unit 2, Lesson 3**; **Unit 3, Lesson 4**; **Unit 5, Lesson 5**; **Unit 6, Lesson 5**
TESTED: **Unit 5 Assessment**

COMPREHENSION

Author's Point of View

Introduced in Grade 2.
Scaffolded throughout Grades 3–5.

REINTRODUCED: **Unit 1, Lesson 6**
REINFORCED: **Unit 3, Lesson 1**; **Unit 6, Lesson 4**
TESTED: **Unit 5 Assessment**

Professional Development: Comprehension

Fluency

Decoding is the process of analyzing graphic symbols to determine their intended meaning. To learn to read, a child must learn the code in which something is written in order to decode the written message. Reading fluency is the freedom from word-identification problems that hinder reading comprehension.

Gaining reading fluency automatically allows students to use their time and energy to comprehend the whole text rather than using up all their energy in simple word-by-word decoding. Becoming fluent is essential to comprehension. Without fluency there is no comprehension.

The best way for students to gain fluency is to practice reading—even when they have a limited knowledge of sounds and spellings. Practice reading is most effective when the material is decodable with sounds and spellings students already know and sight words they have learned.

Truly decodable books are those in which more than 75% of the words in the book either

- contain only sound/spellings that have been explicitly taught.
- are high-frequency words that have been taught.
- are nondecodable (irregular) words that have been explicitly taught.

Even high-frequency words such as *and* are considered nondecodable until each and every sound/symbol relationship has been explicitly taught.

Decodable books help students who have learned only a limited number of sounds and spellings practice reading. Most importantly, they help students grasp the idea that learning to use sound/spelling correspondences and a blending strategy unlocks the words of written language.

Applying their growing knowledge of words and phonic elements, students can read these simple, engaging stories themselves and thereby experience early success with reading. As students read and reread these materials, they gain crucial practice in reading and develop fluency, which is the gateway to comprehension.

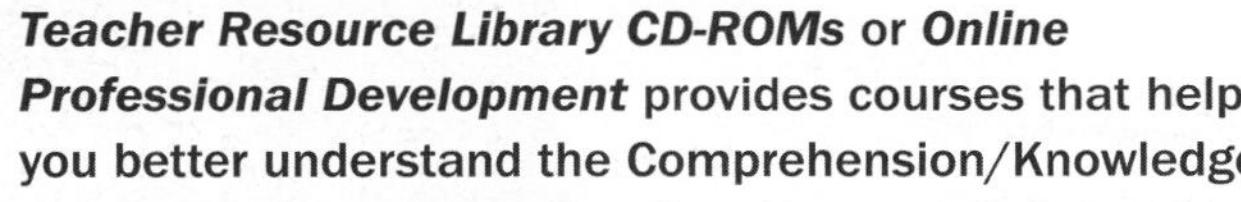

Professional Development

Teacher Resource Library CD-ROMs or ***Online Professional Development*** provides courses that help you better understand the Comprehension/Knowledge Building instruction in ***Open Court Reading.*** For more information about this program, visit SRAonline.com.

Additional information about comprehension, as well as resource references, can be found in the ***Professional Development Guide: Comprehension.***

SELECTION INTRODUCTION

Selection Summary

Genre: Biography

Written with rich background and dialect, this story begins as Bill's grandparents, who were slaves, travel with their masters across the United States. Two generations later and after the slaves have been freed, Bill Pickett is raised on a small farm in Texas in the thick of cattle country. As he fulfills his dreams of becoming an expert cowboy, his talent and unusual bulldogging style lead him to become a rodeo legend.

Some of the elements of biography are listed below. Biography may have one or more of these elements.

- It is written about a real person's life by someone else.
- It contains important information about a person's life, including details about how the person talks, feels, and thinks about things.
- It may span the person's life or tell about only an important part of the person's life.
- It is almost always told in chronological order.
- It often focuses on the most important events in the person's life, and describes the person's achievements or talents.

About the Author

ANDREA DAVIS PINKNEY has a rich writing background. She and her husband, illustrator Brian Pinkney, have teamed up for several books for children. Her awards include the Best Arts Feature Award by the Highlights for Children Foundation, a Notable Book of the Society of School Librarians International, a Booklist Top 25 Black History Picks, and a Reading Rainbow honor.

Students can read more about Andrea Davis Pinkney on page 495 of the ***Student Anthology.***

Other Books by Andrea Davis Pinkney:

- *Alvin Ailey*
- *Raven in a Dove House*
- *Duke Ellington: The Piano Prince and his Orchestra*

About the Illustrator

BRIAN PINKNEY is a highly acclaimed illustrator of books for children. His many awards include the Boston Globe-Horn Book Award, a Caldecott Honor, a Parent's Choice Award, two Coretta Scott King Honors, and a Newbery Honor Book.

Students can read more about Brian Pinkney on page 495 of the ***Student Anthology.***

Other Books Illustrated by Brian Pinkney:

- *Alvin Ailey*
- *Cut from the Same Cloth*
- *Sukey and the Mermaid*

Inquiry Connections

A major aim of ***Open Court Reading*** is knowledge building. Because inquiry is at the root of knowledge building, students are encouraged to investigate topics and questions within each selection that relate to the unit theme.

"Bill Pickett: Rodeo-Ridin' Cowboy" is the true tale of a hero of the American West.

Through this biography the reader sees glimpses of family and farm life, life as a rodeo star, and the growing cattle business.

Key concepts to be explored are:

- After the Civil War, about eight thousand former slaves headed west to become cowboys. Nearly one-fourth of all cowboys were African-Americans.
- Cowboys and ranch hands participated in rodeo competitions in which they showed off their riding and roping skills for recreation and cash prizes.

Before reading the selection:

- Point out that students may post a question, concept, word, illustration, or object on the Concept/Question Board at any time during the course of their unit investigation. Be sure that students include their names or initials on the items they post so that others will know whom to go to if they have an answer or if they wish to collaborate on a related activity.
- Students should feel free to write an answer or a note on someone else's question or to consult the Board for ideas for their own investigations throughout the unit.
- Encourage students to read about the American West at home and to bring in articles or pictures that are good examples to post on the Board.

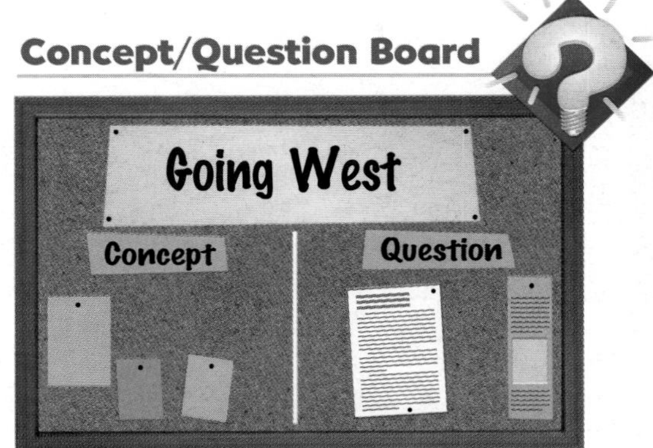

PROGRAM RESOURCES

Leveled Practice

Reteach
Pages 166–170

Challenge
Pages 146–149

English Learner Support Activities

Intervention Workbook

Leveled Classroom Library*

Have students read at least 30 minutes daily outside of class. Have them read books from the ***Leveled Classroom Library,*** which supports the unit theme and helps students develop their vocabulary by reading independently.

Striking It Rich: The Story of the California Gold Rush

BY STEPHEN KRENSKY. ALADDIN, 1996.

A concise history of the Gold Rush, simply told, including how the miners came West, how they panned for gold, how some got rich without finding gold, and the Rush's effect on the growth of California. **(Easy)**

By the Great Horn Spoon!

BY SID FLEISCHMAN. LITTLE, BROWN AND COMPANY, 1963.

Narrated with flair, these are the adventures of young Jack Flagg and his unflappable butler Praiseworthy as they hop a gold ship bound from Boston to California to save Jack's aunt's fortune by striking gold. **(Average)**

Children of the Wild West

BY RUSSELL FREEDMAN. CLARION, 1983.

Historic and fascinating photographs accompany Freedman's details about the experiences of pioneer and Native American children in the West, including the journey west, schools, work, and play. **(Advanced)**

* These books, which all support the unit theme Going West, are part of a 36-book ***Leveled Classroom Library*** available for purchase from SRA/McGraw-Hill. Note: Teachers should preview any trade books for appropriateness in their classrooms before recommending them to students.

SRA TECHNOLOGY

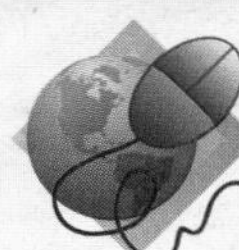

Web Connections

- Going West Web site
- Online Professional Development
- Online Assessment

CD-ROMs

- Research Assistant
- Ultimate Writing and Creativity Center
- Teacher Resource Library

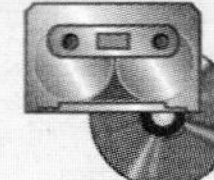

Audiocassettes/CDs

- Listening Library: Going West

Computer Skills

- TechKnowledge

Materials are available through SRA/McGraw-Hill.

LESSON PLANNER

Suggested Pacing: 3–5 days

	DAY 1	DAY 2
1 Preparing to Read **Materials** ■ Routine Card 1	**Word Knowledge,** p. 474K ■ Hyphenated Compound Words ■ Long a Spelled *ai* ■ Inflectional Ending *-ed* ■ Endings *-er* and *-est* **About the Words and Sentences,** p. 474K	**Developing Oral Language,** p. 474L
2 Reading & Responding **Materials** ■ Student Anthology, pp. 474–495 ■ Routine Card 1 ■ Reading Transparencies 45, 54, 58, 68 ■ Comprehension and Language Arts, pp. 166–167 ■ Program Assessment ■ Home Connection, pp. 73–74 ■ Inquiry Journal, p. 115 ■ Unit 5 Assessment, pp. 22–25 ■ Reteach, pp. 166–167 ■ Challenge, p. 146	**Build Background,** p. 474M **Preview and Prepare,** pp. 474M–474N **Selection Vocabulary,** p. 474N **Reading Recommendations,** pp. 474O–474P **Student Anthology,** pp. 474–493 First Read ✓ **Comprehension Strategies** ■ Predicting, pp. 474, 480, 482, 484, 486, 488 ■ Summarizing, pp. 476, 480, 484, 488, 492 ■ Visualizing, pp. 478, 490 **Discussing Strategy Use,** p. 492 **Discussing the Selection,** p. 493A	**Student Anthology,** pp. 474–493 Second Read **Comprehension Skills** ■ Fact and Opinion, pp. 475, 477, 479, 481, 483, 485, 487, 489, 491, 493 **Supporting the Reading** ■ Fact and Opinion, pp. 493C–493D ✓ **Checking Comprehension,** p. 493
Inquiry **Materials** ■ Student Anthology, pp. 474–495 ■ Inquiry Journal, pp. 135–136 ■ Research Assistant	**Investigation** ■ Investigating Concepts Beyond the Text, p. 495A	**Investigation** ■ Concept/Question Board, p. 495B
3 Language Arts **Materials** ■ Comprehension and Language Arts Skills, pp. 168–169 ■ Language Arts Handbook ■ Language Arts Transparency 35 ■ Spelling and Vocabulary Skills, pp. 126–129 ■ Routine Card 2 ■ Student Anthology ■ Student Writing and Research Center ■ Writer's Workbook, pp. 98–101 ■ Unit 5 Assessment, pp. 40–41 ■ Reteach, pp. 168–170 ■ Challenge, pp. 147–149	**Word Analysis** ✓■ Spelling: Words with *-er* and *-est* Pretest, p. 495F **Writing Process Strategies** ■ Personal Writing: Letter of Request, Getting Ideas, p. 495F **English Language Conventions** ■ Mechanics: Commas and Quotations, p. 495F	**Word Analysis** ■ Spelling: Words with *-er* and *-est*, p. 495G ■ Vocabulary: Compound Words, p. 495G **Writing Process Strategies** ■ Personal Writing: Letter of Request, Prewriting, p. 495G **English Language Conventions** ■ Mechanics: Commas and Quotations, p. 495G

✓ Informal Assessment Available ✓ Formal Assessment Available

DAY 2 continued	DAY 3	
DAY 3	**DAY 4**	**DAY 5**
General Review	**General Review**	**Review Word Knowledge**
Student Anthology, pp. 494–495 ✓■ Concept Connections ■ Meet the Author/Illustrator	**Review Selection Vocabulary,** p. 493B **Literary Elements** ■ Biography, p. 493E	✓ **Lesson Assessment** ■ *Unit 5 Assessment:* Lesson Assessment, "Bill Pickett: Rodeo-Ridin' Cowboy," pp. 22–25 **Home Connection,** p. 493B **Social Studies Connection** ■ Moving West, p. 493F
Investigation ✓■ Continuing Investigation and Getting Feedback, p. 495C	**Supporting the Investigation** ■ Technology in Presentations, p. 495D	**Investigation** ■ Unit Investigation Continued ■ Update Concept/Question Board
Word Analysis ■ Spelling: Words with *-er* and *-est,* p. 495H ■ Vocabulary: Compound Words, p. 495H **Writing Process Strategies** ■ Personal Writing: Letter of Request, Drafting, p. 495H **English Language Conventions** ✓■ Mechanics: Commas and Quotations, p. 495H	**Word Analysis** ■ Spelling: Words with *-er* and *-est,* p. 495I ■ Vocabulary: Compound Words, p. 495I **Writing Process Strategies** ■ Personal Writing: Letter of Request, Revising, p. 495I **English Language Conventions** ✓■ Listening, Speaking, Viewing Interacting: Group Presentations, p. 495I	**Word Analysis** ✓■ Spelling: Words with *-er* and *-est* Final Test, p. 495J ✓■ Vocabulary: Compound Words, p. 495J **Writing Process Strategies** ✓■ Personal Writing: Letter of Request, Editing/Proofreading and Publishing, p. 495J **English Language Conventions** ✓■ Penmanship: Joining with *N* and *t,* p. 495J

Below are suggestions for differentiating instruction to meet the individual needs of students. These are the same skills shown on the Lesson Planner; however, these pages provide extra practice opportunities or enriching activities to meet the varied needs of students.

WORKSHOP

Differentiating Instruction

Teacher: Individual and Small-Group Instruction

Spend time each day with individuals and small groups to individualize instruction. Each day:

- preteach students who need help with the next lesson.
- reteach students who need to solidify their understanding of content previously taught.
- listen to students read to check their fluency.
- hold writing and inquiry conferences.

Use the following program components to support instruction:

- ***Reteach*** with students who need a bit more practice.
- ***Intervention*** with students who exhibit a lack of understanding of the lesson concepts.
- ***English Learner Support*** with students who need language help.

Student: Independent Activities

Students can work alone, with a partner, or in small groups on such activities as:

- Review sound/spellings
- Partner Reading
- Practice fluency
- Independent Reading
- Reading Roundtable
- Concept vocabulary
- Selection vocabulary
- Writing in progress
- Conference
- Language Arts
- ***Challenge*** Activities
- Inquiry and Investigation Activities
- Listening Library

Professional Development

Teacher Resource Library CD-ROMs or ***Online Professional Development*** provides courses that help you better understand the Workshop/Intervention instruction in ***Open Court Reading.*** For more information about this program, visit SRAonline.com.

	DAY 1
Word Knowledge	**Teacher Directed** ▪ Teach meanings of blended words ▪ Reading Words and About the Words, ***Intervention Guide***, p. 273
Fluency	**Independent Activities** ▪ Self-test fluency rate
Comprehension	**Teacher Directed** ▪ Preteach "Bill Pickett: Rodeo-Ridin' Cowboy," ***Intervention Guide***, pp. 274–275 ▪ Intervention Selection 1, ***Intervention Guide***, pp. 275–276 ▪ ***English Learner Support Guide***, pp. 438–440 **Independent Activities** ▪ Record response to selection in Writer's Notebook ▪ ***Listening Library Audiocassette/CD*** ▪ Add vocabulary in Writer's Notebook
Inquiry	**Independent Activities** ▪ Concept/Question Board ▪ Explore OCR Web site for theme connections
Language Arts	**Teacher Directed** ▪ Seminar: Select a Topic for a Letter of Request, p. 495F ▪ Commas with Appositives, ***Intervention Guide,*** p. 278 **Independent Activities** ▪ Commas with Quotation Marks, Appositives, Interrupters, and Introductory Words, ***Comprehension and Language Arts Skills,*** p. 168–169

DAY 2	DAY 3	DAY 4	DAY 5
Teacher Directed ▪ Developing Oral Language, ***Intervention Guide***, p. 273	**Teacher Directed** ▪ Dictation and Spelling, ***Intervention Guide,*** pp. 273–274	**Independent Activities** ▪ Add words to Word Bank	**Teacher Directed** ▪ General review as necessary
Independent Activities ▪ Oral reading of "Bill Pickett: Rodeo-Ridin' Cowboy"	**Independent Activities** ▪ Partner read "Bill Pickett: Rodeo-Ridin' Cowboy"	**Independent Activities** ▪ Fluency rate check ▪ Reread "Bill Pickett: Rodeo-Ridin' Cowboy"	**Teacher Directed** ▪ Repeated Readings, ***Intervention Guide,*** p. 277 **Independent Activities** ▪ Fluency rate check
Teacher Directed ▪ Preteach "Bill Pickett: Rodeo-Ridin' Cowboy," ***Intervention Guide***, pp. 274–275 ▪ Reread Intervention Selection 1 ▪ Teach Comprehension Strategies, ***Intervention Guide***, p. 276 ▪ ***English Learner Support Guide***, pp. 441–444 ▪ Review Fact and Opinion ▪ Fact and Opinion, ***Reteach***, pp. 166–167 **Independent Activities** ▪ Fact and Opinion • ***Comprehension and Language Arts Skills***, pp. 166–167 • ***Challenge***, p. 146 • Challenge Tip, 146 ▪ ***English Learner Support Activities***, p. 64	**Teacher Directed** ▪ Teach Intervention Selection 2, ***Intervention Guide***, pp. 276–277 ▪ ***English Learner Support Guide***, pp. 444–446 ▪ Discuss Concept Connections, p. 494 **Independent Activities** ▪ ***Listening Library Audiocassette/CD*** ▪ Independent reading ▪ Supporting the Reading: Link to Writing, p. 493D ▪ Recording Concept Information, ***Inquiry Journal***, p. 115	**Teacher Directed** ▪ Teach Comprehension Strategies, ***Intervention Guide***, p. 277 ▪ Reread Intervention Selection 2 ▪ ***English Learner Support Guide***, pp. 447–450 **Independent Activities** ▪ Literary Elements: Independent Practice, p. 493E	**Teacher Directed** ▪ Reading Roundtable ▪ ***English Learner Support Guide,*** pp. 450–451 **Independent Activities** ▪ Social Studies Connection, p. 493F ▪ ***English Learner Support Activities***, p. 65
Independent Activities ▪ Concept/Question Board ▪ Explore OCR Web site for theme connections	**Teacher Directed** ▪ Begin informal presentations **Independent Activities** ▪ Concept/Question Board ▪ Use ***Research Assistant*** to continue investigation ▪ Feedback, ***Inquiry Journal***, p. 135	**Teacher Directed** ▪ Continue informal presentations **Independent Activities** ▪ Concept/Question Board ▪ Feedback, ***Inquiry Journal***, p. 135	**Independent Activities** ▪ Concept/Question Board ▪ Using Technology, ***Inquiry Journal***, p. 136 ▪ Continue research
Teacher Directed ▪ Commas with Appositives, ***Intervention Guide***, p. 278 ▪ Spelling: Word Sort, p. 495G ▪ Seminar: Plan a Letter of Request, p. 495G ▪ Commas with Quotation Marks, Appositives, Interrupters, and Introductory Words, ***Reteach***, p. 170 **Independent Activities** ▪ Vocabulary: Compound Words, ***Spelling and Vocabulary Skills***, p. 128 ▪ Commas, ***Challenge***, p. 149	**Teacher Directed** ▪ Seminar: Revise a Letter of Request, p. 495H ▪ Writing Activity, ***Intervention Guide***, p. 279 ▪ Vocabulary: Compound Words, ***Reteach***, p. 169 **Independent Activities** ▪ Spelling: Words with *-er* and *-est*, ***Spelling and Vocabulary Skills***, p. 128 ▪ Vocabulary: Compound Words, ***Challenge***, p. 148	**Teacher Directed** ▪ Seminar: Revise a Letter of Request, p. 495I ▪ Writing Activity, ***Intervention Guide***, p. 279 ▪ Spelling: Words with *-er* and *-est*, ***Reteach***, p. 168 **Independent Activities** ▪ Spelling: Words with *-er* and *-est* • ***Spelling and Vocabulary Skills***, p. 129 • ***Challenge***, p. 147	**Teacher Directed** ▪ Seminar: Edit and Publish a Letter of Request, p. 495J **Independent Activities** ▪ Penmanship: Cursive Letters *N* and *t*, p. 495J

ASSESSMENT

Formal Assessment Options

Use these summative assessments along with your informal observations to assess student progress.

Name ______________________ Date ________ Score _____

UNIT 5 Going West • Lesson 6

Bill Pickett: Rodeo-Ridin' Cowboy

Read the following questions carefully. Then completely fill in the bubble of each correct answer. You may look back at the story to find the answer to each of the questions.

1. Which of these is a fact from the story?
   Ⓐ Willie Pickett was more active than most children.
   Ⓑ Being in a rodeo is one of the most dangerous jobs.
   ● Bill Pickett's parents came from South Carolina.
2. The author compares freedom to
   ● bluebonnet blossoms
   Ⓑ the Texas prairie
   Ⓒ parched soil

Read the following questions carefully. Use complete sentences to answer the questions.

3. How does the author describe Willie Pickett as a child?
   The author says that Willie Pickett was quick as a jackrabbit, more wide-eyed than a hooty owl, and curious.
4. How did the Pickett family spend their evenings?
   The Pickett family spent their evenings by swapping stories.
5. What interested Bill most at an early age?
   Bill was most interested in the cowboys who drove thousands of longhorn steers past his parents' farm.

22 Unit 5 • Lesson 6 *Bill Pickett* • Unit 5 Assessment

LESSON ASSESSMENT

Unit 5 Assessment p. 22

Bill Pickett *(continued)*

6. Why was it hard at first for Bill to join the rodeo?
   It was hard for him because he had to leave his family, and some people didn't want an African-American cowboy.
7. Why did the Millers want to hire Bill?
   The Millers wanted to hire Bill because he could draw a crowd and put on a good show.
8. What did people do to show that they liked Bill's riding skills?
   To show Bill they liked his skills, the people dropped coins in his hat.

Read the following questions carefully. Then completely fill in the bubble of each correct answer.

9. Where does this story take place?
   Ⓐ Utah
   Ⓑ Arizona
   ● Texas
10. How did Bill get a bull to go down without a fight?
   ● He bit the animal's lip.
   Ⓑ He pushed the animal over.
   Ⓒ He sang a song to the animal.

Unit 5 Assessment • *Bill Pickett* Unit 5 • Lesson 6 23

LESSON ASSESSMENT

Unit 5 Assessment p. 23

Bill Pickett *(continued)*

Read the question and statement below. Use complete sentences in your answers.

Linking to the Concepts Write about how Bill's early life led to his career.
Answers will vary. Accept all reasonable answers.

Personal Response Bill worked hard to develop his talents and become successful. What talents would you like to develop, and how would they help you become successful?
Answers will vary. Accept all reasonable answers.

24 Unit 5 • Lesson 6 *Bill Pickett* • Unit 5 Assessment

LESSON ASSESSMENT

Unit 5 Assessment p. 24

Bill Pickett *(continued)*

Vocabulary

Read the following questions carefully. Then completely fill in the bubble of each correct answer.

1. To pass the time on the slow, steady trek, the southerners sang traveling songs. Another word for **trek** is
   Ⓐ meal
   ● journey
   Ⓒ race
2. The cowboys looked at this brazen boy and went back to their work. **Brazen** means
   ● pushy
   Ⓑ thin
   Ⓒ shy
3. According to the story, bulldogging was invented by feisty Bill Pickett. Someone who is **feisty** is
   Ⓐ smart and proud
   Ⓑ calm and wise
   ● frisky and brave
4. One of the cowboys put forth a challenge. In this sentence, a **challenge** is
   Ⓐ something everyone already knows
   ● something that may be difficult to do
   Ⓒ something that makes people angry
5. Even when Bill Pickett was very young, he was itching for adventure. **Adventure** means
   ● a fun or exciting experience
   Ⓑ a place to call your very own
   Ⓒ a treasure that makes you rich

Unit 5 Assessment • *Bill Pickett* Unit 5 • Lesson 6 25

LESSON ASSESSMENT

Unit 5 Assessment p. 25

Name ______________________ Date ________ Score _____

UNIT 5 Going West • Lesson 6 *Bill Pickett: Rodeo-Ridin' Cowboy*

Spelling Pretest: Words with *-er* and *-est*

Fold this page back on the dotted line. Take the Pretest. Then correct any word you misspelled by crossing out the word and rewriting it next to the incorrect spelling.

1.	________	1.	happiest
2.	________	2.	wiser
3.	________	3.	slimmer
4.	________	4.	calmest
5.	________	5.	dishonest
6.	________	6.	container
7.	________	7.	scariest
8.	________	8.	daughter
9.	________	9.	easiest
10.	________	10.	saltier
11.	________	11.	cheaper
12.	________	12.	dirtiest
13.	________	13.	farthest
14.	________	14.	nearest
15.	________	15.	loser
16.	________	16.	loudest
17.	________	17.	feistiest
18.	________	18.	closer
19.	________	19.	greater
20.	________	20.	harshest

40 Unit 5 • Lesson 6 *Spelling Pretest: Words with -er and -est* • Unit 5 Assessment

LESSON ASSESSMENT

Unit 5 Assessment p. 40

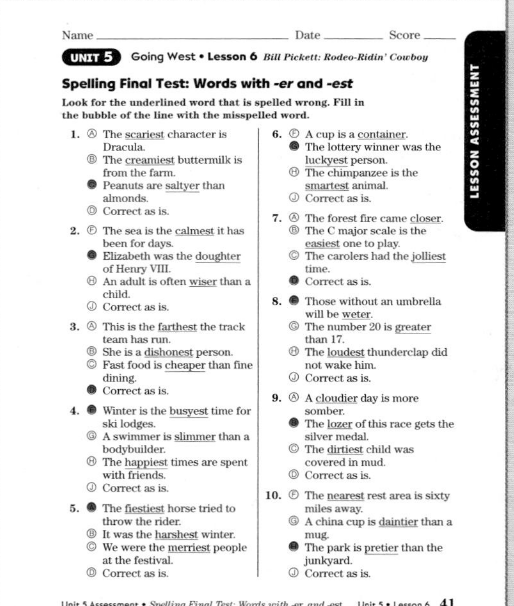

Name ______________________ Date ________ Score _____

UNIT 5 Going West • Lesson 6 *Bill Pickett: Rodeo-Ridin' Cowboy*

Spelling Final Test: Words with *-er* and *-est*

Look for the underlined word that is spelled wrong. Fill in the bubble of the line with the misspelled word.

1. Ⓐ The scariest character is Dracula.
   Ⓑ The creamiest buttermilk is from the farm.
   ● Peanuts are saltyer than almonds.
   Ⓓ Correct as is.
2. Ⓕ The sea is the calmest it has been for days.
   ● Elizabeth was the doughter of Henry VIII.
   Ⓗ An adult is often wiser than a child.
   Ⓙ Correct as is.
3. Ⓐ This is the farthest the track team has run.
   Ⓑ She is a dishonest person.
   Ⓒ Fast food is cheaper than fine dining.
   ● Correct as is.
4. ● Winter is the busyest time for ski lodges.
   Ⓖ A swimmer is slimmer than a bodybuilder.
   Ⓗ The happiest times are spent with friends.
   Ⓙ Correct as is.
5. ● The fiestiest horse tried to throw the rider.
   Ⓑ It was the harshest winter.
   Ⓒ We were the merriest people at the festival.
   Ⓓ Correct as is.
6. Ⓕ A cup is a container.
   ● The lottery winner was the luckyest person.
   Ⓗ The chimpanzee is the smartest animal.
   Ⓙ Correct as is.
7. Ⓐ The forest fire came closer.
   Ⓑ The C major scale is the easiest one to play.
   Ⓒ The carolers had the jolliest time.
   ● Correct as is.
8. ● Those without an umbrella will be weter.
   Ⓖ The number 20 is greater than 17.
   Ⓗ The loudest thunderclap did not wake him.
   Ⓙ Correct as is.
9. Ⓐ A cloudier day is more somber.
   ● The lozer of this race gets the silver medal.
   Ⓒ The dirtiest child was covered in mud.
   Ⓓ Correct as is.
10. Ⓕ The nearest rest area is sixty miles away.
   Ⓖ A china cup is daintier than a mug.
   ● The park is pretier than the junkyard.
   Ⓙ Correct as is.

Unit 5 Assessment • *Spelling Final Test: Words with -er, and -est* Unit 5 • Lesson 6 41

LESSON ASSESSMENT

Unit 5 Assessment p. 41

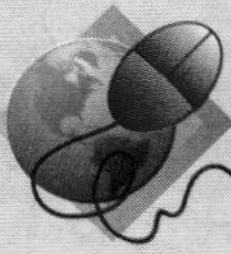

Online Assessment for ***Open Court Reading*** helps teachers differentiate classroom instruction based on students' scores from the weekly and end-of-unit assessments. It provides exercises best suited to meet the needs of each student. For more information visit SRAonline.com.

Informal Comprehension Strategies Rubrics

Predicting

- The student makes predictions about what the text is about.
- The student updates predictions during reading, based on information in the text.

Summarizing

- The student paraphrases text, reporting main ideas and a summary of what is in text.
- The student decides which parts of the text are important in his or her summary.
- The student draws conclusions from the text.
- The student makes global interpretations of the text, such as recognizing the genre.

Visualizing

- The student visualizes ideas or scenes described in the text.

Research Rubrics

During Workshop, assess students using the rubrics below. The rubrics range from 1–4 in most categories, with 1 being the lowest score. Record each student's score on the inside back cover of his or her ***Inquiry Journal.***

Revising Problems and Conjectures

1 No revision.
2 Produces new problems or conjectures with little relation to earlier ones.
3 Tends to lift problems and conjectures directly from reference material.
4 Progresses to deeper, more refined problems and conjectures.

Objectives

- Students determine the relationships between hyphenated compounds and the words they modify.
- Students identify and decode words containing the /ā/ sound spelled *ai.*
- Students identify words that have the *-ed* ending.
- Students recognize and spell words with *-er* and *-est.*

Materials

- Routine Card 1

Routine Card Refer to Routine 1 for the Reading the Words and Sentences procedure.

Teacher Tip SYLLABICATION To help students blend words and build fluency, use the syllabication below of the decodable multisyllabic words in the word lines.

free-spir • it • ed	feist • i • est
a • vai • la • ble	clos • er
per • formed	great • er
bull • dogged	harsh • est
loud • est	

The hyphens in the last three words in Line 1 separate the first and last syllables of the words.

Differentiating Instruction

If...	Then...
Students need extra help with words containing the inflectional ending *-ed*	Use ***Intervention Guide***, pages 273–274

Teacher Tip INFLECTIONAL ENDINGS Check that students' reading and writing reflect an understanding of how the inflectional ending *-ed* is used to change a verb's tense or its part of speech. Remind students to use context clues to determine the meaning of words with this ending. Also remind them to edit their writing for standard use of inflections.

WORD KNOWLEDGE

Word Knowledge

Reading the Words and Sentences

Use direct teaching to teach the Word Knowledge lesson. Write each word and sentence on the board. Have students read each word together. After all the words have been read, have students read each sentence in natural phrases or chunks. Use the suggestions in About the Words and Sentences to discuss the different features of the listed words.

Line 1:	free-spirited full-scale small-time best-loved
Line 2:	trail raise plain available
Line 3:	worked performed cheered bulldogged
Line 4:	loudest feistiest closer greater harshest
Sentence 1:	Bill Pickett performed in a full-scale rodeo.
Sentence 2:	The horses worked their way down the rocky trail.
Sentence 3:	The crowds cheered as the free-spirited rodeo star rode into the ring.
Sentence 4:	Mr. Sanchez concluded that Pedro's friends were the loudest and feistiest he had ever seen.

About the Words and Sentences

- **Line 1:** This line contains hyphenated compound words. Have students determine the meaning of each compound by separating each into two words, determining the meaning of each word separately, then putting the two words and meanings back together to form a new meaning. Explain that when hyphenated compounds function as adjectives, they work together to modify a noun. The first word in the hyphenated compound modifies the second and together they modify the noun. For example, in a *best-loved book*, the word *best* describes *loved*, not *book.*
- **Line 2:** The words in this line have /ā/ spelled *ai.* Have students brainstorm a list of additional words that have long a spelled *ai.* Then, have students make a list of the other spellings of /ā/.
- **Line 3:** All of the words in this line have the inflectional ending *-ed.* Have students identify each root word. Ask students how adding the ending to each root word changes its meaning.
- **Line 4:** The words in the last line review the word endings *-er* and *-est.*

- **Sentences 1 and 3:** Have students read the sentences aloud. Then, have students read the words ending in *-ed (performed, cheered, free-spirited)* and identify the hyphenated compounds.
- **Sentence 2:** Have them read the sentence aloud. Then, have students identify the word containing the long a sound spelled *ai.*
- **Sentence 4:** Have students read the words in the last sentence that contain the ending *-est.* Have them give the root and comparative forms of each. *(loud, louder, feisty, feistier)*

Developing Oral Language

Use direct teaching to review the words. Have students do one or both of the following activities:

- Have students use each of the hyphenated compounds in a sentence. Then have the students identify the noun that the hyphenated compound modifies.
- Students choose words from the board and give clues to one another for their chosen word. The person who figures out the word then picks a new word and gives clues to the rest of the class. Students should use complete sentences and vivid descriptions when possible.

WORD KNOWLEDGE

Teacher Tip BUILDING FLUENCY By this time in grade 5 students should be reading approximately 151 words per minute with fluency and expression. Gaining a better understanding of the spellings of sounds and structure of words will help students as they encounter unfamiliar words in their reading. As students read, you may notice that some need work in building fluency. During Workshop, have these students choose a section of the text (a minimum of 160 words) to read several times in order to build fluency.

Differentiating Instruction

If...	Then...
Students need extra fluency practice	Use the Intervention Selections activities, ***Intervention Guide***, pages 475–477

Spelling
See pages 495F–495J for the corresponding spelling lesson for the endings *-er* and *-est.*

Objectives

- Students will understand the selection vocabulary before reading.
- Students will identify and decode words with the long a spelled *ai* and words ending in *-ed.*
- Students will use the comprehension strategies Predicting, Summarizing, and Visualizing as they read the story the first time.
- Students will use the comprehension skill Fact and Opinion as they read the story the second time.

Materials

- Student Anthology, pp. 474–495
- Reading Transparencies 45, 54, 58, 68
- Comprehension and Language Arts Skills, pp. 166–167
- Inquiry Journal, p. 115
- Listening Library
- Program Assessment
- Unit 5 Assessment, pp. 22–25
- Home Connection, pp. 73–74

Differentiating Instruction

If...	Then...
Students need extra help with the selection vocabulary	Use ***Intervention Guide,*** page 274

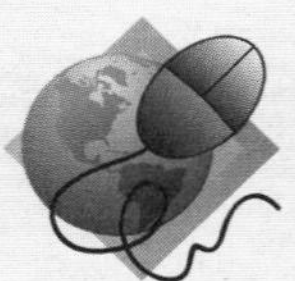

www.sra4kids.com
Web Connection
Students can use the connections to Going West in the Reading link of the SRA Web page for more background information about the American West.

Build Background

Activate Prior Knowledge

Discuss the following with students to find out what they may already know about the selection and have already learned about the theme Going West.

- Preteach "Bill Pickett: Rodeo-Ridin' Cowboy" by first determining students' prior knowledge about cowboys. Ask them, "What do cowboys do?" *(They herd and take care of cattle on a ranch.)*

Background Information

The following information may help students better understand the selection they are about to read.

- The first cowboys were from the Mexican and Texan ranches where *vaqueros*, or Mexican ranch hands, devised the equipment and techniques of the cowboy.
- Rodeos began around 1882. Buffalo Bill Cody was one of the first famous cowboys to arrange rodeos; his first attracted 1,000 cowboys as contestants. This inspired Buffalo Bill's Wild West Shows that traveled the country showing off the skills of the cowboys. These shows continued for 55 years.
- Explain to students that bulldogging was a skill that cowboys often used while working with cattle. To *bulldog* is to throw a steer by seizing the horns and twisting the neck to gain control of the animal. Discuss why this might be an important skill for a cowboy in the American West.
- Be aware that Bill Pickett's unique bulldogging technique may be a sensitive issue in your classroom.
- Have the students discuss what they know about the genre of this selection. Refer to page 474A of the ***Teacher's Edition*** for elements of this selection's genre.

Preview and Prepare

Browse

- Have a student read the title and the names of the author and illustrator aloud. Demonstrate how to browse. Then, since this is a nonfiction piece, have the students preview the selection by browsing the illustrations and text in the entire piece. This helps them to establish what they want to learn from the selection and activate prior knowledge in a way that is relevant to the selection. Then discuss what they think this story might have to do with going west.

- Have the students search for clues that tell them something about the story. Also, have them look for any problems, such as unfamiliar words, that they notice while reading. Use ***Reading Transparency 54*** to record their observations as they browse. For example, the word *rodeo* might be a clue as to where the story is set. For the Problems column, students might say they don't know the meaning of the word *bulldogging.* They might wonder how Bill gets into the rodeo. To save time and model note taking, write students' observations as brief notes rather than complete sentences.
- As students prepare to read the selection, have them browse the Focus Questions on the first page of the selection. Tell them to keep these questions in mind as they read.

Set Purposes

Have students set their own purposes before they begin reading. As they read, have students think about the cowboy way of life, both past and present. Remind students that good readers have a purpose when they read. Let them know that they should make sure they know the purpose for reading whenever they read.

Selection Vocabulary

As students study vocabulary, they will use a variety of skills to determine the meaning of a word. These include context clues, word structure, and apposition. Students will apply these same skills while reading to clarify additional unfamiliar words.

Display ***Transparency 45*** before reading the selection to introduce the following words and their meanings.

trek: a long, slow journey (page 475)
ravage: to destroy (page 476)
brazen: bold, fearless (page 482)
challenge: something that may be difficult to do (page 482)
feisty: frisky and brave, eager for excitement (page 482)
adventure: a fun or exciting experience (page 483)

Have students read the words in the Word Box, stopping to blend any words that they have trouble reading. Demonstrate how to decode multisyllabic words by breaking them into syllables and blending the syllables. Then, have the students try. If the word is not decodable, give the students the pronunciation.

Have students read the sentences on ***Reading Transparency 45*** and use the skills of context, word structure (structural analysis), or apposition to figure out the meanings of the words. Be sure students explain which skill(s) they are using and how they figured out the meanings of the words.

Clues	Problems	Wonderings
Enslaved Cowboy Rodeo Biography	Wagon train Bulldogging	How does Bill get into the rodeo?

Open Court Reading — Reading Transparency 54

Reading Transparency 54

Teacher Tip SELECTION VOCABULARY To help students decode words, divide them into the syllables shown below. The information following each word tells how students can figure out the meaning of each word from the sentences on the transparency.

trek	context clues
rav • age	context clues, word structure
bra • zen	context clues
chal • lenge	context clues
feist • y	context clues
ad • ven • ture	context clues

Routine Card
Refer to Routine 2 for the Selection Vocabulary procedure. Refer to Routine 3 for the Clues, Problems, and Wonderings procedure.

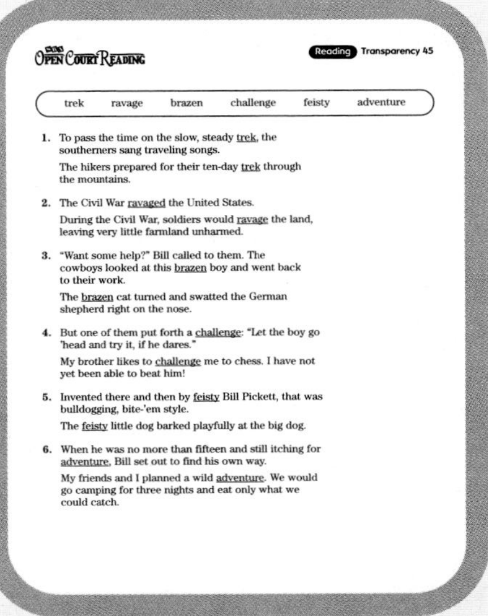

Open Court Reading — Reading Transparency 45

trek ravage brazen challenge feisty adventure

1. To pass the time on the slow, steady trek, the southerners sang traveling songs.
   The hikers prepared for their ten-day trek through the mountains.
2. The Civil War ravaged the United States.
   During the Civil War, soldiers would ravage the land, leaving very little farmland unharmed.
3. "Want some help?" Bill called to them. The cowboys looked at this brazen boy and went back to their work.
   The brazen cat turned and swatted the German shepherd right on the nose.
4. But one of them put forth a challenge: "Let the boy go 'head and try it, if he dares."
   My brother likes to challenge me to chess. I have not yet been able to beat him!
5. Invented there and then by feisty Bill Pickett, that was bulldogging, bite-'em style.
   The feisty little dog barked playfully at the big dog.
6. When he was no more than fifteen and still itching for adventure, Bill set out to find his own way.
   My friends and I planned a wild adventure. We would go camping for three nights and eat only what we could catch.

Reading Transparency 45

Students will enjoy using the ***Listening Library Audiocassette/CD*** and listening to the selection they are about to read. Encourage them to listen to the selection during Workshop. Have students discuss with each other and with you their personal listening preferences (for example, nonfiction, poetry, drama, and so on).

Routine Card
Refer to Routine 4 for the Reading the Selection procedure.

Differentiating Instruction

If...	Then...
Students need extra help with the comprehension strategy Visualizing	Use ***Intervention Guide,*** page 276

Reading Recommendations

Silent Reading

Because of this selection's rich, descriptive language, it is a good selection to have students read silently. Have students read silently for at least fifteen minutes at a time. As they become better readers, students will read silently with increasing ease over longer periods of time. Have them make use of the strategies listed below by recording in their Writer's Notebooks the strategies they used while reading silently. You may want to stop periodically to discuss the selection and strategies used. You may prefer to talk about strategies after the students have read the selection. After the students have finished reading the selection, use the "Discussing the Selection" questions on page 493A to see if they understand what they have read.

Using Comprehension Strategies 

Comprehension strategy instruction allows students to become aware of how good readers read. Good readers constantly check their understanding as they are reading and ask themselves questions. In addition, skilled readers recognize when they are having problems and stop to use various comprehension strategies, to help them make sense of what they are reading.

During the first reading of "Bill Pickett: Rodeo-Ridin' Cowboy," model and prompt the use of the following comprehension strategies. Take turns reading the story aloud with the students.

- **Predicting** causes readers to analyze information given about story events and characters in the context of how it may logically connect to the story's conclusion.
- **Summarizing** prompts readers to keep track of what they are reading and to focus their minds on important information.
- **Visualizing** helps readers to understand descriptions of settings, characters, and events in a story.

As students read, they should be using a variety of strategies to help them understand the selection. Encourage students to use the strategies listed on the previous page as the class reads the story aloud. Do this by stopping at the points indicated by the numbers in magenta circles on the reduced student page and using a particular strategy. Students can also stop reading periodically to discuss what they have learned and what problems they may be having.

In Unit 5, students should be assuming more responsibility for the use of comprehension strategies. Continue Modeling and Prompting as needed. Prompting provides a springboard for students to respond using the strategy mentioned in the prompt. The Student Sample is written in the language that students might use in their actual responses.

The Student Sample may be one of many possible student responses. Accept other responses that are reasonable and appropriate. If student responses indicate that the students do not understand the strategy, be ready to discuss their responses and to provide additional instruction. As students proceed through the lessons, teacher modeling and prompting of strategy use should become less and less necessary.

Building Comprehension Skills Second Read

Revisiting or rereading a selection allows students to apply skills that give them a more complete understanding of the text. Some follow-up comprehension skills help students organize information. Others lead to deeper understanding—to "reading between the lines," as mature readers do. An extended lesson on the comprehension skill Fact and Opinion can be found in the Supporting the Reading section on pages 493C–493D. This lesson is intended to give students extra practice with Fact and Opinion. However, the Teach portion of the lesson may be used at this time to introduce the comprehension skill to students.

- **Fact and Opinion (Review):** Readers determine the validity of the ideas presented in their reading by assessing whether or not a statement is provable.

Reading with a Purpose

Have students think about life as a cowhand as they read and record their thoughts in the Response Journal section of their Writer's Notebooks.

Teacher Tip **GENRE** Remind students that since this is a biography, it was written about the life of a real person by someone else, and may include details about how that person speaks, thinks, and feels.

Differentiating Instruction

If...	Then...
Students need extra help with reading "Bill Pickett: Rodeo-Ridin' Cowboy"	• Preread the selection during Workshop; use the ***Listening Library*** to give students a good reading model • Use ***English Learner Support Guide,*** pages 436–451 • Use ***Intervention Guide,*** pages 274–275

COMPREHENSION

Read pages 474–493.

Comprehension Strategies

Teacher Modeling

1 Predicting *Good readers make predictions to help them focus on the outcomes of events in their reading. This poem is a sort of introduction to the story of "Bill Pickett: Rodeo-Ridin' Cowboy." From the information here, I'd guess that we're going to read about a man named Bill Pickett who rides in rodeos. Because people keep talking about him, I'd guess that he's pretty special, too. Let's keep reading and see if I'm right.*

Word Knowledge

SCAFFOLDING The skills students are reviewing in Word Knowledge should help them in reading the story. This lesson focuses on the long a sound spelled *ai.* These words will be found in boxes similar to this one throughout the selection.

Long a spelled *ai:*

train plains

Teacher Tip MONITORING AND CLARIFYING Some students may need help in clarifying difficult terms in this selection such as *croaker sacks.* Encourage them to share their knowledge about wagon trains and cowboys.

First Reading Recommendation

ORAL • CHORAL • **SILENT**

Focus Questions How did Bill Pickett's family come to live on the Texas plains? What skills did Bill learn by working on the ranch? For what rodeo stunt was Bill famous?

Bill Pickett
Rodeo-Ridin' Cowboy

Andrea D. Pinkney
illustrated by Brian Pinkney

1 *Folks been tellin' the tale*
since way back when.

They been talkin' 'bout
that Pickett boy.

Growed up to be a rodeo-ridin' man.

His story keeps spreadin' on
like swollen waters in the wide Red River.

Yeah, folks been tellin' the tale
since way back when.

And they'll keep on tellin' it
till time's time ends.

—A.D.P.

474

Informal Assessment

Observe individual students as they read and use the Teacher Observation Log found in the ***Program Assessment Teacher's Edition*** to record anecdotal information about each student's strengths and weaknesses.

Differentiating Instruction

If...	Then...
English Learners need extra support with reading "Bill Pickett: Rodeo-Ridin' Cowboy" and using the skill Fact and Opinion	Preteach ***Student Anthology*** pages 474–479 using Day 1 of the "Bill Pickett: Rodeo-Ridin' Cowboy" lesson, found on ***English Learner Support Guide,*** pages 438–441

Long before Bill Pickett was born, a wagon train traveled west, all the way from South Carolina. It was 1854. Eager Americans were packing up their belongings and wheeling on to the Great Plains. Some of these pioneers were white folks, looking for a new life in a new land. The rest were black—enslaved people forced to follow their masters.

The men, women, and children loaded everything they owned into those covered wagons: croaker-sacks, homespun duds, and bedclothes bundled tight. To pass the time on the slow, steady trek, the southerners sang traveling songs:

Westward ho, where the gettin's good.
On to the land of opportunity.
Westward ho, gonna stake my claim.
On to Texas, the Lone Star State.

475

Teacher Tip FACT AND OPINION If students are unclear about the difference between fact and opinion, give examples of each from everyday circumstances. Discuss with students what makes a statement a fact and what makes it an opinion.

COMPREHENSION

Comprehension Skills

Fact and Opinion

Explain to the students that writers often include both *facts* and *opinions* in their writing. Good readers learn to recognize the difference between the two. A fact is something that can be proven true. An opinion is someone's idea; it cannot be proven one way or the other. Opinions can be based on facts.

Tell the students to find a fact on page 475. *(Fact: The men, women, and children loaded everything they owned into those covered wagons.)* Discuss why this is a fact. How could this fact be turned into an opinion?

Word Knowledge

SCAFFOLDED The skills students are reviewing in Word Knowledge should help them in reading the story. This lesson focuses on words ending in *-ed*. These words will be found in boxes similar to this one throughout the selection.

Ending in *-ed:*

traveled **loaded** **owned**

Fact and Opinion

Introduced in Grade 2.
Scaffolded throughout Grades 3–5.

REINTRODUCED: Unit 4, Lesson 6
REINFORCED: Unit 5, Lesson 6
Unit 6, Lesson 3
TESTED: Unit 5 Assessment

Second Reading Recommendation

ORAL • **SILENT**

COMPREHENSION

Comprehension Strategies

Prompting

2 Summarizing *This looks like a good place to stop and sum up the information we have read so far. Who wants to summarize the selection up to this point so that we can be sure we understand it?*

Student Sample

Summarizing *Thomas Jefferson Pickett was born on a wagon train. He and his parents were slaves traveling to Texas. But during the Civil War, Thomas Pickett was freed. He married a woman named Mary Virginia Elizabeth Gilbert. They settled in Jenks-Branch and had 13 children. The second child was named Bill.*

Word Knowledge

Ending in *-ed*:

free-spirited **worked** **parched**

Teacher Tip TALL TALES The author uses tall-tale language in describing Bill Pickett. Some students might enjoy learning about other western tall-tale folk heroes, such as Pecos Bill or John Henry.

During this long journey a baby boy was born. His name was Thomas Jefferson Pickett. He was a free-spirited young'un. But he wasn't free. Born into slavery, he had to wake when his master said *wake*, work when his master said *work*, sleep when his master said *sleep*.

On the Texas plains Thomas grew up learning to brand cattle and swing a lariat. He and his family worked for the white folks, helping them tame the parched soil into prospering feed crops.

Then the Civil War ravaged the United States. And when the war ended, all enslaved people were declared free—as free as the bluebonnet blossoms that covered the Texas prairie.

Thomas married a woman named Mary Virginia Elizabeth Gilbert. They settled with other freed slaves at Jenks-Branch, a small community just north of Austin, Texas. Heaven blessed Thomas and Mary with thirteen children.

Their second-born child was Willie M. Pickett, but folks called him Bill. A young'un who took after his father, Bill was the feistiest boy south of Abilene. He was quick as a
2 jackrabbit, more wide-eyed than a hooty owl—and curious.

476

Informal Assessment

Use the Informal Comprehension Strategies Rubrics on page 474J to determine whether a student is using the strategies being taught.

Differentiating Instruction

If...	Then...
Students are having difficulty summarizing	Remind them to include only main and supporting information; trivial and repetitive information should be left out of summaries

477

Comprehension Skills

Fact and Opinion

Draw the students' attention to some of the facts presented on page 476.

- Thomas Jefferson Pickett was born on a wagon train.
- Some of the people on the wagon train were slaves.
- The slaves were freed during the Civil War.

What opinions can the students find on these pages? *(Bill was the feistiest boy south of Abilene. He was quick as a jackrabbit, more wide-eyed than a hooty owl—and curious.)* (Page 476)

Discuss how combining both facts and opinions in a selection makes the selection interesting, entertaining, and informative.

Teacher Tip **DIALECT** As they read, have students note the cowboy dialect that helps to create the atmosphere of the story (for example, *quick as a jackrabbit* and *more wide-eyed than a hooty owl*).

COMPREHENSION

Differentiating Instruction

Intervention Tip

FACT AND OPINION Remind students that a fact is something that can be proven true. An opinion is what someone thinks or believes. For students having difficulty identifying statements of opinion, review with them the examples of opinion shown in the Comprehension Skills exercise. Help students see that they are all examples of judgments that were not necessarily based on fact.

COMPREHENSION

Comprehension Strategies

First Read

Prompting

③ **Visualizing** *Let's try to form a mental image of what we are reading to help us remember it later. How do you visualize the cattle drives described here?*

Student Sample

Visualizing *I picture cowboys on horses riding alongside huge herds of cattle. I picture big clouds of dust rising from the ground as the thousands of cattle go by and young Bill sitting on the fence watching the scene, waving his hand in greeting.*

Word Knowledge

Ending in *-ed*:

owned helped

Teacher Tip HISTORICAL CONNECTION Some students might enjoy researching more about the Chisholm Trail and the role of the cowboys in the history of that area.

Bill's parents now owned a small plot of land, where they raised chickens and pigs and grew sweet corn, tomatoes, and collards. They sold the vegetables and fruits in town to earn their living.

Bill's brothers and sisters helped tend the crops. But Bill was always wandering off. Most days he straddled the rickety corral gate to watch cattle drives tramp along the Chisholm Trail, a gritty stretch of road that snaked from the Rio Grande to the heart of Kansas.

478

Bill watched as the cowboys drove thousands of ornery longhorn steers past his parents' farm to stockyards in Kansas. Each trail crew had a trail boss, a cook, and a slew of cowboys. Bill always offered them a friendly "How do?" Some cowboys tipped their hats to signal hello. But they hardly ever stopped. And behind them they left hoof-
3 beaten dirt and the smell of adventure.

479

Differentiating Instruction

Challenge Tip

FACT AND OPINION Have students find three examples of fact and three examples of opinion from one of the selections in Unit 5 and write down their examples.

Comprehension Skills

Fact and Opinion

- Have the students identify a fact on pages 478–479. *(They sold the vegetables and fruits in town to earn their living.)* (Page 478)
- Have students identify an opinion on these pages. *(And behind them they left hoof-beaten dirt and the smell of adventure.)* (Page 479)

Discuss how to differentiate a fact from an opinion.

Word Knowledge

Long a spelled *ai*:

trail

COMPREHENSION

COMPREHENSION

Comprehension Strategies

Prompting

4 **Predicting** *What do you predict we will find out about Bill Pickett?*

Student Sample

Predicting *Bill sure wants to be a cowboy. I think he'll run off soon and join a cattle drive. Maybe he'll do something really brave like save somebody during a stampede. I hope so.*

Prompting

5 **Summarizing** *Since we are just now getting to know a little about Bill Pickett, how could we sum up what we've learned so far?*

Student Sample

Summarizing *Bill's family had a small farm, and all his brothers and sisters helped grow things. But Bill was always going off to watch the cowboys drive the cattle along the Chisholm Trail. His cousins would come visit and talk about cattle driving, and Bill would go to sleep and dream about being a cowboy.*

Word Knowledge

Ending in *-ed*:

bragged **sparked**

In the evenings, after the last batch of corn pone had been eaten, Bill and his family would gather round the stove fire for a night of story swapping.

Bill had two cousins, Anderson Pickett and Jerry Barton, who were trail-driving horsemen. When they came to visit, they bragged about roping steer, breaking ponies, and protecting their trail crews against buffalo stampedes. Bill and his family loved to learn their campfire songs about nights on the trail, when Anderson and Jerry slept under the black western sky with nobody watching them but the stars.

All these songs and stories sparked Bill's imagination.
4 They made him more up-jumpy than ever. He would lie in his bed and dream of the day when he'd be old enough to rope mossback cattle and help stray dogies keep up with
5 the herd.

480

Differentiating Instruction

If...	Then...
English Learners need extra support with reading "Bill Pickett: Rodeo-Ridin' Cowboy" and using the skill Fact and Opinion	Preteach ***Student Anthology*** pages 480–485 using Day 2 of the "Bill Pickett: Rodeo-Ridin' Cowboy" lesson, found on ***English Learner Support Guide,*** pages 441–444

One afternoon Bill was straddling the gate as usual when he spotted an eye-popping sight. A bulldog was holding a restless cow's lower lip with its fangs. Bill moved closer to get a good look at how the dog's bite kept the squirming cow down. Soon Bill got to wondering: *If a small bulldog can bite-hold a big-lipped cow, why can't I do the same?*

481

Comprehension Skills

Fact and Opinion

- What fact can the students find on page 480? *(Bill had two cousins, Anderson Pickett and Jerry Barton, who were trail-driving horsemen.)*

  Continue to discuss the differences between fact and opinion.

Word Knowledge

Ending in *-ed:*

spotted **big-lipped**

Teacher Tip MUSICAL CONNECTION Campfire and cowboy songs are an interesting part of our musical heritage. Encourage the students to share campfire or cowboy songs they know with the rest of the class. If possible, share one or two that you know to encourage shy students to participate.

COMPREHENSION

COMPREHENSION

Comprehension Strategies

Prompting

6 Confirming Predictions *We made some predictions earlier about what we might find out about Bill Pickett. How might we revise our predictions?*

Student Sample

Confirming Predictions *Well, this wasn't what I thought would happen. I thought Bill would run off and go on a cattle drive. Instead he's just doing chores on ranches. But he did invent bulldogging. That was pretty special, especially since he was still a child.*

Word Knowledge

Ending in *-ed:*

passed called looked

Days later, on his way to school, Bill passed a band of cowboys from the Littlefield Cattle Company. The men were having a hard time branding their calves.

"Want some help?" Bill called to them. The cowboys looked at this brazen boy and went back to their work.

"I can hold one of them calves by the lip with my teeth, just like a bulldog," Bill went on. "I can do it sure as my name's Bill Pickett."

The cowboys turned out a rip-roarin' laugh.

But one of them put forth a challenge: "Let the boy go 'head and try it, if he dares."

The men roped the calf and threw it to the ground. Bill put his face down and sunk his teeth into the animal's lip. Then Bill held the calf firm while the cowboys pressed a hot branding iron into its side.

"Bulldoggin'—done by a young'un!" The cowboys
6 cheered. Invented there and then by feisty Bill Pickett, that was bulldogging, bite-'em style.

When he was no more than fifteen and still itching for adventure, Bill set out to find his own way. Like many young'uns who came from large families, Bill had to go out and earn a living to help make ends meet.

Bill found work as a cowhand on ranches all over Texas. He spent long days saddling horses and mucking out their stalls. During the winter it was Bill's job to watch for wolves that crept up to the henhouses.

Bill learned to lasso and ride like the cowboys he'd seen pass by on the Chisholm Trail. He practiced bulldogging by catching steers that charged off into the mesquite brush. Soon Bill could tame broncs better than almost any other ranch hand. And every now and then, when work was slow, Bill went home to his mama and daddy's farm. Each time he had a new story of his own to tell his family.

Word of Bill's fearless riding spread from ranch to ranch. On Sundays folks gathered at local barnyards to watch Bill snatch a fire-eyed steer by the horns. Men, women, and young'uns rode on horseback and in their buggies to admire Bill's skill. They dropped coins in his hat to show how much they liked his horsemanship.

483

Comprehension Skills

Fact and Opinion

Have volunteers explain the difference between a *fact* and an *opinion.* Guide them to see that facts can be proven, while opinions cannot.

Help the students identify the facts on page 483. For example:

- Bill was fifteen when he left home to find work.
- Bill worked on many ranches.
- He saddled horses, mucked out stalls, and watched for wolves that crept up to the henhouses.

Tell them to explain how they know that these are facts.

What opinion can they find on this page?

- *"Soon Bill could tame broncos better than almost any ranch hand."*

What makes this an opinion?

Word Knowledge

Ending in *-ed:*

learned **gathered**

Teacher Tip ART CONNECTION Bill Pickett was one of many African-American cowboys. Students might enjoy creating portraits of Bill Pickett and other notable cowboys for display in the classroom or hall. Have them first research these cowboys and then create their portraits.

COMPREHENSION

COMPREHENSION

Comprehension Strategies

First Read

Prompting

7 Summarizing *I think we should stop here and sum up. Can anyone tell me why this is a good place to summarize and then model a summary for the class?*

Student Sample

Summarizing *This is a good place to summarize because there is a break in the action of the story. When he was still a child, Bill Pickett invented bulldogging, which was biting a cow in the lip to make it lie down on the ground. When he got a little older, he went from ranch to ranch working. Then one day, Bill competed in the rodeo. The audience was impressed!*

Prompting

8 Predicting *People seem to be pretty impressed by Bill's bulldogging trick. What do you predict Bill will do now?*

Student Sample

Predicting *I think everyone will love his act and he will become a big rodeo star.*

Word Knowledge

Long a spelled *ai*:

fair

Teacher Tip CHECKING COMPREHENSION Ask students one or more of the following questions to make sure they understand what they are reading: "Is anyone confused? Do you need clarification? Can you summarize what you have read so far? Does what you are reading make sense to you?"

One morning, while he was working at a ranch in Taylor, Texas, Bill heard that the Williamson County Livestock Association had brought a fair to town. The fair included a full-scale rodeo. Men from the association had parked their wagons on a hill a few miles south of Taylor. Their rodeo was going to be a big event. Bill was determined to compete.

For the first time Bill performed his bulldogging stunt before a large rodeo crowd. As the steer thundered into the arena, Bill jumped from the back of his horse and grabbed it by the horns. Then, before the beast knew what was coming, Bill dug his teeth into the animal's tender upper lip. He raised his hands in victory as the grizzly critter went down without a fight.

Somebody let out a holler. "*Hooeee! Hooeee-hi-ooooh!*" All the folks watching the rodeo clapped and stomped.

"He throwed that beast but good!"

"That cowboy's brave clear down to his gizzards!"

7 8 "*Hot-diggity-dewlap!*"

After that Bill bulldogged at rodeos throughout the West. When he wasn't bulldogging for show, he still worked on ranches to make ends meet. But stories about Bill's rodeo ridin' kept on keeping on—from Texas to Arkansas to Oklahoma to Kansas to Colorado and on up through the hills of Wyoming. Now everybody wanted to see Bill perform his special bulldogging feat.

484

Differentiating Instruction

English Learner Tip

SHARING KNOWLEDGE Explain to the English Learners that rodeos are special fairs that sprang up in the West to let people see the displays of strength and skill that cowboys needed to do their jobs. These rodeos were a way of celebrating the skills of the trade. Ask the students to describe what kinds of fairs might showcase the skills of workers today.

Comprehension Skills

Fact and Opinion

Have students find examples of opinion on page 484:

- "Their rodeo was going to be a big event."
- "He throwed that beast but good!"
- "Now everybody wanted to see Bill perform his special bulldogging feat."

Remind the students to look for facts and opinions as they read the selection.

Word Knowledge

Ending in *-ed:*

parked **performed** **jumped**

COMPREHENSION

COMPREHENSION

Comprehension Strategies

Prompting

9 Confirming Predictions *Earlier we made some predictions about what Bill would do with his talent. Does anyone need to revise your predictions?*

Student Sample

Confirming Predictions *I think my prediction is right. Bill is starting to be more and more famous as a rodeo bulldogger, but it's taking more time than I thought it would. I thought he'd get famous right away. Maybe it isn't that easy to become famous in the rodeo.*

Word Knowledge

Ending in *-ed*:

birthed **bulldogged** **turned**

Two years later, in 1890, Bill married Maggie Turner. Bill and Maggie made Taylor, Texas, their home, and together they birthed two boys and seven girls. Sometimes Maggie and the young'uns came to watch Bill perform when he bulldogged at rodeos near their small farm. They cheered the loudest of all.

Finally Bill decided to trade ranch work for rodeo. At first it wasn't easy. He had to leave Maggie and his children for weeks at a time. And some rodeos turned Bill away. Many rodeo owners believed black cowboys should ride with their own kind.

But the newspapers didn't seem to care if Bill was black or white—Bill's *bulldogging* was news! The *Wyoming Tribune* and the *Denver Post* printed stories about the wild-riding South Texas brushpopper who could tackle a steer with his bare hands, and his bite. Slowly Bill began to earn his living as a bulldogger.

486

Differentiating Instruction

If...	Then...
English Learners need extra linguistic support with reading "Bill Pickett: Rodeo-Ridin' Cowboy" and using the skill Fact and Opinion	Preteach ***Student Anthology*** pages 486–491 using Day 3 of the "Bill Pickett: Rodeo-Ridin' Cowboy" lesson, found on ***English Learner Support Guide,*** pages 444–446

9 Whenever Bill came home after time on the road, he would sit his family down and let loose his tales of the rodeo. He told Maggie and their children how, everywhere he went, folks called him the Dusky Demon on account of the dusty dirt cloud that billowed behind him whenever he performed his fearless riding. All his young'uns listened close, the same way their daddy had done to his cousins' stories when he was a boy.

487

Comprehension Skills

COMPREHENSION

Fact and Opinion

Explain that an opinion usually involves a judgment of some kind. Point out these examples on page 486:

- "They cheered loudest of all."
- "At first it wasn't easy."
- "Many rodeo owners believed black cowboys should ride with their own kind."
- "But the newspapers didn't seem to care if Bill was black or white—Bill's *bulldogging* was news!"

Discuss if the opinions that the students found in the other sections involved a judgment.

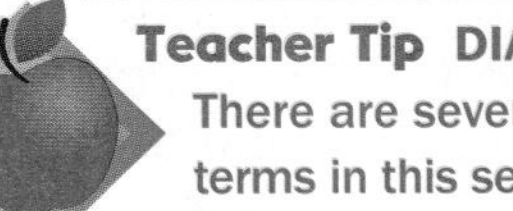

Word Knowledge

Ending in *-ed*:
called **billowed** **listened**

Teacher Tip DIALECT AND JARGON There are several cowboy-specific terms in this selection. Some students might enjoy collecting these terms such as *mossback cattle* or *doggies* into a glossary.

COMPREHENSION

Comprehension Strategies

Prompting

10 Predicting *Okay, now Bill is sure to get really famous. I think that Bill will join the 101 Ranch Wild West Show and become really famous, too, because it sounds like a big show. What do you think?*

Student Sample

11 Confirming Predictions *You were right. Bill did join the show. Not only that, but he was a star attraction. I'm sure Bill became really famous.*

Prompting

12 Summarizing *How would you summarize the events that took place in Bill's life after that first rodeo?*

Student Sample

Summarizing *Bill got married and then decided to be a rodeo cowboy full time. He slowly started to become well-known and earn a living. Then he joined the 101 Ranch Wild West Show and became the star attraction. He played in the show in New York City, Mexico City, and even England for the king and queen.*

Word Knowledge

Ending in *-ed:*

approached **owned** **performed**

Teacher Tip DISCUSSION Allow students to express their ideas without interruption.

In 1905, when Bill was performing in the Texas Fort Worth Fat Stock Show, he was taken by surprise. After the rodeo a fine-talkin' man named Zack Miller approached Bill and shook his hand.

Zack Miller and his brothers, Joe and George, owned one of the biggest ranches in the West. Their 101 Ranch spread over three towns—White Eagle, Red Rock, and Bliss—in Oklahoma. The Miller brothers also owned a traveling Wild West show, a spectacle greater than the small-time rodeos where Bill usually performed. The 101 Ranch Wild West Show had ninety cowboys and cowgirls, three hundred animals, and sixteen acts.

The Millers' show was famous. But to make it the best, they had to have a cowboy who could draw crowds and keep folks yip-yapping for more. The Millers had heard about Bill Pickett. After seeing Bill perform that day, Zack knew Bill was just the cowboy they needed. He asked Bill to join the 101 Ranch Wild West Show. He even told Bill
10 that Maggie and their children would be welcome to live at the 101 Ranch while Bill traveled.

Bill didn't have to think twice. Zack's offer was the best
11 he'd ever got. It wasn't long before Bill and his show horse, Spradley, became the 101's star attraction.

488

Soon Bill began to take his bulldogging to the far corners of the world. Crowds stood up and cheered when Bill bulldogged at Madison Square Garden in New York City.

In Mexico City townspeople filled the stands at El Toro, the national building, to watch the Dusky Demon face a fighting bull that was meaner than ten bulls in one.

Bill bulldogged in Canada and in South America, too. And in 1914 he performed in England for King George V
12 and Queen Mary!

Bill's bulldog act helped turn the 101 Ranch Wild West Show into a high-falutin' wonder. Even more important, Bill helped make rodeo one of the best-loved sports of his time.

489

COMPREHENSION

Comprehension Skills

Fact and Opinion

Help the students distinguish *fact* from *opinion* by having them point out some fine distinctions:

- It's a fact that Zack Miller offered a job to Bill Pickett in his rodeo, but it's a matter of opinion whether that was the best offer Bill ever got.
- It's a fact that Bill Pickett performed at El Toro, but it is an opinion that the bull he faced was "meaner than ten bulls in one." (Page 489)

Have the students find other examples of fact and opinion on these pages.

Word Knowledge

Ending in *-ed:*

cheered **filled** **helped**

Teacher Tip **CLASS DISCUSSION** Call on students to comment on one another's ideas.

COMPREHENSION

Comprehension Strategies

First Read

Prompting

13 Visualizing *Now that we have read the complete story of Bill's life, how do you picture Bill through all the stages of his life?*

Student Sample

Visualizing *I picture him first as a boy dreaming about being a cowboy, and then as a young man wrestling steer in front of amazed spectators, and then as an old man, perhaps telling stories of when he was a famous rodeo cowboy.*

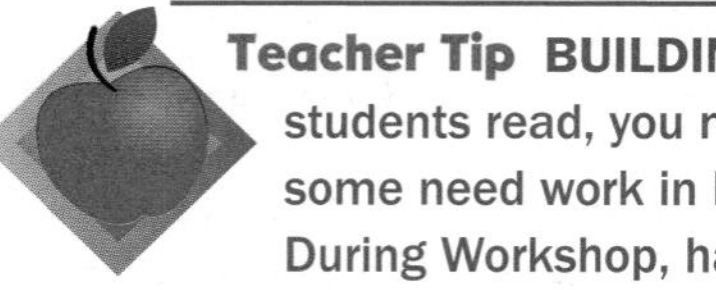

Word Knowledge

Ending in *-ed*:

wanted **returned** **worked**

Teacher Tip BUILDING FLUENCY As students read, you may notice that some need work in building fluency. During Workshop, have these students choose a section of text (a minimum of 160 words) to read several times in order to build fluency.

After years of bulldogging with the 101 show, Bill decided to give traveling a rest. He wanted to spend more time with Maggie and their children. So he returned to the 101 Ranch, where he lived and worked as a cowhand. To keep his skills strong, he bulldogged in rodeos closer to home.

490

Bulldogging lived on long after Bill died in 1932. But nobody could snatch a steer the way Bill did. When Bill's children were grown, they gathered up their own young'uns and told them about their grandfather, Bill Pickett——the feisty cowboy-child from south of Abilene
13 who grew up to be the Dusky Demon.

491

COMPREHENSION

Comprehension Skills

Fact and Opinion

Review with students the definitions of fact and opinion. Then, ask them to identify whether the following statements are fact or opinion.

- Bill died in 1932. *(fact)*
- Bill worked for the 101 Show for years. *(fact)*
- Bill returned to the 101 Ranch and worked as a cowhand. *(fact)*

Word Knowledge

Ending in *-ed:*
gathered

Teacher Tip FLUENCY By this time in grade 5 good readers should be reading approximately 151 words per minute with fluency and expression. The only way to gain this fluency is through practice. Have students reread the selection to you and to one another during Workshop to help build fluency.

COMPREHENSION

Comprehension Strategies

Prompting

14 Summarizing *There's a lot of information in the last two pages, so we should try to sum it up. Who will volunteer to summarize the key points for the class?*

Student Sample

Summarizing *About one-fourth of the cowboys in the old West were African-American. After the Civil War, lots of cowboys were needed to drive cows north to Kansas. Cowboys also competed in rodeos. Bill Pickett created a kind of steer wrestling. He was the first African-American in the Cowboy Hall of Fame.*

Discussing Strategy Use

While students are reading the selection, encourage them to share any problems they encountered and tell what strategies they used.

- How did they make, confirm, and revise predictions as they read?
- What did they visualize as they were reading?
- Where did they pause in the reading to summarize?

Remind students that good readers use all of the strategies listed above and that they should be using them whenever they read. Make sure that students explain how using the strategies helped them understand the selection. For example, "Summarizing forced me to think about what I had read and remember it so that I could read on and use what I already knew to make predictions."

Word Knowledge

Ending in *-ed*:
ended gained worked

More About Black Cowboys

America's history is rich with heroes. Cowboys—the men who tamed the Wild West during the late 1800s—are perhaps the most celebrated of all American legends. Nearly thirty-five thousand cowboys drove cattle when the Old West was in its prime. About one in four of these pioneers was African American.

While many enslaved black people migrated west with their masters before the Civil War, others came after the war ended in 1865 to take advantage of the work opportunities they hoped would come with their newly gained freedom. With their families these courageous people sometimes built self-sufficient, all-black towns. They became cavalrymen, trail bosses, barbers, trappers, nurses, state legislators—and cowboys.

When black men and women arrived on the western plains, they brought with them their own tradition of working with livestock and tending the land. Under the lash of slavery they had cultivated the skills of branding cattle and rounding up and taming horses. They'd worked long hours in plantation fields and had made an art of growing crops from seed to stalk under the harshest conditions.

Their knowledge—along with the care and dignity with which they performed their work—was well suited to the needs of the growing cattle business in the western states from 1865 to the turn of the century.

When the Civil War ransacked the nation, many Texans went off to fight, leaving their ranches to ruin. After the war, longhorn steers wandered wild throughout Texas, while in the northern and eastern states a demand for beef grew. During the Reconstruction period, some Texans saw a business opportunity to turn the Southwest into what came to be called the Cattle Kingdom. To make this empire grow, these businessmen needed strong, capable cowboys to work on their ranches. Black cowboys were willing and eager to take on the challenge.

492

Differentiating Instruction

If...	Then...
English Learners need extra linguistic support with reading "Bill Pickett: Rodeo-Ridin' Cowboy" and using the skill Fact and Opinion	Preteach ***Student Anthology*** pages 492–493 using Day 4 of the "Bill Pickett: Rodeo-Ridin' Cowboy" lesson, found on ***English Learner Support Guide,*** pages 447–449

In the Cattle Kingdom, skill, not skin color, was the primary concern. Along with white cowboys African Americans drove longhorn cattle for hundreds of miles to railroad cars stationed in Abilene, Kansas. Once the steers reached the Kansas railroad, they were shipped to stockyards in Chicago, Illinois, and Kansas City, Missouri.

Cowboys paid tribute to their workaday world by competing in rodeos. Rodeos began as small contests among cowboys to see who could rope and ride the best. By 1870 rodeo competitions were common and popular throughout the Southwest. They eventually became large spectator events that charged admission and paid cash prizes to participants.

Today seven standard contest events make up a rodeo: saddle bronc riding, bareback riding, bull riding, calf roping, team roping, barrel racing, and steer wrestling, which is also called bulldogging.

Bill Pickett's one-of-a-kind bulldogging established steer wrestling as a rodeo event. Today's "doggers" don't sink their teeth into a steer's lip like Bill did in his heyday. But they do try—with all the might and muscle they can muster—to wrestle the snorting beast to the dirt.

In 1971 Bill Pickett became the first African American inducted into the National Cowboy Hall of Fame and Western Heritage Center in Oklahoma City, Oklahoma. A bronze statue that depicts Bill bulldogging was unveiled in 1987 at the Fort Worth Cowtown Coliseum in Fort Worth, Texas. Today folks still praise Bill as Zack Miller, owner of the 101 Ranch, once did: "Bill Pickett was the
14 greatest sweat-and-dirt cowhand that ever lived—bar none."

—*Andrea Davis Pinkney*

493

Comprehension Skills

Fact and Opinion

Explain to students that pages 492–493 are informational text. Therefore, most of the ideas included are fact, not opinion. Discuss how the form of writing influences the inclusion of fact and opinion.

Checking Comprehension

Ask students the following questions to check their comprehension of the selection.

- What is the most surprising thing you learned in this selection about the old West? *(Answers may vary, but some students may express surprise at learning how many cowboys were African-American.)*
- How did Bill Pickett change western rodeos? *(He helped make "bulldogging" a rodeo event.)*
- How did Bill Pickett come to live in the Southwest? *(His father was born on a wagon train on which his grandparents were traveling to Texas as slaves.)*
- How has this selection connected with your knowledge of the unit theme? *(Answers will vary—students should compare/contrast examples of life in the American West from this selection with their own experiences or past reading and use these connections to make a general statement about the unit theme.)*

COMPREHENSION

Differentiating Instruction

If...	Then...
English Learners have been participating in the "Bill Pickett: Rodeo-Ridin' Cowboy" ***English Learner Support Guide*** activities	Review the selection and the skill Fact and Opinion using Day 5 of the "Bill Pickett: Rodeo-Ridin' Cowboy" lesson, found on ***English Learner Support Guide***, pages 450–451

Formal Assessment

See pages 22–25 in ***Unit 5 Assessment*** to test students' comprehension of "Bill Pickett: Rodeo-Ridin' Cowboy."

Word Knowledge

Long a spelled *al*:
railroad paid praise

Routine Card
Refer to Routine 5 for the *handing-off process.*

Clues	Problems	Wonderings
Enslaved Cowboy Rodeo Biography	Wagon train Bulldogging	How does Bill get into the rodeo?

Reading Transparency 54

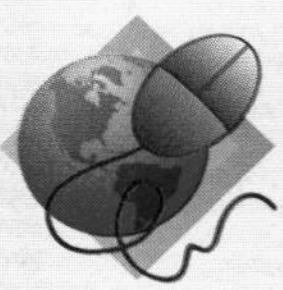

www.sra4kids.com
Web Connection
Some students may choose to conduct a computer search for additional books or information about the American West. Invite them to make a list of these books and sources of information to share with classmates and the school librarian. Check the Reading link of the SRA Web page for additional links to theme-related Web sites.

Teacher Tip LOCATING AND RECALLING INFORMATION Tell students that they will begin today's discussion with a class summary of the selection. Have students scan the selection, looking at each illustration and telling how the illustration relates to the text it accompanies. Tell students that recapping the selection in this way will help them recall details that may be important to the discussion later. Students can also use the illustrations during discussion, to help them locate and share pieces of text that support ideas being discussed.

Discussing the Selection

After the first read, the whole group discusses the selection and any personal thoughts, reactions, problems, or questions that it raises. To stimulate discussion, students can ask one another the kinds of questions that good readers ask themselves about a text: *How does it connect to going west? What have I learned that is new? What did I find interesting? What is important here? What was difficult to understand? Why would someone want to read this?* It is important for students to see you as a contributing member of the group.

Routine 5 To emphasize that you are part of the group, actively participate in the *handing-off process:* Raise your hand to be called on by the last speaker when you have a contribution to make. Point out unusual and interesting insights verbalized by students so that these insights are recognized and discussed. As the year progresses, students will take more and more responsibility for the discussion of selections.

Engage students in a discussion to determine whether they have grasped the following ideas:

- many cowhands were African-Americans who had been freed after the Civil War
- rodeos were popular forms of entertainment in the West

During this time, have students return to the clues, problems, and wonderings that they noted during browsing to determine whether the clues were borne out by the selection, whether and how their problems were solved, and whether their wonderings were answered or deserve further discussion and investigation. Let the students decide which items deserve further discussion. Also have students return to the Focus Questions on the first page of the selection. Select a student to read the questions aloud, and have volunteers answer the questions. If students do not know the answers to the questions, have them return to the text to find the answers.

You may also want to review the elements of biography with the students. Discuss with them how they can tell that "Bill Pickett: Rodeo-Ridin' Cowboy" is a biography.

Have students break into small groups to discuss how the story reflects the theme. Groups can then share their ideas with the rest of the class.

Students may wish to record their thoughts about and reactions to this selection. Encourage students to discuss the exploits of Bill Pickett. Have them also record colorful words and expressions they attribute to ranchers and cowboys. Tell students to write sentences showing context for the words if dictionary definitions can't be found.

Review Selection Vocabulary

Have students review the definitions of the selection vocabulary words that they wrote in the vocabulary section of their Writer's Notebooks. Remind them that they discussed the meanings of these words before reading the selection. Students can use these definitions to study for the vocabulary portion of their Lesson Assessment. Have them add to the personal dictionary section of their Writer's Notebook any other interesting words that they clarified while reading. Encourage students to refer to the selection vocabulary words throughout the unit. The words from the selection are:

brazen **ravage** **challenge** **feisty** **adventure** **trek**

Have students place the words under the appropriate endings in the Word Bank. Encourage the students to find other words related to the unit theme and add them to the Word Bank.

Home Connection

Distribute ***Home Connection,*** page 73. Encourage students to discuss "Bill Pickett: Rodeo-Ridin' Cowboy" with their families. Students can write a paragraph about the reasons for the legendary status of cowboys and cowgirls and discuss how their role has changed over the years. ***Home Connection*** is also available in Spanish, page 74.

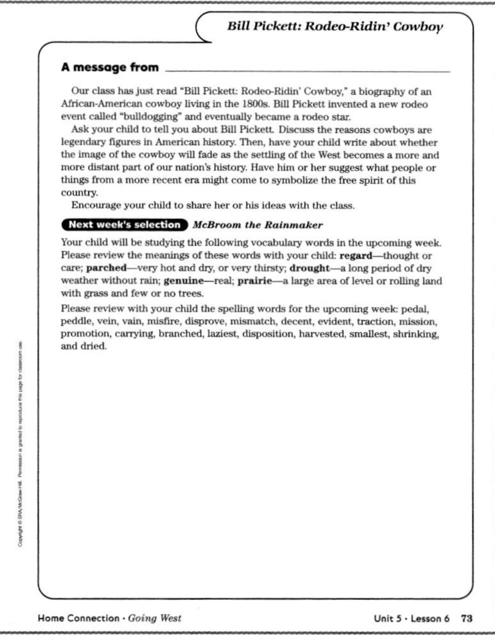

Bill Pickett: Rodeo-Ridin' Cowboy

A message from ____________

Our class has just read "Bill Pickett: Rodeo-Ridin' Cowboy," a biography of an African-American cowboy living in the 1800s. Bill Pickett invented a new rodeo event called "bulldogging" and eventually became a rodeo star.

Ask your child to tell you about Bill Pickett. Discuss the reasons cowboys are legendary figures in American history. Then, have your child write about whether the image of the cowboy will fade as the settling of the West becomes a more and more distant part of our nation's history. Have him or her suggest what people or things from a more recent era might come to symbolize the free spirit of this country.

Encourage your child to share her or his ideas with the class.

Next week's selection ***McBroom the Rainmaker***

Your child will be studying the following vocabulary words in the upcoming week. Please review the meanings of these words with your child: **regard**—thought or care; **parched**—very hot and dry, or very thirsty; **drought**—a long period of dry weather without rain; **genuine**—real; **prairie**—a large area of level or rolling land with grass and few or no trees.

Please review with your child the spelling words for the upcoming week: pedal, peddle, vein, vain, misfire, disprove, mismatch, decent, evident, traction, mission, promotion, carrying, branched, laziest, disposition, harvested, smallest, shrinking, and dried.

Home Connection · *Going West* Unit 5 · Lesson 6 73

Home Connection p. 73

Teacher Tip **SELECTION VOCABULARY** Have students write sentences using the selection vocabulary words. In order to provide additional help in remembering words, students can write synonyms or antonyms for the words if it is appropriate.

Differentiating Instruction

If...	Then...
Students would benefit from repeated readings of "Bill Pickett: Rodeo-Ridin' Cowboy" or the Intervention Selections	Use ***Intervention Guide,*** page 277

Teacher Tip FACT AND OPINION As students read, they should be aware of key words and phrases, such as *I think* and *In my opinion,* that signal that the information is opinion. Students should also be aware of general statements that say someone was "best of all" or the like.

Teacher Tip MAKING CONNECTIONS Remind students of how Henry Wadsworth Longfellow fictionalized historic events in "The Midnight Ride of Paul Revere." The Historical Note included in that selection verified statements from the poem as fact or fiction.

Fact and Opinion

Statement: ____________________

If fact, can cross-reference in this resource: ____________________

Statement: ____________________

If fact, can cross-reference in this resource: ____________________

Statement: ____________________

If fact, can cross-reference in this resource: ____________________

Reading Transparency 68

Reading Transparency 68

Supporting the Reading

Comprehension Skills: Fact and Opinion

Teach Explain to students that a fact is a statement that is verifiable and an opinion is a statement that is not verifiable. Tell students that it is important to distinguish between the two when reading biographies, historical fiction, historical accounts, reviews, and any other forms of writing in which authors take a particular perspective. Explain to students that *verifiable* means that they can support the fact with other sources. For example, that Bill Pickett died in 1932 is a fact. They could verify this information in another book or on the Internet. That Bill's riding was "fearless" (page 483) is an opinion. This cannot be verified by checking sources. If students don't know whether a statement is fact or opinion, they should check other sources to verify the statement.

Explain to students that they should be careful to distinguish facts and opinions from supported inferences made by the author. Point out to students that the author's statement on page 480 that "He would lie in his bed and dream of the day when he'd be old enough to rope mossback cattle and help stray dogies keep up with the herd" is an example of a supported inference. Based on facts about Bill Pickett's life *(Bill heard stories about cowboys and liked to watch them ride past his farm, and later became a cowboy)* and her own prior knowledge *(many young people lie in bed and dream of what they are interested in achieving)* the author infers that Bill dreamed of being a cowboy. Explain to students that in the case of supported inferences, the supporting facts can be verified, but the inferences or conclusions the author draws from them may not.

Explain to students that they should also distinguish facts and opinions from fiction, which may be added by the author, even to nonfiction, to make the selection more interesting or fill in gaps in the factual record. Explain to students that it is the reader's responsibility to verify statements from sources before accepting them as fact.

Guided Practice Use ***Reading Transparency 68*** to help students identify fact and opinion. On the Statement lines, write statements from "Bill Pickett: Rodeo-Ridin' Cowboy." Have students identify each statement as a fact, an opinion, a supported inference, or a fictional statement. Explain that students will check their identifications by trying to verify the statements. Then, on the Resource lines, write student suggestions for sources to use to verify the factual statements. Discuss the probability of finding the information in the suggested source. Have students search the listed sources to verify the statements.

Independent Practice Read through the **Focus** and **Identify** sections of the ***Comprehension and Language Arts Skills,*** page 166, with students. Guide students through the **Identify** portion, and help them come up with support from the story. Then have students complete the **Practice** and **Apply** portions of the ***Comprehension and Language Arts Skills,*** page 167 as homework.

Link to Writing Explain to students that opinions are often formed by drawing conclusions or making inferences from facts. Tell students that part of the inquiry process of researching to support conjectures is actually examining facts in order to form opinions. Have students look over the facts they have gathered for their unit activities and state opinions about their problems based on and supported by those facts.

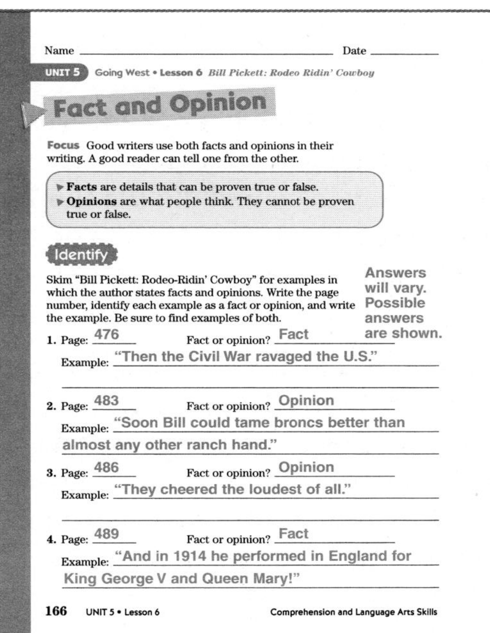

Name ______ Date ______

UNIT 5 Going West • Lesson 6 *Bill Pickett: Rodeo Ridin' Cowboy*

Fact and Opinion

Focus Good writers use both facts and opinions in their writing. A good reader can tell one from the other.

- **Facts** are details that can be proven true or false.
- **Opinions** are what people think. They cannot be proven true or false.

Identify

Skim "Bill Pickett: Rodeo-Ridin' Cowboy" for examples in which the author states facts and opinions. Write the page number, identify each example as a fact or opinion, and write the example. Be sure to find examples of both. Answers will vary. Possible answers are shown.

1. Page: 476 Fact or opinion? Fact
   Example: "Then the Civil War ravaged the U.S."
2. Page: 483 Fact or opinion? Opinion
   Example: "Soon Bill could tame broncs better than almost any other ranch hand."
3. Page: 486 Fact or opinion? Opinion
   Example: "They cheered the loudest of all."
4. Page: 489 Fact or opinion? Fact
   Example: "And in 1914 he performed in England for King George V and Queen Mary!"

166 UNIT 5 • Lesson 6 Comprehension and Language Arts Skills

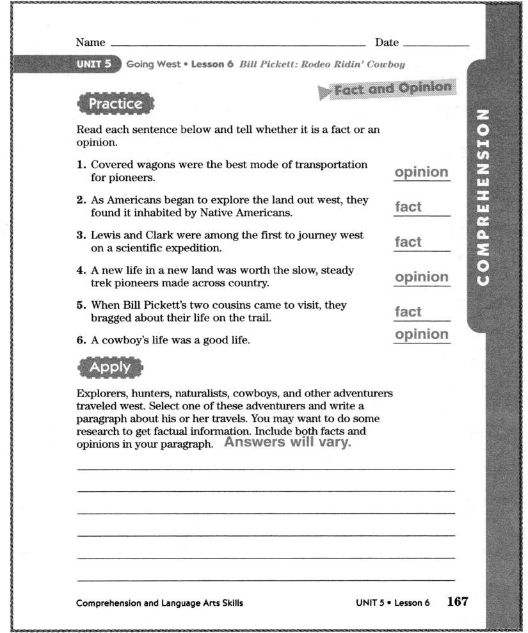

Name ______ Date ______

UNIT 5 Going West • Lesson 6 *Bill Pickett: Rodeo Ridin' Cowboy*

Fact and Opinion

COMPREHENSION

Practice

Read each sentence below and tell whether it is a fact or an opinion.

1. Covered wagons were the best mode of transportation for pioneers. opinion
2. As Americans began to explore the land out west, they found it inhabited by Native Americans. fact
3. Lewis and Clark were among the first to journey west on a scientific expedition. fact
4. A new life in a new land was worth the slow, steady trek pioneers made across country. opinion
5. When Bill Pickett's two cousins came to visit, they bragged about their life on the trail. fact
6. A cowboy's life was a good life. opinion

Apply

Explorers, hunters, naturalists, cowboys, and other adventurers traveled west. Select one of these adventurers and write a paragraph about his or her travels. You may want to do some research to get factual information. Include both facts and opinions in your paragraph. Answers will vary.

Comprehension and Language Arts Skills UNIT 5 • Lesson 6 167

Comprehension and Language Arts Skills pp. 166–167

Differentiating Instruction

If...	Then...
Students need extra help with Fact and Opinion	• Use ***Reteach,*** pages 166–167 • Use ***English Learner Support Guide,*** pages 436–451
Students would enjoy a challenge with Fact and Opinion	Use ***Challenge,*** page 146

Fact and Opinion

Introduced in Grade 2.

Scaffolded throughout Grades 3–5.

REINTRODUCED: Unit 4, Lesson 6

REINFORCED: Unit 5, Lesson 6

Unit 6, Lesson 3

TESTED: Unit 5 Assessment

Professional Development

Teacher Resource Library CD-ROMs or ***Online Professional Development*** provides courses that help you better understand the Comprehension/Knowledge Building instruction in ***Open Court Reading.*** For more information about this program, visit SRAonline.com.

Teacher Tip **BIOGRAPHY** You might have students interview a relative, perhaps a grandparent or older caregiver, to practice gathering the types of information needed to write a biography. Have students ask questions that prompt responses with lots of details about the era being discussed.

Differentiating Instruction

Intervention Tip

BIOGRAPHY Some students may confuse biographies with autobiographies. You may wish to explain that autobiographies have the same characteristics as biographies, *except* autobiographies are written by the main subject of the biography. The author actually writes a book or paper about his or her own life.

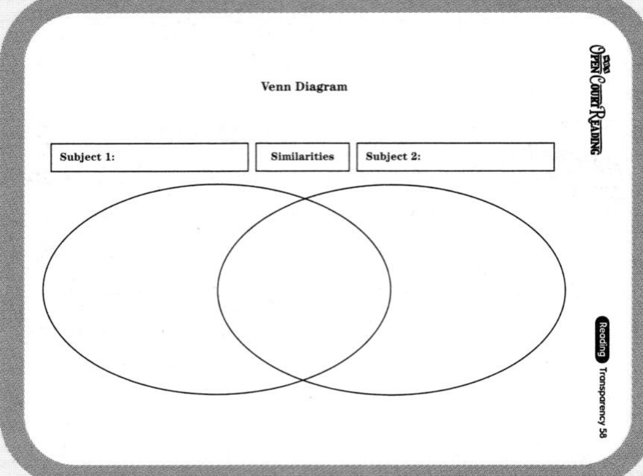

Reading Transparency 58

Literary Elements

Genre: Biography

Teach Ask students to recall what they know about biographies. If necessary, review these elements of biography with students.

- A biography is written about a real person's life by someone else.
- A biography contains important information about the person's life. The stories include details about how the person talks, feels, and thinks about things.
- A biography may span the person's life, or it may tell about only an important part of the person's life. An account that spans the person's entire life is almost always told in chronological order—the order in which the events occurred in time.
- A biography often focuses on the most important events in a person's life. It usually describes a person's achievements or talents.

Tell students that, unlike historical fiction in which many of the characters are creations of the author's imagination, the events and details in a biography are actual facts, and the characters in the biography actually lived and did the things attributed to them in the story. Therefore, writing a biography requires lots of research. However, biography writers often include and try to assign emotions or thoughts to their subject.

Guided Practice Ask the students to reflect on the selection "Bill Pickett: Rodeo-Ridin' Cowboy." What would an author have to do to write a story like this one? Then, ask students to compare and contrast a fictional story such as "Old Yeller and the Bear" from this unit and a biography such as "Bill Pickett: Rodeo-Ridin' Cowboy" using ***Reading Transparency 58.*** Assign each oval a selection title. Have students tell what aspects of each selection's genre are individual to that selection, and which are shared by both selections. Write shared aspects in the overlap area on the Venn diagram.

Independent Practice Have students brainstorm a list of people who once lived in the American West who would make good subjects for a biography. Students should mention names of people they remember from their reading and investigations. Then, have students search the library for biographies of these people.

Social Studies Connection: Moving West

Remind students that Bill Pickett's father rode west in a covered wagon as a slave before the Civil War. Tell them that many slaves and former slaves, as well as people newly emigrated to the United States, made the trip west during this time.

Break students into groups. Assign each group one of the following topics: European immigrants and their modes of transportation into the Ohio and Mississippi Valleys (e.g. wagons, canals, flatboats, steamboats); the overland journey west; locations of principal routes; people who made the journey; reasons for going west; and the geographical features the travelers encountered.

Have each group break down their topics further if necessary and assign different aspects of the topic to different group members. Give each group time to lead a lesson for other groups about what they have learned.

Teacher Tip **MATERIALS** To complete this activity, students will need Internet or library access.

Concept Connections

Linking the Selection

- Many African Americans were taken west as slaves before the Civil War.
- He was separated from his family for long periods of time, and some rodeos turned him away because he was African American.
- Texas was full of cowboys who wanted to show off their skills, and people enjoyed watching them compete.

Exploring Concept Vocabulary

The concept word for this lesson is ***spirited.*** Write the word on the board. Work with the students to develop a definition that clearly links to the unit theme. Have students copy the word and definition into the Vocabulary section of their Writer's Notebooks.

Spirited: full of life. For example, Bill Pickett was able to bring even the most spirited bull to the ground.

- Cowboys represented the courage and energy necessary to survive in the West. They also symbolized a sense of adventure that many frontier settlers shared.
- Cowboy songs and tales sparked his imagination, and he dreamed of the day he could join a cattle drive.

The students' sentences should show an understanding of both vocabulary words.

Expanding the Concept

Have students carry on dialogues in small groups. After the small-group discussions, bring students together to share their ideas with the whole class.

As students complete their discussion, have them record their ideas on page 115 of their ***Inquiry Journal.***

Bill Pickett
Rodeo-Ridin' Cowboy

Concept Connections

Linking the Selection

Think about the following questions, and then record your responses in the Response Journal section of your Writer's Notebook.

- Why did Bill Pickett's family and many other African Americans move west to Texas?
- In what ways was rodeo life difficult for Bill Pickett?
- Why did the rodeo become a popular sport in Texas?

Exploring Concept Vocabulary

The concept word for this lesson is ***spirited.*** If you do not know what this word means, look it up in a dictionary. Answer these questions.

- Why did ***spirited*** cowboys become a symbol of the American West?
- What influence did cowboy stories have on Bill Pickett when he was a ***spirited*** young boy?

In the Vocabulary section of your Writer's Notebook, write a sentence that includes the word ***spirited*** and a word from the selection vocabulary.

Expanding the Concept

Consider how Bill Pickett's young life was different from that of his parents. Compare the ideas the two generations might have had about life in the West. Try to use the word ***spirited*** in your discussion. Add new ideas about the American West to the Concept/Question Board.

494

Teacher Tip INVESTIGATION AND INQUIRY Have groups report and discuss their ideas with the class. As these ideas are stated, have students add them to the Concept/Question Board. As students complete their discussions, have them sum up what they have learned and tell how they might use this information in further investigations.

Informal Assessment

This may be a good time to observe students working in small groups and to mark your observations in the Teacher Observation Log found in the ***Program Assessment Teacher's Edition.***

Meet the Author and Illustrator

Andrea and Brian Pinkney are the husband-and-wife team that worked together to publish "Bill Pickett: Rodeo-Ridin' Cowboy." Andrea did the writing and Brian did the illustrating. Andrea has a degree in journalism. She has been a novelist, a picture-book writer, and the author of articles for *The New York Times* and *Highlights for Children.*

Brian always wanted to be an illustrator because his father, Jerry Pinkney, is a children's book illustrator, and his mother, Gloria Jean Pinkney, is a children's book writer. He earned two degrees in art, and today he works on books both with his wife and on his own. He has taught at the Children's Art Carnival in Harlem and at the School of Visual Arts.

Andrea and Brian Pinkney have worked together on other books including *Alvin Ailey* and *Duke Ellington: The Piano Prince and His Orchestra.*

495

Meet the Author and Illustrator

After the students read the information about Andrea and Brian Pinkney, discuss the following questions with them.

- Why might it be useful for a husband and wife to work together as a team to write a story? *(Possible answer: They can ask each other questions, give each other ideas, and clarify any details within the story or the drawings.)*
- Andrea Pinkney interviewed Bill Pickett's great-grandson to get information for this story. Why do you think she did this? *(Possible answer: She did this so that she would have personal information about Bill Pickett that would help to bring him to life for readers.)*
- Brian Pinkney's father was an illustrator, and his mother was a writer. How do you think this influenced his decision to become an illustrator as an adult? *(Possible answer: He grew up around creativity, stories, and drawing. It became a part of him, and probably felt like a natural thing to do and share with his parents.)*

Objectives

- Students gain a deeper understanding of the American West.
- Students continue to investigate and begin to organize their activities for presentation.
- Students participate in investigation activities.
- Students use technology to enhance presentations.

Materials

- Student Anthology, pp. 474–495
- Inquiry Journal, pp. 135–136
- Research Assistant

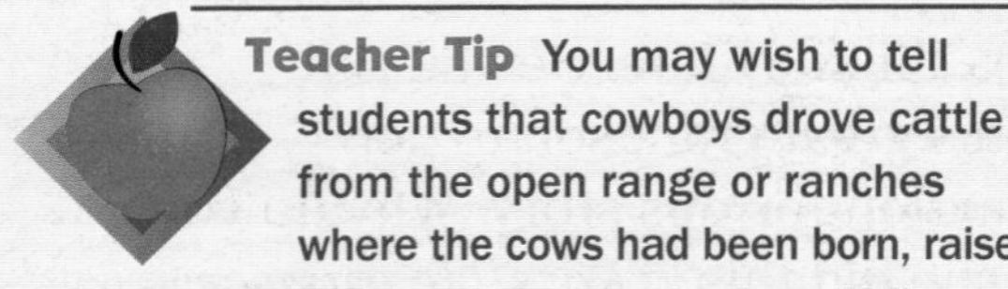

Teacher Tip You may wish to tell students that cowboys drove cattle from the open range or ranches where the cows had been born, raised, and fattened for market to cities such as Abilene. While this was the end of the trail for some of the cows, most of the cows were herded onto railcars and carried by train to the stockyards of Chicago. At first, the cows would be transferred in Chicago to other trains headed to the markets in the East. Later, after the invention of refrigerated freight cars, the cows would be butchered in Chicago, with the beef shipped east to the hungry urban crowds.

Professional Development

Teacher Resource Library CD-ROMs or ***Online Professional Development*** provides courses that help you better understand the Inquiry and Investigation instruction in ***Open Court Reading.*** For more information about this program, visit SRAonline.com.

INVESTIGATION

Investigating Concepts Beyond the Text

To facilitate students' investigation of the American West, you might have them participate in the following activities. Tell students that if they have activity ideas of their own that they would like to pursue, they are free to do so as an alternative to these activity suggestions. For example, students may want to pursue activities of their own choosing that relate more directly to the problems and questions they are investigating with their groups. Tell students that they may work on these activities alone, in pairs, or in small groups, with an option to write about them or to present them to the group upon completion.

The activity suggestions for this lesson are:

- With the students, locate books and photographs of cowboys who lived in the American West. Share these resources, discussing the clothes and equipment used by the cowboys. If possible, locate and display various articles they used, such as saddles, chaps, spurs, and lassos. Encourage the students to share what they know about cowboys today.
- Some students may know that the first cowboys were the Hispanic *vaqueros.* Encourage students to find out more about the history of the vaqueros, at the library and on the Internet.

Upon completion of their activities, have students share with the group anything new they learned about the American West through discussion and by adding information to the Concept/Question Board.

Concept/Question Board

After reading each selection, students should use the Concept/Question Board to

- post any questions they asked about a selection before reading that have not yet been answered.
- refer to as they formulate statements about concepts that apply to their investigations.
- post general statements formulated by each collaborative group.
- continue to post news articles, or other items that they find during the unit investigation.
- read and think about posted questions, articles, or concepts that interest them and provide answers to the questions.

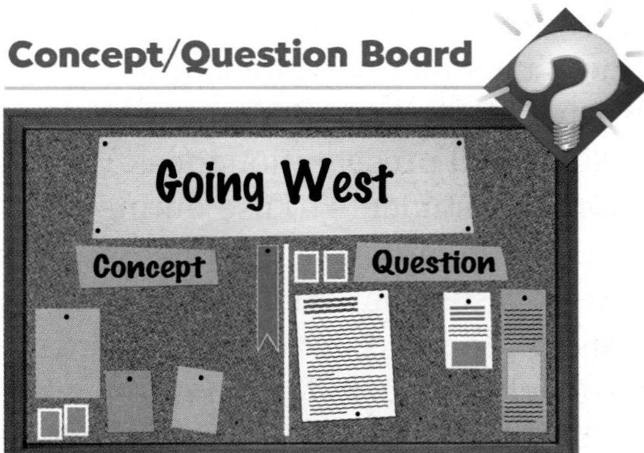

Unit 5 Research Management	
Lesson 1	Students generate questions and ideas for investigation.
Lesson 2	Students formulate questions and problems for investigation.
Lesson 3	Students make conjectures.
Lesson 4	Students establish investigation needs.
Lesson 5	Students establish investigation plans.
Lesson 6	Collaborative Investigation **Students continue investigation and get feedback from other groups.** Supplementary Activities **Students participate in investigation activities and learn to use technology in presentations.**
Lesson 7	Students present their investigation findings to the class.

INVESTIGATION

www.sra4kids.com
Web Connection
Students can use the connections to Going West in the Reading link of the SRA Web page for more background information about Going West.

Research Assistant

The Research Assistant helps students in their investigations.

Teacher Tip ULTIMATE WRITING AND CREATIVITY CENTER Have students use the ***Ultimate Writing and Creativity Center CD-ROM*** as they work on their investigation activities.

Teacher Tip INFORMAL PRESENTATION You may want to suggest to interested students the following options for informal presentation of investigation findings.

- Mini-debate—Group members who have opposing conjectures present them, along with evidence and arguments, for the rest of the class to react to.
- Problem presentations—Groups who are stuck, not able to find relevant material, or who are finding something puzzling or inconsistent, present their problem for suggestions from their peers.
- Poster session—When not enough time is available, groups put up small displays (including posters, graphs, and summaries) of any kind showing their preliminary findings. The students examine these displays during Workshop and give feedback to their peers.

Formal Assessment

Use the Research Rubrics on page 474J to assess students' ability to revise problems and conjectures.

Name ____________ Date ______

Going West UNIT 5

Feedback

If you gave an informal presentation of your investigation findings, record notes on the feedback you received on the lines provided. Reference these notes as you make decisions about how to revise your presentation.

Answers will vary.

Inquiry Journal • *Feedback* UNIT 5 135

***Inquiry Journal* p. 135**

INVESTIGATION

Continuing Investigation and Getting Feedback

By now, students should be in the midst of carrying out the job assignments they were given in their investigation groups. Tell groups that it is time for them to begin compiling their findings to present to the class. Remind them that they may present their findings either orally or in written form. Have groups consider how they might enhance their presentations by using visual aids, technology, or demonstrations. Meet with individual groups to discuss which options might provide the best support for their presentations and to offer guidance on how to use available equipment. Tell students who decide to use special visuals or equipment to list the supplies they will need. Also, help them to work into their project schedules time to create their visuals or practice using the equipment.

Allow groups time to organize their presentations. Groups who finish early or who hit a stumbling block may benefit from giving informal presentations to receive feedback and ideas from other groups. (See the Teacher Tip to the left for informal presentation ideas.) Set aside a special area in the classroom for interested students to use during Workshop. Tell them that the purpose of participating in these informal presentations is both to help and to teach each other. Presenters should respect the time of their audience members by coming prepared. In turn, audience members should be attentive and give feedback that includes things they liked about their peers' presentation as well as things they had trouble understanding or that they think could be better. Remind students that when giving feedback, they must

- be polite and think about the presenters' feelings.
- always begin their comments with a positive statement.
- be specific—if something about the presentation is unclear, they should say what it is.

As students meet, circulate among the groups and model making appropriate comments. Have presenters take notes on the feedback on ***Inquiry Journal***, page 135. They may reference these notes later when making revisions. Tell presenters that they should revise their presentations only as they see fit.

Throughout the remaining time, meet with each group for the following purposes:

- To arrange schedules and update calendars.
- To discuss problems that the students are encountering during their investigation.
- To provide guidance to ensure that groups progress through the process of formulating questions and problems, making conjectures, establishing investigation needs and plans, and proceeding to another cycle of problem, conjecture, and so forth.

SUPPORTING THE INVESTIGATION

Using Technology in Presentations

Teach Ask students what they know about using technology to enhance presentations. Explain to students that word processing programs can be used to add visual appeal to a presentation and to make the information presented more usable and accessible. Tell students that in addition to documents, word processing programs can help them produce charts and other graphics. Demonstrate using pull-down menus, toolbars, the Help function, and other features of a word processing program to manipulate text and create tables and charts.

Guided Practice Once students have observed the manipulation of text in the program, allow them to experiment with

- creating and saving new documents and accessing documents that already have been created.
- making text boldface, italic, or underlined; manipulating the size and type of the font.
- cutting and pasting text in order to manipulate the sequence of words and sentences in a document.
- using the thesaurus and spell check functions.
- manipulating the format of text on the page, by using columns, tab stops, or bullets.
- creating charts or tables to format information and make it more accessible.
- inserting clip art or graphics into text.

Then have students complete ***Inquiry Journal,*** page 136.

Independent Practice Have students use a word processing program to make information they are presenting in their formal presentations more usable and accessible to their audiences. Have them create charts, tables, posters, or handouts made easy to read with columns or bullets. Remind students to focus on enhancing their presentation and be careful not to overwhelm their audience with too much information.

Differentiating Instruction

If...	Then...
Students are having difficulty with their Inquiry activities	Have them use ***TechKnowledge*** to help them learn how to use a word processing program

Encourage students to use ***TechKnowledge*** to help them create visual aids for use during their investigation presentations.

Name______________________ Date__________

UNIT 5 Going West

Using Technology

Write instructions for completing the following operations on your word processing program. If needed, use the Help function to assist you in writing the instructions. Note that the directions for completing a function may differ from one word processing program to another. **Answers will vary.**

Example: **Make a word boldface: Highlight the word and click the Boldface button on the menu bar.**

Operation	Instructions
Create a new document.	
Save a new document.	
Print a document.	
Delete a piece of text.	
Move a piece of text.	
Find and replace misspelled words.	
Find a word's synonym.	
Create a table.	
Insert clipart.	
Make a bulleted list.	

136 UNIT 5 *Using Technology* • Inquiry Journal

Inquiry Journal p. 136

Objectives

Word Analysis

Spelling
- **Spelling Patterns for Words with *-er* or *-est*.** Develop understanding of spelling patterns for words with *-er* or *-est* introduced in Word Knowledge in Part 1.

Vocabulary
- Using words from "Bill Pickett: Rodeo-Ridin' Cowboy," give students practice defining compound words.

Writing Process Strategies
- **Personal Writing: Letter of Request.** Students will learn to write a letter of request.

English Language Conventions

Mechanics
- **Commas and Quotations.** Students will learn the proper use of commas in appositives, introductory words, and interrupters. They will also learn about end marks and quotation marks in dialogue.

Listening, Speaking, Viewing
- **Interacting: Group Presentations.** Give a group presentation.

Penmanship
- **Joining with *N* and *t*.** Review handwriting skills by practicing joining letters with *N* and *t*.

Materials

- Comprehension and Language Arts Skills, pp. 168–169
- Language Arts Handbook
- Language Arts Transparency 35
- Routine Card 2
- Spelling and Vocabulary Skills, pp. 126–129
- Student Anthology
- Writer's Workbook, pp. 98–101
- Unit 5 Assessment, pp. 40–41

Differentiating Instruction

Reteach, Challenge, and ***Intervention*** lessons are available to support the language arts instruction in this lesson.

Research in Action

Phonological awareness, letter recognition facility, familiarity with spelling patterns, spelling-sound relations, and individual words must be developed in concert with real reading and real writing and with deliberate reflection on the forms, functions, and meanings of texts. (*Marilyn Adams*, Beginning to Read: Thinking and Learning About Print)

OVERVIEW

Language Arts Overview

Word Analysis

Spelling The spelling activities on the following pages support the Word Knowledge introduction of words ending in *-er* and *-est* by developing understanding of the spelling patterns for these endings.

Selection Spelling Words

These words from "Bill Pickett: Rodeo-Ridin' Cowboy" contain *-er* or *-est.*

loudest feistiest closer greater harshest

Vocabulary The vocabulary activities introduce students to compound words. Students will construct and define compound words from the selection "Bill Pickett: Rodeo-Ridin' Cowboy."

Vocabulary Skill Words

homespun bedclothes bluebonnet stockyards cowhand

Writing Process Strategies

This Writing Process Strategies lesson will teach students about the form and function of writing a letter of request. A letter of request is a type of business letter and should follow the general business letter format.

To help students identify the Internet as a source of information for writing, show students how to use signatures in e-mail. ***TechKnowledge*** Level 5 Lesson 95 teaches this Internet and electronic reference skill.

Professional Development

Teacher Resource Library CD-ROMs or ***Online Professional Development*** provides courses that help you better understand the Writing instruction in ***Open Court Reading.*** For more information about this program, visit SRAonline.com.

English Language Conventions

Mechanics **Commas and Quotations.** This lesson develops understanding of the use of commas in appositives, introductory words, and interrupters. Students will also learn about end marks and quotation marks in dialogue.

Listening, Speaking, Viewing **Interacting: Group Presentations.** In this Interacting lesson, students give a group presentation on a literature selection. If necessary, set aside additional time on Day 4, or during the next week, to allow students to deliver their group presentations in class.

Penmanship **Joining with *N* and *t*.** This lesson continues the development of handwriting skills. Students join letters with *N* and *t* and then write paragraphs from the literature, focusing on joining letters.

DAY 1

Word Analysis

Spelling

Assessment: Pretest

Spelling Patterns for Words with *-er* or *-est*

Give students the Pretest on page 40 of ***Unit 5 Assessment.*** Have them proofread and correct any misspellings.

Pretest Sentences

1. **happiest** Workers and students are often **happiest** on Fridays.
2. **wiser** Most adults will say that you will become **wiser** with experience.
3. **slimmer** A model is **slimmer** than the average man or woman.
4. **calmest** It is best to swim in the ocean when it is at its **calmest.**
5. **dishonest** Al Capone was **dishonest** in filing his tax returns.
6. **container** Put the leftovers in a plastic **container.**
7. **scariest** The first fall is the **scariest** part of a roller coaster.
8. **daughter** Anastasia was the **daughter** of Tsar Nicholas II.
9. **easiest** We took the **easiest** route.
10. **saltier** The Dead Sea is **saltier** than most any body of water.
11. **cheaper** The **cheaper** items at a bakery are at least a day old.
12. **dirtiest** Those household cleaners can tackle the **dirtiest** messes.
13. **farthest** Of all the explorers, Magellan traveled the **farthest.**
14. **nearest** The shop owners **nearest** to the railroad were successful.
15. **loser** A gracious **loser** will take the time to congratulate the winner.
16. **loudest** The **loudest** singers in a choir must try to blend their voices.
17. **feistiest** The runt in a litter of puppies might be the **feistiest.**
18. **closer** Mercury is **closer** to the Sun than Venus.
19. **greater** An old coin can have a **greater** value than a new one.
20. **harshest** Washington's troops endured the **harshest** of winters.

Writing Process Strategies

Getting Ideas

Letter of Request

Teach

Introduce Writing Form

Have students read ***Language Arts Handbook*** pages 86–91 on business letters.

Inspiration

Teacher Model inspiration: *I want to write a letter of request to the National Cowboy Hall of Fame and Western Heritage Museum to ask them for information about Bill Pickett and the lives of cowboys in 1854.*

Brainstorming

Encourage students to suggest ideas, thoughts, or details that they might use in a letter of request about Bill Pickett and the lives of cowboys in 1854.

Guided Practice

Selecting a Topic

Have each student choose a topic for the letter of request. Suggest that students choose their topic based on information from the Going West unit. For example, they may wish to get information about Sacagawea or the California gold miners. Allow students time in the media center to research where to send their letters of request.

Business Letters

A **business letter** is a formal letter written to a company, organization, or professional person for a specific reason. Your tone should be less personal and even more polite and direct than that normally used for a friendly letter. Below are the parts of a business letter:

Heading

The heading consists of the sender's address and the date. It goes in the upper left corner.

Inside Address

The inside address includes the name and address of the person receiving the letter. It goes two lines below the heading.
Ms. Greta Frederick, Ph.D.

Salutation

The salutation is the greeting. Put a colon after it.
Dear Ms. Samartino:
You may use salutations like these when you don't know the person's name:
To Whom It May Concern: Dear Sir or Madam:
Dear National Geographic Society:

Body

The body includes what you want to say. Be brief and polite but not overly formal or stiff. Begin the body two lines below the salutation. Leave a single line of space between each paragraph. Do not indent.

Closing

The closing goes two lines below the body, at the left margin.
Yours truly, Sincerely,

Signature

Sign your name under the closing.

86 Personal Writing ▲ Business Letters

***Language Arts Handbook* p. 86**

English Language Conventions

Mechanics

Commas and Quotations

Teach

- Use ***Language Arts Handbook*** pages 384–387 for examples of the use of commas in appositives, introductory words, and interrupters; and end marks and quotation marks in dialogue.
- Remind students that commas are often used to set off an appositive, a word or phrase placed next to a noun to provide extra information. *I know many Phoenicians, citizens of Phoenix. Phoenicians, citizens of Phoenix, are proud of their city.*
- Explain that commas are used to set off interrupters, words or phrases that interrupt the main idea of a sentence, and introductory words such as *yes, no, oh, well,* and *now. Paul, on the other hand, has the floor. Oh, I didn't know that.*

Independent Practice

Use ***Comprehension and Language Arts Skills*** pages 168–169 to practice the correct use of commas in appositives, introductory words, and interrupters; and end marks and quotation marks in dialogue.

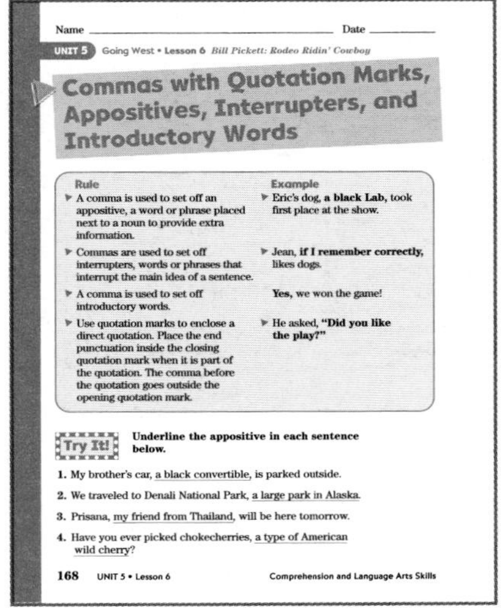

Name ____________ Date ______

UNIT 5 Going West • Lesson 6 *Bill Pickett: Rodeo Ridin' Cowboy*

Commas with Quotation Marks, Appositives, Interrupters, and Introductory Words

Rule	Example
A comma is used to set off an appositive, a word or phrase placed next to a noun to provide extra information.	Eric's dog, **a black Lab,** took first place at the show.
Commas are used to set off interrupters, words or phrases that interrupt the main idea of a sentence.	Jean, **if I remember correctly,** likes dogs.
A comma is used to set off introductory words.	**Yes,** we won the game!
Use quotation marks to enclose a direct quotation. Place the end punctuation inside the closing quotation mark when it is part of the quotation. The comma before the quotation goes outside the opening quotation mark.	He asked, **"Did you like the play?"**

Try It! **Underline the appositive in each sentence below.**

1. My brother's car, a black convertible, is parked outside.
2. We traveled to Denali National Park, a large park in Alaska.
3. Prisana, my friend from Thailand, will be here tomorrow.
4. Have you ever picked chokecherries, a type of American wild cherry?

168 UNIT 5 • Lesson 6 Comprehension and Language Arts Skills

***Comprehension and Language Arts Skills* p. 168**

DAY 2

Word Analysis

Spelling

Word Sorting

Open Word Sort Have students sort the spelling words according to their endings. Have the students explain their answers.

Vocabulary

Compound Words

Teach

- Introduce compound words as words created by combining two individual words. Examples of compound words include *fireplace*, *filmstrip*, *bedspread*, *airport*, and *nightgown*. Explain to students that often they can figure out the meaning of a compound word by breaking it down into two words and defining each word.
- Ask students to brainstorm compound words and make a list on the board.

Guided Practice

Assign page 126 of ***Spelling and Vocabulary Skills.*** Students can complete page 127 of ***Spelling and Vocabulary Skills*** for homework.

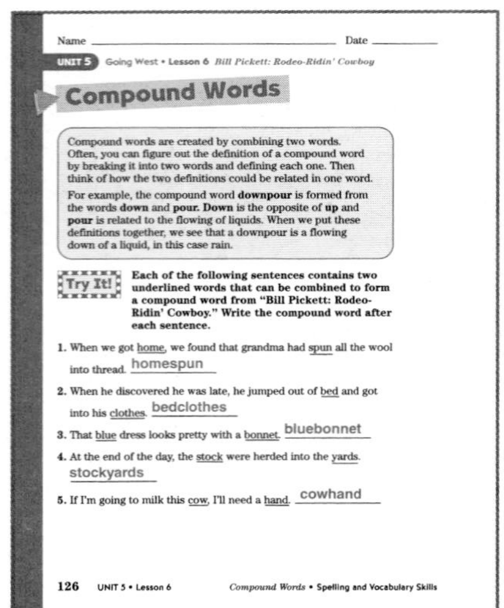
Name ______ Date ______

UNIT 5 Going West • Lesson 6 *Bill Pickett: Rodeo-Ridin' Cowboy*

Compound Words

Compound words are created by combining two words. Often, you can figure out the definition of a compound word by breaking it into two words and defining each one. Then think of how the two definitions could be related in one word.

For example, the compound word **downpour** is formed from the words **down** and **pour. Down** is the opposite of **up** and **pour** is related to the flowing of liquids. When we put these definitions together, we see that a downpour is a flowing down of a liquid, in this case rain.

Try It! **Each of the following sentences contains two underlined words that can be combined to form a compound word from "Bill Pickett: Rodeo-Ridin' Cowboy." Write the compound word after each sentence.**

1. When we got home, we found that grandma had spun all the wool into thread. homespun
2. When he discovered he was late, he jumped out of bed and got into his clothes. bedclothes
3. That blue dress looks pretty with a bonnet. bluebonnet
4. At the end of the day, the stock were herded into the yards. stockyards
5. If I'm going to milk this cow, I'll need a hand. cowhand

126 UNIT 5 • Lesson 6 *Compound Words* • Spelling and Vocabulary Skills

Spelling and Vocabulary Skills p. 126

Writing Process Strategies

Prewriting

Letter of Request

Teach

- Remind students that in a letter of request, they contact a company, organization, or professional person for the purpose of seeking information about a job, product, service, policy, or procedure.
- The writing of this type of letter involves some detective work. Students should ask themselves these questions:
  - What do they want or need? Why? When do they need it?
  - Where can they get it? From whom can they get it?
- The letter needs to be exact to get what is requested. In letters of request, students should
  - introduce themselves and explain why they are writing.
  - include any specific questions they want to have answered.
  - inform the reader of any dates or deadlines the writer must meet.
  - thank the reader for his or her help.

Independent Practice

Have students complete the exercise for writing a letter of request on ***Writer's Workbook*** page 98.

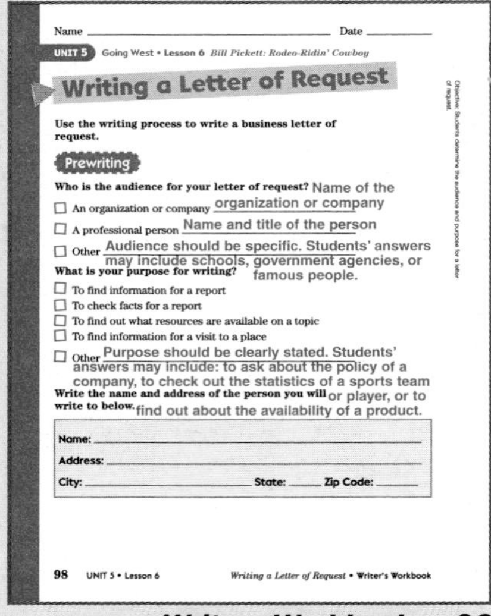
Name ______ Date ______

UNIT 5 Going West • Lesson 6 *Bill Pickett: Rodeo-Ridin' Cowboy*

Writing a Letter of Request

Use the writing process to write a business letter of request.

Prewriting

Who is the audience for your letter of request? Name of the
- ☐ An organization or company organization or company
- ☐ A professional person Name and title of the person
- ☐ Other Audience should be specific. Students' answers may include schools, government agencies, or famous people.

What is your purpose for writing?
- ☐ To find information for a report
- ☐ To check facts for a report
- ☐ To find out what resources are available on a topic
- ☐ To find information for a visit to a place
- ☐ Other Purpose should be clearly stated. Students' answers may include: to ask about the policy of a company, to check out the statistics of a sports team or player, or to find out about the availability of a product.

Write the name and address of the person you will write to below.

Name: ______
Address: ______
City: ______ State: ______ Zip Code: ______

Objective: Students determine the audience and purpose for a letter of request.

98 UNIT 5 • Lesson 6 *Writing a Letter of Request* • Writer's Workbook

Writers Workbook p. 98

English Language Conventions

Mechanics

Commas and Quotations

Teach

- Explain that an appositive can be placed at the beginning of a sentence, before the noun it is identifying or explaining. *A substitute, Ms. Andrews, looked around the room.*
- Write this sentence on the board: *"Now, wouldn't you like to hear my story?" asked Mr. Rabbit.* Then have students come one at a time to the board and write a sentence continuing the story according to your directions: a sentence with an appositive, a sentence with an introductory word, a sentence that is a quoted question, a sentence that is an exclamatory quotation, and so on.
- Use quotation marks to enclose a direct quotation. Periods and commas always go inside quotation marks.
- Place a question mark or an exclamation point inside the closing quotation marks when it is part of the quotation. *He asked, "Did you like the play?"*
- Place a quotation mark or an exclamation point outside the closing quotation marks when it is part of the entire sentence. *Why did she say, "I need a red pen"?*

Guided Practice in Reading

Have students identify commas in appositives, introductory words, and interrupters. Also have them identify end marks and quotation marks in dialogue in "Bill Pickett: Rodeo-Ridin' Cowboy." Point out the introductory word *yeah* on the first page and the appositive phrase that provides extra information about the Chisholm Trail at the bottom of page 478. Explain that sometimes a quotation is set off by a colon, as on page 481.

DAY 3

Word Analysis

Spelling

Spelling Patterns for Words with *-er* or *-est*

Teach

Introduce the spelling patterns for adding the endings *-er* and *-est* to base words. Explain to students that when a word ends in *e*, they should drop the *e* before adding *-er* or *-est.* When a word ends with a short vowel and a consonant, double the consonant before adding the *-er* or *-est.* Also, when a word ends in *y*, students should change the *y* to *i* before adding *-er* or *-est.* Have students generate a list of adjectives and then add *-er* and *-est* to each word.

Guided Practice

Have students complete page 128 from ***Spelling and Vocabulary Skills.***

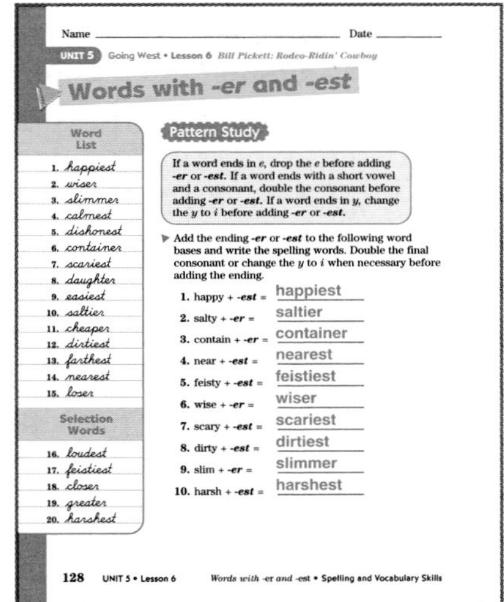

***Spelling and Vocabulary Skills* p. 128**

Vocabulary (continued)

Compound Words

Write the following compound words on the board: *pushover, overpass, pinpoint, timetable, moonwalk, airmail,* and *drawbridge.* Have students break these words into parts. Discuss the meanings of the two parts, and then have students define the entire compound word.

Writing Process Strategies

Drafting

Writing Letter of Request

Teach

Troubleshooting. Caution students about the common pitfalls to avoid when writing a letter of request:

- Students often try to use phrasing that is too formal and awkward. Encourage students to trust their own voices when writing.
- Students tend to use wordy and repetitive phrasing such as "in the near future" instead of "soon."
- Students often use clichés. These are worn-out phrases and should not be used. They should be replaced with clear, simple statements. Instead of saying, "At this point in time," for example, students should use "now."

Independent Practice

Have students complete ***Writer's Workbook,*** page 99. Have students use the page as a guide for drafting their letters. Include the drafts in the students' ***Writing Folders.***

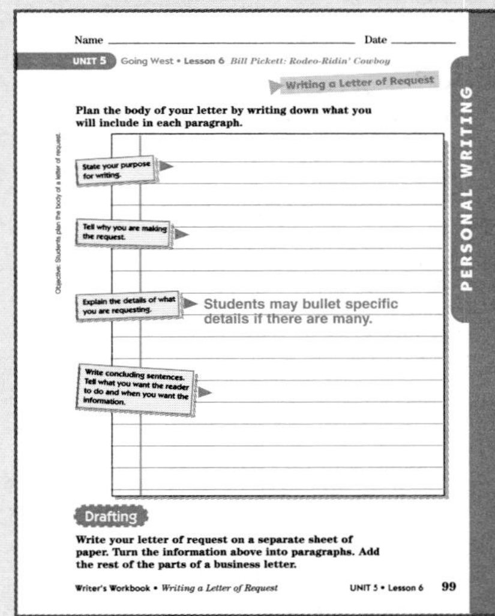

***Writer's Workbook* p. 99**

English Language Conventions

Mechanics

Commas and Quotations

Teach

- Explain that if both the sentence and the quotation at the end of the sentence need a question mark or an exclamation point, students should use only one punctuation mark and place it inside the closing quotation marks: *"When did she ask, 'What's for dinner?'"*
- Tell students that a comma should not be used after a quotation that ends with a question mark or an exclamation point: *"Can you be here on time?" he asked.*

Guided Practice in Writing

Remind students that checking sentences for correct usage of commas in appositives, introductory words, and interrupters and end marks and quotation marks in dialogue is an important part of proofreading their personal writing.

Informal Assessment

Check students' progress in understanding proper comma usage. Also make sure that students are using end marks and quotation marks in dialogue correctly.

DAY 4

Word Analysis

Spelling

Spelling Patterns for Words with *-er* or *-est*

Teach

Remind students of the *e*-drop, changing *y* to *i*, and consonant doubling rules discussed in this lesson. Model the meaning strategy by writing the following sentence on the board: *Potato chips are _____ than plain crackers.* Have students identify and spell the word that fits in the blank, *saltier.*

Guided Practice

Have students complete the Spelling Strategies exercise on page 129 of ***Spelling and Vocabulary Skills.***

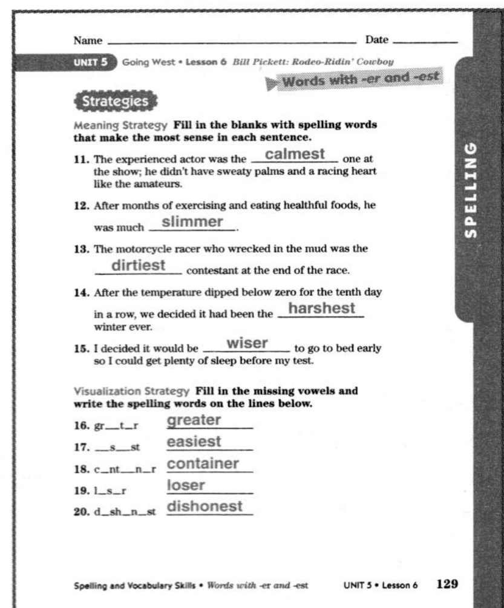

Name ____________ Date ______

UNIT 5 Going West • Lesson 6 *Bill Pickett: Rodeo-Ridin' Cowboy*

Words with -er and -est

Strategies

Meaning Strategy **Fill in the blanks with spelling words that make the most sense in each sentence.**

11. The experienced actor was the calmest one at the show; he didn't have sweaty palms and a racing heart like the amateurs.
12. After months of exercising and eating healthful foods, he was much slimmer.
13. The motorcycle racer who wrecked in the mud was the dirtiest contestant at the end of the race.
14. After the temperature dipped below zero for the tenth day in a row, we decided it had been the harshest winter ever.
15. I decided it would be wiser to go to bed early so I could get plenty of sleep before my test.

Visualization Strategy **Fill in the missing vowels and write the spelling words on the lines below.**

16. gr__t_r greater
17. __s__st easiest
18. c_nt__n_r container
19. l_s_r loser
20. d_sh_n_st dishonest

SPELLING

Spelling and Vocabulary Skills • *Words with -er and -est* UNIT 5 • Lesson 6 129

***Spelling and Vocabulary Skills* p. 129**

Vocabulary (continued)

Compound Words

Have students make up their own compound words. Students should write the word and a dictionary entry for the word including the definition, part of speech, and an example sentence. Students can draw a picture of their word if desired. (Examples: *raincat, noun: A cat that enjoys being out in the rain.*)

Writing Process Strategies

Revising

Letter of Request

Teach

Explain to students the importance of revising their letters to make sure they make sense.

- If the sentences stray from the main idea presented in each paragraph, the reader may become confused and the request may not be granted.
- The tone of the letters should be polite and straightforward. They should not be stuffy or full of awkward words, phrases, and clichés.

Routine Card
Refer to Routine 6 for Writing Conferences.

Independent Practice

Have students use the checklist on ***Writer's Workbook*** page 100 to revise their letters.

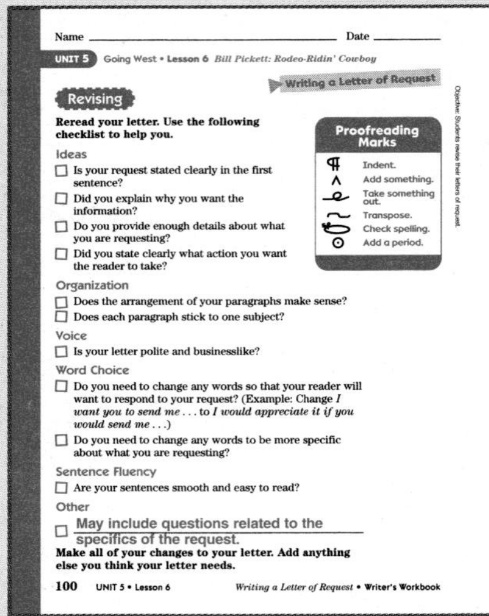

Name ____________ Date ______

UNIT 5 Going West • Lesson 6 *Bill Pickett: Rodeo-Ridin' Cowboy*

Writing a Letter of Request

Revising

Reread your letter. Use the following checklist to help you.

Ideas
- ☐ Is your request stated clearly in the first sentence?
- ☐ Did you explain why you want the information?
- ☐ Do you provide enough details about what you are requesting?
- ☐ Did you state clearly what action you want the reader to take?

Organization
- ☐ Does the arrangement of your paragraphs make sense?
- ☐ Does each paragraph stick to one subject?

Voice
- ☐ Is your letter polite and businesslike?

Word Choice
- ☐ Do you need to change any words so that your reader will want to respond to your request? (Example: Change *I want you to send me . . .* to *I would appreciate it if you would send me . . .*)
- ☐ Do you need to change any words to be more specific about what you are requesting?

Sentence Fluency
- ☐ Are your sentences smooth and easy to read?

Other
- ☐ May include questions related to the specifics of the request.

Make all of your changes to your letter. Add anything else you think your letter needs.

Proofreading Marks
- ¶ Indent.
- ^ Add something.
- Take something out.
- Transpose.
- Check spelling.
- ⊙ Add a period.

Objective: Students revise their letters of request.

100 UNIT 5 • Lesson 6 *Writing a Letter of Request* • Writer's Workbook

***Writer's Workbook* p. 100**

English Language Conventions

Listening, Speaking, Viewing

Interacting: Group Presentations

Teach

- Instruct students to review the assigned roles from Lesson 5. Remind each group to properly use the talents and interests of each of the group members. Some members may enjoy speaking. Some may want to draw visual aids while others may feel drawn to the research aspects of a group presentation.
- Remind students that group presentations can consist of the actual oral report as well as visual aids, role playing, and other creative or dramatic presentations.

Guided Practice

- Have students give short group presentations on the literature "Old Yeller and the Bear" or "Bill Pickett: Rodeo-Ridin' Cowboy." Give students the freedom to dramatize part of the story, show time lines of events, do a critical review of the literature, or report on the historical events of the period.
- Have students turn in a list of the roles and responsibilities of each of the group members before the presentation is given.

Independent Practice

If necessary, schedule additional time for students to give their group presentations. Student presentations should be organized, include content appropriate for the audience, and should summarize main points.

Informal Assessment

Observe whether students can give an effective group presentation, fulfilling assigned roles.

DAY 5

Word Analysis

Spelling

Assessment: Final Test

Spelling Patterns for Words with *-er* or *-est*

Teach

Repeat the Pretest for this lesson or use the Final Test on page 41 of ***Unit 5 Assessment.***

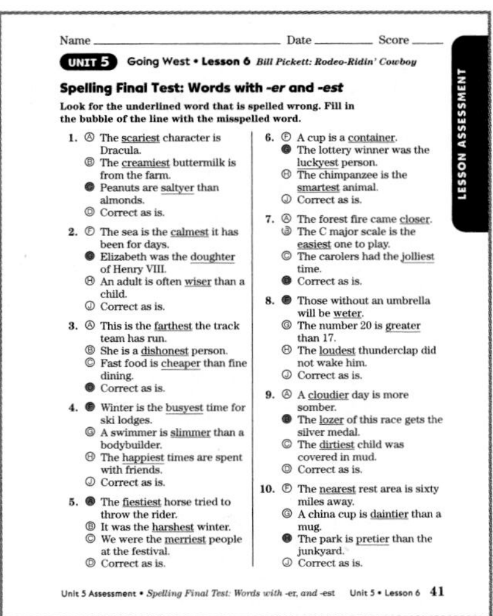

Name ______________ Date ________ Score ______

UNIT 5 Going West • Lesson 6 *Bill Pickett: Rodeo-Ridin' Cowboy*

LESSON ASSESSMENT

Spelling Final Test: Words with *-er* and *-est*

Look for the underlined word that is spelled wrong. Fill in the bubble of the line with the misspelled word.

1. Ⓐ The scariest character is Dracula.
   Ⓑ The creamiest buttermilk is from the farm.
   ● Peanuts are saltyer than almonds.
   Ⓓ Correct as is.
2. Ⓕ The sea is the calmest it has been for days.
   ● Elizabeth was the doughter of Henry VIII.
   Ⓗ An adult is often wiser than a child.
   Ⓙ Correct as is.
3. Ⓐ This is the farthest the track team has run.
   Ⓑ She is a dishonest person.
   Ⓒ Fast food is cheaper than fine dining.
   ● Correct as is.
4. ● Winter is the busyest time for ski lodges.
   Ⓖ A swimmer is slimmer than a bodybuilder.
   Ⓗ The happiest times are spent with friends.
   Ⓙ Correct as is.
5. ● The fiestiest horse tried to throw the rider.
   Ⓑ It was the harshest winter.
   Ⓒ We were the merriest people at the festival.
   Ⓓ Correct as is.
6. Ⓕ A cup is a container.
   ● The lottery winner was the luckyest person.
   Ⓗ The chimpanzee is the smartest animal.
   Ⓙ Correct as is.
7. Ⓐ The forest fire came closer.
   Ⓑ The C major scale is the easiest one to play.
   Ⓒ The carolers had the jolliest time.
   ● Correct as is.
8. ● Those without an umbrella will be weter.
   Ⓖ The number 20 is greater than 17.
   Ⓗ The loudest thunderclap did not wake him.
   Ⓙ Correct as is.
9. Ⓐ A cloudier day is more somber.
   ● The lozer of this race gets the silver medal.
   Ⓒ The dirtiest child was covered in mud.
   Ⓓ Correct as is.
10. Ⓕ The nearest rest area is sixty miles away.
    Ⓖ A china cup is daintier than a mug.
    ● The park is pretier than the junkyard.
    Ⓙ Correct as is.

Unit 5 Assessment • *Spelling Final Test: Words with -er, and -est* Unit 5 • Lesson 6 41

Unit 5 Assessment p. 41

Guided Practice

Have students categorize any mistakes they made on the Final Test.

Are they careless errors?
Are they lesson pattern problems?

Vocabulary

Compound Words

Informal Assessment

- Have students write two sentences containing the vocabulary words for this lesson. Periodically check to see if students can break compound words into two parts to discover their meanings.
- Encourage students to list compound words in their Writer's Notebooks.

Writing Process Strategies

Editing/Proofreading and Publishing

Letter of Request

Teach

Teacher Model using editing marks by addressing each of the Editing checklist items on ***Writer's Workbook*** page 101. Also use ***Language Arts Transparency 25,*** All Conventions to assist in editing.

Independent Practice

- Have students use the checklist on page 101 of the ***Writer's Workbook*** to proofread and edit their letters.
- Have students choose a method for publishing.

Formal Assessment

Total Point Value: 10

1. The tone of the letter is polite and suitable for the purpose and the audience. (2 points)
2. The sentences do not stray from the main idea. (2 points)
3. The phrasing is not wordy or awkward. (2 points)
4. The first part of the letter introduces the writer and explains why he or she is writing. (2 points)
5. The correct format for a business letter is followed. (2 points)

Name ______________ Date ________

UNIT 5 Going West • Lesson 6 *Bill Pickett: Rodeo-Ridin' Cowboy*

Writing a Letter of Request

PERSONAL WRITING

Editing/Proofreading

Objective: Students get their letters of request ready for mailing.

Proofread your letter. Letters with mistakes do not make a good impression. Use this checklist to help you.

Conventions

- ☐ Did you follow the correct format for writing a business letter?
- ☐ Did you capitalize names of streets, cities, months, and people?
- ☐ Did you capitalize the title of the recipient and the company in the inside address?
- ☐ Did you capitalize the word *Dear,* all nouns in the salutation, and the first word of the closing?
- ☐ Did you check for spelling errors, including those missed by a spell checker?
- ☐ Other May include questions about grammar, usage, and mechanics related to a business letter.

Publishing

Use this checklist to get your letter ready to mail.

Presentation — You may want to discuss conventions for signing business letters.

- ☐ Write your letter on a clean sheet of paper. Use only one side of the page. You may want to type and print your letter. Leave space between your closing and your name so that you can sign the letter.
- ☐ Reread your letter again for errors.
- ☐ Sign your letter.
- ☐ Address and proofread the envelope. Put the person's name and title on the envelope.
- ☐ Fold the letter and place it in the envelope. Put the correct postage on the envelope and mail it.
- ☐ Other You may want to read students' letters before they mail them.

Writer's Workbook • *Writing a Letter of Request* UNIT 5 • Lesson 6 101

Writer's Workbook p. 101

English Language Conventions

Penmanship

Joining with *N* and *t*

Teach

- **Teacher Model:** Review formation of uppercase *N* and lowercase *t* on the board.

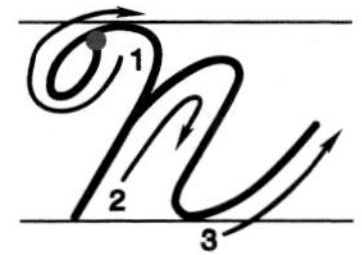

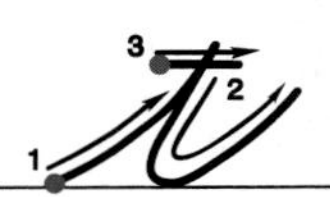

N Starting point, loop
Curve forward
Slant down
Retrace up slant
Overcurve down
Undercurve: capital *N*

t Starting point, undercurve
Slant down, undercurve to endpoint
Starting point, straight across: small *t*

- **Teacher Model:** Write the following sentence to model proper joining of letters: *Nothing bad ever happened to Nate.*

Guided Practice

- In the Writer's Notebook, have students join *N* with the letters *a, o, i,* and *e* and join *t* with *o, e, a,* and *u.*
- From "Bill Pickett: Rodeo-Ridin' Cowboy," ask students to write two paragraphs to practice joining letters.

Informal Assessment

Check students' handwriting for proper slant to the right and joining of letters.

Reading and Language Arts Skills Traces

Language Arts

WORD ANALYSIS

Skills Trace

Spelling: Words with -er and -est

Introduced in Grade 2.
Scaffolded throughout Grades 3–5.

REINTRODUCED: **Unit 5, Lesson 6,** p. 495F
PRACTICED: **Unit 5, Lesson 6,** pp. 495G–495I
Spelling and Vocabulary Skills, pp. 128–129
TESTED: **Unit 5, Lesson 6,** p. 495J
Unit 5 Assessment

Skills Trace

Vocabulary: Compound Words

Introduced in Grade 1.
Scaffolded throughout Grades 2–5.

REINTRODUCED: **Unit 5, Lesson 6,** p. 495G
PRACTICED: **Unit 5, Lesson 6,** pp. 495H–495I
Spelling and Vocabulary Skills, pp. 126–127
TESTED: **Informal Assessment**
Unit 5 Assessment

Reading

COMPREHENSION

Fact and Opinion

Introduced in Grade 2.
Scaffolded throughout Grades 3–5.

REINTRODUCED: **Unit 4, Lesson 6**
REINFORCED: **Unit 5, Lesson 6**
Unit 6, Lesson 3
TESTED: **Unit 5 Assessment**

WRITING PROCESS STRATEGIES

Skills Trace

Letter of Request

Introduced in Grade 4.
Scaffolded throughout Grades 4–5.

REINTRODUCED: **Unit 5, Lesson 6,** p. 495F
PRACTICED: **Unit 5, Lesson 6,** pp. 495F–495J
Writer's Workbook, pp. 98–101
TESTED: **Formal Assessment**
Unit 5, Lesson 6, p. 495J
Unit 5 Assessment

ENGLISH LANGUAGE CONVENTIONS

Skills Trace

Grammar and Usage: Commas and Quotations

Introduced in Grade 3.
Scaffolded throughout Grades 3–5.

REINTRODUCED: **Unit 5, Lesson 6,** p. 495F
PRACTICED: **Unit 5, Lesson 6,** pp. 495F–495H
Comprehension and Language Arts Skills, pp. 168–169
TESTED: **Unit 5 Assessment**

Skills Trace

Listening, Speaking, Viewing Interacting: Group Presentations

Introduced in Grade 5.
Scaffolded throughout Grade 5.

INTRODUCED: **Unit 5, Lesson 6,** p. 495I
PRACTICED: **Unit 5, Lesson 6,** p. 495I
TESTED: **Informal Assessment,** p. 495I

Skills Trace

Penmanship: Joining with N and t

Introduced in Grade 3 (*N*) and Grade 2 (*t*).
Scaffolded throughout Grades 4–5 and Grades 3–5.

REINTRODUCED: **Unit 5, Lesson 6,** p. 495J
PRACTICED: **Unit 5, Lesson 6,** p. 495J
TESTED: **Informal Assessment,** p. 495J

Professional Development: Comprehension

Comprehension Strategies and Skills

The primary aim of reading is comprehension. Experienced readers generally understand most of what they read. They also recognize when they do not understand, and they have various comprehension strategies for monitoring and furthering their understanding. Research has shown that students do not develop comprehension skills and strategies on their own. These strategies need to be taught and modeled before students begin to use them effectively.

Set Reading Goals

Good readers usually know what they want from a text. They

- activate prior knowledge, considering what they already know about the subject.
- browse the text to get an idea of what to expect from a text.
- consider the purpose of reading, whether for pleasure or to learn something specific.

Use Comprehension Strategies to Respond to Text

Good readers continually respond to the text they are reading and check to make sure they understand what they are reading. They

- **ask questions** about what they are reading to monitor comprehension.
- **monitor** what they read and **clarify** the meanings of words, phrases, and longer pieces of text by rereading, using context, or asking someone else.
- make connections between what they read and what they already know.
- make predictions about what they are reading and confirm or revise those predictions as they read.
- summarize periodically to check their understanding.
- visualize, or picture, what is happening in the text to comprehend descriptions.
- monitor their reading and adjust their reading speed to the content of their reading.

Develop Comprehension Skills

Good readers try to understand what the author is saying. Good readers have learned to

- consider the **author's point of view.**
- understand the **author's purpose.**
- comprehend **cause-and-effect relationships.**
- **compare and contrast** items and events.
- **draw conclusions** from what is read.
- distinguish **fact from opinion.**
- identify **main idea and details.**
- **make inferences** that help them understand what they are reading.
- **classify** information into **categories.**
- understand the **sequence** of events.

Professional Development

Teacher Resource Library CD-ROMs or ***Online Professional Development*** provides courses that help you better understand the Comprehension/Knowledge Building instruction in ***Open Court Reading.*** For more information about this program, visit SRAonline.com.

Additional information about comprehension, as well as resource references, can be found in the ***Professional Development Guide: Comprehension.***

Focus Questions How does McBroom plan to create a rainstorm? Why do you think this type of story was popular with frontier people?

Sid Fleischman
illustrated by Bill Ogden

I dislike to tell you this, but some folks have no regard for the truth. A stranger claims he was riding a mule past our wonderful one-acre farm and was attacked by woodpeckers.

Well, there's no truth to that. No, indeed! Those weren't woodpeckers. They were common prairie mosquitoes.

Small ones.

Why, skeeters grow so large out here that everybody uses chicken wire for mosquito netting. But I'm not going to say an unkind word about those zing-zanging, hot-tempered, needle-nosed creatures. They rescued our farm from ruin. That was during the Big Drought we had last year.

Dry? Merciful powers! Our young'uns found some tadpoles and had to teach them to swim. It hadn't rained in so long those tadpoles had never seen water.

That's the sworn truth—certain as my name's Josh McBroom. Why, I'd as soon grab a skunk by the tail as tell a falsehood.

Now, I'd best creep up on the Big Drought the way it crept up on us. I remember we did our spring plowing, as usual, and the skeeters hatched out, as usual. The bloodsucking rapscallions could be mighty pesky, but we'd learned to distract them.

"Will*jill*hester*chester*peter*polly*tim*tom*mary*larry*and-little*clarinda!*" I called out. "I hear the whine of gallinippers. We'd better put in a patch of beets."

496

SELECTION INTRODUCTION

Selection Summary

Genre: Tall Tale

Drought was a serious problem for the homesteaders of the American West, but in this tall tale, the wily Josh McBroom breaks "the big dry." It's so dry, says McBroom, that his cows are giving powdered milk, and his string of children, "Will*jill*hester*chester*peter-*polly*tim*tom*mary*larry*andlittle*clarinda*," may not be able to grow firecrackers for the Fourth of July. So McBroom puts his mind to hatching a plot to create a rainstorm—a plot that involves "zing-zanging, hot-tempered, blood-sucking prairie mosquitoes" that are as big as woodpeckers. And that's the sworn truth.

The tall tale became popular on the American frontier, where isolation and loneliness led to exaggerated stories often told by pioneers. In this way, pioneers expressed their astonishment at their new surroundings.

Some of the elements of tall tales are listed below. A tall tale may have one or more of these elements.

- It uses humor and exaggeration to tell the adventures of a fictional character, such as Paul Bunyan.
- It tells about unusual incidents that are handled in clever ways, such as Alfred Bulltop Stormalong's putting hinges on the tall masts of his ship to let the moon go by.

About the Author

Sid Fleischman is a master of creating suspense and keeping his readers guessing. "McBroom the Rainmaker" was a Golden Kite Award Honor Book, and Fleischman's more serious novel, *The Whipping Boy*, won a Newbery Medal.

Students can read more about Sid Fleischman on page 507 of the ***Student Anthology.***

Other Books by Sid Fleischman:

- *By the Great Horn Spoon!*
- *Chancy and the Grand Rascal*
- *Here Comes McBroom*
- *McBroom Tells the Truth (The Adventures of McBroom)*

About the Illustrator

Bill Ogden majored in illustration at the California Institute of the Arts. When he is not drawing, he can be found in the great outdoors, "stalking the wild mushroom, catching the wily bass, and chasing the dreaded, garden-eating woodchuck."

Students can read more about Bill Ogden on page 507 of the ***Student Anthology.***

Other Books Illustrated by Bill Ogden:

- *The Dog that Stole Football Plays*
- *The Dog that Called the Signals*
- *The Great McGoniggle Switches Pitches*

Inquiry Connections

A major aim of ***Open Court Reading*** is knowledge building. Because inquiry is at the root of knowledge building, students are encouraged to investigate topics and questions within each selection that relate to the unit theme.

"McBroom the Rainmaker" illustrates how adversity can be countered with humor and fun, as it often was in the American West. The tale tells about a serious problem faced by settlers of the American West told in true American West style—with sass and exaggeration.

Key concepts explored are:

- Drought was a serious problem for the homesteaders of the American West, but storytellers were able to find humor in the hardships.
- Tall tales are characterized by unique language, fast pacing, and humorous logic.

Before reading the selection:

- Point out that students may post a question, concept, word, illustration, or object on the Concept/Question Board at any time during the course of their unit investigation. Be sure that students include their names or initials on the items they post so that others will know whom to go to if they have an answer or if they wish to collaborate on a related activity.
- Students should feel free to write an answer or a note on someone else's question or to consult the Board for ideas for their own investigations throughout the unit.
- Encourage students to read about the American West at home and to bring in articles or pictures that are good examples to post on the Board.

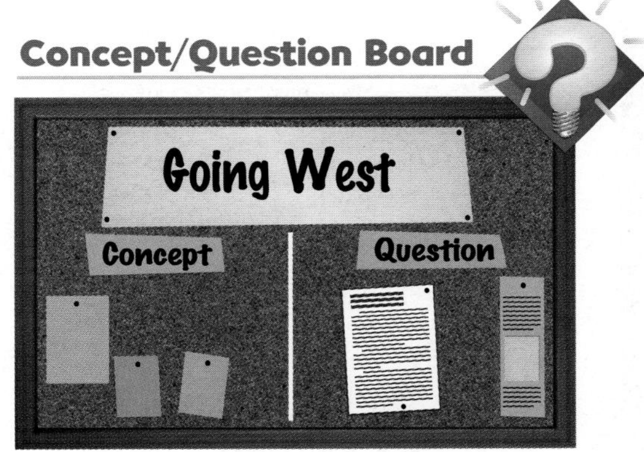

Leveled Practice

Reteach
Pages 171–176

Challenge
Pages 150–154

English Learner Support Activities

Intervention Workbook

Leveled Classroom Library*

Have students read at least 30 minutes daily outside of class. Have them read books from the ***Leveled Classroom Library,*** which supports the unit theme and helps students develop their vocabulary by reading independently.

Striking It Rich: The Story of the California Gold Rush

BY STEPHEN KRENSKY. ALADDIN, 1996.

A concise history of the Gold Rush, simply told, including how the miners came West, how they panned for gold, how some got rich without finding gold, and the Rush's effect on the growth of California. **(Easy)**

Black-Eyed Susan

BY JENNIFER ARMSTRONG. KNOPF, 1995.

While her father builds their homestead, Susie's efforts to cure her mother's prairie loneliness are helped by the arrival of some visitors to the isolated sod house. **(Average)**

Caddie Woodlawn

BY CAROL RYRIE BRINK. ALADDIN, 1990.

Based on the author's grandmother, the real Caddie Woodlawn, this is the story of a misunderstood prairie girl who is friends with the Indians and loves to play outside. (Newbery Medal Winner) **(Advanced)**

* These books, which all support the unit theme Going West, are part of a 36-book ***Leveled Classroom Library*** available for purchase from SRA/McGraw-Hill. Note: Teachers should preview any trade books for appropriateness in their classrooms before recommending them to students.

SRA TECHNOLOGY

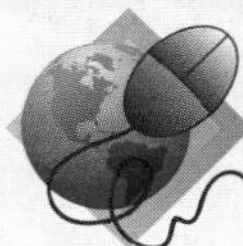

Web Connections

- Going West Web site
- Online Professional Development
- Online Assessment

CD-ROMs

- Research Assistant
- OCR Spelling
- Ultimate Writing and Creativity Center
- Teacher Resource Library

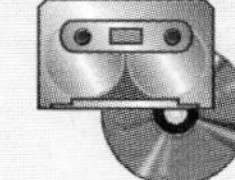

Audiocassettes/CDs

- Listening Library: Going West

Computer Skills

- TechKnowledge

Materials are available through SRA/McGraw-Hill.

McBroom the Rainmaker

Suggested Pacing: 3–5 days

LESSON PLANNER

	DAY I	DAY 2
1 Preparing to Read **Materials** ■ Routine Card 1	**Word Knowledge,** p. 496K ■ Short u Sound ■ /z/ Sound Spelled s or z ■ /k/ Sound Spelled *k, c,* or *ck* ■ Endings *-tion, -ed,* and *-est* **About the Words and Sentences,** p. 496K	**Developing Oral Language,** p. 496L
2 Reading & Responding **Materials** ■ Student Anthology, pp. 496–507 ■ Routine Card 1 ■ Reading Transparencies 46, 54, 64 ■ Comprehension and Language Arts Skills, pp. 170–171 ■ Program Assessment ■ Home Connection, pp. 75–76 ■ Inquiry Journal, p. 115 ■ Unit 5 Assessment, pp. 26–29 ■ Reteach, pp. 171–172 ■ Challenge, p. 150	**Build Background,** p. 496M **Preview and Prepare,** pp. 496M–496N **Selection Vocabulary,** p. 496N **Reading Recommendations,** pp. 496O–496P **Student Anthology,** pp. 496–505 First Read ✓ **Comprehension Strategies** ■ Making Connections, p. 496 ■ Monitoring and Adjusting Reading Speed, p. 496 ■ Monitoring and Clarifying, p. 498 ■ Predicting, pp. 500, 502, 504 **Discussing Strategy Use,** p. 504 **Discussing the Selection,** p. 505A	**Student Anthology,** pp. 496–505 Second Read **Comprehension Skills** ■ Cause and Effect, pp. 497, 499, 501, 503, 505 **Supporting the Reading,** pp. 505C–505D ■ Cause and Effect ✓ **Checking Comprehension,** p. 505
Inquiry **Materials** ■ Student Anthology, pp. 496–507 ■ Inquiry Journal, pp. 137–138 ■ Research Assistant	**Investigation** ■ Investigating Concepts Beyond the Text, p. 507A	**Investigation** ■ Concept/Question Board, p. 507B
3 Language Arts **Materials** ■ Comprehension and Language Arts Skills, pp. 172–175 ■ Language Arts Handbook ■ Language Arts Transparencies 15, 25 ■ Spelling and Vocabulary Skills, pp. 130–133 ■ Spelling Software ■ Student Anthology ■ Student Writing and Research Center ■ Writer's Workbook, pp. 102–105 ■ Unit 5 Assessment, pp. 42–43 ■ Reteach, pp. 173–176 ■ Challenge, pp. 151–154	**Word Analysis** ✓■ Spelling: Review Pretest, p. 507F **Writing Process Strategies** ■ Personal Writing: Memo, Getting Ideas, p. 507F **English Language Conventions** ■ Grammar, Usage, and Mechanics: Review, p. 507F	**Word Analysis** ■ Spelling: Review, p. 507G ■ Vocabulary: Review, p. 507G **Writing Process Strategies** ■ Personal Writing: Memo, Prewriting, p. 507G **English Language Conventions** ■ Grammar, Usage, and Mechanics: Review, p. 507G

✓ Informal Assessment Available ✓ Formal Assessment Available

DAY 2 continued	DAY 3	
DAY 3	**DAY 4**	**DAY 5**
General Review	**General Review**	**Review Word Knowledge**
Student Anthology, pp. 506–507 ✓■ Concept Connections ■ Meet the Author/Illustrator	**Review Selection Vocabulary,** p. 505B **Literary Elements,** p. 505E ■ Tall Tale	✓ **Lesson Assessment** ■ *Unit 5 Assessment:* Lesson Assessment, "McBroom the Rainmaker," pp. 26–29 **Home Connection,** p. 505B **Science Connection,** p. 505F ■ Water Conservation
Investigation ✓✓■ Presenting Investigation Findings, p. 507C	**Supporting the Investigation,** p. 507D ■ Reading and Using Graphic Sources of Information	**Investigation** ■ Unit Investigation Continued ■ Update Concept/Question Board
Word Analysis ■ Spelling: Review, p. 507H ■ Vocabulary: Review, p. 507H **Writing Process Strategies** ■ Personal Writing: Memo, Drafting, p. 507H ■ Writer's Craft: Structure of a Memo, p. 507H **English Language Conventions** ✓■ Grammar, Usage, and Mechanics: Review, p. 507H	**Word Analysis** ■ Spelling: Review, p. 507I ■ Vocabulary: Review, p. 507I **Writing Process Strategies** ■ Personal Writing: Memo, Revising, p. 507I **English Language Conventions** ✓■ Listening, Speaking, Viewing: Presenting: Oral Presentations, p. 507I	**Word Analysis** ✓■ Spelling: Review Final Test, p. 507J ✓■ Vocabulary: Review, p. 507J **Writing Process Strategies** ✓■ Personal Writing: Memo, Editing/Proofreading and Publishing, p. 507J **English Language Conventions** ✓■ Penmanship: Joining with *R* and *s*, p. 507J ✓✓ **Unit 5 Wrap-Up**

Below are suggestions for differentiating instruction. These are the same skills shown on the Lesson Planner; however, these pages provide extra practice opportunities or enriching activities to meet the varied needs of students.

WORKSHOP

Differentiating Instruction

Teacher: Individual and Small-Group Instruction

Spend time each day with individuals and small groups to individualize instruction. Each day:

- preteach students who need help with the next lesson.
- reteach students who need to solidify their understanding of content previously taught.
- listen to students read to check their fluency.
- hold writing and inquiry conferences.

Use the following program components to support instruction:

- ***Reteach*** with students who need a bit more practice.
- ***Intervention*** with students who exhibit a lack of understanding of the lesson concepts.
- ***English Learner Support*** with students who need language help.
- ***Differentiating Instruction Support Activities*** with students who need alternative activities to strengthen skill and strategy instruction.

Student: Independent Activities

Students can work alone, with a partner, or in small groups on such activities as:

- Review sound/spellings
- Partner Reading
- Practice fluency
- Independent Reading
- Reading Roundtable
- Concept vocabulary
- Selection vocabulary
- Writing in progress
- Conference
- Language Arts
- ***Challenge*** Activities
- Inquiry and Investigation Activities
- Listening Library

Professional Development

Teacher Resource Library CD-ROMs or ***Online Professional Development*** provides courses that help you better understand the Workshop/Intervention instruction in ***Open Court Reading***.

For more information on this program, visit SRAonline.com.

	DAY I
Word Knowledge	**Teacher Directed** ▪ Teach meanings of blended words ▪ Reading Words and About the Words, ***Intervention Guide,*** p. 281
Fluency	**Independent Activities** ▪ Self-test fluency rate
Comprehension	**Teacher Directed** ▪ Preteach "McBroom the Rainmaker," ***Intervention Guide,*** pp. 282–283 ▪ Intervention Selection 1, ***Intervention Guide,*** pp. 283–284 ▪ ***English Learner Support Guide,*** pp. 454–457 **Independent Activities** ▪ Record response to selection in Writer's Notebook ▪ Browse ***Leveled Classroom Library*** ▪ ***Listening Library Audiocassette/CD*** ▪ Add vocabulary in Writer's Notebook
Inquiry	**Independent Activities** ▪ Concept/Question Board ▪ Explore OCR Web site for theme connections
Language Arts	**Teacher Directed** ▪ Seminar: Select a Topic for Memo, p. 507F ▪ Review Capitalization and Punctuation, ***Intervention Guide,*** p. 286 **Independent Activities** ▪ Grammar, Usage, and Mechanics: Review, ***Comprehension and Language Arts Skills,*** pp. 172–173

DAY 2	DAY 3	DAY 4	DAY 5
Teacher Directed ▪ Developing Oral Language, ***Intervention Guide,*** p. 281	**Teacher Directed** ▪ Dictation and Spelling, ***Intervention Guide,*** pp. 281–282	**Independent Activities** ▪ Add words to Word Bank	**Teacher Directed** ▪ General review as necessary
Independent Activities ▪ Oral reading of "McBroom the Rainmaker"	**Independent Activities** ▪ Partner read "McBroom the Rainmaker"	**Independent Activities** ▪ Fluency rate check ▪ Reread "McBroom the Rainmaker"	**Teacher Directed** ▪ Repeated Readings, ***Intervention Guide,*** p. 285 **Independent Activities** ▪ Fluency Rate Check
Teacher Directed ▪ Preteach "McBroom the Rainmaker," ***Intervention Guide,*** pp. 282–283 ▪ Reread Intervention Selection 1 ▪ Teach Comprehension Strategies, ***Intervention Guide,*** p. 284 ▪ ***English Learner Support Guide,*** pp. 457–459 ▪ Review Cause and Effect ▪ Cause and Effect, ***Reteach,*** pp. 171–172 **Independent Activities** ▪ Cause and Effect • ***Comprehension and Language Arts Skills,*** pp. 170–171 • ***Challenge,*** p. 150 ▪ Choose ***Leveled Classroom Library*** book	**Teacher Directed** ▪ Teach Intervention Selection 2, ***Intervention Guide,*** pp. 284–285 ▪ ***English Learner Support Guide,*** pp. 459–461 ▪ Discuss Concept Connections, p. 506 **Independent Activities** ▪ ***English Learner Support Activities,*** p. 66 ▪ Read ***Leveled Classroom Library*** book ▪ ***Listening Library Audiocassette/CD*** ▪ Recording Concept Information, ***Inquiry Journal,*** p. 115 ▪ Complete Supporting the Reading: Link to Writing, p. 505D	**Teacher Directed** ▪ Teach Comprehension Strategies, ***Intervention Guide,*** p. 285 ▪ Reread Intervention Selection 2 ▪ ***English Learner Support Guide,*** pp. 462–464 **Independent Activities** ▪ Read ***Leveled Classroom Library*** book ▪ Literary Elements: Independent Practice, p. 505E	**Teacher Directed** ▪ Reading Roundtable ▪ ***English Learner Support Guide,*** pp. 464–465 ▪ ***Differentiating Instruction Support Activities,*** pp. 31–32 **Independent Activities** ▪ Read ***Leveled Classroom Library*** book ▪ Science Connection, p. 505F ▪ ***English Learner Support Activities,*** p. 67
Independent Activities ▪ Concept/Question Board ▪ Explore OCR Web site for theme connections	**Teacher Directed** ▪ Begin presentations of investigation findings **Independent Activities** ▪ Concept/Question Board ▪ Use ***Research Assistant*** to continue investigation	**Teacher Directed** ▪ Continue presentations of investigation findings **Independent Activities** ▪ Concept/Question Board	**Independent Activities** ▪ Concept/Question Board ▪ Interpreting Graphs, ***Inquiry Journal,*** pp. 137–138 ▪ Continue research
Teacher Directed ▪ Review Capitalization and Punctuation, ***Intervention Guide,*** p. 286 ▪ Spelling: Word Sort, p. 507G ▪ Seminar: Plan a Memo, p. 507G ▪ Grammar, Usage, and Mechanics: Review, ***Reteach,*** p. 175 **Independent Activities** ▪ Vocabulary: Review, ***Spelling and Vocabulary Skills,*** pp. 130–131 ▪ Grammar, Usage, and Mechanics: Review, ***Challenge,*** p. 153	**Teacher Directed** ▪ Seminar: Draft a Memo, p. 507H ▪ Writing Activity, ***Intervention Guide,*** p. 287 ▪ Vocabulary: Review, ***Reteach,*** p. 174 **Independent Activities** ▪ Spelling: Review, ***Spelling and Vocabulary Skills,*** p. 132 ▪ Vocabulary: Review, ***Challenge,*** p. 152 ▪ Writer's Craft: Structure of a Memo, ***Comprehension and Language Arts,*** pp. 174–175	**Teacher Directed** ▪ Seminar: Revise a Memo, p. 507I ▪ Writing Activity, ***Intervention Guide,*** p. 287 ▪ Spelling: Review, ***Reteach,*** p. 173 **Independent Activities** ▪ Spelling: Review • ***Spelling and Vocabulary Skills,*** p. 133 • ***Challenge,*** p. 151	**Teacher Directed** ▪ Seminar: Edit and Publish a Memo, p. 507J ▪ Writer's Craft: Structure of a Memo, ***Reteach,*** p. 176 ▪ ***Differentiating Instruction Support Activities,*** pp. 33–36 **Independent Activities** ▪ Penmanship: Cursive Letters *R* and *s*, p. 507J ▪ Writer's Craft: Structure of a Memo, ***Challenge,*** p. 154 ▪ Unit Wrap-Up, ***Inquiry Journal,*** pp. 139–140

ASSESSMENT

Formal Assessment Options

Use these summative assessments along with your informal observations to assess student progress.

Name ______________________ Date ________ Score ______

UNIT 5 Going West • Lesson 7

McBroom the Rainmaker

Read the following questions carefully. Then completely fill in the bubble of each correct answer. You may look back at the story to find the answer to each of the questions.

1. McBroom says that what the stranger thought were woodpeckers were really
   - Ⓐ vultures
   - ● mosquitoes
   - Ⓒ helicopters
2. How many children do the McBrooms have?
   - Ⓐ nine
   - ● eleven
   - Ⓒ thirteen

Read the following questions carefully. Use complete sentences to answer the questions.

3. Why did McBroom decide to go hunting for a rain cloud?
   McBroom decides to go hunting for a rain cloud because the topsoil and all the plants are drying up.
4. What happened to the pocket watch McBroom dropped?
   The pocket watch he dropped put down roots and grew into a three-dollar alarm clock.
5. How do the young McBrooms make fireworks?
   They shoot radish seeds with their bean shooters.

26 Unit 5 • Lesson 7 *McBroom the Rainmaker* • Unit 5 Assessment

Unit 5 Assessment p. 26

McBroom the Rainmaker *(continued)*

6. How did the skeeters help the McBrooms?
   They cried so much from the onions that the McBrooms had plenty of water.
7. What did the mosquitoes do to the beets?
   The mosquitoes sucked the beets dry until they went from red to white.
8. What was the first sign that there was going to be a dry spell?
   The first sign of a dry spell came when the vegetable clocks that grew on the farm started running slowly.

Read the following questions carefully. Then completely fill in the bubble of each correct answer.

9. What does McBroom plant to end the drought?
   - Ⓐ a raintree
   - Ⓑ watermelon
   - ● onions
10. What caused the handkerchiefs to be as wet as dishrags?
   - Ⓐ The rain fell so hard it got into the farm house.
   - ● The onions made everyone cry.
   - Ⓒ The river rose so high it reached their heads.

Unit 5 Assessment • *McBroom the Rainmaker* Unit 5 • Lesson 7 27

Unit 5 Assessment p. 27

McBroom the Rainmaker *(continued)*

Read the questions and statement below. Use complete sentences in your answers.

Linking to the Concepts How are the McBrooms like other pioneer families?

Answers will vary. Accept all reasonable answers.

Personal Response McBroom says that "some folks have no regard for the truth." Is that a good introduction to this story? Why or why not?

Answers will vary. Accept all reasonable answers.

28 Unit 5 • Lesson 7 *McBroom the Rainmaker* • Unit 5 Assessment

Unit 5 Assessment p. 28

McBroom the Rainmaker *(continued)*

Vocabulary

Read the following questions carefully. Then completely fill in the bubble of each correct answer.

1. McBroom says that some folks have no regard for the truth. **Regard** means
   - Ⓐ friendship
   - Ⓑ humor
   - ● concern
2. The earth was so parched, they couldn't raise a crop of beets. In this sentence, **parched** means
   - ● very hot and dry
   - Ⓑ moist and rich
   - Ⓒ filled with bugs
3. In this story, the "Big Dry" is what McBroom calls the drought. A **drought** is
   - Ⓐ a period with very few insects
   - ● a long period of dry weather
   - Ⓒ a rainy spell that causes floods
4. McBroom found a genuine rain crow hiding from the skeeters under a milk pail. Another word for **genuine** is
   - Ⓐ young
   - Ⓑ friendly
   - ● real
5. Those hot-tempered prairie mosquitoes were returning from town. A **prairie** is
   - Ⓐ an area in town where people play sports
   - Ⓑ a pond where large numbers of wildlife live
   - ● a large area of flat land covered with grass

Unit 5 Assessment • *McBroom the Rainmaker* Unit 5 • Lesson 7 29

Unit 5 Assessment p. 29

Name ______________________ Date ________ Score ______

UNIT 5 Going West • Lesson 7 *McBroom the Rainmaker*

Spelling Pretest: Review

Fold this page back on the dotted line. Take the Pretest. Then correct any word you misspelled by crossing out the word and rewriting it next to the incorrect spelling.

1. pedal
2. vain
3. promotion
4. laziest
5. evident
6. misfire
7. mission
8. peddle
9. disprove
10. carrying
11. vein
12. traction
13. mismatch
14. decent
15. branched
16. disposition
17. harvested
18. smallest
19. shrinking
20. dried

42 Unit 5 • Lesson 7 *Spelling Pretest: Review* • Unit 5 Assessment

Unit 5 Assessment p. 42

Name ______________________ Date ________ Score ______

UNIT 5 Going West • Lesson 7 *McBroom the Rainmaker*

Spelling Final Test: Review

Look for the underlined word that is spelled wrong. Fill in the bubble of the line with the misspelled word.

1. Ⓐ A promotion means more responsibility.
   ● The discusion group meets every Friday.
   Ⓒ His mission was to eat a whole turkey.
   Ⓓ Correct as is.
2. Ⓔ A vain person looks in the mirror often.
   Ⓖ The runners shoes have a lot of traction.
   Ⓗ His tooth ached.
   ● Correct as is.
3. ● Two vertions of the poem were published.
   Ⓑ The laziest worker is likely to be fired.
   Ⓒ Pedal faster if you want to get up the hill.
   Ⓓ Correct as is.
4. Ⓕ The vein carries blood.
   ● Which word did you mispell on the test?
   Ⓗ The river branched out into smaller streams.
   Ⓙ Correct as is.
5. Ⓐ People at the market peddle various fruits.
   ● The aide is the teacher's assistent.
   Ⓒ Copernicus would disprove ideas.
   Ⓓ Correct as is.
6. Ⓔ The height of a horse is measured in hands.
   Ⓖ Insects are found crawling in the cellar.
   Ⓗ That old building is a Spanish mission.
   ● Correct as is.
7. Ⓐ American colonists harvested tobacco.
   Ⓑ Don't mismatch the gloves.
   ● This job may be temporary or permenant.
   Ⓓ Correct as is.
8. Ⓕ Her behavior will displease her parents.
   Ⓖ A hummingbird is one of the smallest birds.
   ● It is evidant that the students are distracted.
   Ⓙ Correct as is.
9. Ⓐ Cinderella didn't have a decent dress.
   Ⓑ The clothes are shrinking in the dryer.
   Ⓒ A grouchy disposition is unappealing.
   ● Correct as is.
10. ● Dryed flowers make a nice wreath.
   Ⓖ The woman is carrying the jar on her head.
   Ⓗ Have a lozenge if your throat is hoarse.
   Ⓙ Correct as is.

Unit 5 Assessment • *Spelling Final Test: Review* Unit 5 • Lesson 7 43

Unit 5 Assessment p. 43

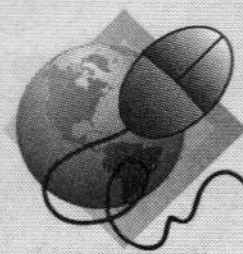

Online Assessment for ***Open Court Reading*** helps teachers differentiate classroom instruction based on students' scores from the weekly and end-of-unit assessments. It provides exercises best suited to meet the needs of each student. For more information visit SRAonline.com.

Informal Comprehension Strategies Rubrics

Making Connections

- The student activates prior knowledge and related knowledge.
- The student uses prior knowledge to explain something encountered in the text.
- The student connects ideas presented later in the text to ideas presented earlier in the text.
- The student notes ideas in the text that are new to him or her or conflict with what he or she thought previously.

Predicting

- The student makes predictions about what the text is about.
- The student updates predictions during reading, based on information in the text.

Monitoring and Adjusting Reading Speed

The student changes reading speed in reaction to text, exhibiting such behavior as

- Skimming parts of the text that are not important or relevant.
- Purposely reading more slowly because of difficulty in comprehending the text.

Research Rubrics

During Workshop, assess students using the rubrics below. The rubrics range from 1–4 in most categories, with 1 being the lowest score. Record each student's score on the inside back cover of his or her ***Inquiry Journal.***

Communicating Research Progress and Results

This rubric may apply to oral, written, or multimedia reports.

1 Reporting is sparse and fragmentary.

2 Report is factual; communicates findings but not the thinking behind them.

3 Report provides a good picture of the research problem, of how original conjectures were modified in light of new information, and of difficulties and unresolved issues.

4 A report that not only interests and informs the audience but also draws helpful commentary from them.

Overall Assessment of Research

1 A collection of facts related in miscellaneous ways to a topic.

2 An organized collection of facts relevant to the research problem.

3 A thoughtful effort to tackle a research problem, with some indication of progress toward solving it.

4 Significant progress on a challenging problem of understanding.

WORD KNOWLEDGE

Objectives

- Students recognize and decode words with the short u sound.
- Students recognize and decode words with the /z/ sound spelled *s* or *z*.
- Students recognize and read words with the /k/ sound spelled *k*, *c*, or *ck*.
- Students recognize and spell words with various endings.

Materials

- Routine Card 1

Routine Card
Refer to Routine 1 for the Reading the Words and Sentences procedure.

Teacher Tip SYLLABICATION To help students blend words and build fluency, demonstrate syllabication using decodable multisyllabic words in the word lines.

us • es	dis • po • si • tion	smal • lest
pic • nic	har • vest • ed	shrink • ing

Differentiating Instruction

If...	Then...
Students need extra help with words containing the suffixes *-ed*, *-est*, and *-tion*	Use ***Intervention Guide***, pages 281–282

Word Knowledge

Reading the Words and Sentences

Use direct teaching to teach the Word Knowledge lesson. Write each word and sentence on the board. Have students read each word together. After all the words have been read, have students read each sentence in natural phrases. Use the suggestions in About the Words and Sentences to discuss the different features of the listed words.

Line 1:	skunk	mud	stuck	run	
Line 2:	raise	please	gazed	size	uses
Line 3:	kind	keep	picnic	track	
Line 4:	disposition	harvested	smallest	shrinking	dried

Sentence 1: Our tires keep getting stuck in the mud.
Sentence 2: Please raise your hand if you have an idea to share.
Sentence 3: Do you remember when that skunk ruined our picnic?
Sentence 4: After the lavender was harvested, it was dried and used for flower arrangements.

About the Words and Sentences

- **Line 1:** Each of these words have the short u sound. Explain to students that when a word or syllable has one vowel and ends in one or two consonants, the vowel is usually short. Have students say these words aloud. Encourage them to think of other common words with the short u sound.
- **Line 2:** These words have the /z/ sound spelled *s* or *z*. Say the words aloud for students, stressing the /z/ sound in each. Then have students pronounce the words aloud. Ask students to identify the word in Line 2 that has the /z/ sound in two places *(uses)*. Point out that the *s* in *size* has the /s/ sound. Ask students how they might give *size* another /z/ sound *(add an -s to make it plural)*. Explain that in many plural words that end in *-s*, the *s* has the /z/ sound. Ask students to think of other words with the /z/ sound spelled *s* or *z* and say them aloud.
- **Line 3:** These words have the /k/ sound spelled *k*, *c*, or *ck*. Have students say the words aloud. Ask students to identify the sound that each word has in common. Once students are aware of the /k/ sound, ask them to identify the letter(s) in each word that makes the /k/ sound.
- **Line 4:** The words in the last line review the word endings *-tion*, *-ed*, *-ing*, and *-est*.

- **Sentence 1:** Have students read the sentence aloud. Ask students to identify the words in the sentence that have the short u sound *(stuck, mud)*. Remind students of the rules for short vowel sounds that you previously shared with them. Lead students to understand that *stuck* follows both rules, while *mud* follows the rule about a word that has one vowel and ends in one consonant.
- **Sentence 2:** Have students read the sentence aloud. Have students identify the words in the sentence that include the /z/ sound *(please, raise)*. Point out that the /z/ sound is spelled *s* in both of these words. Ask students to think of other words with the /z/ sound spelled *s* or *z*. Have students use these words in sentences and say them aloud. Other students should listen closely and identify the word with the /z/ sound in students' sentences.
- **Sentence 3:** Read the sentence aloud for students. Ask students to identify the word in the sentence that has both the /k/ sound and the short u sound *(skunk)*. Now ask students to find the word that has the /k/ sound twice *(picnic)*. Finally, have students read the sentence aloud.
- **Sentence 4:** Have students identify the words in the last sentence that contain the ending *-ed (harvested, dried, used)*.

Developing Oral Language

Using direct teaching to review the words, do one or both of the following activities.

- You might challenge students to create tongue twisters in which each word begins with or includes the /k/ sound. Write several tongue twisters on the board and work with students to identify the spellings that make the /k/ sound.
- Point to one word in the lines above and select a student to read the word and use it in a sentence. Have other students expand the sentence using more words from the board. Challenge students to make the sentence as long as possible while still making sense. Then challenge students to create a new sentence using all of the words from their "longest possible" sentence.

Teacher Tip BUILDING FLUENCY By this time in grade 5 students should be reading approximately 151 words per minute with fluency and expression. Gaining a better understanding of the spellings of sounds and structure of words will help students as they encounter unfamiliar words in their reading. As students read, you may notice that some need work in building fluency. During Workshop, have these students choose a section of the text (a minimum of 160 words) to read several times in order to build fluency.

Differentiating Instruction

If...	Then...
Students need extra fluency practice	Use the Intervention Selections activities, ***Intervention Guide,*** pages 283–285

Spelling
See pages 507F–507J for the corresponding spelling lesson for review of word endings.

Objectives

- Students will understand the selection vocabulary before reading.
- Students will recognize and read words with the /k/ sound spelled *k, c,* or *ck.*
- Students will recognize and read words with the /z/ sound spelled *s* or *z.*
- Students will use the comprehension strategies Making Connections, Monitoring and Clarifying, Monitoring and Adjusting Reading Speed, and Predicting as they read the story the first time.
- Students will use the comprehension skill Cause and Effect as they read the story the second time.

Materials

- Student Anthology, pp. 496–507
- Comprehension and Language Arts Skills, pp. 170–171
- Inquiry Journal, p. 115
- Reading Transparencies 46, 54, 64
- Listening Library
- Program Assessment
- Unit 5 Assessment, pp. 26–29
- Home Connection, p. 75

Differentiating Instruction

English Learner Tip

SHARING EXPERIENCES Explain that America has a history of telling tall tales and spinning yarns. This story is funny because the author exaggerates and uses colorful, descriptive language. Ask English Learners to tell a folktale or tall tale that they know from their native countries.

If...	Then...
Students need extra help with the selection vocabulary	Use ***Intervention Guide,*** page 282

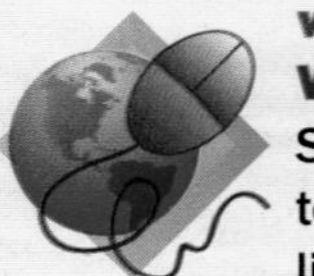

www.sra4kids.com
Web Connection
Students can use the connections to Going West in the Reading link of the SRA Web page for more background information about the American West.

Build Background

Activate Prior Knowledge

Discuss the following with students to find out what they may already know about the selection and have already learned about the theme Going West.

- Preteach "McBroom the Rainmaker" by first determining students' prior knowledge about the Big Dry. Ask them, what does "Big Dry" mean? *("Big Dry" is the name given to a long period of drought.)*
- Have students recall the rural life of settlers in the American West that was portrayed in "Old Yeller and the Bear."

Background Information

The following information may help students understand the selection they are about to read.

- Tell students that tall tales are closely associated with rural America. They became popular on the American frontier where isolation and loneliness led to the exaggerated stories often told by the pioneers. These tall tales were one way pioneers conveyed their astonishment at their amazing new surroundings and the events that occurred in this region.
- Students may already be familiar with tall tale characters. Remind them of these examples of tall tales that they may have read or heard before: Paul Bunyan, Pecos Bill, Johnny Appleseed, Davy Crockett, and John Henry.
- Have the students discuss what they know about the genre of this selection. Refer to page 496A of the ***Teacher's Edition*** for elements of this selection's genre.

Preview and Prepare

Browse

- Have a student read aloud the title and the names of the author and illustrator. Demonstrate how to browse. Since this is a fiction piece, have the students browse only its first couple of pages, so that the ending will not be spoiled. This helps them to activate prior knowledge in a way that is relevant to the selection. Then discuss what they think this story might have to do with going west.

- Have the students search for clues that tell them something about the story. Also, have them look for any problems, such as unfamiliar words or long sentences, that they notice while reading. Use ***Reading Transparency 54*** to record their observations as they browse. For example, the fact that this is a tall tale might be a clue that the events will be humorous and exaggerated. For the Problems column, students might say they don't know the meaning of the term *Big Dry*. They might wonder what mosquitoes have to do with a drought. To save time and model note taking, write students' observations as brief notes rather than complete sentences.
- As students prepare to read the selection, have them browse the Focus Questions on the first page of the selection. Tell them to keep these questions in mind as they read.

Set Purposes

Have students set their own purpose for reading this selection. You might suggest that they think about how amazed new settlers must have been when they encountered the American West. Remind students that good readers have a purpose when they read. Let them know that they should make sure they know the purpose for reading whenever they read.

Selection Vocabulary

As students study vocabulary, they will use a variety of skills to determine the meaning of a word. These include context clues, word structure, and apposition. Students will apply these same skills while reading to clarify additional unfamiliar words.

Display ***Reading Transparency 46*** before reading the selection to introduce and discuss the following words and their meanings.

regard: thought or care (page 496)
parched: very hot and dry, or very thirsty (page 499)
drought: a long period of dry weather without rain (page 500)
genuine: real (page 501)
prairie: a large area of level or rolling land with grass and few or no trees (page 501)

Have students read the words in the Word Box, stopping to blend any words that they have trouble reading. Help students decode multisyllabic words by breaking them into syllables and blending the syllables. If the word is not decodable, give the students the pronunciation.

Have students read the sentences on ***Reading Transparency 46*** and use the skills of context, word structure (structural analysis), or apposition to figure out the meanings of the words. Be sure students explain which skill(s) they are using and how they figured out the meanings of the words.

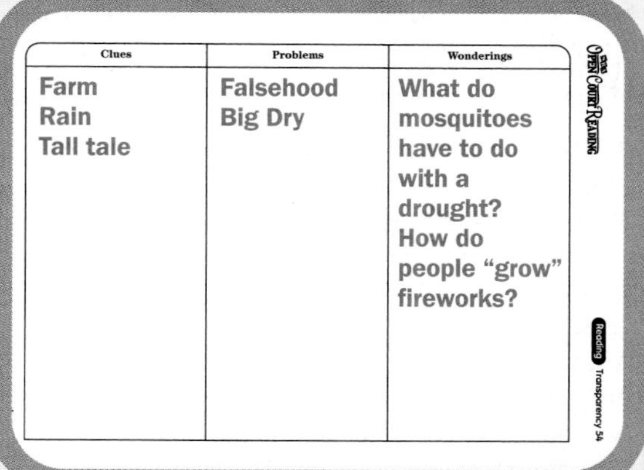

Open Court Reading — Reading Transparency 54

Clues	Problems	Wonderings
Farm Rain Tall tale	Falsehood Big Dry	What do mosquitoes have to do with a drought? How do people "grow" fireworks?

Reading Transparency 54

Teacher Tip SELECTION VOCABULARY To help students decode words, divide them into the syllables shown below. The information following each word tells how students can figure out the meaning of each word from the sentences on the transparency.

re • gard	context clues
parched	context clues, word structure
drought	context clues
gen • u • ine	context clues
prair • ie	context clues

Routine Card
Refer to Routine 2 for the Selection Vocabulary procedure. Refer to Routine 3 for the Clues, Problems, and Wonderings procedure.

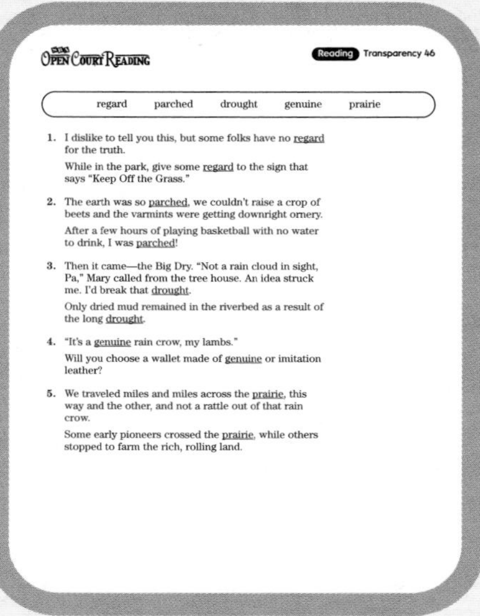

Open Court Reading — Reading Transparency 46

regard parched drought genuine prairie

1. I dislike to tell you this, but some folks have no regard for the truth.
   While in the park, give some regard to the sign that says "Keep Off the Grass."
2. The earth was so parched, we couldn't raise a crop of beets and the varmints were getting downright ornery.
   After a few hours of playing basketball with no water to drink, I was parched!
3. Then it came—the Big Dry. "Not a rain cloud in sight, Pa," Mary called from the tree house. An idea struck me. I'd break that drought.
   Only dried mud remained in the riverbed as a result of the long drought.
4. "It's a genuine rain crow, my lambs."
   Will you choose a wallet made of genuine or imitation leather?
5. We traveled miles and miles across the prairie, this way and the other, and not a rattle out of that rain crow.
   Some early pioneers crossed the prairie, while others stopped to farm the rich, rolling land.

Reading Transparency 46

Differentiating Instruction

English Learner Tip

EXAGGERATION Before reading the selection, tell English Learners that the story is meant to be humorous. Read the first paragraph. Then show students a picture of a mosquito and a woodpecker. Explain the meaning of *exaggeration,* and that the author is using it when he says that the common prairie mosquito is big enough to be mistaken for a woodpecker. Continue through the story explaining as you read. Ask the students to illustrate the part of the story they found to be the funniest.

Routine Card
Refer to Routine 4 for the Reading the Selection procedure.

Students will enjoy using the ***Listening Library Audiocassette/CD*** and listening to the selection they are about to read. Encourage them to listen to the selection during Workshop. Have students discuss with each other and with you their personal listening preferences (for example, nonfiction, poetry, drama, and so on).

Reading Recommendations

Oral Reading

This selection's colorful language and humor make it a good choice for reading aloud. Have students help each other with unfamiliar words and difficult ideas. As students read aloud, have them read expressively, at an appropriate pace, in natural phrases and chunks. Remind students to keep their audience in mind as they read aloud, adjusting volume as necessary and enunciating words clearly. Reading the selection with fluency and accuracy will help students comprehend the text. If students have trouble reading decodable words, have them break the words into sounds or syllables and then blend them together to read the word.

Have students make use of the reading strategies below to help them understand the selection. Have them stop reading periodically or wait until they have completed the selection to discuss the reading strategies. After the students have finished reading the selection, use the "Discussing the Selection" questions on page 505A to see if they understand what they have read.

Using Comprehension Strategies

Comprehension strategy instruction allows students to become aware of how good readers read. Good readers constantly check their understanding as they are reading and ask themselves questions. In addition, skilled readers recognize when they are having problems and stop to use various comprehension strategies to help them make sense of what they are reading.

During the first reading of "McBroom the Rainmaker," model and prompt the use of the following comprehension strategies. Take turns reading the story aloud with the students.

- **Making Connections** deepens students' understanding of what they read by linking it to their own past experiences and previous reading.
- **Predicting** causes readers to analyze information given about story events and characters in the context of how it may logically connect to the story's conclusion.
- **Monitoring and Clarifying** prompts readers to track and immediately clear up unfamiliar words and ideas by using context, word structure, apposition, and outside resources. Stop and check that students understand when something is unclear.
- **Monitoring and Adjusting Reading Speed** prompts readers to assess the difficulty level of a text and adapt their reading pace accordingly.

As students read, they should be using a variety of strategies to help them understand the selection. Encourage students to use the strategies listed on the previous page as the class reads the story aloud. Do this by stopping at the points indicated by the numbers in magenta circles on the reduced student page and using a particular strategy. Students can also stop reading periodically to discuss what they have learned and what problems they may be having.

In Unit 5, students should be assuming more responsibility for the use of comprehension strategies. Continue Teacher Modeling and Prompting as needed. Prompting provides a springboard for students to respond using the strategy mentioned in the prompt. The Student Sample is written in the language that students might use in their actual responses.

The Student Sample may be one of many possible student responses. Accept other responses that are reasonable and appropriate. If student responses indicate that the students do not understand the strategy, be ready to discuss their responses and to provide additional instruction. As students proceed through the lessons, teacher modeling and prompting of strategy use should become less and less necessary as students assume more and more responsibility for using strategies.

Building Comprehension Skills 

Revisiting or rereading a selection allows students to apply skills that give them a more complete understanding of the text. Some follow-up comprehension skills help students organize information. Others lead to deeper understanding—to "reading between the lines," as mature readers do. An extended lesson on comprehension skill Cause and Effect can be found in the Supporting the Reading section on pages 505C–505D. This lesson is intended to give students extra practice with Cause and Effect. However, the Teach portion of the lesson may be used at this time to introduce the comprehension skill to students.

- **Cause and Effect (Review):** Readers identify an event's reasons and results and understand how they are related.

Reading with a Purpose

Have students list aspects of the American West that might have amazed the new settlers in the Response Journal section of their Writer's Notebooks.

Teacher Tip **CAUSE AND EFFECT** Encourage students to use a graphic organizer to keep track of the causes and effects they identify while reading "McBroom the Rainmaker." They might list each cause on the left-hand side of a paper, place an arrow in the center, and list its effect(s) on the right-hand side.

DIFFERENTIATING INSTRUCTION

If...	Then...
Students need extra help with reading "McBroom the Rainmaker"	• Preread the selection during Workshop; use the ***Listening Library*** to give students a good reading model • Use ***English Learner Support Guide,*** pages 452–465 • Use ***Intervention Guide,*** pages 282–283

Research in Action
Metacognition

Helping students become aware of how they comprehend is an important part of comprehension instruction. *Cognition* refers to functions of the mind, such as remembering, focusing attention, and processing information. *Metacognition* refers to our awareness of our cognition—it is thinking about thinking. When it is applied to reading, the term *metacognitive awareness* means that readers are aware of what they do when they read, what to do when they encounter difficulties, and how to select strategies to accomplish their purposes for reading. *(Ann L. Brown)*

COMPREHENSION

Read pages 496–505.

Comprehension Strategies

Read the story aloud, taking turns with the students. Model and prompt the use of strategies for the students.

Student Sample

1 Making Connections *I've read stories like this before. This is a tall tale like the stories about Pecos Bill or Paul Bunyan, that always start out with people saying that they are going to tell you the truth, and then exaggerating until it seems that what they're saying really couldn't happen.*

Teacher Modeling

2 Monitoring and Adjusting Reading Speed *I am seeing some words that I am unaccustomed to, like skeeters. If I slow down a bit, I will be more likely to pick up on the context clues that tell me their meanings.*

Teacher Modeling

3 Making Connections *I know that beets and turnips are the same shape, and that beets are red and turnips are white. The mosquitoes must think that the red in the beets is blood, and they suck it all out of the beets turning them white like turnips.*

Word Knowledge

SCAFFOLDING The skills students are reviewing in Word Knowledge should help them in reading the story. This lesson focuses on the /z/ sound spelled s or z. These words will be found in boxes similar to this one throughout the selection.

/z/ sound spelled:

s **mosquitoes, uses, needle-nosed**

z **zing-zanging**

First Reading Recommendation

ORAL • CHORAL • SILENT

Focus Questions How does McBroom plan to create a rainstorm? Why do you think this type of story was popular with frontier people?

McBroom the Rainmaker

Sid Fleischman

illustrated by Bill Ogden

1 I dislike to tell you this, but some folks have no regard for the truth. A stranger claims he was riding a mule past our wonderful one-acre farm and was attacked by woodpeckers.

2 Well, there's no truth to that. No, indeed! Those weren't woodpeckers. They were common prairie mosquitoes.

Small ones.

Why, skeeters grow so large out here that everybody uses chicken wire for mosquito netting. But I'm not going to say an unkind word about those zing-zanging, hot-tempered, needle-nosed creatures. They rescued our farm from ruin. That was during the Big Drought we had last year.

Dry? Merciful powers! Our young'uns found some tadpoles and had to teach them to swim. It hadn't rained in so long those tadpoles had never seen water.

That's the sworn truth—certain as my name's Josh McBroom. Why, I'd as soon grab a skunk by the tail as tell a falsehood.

Now, I'd best creep up on the Big Drought the way it crept up on us. I remember we did our spring plowing, as usual, and the skeeters hatched out, as usual. The bloodsucking rapscallions could be mighty pesky, but we'd learned to distract them.

"Will*jill*hester*chester*peter*polly*tim*tom*mary*larry*and-little*clarinda!*" I called out. "I hear the whine of gallinippers. We'd better put in a patch of beets."

496

Informal Assessment

Observe individual students as they read and use the Teacher Observation Log found in the ***Program Assessment Teacher's Edition*** to record anecdotal information about each student's strengths and weaknesses.

Differentiating Instruction

If...	Then...
English Learners need extra support with reading "McBroom the Rainmaker" and using the skill Cause and Effect	Preteach ***Student Anthology*** pages 496–498 using Day 1 of the "McBroom the Rainmaker" lesson, found on ***English Learner Support Guide,*** pages 454–457

Once the beets were up, the thirsty skeeters stuck in their long beaks like straws. Didn't they feast though!
3 They drained out the red juice, the beets turned white, and we harvested them as turnips.

The first sign of a dry spell was when our clocks began running slow. I don't mean the store-bought kind—no one can predict the weather with a tin timepiece. We grew our own clocks on the farm.

Vegetable clocks.

Now, I'll admit that may be hard to believe, but not if you understand the remarkable nature of our topsoil. Rich? Glory be! Anything would grow in it—lickety-bang. Three or four crops a day until the confounded Big Dry came along.

Of course, we didn't grow clocks with gears and springs and a name on the dial. Came close once, though. I dropped my dollar pocket watch one day, and before I could find it, the thing had put down roots and grown into a three-dollar alarm clock. But it never kept accurate time after that.

It was our young'uns who discovered they could tell time by vegetable. They planted a cucumber seed, and once the vine leaped out of the ground, it traveled along steady as a clock.

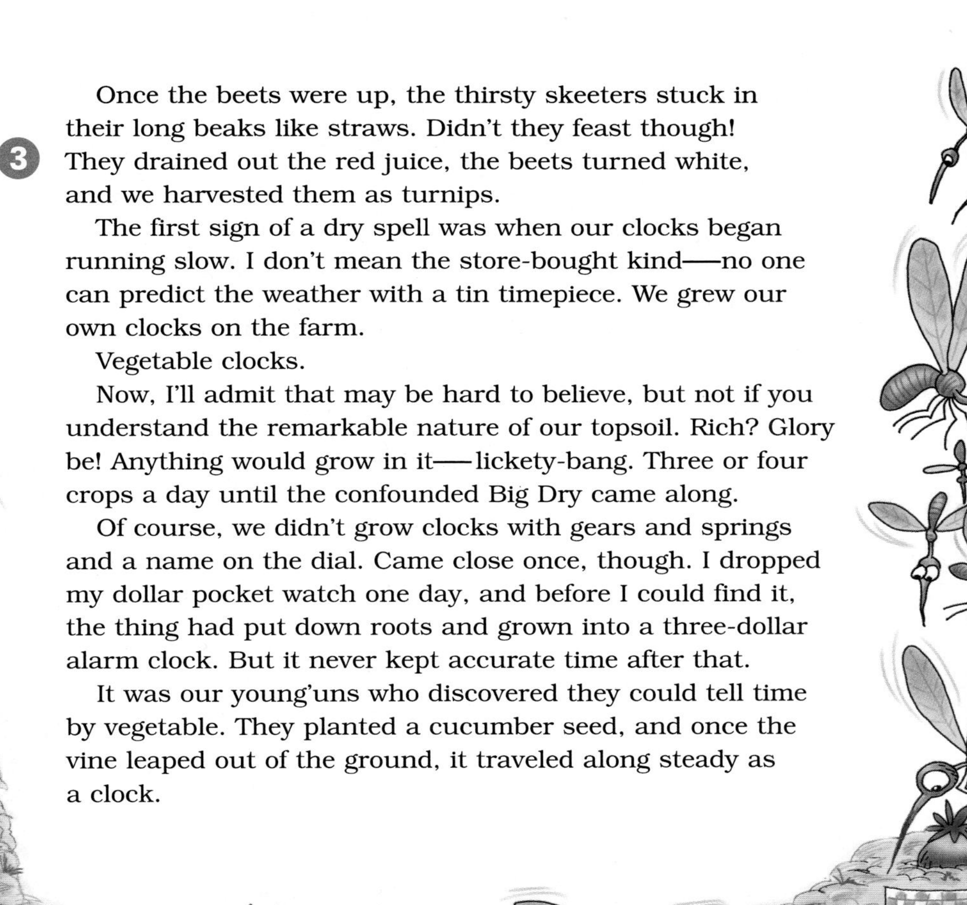

Teacher Tip **COLORFUL LANGUAGE** Remind students that authors often use colorful language to reflect a specific region or culture. Have students identify examples of colorful sayings in "McBroom the Rainmaker." Students can derive the meanings of these terms by using context clues and the glossary. (Possible answers include: skeeters, rapscallions, gallinippers, and young'uns.)

COMPREHENSION

Comprehension Skills

Cause and Effect

Remind students of the concept of *cause and effect.* A cause is *why* something happens. The effect is *what* happens. For example, if a person plants a seedling (cause), a tree will grow (effect). Tell students that a good way to identify cause and effect is to ask questions about events. For example, *Why did a tree grow here? Because someone planted a seedling.* You might also explain that the word *because* often signals a cause-and-effect relationship. Work with students to recognize and understand cause-and-effect relationships in the selection. You might ask them the following questions:

- Effect: Why did the beets turn white and become turnips? *(Cause: Because the mosquitoes drained all the red juice out of them.)*
- Cause: What happened to the homegrown clocks because of the dry spell? *(Effect: The clocks began to run slow.)*

Cause and Effect

Introduced in Grade 2.

Scaffolded throughout Grades 3–4.

REINTRODUCED: Unit 4, Lesson 1

REINFORCED: Unit 5, Lesson 7

Unit 6, Lesson 2

TESTED: Unit 5 Assessment

Second Reading Recommendation

ORAL • **SILENT**

COMPREHENSION

Comprehension Strategies

Prompting

4 Monitoring and Clarifying *In the text it says that chickens were laying fried eggs. To clarify what the author is saying, we can connect it with the way fried eggs are really made, which is on a hot stove. It must be really hot out if the eggs are already fried when the chickens lay them.*

What other ideas can you clarify by making connections?

Student Sample

Monitoring and Clarifying *Prunes are dried plums. It must really be dry for prunes to grow instead of plums.*

Word Knowledge

/z/ sound spelled: s

losing raise rising skies

Teacher Tip SELF-EVALUATING COMPREHENSION Good readers constantly evaluate their understanding of what they read. Stop often to make sure students are doing this.

"An inch a second," Will said. "Kind of like a second hand."

"Blossoms come out on the minute," Jill said. "Kind of like a minute hand."

They tried other vegetable timepieces, but pole beans had a way of running a mite fast and squash a mite slow.

As I say, those homegrown clocks began running down. I remember my dear wife, Melissa, was boiling three-and-a-half-minute eggs for breakfast. Little Clarinda planted a cucumber seed, and before it grew three blossoms and thirty inches, those eggs were hard-boiled.

"Mercy!" I declared. "Topsoil must be drying out."

Well, the days turned drier and drier. No doubt about it—our wonderful topsoil was losing some of its get-up-and-go. Why, it took almost a whole day to raise a crop of corn. The young'uns had planted a plum tree, but all it would grow was prunes. Dogs would fight over a dry bone—for the moisture in it.

"Will*jill*hester*chester*peter*polly*tim*tom*mary*larry*and-little*clarinda!*" I called. "Keep your eyes peeled for rain."

They took turns in the tree house scanning the skies, and one night Chester said, "Pa, what if it doesn't rain by Fourth of July? How'll we shoot off firecrackers?"

Informal Assessment

Use the Informal Comprehension Strategies Rubrics on page 496J to determine whether a student is using the strategies being taught.

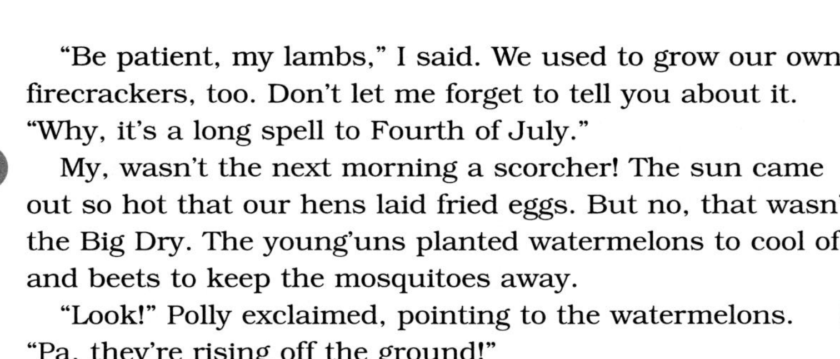

"Be patient, my lambs," I said. We used to grow our own firecrackers, too. Don't let me forget to tell you about it. "Why, it's a long spell to Fourth of July."

4 My, wasn't the next morning a scorcher! The sun came out so hot that our hens laid fried eggs. But no, that wasn't the Big Dry. The young'uns planted watermelons to cool off and beets to keep the mosquitoes away.

"Look!" Polly exclaimed, pointing to the watermelons. "Pa, they're rising off the ground!"

Rising? They began to float in the air like balloons! We could hardly believe our eyes. And gracious me! When we cut those melons open, it turned out they were full of hot air.

Well, I was getting a mite worried myself. Our beets were growing smaller and smaller, and the skeeters were growing larger and larger. Many a time, before dawn, a rapping at the windows would wake us out of a sound sleep. It was those confounded, needle-nosed gallinippers pecking away, demanding breakfast.

Then it came—the Big Dry.

Mercy! Our cow began giving powdered milk. We pumped away on our water pump, but all it brought up was dry steam. The oldest boys went fishing and caught six dried catfish.

"Not a rain cloud in sight, Pa," Mary called from the tree house.

"Watch out for gallinippers!" Larry shouted, as a mosquito made a dive at him. The earth was so parched, we couldn't raise a crop of beets and the varmints were getting downright ornery. Then, as I stood there, I felt my shoes getting tighter and tighter.

499

Differentiating Instruction

If...	Then...
English Learners need extra support with reading "McBroom the Rainmaker" and using the skill Cause and Effect	Preteach ***Student Anthology*** pages 499–501 using Day 2 of the "McBroom the Rainmaker" lesson, found on ***English Learner Support Guide,*** pages 457–459

Comprehension Skills

Cause and Effect

Point out to students that much of this tall tale is built around causes and effects. Explain that pages 498 and 499 describe many of the effects caused by the drought. Have students identify several effects mentioned here and discuss them aloud as a class.

Help students recognize other cause-and-effect relationships on these pages by asking them the following question:

- Why did McBroom's shoes get smaller as he stood on the topsoil? *(Because the topsoil was so dry that it was shrinking things.)*

Word Knowledge

SCAFFOLDING The skills students are reviewing in Word Knowledge should help them in reading the story. This lesson focuses on the /k/ sound spelled *k, c,* or *ck.* These words will be found in boxes similar to this one throughout the selection.

/k/ sound spelled:

k	**look, like**
c	**cool, confounded**
ck	**firecrackers, pecking**

COMPREHENSION

COMPREHENSION

Comprehension Strategies

Prompting

5 Predicting *What do you predict McBroom will do to make it start raining?*

Student Sample

Predicting *I predict it will have something to do with the yellow-billed cuckoo. I predict the cuckoo brings the rain.*

Prompting

6 Predicting *I think we're right so far about the yellow-billed cuckoo being involved. They are using it to look for a raincloud. But I don't know why they are going to wet down the topsoil. What do you predict they'll do with the topsoil once it's wet?*

Student Sample

7 Predicting *I predict they'll bring the soil back to the farm when it's wet, and then try to grow something.*

Word Knowledge

/k/ sound spelled:

k	**awake, took**
c	**cuckoo, birdcage**
ck	**struck, track**

Teacher Tip CONNECT TO UNIT THEME As a class, discuss the challenges the McBrooms and other frontier families faced, and how they dealt with these difficulties. Then have students update the Concept/Question Board.

Teacher Tip VISUALIZING Encourage students to try to visualize the yellow-billed cuckoo, or "rain crow." Students may want to draw pictures of what they think this bird looks like.

"Thunderation!" I exclaimed. "Our topsoil's so dry it's gone in reverse. It's *shrinking* things."

Didn't I lay awake most of the night! Our wonderful one-acre farm might shrink to a square foot. And all night long the skeeters rattled the windows and hammered at the door. Big? The *smallest* ones must have weighed three pounds. In the moonlight I saw them chase a yellow-billed cuckoo.

5 Didn't that make me sit up in a hurry! An idea struck me. Glory be! I'd break that drought.

First thing in the morning I took Will and Chester to town with me and rented three wagons and a birdcage. We drove straight home, and I called everyone together.

"Shovels, my lambs! Heap these wagons full of topsoil!"

But Larry and little Clarinda were still worried about Fourth of July. "We won't be able to grow fireworks, Pa!"

"You have my word," I declared firmly.

Before long, we were on our way. I drove the first wagon, with the young'uns following along behind in the other two. It might be a longish trip, and we had loaded up with picnic hampers of food. We also brought along rolls of chicken wire and our raincoats.

"Where are we going, Pa?" Jill called from the wagon behind.

"Hunting."

"Hunting?" Tom said.

"Exactly, my lambs. We're going to track down a rain cloud and wet down this topsoil."

"But how, Pa?" asked Tim.

500

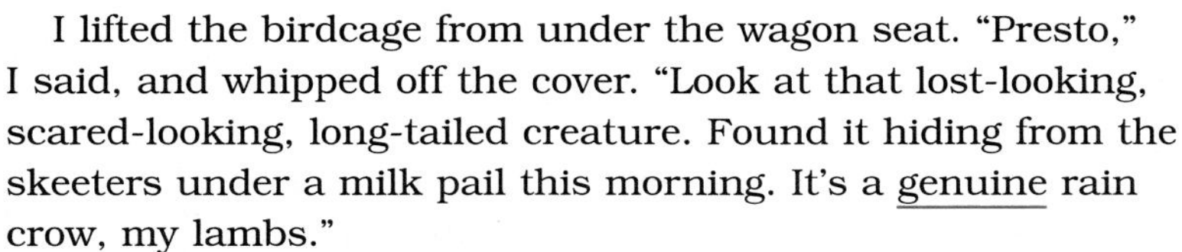

I lifted the birdcage from under the wagon seat. "Presto," I said, and whipped off the cover. "Look at that lost-looking,
6 scared-looking, long-tailed creature. Found it hiding from the skeeters under a milk pail this morning. It's a genuine rain crow, my lambs."

"A rain crow?" Mary said. "It doesn't look like a crow at all."

"Correct and exactly," I said, smiling. "It looks like a yellow-billed cuckoo, and that's what it is. But don't folks call 'em rain crows? Why, that bird can smell a downpour coming sixty miles away. Rattles its throat and begins to squawk. All we got to do is follow that squawk."

But you never heard such a quiet bird! We traveled miles and miles across the prairie, this way and the other, and not a rattle out of that rain crow.

The Big Dry had done its mischief everywhere. We didn't see a dog without his tongue dragging, and it took two of them to bark at us once. A farmer told us he hadn't been able to grow anything all year but baked potatoes!

Of course, we slept under chicken wire—covered the horses, too. My, what a racket the gallinippers made!

7 Day after day we hauled our three loads of topsoil across the prairie, but that rain crow didn't so much as clear its throat.

The young'uns were getting impatient. "Speak up, rain crow," Chester muttered desperately.

"Rattle," Hester pleaded.

"Squawk," said Peter.

"Please," said Mary. "Just a little peep would help."

501

Comprehension Skills

Cause and Effect

Point out to students that a series of causes and effects lead Pa to pursue an idea for ending the drought. Ask students the following questions.

- What *caused* McBroom to get the idea for ending the drought? *(He watched the mosquitoes chase a yellow-billed cuckoo in the moonlight.)*
- What effect did this sudden idea have on Pa? *(He was so struck by it that he acted on it first thing the next day.)*

Word Knowledge

/z/ sound spelled: s

doesn't skeeters miles

COMPREHENSION

COMPREHENSION

Comprehension Strategies

Prompting

Confirming Predictions *How are you doing on your predictions? Are there any that have come true or that need to be revised based on new information?*

Student Sample

8 Confirming Predictions *I see that the prediction that the family would get the topsoil wet and then try to grow something came true. Pa planted onions in the soil—why onions? I know that the smell of onions can make people cry. Maybe that's how Pa will water the rest of the dry soil.*

Word Knowledge

/k/ sound spelled:

k	**weeks, beak**
c	**confess, cage**
ck	**chicken**

Teacher Tip MAKING CONNECTIONS Have students ask themselves, "Does this make sense?" throughout the selection to help locate places where making connections might be helpful.

Not a cloud appeared in the sky. I'll confess I was getting a mite discouraged. And the Fourth of July not another two weeks off!

We curled up under chicken wire that night, as usual, and the big skeeters kept banging into it, so you could hardly sleep. Rattled like a hailstorm. And suddenly, at daybreak, I rose up laughing.

"Hear that?"

The young'uns crowded around the rain crow. We hadn't been able to hear its voice rattle for the mosquitoes. Now it turned in its cage, gazed off to the northwest, opened its yellow beak, and let out a real, ear-busting rain cry.

"K-*kawk*! K-*kawk*! K-*kawk*!"

"Put on your raincoats, my lambs!" I said, and we rushed to the wagons.

"K-*kawk*! K-*kawk*! K-*kawk*!"

Didn't we raise dust! That bird faced northwest like a dog on point. There was a rain cloud out there and before long Jill gave a shout.

"I see it!"

And the others chimed in one after the other. "Me, too!"

"K-*kawk*! K-*kawk*! K-*kawk*!"

We headed directly for that lone cloud, the young'uns yelling, the horses snorting, and the bird squawking.

Glory be! The first raindrops spattered as large as quarters. And my, didn't the young'uns frolic in that cloudburst! They lifted their faces and opened their mouths and drank right out of the sky. They splashed about and felt mud between their toes for the first time in ages. We all forgot to put on our raincoats and got wet as fish.

502

Differentiating Instruction

If...	Then...
English Learners need extra linguistic support with reading "McBroom the Rainmaker" and using the skill Cause and Effect	Preteach ***Student Anthology*** pages 502–503 using Day 3 of the "McBroom the Rainmaker" lesson, found on ***English Learner Support Guide,*** pages 459–461

Our dried-up topsoil soaked up raindrops like a sponge. It was a joy to behold! But if we stayed longer, we'd get stuck in the mud.

"Back in the wagons!" I shouted. "Home, my lambs, and not a moment to lose."

Well, home was right where we left it.

I got a pinch of onion seeds and went from wagon to wagon, sowing a few seeds in each load of moist earth.
8 I didn't want to crowd those onions.

Now, that rich topsoil of ours had been idle a long time—it was rarin' to go. Before I could run back to the house, the greens were up. By the time I could get down my shotgun, the tops had grown four or five feet tall—onions are terrible slow growers. Before I could load my shotgun, the bulbs were finally bursting up through the soil.

We stood at the windows watching. Those onion roots were having a great feast. The wagons heaved and creaked as the onions swelled and lifted themselves—they were already the size of pumpkins. But that wasn't near big enough. Soon they were larger'n washtubs and began to shoulder the smaller ones off the wagons.

503

Comprehension Skills

COMPREHENSION

Cause and Effect

Continue to work with students to help them recognize and understand the cause-and-effect relationships in the selection. Ask students these questions:

- According to McBroom, what caused the chicken wire to rattle like a hail storm? *(The mosquitoes were banging into it.)*
- Why did the McBroom family get "wet as fish"? *(Because they played in the rain without their raincoats on.)*

Encourage students to identify which is the cause and which is the effect in these relationships. *(Mosquitoes cause the chicken wire to rattle. Playing in the rain without their raincoats caused the family to get wet.)*

Word Knowledge

/z/ sound spelled:

s	**lose, onions**
z	**size**

Teacher Tip FLUENCY By this time in grade 5 good readers should be reading approximately 151 words per minute with fluency and expression. The only way to gain this fluency is through practice. Have students reread the selection to you and to one another during Workshop to help build fluency.

COMPREHENSION

Comprehension Strategies

Teacher Modeling

9 Confirming Predictions *We predicted that the onions would make people cry, but the mosquitoes were the ones Pa wanted to make cry!*

Discussing Strategy Use

While they are reading the selection, have students share any problems they encountered and tell what strategies they used.

- How did they make, confirm, and revise predictions as they read?
- How did they clarify confusing passages?
- What connections did they make between the reading and what they already know?

Remind students that good readers use all of the strategies listed above and that they should be using them whenever they read. Make sure that students explain how using the strategies helped them better understand the selection. For example, "Stopping to clarify the strange words and phrases in the story helped me understand them better and see the humor in them."

Word Knowledge

/z/ sound spelled:
- ***s*** **dispositions**
- ***z*** **zing-zanging**

Teacher Tip EXTRA HELP Reread the selection with students who had difficulty understanding it. Continue modeling and prompting the use of strategies and skills as you reread.

Suddenly we heard a distant roaring in the air. Those zing-zanging, hot-tempered, blood-sucking prairie mosquitoes were returning from town with their stingers freshly sharpened. The Big Dry hadn't done their dispositions any good—their tempers were at a boil.

"You going to shoot them down, Pa?" Will asked.

"Too many for that," I answered.

"How big do those onions have to grow?" Chester asked. "How big are they now?"

"A little smaller'n a cow shed."

"That's big enough," I nodded, lifting the window just enough to poke the shotgun through.

Well, the gallinippers spied the onions—I had planted red onions, you know—and came swarming over our farm. I let go at the bulbs with a double charge of buckshot and slammed the window.

504

Differentiating Instruction

If...	Then...
English Learners need extra linguistic support with reading "McBroom the Rainmaker" and using the skill Cause and Effect	Preteach ***Student Anthology*** pages 504–505 using Day 4 of the "McBroom the Rainmaker" lesson, found on ***English Learner Support Guide,*** pages 462–464

Teacher Tip BUILDING FLUENCY As students read, you may notice that some need work in building fluency. During Workshop, have these students choose a section of text (a minimum of 160 words) to read several times in order to build fluency.

"Handkerchiefs, everyone!" I called out. The odor of fresh-cut onion shot through the air, under the door, and through the cracks. Cry? In no time our handkerchiefs were wet as dishrags.

9 "Well! You never saw such surprised gallinippers. They zing-zanged every which way, most of them backwards. And weep? Their eyes began to flow like sprinkling cans. Onion tears! The roof began to leak. Mud puddles formed everywhere. Before long, the downpour was equal to any cloudburst I ever saw. Near flooded our farm!

The skeeters kept their distance after that. But they'd been mighty helpful.

With our farm freshly watered we grew tons of great onions—three or four crops a day. Gave them away to farmers all over the country.

The newspaper ran a picture of the whole family—the rain crow, too.

The young'uns had a splendid Fourth of July. Grew all the fireworks they wanted. They'd dash about with bean shooters—shooting radish seeds. You know how fast radishes come up. In our rich topsoil they grew quicker'n the eye. The seeds hardly touched the ground before they took root and swelled up and exploded. They'd go off like strings of firecrackers.

And, mercy, what a racket! Didn't I say I'd rather catch a skunk by the tail than tell a fib? Well, at nightfall a scared cat ran up a tree, and I went up a ladder to get it down. Reached in the branches and caught it by the tail.

I'd be lying if I didn't admit the truth. It was a skunk.

505

Comprehension Skills

COMPREHENSION

Cause and Effect

Ask students to review what they know about *cause and effect.* Remind them that a cause is why something happened; an effect is what happened.

Work with students to ensure that they recognize and understand some of the main causes and effects in this story. You might discuss the effects of the drought, the effects of McBroom's plan to end the drought, and the effects of the drought ending. During your discussion, have students skim the text and point out these effects. Have students quote lines directly from the text to capture the humor in the effects.

Checking Comprehension

Ask students the following questions to check their comprehension of the story.

- What was Pa's plan to end the Big Drought? *(to get all the mosquitoes to cry by shooting at the onions)*
- What was the funniest part of the story? *(Answers may vary. Some students might mention the big mosquitoes, or the vegetable clocks.)*
- What was believable in this story ? *(Answers may vary. Some students might decide that a drought might have actually happened.)*
- How has this selection connected with your knowledge of the unit theme? *(Answers will vary—students should compare/contrast examples of life in the American West from this selection with their own experiences or past reading and use these connections to make a general statement about the unit theme.)*

Differentiating Instruction

If...	Then...
English Learners have been participating in the "McBroom the Rainmaker" ***English Learner Support Guide*** activities	Review the selection and the skill Cause and Effect using Day 5 of the "McBroom the Rainmaker" lesson, found on ***English Learner Support Guide,*** pages 464–465

Formal Assessment

See pages 26–29 in ***Unit 5 Assessment*** to test students' comprehension of "McBroom the Rainmaker."

Teacher Tip CONNECTING IDEAS Encourage students to tell about anything that they learned from their research that connects to this selection. You might also have them compare and contrast the descriptions of the American West in the unit selections they have read so far.

Routine Card
Refer to Routine 5 for the *handing-off process.*

Differentiating Instruction

English Learner Tip

REVIEWING THE PLOT After English Learners have read and reread the story, ask them to tell you which exaggerations they thought were the most outlandish: the vegetable clocks, the one-acre farm shrinking to a foot, the weeping mosquitoes, and so on. Tell them to illustrate the exaggeration they liked the best.

Clues	Problems	Wonderings
Farm Rain Tall tale	Falsehood Big Dry	What do mosquitoes have to do with a drought? How do people "grow" fireworks?

Reading Transparency 54

Discussing the Selection

After the first read, the whole group discusses the selection and any personal thoughts, reactions, problems, or questions that it raises. To stimulate discussion, students can ask one another the kinds of questions that good readers ask themselves about a text: *How does it connect to going west? What have I learned that is new? What did I find interesting? What is important here? What was difficult to understand? Why would someone want to read this?* It is important for students to see you as a contributing member of the group.

Routine 5 To emphasize that you are part of the group, actively participate in the *handing-off process:* Raise your hand to be called on by the last speaker when you have a contribution to make. Point out unusual and interesting insights verbalized by students so that these insights are recognized and discussed. As the year progresses, students will take more and more responsibility for the discussion of selections.

Engage students in a discussion to determine whether they have grasped the following ideas.

- Early settlers, like McBroom and his family, faced challenges in the American West.
- Some early settlers told about their difficulties in humorous stories called tall tales.

During this time, have students return to the clues, problems, and wonderings that they noted during browsing to determine whether the clues were borne out by the selection, whether and how their problems were solved, and whether their wonderings were answered or deserve further discussion and exploration. Let the students decide which items deserve further discussion. Also have students return to the Focus Questions on the first page of the selection. Select a student to read the questions aloud, and have volunteers answer the questions. If students do not know the answers to the questions, have them return to the text to find the answers.

You may also want to review the elements of tall tales with students. Discuss with them how they can tell that "McBroom the Rainmaker" is a tall tale.

Have students break into small groups to discuss how the story reflects the theme. Groups can then share their ideas with the rest of the class.

Students may wish to record their personal responses to the selection. If they have learned something new about the American West, early settlers, or tall tales, encourage them to record this information.

Review Selection Vocabulary

Have students review the definitions of the selection vocabulary words that they wrote in the vocabulary section of their Writer's Notebooks. Remind them that they discussed the meanings of these words before reading the selection. Students can use these definitions to study for the vocabulary portion of their Lesson Assessment. Have them add to the personal dictionary section of their Writer's Notebook any other interesting words that they clarified while reading. Encourage students to refer to the selection vocabulary words throughout the unit. The words from the selection are:

drought **genuine** **parched** **prairie** **regard**

Have students place the words under the appropriate endings in the Word Bank. Encourage the students to find other words related to the unit theme and add them to the Word Bank.

Home Connection

Distribute ***Home Connection,*** page 75. Encourage students to discuss "McBroom the Rainmaker" with their families. Students can work with their families to write original tall tales that include a lot of exaggeration. ***Home Connection*** is also available in Spanish, page 76.

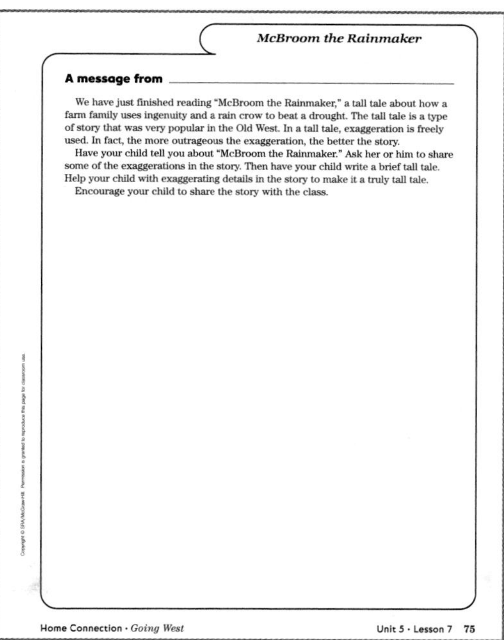
McBroom the Rainmaker

A message from ______

We have just finished reading "McBroom the Rainmaker," a tall tale about how a farm family uses ingenuity and a rain crow to beat a drought. The tall tale is a type of story that was very popular in the Old West. In a tall tale, exaggeration is freely used. In fact, the more outrageous the exaggeration, the better the story.

Have your child tell you about "McBroom the Rainmaker." Ask her or him to share some of the exaggerations in the story. Then have your child write a brief tall tale. Help your child with exaggerating details in the story to make it a truly tall tale.

Encourage your child to share the story with the class.

Home Connection • *Going West* Unit 5 • Lesson 7 75

Home Connection p. 75

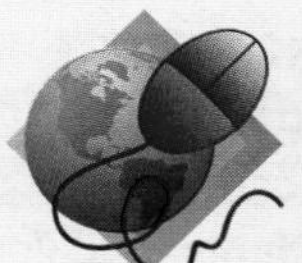

www.sra4kids.com
Web Connection
Some students may choose to conduct a computer search for additional books or information about the American West. Invite them to make a list of these books and sources of information to share with classmates and the school librarian. Check the Reading link of the SRA Web page for additional links to theme-related Web sites.

Differentiating Instruction

If...	Then...
Students would benefit from repeated readings of "McBroom the Rainmaker" or the Intervention Selections	Use ***Intervention Guide,*** page 285

Teacher Tip CAUSE AND EFFECT Point out to students that most stories revolve around causes and effects. Encourage students to look for causes and effects in other stories they read. Explain that they will get the most out of their reading if they combine all of their comprehension skills when they read.

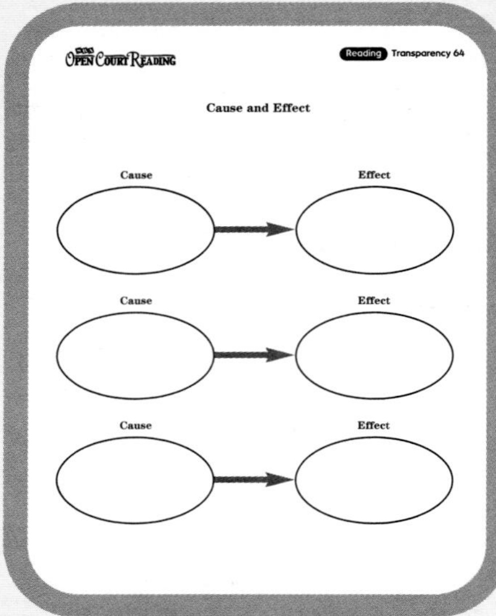

Reading Transparency 64

Supporting the Reading

Comprehension Skill: Cause and Effect

Teach Ask students to explain what they know about cause-and-effect relationships. If necessary, remind them that a cause is *why* something happens, while an effect is *what* happens. Point out that the word *because* often signals a cause-and-effect relationship.

Point out to students that, sometimes, authors might show the effects of something, but leave the reader to figure out the cause. Other times, authors might show a cause, and readers have to use their imaginations to figure out the effects.

Guided Practice Use the graphic organizer on ***Reading Transparency 64*** to help students recognize and understand the causes and effects they find in "McBroom the Rainmaker." For example, under "Cause" you might note that the weather is very hot and dry, and under "Effect" you might note that the cow began to give dried milk. You might start by listing causes on the transparency and having students suggest their effects, then listing effects that have not yet been mentioned and having students name their causes. For causes that have multiple effects, you might connect the boxes to the cause or rewrite the cause next to each effect.

Independent Practice Read through the **Focus** and **Identify** sections of the ***Comprehension and Language Arts Skills,*** page 170 with students. Guide students through the **Identify** portion, and help them come up with examples found in the selection. Then have students complete the **Practice** and **Apply** portions of the ***Comprehension and Language Arts Skills,*** page 171 as homework.

Link to Writing Point out to students that it is a good idea for writers to show causes and effects in their writing. Have students review previous writing assignments. Ask them to choose several writing pieces and identify the causes and effects they contained. They might also like to revise certain pieces to make the causes and effects more apparent to the reader.

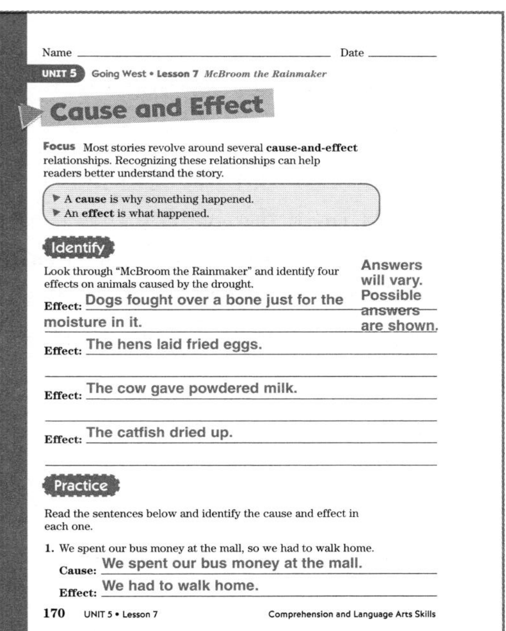

Name ______ Date ______

UNIT 5 Going West • Lesson 7 *McBroom the Rainmaker*

Cause and Effect

Focus Most stories revolve around several **cause-and-effect** relationships. Recognizing these relationships can help readers better understand the story.

- A **cause** is why something happened.
- An **effect** is what happened.

Identify

Look through "McBroom the Rainmaker" and identify four effects on animals caused by the drought. Answers will vary. Possible answers are shown.

Effect: Dogs fought over a bone just for the moisture in it.

Effect: The hens laid fried eggs.

Effect: The cow gave powdered milk.

Effect: The catfish dried up.

Practice

Read the sentences below and identify the cause and effect in each one.

1. We spent our bus money at the mall, so we had to walk home.
   Cause: We spent our bus money at the mall.
   Effect: We had to walk home.

170 UNIT 5 • Lesson 7 Comprehension and Language Arts Skills

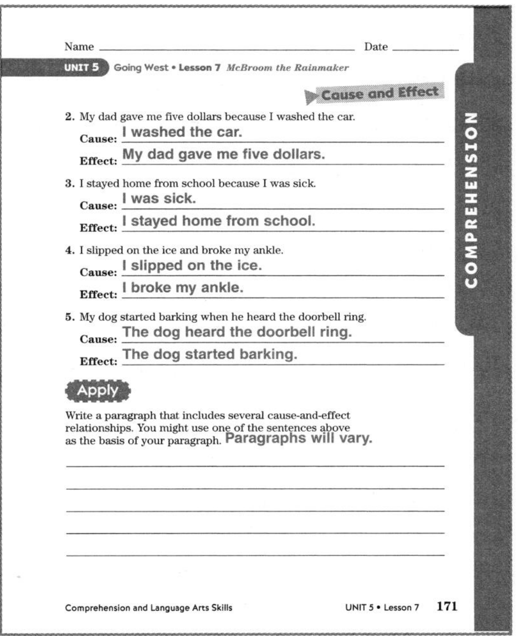

Name ______ Date ______

UNIT 5 Going West • Lesson 7 *McBroom the Rainmaker*

Cause and Effect

COMPREHENSION

2. My dad gave me five dollars because I washed the car.
   Cause: I washed the car.
   Effect: My dad gave me five dollars.
3. I stayed home from school because I was sick.
   Cause: I was sick.
   Effect: I stayed home from school.
4. I slipped on the ice and broke my ankle.
   Cause: I slipped on the ice.
   Effect: I broke my ankle.
5. My dog started barking when he heard the doorbell ring.
   Cause: The dog heard the doorbell ring.
   Effect: The dog started barking.

Apply

Write a paragraph that includes several cause-and-effect relationships. You might use one of the sentences above as the basis of your paragraph. Paragraphs will vary.

Comprehension and Language Arts Skills UNIT 5 • Lesson 7 171

Comprehension and Language Arts Skills pp. 170–171

Differentiating Instruction

If...	Then...
Students need extra help with Cause and Effect	• Use ***Reteach,*** pages 171–172 • Use ***English Learner Support Guide,*** pages 452–465
Students would enjoy a challenge with Cause and Effect	Use ***Challenge,*** page 150

Cause and Effect

Introduced in Grade 1.
Scaffolded throughout Grades 2–5.

REINTRODUCED: Unit 4, Lesson 1
REINFORCED: Unit 5, Lesson 7
Unit 6, Lesson 2
TESTED: Unit 5 Assessment

Professional Development

Teacher Resource Library CD-ROMs or ***Online Professional Development*** provides courses that help you better understand the Comprehension/Knowledge Building instruction in ***Open Court Reading.*** For more information about this program, visit SRAonline.com.

Teacher Tip **TALL TALES** Have students do a library search of other tall tales from or about the American West. Have them create book reports on the tales they read that include a summary of the story and their opinions about it. As part of their response to the tale have students analyze them for information that is based on true events.

Literary Elements

Genre: Tall Tale

Teach Have students tell you what they know about tall tales. If necessary, tell them that a tall tale, using humorous exaggeration, tells the adventures of a fictional character such as Paul Bunyan. Such stories relate a series of extraordinary events and challenges that are solved in inventive ways. List and review some of these other characteristics of tall tales.

- an ordinary setting
- a grain of truth
- improbable incidents
- unpredictable or surprise endings
- frequent pleas by narrator asking the reader to believe what is being told
- competition against nature or humankind

Guided Practice Have students work in small groups to identify and list examples of the tall tale elements in the selection "McBroom the Rainmaker." For example, this story has an ordinary setting of a farm in rural America, and McBroom is a humorous character, as expressed in how he calls his eleven children. Have students identify the characteristics of fiction stories, and describe how tall tales are similar or differ from realistic or historical fiction stories they have read.

Independent Practice Have students write tall tales of their own in their Writer's Notebooks. Encourage students to use the list on the board, as well as "McBroom the Rainmaker" as guides. Tell them that their tall tales can be as short as a few paragraphs or as long as a few pages. Have students analyze classmates' stories, identifying characteristics of tall tales.

Science Connection: Water Conservation

Have students recall McBroom's experiences with the Big Dry in "McBroom the Rainmaker." Tell students that, though McBroom's story is humorous, the depletion of fresh-water supplies can be a real concern during times of drought. Divide the students into groups. Have each group brainstorm a list of places fresh water can be found. Have the groups share their lists with the whole class. Prompt students to tell you why the amount of water in each source is limited, rather than inexhaustible.

Have the groups conduct library or Internet research to discover how the availability of water can be extended (for example, through recycling and conservation).

Have the groups conduct personal interviews with a representative of their local water utility to discover the source of their water, what happens to used water, and what steps their local utility takes to extend water's utility.

Have each group compile their information into a persuasive letter to city council. Their letters should state a clear position in favor of measures to increase water availability, include relevant evidence supporting their position, and follow a formal organizational pattern. Letters should address the concerns of the audience by telling quantity of water available and suggesting ways to extend water availability, such as by finding new sources of water and new ways to recycle and reduce consumption.

Teacher Tip Maps, atlases, and other resources for geographic and climatic conditions are available from the school or public library. Encourage students to visit their local library for other resources for their investigations.

Concept Connections

Linking the Selection

- Plagues of insects and drought were real concerns to the settlers.
- Having a large family meant there were more people to help work the land and run the farm.

Exploring Concept Vocabulary

The concept word for this lesson is ***vast.*** Write the word on the board. Work with the students to develop a definition that clearly links to the unit theme. Have students copy the word and definition into the Vocabulary section of their Writer's Notebooks.

Vast: very great in size or amount. For example, the McBrooms traveled many miles across the vast prairie searching for a rain cloud.

- The exaggerations of a tall tale are a good match for the West's "bigness."
- McBroom's descriptions of plowing the land and of growing a variety of crops make the farm seem larger.

The students' sentences should show an understanding of both vocabulary words.

Expanding the Concept

Have students carry on dialogues in small groups. After the small-group discussions, bring students together to share their ideas with the whole class.

As students complete their discussion, have them record their ideas about the selection on page 115 of their ***Inquiry Journal.***

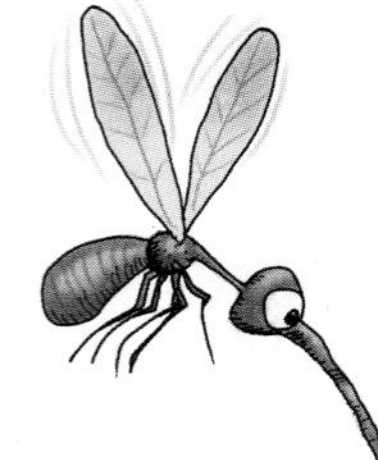

McBroom the Rainmaker

Concept Connections

Linking the Selection

Think about the following questions, and then record your responses in the Response Journal section of your Writer's Notebook.

- What things in this story were actual challenges to settlers?
- Why did farmers who settled the West have large families, as the McBrooms did?

Exploring Concept Vocabulary

The concept word for this lesson is ***vast.*** If you do not know what this word means, look it up in a dictionary. Answer these questions.

- Why are many tall tales set in the ***vast*** landscape of the West?
- How does McBroom's tale make his small, one-acre farm seem ***vast?***

Make up an oral sentence that includes both the word ***vast*** and a word from the selection vocabulary.

Expanding the Concept

This unit included many stories of hardship set in the American West. What conclusions can you draw about the consequences and rewards of America's westward expansion? Try to use the word ***vast*** in your discussion of the unit selections. Add new ideas about the American West to the Concept/Question Board.

506

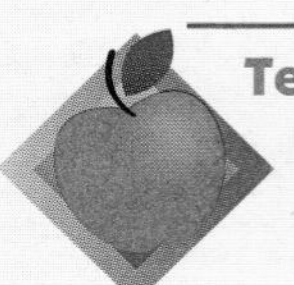

Teacher Tip INQUIRY AND INVESTIGATION Have groups report and discuss their ideas with the class. As these ideas are stated, have students add them to the Concept/Question Board. As students complete their discussions, have them sum up what they have learned and tell how they might use this information in further investigations.

Informal Assessment

This may be a good time to observe students working in small groups and to mark your observations in the Teacher Observation Log found in the ***Program Assessment Teacher's Edition.***

Meet the Author

Sid Fleischman was fascinated with sleight of hand performers during his school years. After graduating at the age of seventeen, he had a traveling act of his own, performing tricks countrywide. He later went to college, after which he became a reporter and writer for the San Diego paper. He started writing for young readers by making up stories for his own children. He writes at a huge table stacked with story ideas, library books, research, letters, notes, pens, pencils, and a typewriter. His cat, Nora, sits close by to help him when he needs it. One of his most popular book characters is McBroom, who is the star of several tall tales.

Meet the Illustrator

Bill Ogden lives on five acres of land in New Hampshire, with his wife and his son. He is a true nature lover, who shares his land with a wide variety of animals, such as deer, foxes, beavers, coyotes, hawks, mice, ducks, geese, raccoons, otters, owls, giant blue herons, crows, and *"extremely large tomato horn worms."* When he's not drawing, he says he can be found in the great outdoors, *"stalking the wild mushroom, catching the wily bass, and chasing the dreaded, garden-eating woodchuck."*

507

Meet the Author

After the students read the information about Sid Fleischman, discuss the following question with them.

- When he writes, Sid Fleischman sits at a huge table surrounded by ideas, books, research, letters, notes, pens, pencils, and his typewriter. Why might it be a good idea for him to have all of these things at hand while he is writing? *(Possible answer: If he keeps all of these things with him, he doesn't risk being distracted from his writing by having to go in search of a pencil or information he needs for his story.)*

Meet the Illustrator

After the students read the information about Bill Ogden, discuss the following question with them.

- Bill Ogden lives on a land surrounded by various types of wildlife. How do you think this has influenced his illustrations? *(Possible answer: He probably enjoys incorporating the nature around him into his illustrations. Being surrounded by wildlife would be very useful as he illustrates stories with different types of animals.)*

Objectives

- Students wrap up their investigations and present their findings.
- Students participate in investigation activities.
- Students read and use graphic sources of information.

Materials

- Student Anthology, pp. 496–507
- Inquiry Journal, pp. 137–138
- Research Assistant

INVESTIGATION

Investigating Concepts Beyond the Text

To facilitate students' investigation of the American West, you might have them participate in the following activity. Tell students that if they have activity ideas of their own that they would like to pursue, they are free to do so as an alternative to this activity suggestion. For example, students may want to pursue activities of their own choosing that relate more directly to the problems and questions they are investigating with their groups. Tell students that they may work on this activity alone, in pairs, or in small groups, with an option to write about it or to present it to the group upon completion.

The activity suggestion for this lesson is:

- Engage students in a discussion about the geography of the American West and the challenges the region's terrain and severe weather posed to the settlers. For example, droughts were common on the plains. The heat and lack of water in the Southwest desert posed other problems. Encourage the students to discuss and explore the different ways these conditions may have affected the various groups in the American West. For example, were the geographic conditions harder on the settlers from New England than on the Native Americans who had lived there for generations?

Upon completion of their activities, have students share with the group anything new they learned about the American West through discussion and by adding information to the Concept/Question Board.

Concept/Question Board

After reading each selection, students should use the Concept/Question Board to

- post any questions they asked about a selection before reading that have not yet been answered.
- refer to as they formulate statements about concepts that apply to their investigations.
- post general statements formulated by each collaborative group.
- continue to post news articles, or other items that they find during the unit investigation.
- read and think about posted questions, articles, or concepts that interest them and provide answers to the questions.

Unit 5 Investigation Management

Lesson 1	Students generate questions and ideas for investigation.
Lesson 2	Students formulate questions and problems for investigation.
Lesson 3	Students make conjectures.
Lesson 4	Students establish investigation needs.
Lesson 5	Students establish investigation plans.
Lesson 6	Students continue investigation and get feedback from other groups.
Lesson 7	Collaborative Investigation **Students present their investigation findings to the class.** Supplementary Activities **Students participate in investigation activities and learn to read and use graphic sources of information.**

INVESTIGATION

www.sra4kids.com
Web Connection
Students can use the connections to Going West in the Reading link of the SRA Web page for more background information about Going West.

Research Software

The *Research Assistant* helps students in their investigations.

Teacher Tip ULTIMATE WRITING AND CREATIVITY CENTER Have students use the ***Ultimate Writing and Creativity Center CD-ROM*** as they work on their investigation activities.

Teacher Tip PRESENTATION TIPS Remind students to practice their presentations several times before they speak in front of the class. Encourage them to read expressively and at an appropriate pace. Explain that they should speak loudly, if necessary, and use gestures and facial expressions to keep the audience's attention. Have them use the Informal Assessment criteria below to evaluate their performance as well as that of their peers.

Differentiating Instruction

If...	Then...
Students are having difficulty with their Inquiry activities	Remind them that new findings give rise to new problems and conjectures and, therefore, to new cycles of investigation

Informal Assessment

As students give oral presentations, note your observations as to the organization of their presentations. For example,

- Is it apparent that the presenters prepared for the presentation?
- Is the presentation focused and organized?
- If the presentation is informational, does it contain a controlling idea developed and clarified with simple facts, details, examples, and explanations?
- If the presentation is narrative, do the presenters establish a situation, plot, point of view, and setting with descriptive words and phrases?
- Are visual aids, technology, or demonstrations effectively used to support the presentation?

Also note your observations of students' ability to speak effectively. For example,

- Do they use strategies to speak clearly?
- Do they use both verbal and nonverbal strategies to engage the audience?
- Do they correctly use grammar, sentence structure, and sentence variety in speech?
- Do they use concise language that is appropriate to the situation, audience, and purpose of the presentation?
- Do they use appropriate words to shape reactions, perceptions, and beliefs?

Finally, observe audience members and note their use of listening strategies and their ability to comprehend, respond to, and evaluate the presentations.

INVESTIGATION

Presenting Investigation Findings

By now, groups should be wrapping up compilation of their investigation findings for presentation to the class. Some groups may also be revising their presentations based on feedback they received from their peers during Workshop. Tell students that the time has come to formally present their findings to the class, so that they may contribute to their peers' understanding of the American West. Encourage those who will be using audiovisual equipment, making oral presentations, or performing demonstrations to practice a few times before presenting to the class. Then, allow time for groups to give their presentations.

Tell students who will be making oral presentations to be sure that they speak clearly, being mindful that the rate and volume at which they speak is appropriate for the audience. Tell them that they should also use nonverbal strategies to engage their audience, such as making eye contact, incorporating hand gestures, and practicing good posture. Tell audience members that they should use listening strategies to help them comprehend what they are hearing. They should face the speaker, making eye contact with him or her, and take notes on information that they find interesting or would like to know more about.

Following each presentation, allow students time to respond to the presenters. Have them ask questions and paraphrase parts of the presentation to confirm their understanding. Have them contribute new ideas and share conclusions they have come to as a result of the presented material. Have them also offer feedback, telling what they especially liked about the presentation or offering constructive criticism. Allow presenters to respond to this feedback by answering questions and sharing their ideas. Finally, have students share new problems or questions raised by the presented material that have not previously been discussed. Then have the students add information to the Concept/Question Board. Encourage interested students to continue investigating and learning about their problems.

Professional Development

Teacher Resource Library CD-ROMs or ***Online Professional Development*** provides courses that help you better understand the Inquiry and Investigation instruction in ***Open Court Reading.*** For more information about this program, visit SRAonline.com.

Reading and Using Graphic Sources of Information

Teach Explain to the students that information can be made more usable and accessible by organizing it in graphs, charts, and diagrams. Tell students that graphic organizers often can be found in expository texts. Authors use them to help clarify ideas for readers. Students can also use them to organize information from their investigations. Have students name some examples of graphic organizers they have seen in their workbooks and used in their group work. Have them tell how these organizers made information easier to use and access as they studied for a test, compiled notes from their investigations, or presented their findings.

Guided Practice Tell students that one type of graphic organizer they might find useful is a line graph. Use page 137 in the ***Inquiry Journal*** and complete it as a group. Review the line graph for the type of information it gives. Remind students that it is important to read the title of the graph so they know what information it contains. Have the class answer the questions orally, accepting any reasonable answers they can infer from the other selections and activities in Unit 5. Then have students complete Part 2 of ***Inquiry Journal,*** page 138.

Independent Practice Have students select at least one source containing graphic organizers for use in their investigations. Have them make note in the Writer's Notebooks of what the name of the source is, what type of graphic organizer was used, and how the graphic organizer made the information in the text easier to understand. Have students also use a graphic organizer to present findings from their investigations.

SUPPORTING THE INVESTIGATION

Name ______ Date ______

Going West UNIT 5

Interpreting Graphs

Study the following graph. Then, use information in the graph and what you have learned from the stories and activities in this unit to answer the questions.

Population Growth in Selected Western States, 1860–1900

Texas
California
Colorado

- Which state probably had the most opportunities for making a living between 1860 and 1900? Explain your answer.
  Texas. This state had the greatest increase in population. The cattle industry attracted many people to Texas.
- Many families lived on farms in the 1800s. Which state may not have been good for farming? Explain.
  Colorado. This state had the smallest population growth. Mountainous land may have made farming difficult.

Inquiry Journal • *Interpreting Graphs* UNIT 5 137

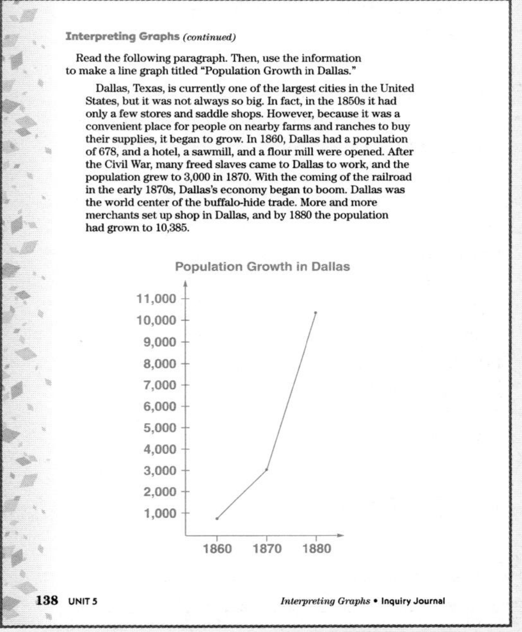

Interpreting Graphs *(continued)*

Read the following paragraph. Then, use the information to make a line graph titled "Population Growth in Dallas."

Dallas, Texas, is currently one of the largest cities in the United States, but it was not always so big. In fact, in the 1850s it had only a few stores and saddle shops. However, because it was a convenient place for people on nearby farms and ranches to buy their supplies, it began to grow. In 1860, Dallas had a population of 678, and a hotel, a sawmill, and a flour mill were opened. After the Civil War, many freed slaves came to Dallas to work, and the population grew to 3,000 in 1870. With the coming of the railroad in the early 1870s, Dallas's economy began to boom. Dallas was the world center of the buffalo-hide trade. More and more merchants set up shop in Dallas, and by 1880 the population had grown to 10,385.

138 UNIT 5 *Interpreting Graphs* • Inquiry Journal

***Inquiry Journal* pp. 137–138**

Encourage students to use ***TechKnowledge*** to help them create graphic representations of their investigation findings.

Objectives

Word Analysis

Spelling

- **Review.** Review spelling patterns for homophones and words with *dis-*, *mis-*, *-ent*, *-ant*, *-tion*, *-sion*, *-sure*, *-ed*, *-ing*, *-er*, or *-est* introduced in Word Knowledge in Part 1.

Vocabulary

- Using words from "McBroom the Rainmaker," review the vocabulary concepts discussed in Unit 5.

Writing Process Strategies

- **Personal Writing: Memo.** Building from an idea from "McBroom the Rainmaker," students will learn the form and function of a memo. Students will then draft their own memo.

English Language Conventions

Grammar, Usage, and Mechanics

- **Review.** Students will review skills practiced in this unit.

Listening, Speaking, Viewing

- **Presenting: Oral Presentations.** Identify and implement appropriate styles of oral presentations.

Penmanship

- **Joining with *R* and *s*.** Review handwriting skills by practicing joining letters with *R* and *s*.

Materials

- Comprehension and Language Arts Skills, pp. 172–175
- Language Arts Handbook
- Language Arts Transparencies 15, 25
- Unit 5 Assessment, pp. 42–43
- Spelling Software
- Spelling and Vocabulary Skills, pp. 130–133
- Student Anthology
- Writer's Workbook, pp. 102–105

Differentiating Instruction

Reteach*, *Challenge*,** and ***Intervention lessons are available to support the language arts instruction in this lesson.

Research in Action

Each invented spelling is a permanent record of an individual's journey to spelling competence.
(*J. Richard Gentry and Jean Wallace Gillet*, Teaching Kids to Spell)

OVERVIEW

Language Arts Overview

Word Analysis

Spelling The spelling activities on the following pages support the Word Knowledge introduction of homophones, words with *dis-* and *mis-*, words with *-ent* or *-ant*, words with *-tion*, *-sion*, or *-sure*, and words with the endings *-ed*, *-ing*, *-er*, and *-est* by developing understanding of the spelling patterns for these words.

Selection Spelling Words

These words from "McBroom the Rainmaker" contain *-tion*, *-ed*, *-ing*, and *-est*.

disposition harvested smallest shrinking dried

Vocabulary The vocabulary activities review the concepts discussed in Unit 5.

Vocabulary Skill Words

rapscallions parched* confounded ornery splendid

**Also Selection Vocabulary.*

Writing Process Strategies

This Writing Process Strategies lesson involves instruction in writing a memo. A *memo*, or *memorandum*, is a written message from one person to one or more people in the same organization.

To help students understand that CD-ROMs contain information that can be used for writing, review steps to search CD-ROMs. You might want to help students search for information about the president of the United States. ***TechKnowledge*** Level 5 Lesson 79 teaches these electronic reference skills.

English Language Conventions

Grammar, Usage, and Mechanics **Review.** This lesson reviews sentence structure; punctuation and capitalization in letters; commas with appositives and clauses; and end and quotation marks in dialogue.

Listening, Speaking, Viewing **Presenting: Oral Presentations.** In this Presenting lesson, students identify and implement appropriate styles of oral presentations for specific purposes. Set aside additional time on Day 4, or during the next week, to allow students to deliver their presentations in class.

Penmanship **Joining with *R* and *s*.** This lesson continues the development of handwriting skills. Students join letters with *R* and *s* and then write paragraphs from the literature, focusing on joining letters.

DAY 1

Word Analysis

Spelling

Assessment: Pretest

Review

Give students the Pretest on page 42 of ***Unit 5 Assessment.*** Have them proofread and correct any misspellings.

Pretest Sentences

1. **pedal** A bicycle **pedal** could be made of titanium.
2. **vain** A **vain** person might spend a lot of time in front of the mirror.
3. **promotion** An assistant manager will probably seek a **promotion.**
4. **laziest** The sloth is said to be one of the **laziest** animals.
5. **evident** When sirens sound, it is **evident** that a tornado is near.
6. **misfire** Target shooters hope their rifles will not **misfire.**
7. **mission** An astronaut might go on more than one space **mission.**
8. **peddle** A traveling salesperson might **peddle** vacuum cleaners.
9. **disprove** Scientists often try to **disprove** each other's theories.
10. **carrying** Llamas were used for **carrying** supplies.
11. **vein** A **vein** carries blood.
12. **traction** New tires have better **traction.**
13. **mismatch** It is easy to **mismatch** black and navy socks.
14. **decent** Striking workers will often demand **decent** wages.
15. **branched** The river **branched** off into smaller streams.
16. **disposition** A cheerful **disposition** is an advantage for a teacher.
17. **harvested** The crops had to be **harvested.**
18. **smallest** Rhode Island is the **smallest** state in the United States.
19. **shrinking** The Brazilian rain forest is **shrinking.**
20. **dried** A raisin is a **dried** grape.

Writing Process Strategies

Getting Ideas

Memo

Teach

Introduce the Writing Form

Read ***Language Arts Handbook*** pages 92–93 on memos. Point out that a memo is a form of business letter that is meant to inform, explain, or make a request.

Inspiration

Teacher Model: *I will imagine I am the President of the United States and I will write a memo to the Agriculture Committee suggesting drought relief for farmers whose crops are suffering.*

Brainstorming

Encourage students to suggest ideas, thoughts, or details that they might use to write a memo as President of the United States to the Agriculture Committee asking for drought-relief aid.

Independent Practice

Selecting a Topic

Have students select their own memo topics. For this assignment, students may choose to write memos that pertain to things happening in their own lives. For example, a student may choose to write a memo to his or her soccer team about practice times.

Memos

A **memo** is a short message that communicates something to a person or a group of people with whom you are working. The word memo is short for **memorandum**, which means "written reminder." Memos do not have closings or signatures. Instead, writers may initial their names by the headings. The format of a memo is much different from the format of a business letter.

Take a Look

Fun Fact: *Re* comes from Latin. It means "in regard to the thing."

Heading ▸
Memo
Date: April 14, 2003
To: Dogwood Festival Float-Building Committee
From: Ava Gregorio, Chair AV
Subject: Donations
CC: Fred Cushing and all Community Center Maintenance Staff

Body ▸
Please collect large- and medium-sized cardboard boxes. We will need them for building our float. Also, we need the following donations: white sheets; brown felt; cans of blue, green, and yellow latex paint. Items may be left Tuesday through Friday, April 15–18, at the Community Center garage between 3 p.m. and 8 p.m.

Memos sometimes use the label *CC*. *CC* stands for carbon copy (even though most memos today are photocopied). Write *CC:* at the end of the heading before a list of other people who will receive copies.
The label *Re:* is sometimes used in place of *Subject:* to describe the topic.

92 Personal Writing ▲ Memos

Language Arts Handbook p. 92

English Language Conventions

Grammar, Usage, and Mechanics

Review

Teach

- Use ***Language Arts Handbook*** to review the following:
  - Sentence structure and fragments.
  - Punctuation and capitalization in letters.
  - Commas with appositives and clauses.
  - End marks and quotation marks in dialogue.
- Remind students that every sentence needs to have unity: a single thought or a group of closely related thoughts.

Guided Practice

Use ***Comprehension and Language Arts Skills*** pages 172–173 to practice the skills that were reviewed.

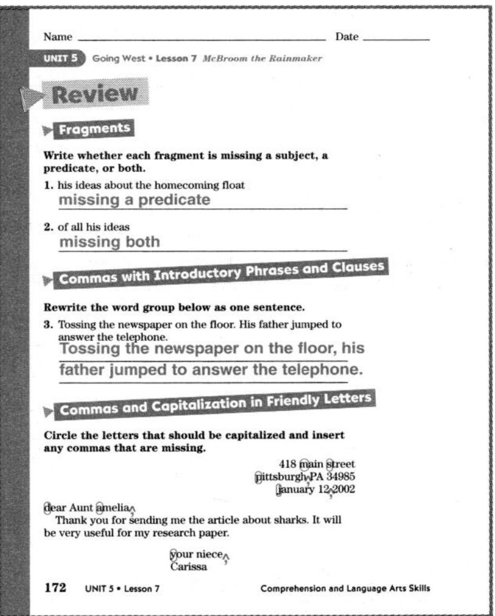

Name ______ Date ______

UNIT 5 Going West • Lesson 7 *McBroom the Rainmaker*

Review

Fragments

Write whether each fragment is missing a subject, a predicate, or both.

1. his ideas about the homecoming float
missing a predicate
2. of all his ideas
missing both

Commas with Introductory Phrases and Clauses

Rewrite the word group below as one sentence.

3. Tossing the newspaper on the floor. His father jumped to answer the telephone.
Tossing the newspaper on the floor, his father jumped to answer the telephone.

Commas and Capitalization in Friendly Letters

Circle the letters that should be capitalized and insert any commas that are missing.

418 main street
pittsburgh PA 34985
january 12 2002

dear Aunt amelia
Thank you for sending me the article about sharks. It will be very useful for my research paper.

your niece
Carissa

172 UNIT 5 • Lesson 7 Comprehension and Language Arts Skills

Comprehension and Language Arts Skills p. 172

DAY 2

Word Analysis

Spelling

Review

Have students complete the Spelling Bee activity for Unit 5 on the ***Spelling Software.***

Vocabulary

Review

Teach

- Answer questions from students about the concepts discussed in Unit 5. Clarify any discussions about foreign words, concept words, similes, and compound words.
- Have students look for examples of compound words, similes, or words with multiple meanings in "McBroom the Rainmaker." Examples include *rainmaker, claims, woodpeckers, timepiece, second, homegrown, topsoil, float in the air like balloons, birdcage, rattled like a hailstorm,* and *raincoats.*

Guided Practice

Assign page 130 of ***Spelling and Vocabulary Skills.*** Students can complete page 131 of ***Spelling and Vocabulary Skills*** for homework.

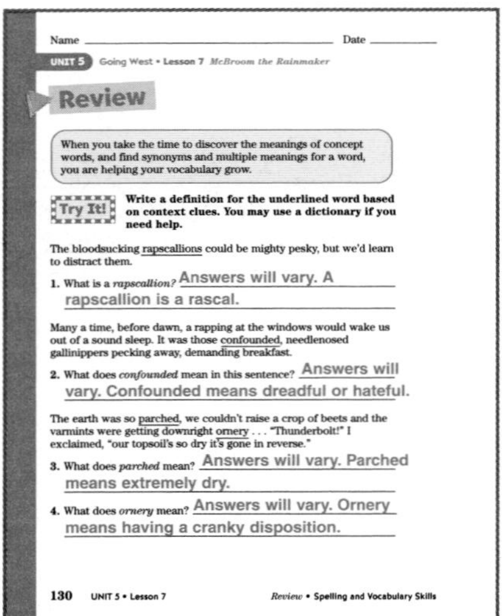

Name ________________ Date ________

UNIT 5 Going West • Lesson 7 *McBroom the Rainmaker*

Review

When you take the time to discover the meanings of concept words, and find synonyms and multiple meanings for a word, you are helping your vocabulary grow.

Try It! **Write a definition for the underlined word based on context clues. You may use a dictionary if you need help.**

The bloodsucking rapscallions could be mighty pesky, but we'd learn to distract them.

1. What is a *rapscallion?* Answers will vary. A rapscallion is a rascal.

Many a time, before dawn, a rapping at the windows would wake us out of a sound sleep. It was those confounded, needlenosed gallinippers pecking away, demanding breakfast.

2. What does *confounded* mean in this sentence? Answers will vary. Confounded means dreadful or hateful.

The earth was so parched, we couldn't raise a crop of beets and the varmints were getting downright ornery . . . "Thunderbolt!" I exclaimed, "our topsoil's so dry it's gone in reverse."

3. What does *parched* mean? Answers will vary. Parched means extremely dry.
4. What does *ornery* mean? Answers will vary. Ornery means having a cranky disposition.

130 UNIT 5 • Lesson 7 *Review* • Spelling and Vocabulary Skills

***Spelling and Vocabulary Skills* p. 130**

Writing Process Strategies

Prewriting

Memo

Teach

- Review ideas and thoughts discussed on Day 1.
- If possible, bring in copies of memos so students can view them.
- Remind students to consider audience and purpose when writing their memos. Tell students that because a memo is a form of business letter, it will always have a formal tone.

Independent Practice

- Have students describe the audience and purpose for their memos in their Writer's Notebooks.
- Have students complete the prewriting for writing a memo on ***Writer's Workbook*** page 102.

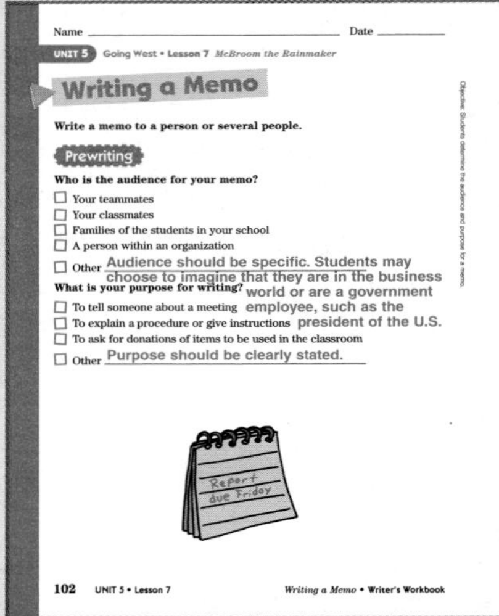

Name ________________ Date ________

UNIT 5 Going West • Lesson 7 *McBroom the Rainmaker*

Writing a Memo

Write a memo to a person or several people.

Prewriting

Who is the audience for your memo?

- ☐ Your teammates
- ☐ Your classmates
- ☐ Families of the students in your school
- ☐ A person within an organization
- ☐ Other Audience should be specific. Students may choose to imagine that they are in the business world or are a government employee, such as the president of the U.S.

What is your purpose for writing?

- ☐ To tell someone about a meeting
- ☐ To explain a procedure or give instructions
- ☐ To ask for donations of items to be used in the classroom
- ☐ Other Purpose should be clearly stated.

Objective: Students determine the audience and purpose for a memo.

102 UNIT 5 • Lesson 7 *Writing a Memo* • Writer's Workbook

***Writer's Workbook* p. 102**

Professional Development

Teacher Resource Library CD-ROMs or ***Online Professional Development*** provides courses that help you better understand the Writing instruction in ***Open Court Reading.*** For more information about this program, visit SRAonline.com.

English Language Conventions

Grammar, Usage, and Mechanics

Review

Teach

- Review commas with appositives and clauses.
- Write these words on the board. Have students suggest corrections.
  - We went to visit them but they weren't home. *(We went to visit them, but they weren't home.)*
  - Although they said, they could go we discovered they were wrong. *(Although they said they could go, we discovered they were wrong.)*
  - He was born on january 4, 1998 I believe. *(He was born on January 4, 1998, I believe.)*
  - I know that most Californians, citizens of California love the ocean. *(I know that most Californians, citizens of California, love the ocean.)*

Guided Practice in Reading

Have students look for fragments and commas used with appositives and clauses in "McBroom the Rainmaker." Point out that the style of the author is more informal than that of other stories they have been reading. There are many instances of fragments written intentionally for effect.

DAY 3

Word Analysis

Spelling

Review

Teach

Review the spelling patterns and conventions discussed in Unit 5. Answer any questions students may have about prefixes, suffixes, adding endings to words, and homophones. Have students locate words that display these patterns and conventions in the selection "McBroom the Rainmaker."

Guided Practice

Have students complete page 132 from ***Spelling and Vocabulary Skills*** to review the spelling patterns and conventions discussed in Unit 5.

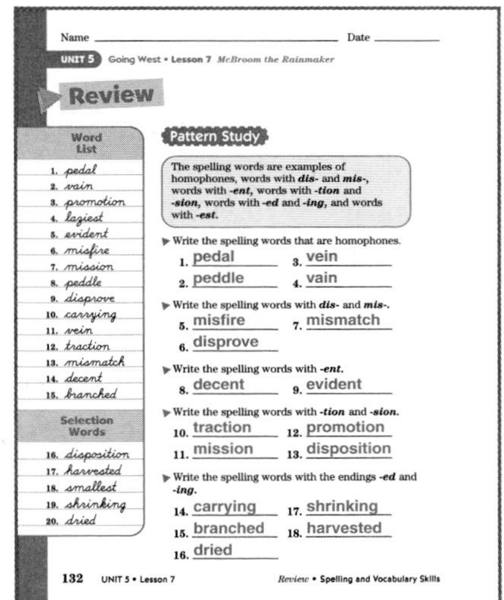

Name ______________ Date ________

UNIT 5 Going West • Lesson 7 *McBroom the Rainmaker*

Review

Word List

1. pedal
2. vain
3. promotion
4. laziest
5. evident
6. misfire
7. mission
8. peddle
9. disprove
10. carrying
11. vein
12. traction
13. mismatch
14. decent
15. branched

Selection Words

16. disposition
17. harvested
18. smallest
19. shrinking
20. dried

Pattern Study

The spelling words are examples of homophones, words with ***dis-*** and ***mis-***, words with ***-ent***, words with ***-tion*** and ***-sion***, words with ***-ed*** and ***-ing***, and words with ***-est***.

▶ Write the spelling words that are homophones.

1. pedal 3. vein
2. peddle 4. vain

▶ Write the spelling words with ***dis-*** and ***mis-***.

5. misfire 7. mismatch
6. disprove

▶ Write the spelling words with ***-ent***.

8. decent 9. evident

▶ Write the spelling words with ***-tion*** and ***-sion***.

10. traction 12. promotion
11. mission 13. disposition

▶ Write the spelling words with the endings ***-ed*** and ***-ing***.

14. carrying 17. shrinking
15. branched 18. harvested
16. dried

132 UNIT 5 • Lesson 7 *Review* • Spelling and Vocabulary Skills

***Spelling and Vocabulary Skills* p. 132**

Vocabulary (continued)

Review

Have students write similes about any of the objects or characters encountered in the reading selections for Unit 5. Possible topics could include Native Americans, wild animals, buffalo, Lewis and Clark and Sacagawea, gold, horses, cattle, elements of the rodeo, and farming.

Writing Process Strategies

Drafting

Memo

Teach

Writer's Craft

Structure of a Memo

- Begin by noting that the **heading** of a memo includes the date, to and from whom the memo is sent, the subject of the memo, and who receives copies of the memo.
  - The subject line is within the heading. It should be precise so that the topic is clear and the memo is easy to file.
  - *Re:* is a label sometimes used in place of *Subject:* to describe the topic or main point of the memo.
- The **body** states what the writer wants to say. Tell students that it is important to get right to the point in the body. Then give the necessary details and let the readers know the response needed.
- Have students use ***Comprehension and Language Arts Skills*** pages 174–175 to practice correct memo form.

Independent Practice

- Have students complete ***Writer's Workbook,*** page 103.
- Have students write a draft of their memo and keep it in their ***Writing Folders.***

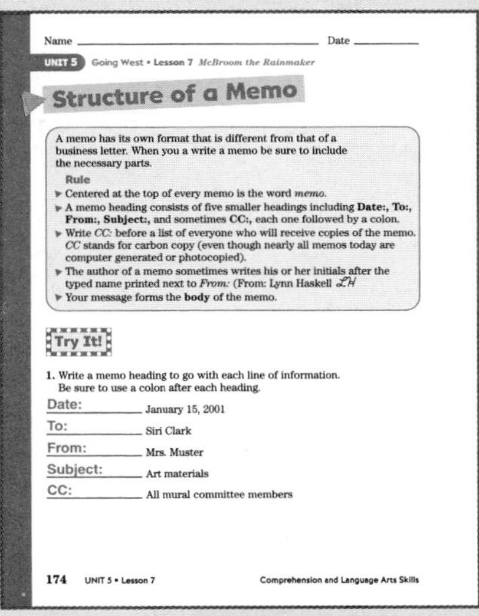

Name ______________ Date ________

UNIT 5 Going West • Lesson 7 *McBroom the Rainmaker*

Structure of a Memo

A memo has its own format that is different from that of a business letter. When you a write a memo be sure to include the necessary parts.

Rule

▶ Centered at the top of every memo is the word *memo.*

▶ A memo heading consists of five smaller headings including **Date:, To:, From:, Subject:,** and sometimes **CC:**, each one followed by a colon.

▶ Write *CC:* before a list of everyone who will receive copies of the memo. *CC* stands for carbon copy (even though nearly all memos today are computer generated or photocopied).

▶ The author of a memo sometimes writes his or her initials after the typed name printed next to *From:* (From: Lynn Haskell *LH*

▶ Your message forms the **body** of the memo.

Try It!

1. Write a memo heading to go with each line of information. Be sure to use a colon after each heading.

Date: January 15, 2001
To: Siri Clark
From: Mrs. Muster
Subject: Art materials
CC: All mural committee members

174 UNIT 5 • Lesson 7 Comprehension and Language Arts Skills

***Comprehension and Language Arts Skills* p. 174**

English Language Conventions

Grammar, Usage, and Mechanics

Review

Teach

- Review end punctuation and quotation marks in dialogue.
- Write these sentences on the board. Have students suggest corrections.
  - Did you ask, "Where are the students?"? *(Did you ask, "Where are the students?")*
  - Jackie replied I don't know but I saw him yesterday *(Jackie replied, "I don't know, but I saw him yesterday.")*
  - Alex Leslie asked will you please take out the trash *("Alex," Leslie asked, "will you please take out the trash?")*
- Remind students that a salutation in a friendly letter is followed by a comma; a greeting in a business letter or memo is followed by a colon.

Guided Practice in Writing

Have students rewrite their memos in business-letter format. They may insert an address. Remind students that checking for sentence fragments, punctuation, and capitalization is an important part of editing their memos.

Informal Assessment

While students are writing their memos, check to see that they are using correct punctuation and capitalization. Also make certain that there are no sentence fragments in their memos. Make certain students are continuing to make progress with all the skills taught in this unit.

DAY 4

Word Analysis

Spelling

Review

Teach

Model the family strategy exercise for students by writing the word *peddling* on the board and asking students to identify and spell the spelling word that is in the same word family, *peddle.*

Guided Practice

Have students complete the Spelling Strategies exercise on page 133 of ***Spelling and Vocabulary Skills.***

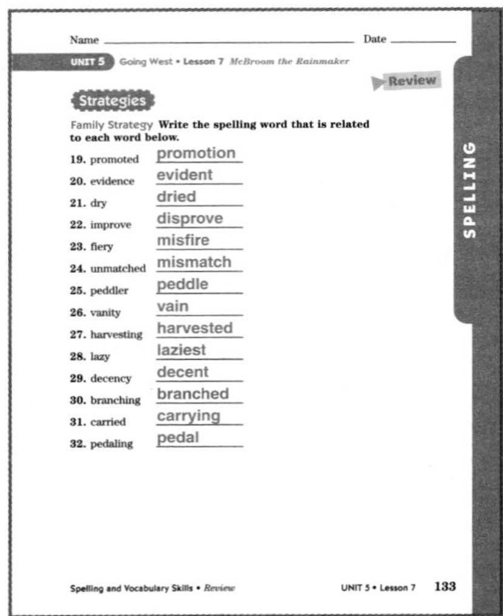

Name ______ Date ______

UNIT 5 Going West • Lesson 7 *McBroom the Rainmaker*

Review

Strategies

Family Strategy **Write the spelling word that is related to each word below.**

19. promoted promotion
20. evidence evident
21. dry dried
22. improve disprove
23. fiery misfire
24. unmatched mismatch
25. peddler peddle
26. vanity vain
27. harvesting harvested
28. lazy laziest
29. decency decent
30. branching branched
31. carried carrying
32. pedaling pedal

SPELLING

Spelling and Vocabulary Skills • *Review* UNIT 5 • Lesson 7 133

***Spelling and Vocabulary Skills* p. 133**

Vocabulary (continued)

Review

Now that students have learned many concept words related to the American West, have them create another word map of concept words used to speak and write about this topic. Students can work in small groups or individually.

Writing Process Strategies

Revising

Memo

Teach

- **Teacher Model** revising by using ***Language Arts Transparency 15,*** Revising for Clarity. Tell students that clarity is particularly important in memos because their purpose is to inform, explain, or request. If the language in a memo is not clear, the reader may not know how to respond.
- Point out to students that memos should be written only when necessary.
  - They are written to create a *flow of information* within an organization.
  - They should be sent only to those who need them. They are written to ask and answer questions, describe procedures and policies, and to remind people of appointments and meetings.
  - Details that the reader needs are often listed in bullet form rather than buried in a paragraph.
  - It is best to close on a positive note.

Independent Practice

Have students use the checklist in their ***Writer's Workbooks*** on page 104 to revise their memos.

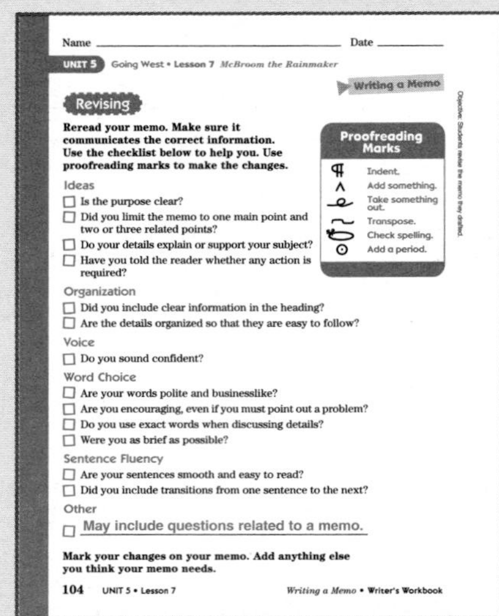

Name ______ Date ______

UNIT 5 Going West • Lesson 7 *McBroom the Rainmaker*

Writing a Memo

Revising

Reread your memo. Make sure it communicates the correct information. Use the checklist below to help you. Use proofreading marks to make the changes.

Proofreading Marks
- ¶ Indent.
- ^ Add something.
- Take something out.
- Transpose.
- Check spelling.
- ⊙ Add a period.

Ideas
- ☐ Is the purpose clear?
- ☐ Did you limit the memo to one main point and two or three related points?
- ☐ Do your details explain or support your subject?
- ☐ Have you told the reader whether any action is required?

Organization
- ☐ Did you include clear information in the heading?
- ☐ Are the details organized so that they are easy to follow?

Voice
- ☐ Do you sound confident?

Word Choice
- ☐ Are your words polite and businesslike?
- ☐ Are you encouraging, even if you must point out a problem?
- ☐ Do you use exact words when discussing details?
- ☐ Were you as brief as possible?

Sentence Fluency
- ☐ Are your sentences smooth and easy to read?
- ☐ Did you include transitions from one sentence to the next?

Other
- ☐ May include questions related to a memo.

Mark your changes on your memo. Add anything else you think your memo needs.

Objective: Students revise the memo they drafted.

104 UNIT 5 • Lesson 7 *Writing a Memo* • Writer's Workbook

***Writer's Workbook* p. 104**

English Language Conventions

Listening, Speaking, Viewing

Presenting: Oral Presentations

Teach

- Delineate for students the most common purposes of oral presentations: to persuade, to inform or explain, to report an event, or to provide entertainment.
- Point out to students that the style of an oral presentation is driven by the purpose. Explain that an informational presentation is usually a serious one that contains factual information. A persuasive presentation usually contains opinions based on facts. An entertaining presentation can be humorous or dramatic. Some presentations may invite participation from the audience as well.

Guided Practice

- Have students give an extemporaneous oral presentation on one of the following: news report of a local or national event, dramatic reading of a piece of literature or play, or a persuasive speech about a topic of the student's choice. You may wish to allow students to work in pairs or in groups, depending on their choices of oral presentations.
- Remind students that their style of presentation should be appropriate for the particular purpose of the presentation.

Independent Practice

- Set aside time for a special assembly during which students will give their presentations.

Informal Assessment

Observe whether students can identify and implement appropriate styles of oral presentations for specific purposes.

DAY 5

Word Analysis

Spelling

Assessment: Final Test

Review

Teach

Repeat the Pretest for this lesson or use the Final Test on page 43 of ***Unit 5 Assessment***.

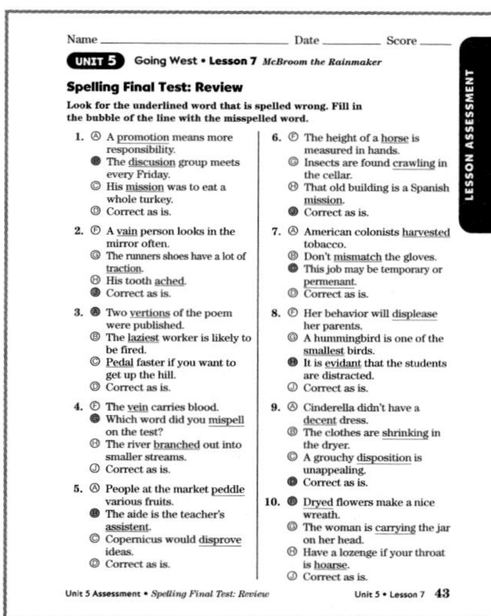

Name ____________ Date ________ Score ____

UNIT 5 Going West • Lesson 7 *McBroom the Rainmaker*

LESSON ASSESSMENT

Spelling Final Test: Review

Look for the underlined word that is spelled wrong. Fill in the bubble of the line with the misspelled word.

1. Ⓐ A promotion means more responsibility.
   ● The discusion group meets every Friday.
   Ⓒ His mission was to eat a whole turkey.
   Ⓓ Correct as is.
2. Ⓕ A vain person looks in the mirror often.
   Ⓖ The runners shoes have a lot of traction.
   Ⓗ His tooth ached.
   ● Correct as is.
3. ● Two vertions of the poem were published.
   Ⓑ The laziest worker is likely to be fired.
   Ⓒ Pedal faster if you want to get up the hill.
   Ⓓ Correct as is.
4. Ⓕ The vein carries blood.
   ● Which word did you mispell on the test?
   Ⓗ The river branched out into smaller streams.
   Ⓙ Correct as is.
5. Ⓐ People at the market peddle various fruits.
   ● The aide is the teacher's assistent.
   Ⓒ Copernicus would disprove ideas.
   Ⓓ Correct as is.
6. Ⓕ The height of a horse is measured in hands.
   Ⓖ Insects are found crawling in the cellar.
   Ⓗ That old building is a Spanish mission.
   ● Correct as is.
7. Ⓐ American colonists harvested tobacco.
   Ⓑ Don't mismatch the gloves.
   ● This job may be temporary or permenant.
   Ⓓ Correct as is.
8. Ⓕ Her behavior will displease her parents.
   Ⓖ A hummingbird is one of the smallest birds.
   ● It is evidant that the students are distracted.
   Ⓙ Correct as is.
9. Ⓐ Cinderella didn't have a decent dress.
   Ⓑ The clothes are shrinking in the dryer.
   Ⓒ A grouchy disposition is unappealing.
   ● Correct as is.
10. ● Dryed flowers make a nice wreath.
    Ⓖ The woman is carrying the jar on her head.
    Ⓗ Have a lozenge if your throat is hoarse.
    Ⓙ Correct as is.

Unit 5 Assessment • *Spelling Final Test: Review* Unit 5 • Lesson 7 43

Unit 5 Assessment p. 43

Guided Practice

Have students categorize any mistakes they made on the Final Test.

- Are they careless errors?
- Are they lesson pattern problems?

Vocabulary

Review

Informal Assessment

- Periodically check to see if students remember the concepts discussed in Unit 5 and can identify word examples in texts.
- Remind students to continue adding vocabulary words to their Writer's Notebooks.

Writing Process Strategies

Editing/Proofreading and Publishing

Memo

Teach

Using ***Language Arts Transparency 25,*** All Conventions, **teacher model** editing. Address each of the checklist items on ***Writer's Workbook*** page 105.

Independent Practice

- Have students use the checklist on page 105 of the ***Writer's Workbook*** to proofread and edit their memos.
- Have students choose a method for publishing.

Formal Assessment

Share this rubric with students before they begin the assignment to give them a foundation from which to work.

Total Point Value: 10

1. The subject line of the memo is precise so that the topic is clear. (2 points)
2. The body of the memo gets right to the point by stating the subject. (2 points)
3. The details support the subject. (2 points)
4. The sentences flow smoothly. (2 points)
5. The format is correct. (2 points)

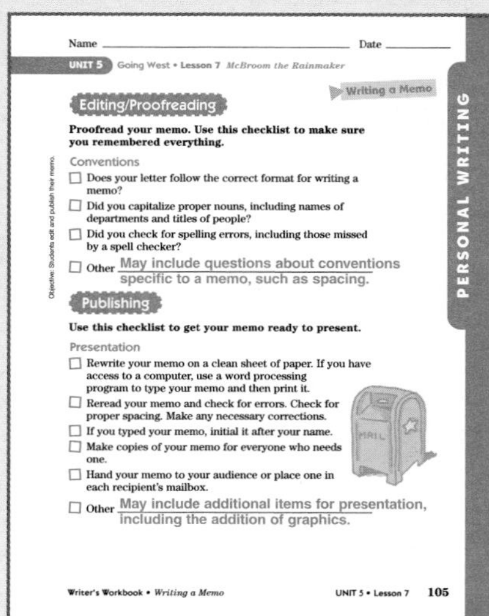

Name ____________ Date ________

UNIT 5 Going West • Lesson 7 *McBroom the Rainmaker*

Writing a Memo

PERSONAL WRITING

Editing/Proofreading

Proofread your memo. Use this checklist to make sure you remembered everything.

Objective: Students edit and publish their memo.

Conventions

- ☐ Does your letter follow the correct format for writing a memo?
- ☐ Did you capitalize proper nouns, including names of departments and titles of people?
- ☐ Did you check for spelling errors, including those missed by a spell checker?
- ☐ Other May include questions about conventions specific to a memo, such as spacing.

Publishing

Use this checklist to get your memo ready to present.

Presentation

- ☐ Rewrite your memo on a clean sheet of paper. If you have access to a computer, use a word processing program to type your memo and then print it.
- ☐ Reread your memo and check for errors. Check for proper spacing. Make any necessary corrections.
- ☐ If you typed your memo, initial it after your name.
- ☐ Make copies of your memo for everyone who needs one.
- ☐ Hand your memo to your audience or place one in each recipient's mailbox.
- ☐ Other May include additional items for presentation, including the addition of graphics.

Writer's Workbook • *Writing a Memo* UNIT 5 • Lesson 7 105

Writer's Workbook p. 105

English Language Conventions

Penmanship

Joining with *R* and *s*

Teach

- **Teacher Model:** Review formation of uppercase *R* and lowercase *s* on the board.

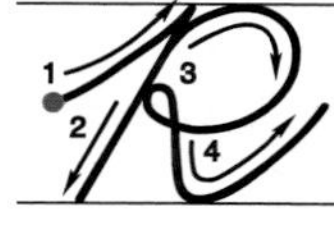

R Starting point, undercurve
Slant down, retrace up
Curve forward to slant
Curve forward
Undercurve: capital *R*

S Starting point, undercurve
Curve down and back
Undercurve: small *s*

- **Teacher Model:** Write the following sentence to model proper joining of letters: *Ramon is from a little town scarcely nine miles from Reims.*

Guided Practice

- In the Writer's Notebook, have students join *R* with the letters *a*, *o*, *e*, and *i* and join *s* with *l*, *p*, *w*, and *c*.
- From "McBroom the Rainmaker," have students write two paragraphs to practice joining letters.

Informal Assessment

Check students' handwriting for legibility and proper joining of letters.

Reading and Language Arts Skills Traces

Language Arts

WORD ANALYSIS

Skills Trace

Spelling: Review

Introduced in Grade 2.
Scaffolded throughout Grades 3–5.

REINTRODUCED: Unit 5, Lesson 7, p. 507F
PRACTICED: Unit 5, Lesson 7, pp. 507G–507I
Spelling and Vocabulary Skills, pp. 132–133
TESTED: Unit 5, Lesson 7, p. 507J
Unit 5 Assessment

Skills Trace

Vocabulary: Review

Introduced in Grade 2.
Scaffolded throughout Grades 3–5.

REINTRODUCED: Unit 5, Lesson 7, p. 507G
PRACTICED: Unit 5, Lesson 7, pp. 507H–507I
Spelling and Vocabulary Skills, pp. 130–131
TESTED: Informal Assessment, p. 507J
Unit 5 Assessment

Reading

COMPREHENSION

Cause and Effect

Introduced in Grade 1.
Scaffolded throughout Grades 2–5.

REINTRODUCED: Unit 4, Lesson 1
REINFORCED: Unit 5, Lesson 7
Unit 6, Lesson 2
TESTED: Unit 5 Assessment

WRITING PROCESS STRATEGIES

Skills Trace

Personal Writing: Memo

Introduced in Grade 5.
Scaffolded throughout Grade 5.

INTRODUCED: Unit 5, Lesson 7, p. 507F
PRACTICED: Unit 5, Lesson 7, pp. 507F–507J
Writer's Workbook, pp. 102–105
TESTED: Formal Assessment
Unit 5, Lesson 7, p. 507J
Unit 5 Assessment

Skills Trace

Writer's Craft: Structure of a Memo

Introduced in Grade 5.
Scaffolded throughout Grade 5.

INTRODUCED: Unit 5, Lesson 7, p. 507H
PRACTICED: Unit 5, Lesson 7, p. 507H
Comprehension and Language Arts Skills, pp. 174–175
TESTED: Unit 5 Assessment

ENGLISH LANGUAGE CONVENTIONS

Skills Trace

Grammar and Usage: Review

Skills Trace

Listening, Speaking, Viewing Presenting: Oral Presentations

Introduced in Grade 2.
Scaffolded throughout Grades 3–5.

REINTRODUCED: Unit 5, Lesson 7, p. 507I
PRACTICED: Unit 5, Lesson 7, p. 507I
TESTED: Informal Assessment, p. 507I

Penmanship: Joining with R and s

Introduced in Grade 3.
Scaffolded throughout Grades 4–5.

REINTRODUCED: Unit 5, Lesson 7, p. 507J
PRACTICED: Unit 5, Lesson 7, p. 507J
TESTED: Informal Assessment, p. 507J

Professional Development: Assessment

Assessment

The goal of true assessment is to provide information for instruction. It helps determine what students know and how to change the instruction to help students learn what they need to know.

Assessment in any form is most valuable when it leads to changes in classroom instruction. Assessment tasks should reflect classroom practice and the abilities students are expected to acquire. When the results of assessment suggest that students are having a difficult time mastering a skill, the teacher should implement alternate instructional strategies and materials.

Informal teacher observations, structured assessments, and on-demand reading and writing evaluations provide a comprehensive picture of student growth and progress and avoid the more limited view of performance that results from basing assessment on just one or two measures.

The teacher's professional judgment is the keystone of the evaluation process. The teacher is the person who knows the student best, and teacher observations are the single most important source of information about student growth and potential.

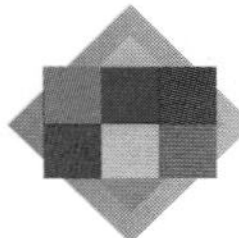

Professional Development

Teacher Resource Library CD-ROMs or ***Online Professional Development*** provides courses that help you better understand the Assessment instruction in ***Open Court Reading.*** For more information about this program, visit SRAonline.com.

Additional information about assessment, as well as resource references, can be found in the ***Professional Development Guide: Assessment.***

Review the Concepts

After all the groups have presented their findings, lead students in a large-group discussion about the unit activities. Ask students which part of the investigation they enjoyed most. Which part was the most challenging? What part of their investigations can they use in their everyday lives?

Review with students the following key concepts.

- The Louisiana Purchase doubled the size of the United States. Lewis and Clark explored this territory in hopes of finding a route to the Pacific Ocean.
- Native Americans' way of life was changed forever by the coming of the white settlers.
- People who lived on the frontier were hard working and resourceful.

Tips for Reviewing Concepts

- Students' ideas should determine the discussion.
- Remind students that they can continue to investigate the American West even though they have completed the unit.

Have students refer to page 112 of their ***Inquiry Journals*** to remind themselves of what their ideas were when the unit began and also of what they expected to learn from the unit. Ask them to describe the new ideas they have acquired and the new information they have learned.

Name________________ Date________

UNIT 5 Going West

Knowledge about Going West

- This is what I know about the American West before reading the unit.

Answers will vary.

- These are some things I would like to know about the American West.

Answers will vary.

Reminder: I should read this page again when I get to the end of the unit to see how much I've learned about Going West.

112 UNIT 5 *Knowledge about Going West* • Inquiry Journal

Inquiry Journal p. 112

Evaluating the Unit

- Have students conduct an evaluation of the unit selections, identifying those selections they found most interesting and those they found least interesting.
- Have students evaluate the different activities in which they participated throughout the unit. Which activities did they find the most enjoyable and informative?
- Ask students to evaluate the overall unit. Have them answer questions such as the following: How well did the unit cover the theme? Which selections added something new to your knowledge of the American West?
- Have students suggest ideas related to the American West to explore further, possibly beginning with any questions left on the Concept/Question Board.

Evaluating the Groups

In their small groups, have students discuss the unit activity. Encourage them to talk about the importance of teamwork. Have the groups consider the following: What things did we do well as a team? What things could we do better next time? Why is teamwork important?

Throughout this unit investigation into Going West, you have been informally assessing student progress. Go over your notes to see who has been contributing to the group's investigation and how students have helped each other during this process. Talk with each group to get their feedback about how they felt working as a team. Use your observation notes, feedback from the group, and the Research Rubrics to assess the groups as well as individual student participation in the groups. Record each student's score on the inside back cover of the ***Inquiry Journal.***

Research Rubrics

Collaborative Group Work (this rubric is applied to groups, not individuals)

1 Group members work on separate tasks with little interaction.

2 Work-related decisions are made by the group, but there is little interaction related to ideas.

3 Information and ideas are shared, but there is little discussion concerned with advancing understanding.

4 The group clearly progresses in its thinking beyond where individual students could have gone.

Participation in Collaborative Inquiry (this rubric is applied to individual students)

1 Does not contribute ideas or information to team or class.

2 Makes contributions to Concept/Question Board or class discussions when specifically called upon to do so.

3 Occasionally contributes ideas or information to other students' inquiries.

4 Takes an active interest in the success of the whole class's knowledge-building efforts.

Informal Assessment

Self-Evaluation

- Give students the opportunity to evaluate their personal learning experiences during this unit by completing ***Inquiry Journal,*** pages 139–140.
- The students could also complete the self-evaluation questions on the ***Research Assistant CD–ROM.***

Name__________ Date______

Going West UNIT 5

Unit Wrap-Up

- How did you feel about this unit?
  - ☐ I enjoyed it very much. ☐ I liked it.
  - ☐ I liked some of it. ☐ I didn't like it.
- How would you rate the difficulty of this unit?
  - ☐ easy ☐ medium ☐ hard
- How would you rate your performance during this unit?
  - ☐ I learned a lot about the American West.
  - ☐ I learned some new things about the American West.
  - ☐ I didn't learn much about the American West.
- Why did you choose this rating?
  Answers will vary.
- What was the most interesting thing you learned about the American West?
  Answers will vary.
- Is there anything else about the American West that you would like to learn? What?
  Answers will vary.

Inquiry Journal • *Unit Wrap-Up* UNIT 5 139

Unit Wrap-Up *(continued)*

- What did you learn about the American West that you didn't know before?
  Answers will vary.
- What did you learn about yourself as a learner?
  Answers will vary.
- What do you need to work on as a learner?
  Answers will vary.
- What resources (books, films, magazines, interviews, other) did you use on your own during this unit? Which of these were the most helpful? Why?
  Answers will vary.

140 UNIT 5 *Unit Wrap-Up* • Inquiry Journal

Inquiry Journal pp. 139–140

Formal Assessment

Use these summative assessments along with your informal observations to assess student mastery.

Name ________ Date ________ Score ____

UNIT 5 Going West

Connecting Unit Selections

Read the following questions carefully. Then answer each one in complete sentences. You may want to refer back to the stories.

1. Native American life changed when the buffalo almost disappeared. Today, the buffalo is returning, but Native Americans have not gone back to their old way of life. Why is this true?
   The West has changed so much and Native American life has changed so much that they can never go back to the old ways.

2. How were the lives of Bill Pickett and other African-American cowboys similar to the lives of Native Americans?
   Both groups helped settle the West, and both groups suffered from prejudice. Native Americans lost their lands, and the African-American cowboys were not given an equal chance to own property.

END OF UNIT ASSESSMENT Short Answer

44 *Connecting Unit Selections* • Unit 5 Assessment

Unit 5 Assessment p. 44

Connecting Unit Selections *(continued)*

3. Many tall tales like "McBroom the Rainmaker" have come out of the West. Why do you think this is so?
   The American West is a place with huge mountains, deserts, rivers, and forests. It was a wild place until recently, and this is the type of place that leads to the creation of tall tales.

4. What do the stories in this unit say about the expansion of the West?
   Answers will vary.

END OF UNIT ASSESSMENT Short Answer

Unit 5 Assessment • *Connecting Unit Selections* 45

Unit 5 Assessment p. 45

Name ________ Date ________ Score ____

UNIT 5 Going West

Comprehension Assessment

Read the following selection and questions carefully. Then completely fill in the bubble of each correct answer.

Going West

A fire crackled cheerfully in the kitchen fireplace as Nathan, Isaac, Rachel, Mother, and Father sat down for dinner. Father seemed excited as he ladled stew into each bowl.

When everyone was served, he cleared his throat. "Your mother and I have some news. We are thinking about joining the wagon train going West."

Wide-eyed, Nathan and Isaac turned to one another and started whooping with excitement. Rachel, the youngest, was quiet. She was too young to understand what a trip like this meant.

"We could finally have some land of our own," said Mother.

Nathan stood up. "When do we start packing?" he asked.

"Sit down, young man," Father chuckled. "If we go, we'll need to pack very thoughtfully, keeping in mind we can only bring the bare essentials. We'd need a rifle so we could hunt for food and an axe to cut wood and clear land." Mother would bring a couple of pots and pans and her spinning wheel to make fabric for clothing.

They could only bring what fit in their wagon, which would be pulled by a pair of oxen. "The lighter you travel, the easier it is," Father said. Bess, their milk cow, and Jack, the family dog, would probably go along. Jack would help with hunting and would warn the family of danger.

They would need basics like blankets and a change of clothing as well as hearty foods that did not spoil, like cornmeal and dried meat. And seeds — they would have to remember to bring seeds for their crops.

"What do you think?" asked Father. "Should we go?" Without a moment's pause, everyone, even Rachel, said, "Yes!"

END OF UNIT ASSESSMENT Multiple Choice

46 *Comprehension Assessment* • Unit 5 Assessment

Unit 5 Assessment p. 46

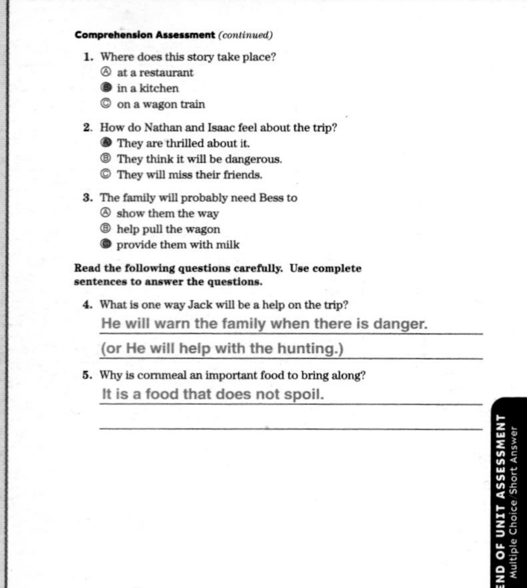

Comprehension Assessment *(continued)*

1. Where does this story take place?
   Ⓐ at a restaurant
   ● in a kitchen
   Ⓒ on a wagon train

2. How do Nathan and Isaac feel about the trip?
   ● They are thrilled about it.
   Ⓑ They think it will be dangerous.
   Ⓒ They will miss their friends.

3. The family will probably need Bess to
   Ⓐ show them the way
   Ⓑ help pull the wagon
   ● provide them with milk

Read the following questions carefully. Use complete sentences to answer the questions.

4. What is one way Jack will be a help on the trip?
   He will warn the family when there is danger. (or He will help with the hunting.)

5. Why is cornmeal an important food to bring along?
   It is a food that does not spoil.

END OF UNIT ASSESSMENT Multiple Choice/Short Answer

Unit 5 Assessment • *Comprehension Assessment* 47

Unit 5 Assessment p. 47

Name ________ Date ________ Score ____

UNIT 5 Going West

Spelling Assessment

Look for the underlined word that is spelled wrong. Fill in the bubble of the line with the misspelled word.

1. Ⓐ The leaders met to discuss world peace.
   ● She was an immigrent from Ireland.
   Ⓒ The army captured the fort.
   Ⓓ Correct as is.

2. Ⓕ The animals could die of starvation.
   ● Breakfast is an importent meal.
   Ⓗ The small print is not very distinct.
   Ⓙ Correct as is.

3. Ⓐ We heard that the meeting was canceled.
   Ⓑ Sudan is a nation in Africa.
   ● I don't mind scrambleing the eggs.
   Ⓓ Correct as is.

4. Ⓕ Her ankle ached when the weather was cold.
   Ⓖ This is the feistiest puppy in the litter.
   Ⓗ The number 20 is greater than 15.
   ● Correct as is.

5. ● All the traffic must go in one direcsion.
   Ⓑ The host poured us glasses of lemonade.
   Ⓒ The final coat of paint is a protectant.
   Ⓓ Correct as is.

6. Ⓕ Do not disturb the lions.
   Ⓖ The plane landed safely.
   ● She tied a colorful scarf around her waiste.
   Ⓙ Correct as is.

7. ● Dad was insistant that I clean my room.
   Ⓑ The goalie is good at catching the ball.
   Ⓒ I was ill for the duration of the trip.
   Ⓓ Correct as is.

8. Ⓕ The harshest storms were north of us.
   Ⓖ Iowa is closer to Chicago than to Maine.
   Ⓗ The loudest fans rooted for the home team.
   ● Correct as is.

9. Ⓐ A tidal wave causes much destruction.
   ● She was hesitent to jump.
   Ⓒ The food will go to waste if it's not eaten.
   Ⓓ Correct as is.

10. Ⓕ Bleach will make the stain disappear.
    Ⓖ She wore a plain, black dress to the funeral.
    Ⓗ He ran a distance of three miles.
    ● Correct as is.

END OF UNIT ASSESSMENT Multiple Choice

48 *Spelling Assessment* • Unit 5 Assessment

Unit 5 Assessment p. 48

Name ________ Date ________ Score ____

UNIT 5 Going West

Vocabulary Assessment

Read each sentence carefully. Then choose the answer in which the underlined word is used in the same way as it is in the sentence.

SAMPLE
My cousin can swim only one lap in the pool. **Which answer shows the word lap used in the same way as it is above?**
Ⓐ I put the napkin in my lap.
Ⓑ I watched the kitten lap up the milk.
● Carmen has one more lap to run.
Ⓓ Listen to the waves lap against the side of the boat.

1. She went to the bank to deposit the money she got for her birthday. **Which answer shows the word deposit used in the same way as it is above?**
   Ⓐ We saw calcium deposits deep inside the cave.
   Ⓑ He watched the river deposit sand on the bank.
   ● Sign that check before you deposit it into your account.
   Ⓓ The land contains a large deposit of coal.

2. The people sat in wooden rockers on the large front porch. **Which answer shows the word rockers used in the same way as it is above?**
   Ⓕ The fans screamed as the rockers came out on stage.
   Ⓖ The rockers used by the miners to search for gold were scattered everywhere.
   Ⓗ The rockers on the cradle needed to be fixed.
   ● There were several rockers in the nursery so mothers could sit with their babies.

3. The settlers traveled hundreds of miles to prospect this land for gold. **Which answer shows the word prospect used in the same way as it is above?**
   ● The old, bearded man had come to Alaska years ago to prospect.
   Ⓑ This student is a good prospect for being admitted into college.
   Ⓒ The prospect of going to Europe excited her.
   Ⓓ The young prospect wore a tie to his interview.

END OF UNIT ASSESSMENT Multiple Choice

Unit 5 Assessment • *Vocabulary Assessment* 49

Unit 5 Assessment p. 49

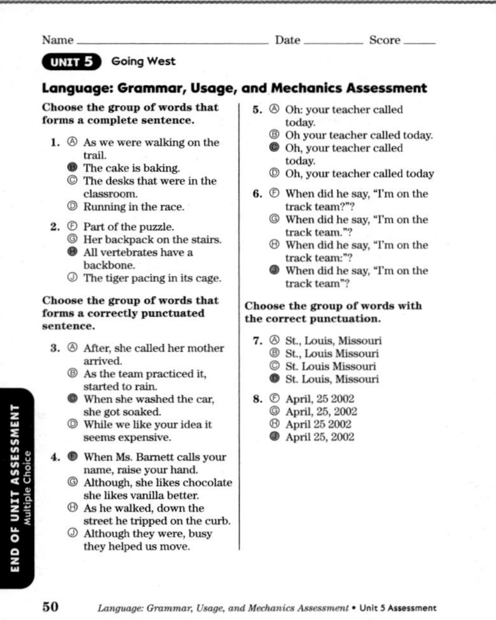

Name ______________ Date ______ Score ______

UNIT 5 Going West

Language: Grammar, Usage, and Mechanics Assessment

Choose the group of words that forms a complete sentence.

1. Ⓐ As we were walking on the trail.
   ● The cake is baking.
   Ⓒ The desks that were in the classroom.
   Ⓓ Running in the race.
2. Ⓕ Part of the puzzle.
   Ⓖ Her backpack on the stairs.
   ● All vertebrates have a backbone.
   Ⓙ The tiger pacing in its cage.

Choose the group of words that forms a correctly punctuated sentence.

3. Ⓐ After, she called her mother arrived.
   Ⓑ As the team practiced it, started to rain.
   ● When she washed the car, she got soaked.
   Ⓓ While we like your idea it seems expensive.
4. ● When Ms. Barnett calls your name, raise your hand.
   Ⓖ Although, she likes chocolate she likes vanilla better.
   Ⓗ As he walked, down the street he tripped on the curb.
   Ⓙ Although they were, busy they helped us move.
5. Ⓐ Oh: your teacher called today.
   Ⓑ Oh your teacher called today.
   ● Oh, your teacher called today.
   Ⓓ Oh, your teacher called today
6. Ⓕ When did he say, "I'm on the track team?"?
   Ⓖ When did he say, "I'm on the track team."?
   Ⓗ When did he say, "I'm on the track team:"?
   ● When did he say, "I'm on the track team"?

Choose the group of words with the correct punctuation.

7. Ⓐ St., Louis, Missouri
   Ⓑ St., Louis Missouri
   Ⓒ St. Louis Missouri
   ● St. Louis, Missouri
8. Ⓕ April, 25 2002
   Ⓖ April, 25, 2002
   Ⓗ April 25 2002
   ● April 25, 2002

END OF UNIT ASSESSMENT Multiple Choice

50 *Language: Grammar, Usage, and Mechanics Assessment* • Unit 5 Assessment

Unit 5 Assessment p. 50

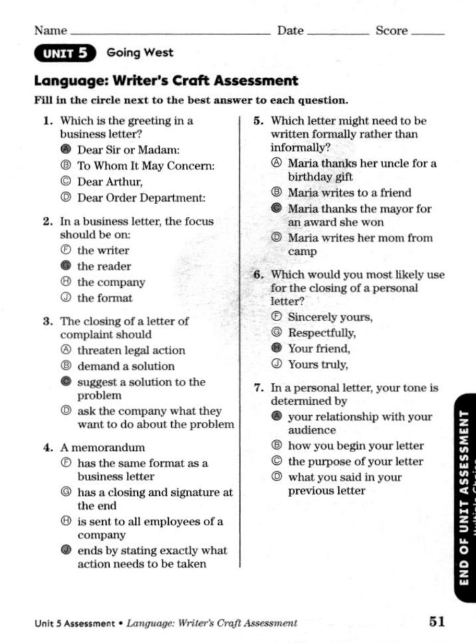

Name ______________ Date ______ Score ______

UNIT 5 Going West

Language: Writer's Craft Assessment

Fill in the circle next to the best answer to each question.

1. Which is the greeting in a business letter?
   ● Dear Sir or Madam:
   Ⓑ To Whom It May Concern:
   Ⓒ Dear Arthur,
   Ⓓ Dear Order Department:
2. In a business letter, the focus should be on:
   Ⓕ the writer
   ● the reader
   Ⓗ the company
   Ⓙ the format
3. The closing of a letter of complaint should
   Ⓐ threaten legal action
   Ⓑ demand a solution
   ● suggest a solution to the problem
   Ⓓ ask the company what they want to do about the problem
4. A memorandum
   Ⓕ has the same format as a business letter
   Ⓖ has a closing and signature at the end
   Ⓗ is sent to all employees of a company
   ● ends by stating exactly what action needs to be taken
5. Which letter might need to be written formally rather than informally?
   Ⓐ Maria thanks her uncle for a birthday gift
   Ⓑ Maria writes to a friend
   ● Maria thanks the mayor for an award she won
   Ⓓ Maria writes her mom from camp
6. Which would you most likely use for the closing of a personal letter?
   Ⓕ Sincerely yours,
   Ⓖ Respectfully,
   ● Your friend,
   Ⓙ Yours truly,
7. In a personal letter, your tone is determined by
   ● your relationship with your audience
   Ⓑ how you begin your letter
   Ⓒ the purpose of your letter
   Ⓓ what you said in your previous letter

END OF UNIT ASSESSMENT Multiple Choice

Unit 5 Assessment • *Language: Writer's Craft Assessment* 51

Unit 5 Assessment p. 51

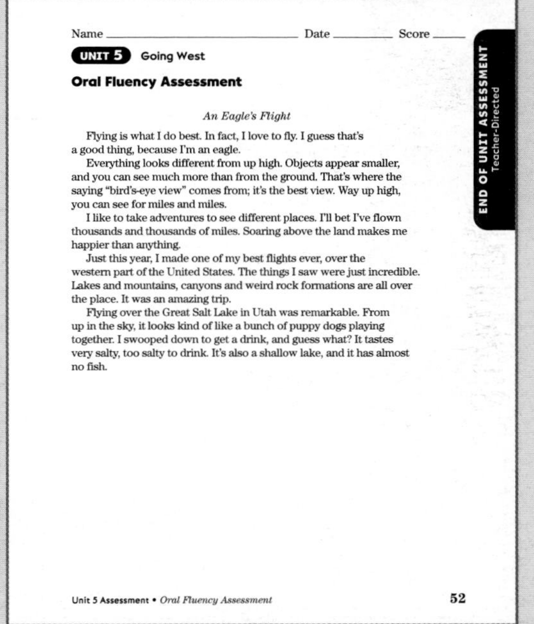

Name ______________ Date ______ Score ______

UNIT 5 Going West

Oral Fluency Assessment

An Eagle's Flight

Flying is what I do best. In fact, I love to fly. I guess that's a good thing, because I'm an eagle.

Everything looks different from up high. Objects appear smaller, and you can see much more than from the ground. That's where the saying "bird's-eye view" comes from; it's the best view. Way up high, you can see for miles and miles.

I like to take adventures to see different places. I'll bet I've flown thousands and thousands of miles. Soaring above the land makes me happier than anything.

Just this year, I made one of my best flights ever, over the western part of the United States. The things I saw were just incredible. Lakes and mountains, canyons and weird rock formations are all over the place. It was an amazing trip.

Flying over the Great Salt Lake in Utah was remarkable. From up in the sky, it looks kind of like a bunch of puppy dogs playing together. I swooped down to get a drink, and guess what? It tastes very salty, too salty to drink. It's also a shallow lake, and it has almost no fish.

END OF UNIT ASSESSMENT Teacher-Directed

Unit 5 Assessment • *Oral Fluency Assessment* 52

Unit 5 Assessment p. 52

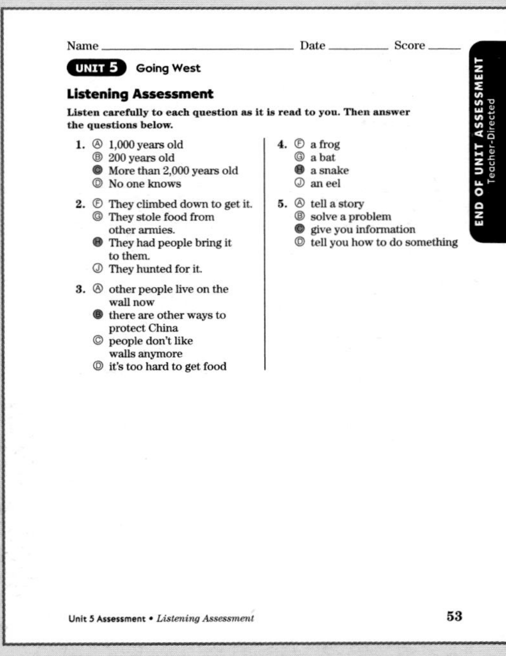

Name ______________ Date ______ Score ______

UNIT 5 Going West

Listening Assessment

Listen carefully to each question as it is read to you. Then answer the questions below.

1. Ⓐ 1,000 years old
   Ⓑ 200 years old
   ● More than 2,000 years old
   Ⓓ No one knows
2. Ⓕ They climbed down to get it.
   Ⓖ They stole food from other armies.
   ● They had people bring it to them.
   Ⓙ They hunted for it.
3. Ⓐ other people live on the wall now
   ● there are other ways to protect China
   Ⓒ people don't like walls anymore
   Ⓓ it's too hard to get food
4. Ⓕ a frog
   Ⓖ a bat
   ● a snake
   Ⓙ an eel
5. Ⓐ tell a story
   Ⓑ solve a problem
   ● give you information
   Ⓓ tell you how to do something

END OF UNIT ASSESSMENT Teacher-Directed

Unit 5 Assessment • *Listening Assessment* 53

Unit 5 Assessment p. 53

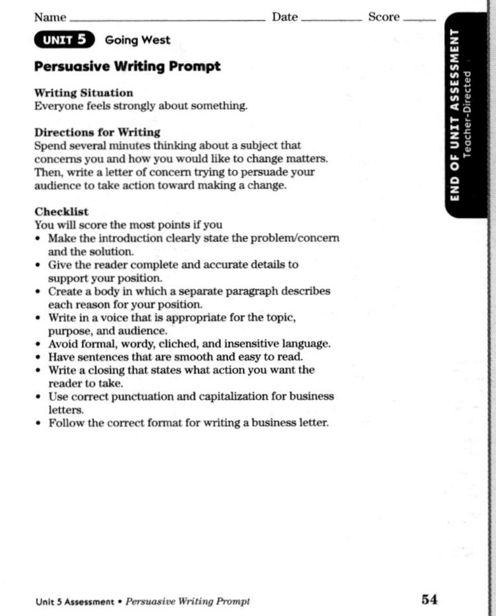

Name ______________ Date ______ Score ______

UNIT 5 Going West

Persuasive Writing Prompt

Writing Situation
Everyone feels strongly about something.

Directions for Writing
Spend several minutes thinking about a subject that concerns you and how you would like to change matters. Then, write a letter of concern trying to persuade your audience to take action toward making a change.

Checklist
You will score the most points if you
- Make the introduction clearly state the problem/concern and the solution.
- Give the reader complete and accurate details to support your position.
- Create a body in which a separate paragraph describes each reason for your position.
- Write in a voice that is appropriate for the topic, purpose, and audience.
- Avoid formal, wordy, clichéd, and insensitive language.
- Have sentences that are smooth and easy to read.
- Write a closing that states what action you want the reader to take.
- Use correct punctuation and capitalization for business letters.
- Follow the correct format for writing a business letter.

END OF UNIT ASSESSMENT Teacher-Directed

Unit 5 Assessment • *Persuasive Writing Prompt* 54

Unit 5 Assessment p. 54

Also included:

- Writing Rubrics (Four Point and Six Point)
- Writing Portfolio Assessment and Rubrics
- Directions for Listening Assessment
- Teacher's Record of Oral Fluency
- Formal Assessment Record

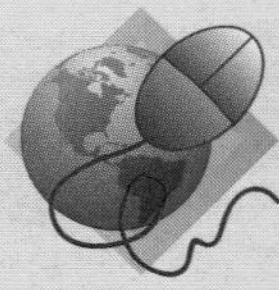

Online Assessment **for *Open Court Reading*** helps teachers differentiate classroom instruction based on students' scores from the weekly and end-of-unit assessments. It provides exercises best suited to meet the needs of each student. For more information visit SRAonline.com.

Responding to Results

Differentiating Instruction Support Activities is designed for students who need quick alternative activities to strengthen or extend their skills.

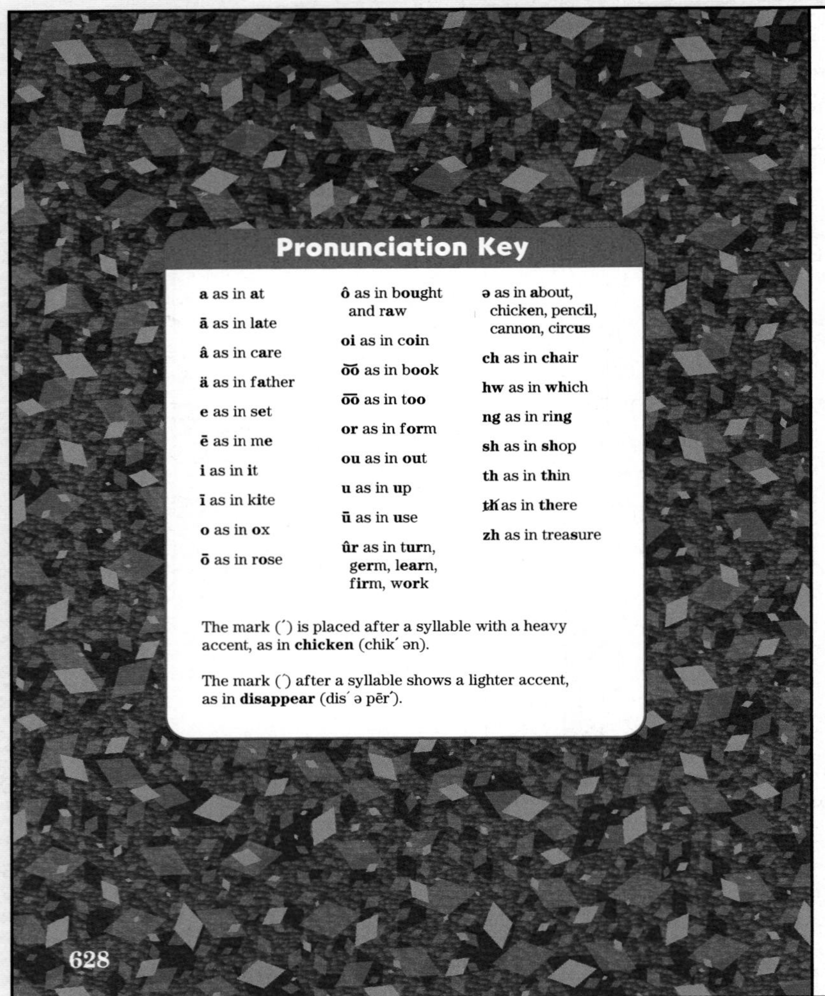

Glossary

A

abacus (a´ bə kəs) *n.* A tool used to figure math problems by sliding counters.
abandon (ə ban´ dən) *v.* Leave something behind forever.
accomplish (ə kom´ plish) *v.* Do something successfully.
accuracy (a´ kyə rə sē) *n.* Freedom from errors or mistakes; correctness.
ace (ās) *v.* To easily get all or most answers correct.
acquit (ə kwit´) *v.* Conduct oneself well, even in a stressful situation.
adjacent (ə jā´ sənt) *adj.* Next to; touching.
adjourn (ə jûrn´) *v.* Bring to a temporary end; end for the present.
admission (əd mish´ ən) *n.* The price paid to attend an event.
adobe (ə dō´ bē) *n.* Sun-dried brick.
adventure (əd ven´ chər) *n.* A fun or exciting experience.
agate (a´ gət) *n.* A striped marble.
aimlessly (ām´ ləs lē) *adv.* Without purpose or direction.
alder (ôl´ dər) *n.* A tree in the birch family.
align (ə līn´) *v.* To place in a straight line.
alignment (ə līn´ mənt) *n.* The arrangement of things in a straight line.
altitude (al´ tə to͞od) *n.* How high something is above Earth.
amiss (ə mis´) *adv.* Wrong; not as expected.
ample (am´ pəl) *adj.* More than enough.
ancestor (an´ ses tər) *n.* A person from whom one is descended.
anticipation (an tisˊ ə pā´ shən) *n.* A feeling of looking forward to something.
apparatus (a´ pə ra´ təs) *n.* A piece of equipment that has a particular use.
appetite (ap´ ə tīt) *n.* Desire for food.
apprehension (apˊ ri hen´ shən) *n.* Fear.
apprentice (ə pren´ tis) *v.* To bind oneself to a craft worker in order to learn a trade.—*n.* A person learning a trade or an art.
apt (apt´) *adj.* Inclined; likely.
arc (ärk) *v.* To move in a curved line. —*n.* A curve.

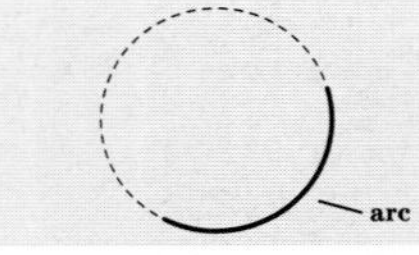

Word Derivations

Below are some words related to *arc.*

arcade	arcading	arcing
arcaded	arced	arcs

archaeoastronomy (ärˊ kē ō ə stron´ ə mē) *n.* The study of ancient astronomical observatories.

629

Pronunciation Key: at; lāte; câre; fäther; set; mē; it; kīte; ox; rōse; ô in bought; coin; bo͝ok; to͞o; form; out; up; ūse; tûrn; ə sound in about, chicken, pencil, cannon, circus; chair; hw in which; ring; shop; thin; t͟here; zh in treasure.

archaeology or **archeology** (är´ kē ol´ ə jē) *n.* The scientific study of people of the past by digging up things they left behind.

Word History

Archaeology, or **archeology,** came into English in the year 1837. It is from the Latin word *archaeologia,* meaning "knowledge gained through the study of ancient objects." This Latin word's origins are with the Greek words *archē,* meaning "beginning," and *logos,* meaning "word."

arm (ärm) *v.* Prepare for war; make weapons ready for use.
aroma (ə rō´ mə) *n.* A smell or odor, usually pleasant.
artifice (är´ tə fis) *n.* A clever trick in the way a story's plot is constructed.
artisan (är´ tə zən) *n.* A person who works at a craft that requires artistic skill or working with the hands.
ascend (ə send´) *v.* To climb up; to rise.

Word Derivations

Below are some words related to *ascend.*

ascension	ascendant	ascent
ascending	ascender	ascendible

ashamed (ə shāmd´) *adj.* Embarrassed; not proud.
astronomical (as´ trə nom´ i kəl) *adj.* Having to do with the study of the stars and planets.
astronomy (ə stron´ ə mē) *n.* The scientific study of stars and planets.
athletic (ath le´ tik) *adj.* Having skill and strength in sports and other physical activities.
atmosphere (at´ mə sfir´) *n.* The gases that surround a planet or moon.

Word History

Atmosphere came into English in the year 1677. It is from the New Latin word *atmosphaera,* which was made from the Greek word *atmos* and the Latin word *sphaera. Atmos* means "vapor," and *sphaera* means "sphere."

attendant (ə ten´ dənt) *n.* A person who waits on someone.
attitude (a´ tə to͞od´) *n.* A way of thinking, acting, or behaving.
avert (ə vûrt´) *v.* To avoid.

B

bamboo (bam´ bo͞o´) *n.* A tropical, grass plant with long, stiff, hollow stems.
bandana (ban dan´ ə) *n.* A large, colorful handkerchief.
barrack (bar´ ək) *n.* A building where soldiers live.
bastion (bas´ chən) *n.* A part of a fortified structure that juts out so that defenders can fire at attackers from several angles.

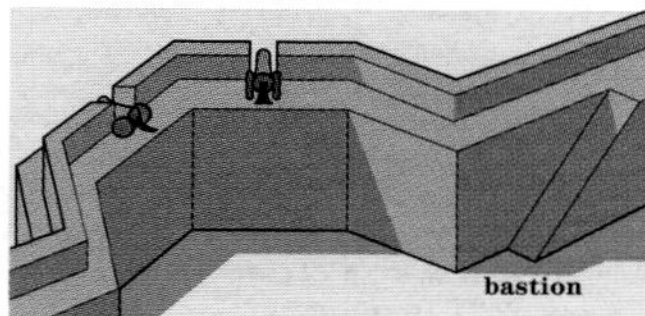

beanie (bē´ nē) *n.* A small bill-less cap worn on the crown of the head.
bedclothes (bed´ klōz) *n.* Items used to cover a bed, such as sheets, blankets, and quilts.
bedrock (bed´ rok) *n.* Solid rock.
benevolent (bə nev´ ə lənt) *adj.* Kind; generous.
berate (bi rāt´) *v.* To scold harshly.
bice (bīs) *adj.* Blue or blue-green.
biologist (bī o´ lə jəst) *n.* A person who studies plant and animal life specific to certain environments.
blemish (blem´ ish) *n.* A stain; a defect.
blintze (blints) *n.* Cheese or fruit wrapped in a thin pancake.
bloody (blu´ dē) *adj.* A word used to indicate an extremely negative feeling.
body (bo´ dē) *n.* An object such as a star or asteroid.
bombard (bom´ bärd) *n.* A leather jug or bottle.
booklet (bo͝ok´ lət) *n.* A small book, usually with a paper cover.
bore (bor) *v.* To drill into; to pierce.
bow (bou) *n.* The front part of a ship.

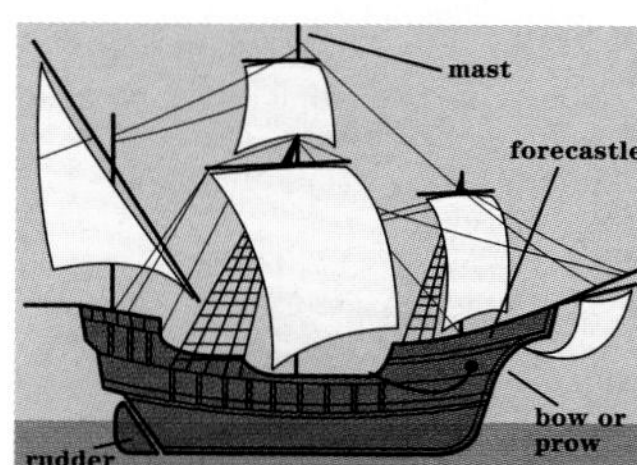

Word History

Bow came into English about 500 years ago. It probably came from the Dutch word *boech,* meaning "bow" or "shoulder." It is also related to *bōg,* a word meaning "bough" (a large tree branch) that dates back more than 800 years.

boycott (boi´ kot´) *v.* Join with others in refusing to buy from or deal with a person, nation, or business.
brazen (brā´ zən) *adj.* Bold; cocky.
breach (brēch) *n.* A violation of a law or agreement.
break (brāk) *v.* To tame a horse.
breakwater (brāk´ wô´ tər) *n.* Any structure that protects a harbor or beach from damage by waves.
brocade (brō kād´) *n.* Woven cloth that has a raised pattern.
bronc (bronk) *n.* A wild or poorly broken horse.
brushpopper (brush´ po pər) *n.* A person who works in an area covered with low-growing bushes and weeds.
bulldog (bo͝ol´ dôg´) *v.* To wrestle a steer, usually by grabbing its horns and twisting its neck.
buttress (bu´ tris) *n.* A structure built outside a wall to give the wall support.

C

cairn (kârn) *n.* A pile of stones left as a landmark or a monument.

Pronunciation Key: **a**t; l**ā**te; c**â**re; f**ä**ther; s**e**t; m**ē**; **i**t; k**ī**te; **o**x; r**ō**se; **ô** in b**ough**t; c**oi**n; b**o͝o**k; t**o͞o**; f**o**rm; **ou**t; **u**p; **ū**se; t**û**rn; **ə** sound in **a**bout, chick**e**n, penc**i**l, cann**o**n, circ**u**s; **ch**air; **hw** in **wh**ich; ri**ng**; **sh**op; **th**in; **th**ere; **zh** in trea**s**ure.

calculation (kal´ kyə lā´ shən) *n.* 1. Counting, computing, or figuring. 2. The result of counting, computing, or figuring.
campaign (kam pān´) *n.* A series of actions planned and carried out to bring about a particular result; an organized effort to accomplish a purpose.
candidate (kan´ də dāt´) *n.* A person who is seeking an office, job, or position.
canyon (kan´ yən) *n.* A deep, narrow valley with high, steep sides.
capable (kā´ pə bəl) *adj.* Skilled or able to do something well.
capsule (kap´ səl) *n.* The top part of a rocket that is self-contained and holds astronauts and equipment.

capsize (kap´ sīz) *v.* To turn upside down.
captivity (kap ti´ və tē) *n.* Being held as prisoner.
carbon dating (kär´ bən dā´ ting) *v.* Using carbon 14 to find out the age of old material.
carcass (kär´ kəs) *n.* The body of a dead animal.
caribou (kar´ ə bo͞o´) *n.* A reindeer.
cease (sēs) *v.* Bring an activity or action to an end.
celandine (sel´ ən dīn´) *n.* A plant in the buttercup family with single yellow flowers.
celestial (sə les´ chəl) *adj.* Relating to the sky.
ceremonial (ser´ ə mō´ nē əl) *adj.* Having to do with a formal celebration.
chance (chans) *v.* To take a risk and try something difficult.
challenge (chal´ ənj) *n.* Something that may be difficult to do.
chaparral (shap´ ə ral´) *n.* An area thick with shrubs and small trees.
cheder (kā´ dər) *n.* Religious school for teaching Judaism.
chives (chīvz) *n.* A food seasoning made from the leaves of a plant related to the onion.
cinder (sin´ dər) *n.* Ash or a piece of partially burnt coal or wood.
circumference (sər kum´ fər əns) *n.* The line that defines a circle.
claim (klām) *n.* A section of land declared as belonging to one person or group of people.
clamber (klam´ bər) *v.* To climb with difficulty.
clarify (klâr´ ə fī´) *v.* To make something clear; to explain.
cloister (kloi´ stər) *n.* A place where religious people live away from the world; a convent or a monastery.
cobbler (kob´ lər) *n.* A person who repairs shoes and boots.
collards (käl´ ərds) *n.* A green, leafy vegetable.
collide (kə līd´) *v.* Crash.

colonel (kûr´ nəl) *n.* A military officer; ranking between lieutenant and general.
commence (kə mens´) *v.* To begin.

Word History

Commence came into English about 600 years ago. It came from the French word *comencer*, and its assumed origin is the Latin word *cominitiare*. This Latin word is a derivative of *initiare*, meaning "to initiate." (Also note that the word *commence* contains the *-ence* suffix, which in this word means "the action of" or "the process of.")

commission (kə mi´ shən) *n.* An important task or assignment.
commotion (kə mō´ shən) *n.* Noise; excitement; disturbance.
communal (kə mū´ nəl) *adj.* Public; shared by all.
compassion (kəm pash´ ən) *n.* Sympathy; pity.
composition (kom´ pə zish´ ən) *n.* What something is made of.
comrade (kom´ rad´) *n.* Friend; companion.
concave (kon kāv´) *adj.* Curved inward; hollow; like the inner curve of a contact lens.

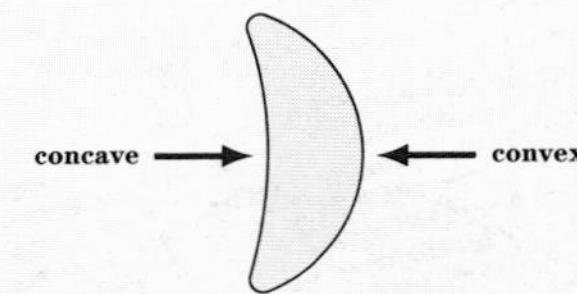

conceive (kən sēv´) *v.* 1. To start something with a certain point of view. 2. To understand.
conciliatory (kən sil´ ē ə tor´ ē) *adj.* Causing peace to be made.
condense (kən dens´) *v.* Change the physical state of something from a gas to a liquid or solid.
confederation (kən fe´ də rā´ shən) *n.* The act of joining states together for a common purpose.
confetti (kən fet´ ē) *n.* Tiny pieces of colored paper that are thrown during celebrations.
confidence (kon´ fə dəns) *n.* A belief in one's ability to do something.
confine (kən fīn´) *v.* 1. To limit. 2. To keep in a place.
confounded (kon foun´ did) *adj.* Darned.
confront (kən frunt´) *v.* To face.

Word Derivations

Below are some words related to *confront.*
confronter confrontation confrontational confrontationist confrontal

congress (kong´ gris) *n.* An assembly of people who make laws.
constellation (kon´ stə lā´ shən) *n.* A group of stars that form shapes in the sky.
constituent (kən stich´ wənt) *n.* A voter in a particular area.
constitution (kon´ sti to͞o´ shən) *n.* The basic principles used to govern a state, country, or organization.
content (kən tent´) *adj.* Happy or satisfied.
contest (kon´ test) *n.* A competition.
convention (kən ven´ shən) *n.* A formal meeting for some special purpose.

Pronunciation Key: at; lāte; câre; fäther; set; mē; it; kīte; ox; rōse; ô in bought; coin; bŏŏk; tōō; form; out; up; ūse; tûrn; ə sound in about, chicken, pencil, cannon, circus; chair; hw in which; ring; shop; thin; there; zh in treasure.

convex (kon veks′) *adj.* Curved outward; like the outer curve of a contact lens.
conveyor belt (kən vā′ ər belt′) *n.* A device with a large looping belt used to move objects.
cordially (kor′ jə lē) *adj.* Sincerely; pleasantly.
corn pone (korn′ pōn′) *n.* Baked or fried corn bread.
cotangent (kō tan′ jənt) *n.* A term used in trigonometry.
course (kors) *v.* To flow.
cradleboard (krād′ l bord′) *n.* A wooden frame that Native American women wore on their backs to carry their babies.

cringe (krinj) *v.* To back away from something unpleasant; to physically shrink because of fear or excessive humility.
croaker-sack (krō′ kər sak) *n.* A sack usually made of burlap.
cultivate (kul′ tə vāt′) *v.* To till the ground; to grow crops.
curvilinear (kur′ və li′ nē ər) *adj.* Having rounded or curving lines.

D

decipher (dē sī′ fər) *v.* To read or translate something written in code; decode.
deduction (di duk′ shən) *n.* A fact or conclusion figured out by reasoning.
defeatist (di fē′ təst) *adj.* Expecting and accepting that one will lose or be defeated.
defect (di fekt′) *v.* To leave one's home country for another.
defiance (di fī′ əns) *n.* Bold refusal to obey or respect authority.
dehydration (dē′ hī drā′ shən) *n.* Loss of water in the body.
delegation (del′ i gā′ shēn) *n.* A group of people chosen to act for others; representatives.
deliberately (di li′ bə rət lē) *adv.* On purpose; meaning to.

Word History

Deliberately came into English about 500 years ago. It is the adverb form of the word *deliberate*, which came from the Latin word *deliberare*, meaning "to consider carefully." It is assumed that the Latin word *libra*, meaning "pound" or "scale," is also in its word history. This brings to mind the modern figure of speech "to weigh one's options." (Also note that *deliberately* contains the *-ly* suffix, which in this word means "in the manner of being.")

delta (del′ tə) *n.* Land formed at the mouth of a river by sediment carried in the water.

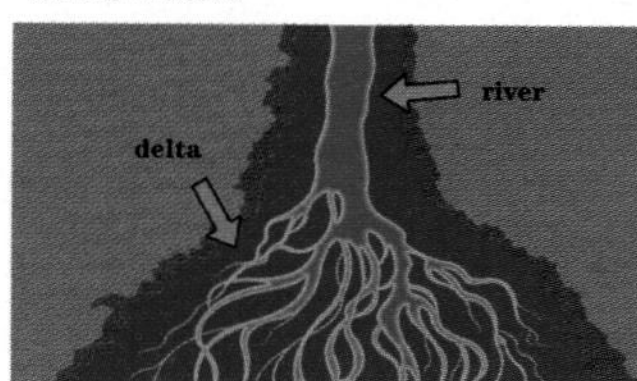

demolish (di mol′ ish) *v.* To do away with.
denounce (di nouns′) *v.* Openly condemn; declare disapproval.
deposits (di poz′ its) *n.* Valuables put away for safekeeping, as in a bank.
depredation (dep′ ri dā′ shən) *n.* The act of attacking and robbing.
descent (di sent′) *n.* A coming from a higher place to a lower one.
desert (dez′ ərt) *n.* A place where little or no rain falls.
deserted (də zər′ təd) *adj.* Not lived in; abandoned.
desist (di sist′) *v.* To stop.
desolation (des′ ə lā′ shən) *n.* Deserted condition.
desperation (des′ pə rā′ shən) *n.* A hopeless feeling, when you are ready to try anything to help the situation.
despotism (des′ pə ti′ zəm) *n.* A government run by a tyrannical ruler.
dialect (dī′ ə lekt′) *n.* A form of language that is spoken in a particular area or by a particular group of people.
diligence (dil′ i jens) *n.* Steady effort put forth to accomplish a task.

Word History

Diligence came into English about 600 years ago. It is a derivative of the word *diligent*, which has origins in the French word *diligere*, meaning "to love" or "to esteem." *Diligere* can also be divided into the word parts *di-*, meaning "apart," and *legere*, meaning "to select." (Also note that *diligence* contains the *-ence* suffix, which in this word means "the quality of" or "the state of.")

diminish (di min′ ish) *v.* To decrease; to lessen; to get smaller.
din (din) *n.* Clamor; uproar; racket.
diplomacy (di plō′ mə sē) *n.* The handling of relations between nations.
discernible (di sûrn′ ə bəl) *adj.* Easy to recognize as different.
disconsolately (dis kon′ sə lit lē) *adv.* In a very unhappy way; hopelessly.
disembodied (dis′ em bod′ ēd) *adj.* Without a body.
dismay (dis mā′) *n.* A sudden feeling of disappointment.
disown (di sōn′) *v.* To deny a connection to; to refuse to admit a relationship to.
distinct (di stingkt′) *adj.* 1. Clear; plain. 2. Separate.
district (dis′ trikt) *n.* A region that is part of some larger entity such as a city or county.
document (dok′ yə mənt) *n.* A written or printed statement that gives official proof and information about something.
dogie (dō′ gē) *n.* A calf with no mother.
domesticated (də mes′ ti kāt′ əd) *adj.* Able to exist closely with humans.

Pronunciation Key: **at**; **lāte**; **câre**; **fäther**; **set**; **mē**; **it**; **kīte**; **ox**; **rōse**; **ô** in **bought**; **coin**; **bo͝ok**; **to͞o**; **form**; **out**; **up**; **ūse**; **tûrn**; **ə** sound in **a**bout, chick**e**n, penc**i**l, cann**o**n, circ**u**s; **ch**air; **hw** in **wh**ich; **ring**; **sh**op; **th**in; **th**ere; **zh** in trea**s**ure.

downpour (doun′ pôr′) *n.* A heavy rain.
dramatization (dram′ ə tə zā′ shən) *n.* An acting out of a story.
draught (draft) *n. chiefly British.* A liquid that is drunk; a dose.
dribble (dri′ bəl) *v.* In soccer, to move a ball down the field with a series of short, controlled kicks.
drill (dril) *n.* An exercise to increase mental or physical skills.
drought (drout) *n.* Dry weather that lasts a very long time.
dubiously (do͞o′ bē əs lē) *adv.* In a doubtful way.
dumpling (dum′ pling) *n.* A small pocket of dough filled with a meat or vegetable mixture and cooked by steaming or boiling it.
dwindle (dwin′ dl) *v.* To get smaller gradually.

E

eclipse (i klips′) *v.* To become more important than; to cover over.
ecstatically (ek stat′ ik lē) *adv.* With great joy.
eddy (ed′ ē) *n.* A small, circling current of water.
edible (ed′ ə bəl) *adj.* Eatable.
election (i lek′ shən) *n.* The act of choosing, by voting, someone to serve in an office, or whether to accept an idea.

Word History

Election came into English in the 1200s. *Election* is a derivative of the word *elect*, which came from the Latin word *electus*. The word *electus* was the past participle of *eligere*, which means "to select." *Eligere* was formed by adding *e-* to *legere*, which means "to choose." (Also note that *election* contains the Latin suffix *-tion*, which in this word means "the act or process of.")

elector (i lek′ tər) *n.* A qualified voter.
embarrassed (im bar′ əsd) *adj.* Feeling bad or silly about something one has done.
embellish (em bel′ ish) *v.* To make something better or more beautiful by adding to it.
emphatically (em fat′ ik lē) *adv.* With spoken firmness or force.
employee (em ploi′ ē′) *n.* One who works for pay.
encampment (en kamp′ mənt) *n.* A camp; a temporary stopping place.
encompass (en kum′ pəs) *v.* To include.
encounter (en koun′ tər) *v.* To meet by chance.
endurance (en dûr′ əns) *n.* The power to put up with hardships or difficulties.
energy (e′ nər jē) *n.* The strength or eagerness to work or do things.
enthusiastic (in tho͞o′ zē as′ tik) *adj.* Filled with excitement.

Equator (i kwā′ tər) *n.* The imaginary line that circles Earth's center; it is perpendicular to Earth's axis and equally distant from Earth's North and South Poles.

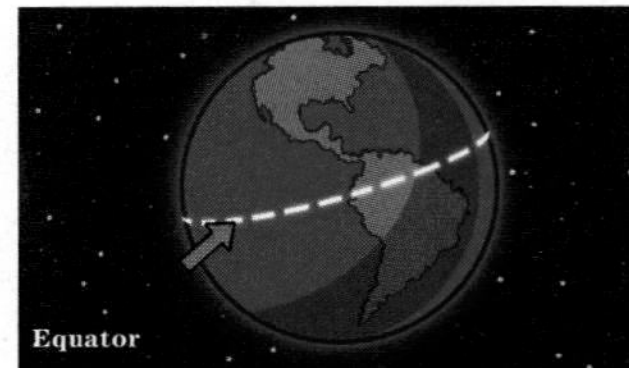
Equator

equinox (ē′ kwə noks′) *n.* The two times of the year when day and night are equal in length.

Word History

Equinox came to English in the 1300s. It came from the Anglo-French word *equinocce*, which came from the Middle Latin word *equinoxium*. *Equinoxium* is a version of the Latin word *aequinoctium*. In *aequinoctium*, *aequi-* means "equal," and *noct-* is taken from the word *nox*, which means "night."

era (er′ ə) *n.* A period of time or of history, often beginning or ending with an historical event.
ermine (ûr′ min) *n.* A valuable white fur; the winter white fur coat of some weasels.
escort (e skort′) *v.* To go with and help or protect.
establish (i stab′ lish) *v.* To settle in a place.

Word Derivations

Below are some words related to *establish*.
establishable establisher establishment established establishes

estate (i stāt′) *n.* A large piece of land owned by one individual or family.
eternal (i tûr′ nl) *adj.* Everlasting; always; endless.
ewe (ū) *n.* A female sheep.
excursion (ik skûr′ zhən) *n.* A pleasure trip; an outing.
exhausted (ig zô′ stəd) *adj.* Very tired.
explorer (ik splor′ ər) *n.* A person who goes to a place one knows nothing about.
extraordinary (ik stror′ dən âr′ ē) *adj.* Unusual or amazing.

F

facility (fə sil′ ə tē) *n.* A place, such as a building, that serves a certain purpose.
Fahrenheit (fâr′ ən hīt) *adj.* Relating to a system for measuring temperature where water freezes at 32 degrees and water boils at 212 degrees.
fare (fâr) *n.* The cost to ride a bus, taxi, or other means of transportation.
feat (fēt) *n.* An act or deed that shows great courage, strength, or skill.
federal (fed′ ər əl) *adj.* Formed by an agreement of states or provinces to join together as one nation.
feisty (fī′ stē) *adj.* Having a lively and aggressive personality.

Pronunciation Key: **a**t; **lā**te; **câ**re; **fä**ther; **s**et; **mē**; **i**t; **kī**te; **o**x; **rō**se; **ô** in b**ou**ght; **coi**n; **bo͝o**k; **to͞o**; **fo**rm; **ou**t; **u**p; **ū**se; **tû**rn; **ə** sound in **a**bout, chick**e**n, penc**i**l, cann**o**n, circ**u**s; **ch**air; **hw** in **wh**ich; ri**ng**; **sh**op; **th**in; **th**ere; **zh** in trea**s**ure.

fervently (fûr′ vənt lē) *adv.* With great feeling; with emotion.
fidelity (fi del′ i tē) *n.* Faithfulness to duties or promises.
fife (fīf) *n.* A musical instrument like a flute that makes a high, clear sound and is often used with drums in a marching band.
floe (flō) *n.* A large sheet of floating ice.
flounder (floun′ dər) *v.* To struggle.—*n.* A type of flatfish that is good to eat.
forlornly (for lorn′ lē) *adv.* Sadly; hopelessly.

Word History

Forlornly is the adverb form of the word *forlorn,* which came into English more than 800 years ago. It is a derivative of the word *forlēosan,* which means "to lose." (Also note that *forlornly* contains the *-ly* suffix, which in this word means "in the manner of being.")

formation (for mā′ shən) *n.* A particular arrangement.
foundry (foun′ drē) *n.* A place where metal is melted and formed.
frantic (fran′ tik) *adj.* Very worried and afraid.
frantically (fran′ ti klē) *adv.* Quickly in a worried way.
frequency (frē′ kwən sē) *n.* The number of times something happens within a set period of time.
frigate (frig′ it) *n.* A type of tropical seabird with a hooked beak, webbed feet, and long wings and tail feathers.

frigate

fume (fūm) *v.* To mumble something in an angry or irritated way.
furrow (fûr′ ō) *n.* A trench cut by a plow.
fuse (fūz) *v.* To join together by melting.

G

gable (gā′ bəl) *n.* A part of a wall that is enclosed by sloping sides of a roof, making a triangle-shaped section on a building.
galaxy (gal′ ək sē) *n.* A large group of stars, dust, and gas.
gallinipper (gal′ ə nip′ ər) *n. informal.* Any of several insects that sting or bite.
garrison (gâr′ i sən) *n.* A military post or station.
genuine (jen′ yə wən) *adj.* Real.
geologist (jē o′ lə jist) *n.* A person who studies the solid matter on a moon or planet.
ginger (jin′ jər) *n.* A strong tasting spice made from ground ginger root.
gizzard (gi′ zərd) *n.* Intestine.
globular (glob′ yə lər) *adj.* Having the shape of a globe.

gore (gor) *v.* To pierce with an animal's horn or tusk.
gourd (gord) *n.* A melon-shaped fruit that can be dried and used as a bowl.
grenadier (gren′ ə dēr′) *n.* A soldier on foot; an infantry soldier.
groschen (grō′ shən) *n.* A form of money worth 1/100 of a schilling. (A schilling is worth about 7½ cents.)
grozing iron (grō′ zing ī′ ərn) *n.* A steel tool for cutting glass.
grueling (gro͞o′ ə ling) *adj.* Very difficult or exhausting.
guide (gīd) *v.* Lead someone along a path or to show the way.

Word Derivations

Below are some words related to *guide.*

guidance	guideline	guidebook
guidable	guide word	guider

H

haberdasher (ha′ bər da′ shər) *n. chiefly British.* One who sells men's clothing.
haint (hānt) *n.* A ghost.
hamlet (ham′ lit) *n.* A small village.
haughtily (hô′ təl ē) *adv.* In an overly proud way.
headquarters (hed′ kwor′ tərz) *n.* A center of operations where leaders work and give orders; a main office.
healer (hē′ lər) *n.* A doctor.
heavens (he′ vəns) *n.* The sky as viewed from earth.
hemisphere (hem′ ə sfir) *n.* Half of a sphere that results from cutting it through the center with a horizontal plane.

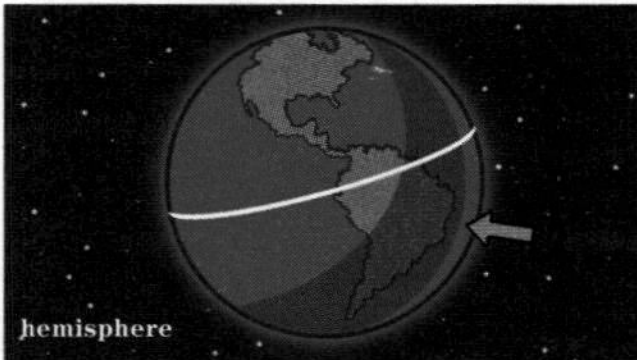
hemisphere

Word History

Hemisphere came into English in the 1300s. *Hemisphere* came from the Middle English word *hemispere,* which came from the Latin word *hemisphaerium.* The word *hemisphaerium* came from the Greek word *hēmisphairion.* In *hēmisphairion, hēmi-* means "half," and *sphaerion* means "small sphere."

hesitate (hez′ ə tāt) *v.* Pause.
high-falutin' (hī′ fə lo͞o′ tn) *adj.* Appealing to a higher class of people; fancy; showy.
hogan (hō′ gôn) *n.* A Navaho dwelling.
homespun (hōm′ spən) *adj.* Made at home.
hone (hōn) *v.* To sharpen.
honor (ä′ nər) *v.* Show respect.
horizon (hə rī′ zən) *n.* A line formed in the distance by an apparent meeting of Earth and sky.
horizontal (hor′ ə zon′ tl) *adj.* Along a line parallel to the horizon.
hospitable (hos pi′ tə bəl) *adj.* Kind and generous to guests.

Pronunciation Key: **at**; **lāte**; **câre**; **fäther**; **set**; **mē**; **it**; **kīte**; **ox**; **rōse**; **ô** in **bought**; **coin**; **b**o͝o**k**; **t**o͞o; **form**; **out**; **up**; **ūse**; **tûrn**; ə sound in **a**bout, chick**e**n, penc**i**l, cann**o**n, circ**u**s; **chair**; **hw** in **wh**ich; **ring**; **shop**; **thin**; **th**ere; **zh** in trea**s**ure.

hover (huv′ ər) *v.* To hang in the air.

Word History

Hover came from an older English word, *hoven*, which may have come into use as many as 800 years ago. Since the earliest records of this word, it has always had the same meaning.

humanity (hū man′ ə tē) *n.* People; all human beings.

hypotenuse (hī po′ tə no͞os′) *n.* In a right triangle, the side opposite the right angle.

I

ice floes (īs′ flōz′) *n.* Large sheets of floating ice.

immigrant (i′ mi grənt) *n.* A person who comes to live in a country in which he or she was not born.

impeach (im pēch′) *v.* Accuse of misconduct.

imperial (im pir′ ē əl) *adj.* Part of, or belonging to, a king's empire.

impetuous (im pech′ wəs) *adj.* Acting or done too quickly, without planning or thought.

impoverished (im pov′ risht) *adj.* Living in poverty.

impressed (im prest′) *adj.* Made to form a high opinion of someone or something.

inexorable (in ek′ sər ə bəl) *adj.* Absolute; unyielding.

infallibility (in fal′ ə bil′ ə tē) *n.* Assuredness or certainty of success.

inferno (in fûr′ nō) *n.* A place of extreme, almost unbearable, heat.

infirm (in fûrm′) *adj.* Weak; feeble; insecure.

ingenious (in jēn′ yəs) *adj.* Clever; skillful.

Word History

Ingenious came into English about 500 years ago. It comes from the Latin word *ingenium*, which means "natural capacity." Some meanings of the word *capacity* are "the amount that can be held in a space" and "ability or power." (Also note that *ingenious* contains the *in-* prefix, which in this word means "within," and the *-ous* suffix, which in this word means "having" or "possessing.")

ingot (ing′ gət) *n.* A piece of metal in the shape of a bar or a block.

ingratiate (in grā′ shē āt′) *v.* To put oneself in the good graces of others.

innovation (in′ ə vā′ shən) *n.* The act of creating something new or original.

insignificant (in′ sig ni′ fə kənt) *adj.* Not important.

intelligence (in tel′ ə jəns) *n.* 1. A network of people and resources working to gather secret information about an enemy. 2. The secret information about an enemy gathered by a spy.

intensity (in ten′ si tē) *n.* Great strength.

internal (in tûr′ nəl) *adj.* On the inside.

interplanetary (in′ tər pla′ nə târ′ ē) *adj.* Shared between the planets.

interrogation (in ter′ ə gā′ shən) *n.* Questioning.

interview (in′ tər vū′) *v.* Ask questions to find out about a person or what a person thinks.

intimacy (in′ tə mə sē) *n.* A closeness.

intricate (in′ tri kit) *adj.* Tangled; complicated.

investment (in vest′ mənt) *adj.* Using money to make a profit.

irrepressible (ir′ i pres′ ə bəl) *adj.* Unwilling to be controlled.

J

jabber (ja′ bər) *v.* Talk a lot and very fast.

journeyman (jûr′ nē mən) *n.* A person who has completed an apprenticeship and can now work in a trade under another person.

juggle (ju′ gəl) *v.* Handle more than one object or activity at one time; perform a clever trick.

juniper (jo͞o′ nə pər) *n.* An evergreen shrub with purple berries.

K

karate (kə rä′ tē) *n.* An Asian art of self-defense.

kasha (kä′ shə) *n.* A soft food made from a grain, usually buckwheat.

kayak (kī′ ak) *n.* A light Eskimo canoe having a wooden or bone framework and covered with skins.

keelboat (kēl′ bōt) *n.* A shallow boat built with a keel, or long beam, on the bottom.

kiln (kiln) *n.* An oven for firing glass, or heating it at very high temperatures, in order to make the color permanent.

kosher (kō′ shər) *adj.* Proper or acceptable according to Jewish law.

L

lambent (lam′ bənt) *adj.* Glowing softly.

lance (lans) *n.* A long-shafted spear.

lariat (lâr′ ē ət) *n.* A rope tied with a movable loop at one end, used to catch cows and horses; a lasso.

learned (lûrnd) *v.* Past tense of **learn:** To gain new knowledge or skill. —*adj.* (lûr′ nid) Educated.

legendary (lej′ ən der′ ē) *adj.* From a story that has been passed down from a people's earlier times.

legislature (lej′ i slā′ chər) *n.* A group of people who make or pass laws.

levee (le′ vē) *n.* An embankment built along a river to keep the river from overflowing.

levity (le′ və tē) *n.* A lighthearted attitude.

Pronunciation Key: **at**; **lāte**; **câre**; **fäther**; **set**; **mē**; **it**; **kīte**; **ox**; **rōse**; **ô** in **bought**; **coin**; **bo͝ok**; **to͞o**; **form**; **out**; **up**; **ūse**; **tûrn**; **ə** sound in **a**bout, chick**e**n, penc**i**l, cann**o**n, circ**u**s; **ch**air; **hw** in **wh**ich; ri**ng**; **sh**op; **th**in; **th**ere; **zh** in trea**s**ure.

lieutenant (lo͞o ten´ ənt) *n.* An officer in the armed forces.
lull (lul) *n.* A period of reduced noise or violence.
lumber (lum´ bər) *n.* Wood that has been cut into boards of various sizes for building.
lunar (lo͞o´ nər) *adj.* Relating to the moon.
luxurious (lug zho͝or´ ē əs) *adj.* Grand; rich; elegant.
lynx (lingks) *n.* A wildcat; a bobcat.

M

macaw (mə kô´) *n.* A large parrot that has bright colors and a long tail.
magnification (mag´ nə fi kā´ shən) *n.* The amount of enlargement possible; the amount something is enlarged.

Word History

Magnification is a derivative of the word *magnify*, which came into English in the 1300s. *Magnify* was derived from the Middle English word *magnifien*, which came from the Anglo-French word *magnifier*. The word *magnifier* was derived from the Latin word *magnificare*, which came from the word *magnificus* meaning "important or splendid." (Also note that *magnification* contains the Latin suffix *-tion*, which in this word means "the state of being.")

magnificent (mag ni´ fə sənt) *adj.* Outstanding or inspiring.
mallet (ma´ lət) *n.* A type of hammer with a head made of wood or other soft material.
manager (ma´ ni gər) *n.* A person who takes care of or organizes something, like an office or a sports team.
maneuvering (mə no͞o´ vər ing) *n.* Planning and then acting according to plans.
manic (man´ ik) *adj.* Overly excited.
mantel (man´ təl) *n.* A shelf over a fireplace.
marrow (mar´ ō) *n.* 1. The soft substance in the hollow parts of bones. 2. The center; the core.
mast (mast) *n.* A pole that supports the sails of a ship or boat. See illustration of **bow.**
match (mach´) *n.* A contest, competition, or race.

Maya or **Mayan** (mä´ yə) or (mä´ yən) *n.* A member of a people who built an ancient civilization in Mexico and Central America. **Mayan** *adj.* Having to do with the civilization of the Mayas.
medley (med´ lē) *n.* A mixture; a jumble.
melodrama (mel´ ə drä´ mə) *n.* A play that exaggerates emotions and encourages the audience to be sympathetic.
menial (mē´ nē əl) *adj.* Humble; lowly; boring; tedious.
merciful (mûr´ si fəl) *adj.* Forgiving.
mesa (mā´ sə) *n.* A small, high plateau that stands alone, like a mountain with a flat top.

mesquite (me skēt´) *n.* A spiny shrub or tree in the legume, or pea and bean, family.
meteorite (mē´ tē ə rīt´) *n.* A piece of matter from the solar system that hits a planet or moon's surface.
microbes (mī´ krōbz) *n.* Living things that can only be seen with a microscope.
militia (mə lish´ ə) *n.* A group of citizens trained to fight and help in emergencies.
mill (mil) *n.* A factory.
mischievous (mis´ chə vəs) *adj.* Causing trouble in a playful way.
mission (mish´ ən) *n.* A special job or task.
module (mä´ jəl) *n.* A separate part of a rocket that is self-contained and serves a specific purpose.
monarch (mon´ ərk) *n.* A ruler; a king or a queen.
morale (mə ral´) *n.* The level of one's confidence.
morose (mə rōs´) *adj.* Sullen; gloomy.
mossback (môs´ bak) *n.* A wild bull or cow.
move (mo͞ov) *v.* To make a motion or a suggestion to act on something in a meeting.
muck (muk) *v.* To clean out.
muff (muf) *v.* To do an action poorly; to miss; to mess up.
musket (mus´ kət) *n.* A weapon, used in early American battles, which was aimed and fired from the shoulder. It fired a small, lead ball.
muster (mus´ tər) *v.* To work up; to gather a group in preparation for battle.
myriad (mir´ ē əd) *n.* An immense number; many.
mystified (mis´ tə fīd´) *adj.* Bewildered; baffled; puzzled.
mythology (mi thol´ ə jē) *n.* A collection of legends or fables.

N

nation (nā´ shən) *n.* A group of people living in a particular area under one government.

Word Derivations

Below are some words related to *nation*.

national	nationalism	nationality
nationally	international	nationwide

Pronunciation Key: **at**; **lāte**; **câre**; **fäther**; **set**; **mē**; **it**; **kīte**; **ox**; **rōse**; **ô** in **bought**; **coin**; **bŏŏk**; **tōō**; **form**; **out**; **up**; **ūse**; **tûrn**; **ə** sound in **about**, chicken, pencil, cannon, circus; **chair**; **hw** in **which**; **ring**; **shop**; **thin**; **th͟ere**; **zh** in treasure.

nebula (ne´ byə lə) *n.* Glowing clouds of gas and dust amidst the stars.
netherworld (neth´ ər wûrld´) *n.* The region below the ground; hell.
nomination (no´ mə nā´ shən) *n.* A proposal that someone could hold a government position or office.

Word History

Nomination is a derivative of the word *nominate*, which came into English about 500 years ago. It came from a derivation of the Latin word *nomen*, which means "name." (Also note that the word *nomination* contains the *-ation* suffix, which means "connected to the process of.")

novelty (no´ vəl tē) *n.* Something new or different.
nuclear reaction (nōō´ klē ər rē ak´ shən) *n.* A process in which the centers or cores of atoms are changed.
nugget (nug´ ət) *n.* A solid lump of gold.
nylon (nī´ lon´) *adj.* A synthetic fiber that is strong and durable.

O

obliterate (ə blit´ ə rāt´) *v.* To destroy completely; to rub out; to erase.

Word Derivations

Below are some words related to *obliterate.*

obliterated	obliterating	obliterative
obliterates	obliteration	obliterator

oblong (ob´ lông) *adj.* Being longer than it is wide.
obscure (əb skyŏŏr´) *adj.* Not well known. —*v.* To hide; to cover up.
observatory (əb zûr´ və tor´ē) *n.* A place that is designed for astronomers to study the stars.

observatory

ocelot (o´ sə lot´) *n.* A small wildcat with black spots and a yellow coat.

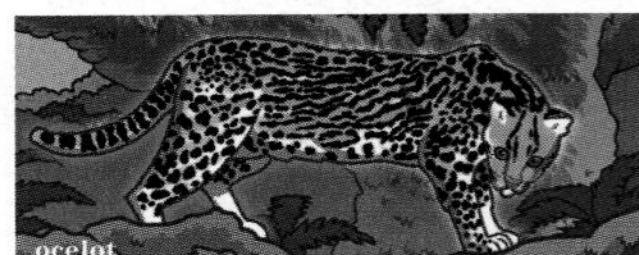
ocelot

optical (op´ ti kəl) *adj.* Having to do with sight.
optimism (op´ tə miz´ əm) *n.* The belief that everything will happen for the best.
optimistic (op´ tə mis´ tik) *adj.* Having a positive outlook.

organic (or gan´ ik) *adj.* Produced by living things; was once alive.
organism (or´ gə niz´ əm) *n.* Any living thing.
ornery (or´ nə rē) *adj.* Mean; grouchy; irritable.
oxlip (oks´ lip) *n.* A flowering herb with pale-colored flowers.

P

pantomime (pan´ tə mīm´) *v.* Use bodily movements or facial expressions, instead of speech, to tell a story.
parched (pärcht) *adj.* Very hot and dry.
parliamentary procedure (pär´ lə men´ trē prə sē´ jər) *n.* A formal way to hold or conduct a meeting, following certain rules.
particle (pär´ ti kəl) *n.* A very small piece or portion of something.
partisan (pär´ tə zən) *n.* A committed supporter of a party, cause, person, or idea.
passion (pash´ ən) *n.* A strong liking or enthusiasm for something.

Word Derivations

Below are some words related to *passion.*

impassioned	passionate
dispassionate	passionately
passionless	disimpassioned

patchwork quilt (pach´ wûrk´ kwilt´) *n.* A blanket made from scraps of material sewn together.
peevishly (pē´ vish lē) *adv.* With irritation or lack of patience.
perimeter (pə rim´ i tər) *n.* The distance around the boundary of something.
persecute (pûr´ si kūt´) *v.* To torment; to oppress; to treat badly.
perspective (pər spek´ tiv) *n.* A way of looking at things in relation to each other.

Word History

Perspective came into English about 600 years ago. It came from the Latin word *perspectivus*, meaning "of sight" or "optical." This Latin word came from a derivation of *perspicere*, which can be broken into the word parts *per-*, meaning "through," and *specere*, meaning "to look." (Also note that the word *perspective* contains the *-ive* suffix, which means "performs the action of.")

persuade (pər swād´) *v.* To get others to think as you do about a subject or topic.

Word Derivations

Below are some words related to *persuade.*

persuasive	persuasion	persuadable
persuasively	unpersuasive	persuasiveness

pester (pes´ tər) *v.* To bother; to annoy.
petition (pə ti´ shən) *v.* Submit a formal request to someone in authority.
petroglyph (pe´ trə glif´) *n.* A drawing or word carved into a rock.

Word History

Petroglyph came to English in 1860. It came from the French word *petroglyphe*, which came from the Greek *petr-*, meaning "stone," and the Middle French *-glyphe*, meaning "hieroglyph, or sign used in a type of writing made with pictures rather than letters."

Pronunciation Key: **a**t; l**ā**te; c**â**re; f**ä**ther; s**e**t; m**ē**; **i**t; k**ī**te; **o**x; r**ō**se; **ô** in b**ou**ght; c**oi**n; b**o͝o**k; t**o͞o**; f**or**m; **ou**t; **u**p; **ū**se; t**û**rn; **ə** sound in **a**bout, chick**e**n, penc**i**l, cann**o**n, circ**u**s; **ch**air; **hw** in **wh**ich; ri**ng**; **sh**op; **th**in; **th**ere; **zh** in trea**s**ure.

peyote (pā ō´ tē) *n.* A cactus plant.
piñon (pin´ yən) *n.* A kind of pine tree with edible seeds.
pity (pi´ tē) *v.* Feel sorry for.
plateau (pla tō´) *n.* A tract of high, flat land; a tableland.
player (plā´ ər) *n.* A person who takes part in, and plays against another person in, a match.
plummet (plum´ it) *v.* Fall suddenly.
pogrom (pō´ grəm) *n.* An organized attack on Jews in Russia in the late 1800s. Pogroms were encouraged by the Russian government at that time.
ponder (pon´ dər) *v.* To think about.
portage (pôr täzh´) *n.* The act of carrying boats and supplies from one waterway to another.

portal (por´ təl) *n.* An entryway.
posterity (po ster´ ə tē) *n.* Future generations.

Word History

Posterity came into English in the 1300s. It came from the Middle English word *posterite*, which came from the Anglo-French word *pusterité*. The word *pusterité* came from the Latin *posteritat-*, which is a Latin word part derived from *posteritas*. In turn, the word *posteritas* comes from the Latin word *posterus*, which means "coming after."

poultice (pōl´ tis) *n.* A wad of something soft and moist that is placed over a wound to heal it.
prairie (prâr´ ē) *n.* A large area of level or rolling land with grass and few or no trees.
prankster (prangk´ stər) *n.* A person who plays tricks on people for fun.
preamble (prē´ am´ bəl) *n.* The section of text at the beginning of a law document that states why the document was written.
precarious (pri kâr´ ē əs) *adj.* Lacking security or stability.
precaution (pri kô´ shən) *n.* Care taken beforehand.
prediction (pri dik´ shən) *n.* A statement about what someone thinks will happen in the future.
preserve (pri zərv´) *v.* 1. Protect and maintain. 2. Prepare food so that it can be eaten in the future.
pressure (pre´ shər) *v.* To force.
prevail (pri vāl´) *v.* To persuade.
primary (prī´ mâr ē) *adj.* Main.
prime (prīm) *n.* The most successful or important period of time.

primitive (prim´ ə tiv) *adj.* 1. Living in the ways of long ago. 2. In the earliest stages of development.
procedure (prə sē´ jər) *n.* The steps to follow in carrying out a routine or method.
proclaim (prō klām´) *v.* To announce publicly.
procure (prə kyûr´) *v.* Obtain by making a special effort.
profound (prə found´) *adj.* Deep.
prominence (prom´ ə nəns) *n.* Fame; importance.
prominent (prom´ ə nənt) *adj.* Famous; well-known.
proportions (prə por´ shənz) *n.* Amounts.
prospect (pros´ pekt´) *v.* Look for gold.
provisions (prə vizh´ ənz) *n.* Supplies, especially food or tools.
ptarmigan (tär´ mi gən) *n.* A bird also known as a grouse.

pun (pun) *n.* A joke made by using words that sound almost the same but have different meanings.
pungent (pun´ jənt) *adj.* Sharp or strong smelling or tasting.

Q

quarantine (kwor´ ən tēn´) *adj.* Involving the isolation of people from others to prevent the spreading of disease.
quiver (kwi´ vər) *v.* To shake slightly.

R

racquetball (ra´ kət bôl´) *n.* A sport played with a racket and small rubber ball in an enclosed room.
radiation (rā´ dē ā´ shən) *n.* Emitted energy that can be harmful.
radical (ra´ di kəl) *n.* A person who favors extreme changes or reforms.
rampart (ram´ pärt) *n.* A wall used as a defense for a city.
rancid (ran´ sid) *adj.* Stale; unpleasant.
rapscallion (rap skal´ yən) *n.* A rascal; a scamp.
ratification (rat´ ə fi kā´ shən) *n.* The formal approval of a law or laws.
ration (rash´ ən) *n.* A limited share of food.
ravage (ra´ vij) *v.* To damage heavily.
ravine (rə vēn´) *n.* A narrow, steep-sided valley worn into the earth by running water.
rebellion (ri bel´ yən) *n.* An uprising against a ruling authority; an act of defiance.
recede (ri sēd´) *v.* To go backward; to back away.

Word Derivations

Below are some words related to *recede*.

receded	recession	recessionary
receding	recessional	recessive
recess		

ANTHOLOGY GLOSSARY

Pronunciation Key: **at**; **lāte**; **câre**; **fäther**; **set**; **mē**; **it**; **kīte**; **ox**; **rōse**; **ô** in **bought**; **coin**; **bŏŏk**; **tōō**; **form**; **out**; **up**; **ūse**; **tûrn**; **ə** sound in **a**bout, chick**e**n, penc**i**l, cann**o**n, circ**u**s; **chair**; **hw** in **wh**ich; **ring**; **shop**; **thin**; **th**ere; **zh** in trea**s**ure.

recognize (re′ kig nīz′) *v.* Know that you have seen someone or something before.
recoil (ri koil′) *v.* To spring back from.
reconciliation (rek′ ən sil′ ē ā′ shən) *n.* A restoration of agreement between two or more parties.
record (re′ kərd) *n.* A written account of the number of games a team won or lost during its season.
refracting (ri frak′ ting) *adj.* Passing through an object and changing direction, as a light ray passing into a lens at one angle and coming out at a different angle.
regard (re gärd′) *n.* Thought or care.
regiment (rej′ ə mənt) *n.* A large body of soldiers.
register (re′ jə stər) *v.* Officially record in order to protect.
rehearse (ri hûrs′) *v.* Practice.
remedy (rem′ ə dē) *n.* A cure; something that will make a sickness better.
remote (ri mōt′) *adj.* Far away and separate from others.
renounce (ri nouns′) *v.* To give up; to reject.
represent (re′ pri zent′) *v.* Speak or act for someone else.
resonance (rez′ ə nəns) *n.* Richness of sound; echoing.
resource (rē′ sors) *n.* Something that can be used.
reunion (rē ūn′ yən) *n.* A coming or bringing together of family, friends, or other groups of people.
reverie (rev′ ə rē) *n.* A daydream.
revolution (rev′ ə lōō′ shən) *n.* The overthrow of a system of government and the setting up of a new system of government.

Word History

Revolution came into English in the 1300s. It came from the Middle English word *revolucioun*, which was derived from the Middle French word *revolution*. The Middle French *revolution* came from the Lower Latin word part *revolution-*, which was derived from *revolutio*. The Lower Latin word *revolutio* came from the Latin word *revolvere*, which means "to revolve, or turn."

revolutionize (re′ və lōō′ shə nīz′) *v.* Cause dramatic change.
rice paper (rīs′ pā′ pər) *n.* A thin paper produced from the stems of rice plants.
riddle (rid′ əl) *n.* A puzzle that appears as a statement or question.
ritual (rich′ ōō əl) *n.* A ceremony of worship; an act always performed on certain occasions.
roam (rōm) *v.* Wander.
rocker (ro′ kər) *n.* A device used to separate gold from sand and dirt.
rotate (rō′ tāt) *v.* To revolve; to turn around; to spin.
rowdy (rou′ dē) *adj.* Rough; disorderly.
rudder (rud′ ər) *n.* A broad, flat blade at the rear of a ship used to steer. See illustration of **bow.**
rutting (rut′ ing) *n.* Mating.

S

saber (sā′ bər) *n.* A heavy sword with a curved blade.
sabotage (sab′ ə täzh′) *v.* To damage purposely.
salutary (sal′ yə ter′ ē) *adj.* Favorable; positive.
salutation (sal′ yə tā′ shən) *n.* Greeting.
samovar (sam′ ə vär′) *n.* A decorative metal container with a spigot, or faucet, often used in Russia to heat water for tea.

Word History

Samovar came into English in the year 1830. It is a Russian word formed by joining the word parts *samo-*, meaning "self," and *varit'*, which means "to boil."

scallion (skal′ yən) *n.* A type of onion.
scout (skout) *v.* Go ahead of the group, while on a journey, to look for information.
scowl (skoul) *v.* Frown.
scythe (sīth) *n.* A tool with a long, curved blade for cutting grass or grain by hand.

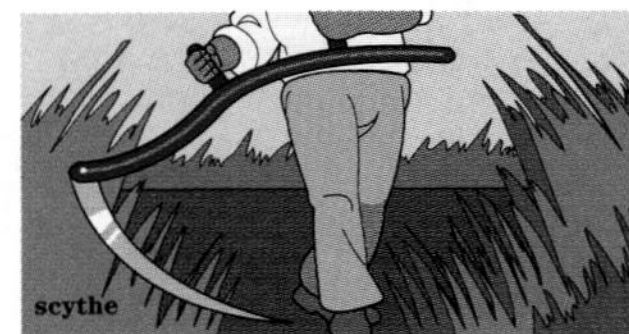
scythe

sear (sēr) *v.* To roast; to burn.
seclude (si klōōd′) *v.* To keep away from others.
second (se′ kənd) *v.* To verbally agree with a motion or suggestion to do something in a meeting.
sect (sekt) *n.* A group of people bound together by common beliefs or ideals.
secure (sə kyŏŏr′) *adj.* Safe from harm or danger.
sentinel (sent′ nəl) *n.* A person who stands watch; a guard.
serve (sûrv) *n.* In volleyball and tennis, a way of putting the ball into play by sending it over the net.
shamefaced (shām′ fāst) *adj.* Embarrassed.
sharecropper (shâr′ krop′ ər) *n.* A farmer who gives part of his or her crop as rent to the owner of the land.
shlemiel (shlə mēl′) *n. slang.* A fool who is both awkward and unlucky.
shmendrick (shmen′ drik) *n. slang.* A nincompoop; a nobody.
short circuit (short′ sûr′ kət) *n.* A condition in which the path of an electrical current is obstructed.
shrill (shril) *adj.* High-pitched; piercing.
shroud (shroud) *n.* A covering for a dead body.
shy (shī′) *adj.* 1. Lacking; falling short. 2. Secretive; protective.
simultaneously (sī′ məl tā′ nē əs lē) *adv.* At exactly the same time.
singsong (sing′ sông′) *adj.* Having a repetitive musical sound.
skeeter (skē′ tər) *n. informal.* A mosquito.
slaughter (slô′ tər) *n.* The killing of a large number of animals.
slew (slōō) *n.* Many.

Pronunciation Key: **at**; **lāte**; **câre**; **fäther**; **set**; **mē**; **it**; **kīte**; **ox**; **rōse**; **ô** in **bought**; **coin**; **bŏŏk**; **tōō**; **form**; **out**; **up**; **ūse**; **tûrn**; **ə** sound in **a**bout, chick**e**n, penc**i**l, cann**o**n, circ**u**s; **chair**; **hw** in **wh**ich; **ring**; **shop**; **thin**; **th**ere; **zh** in trea**s**ure.

slump (slump) *v.* To sit with drooping shoulders.

Word History

Slump came into English in the year 1887. Its origins are probably in the Scandinavian languages. It is related to the Norwegian word *slumpa*, which means "to fall."

smithy (smith′ ē) *n.* A blacksmith's shop; a place where horseshoes are made.
solar system (sō′ lər sis′ təm) *n.* The sun and all the planets and other bodies that revolve around it.

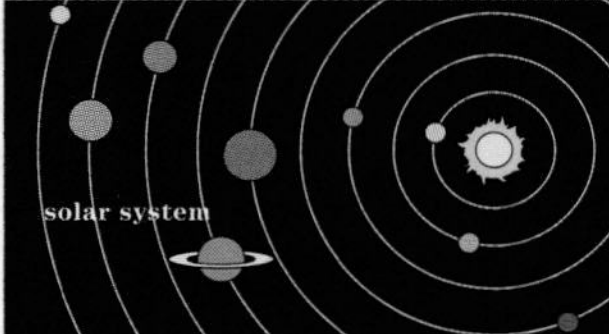
solar system

solder (sod′ ər) *v.* To join metal pieces together by using a highly heated liquid metal at a joint without heating the pieces themselves.
solitary (sol′ i ter′ ē) *adj.* Alone; single.
solstice (sol′ stis) *n.* The day of the year when the sun appears the farthest north and the day when it appears the farthest south in the sky.
sombre (som′ bər) *adj.* Dark or gloomy.
sovereign (so′ vrən) *adj.* Independent; self-governed.
span (span) *v.* To stretch across.
spar (spär) *n.* A pole or beam which supports the rigging on a ship; a mast.
spare (spâr) *adj.* Left over; remaining; extra.
spasm (spaz′ əm) *n.* A seizure; a fit.
spawn (spôn) *v.* To lay eggs and deposit them in water.
spectral (spek′ trəl) *adj.* Ghostly, eerie.
speculation (spek′ yə lā′ shən) *n.* Thinking about a subject; pondering.
spew (spū) *v.* To pour out; to squirt out.
spike (spīk) *v.* To forcefully hit a volleyball down the other side of the net.
spirit (spir′ ət) *n.* Enthusiasm; loyalty.
spirits (spir′ its) *n.* A liquid containing alcohol.
spooked (spŏŏkt) *adj.* Scared.
stance (stans) *n.* A person's mental position on a subject.
staple (stā′ pəl) *n.* A basic, or necessary, food.
stockyard (stok′ yärd′) *n.* A place where livestock such as cattle, sheep, horses, and pigs that are to be bought or sold, slaughtered, or shipped are held.

Stonehenge (stōn´ henj) *n.* A group of large stones in England placed in circular formations around 3,500 years ago, possibly as an astronomical calendar.

straddle (stra´ dəl) *v.* To sit with one's legs on each side of an object.
stroke (strōk) *n.* A sudden attack of illness caused by a blocked or broken blood vessel in or leading to the brain.
succession (sək sesh´ ən) *n.* One thing happening right after another.
substitute (sub´ stə to͞ot) *n.* Anything that could take the place of something else.
succulent (suk´ yə lənt) *adj.* Juicy; tasty.
sufficient (sə fish´ ənt) *adj.* Enough.
suffocate (suf´ ə kāt´) *v.* To smother; to choke.
sull (sul) *v.* To balk; to stop suddenly and refuse to move.
summon (sum´ ən) *v.* Ask to come.
supple (sup´ əl) *adj.* Easily bent; not stiff.
sway (swā) *v.* To influence.

T

tan (tan) *v.* To turn animal hides into leather.

Word History

Tan came into English about 600 years ago, from the French word *tanner*, a derivation of the Latin word *tanum* or *tannum*. The Latin word means "tanbark," a type of bark that contains an astringent, or drying, substance used in the making of leather.

tangled-up (tang´ gəld up´) *adj.* Mixed-up and stuck together.
tantrum (tan´ trəm) *n.* A screaming, crying fit of childish anger.
tapir (tā´ pər) *n.* An animal similar to a pig, but with a long, flexible nose.
tariff (târ´ əf) *n.* A fee charged by a government on imports and exports.
teeming (tē´ ming) *adj.* Overflowing; swarming.
terminal (tûr´ mə nəl) *adj.* Eventually ending in death.
terrace (târ´ əs) *n.* A raised area with a series of level steps or surfaces cut into the side.
terrain (tə rān´) *n.* An area of land that is thought of in terms of its physical features.
tethered (teth´ ərd) *adj.* Tied by rope to a fixed object.
thresh (thresh) *v.* To separate grain from the stalk by beating it.
tidal flat (tī´ dəl flat) *n.* A flat area of land that is sometimes covered by tidal waters.
timpani (tim´ pə nē) *n.* A type of drum.

Pronunciation Key: **a**t; l**ā**te; c**â**re; f**ä**ther; s**e**t; m**ē**; **i**t; k**ī**te; **o**x; r**ō**se; **ô** in b**ou**ght; c**oi**n; b**o͝o**k; t**o͞o**; f**o**rm; **ou**t; **u**p; **ū**se; t**û**rn; **ə** sound in **a**bout, chick**e**n, penc**i**l, cann**o**n, circ**u**s; **ch**air; **hw** in **wh**ich; ri**ng**; **sh**op; **th**in; **th**ere; **zh** in trea**s**ure.

tipi (tē´ pē) *n.* A tent of the Native Americans of the Plains; a tepee.

Word History

Tipi, or tepee, came into English in the year 1743. It is a Native American word, meaning "to dwell," that originated with the Dakota tribe.

toboggan (tə bog´ ən) *n.* A long, narrow sled.
tome (tōm) *n.* One volume of a set of books.
tract (trakt) *n.* A large area of land.
traditional (trə di´ shən əl) *adj.* Passed from one generation to another.
traitor (trā´ tər) *n.* A person who betrays his or her country.
tranquility (tran kwil´ ə tē) *n.* Calmness.
transcribe (tran skrīb´) *v.* To change from one recorded form to another; to translate.
treason (trē´ zən) *n.* The act of betraying someone's trust.
treaty (trē´ tē) *n.* A formal agreement between two countries.
trek (trek) *n.* A long, slow journey.
trench (trench) *n.* A ditch; a long, narrow channel cut in the earth.
tributary (trib´ yə ter´ ē) *n.* A stream or river that flows into a larger one.
tribute (trib´ ūt) *n.* Praise, honor, or gifts given to show respect or to show thanks.
trifling (trī´ fling) *adj.* Small and unimportant.
trinket (tring´ kit) *n.* A small or cheap piece of jewelry.
tripod (trī´ pod) *n.* A three-legged table or stand.

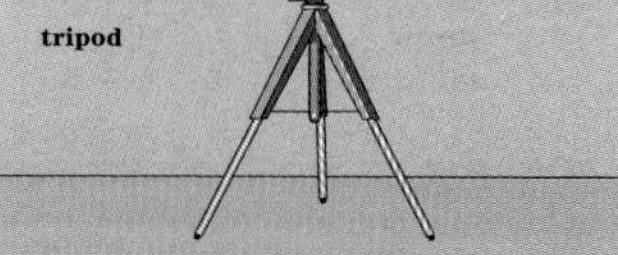

troop (tro͞op) *n.* Soldiers.
tsar (zär) *n.* An emperor of Russia before 1918.
tsarina (zä rē´ nə) *n.* An empress of Russia before 1918.
tumult (to͞o´ mult) *n.* A great disorder; an uproar.
tundra (tun´ drə) *n.* A large, treeless plain in the arctic regions.
tunic (to͞o´ nik) *n.* A short coat.
tyranny (tir´ ə nē) *n.* The unjust use of power; harsh or cruel government.

U

unaccountably (un´ ə koun´ tə blē) *adv.* In a way that cannot be explained.
unalienable (un´ āl´ yə nə bəl) *adj.* Not capable of being given or taken away.
unanimity (ū´ nə ni´ mə tē) *n.* A condition of complete agreement.

unison (ū´ nə sən) *n.* Behaving the same way at the same time. **in unison** *idiom.* Two or more people saying or doing the same thing at the same time.

Word History

Unison came into English about 600 years ago. It came from the Middle English word *unisoun*, which was derived from the Middle French word *unisson*. The word *unisson* came from the Middle Latin word *unisonus*, which means "having the same sound." *Unisonus* came from the Latin *uni-*, meaning "one," and *sonus*, meaning "sound."

universe (ū´ nə vers´) *n.* Everything that exists, including the earth, the planets, the stars, and all of space.
unquenchably (un kwench´ ə blē) *adv.* Endlessly; in a persistent way.

V

vain (vān) *adj.* Conceited.
vagabond (va´ gə bond´) *n.* One who wanders from place to place.
valiant (val´ yənt) *adj.* Brave; fearless.
variable (vâr´ ē´ ə bəl) *adj.* Likely to change.
velocity (və los´ i tē) *n.* Speed.
vindicate (vin´ di kāt´) *v.* To prove innocent.
vintage (vin´ tij) *n.* The grapes or wine produced in a vineyard in one year.
vintner (vint´ nər) *n.* A person who makes wine for a living.
visible (vi´ zə bəl) *adj.* Able to be seen or noticed.

Word Derivations

Below are some words related to *visible.*

visibility	invisible	visibly
invisibility	invisibly	

vocation (vō kā´ shən) *n.* An occupation; a profession.

Word History

Vocation came into English in the 1400s. It came from the Middle English word *vocacioun*, which was derived from the Anglo-French word *vocacium*. The word *vocaciun* came from the Latin word *vocation-*, which was derived from *vocatio*, meaning "summons." *Vocatio* came from the word *vocare*, meaning "to call." *Vocare* came from the word *vox*, meaning "voice."

voyage (voi´ ij) *n.* A journey by water.

W

water buffalo (wô´ tər buf´ ə lō´) *n.* A kind of oxen with large curved horns and a bluish-black hide. Water buffaloes are trained to work in rice fields in Asia.
whim (hwim) *n.* An impulsive thought, idea, or desire.
whopper (hwop´ ər) *n. informal.* A big lie.
wince (wins) *v.* To flinch; to start back from.

Pronunciation Key: **a**t; l**ā**te; c**â**re; f**ä**ther; s**e**t; m**ē**; **i**t; k**ī**te; **o**x; r**ō**se; **ô** in b**ou**ght; c**oi**n; b**o͝o**k; t**o͞o**; f**o**rm; **ou**t; **u**p; **ū**se; t**û**rn; **ə** sound in **a**bout, chick**e**n, penc**i**l, cann**o**n, circ**u**s; **ch**air; **hw** in **wh**ich; ri**ng**; **sh**op; **th**in; **th**ere; **zh** in trea**s**ure.

windlass (wind´ ləs) *n.* A roller turned with a handle used for lifting heavy weights.

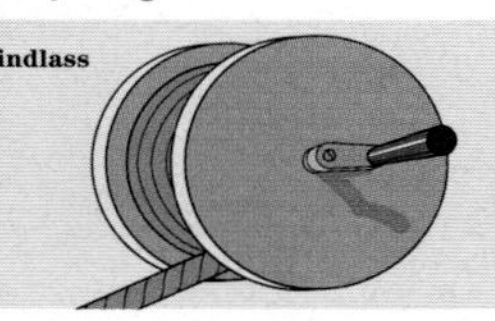

winnow (win´ ō) *v.* To remove the chaff, or husks, from grain.
wrath (rath) *n.* Anger; rage.

Y

yarn (yärn) *n.* A made-up story.
yield (yēld) *v.* To give in; to stop arguing.

Word Derivations

Below are some words related to *yield.*

yielded	yielding	yielder
unyielding	unyieldingly	yieldingly

Z

Zulu (zo͞o´ lo͞o) *n.* A person from KwaZulu Natal in South Africa.

Program Appendix

Program Appendix

The Program Appendix includes a step-by-step explanation of procedures for research-based, effective practices in reading instruction that are repeatedly used throughout ***SRA/Open Court Reading.*** These practices may also be used in other instructional materials.

Table of Contents

Effective Teaching Practices

Teacher References

Reading Materials and Techniques

PROGRAM APPENDIX

Different reading materials and techniques are appropriate at different stages of reading development. The purpose of this section is to discuss different types of reading materials and how they may be used most effectively.

Reading Big Books

Purpose

Many students come from homes where they are read to often, but a significant number of other students have not had this valuable experience. Big Books (Levels K and 1) offer all students crucial opportunities to confirm and expand their knowledge about print and reading. They are especially useful for shared reading experiences in the early grades.

The benefits of reading Big Books include engaging even nonreaders in:

- unlocking the books' messages.
- developing print awareness.
- participating in good reading behaviors.
- observing what a good reader does: remarking on the illustrations and the title, asking questions about the content and what might happen, making predictions, and clarifying words and ideas.
- promoting the insight that a given word is spelled the same way every time it occurs as high-frequency words are pointed out.
- reinforcing the correspondence between spoken and written words and spelling patterns.
- enjoying the illustrations and connecting them to the text to help students learn to explore books for enjoyment and information.
- interpreting and responding to literature and expository text before they can read themselves.

Procedure for Reading Big Books

During the first reading of the Big Books, you will model reading behaviors and comprehension strategies similar to those that will later be taught formally. During the second reading, you will address print awareness and teach comprehension skills such as classifying and categorizing or sequencing, which help the reader organize information. In addition, you will teach skills such as making inferences and drawing conclusions, which help the reader focus on the deeper meaning of the text. At first, teachers should expect to do all of the reading but should not prevent students from trying to read on their own or from reading words they already know.

- **Activate Prior Knowledge.** Read the title of the selection and the author's and illustrator's names. At the beginning of each Big Book, read the title of the book and discuss what the whole book is about before going on to reading the first selection.
- **Discuss Prior Knowledge.** Initiate a brief discussion of any prior knowledge the students have that might help them understand the selection.
- **Browse the Selection.** Ask students to tell what they think the story might be about just from looking at the illustrations. This conversation should be brief so that the students can move on to a prereading discussion of print awareness.

Big Books offer all students crucial opportunities to confirm and expand their knowledge about print and reading.

- **Develop Print Awareness.** The focus of browsing the Big Books is to develop awareness of print. Urge students to tell what words or letters they recognize rather than what they expect the selection to be about.

  To develop print awareness, have students look through the selection page by page and comment on whatever they notice in the text. Some students may know some of the words, while others may only recognize specific letters or sounds. The key is to get the students to look at the print separately from the illustrations even before they have heard the actual text content. This process isolates print awareness so that it is not influenced by content. It also gives you a clearer idea of what your students do or do not know about print.
- **Read Aloud.** Read the selection aloud expressively. The reading enables the students simply to hear and enjoy the text as it is read through once. With this reading, you will model behaviors and comprehension strategies that all students will need to develop to become successful readers—for example, asking questions; clarifying unfamiliar words, first by using the pictures and later by using context; or predicting what might happen next.
- **Reread.** Read the selection expressively again. During the second reading of the stories, you will focus on teaching comprehension skills. Also, to develop print awareness, point to each word as it is read, thus demonstrating that text proceeds from left to right and from top to bottom and helping advance the idea that words are individual spoken and written units. Invite the students to identify the rhyming words in a poem or chime in on repetitive parts of text as you point to the words. Or students can read with you on this second reading, depending on the text.
- **Discuss Print.** Return to print awareness by encouraging discussion of anything the students noticed about the words. Young students should begin to realize that you are reading separate words that are separated by spaces. Later, students will begin to see that each word is made up of a group of letters. The students should be encouraged to discuss anything related to the print. For example, you might ask students to point to a word or count the number of words on a line. Or you might connect the words to the illustrations by pointing to a word and saying it and then asking the students to find a picture of that word.
- **Responding.** Responding to a selection is a way of insuring comprehension. Invite students to tell about the story by asking them what they like about the poem or story or calling on a student to explain in his or her own words what the poem or story tells about. Call on others to add to the telling as needed. For nonfiction selections, this discussion might include asking students what they learned about the topic and what they thought was most interesting.

Tips for Using Big Books

- Make sure the entire group is able to see the book clearly while you are reading.
- If some students are able to read or predict words, encourage them to do so during the rereading.
- Encourage students to present and use their knowledge of print.
- Allow students to look at the Big Books whenever they wish.
- Provide small versions of the Big Books for students to browse through and try to read at their leisure.
- The reader of the Big Book should try to be part of the collaborative group of learners rather than the leader.

Using the Pre-Decodable Books

Purpose

Pre-Decodable Books play an important role in students' early literacy development by providing them with meaningful "reading" experiences before they are actually reading on their own and by expanding their awareness of the forms and uses of print. By following along as you read aloud a **Pre-Decodable Book,** students learn about the left-to-right and top-to-bottom progression of print on a page, the clues that indicate the beginnings and endings of sentences, the connections between pictures and words, and important book conventions, such as front and back covers, authors' and illustrators' names, title pages, and page numbers.

The **Pre-Decodable Books** provide students with opportunities to apply their growing knowledge of letter names, shapes, and sounds, and to become familiar with individual words.

Through retelling the story in a **Pre-Decodable Book,** predicting or wondering about what will happen, and asking and responding to questions about the book, students not only learn about the relationship between spoken and written language, they learn to think about what they have read.

About the Pre-Decodable Books

Each **Pre-Decodable Book** contains a story that engages students' interest as it provides them with opportunities to practice what they are learning in their lessons. These "Pre-Decodable" stories each contain several high-frequency words that most students already have in their spoken vocabularies and that are a basic part of all meaningful stories. Learning to identify high-frequency words quickly, accurately, and effortlessly is a critical part of students' development as fluent, independent readers. The inside back cover of each **Pre-Decodable Book** contains a list of high-frequency words.

How to Read the Pre-Decodable Books

- Before reading a **Pre-Decodable Book,** take time to familiarize students with any new **high-frequency words** in the book and to review previously introduced words. To reinforce the idea that it is important to know these words because they are used so often in print, always point out the words in context. For example, focus students' attention on the words in Big Book selections or on signs and posters around the classroom.
- Give each student a copy of the book. Tell students that you will read the book together. Hold up your book. Read the title. If the title has a rebus picture, point to it and tell the students what it is. Then point to the word beneath it and explain that the picture represents that word. Point to and read the names of the author and illustrator, reminding students that an author writes a book and an illustrator draws the pictures. Page through the book, pointing to and naming the rebus pictures. Have the students say the name of each rebus. To avoid confusion, always *tell* them the *exact* word that a rebus represents. *Don't encourage them to guess at its meaning.*
- Allow students time to browse through the book on their own, commenting on what they see in the illustrations and making predictions about what they think the book will be about. Encourage them to comment on anything special they notice about the story, the illustrations, or the words in the book.
- Help the students to find page 3. Read the book aloud without stopping. As you read, move your hand beneath the words to show the progression of print. Pause at each rebus as you say the word it represents, pointing first to the rebus, then to the word beneath it.
- Reread the book. This time, ask the students to point to and read the high-frequency words.
- Tell the students to follow along in their books as you read the story again. Read the title aloud, and then have the students read it with you. Reread page 3. Point to each rebus picture and ask a volunteer to "read" it. Point to the word beneath the picture and remind students that the picture shows what the word is. Continue through each page of the book, calling on volunteers to "read" and stopping as necessary to clarify and help students with words.
- After reading, answer any questions the students might have about the book. Encourage them to discuss the illustrations and to explain what is happening in each one.

Reading Decodables and Building Fluency

Purpose

The most urgent task of early reading instruction is to make written thoughts intelligible to students. This requires a balanced approach that includes systematic instruction in phonics as well as experiences with authentic literature. Thus, from the very beginning, ***Open Court Reading*** includes the reading of literature. At the beginning of first grade, when students are learning phonics and blending as a tool to access words, the teacher reads aloud. During this time students are working on using comprehension strategies and skills and discussing stories. As students learn the code and blend words, recognize critical sight words, and develop some level of fluency, they take more responsibility for the actual reading of the text.

This program has a systematic instruction in phonics that allows the students to begin reading independently. This instruction is supported by ***Open Court Reading*** **Decodable Books.**

Practice

The ***Open Court Reading*** **Decodable Books** are designed to help the students apply, review, and reinforce their expanding knowledge of sound/spelling correspondences. Each story supports instruction in new phonic elements and incorporates elements and words that have been learned earlier. There are eight page and sixteen page **Decodable Books.** Grade K has eight-page **Decodable Books.** In Grade 1 the eight-page books focus on the new element introduced in the lesson, while the sixteen-page books review and reinforce the elements that have been taught since the last sixteen-page book. They review sounds from several lessons and provide additional reading practice. Grades 2–3 have eight-page **Decodable Books** in Getting Started, and sixteen-page books in the first 4–5 units of the grade level. The primary purpose is to provide practice reading the words. It is important that the students also attach meaning to what they are reading. Questions are often included in the ***Teacher's Edition*** to check both understanding and attention to words.

Fluency

Fluency is the effortless ability to read or access words with seemingly little attention to decoding. It also involves grouping words into meaningful units and using expression appropriately. Fluency is critical but not sufficient for comprehension.

To become proficient readers who fully understand what they read, the whole process of decoding must become as automatic as possible. The students need to be so familiar with the

Reading Materials and Techniques (continued)

sound/spellings and with the most common nondecodable sight words that they automatically process the letters or spellings and expend most of their energy on comprehending the meaning of the text.

While fluency begins in first grade, many students will continue to need practice in building fluency in second and third grades. Initially, students can use the ***Open Court Reading*** **Decodable Books** in grades 2 and 3, but fluency practice should include using materials from actual literature the students are reading.

Procedure

Preparing to Read

- Introduce and write on the board any nondecodable high-frequency or story words introduced or reviewed in the story. Tell the students how to pronounce any newly introduced high-frequency words. Then point to each new word and have the students say it. Have them read any previously introduced sight word in the Word Bank list. All of the ***Open Court Reading*** **Decodable Books** contain high-frequency words that may not be decodable. For example, the word *said* is a very common high-frequency word that is not decodable. Including words like *said* makes the language of the story flow smoothly and naturally. The students need to be able to recognize these words quickly and smoothly.
- Read the title. At the beginning of the year, you may need to read the title of the book to the students, but as the year goes on, you should have a student read it whenever possible. The sixteen-page ***Open Court Reading*** **Decodable Books** contain two related chapters, each using the same sounds and spellings. In such cases, read the title of the **Decodable** book, and then point out the two individual chapter titles. Have volunteers read the title of the chapter you are about to read.
- Browse the story. Have the students look through the story, commenting on whatever they notice in the text or illustrations and telling what they think the story will tell them.

Reading the Story

After this browsing, the students will read the story a page at a time. Again, these books are designed to support the learning of sounds and spellings. The focus should not be on comprehension. Students should understand what they are reading, and they should feel free to discuss anything in the story that interests them. Any areas of confusion are discussed and clarified as they arise, as described below.

- Have the students read a page to themselves. Then call on one student to read the page aloud, or have the whole group read it aloud.
- If a student has difficulty with a word that can be blended, help her or him blend the word. Remind the student to check the **Sound/Spelling Cards** for help. If a word cannot be blended using the sound/spellings learned so far, pronounce the word for the student.
- If a student has trouble with a word or sentence, have the reader call on a classmate for help, and then continue reading after the word or sentence has been clarified. After something on a page has been clarified or discussed, have that page reread by a different student before moving on to the next page.
- Repeat this procedure for each page.
- Reread the story twice more, calling on different students to read or reading it in unison. These readings should go more quickly, with fewer stops for clarification.

Responding to the Story

Once the story has been read aloud a few times, have the students respond as follows:

- Ask the students what hard words they found in the story and how they figured them out. They may mention high-frequency words they didn't recognize, words they had to blend, and words whose meanings they did not know.
- Invite the students to tell about the story, retelling it in their own words, describing what they liked about it, or citing what they found interesting or surprising. Specific suggestions to use are listed in the ***Teacher's Edition.***
- Questions are provided in the ***Teacher's Edition.*** They are designed to focus the students' attention on the words and not just the pictures. The questions require answers that cannot be guessed by looking at the pictures alone, such as a name, a bit of dialogue, or an action or object that is not pictured. Have the students point to the words, phrases, or sentences that answer the questions.

Building Fluency

Buiding fluency is essential to gaining strong comprehension. The more fluent the students become, the more they can attend to the critical business of understanding the text. Opportunities for students to build fluency may include:

- Have students "partner read" the most recent ***Open Court Reading*** **Decodable Book** twice, taking turns reading a page at a time. The partners should switch the second time through so they are reading different pages from the ones they read the first time. If there is time left, the partners should choose any of the previously read stories to read together. Use this time for diagnosis, having one student at a time read with you.
- Making sure that the ***Open Court Reading*** **Decodable Books** are readily available in the classroom.
- Reading **Decodable Books** with as many students as possible one at a time.
- Reminding the students that they may read with partners during Workshop.

The only way the students can become fluent readers is to read as much and as often as possible.

Reading the Student Anthologies

Purpose

Reading is a complex process that requires students not only to decode what they read but also to understand and respond to it. The purpose of this section is to help you identify various reading behaviors used by good readers and to encourage those behaviors in your students.

Reading Behaviors and Comprehension Strategies

There are four basic behaviors that good readers engage in during reading. These behaviors include the application of certain comprehension strategies, which are modeled while reading the Student Anthology (Levels 1–6).

Setting Reading Goals and Expectations

Good readers set reading goals and expectations before they begin reading. This behavior involves a variety of strategies that will help students prepare to read the text.

- **Activate prior knowledge.** When good readers approach a new text, they consider what they already know about the subject or what their experiences have been in reading similar material.
- **Browse the text.** To get an idea of what to expect from a text, good readers look at the title and the illustrations. They may look for potential problems, such as difficult words. When browsing a unit, have students glance quickly at each selection, looking briefly at the illustrations and the print. Have them tell what they think they might be learning about as they read the unit.
- **Decide what they expect from the text.** When reading for pleasure, good readers anticipate enjoying the story or the language. When reading to learn something, they ask themselves what they expect to find out.

Responding to Text

Good readers are active readers. They interact with text by using the following strategies:

- **Making connections.** Good readers make connections between what they read and what they already know. They pay attention to elements in the text that remind them of their own experiences.
- **Visualizing, or picturing.** Good readers visualize what is happening in the text. They form mental images as they read. They picture the setting, the characters, and the action in a story. When reading expository text, good readers picture the objects, processes, or events described. Visualizing helps readers understand descriptions of complex activities or processes.
- **Asking questions.** Good readers ask questions that may prepare them for what they will learn. If their questions are not answered in the text, they may try to find answers elsewhere and thus add even more to their store of knowledge.
- **Predicting.** Good readers predict what will happen next. When reading fiction, they make predictions about what they are reading and then confirm or revise those predictions as they go.
- **Thinking about how the text makes you feel.** Well-written fiction touches readers' emotions; it sparks ideas.

Checking Understanding

One of the most important behaviors good readers exhibit is the refusal to continue reading when something fails to make sense. Good readers continually assess their understanding of the text with strategies such as:

- **Interpreting.** As they read, good readers make inferences that help them understand and appreciate what they are reading.
- **Summing up.** Good readers sum up to check their understanding as they read. Sometimes they reread to fill in gaps in their understanding.
- **Monitoring and adjusting reading speed.** Good readers monitor their understanding of what they read. They slow down as they come to difficult words and passages. They speed up as they read easier passages.

Monitoring and Clarifying Unfamiliar Words and Passages

- **Apply decoding skills** to sound out unknown words.
- **Determine what is unclear** to find the source of the confusion.
- **Apply context clues** in text and illustrations to figure out the meanings of words or passages.
- **Reread the passage** to make sure the passage makes sense.
- **Check a dictionary or the glossary** to understand the meanings of words not clarified by clues or rereading.

Procedures

Modeling and Thinking Aloud

Modeling and encouraging students to think aloud as they attempt to understand text can demonstrate for everyone how reading behaviors are put into practice. The most effective models will be those that come from your own reading. Using questions such as the following, as well as your students' questions and comments, will make both the text and the strategic reading process more meaningful to students.

- What kinds of things did you wonder about?
- What kinds of things surprised you?
- What new information did you learn?
- What was confusing until you reread or read further?

Model comprehension strategies in a natural way, and choose questions and comments that fit the text you are reading. Present a variety of ways to respond to text.

- Pose questions that you really do wonder about.
- Identify with characters by comparing them with yourself.
- React emotionally by showing joy, sadness, amusement, or surprise.
- Show empathy with or sympathy for characters.
- Relate the text to something that has happened to you or to something you already know.
- Show interest in the text ideas.
- Question the meaning or clarity of the author's words and ideas.

Encouraging Students' Responses and Use of Strategies

Most students will typically remain silent as they try to figure out an unfamiliar word or a confusing passage. Encourage students to identify specifically what they are having difficulty with. Once the problem has been identified, ask the students to suggest a strategy for dealing with the problem. Remind students to:

- Treat problems encountered in text as interesting learning opportunities.
- Think out loud about text challenges.
- Help each other build meaning. Rather than tell what a word is, students should tell how they figured out the meanings of challenging words and passages.
- Consider reading a selection again with a partner after reading it once alone. Partner reading provides valuable practice in reading for fluency.
- Make as many connections as they can between what they are reading and what they already know.
- Visualize to clarify meanings or enjoy descriptions.
- Ask questions about what they are reading.
- Notice how the text makes them feel.

PROGRAM APPENDIX

Reading Techniques

Reading Aloud

Purpose

Adults read a variety of materials aloud to students. These include Big Books, picture books, and novels. Research has shown that students who are read to are more likely to develop the skills they need to read successfully on their own.

In every grade level of **Open Court Reading** there are opportunities for teachers to read aloud to students. At the beginning of each unit is a Read-Aloud selection tied to the unit theme. This Read-Aloud selection allows students the opportunity to think about the unit theme before reading selections on their own.

Reading aloud at any age serves multiple purposes. Reading aloud:

- Provokes students' curiosity about text.
- Conveys an awareness that text has meaning.
- Demonstrates the various reasons for reading text (to find out about the world around them, to learn useful new information and new skills, or simply for pleasure).
- Exposes students to the "language of literature," which is more complex than the language they ordinarily use and hear.
- Provides an opportunity to teach the problem-solving strategies that good readers employ. As the students observe you interacting with the text, expressing your own enthusiasm, and modeling your thinking aloud, they perceive these as valid responses and begin to respond to text in similar ways.

Procedures

The following set of general procedures for reading aloud is designed to help you maximize the effectiveness of Read-Aloud sessions.

- **Read-aloud sessions.** Set aside time each day to read aloud.
- **Introduce the story.** Tell the students that you are going to read a story aloud to them. Tell its title and briefly comment on the topic. To allow the students to anticipate what will happen in the story, be careful not to summarize.
- **Activate prior knowledge.** Ask whether anyone has already heard the story. If so, ask them to see if this version is the same as the one they have heard. If not, activate prior knowledge by saying, "First, let's talk a little about _____." If the story is being read in two (or more) parts, before reading the second part, ask the students to recall the first part.
- **Before reading.** Invite students to interrupt your reading if there are any words they do not understand or ideas they find puzzling. Throughout the reading, encourage them to do this.
- **Read the story expressively.** Occasionally react verbally to the story by showing surprise, asking questions, giving an opinion, expressing pleasure, or predicting events. Think-aloud suggestions are outlined below.
- **Use Comprehension Strategies.** While reading aloud to the students, model the use of comprehension strategies in a natural, authentic way. Remember to try to present a variety of ways to respond to text. These include visualizing, asking questions, predicting, making connections, clarifying, and summarizing.
- **Retell.** When you have finished reading the story, call on volunteers to retell it.
- **Discuss.** After reading, discuss with the students their own reactions: how the story reminded them of things that have happened to them, what they thought of the story, and what they liked best about the story.
- **Reread.** You may wish to reread the selection on subsequent occasions focusing the discussion on the unit theme.

Think-Aloud Responses

The following options for modeling thinking aloud will be useful for reading any story aloud. Choose responses that are most appropriate for the selection you are reading.

- **React emotionally** by showing joy, sadness, amusement, or surprise.
- **Ask questions** about ideas in the text. This should be done when there are points or ideas that you really do wonder about.
- **Identify with characters** by comparing them to yourself.
- **Show empathy with or sympathy for** characters.
- **Relate the text to something** you already know or something that has happened to you.
- **Show interest** in the text ideas.
- **Question the meaning and/or clarity** of the author's words and ideas.

Questions to Help Students Respond

At reasonable stopping points in reading, ask the students general questions in order to get them to express their own ideas and to focus their attention on the text.

- What do you already know about this?
- What seems really important here? Why do you think so?
- Was there anything that you didn't understand? What?
- What did you like best about this?
- What new ideas did you learn from this?
- What does this make you wonder about?

Reading Roundtable

Purpose

Adult readers discuss their reading, give opinions on it, and recommend books to each other. Reading Roundtable, an activity students may choose to participate in during **Workshop**, provides the same opportunity for students in the classroom. Sessions can be small or large. During Reading Roundtable, students share the reading they do on their own. They can discuss a book they have all read, or one person can review a book for the others and answer questions from the group.

During Reading Roundtable, students can discuss and review a variety of books:

- Full-length versions of Anthology selections.
- Classroom Library selections.
- Books that students learn about when discussing authors and illustrators.
- Books related to the investigations of unit concepts can be shared with others who might want to read them.
- Interesting articles from magazines, newspapers, and other sources.

Procedures

Encouraging Reading

- Read aloud to your students regularly. You can read Classroom Library selections or full-length versions of Student Anthology selections.
- Provide a time each day for students to read silently. This time can be as short as 10–15 minutes but should be strictly observed. You should stop what you are doing and read. Students should be allowed to choose their own reading materials during this time and record their reactions in the Response Journal section of their Writer's Notebook.
- Establish a classroom library and reading center with books from the school or local library or ask for donations of books from students, parents, and community members.
- Take your students to the school library or to the public library.

Conducting a Reading Roundtable

- When a student reviews a book others have not read, he or she can use some of the sentence starters to tell about the book. These may include, "This book is about . . . , I chose this book because. . . , What I really like/don't like about this book is . . . " and so on.
- When several students read the same book and discuss it during Reading Roundtable, they can use discussion starters. If the book is from the Classroom Library, they can discuss how it relates to the unit concepts.

Introducing Sounds and Letters

Purpose

In ***SRA/Open Court Reading***, students learn to relate sounds to letters in Kindergarten through the use of thirty-one **Alphabet Sound Cards** (Level K). In the upper grade levels, **Sound Spelling Cards** (Levels 1–3) are used to relate sounds and spellings. The purpose of the **Alphabet Sound Cards** is to remind the students of the sounds of the English language and their letter correspondences. These cards are a resource for the students to use to remember sound-letter associations for both reading and writing.

Each card contains the capital and small letter, and a picture that shows the sound being produced. For instance, the **Monkey** card introduces the /m/ sound and shows a monkey looking at bananas and saying */m/ /m/ /m/*. The name of the picture on each card contains the target sound at the beginning of the word for the consonants and in the middle for most of the vowels. Vowel letters are printed in red and consonants are printed in black. In addition, the picture associates a sound with an action. This action-sound association is introduced through a short, interactive story found in the ***Teacher's Edition*** in which the pictured object or character "makes" the sound of the letter. Long vowels are represented by a tall—or "long"—picture of the letters themselves, rather than by a picture for action-sound association.

Procedures

- Display the cards 1–26 with the picture sides to the wall. Initially post the first twenty-six cards in alphabetical order so that only the alphabet letters show. The short vowel cards may be posted as they are introduced later. As you introduce the letter sound, you will turn the card to show the picture and the letter on the other side. Once the cards are posted, do not change their positions so that the students can locate the cards quickly.
- Before turning a card, point to the letter. Ask students to tell what they know about the letter. For example, they are likely to know its name and possibly its sound if the letter is one they have already worked with.
- Turn the card and show the picture. Tell the students the name of the card, and explain that it will help them to remember the sound the letter makes.
- Read the story that goes with the letter. Read it expressively, emphasizing the words with the target sound and the isolated sound when it occurs. Have the students join in to produce the sound.
- Repeat the story a few times, encouraging all students to say the sound along with you.
- Follow the story with the cards for the target sound. (These are listed within the lessons.)
- Name each picture, and have students listen for the target sound at the beginning of the word. Ask students to repeat the words and the sound.
- For every letter sound, a listening activity follows the introduction of the cards. Lead the students in the "Listening for the Sound" activity to reinforce the letter sound.
- To link the sound and the letter, demonstrate how to form the uppercase and lowercase letter by writing on the board or on an overhead transparency. The students practice forming the letter and saying the sound as they write.

Alphabet Sound Cards

The pictures and letters on the **Alphabet Sound Cards (Wall Cards)** also appear on the small sets of **Alphabet Sound Cards (Individual)**. The Teacher's Edition specifically suggests that you use the **Individual Alphabet Sound Cards** for some activities. You may also use the small cards for review and for small-group reteaching and practice sessions. Have sets of the cards available for the students to use during **Workshop** either alone or with partners. Add each small card to the Activity Center after you have taught the lesson in which the corresponding **Alphabet Sound Card** is introduced. Here are some suggestions for activities using the **Alphabet Sound Cards**:

1. **Saying sounds from pictures.** The leader flashes pictures as the others say the sound each picture represents.
2. **Saying sounds.** The leader flashes the letters on the cards as the others say the sound that the letters represent.
3. **Naming words from pictures.** The leader flashes pictures. The others say the sound, and then say a word beginning with that sound.
4. **Writing letters from the pictures.** Working alone, a student looks at a picture and then writes the letter for the sound that picture represents.

Tips

- Throughout the beginning lessons, help students remember that vowels are special by reminding them that vowels sometimes say their names in words. For example, the picture of the *a* on the long *a* **Alphabet Sound Card** is long because the long *a* says its name. The short *a* **Alphabet Sound Card** pictures the lamb, because the lamb makes the short *a* sound, and you can hear the sound in the word, *lamb*. In the later lessons, students will use both sets of cards to help them remember that the vowels have both a short and a long sound.
- From the very beginning, encourage students to use the **Alphabet Sound Cards** as a resource to help them with their work.
- Mastery of letter recognition is the goal students should reach so that they will be prepared to link each letter with its associated sound. If students have not yet mastered the names of the letters, it is important to work with them individually in **Workshop**, or at other times during the day.
- The *Kk* card is a little tricky. A camera makes the /k/ sound when it clicks, and the word *camera* begins with the /k/ sound. However, the word *camera* is not spelled with a *k*. While you need not dwell on this, be aware that some students may be confused by the fact that the *Cc* and *Kk* cards have the same picture.
- The picture on the *Qq* card depicts ducks, *quacking ducks*. Make sure that the students consistently call them *quacking ducks*, not *ducks*, and that they focus on the /kw/ sound.

The Alphabetic Principle: How the Alphabet Works

PROGRAM APPENDIX

The Alphabetic Principle

Purpose

A major emphasis in the kindergarten program is on letter recognition and attending to sounds. Students need to learn the alphabetic principle: that letters work together in a systematic way to connect spoken language to written words. This understanding is the foundation for reading. Students are not expected to master letter/sound correspondence at the beginning of kindergarten, nor are they expected to blend sounds into words themselves. They are only expected to become an "expert" on their Special Letter as they learn how the alphabet works. Through this introduction to the alphabetic principle, the students will have the basic understanding required to work through the alphabet letter by letter, attaching sounds to each.

Key concepts of the Alphabetic Principle include:

- A limited number of letters combine in different ways to make many different words.
- Words are composed of sounds and letters represent those sounds.
- Anything that can be pronounced can be spelled.
- Letters and sounds can be used to identify words.
- Meaning can be obtained by using letters and sounds to figure out words.

Procedures for Kindergarten

The following steps can be used for introducing letters and sounds in Kindergarten. These steps may be adapted for students at other grades if they do not understand the alphabetic principle. The tone of these activities should be informal, fun, and fast-paced. The purpose of these activities is to familiarize the students with how the alphabet works by having them participate in group play with letters and sounds.

Introducing Letters

- Reinforce the idea that anything that can be pronounced can be spelled with the letters of the alphabet.
- Tell the students that you can spell any word. Have them give you words to spell.
- Write the words on the board, and show students that the words contain the letters displayed on the **Alphabet Sound Cards**.
- Have students help you spell the words by pointing to letters as you say them and then write them.
- Encourage students to spell each word letter by letter.

Letter Expert Groups

- Have **Letter Cards** (Levels K and 1) available for the following set of letters: *b, d, f, h, l, m, n, p, s, t*. You will need two or three cards for each letter. (You will not need the **Alphabet Sound Cards** until later.)
- You will be the letter expert for the vowels.
- Divide the class into groups of two or three and assign each group a letter. Give each student the appropriate **Letter Card**.
- Tell the students that they are now in their Letter Expert groups and that they are going to become experts on their Special Letter's name, shape, and sound.

Students need to learn the alphabetic principle: that letters work together in a systematic way to connect spoken language to written words. This understanding is the foundation for reading.

Making Words

- Begin each lesson with a rehearsal of each group's letter name.
- Demonstrate how letters work by writing a word in large letters on the board.
- Tell the students the experts for each letter in the word should hold up their **Letter Cards** and name the letter. One member of the group should stand in front of their letter on the board.
- Continue until all letters in the word are accounted for. Remember that you are responsible for the vowels.
- Demonstrate that you can make different words by changing a letter or by changing the letter order.

Identifying Sounds in Words

- Use the **Alphabet Sound Cards** to demonstrate that every letter has at least one sound.
- Give each student the **Alphabet Sound Card** for his or her Special Letter.
- Point out the pictures on the cards. Explain that each card has a picture of something that makes the letter's sound. The picture will help them remember the sound.
- Tell each group the sound for its letter. (Remember, you are the expert for the vowels.)
- Quickly have each group rehearse its letter's name and sound.
- Write a word on the board in large letters. Say the word first sound-by-sound and then blend the word.
- For each letter/sound in the word, have one student from each Letter Expert group come forward, stand in front of the appropriate letter, and hold their cards. Although only one member of the group may come forward with the **Letter Card** or **Alphabet Sound Card,** all students in a Special Letter group should say the name and/or sound of their letter when it occurs in words.
- Say the word again, pointing to the **Alphabet Sound Cards**.
- Ask students who are not already standing to help you hold the vowel cards.
- Vary the activity by changing one letter sound and having an expert for that letter come forward.
- End the activity for each word by saying the sounds in the words one by one and then saying the entire word. Encourage the students to participate.

Tips

- Remind the students to use the picture on the **Alphabet Sound Card** for their Special Letter to help them remember the letter's sound. The students are expected only to "master" their own Special Letter and share the information with their classmates. At this point in the year, they are not expected to blend and read the words by themselves. These are group activities in which you work with the students to help them gain insight into the alphabet.
- Have students note that what they learn about the letters and words applies to the words they work with in Big Book selections.
- Occasionally, have students find their special letters in a Big Book selection. Play some of the letter replacement and rearrangement games with words encountered in the Big Books.

Developing the Alphabetic Principle

Purpose

The following activities are extended to provide kindergarten students with a more thorough understanding of how sounds "work" in words. In this group of exercises, the students are introduced to specific letter/sound correspondences, consonants and short vowels. The students have previously been introduced to vowels and their special characteristics. This understanding is extended by introducing students to the convention that a vowel has a short sound in addition to its long sound. With this information and a carefully structured set of activities, the students can begin to explore and understand the alphabetic principle in a straightforward and thorough manner. The students not only listen for sounds in specified positions in words; they also link sounds to their corresponding letters. The activities in this group of lessons lay the groundwork for students to work their way through the entire alphabet as they learn letter-sound associations and to understand the purpose and the value of this learning.

Move the students quickly through these activities. Do not wait for all the students to master each letter/sound correspondence before going on. The students will have more opportunities to achieve mastery. The goal of these activities is for the students to obtain a basic understanding of the alphabetic principle.

Procedures

Introducing Consonant Letters and Sounds

- Point to the **Alphabet Sound Card** and name the letter.
- Point to the picture. Tell the students the sound of the letter and how the picture helps them to remember the sound. Repeat the sound several times.
- Tell the students you will read them the short story or an alliterative sentence to help them remember the sound of the letter. Read the story several times, emphasizing the words with the target sound. Have the students join in and say the sound.
- After introducing and reviewing a letter/sound correspondence, summarize the information on the **Alphabet Sound Card**.

Generating Words with the Target Sound

- Brainstorm to create a list of words that begin with the target sound. Write the words on the board or on a chart. Include any of the students' names that begin with the target sound.
- Play the *I'm Thinking of Something That Starts With* game. Begin with the target sound and add clues until the students guess the word. If the students guess a word that does not begin with the target sound, emphasize the beginning sound and ask if the word begins with the target sound.
- Silly Sentences. Make silly sentences with the students that include many words with the target sound. Encourage the students to participate by extending the sentences: *Mary mopes. Mary mopes on Monday. Mary and Michael mope on Monday in Miami.*

Listening for Initial Sounds

- Give each student a **Letter Card** for the target sound, /s/.
- Point to the picture on the **Alphabet Sound Card**, and have the students give the sound, /s/.
- Tell the students to listen for the first sound in each word you say. If it is /s/, they should hold up their *s* cards. Establish a signal so that the students know when to respond.
- Read a list of words, some beginning with /s/, some beginning with other sounds.

Listening for Final Sounds

The procedure for listening for the final sound of a word is the same as that for listening for the initial sound. The students may need to be reminded throughout the activity to pay attention to the *final* sound.

- Read a list of words, some ending with the target sound and some ending with other sounds. Avoid words that begin with the target sound.

Linking the Sound to the Letter

- **Word Pairs (initial sounds).** Write pairs of words on the board. One of each pair should begin with the target sound. Say the word beginning with the target sound, and ask the students to identify it. Remind them to listen for the target sound at the beginning of the word, to think about which letter makes that sound, and to find the word that begins with that letter. For example,
  Target sound: /s/
  Word pair: *fit sit*
  Which word is *sit*?
- **Word Pairs (final sounds).** Follow the same procedure used for initial sounds, and direct the students to think about the sound that they hear at the end of the word. Since it is often more difficult for the students to attend to the ending sound, you may need to lead them through several pairs of words. Remind the students to listen for the target sound and to think about which letter makes that sound.
- **Writing Letters.** Using either of the handwriting systems outlined in the Program Appendix of ***SRA/Open Court Reading***, or the system in use at your school, have students practice writing uppercase and lowercase letters. Remind the students about the letter sound, and have them repeat it.

Comparing Initial Consonant Sounds

This activity is exactly like **Listening for Initial Sounds** except that the students must discriminate between two sounds. They are given **Letter Cards** for both sounds and must hold up the appropriate card when they hear the sound.

Comparing Final Consonant Sounds

This activity is exactly like listening for final sounds except that the students must discriminate between two sounds. They are given **Letter Cards** for both sounds and must hold up the appropriate card when they hear the sound.

Linking the Consonant Sound to the Letter

In this activity to help students link sounds and letters, the students will make words either by adding initial consonants to selected word parts or by adding a different final consonant to a consonant-vowel-consonant combination.

The Alphabetic Principle: How the Alphabet Works (continued)

Introducing Short Vowel Sounds

- Tell the students that the vowels are printed in red to remind them that they are special letters. (They are not special because they are printed in red.) They are special because they have more than one sound, and every word must have a vowel sound.
- Point to the long *Aa* **Alphabet Sound Card,** and remind the students that this letter is called a *vowel*. Vowels sometimes say their names in words: for example, *say, day, tray.* This vowel sound is called long *a*.
- Have the students repeat the sound.
- Sometimes vowels say different sounds. Point to the picture of the lamb on the short *Aa* card, and tell students that *a* also makes the sound heard in the middle of *lamb*. This is the short *a*. Read the short vowel story to help the students remember the short *a*.
- Have all the students join in saying /a/ /a/ /a/.

Listening for Short Vowel Sounds Versus Long Vowel Sounds

- Tell the students that you will read words with long *a* and short *a*. Review the two sounds.
- Give the students a signal to indicate when they hear the vowel sound. You may want one signal for short *a*, such as scrunching down, and another for long *a*, such as stretching up tall.
- Continue with lists of words such as: *add, back, aid, tan, bake, tame.*

Linking the Vowel Sound to the Letter

- Writing Letters. Have students practice writing the letter and review the sound of the letter.
- In this activity to help students link sounds and letters, the students will make words either by adding initial consonants to selected word parts or by adding a different final consonant to a consonant-vowel-consonant combination. Change the beginning of the word or the word ending, but retain the vowel sound to make new words:

at	*hat*	*mat*	*pat*
ap	*map*	*tap*	*sap*
am	*Sam*	*Pam*	*ham*

Comparing Short Vowel Sounds

This activity requires students to discriminate between short vowel sounds in the middle of words. Review the vowel sounds.

- Say a word, and have the students repeat it. Establish a signal to indicate whether they hear short *a* or short *o* in the middle of the word. For example, they can hold up the appropriate **Letter Card** when they hear a sound. Sample words: *cap, cot, rat, rot, rack, rock.*

Linking the Sound to the Letter

- In this activity write a word on the board, and help the students say it.
- Change the word by changing the vowel. Help the students say the new word, for example, *map, mop; hot, hat; pot, pat.*
- For a variation of this activity, write the pairs of words, and simply have the students say which word is the target word. For example, the students see *tap* and *top*. Ask which word *top* is, directing the students' attention to the vowel.

Tips

- Lead and model the exercises as necessary until the students begin to catch on and can participate with confidence.
- To keep the students focused on the various activities, have them tell you the task for each activity. For example, after telling the students to listen for final sounds, ask the students what they will be listening for.
- Actively involve the students by giving them opportunities to tell what they know rather than supplying the information for them. Do they know the letter name? Do they know the sound? Can they think of words that begin with the sound?
- Keeping the students focused on the idea that they are learning about sounds and letters so they can read these books themselves makes the lessons more relevant for the students.

Phonemic Awareness

The basic purpose of providing structured practice in phonemic awareness is to help the students hear and understand the sounds from which words are made. Before students can be expected to understand the sound/symbol correspondence that forms the base of written English, they need to have a strong working knowledge of the sound relationships that make up the spoken language. This understanding of spoken language lays the foundation for the transition to written language.

Phonemic awareness activities provide the students with easy practice in discriminating the sounds that make up words. Phonemic awareness consists of quick, gamelike activities designed to help students understand that speech is made up of distinct, identifiable sounds. The playful nature of the activities makes them appealing and engaging, while giving the students practice and support for learning about language. Once the students begin reading and writing, this experience with manipulating sounds will help them use what they know about sounds and letters to sound out and spell unfamiliar words when they read and write.

The two main formats for teaching phonemic awareness are oral blending and segmentation. These are supported by occasional discrimination activities and general wordplay. Oral blending encourages students to combine sounds to make words. Segmentation, conversely, requires them to isolate sounds from words. Other activities support discrimination, or recognition, of particular sounds. Sometimes simple songs, rhymes, or games engage students in wordplay. In these, the students manipulate words in a variety of ways. From these playful activities, the students derive serious knowledge about language.

As the students progress through different phonemic awareness activities, they will become proficient at listening for and reproducing the sounds they hear. It is essential for their progression to phonics and reading that they are able to hear the sounds and the patterns used to make up recognizable words. The phonemic awareness activities support the phonics instruction, but the activities are oral and do not focus on sound/spelling correspondences. Because the students are not expected to read the words they are experimenting with, any consonant and vowel sounds may be used, even if the students have not been formally taught the sound and its spellings.

Oral Blending

Purpose

In oral blending, the students are led through a progression of activities designed to help them hear how sounds are put together to make words.

Until students develop an awareness of the component parts of words, they have no tools with which to decode words or put letters together to form words. Oral blending helps students master these component parts of words, from syllables down to single sounds, or phonemes. Oral blending is not to be confused with the formal blending of specific sounds whose spellings the students will be taught through phonics instruction. Oral blending does not depend on the recognition of written words; it focuses instead on hearing the sounds.

Oral blending focuses on hearing sounds through a sequence that introduces the most easily distinguished word parts and then systematically moves to sound blending that contains all the challenges of phonic decoding (except letter recognition). This sequence provides support for the least-prepared student—one who comes to school with no concept of words or sounds within words. At the same time, the lively pace and playful nature of oral blending activities hold the interest of students who already have some familiarity with words and letters.

Oral blending prepares students for phonics instruction by developing an awareness of the separate sounds that make up speech. Oral blending activities then continue in concert with phonics instruction to reinforce and extend new learning. And, because these activities involve simply listening to and reproducing sounds, oral blending need not be restricted to the sounds students have been or will be taught in phonics.

The tone of the activities should be playful and informal and should move quickly. Although these activities will provide information about student progress, they are not diagnostic tools. Do not expect mastery. Those students who have not caught on will be helped more by varied experiences than by more drilling on the same activity.

Procedures

Following is a description of the progression of oral blending activities.

Syllable Blending

Syllables are easier to distinguish than individual sounds (phonemes), so students can quickly experience success in forming meaningful words. Tell the students that you are going to say some words in two parts. Tell them to listen carefully so that they can discover what the words are. Read each word, pronouncing each part distinctly with a definite pause between syllables broken by. . . . The lists of words that follow are arranged in sequence from easy to harder. They cover different types of cues. At any point where they fit in the sequence, include multisyllable names of students in the class.

Model

Teacher: *dino . . . saur. What's the word?*

Students: *dinosaur*

Example Words

- First part of the word cues the whole word:
  vita . . . min *vaca . . . tion*
  hippopot . . . amus *ambu . . . lance*
- Two distinct words easily combined:
  butter. . . fly *straw. . . berry*
  surf . . . board *basket . . . ball*

Phonemic Awareness (continued)

- Two distinct words, but first word could cue the wrong ending:
  tooth . . . ache *tooth . . . paste*
  water . . . fall *water . . . melon*
- First part, consonant + vowel, not enough to guess whole word:
  re . . . member *re . . . frigerator*
  bi . . . cycle *bi . . . ology*
- Identifying clues in second part:
  light . . . ning *sub . . . ject* *in . . . sect*
- Last part, consonant + vowel sound, carries essential information:
  yester . . . day *rain . . . bow*
  noi . . . sy *pota . . . to*
- Changing the final part changes the word:
  start . . . ing *start . . . er* *start. . . ed*

Initial Consonant Sounds

Initial consonant blending prepares students for consonant replacement activities that will come later. Tell the students that you will ask them to put some sounds together to make words. Pronounce each word part distinctly, and make a definite pause at the breaks indicated. When a letter is surrounded by slash marks, pronounce the letter's sound, not its name. When you see /s/, for example, you will say "ssss," not "ess." The words that follow are arranged from easy to harder. At any point where they fit in the sequence, include names of students in the class.

Model

TEACHER: /t/ . . . iger. What's the word?

STUDENTS: tiger

Example Words

- Separated consonant blend, with rest of word giving strong cue to word identity:
  /b/ . . . *roccoli* /k/ . . . *racker*
  /f/ . . . *lashlight* /k/ . . . *reature*
- Held consonant that is easy for students to hear, with rest of word giving strong cue:
  /s/ . . . *innamon* /l/ . . . *adybug*
  /s/ . . . *eventeen* /n/ . . . *ewspaper*
- Stop consonant that is harder for students to hear preceding vowel, with rest of word giving strong cue:
  /t/. . . *adpole* /p/ . . . *iggybank*
  /d/ . . . *ragonfly* /b/ . . . *arbecue*
- Single-syllable words and words in which the second part gives a weaker cue:
  /s/ . . . *ing* /l/ . . . *augh* /v/ . . . *ase*

Final Consonant Sounds

In this phase of oral blending, the last sound in the word is separated.

Model

TEACHER: cabba . . . /j/. What's the word?

STUDENTS: cabbage

Example Words

- Words that are easily recognized even before the final consonant is pronounced:
  bubblegu . . . /m/ *Columbu . . .* /s/
  crocodi . . . /l/ *submari . . .* /n/
- Multisyllable words that need the final consonant for recognition:
  colle . . . /j/ *(college)* *come . . .* /t/ *(comet)*
- Single-syllable words:
  sa . . . /d/ *gra . . .* /s/ *snai . . .* /l/

Initial Consonant Sound Replacement

This level of oral blending further develops awareness of initial consonant sounds. The activity begins with a common word, then quickly changes its initial consonant sound. Most of the words produced are nonsense words, which helps keep the focus on the sounds in the word. Note that the words are written on the board, but the students are not expected to read them. The writing is to help the students see that when the sounds change, the letters change, and vice versa.

Model

TEACHER: [Writes word on board.] This word is *magazine*. What is it?

STUDENTS: *magazine*

TEACHER: Now I'm going to change it. [Erases initial consonant.] Now it doesn't start with /m/, it's going to start with /b/. What's the new word?

STUDENTS: *bagazine*

TEACHER: That's right . . . [Writes b where m had been.] It's *bagazine*. Now I'm going to change it again. . . .

Repeat with different consonant sounds. Then do the same with other words, such as: *remember, Saturday, tomorrow, lotion*, and *million*. Continue with single-syllable words, such as: *take, big, boot, cot, seat, look, tap, ride*, and *late*. There are two stages in using written letters:

- The replacement letter is not written until *after* the new "word" has been identified.
- Later, the replacement letter is written *at the same time* the change in the initial phoneme is announced. For example, the teacher erases *d* and writes *m* while saying, "Now it doesn't start with /d/, it starts with /m/."

You may wish to alter the procedure when the consonants used have already been introduced in phonics by writing the replacement letter and having students sound out the new word. Feel free to switch between the two procedures within a single exercise. If the students are not responding orally to written spellings that have been introduced in phonics, don't force it. Proceed by saying the word before writing the letter, and wait until another time to move on to writing before pronouncing.

One-Syllable Words

The students now begin blending individual phonemes to form words. This important step can be continued well into the year. Continued repetitions of this activity will help the students realize how they can use the sound/spellings they are learning to read and write real words.

At first, the blended words are presented in a story context that helps the students identify the words. They soon recognize that they are actually decoding meaningful words. However, the context must not be so strong that the students can guess the word without listening to the phonemic cues. Any vowel sounds and irregularly spelled words may be used, since there is no writing involved.

Model

TEACHER: *When I looked out the window, I saw a /l/ /ī/ /t/. What did I see?*

STUDENTS: *A light.*

TEACHER: *Yes, I saw a light. At first I thought it was the /m/ /o͞o/ /n/. What did I think it was?*

STUDENTS: *The moon.*

TEACHER: *But it didn't really look like the moon. Suddenly I thought, maybe it's a space /sh/ /i/ /p/. What did I think it might be?*

STUDENTS: *A space ship!*

Once the students are familiar with this phase of oral blending, they can move to blending one-syllable words without the story context.

Example Words

- CVC (consonant/vowel/consonant) words beginning with easily blended consonant sounds (/sh/, /h/, /r/, /v/, /s/, /n/, /z/, /f/, /l/, /m/):
  nip *nap*
- CVC words beginning with any consonant:
  ten *bug* *lip*
- Add CCVC words:
  flap *step*
- Add CVCC words:
  most *band* *went*
- Add CCVCC words:
  stamp *grand* *scuffs*

Final Consonant Sound Replacement

Final consonant sounds are typically more difficult for students to use than initial consonants.

- Begin with multisyllable words, and move to one-syllable words.
- As with initial consonants, first write the changed consonant after students have pronounced the new word.
- Then write the consonant as they pronounce it.
- For sound/spellings introduced in phonics instruction, write the new consonant spelling, and have students identify and pronounce it.

Model

Teacher: *[Writes word on board.] This word is* teapot*. What is it?*

Students: *teapot*

Teacher: *Now I'm going to change it.* [Erases final consonant.] *Now it doesn't end with /t/, it ends with /p/. What's the word now?*

Students: *teapop*

Teacher: *That's right . . .* [Writes *p* where *t* had been.] *It's* teapop. *Now I'm going to change it again. . . .*

Example Words

- Words that are easily recognized even before the final consonant is pronounced:
  picnic picnit picnis picnil picnid
  airplane airplate airplabe airplafe
- Multisyllable words that need the final consonant for recognition:
  muffin muffil muffim muffip muffit
  amaze amate amake amale amade
- Single-syllable words:
  neat nean neap neam neaj nead neaf
  broom broot brood broof broop broon

Initial Vowel Replacement

Up to now, oral blending has concentrated on consonant sounds because they are easier to hear than vowels. As you move to vowel play, remember that the focus is still on the sounds, not the spellings. Use any vowel sounds.

Model

Teacher: [Writes word on board.] *This word is* elephant*. What is it?*

Students: *elephant*

Teacher: *Now I'm going to change it.* [Erases initial vowel.] *Now it doesn't start with /e/, it starts with /a/. What's the word now?*

Students: *alephant*

Teacher: *That's right . . .* [Writes *a* where *e* had been.] *It's alephant. Now I'm going to change it again. . . .*

Example Words

- Multisyllable words:
  angry ingry oongry ungry engry
  ivy avy oovy evy ovy oivy
- One-syllable words:
  ink ank oonk unk onk oink
  add odd idd oudd edd udd

Segmentation

Purpose

Segmentation and oral blending complement each other: Oral blending puts sounds together to make words, while segmentation separates words into sounds. Oral blending will provide valuable support for decoding when students begin reading independently.

Procedure

Syllables

The earliest segmentation activities focus on syllables, which are easier to distinguish than individual sounds, or phonemes. Start with students' names, then use other words. As with the oral blending activities, remember to move quickly through these activities. Do not hold the class back waiting for all students to catch on. Individual progress will vary, but drilling on one activity is less helpful than going on to others. Return to the same activity often. Frequent repetition is very beneficial and allows students additional opportunities to catch on.

- Say, for example, "Let's clap out Amanda's name. A-man-da."
- Have the students clap and say the syllables along with you. Count the claps.
- Tell the students that these word parts are called *syllables*. Don't try to explain; the idea will develop with practice. Once you have provided the term, simply say, "How many syllables?" after the students clap and count.
- Mix one-syllable and multisyllable words:
  fantastic tambourine good
  imaginary stand afraid

Comparative Length of Words

Unlike most phonemic awareness activities, this one involves writing on the board or on an overhead transparency. Remember, though, that the students are not expected to read what is written. They are merely noticing that words that take longer to say generally look longer when written.

- Start with students' names. Choose two names, one short and one long, with the same first initial (for example, *Joe* and *Jonathan*).
- Write the two names on the board, one above the other, so that the difference is obvious.
- Tell the students that one name is *Jonathan* and one is *Joe*. Have them pronounce and clap each name. Then, have them tell which written word they think says *Joe*.
- Move your finger under each name as they clap and say it, syllable by syllable.
- Repeat with other pairs of names and words, such as: *tea/telephone, cat/caterpillar, butterfly/bug*. Be sure not to give false clues. For example, sometimes write the longer word on top, sometimes the shorter one; sometimes ask for the shorter word, sometimes the longer; sometimes ask for the top word, sometimes the bottom; sometimes point to a word and ask the students to name it, and sometimes name the word and ask the students to point to it.

Listen for Individual Sounds

Activities using a puppet help the students listen for individual sounds in words. Use any puppet you have on hand. When you introduce the puppet, tell the students that it likes to play word games. Each new activity begins with the teacher speaking to and for the puppet until the students determine the pattern. Next, students either speak for the puppet or correct the puppet. To make sure all the students are participating, alternate randomly between having the whole group or individuals respond. The activities focus on particular parts of words, according to the following sequence:

1. **Repeating last part of word.** Use words beginning with easy-to-hear consonants, such as *f, l, m, n, r, s,* and *z*. The puppet repeats only the rime, the part of the syllable after the initial consonant.

Model

Teacher: *farm*

Puppet: *arm*

Once the pattern is established, the students respond for the puppet.

Teacher: *rope*

Students: *ope*

Example Words

Use words such as the following: *mine . . . ine soup . . . oup feet . . . eet*

2. **Restoring initial phonemes.** Now the students correct the puppet. Be sure to acknowledge the correction.

Model

Teacher: *lake*

Puppet: *ake*

Teacher: *No, llllake. You forgot the /l/.*

Teacher: *real*

Puppet: *eal*

Teacher: *What did the puppet leave off?*

Students: */r/. It's supposed to be* real.

Teacher: *That's right. The word is* real.

Example Words

Use words such as the following:

look . . . ook mouse . . . ouse sand . . . and

3. **Segmenting initial consonants.** The puppet pronounces only the initial consonant.

Phonemic Awareness (continued)

PROGRAM APPENDIX

Model

Teacher: *pay*

Puppet: */p/*

Example Words

Use words such as the following:

moon . . . /m/ *nose . . . /n/* *bell . . . /b/*

4. **Restoring final consonants.** The students correct the puppet. Prompt if necessary: *"What's the word? What did the puppet leave off?"*

Model

Teacher: *run*

Puppet: *ru*

Students: *It's run! You left off the /n/.*

Teacher: *That's right. The word is* run.

Example Words

Use words such as the following:

meet. . . mee *cool . . . coo* *boot. . . boo*

5. **Isolating final consonants.** The puppet pronounces only the final consonant.

Model

Teacher: *green*

Puppet: */n/*

Example Words

Use words such as the following:

glass . . . /s/ *boom . . . /m/* *mice . . . /s/*

6. **Segmenting initial consonant blends.** The sounds in blends are emphasized.

Model

Teacher: *clap*

Puppet: *lap*

Next have students correct the puppet.

Teacher: *stain*

Puppet: *tain*

Students: *It's* stain! *You left off the /s/.*

Teacher: *That's right. The word is stain.*

Example Words

Use words such as the following:

blaze . . . laze *draw. . . raw* *proud . . . roud*

Discrimination

Purpose

Discrimination activities help students focus on particular sounds in words.

Listening for long vowel sounds is the earliest discrimination activity. Vowel sounds are necessary for decoding, but young students do not hear them easily. This is evident in students' invented spellings, where vowels are often omitted. Early in the year, the students listen for long vowel sounds, which are more easily distinguished than short vowel sounds:

- Explain to the students that vowels are special, because sometimes they say their names in words.
- Tell the students which vowel sound to listen for.
- Have them repeat the sound when they hear it in a word. For example, if the target vowel sound is long e, the students will say long e when you say *leaf* but they should not respond when you say *loaf*.
- Initially the students should listen for one long vowel sound at a time. Later they can listen for two vowel sounds. All **Example Words**, however, should contain one of the target vowels.

Procedure

Listening for short vowel sounds discrimination activities should be done once the short vowels /a/ and /i/ have been introduced. Short vowels are very useful in reading. They are generally more regular in spelling than long vowels, and they appear in many short, simple words. However, their sounds are less easily distinguished than those of long vowels. Thus, the activities focus only on /a/ and /i/. All the words provided have one or the other of these sounds. Either have the students repeat the sound of a specified vowel, or vary the activity as follows: Write an *a* on one side of the board and an *i* on the other. Ask the students to point to the *a* when they hear a word with the /a/ sound and point to the *i* when they hear a word with the /i/ sound. Use words such as the following:

bat *mat* *sat* *sit* *spit*
pit *pat* *pan* *pin* *spin*

Consonant sounds in multisyllable words. Discriminating these sounds helps students attend to consonant sounds in the middle of words.

- Say the word *rib*, and have the students repeat it. Ask where they hear the /b/ in *rib*.
- Then say *ribbon* and ask the students where they hear the /b/ in *ribbon*.
- Tell the students that you will say some words and they will repeat each word.
- After they repeat each word, ask what consonant sound they hear in the middle of that word. Use words such as the following:
  famous *message* *picky*
  jogger *flavor* *zipper*

Phonemic Play

Purpose

Wordplay activities help the students focus on and manipulate sounds, thus supporting the idea that words are made of specific sounds that can be taken apart, put together, or changed to make new words. Through wordplay, students gain important knowledge about language.

Procedure

Producing rhymes. Many phonemic play activities focus on producing rhymes. A familiar or easily learned rhyme or song is introduced, and the students are encouraged to substitute words or sounds. An example is "*Willaby Wallaby Woo*," in which students change the rhyming words in the couplet "*Willaby Wallaby Woo/An elephant sat on you*" so that the second line ends with a student's name and the first line ends with a rhyme beginning with W (for example, "*Willaby Wallaby Wissy/An elephant sat on Missy*").

Generate alliterative words. Students can also say as many words as they can think of that begin with a given consonant sound. This is a valuable complement to discrimination activities in which the teacher produces the words and the students identify them.

Explicit, Systematic Phonics

The purpose of phonics instruction is to teach students the association between the sounds of the language and the written symbols—spellings—that have been chosen to represent those sounds.

As with all alphabetic languages, English has a limited number of symbols—twenty-six—that are combined and recombined to make the written language. These written symbols are a visual representation of the speech sounds we use to communicate. This is simply a code. The faster the students learn the code and how it works, the faster the whole world of reading opens to them.

Students are introduced to the sounds and spellings of English in a very systematic, sequential manner. This allows them to continually build on what they learned the day before. As each sound/symbol relationship is introduced, students learn about and practice with words containing the target sound/spelling and then reinforce their learning through the use of engaging text specifically written for this purpose.

It can be very difficult for students to hear the individual sounds, or phonemes, that make up words. When phonics instruction is explicit—students are told the sounds associated with the different written symbols—there is no guesswork involved. They know that this sound /b/ is spelled *b*. Therefore, students in an SRA/Open Court Reading classroom spend time learning to discriminate individual speech sounds, and then they learn the spellings of those sounds. This systematic, explicit approach affords students the very best chance for early and continuing success.

Sound/Spelling Cards

Purpose

The purpose of the **Sound/Spelling Cards** (Levels 1–3) is to remind the students of the sounds of English and their spellings. The name of the picture on each card contains the target sound at the beginning for the consonants and in the middle for most vowels. In addition, the picture associates a sound with an action. This association is introduced through an interactive story in which the pictured object or character "makes" the sound. These cards are a resource for the students to use to remember sound/spelling associations for both reading and writing.

Procedure

Posting the Cards

Initially, post the first twenty-six cards with the picture to the wall so that only the alphabet letters on the backs show. As you introduce each card, you will turn it to show the picture and the spellings on the front of the card. If, however, most of your students already have some knowledge of the letters—this is a second- or third-grade classroom and students are reviewing what they learned the year before—you may want to go ahead and place the cards with the picture and the spellings facing forward to provide support as they begin writing. Make sure that the cards are positioned so that you can touch them with your hand or with a pointer when you refer to them and so that all of the students can see them easily. The cards should be placed where the students can readily see them during reading and writing.

Special Devices

- Vowel spellings are printed in red to draw attention to them. Consonants are printed in black. The blank line in a spelling indicates that a letter will take the place of the blank in a word. For example, the replacement of the blank with *t* in the spelling *a_e* makes the word *ate*. The blank lines may also indicate the position of a spelling in a word or a syllable. The blank in *h_* for example, means that the spelling occurs at the beginning of a word or a syllable.
- The blanks in *_ie_* indicate that the *ie* spelling comes in the middle of a word or a syllable, while the blank in *_oy* shows that the *oy* spelling comes at the end of a word or a syllable. Uses of blanks in specific spellings are in the lessons. Please note now, however, that when you write a spelling of a sound on the board or an overhead transparency, you should include the blanks.
- The color of the background behind the spellings also has a meaning. Consonants have a white background. The colors behind vowel spellings are pronunciation clues. Short vowel spellings have a green background, which corresponds to the green box that appears before some consonant spellings. Thus, before *ck* or *x* you will see a green box, which indicates that a short vowel always precedes that spelling. Long vowel spellings have a yellow background; other vowel spellings, such as r-controlled vowels and diphthongs, have a blue background. The color code reinforces the idea that vowels are special and have different pronunciations.

Introducing the Sound/Spelling Cards

In first grade, each sound and spelling is introduced by using a see/hear/say/write sequence. In grades two and three the same sequence is used in the review of the cards.

1. **See:** Students see the spelling or spellings on the **Sound/Spelling Card** and the board or an overhead transparency.
2. **Hear:** Students hear the sound used in words and in isolation in the story. The sound is, of course, related to the picture (and the action) shown on the **Sound/Spelling Card.**
3. **Say:** Students say the sound.
4. **Write:** Students write the spelling(s) for the sound.

There are a number of important points to remember about this technique.

- The first item written on the board or an overhead transparency is the spelling of the sound being introduced. This gives the spelling a special emphasis in the mind of the student. It is the "see" part of the sequence.
- One of the causes of blending failure is the failure to teach sounds thoroughly during introduction of the **Sound/Spelling Card** and during initial sounding and blending. To help ensure success for all students, make certain that every student is able to see the board or screen.
- After you present the sound and spelling, have several students go to the board to write the spelling. Have them say the sound as they write the spelling. After they have written the spelling of the sound, give them a chance to proofread their own work. Then give the other

students the opportunity to help with proofreading by noting what is good about the spelling and then suggesting how to make it better.

Sample Lesson, Using the Letter m and the Sound /m/

- Point to the **Sound/Spelling Card 13 Monkey** and have students tell you whether it is a vowel or a consonant. Have them tell the name of the card. If they do not know it, tell them it is Monkey. Point to the *monkey* in the picture and say the word monkey, emphasizing the initial consonant sound—*mmmonkey*.
- Point to the spelling *m*. Tell students that /m/ is spelled *m*.
- If you wish, make up an alliterative sentence about the Monkey, or use the alliterative story that accompanies the card. (In first grade this story is printed on the page on which the card is introduced and in the Appendix. In grades two and three, the cards are printed in the Appendix of the ***Teacher's Edition.***) For example, *When Muzzie the monkey munches bananas, the sound she makes is /mmmmmm/.*
- If students had ***SRA/Open Court Reading*** before, you can ask them if they learned an action such as rubbing their tummies to help them remember the sound. If your students don't have an action they associate with the cards already, make some up with your students. They will have fun, and it will be another way for them to remember the sound/spelling relationships.
- Write *m* on the board or on an overhead transparency and say the sound. Write the letter again and ask the students to say the sound with you as they write the letter on slates, on paper, or with their index finger on a surface. Repeat this activity several times.
- Have the students listen for words beginning with /m/, indicating by some signal, such as thumbs-up or thumbs-down, whether they hear the /m/ sound and saying /m/ when they hear it in a word. Repeat with the sound in various positions in words. Encourage students to tell you and the class words with /m/ at the beginning and end as well as in the middle of words.
- Check students' learning by pointing to the card. Have students identify the sound, name the spelling, and discuss how the card can help them remember the sound.

Individual Sound/Spelling Cards

Use the **Individual Sound/Spelling Cards** for review and for small-group reteaching and practice sessions. Students can use them alone or with partners. Here are some suggestions for activities using the **Individual Sound/Spelling Cards**:

1. **Saying sounds from pictures.** The leader flashes pictures as the others say the sound each picture represents.
2. **Saying sounds.** The leader flashes the spellings on the cards as the others say the sound that the spellings represent.

The faster the students learn the code and how it works, the faster the whole world of reading opens to them.

3. **Naming spellings from pictures.** The leader flashes pictures. The others name the card, say the sound, and then name as many spellings as they can.
4. **Writing spellings from the pictures.** Working alone, a student looks at a picture and then writes as many spellings for that **Sound/Spelling Card** as he or she can remember.
5. **Saying words from pictures.** The leader presents a series of pictures. The others form words by blending the sounds represented.

Blending

Purpose

The purpose of blending is to teach the students a strategy for figuring out unfamiliar words. Initially, students will be blending sound by sound. Ultimately, the students will sound and blend only those words that they cannot read. Eventually, the blending process will become quick and comfortable for them.

Procedure

Learning the sounds and their spellings is only the first step in learning to read and write. The second step is learning to blend the sounds into words.

Blending Techniques

Blending lines are written on the board or an overhead transparency as the students watch and participate. The lines and sentences should not be written out before class begins. It is through the sound-by-sound blending of the words and the sentences that the students learn the blending process.

Sound-by-Sound Blending

- Write the spelling of the first sound in the word. Point to the spelling, and say the sound.
- Have the students say the sound with you as you say the sound again. Write the spelling of the next sound. Point to the spelling, and say the sound. Have the students say the sound with you as you say the sound again. After you have written the vowel spelling, blend through the vowel (unless the vowel is the first letter of the word), making the blending motion—a smooth sweeping of the hand beneath the sounds, linking them from left to right, for example, *ba*. As you make the blending motion, make sure that your hand is under the letter that corresponds to the sound you are saying at the moment.
- Have the students blend through the vowel. Write the spelling of the next sound. Point to the spelling and say the sound. Have the students say the sound with you as you touch the letter and say the sound again.
- Continue as described above through the word. After pronouncing the final sound in the word, make the blending motion from left to right under the word as you blend the sounds. Then have the students blend the word. Let them be the first to pronounce the word normally.
- Ask a student to read the word again and use it in a sentence. Ask another student to extend the sentence—that is, make it longer by giving more information. Help the student by asking an appropriate question about the sentence, using, for example, *How? When? Where?* or *Why?* Continue blending the rest of the words.

Whole-Word Blending

Once students are comfortable with sound-by-sound blending, they are ready for whole-word blending.

- Write the whole word to be blended on the board or an overhead transparency.
- Ask the students to blend the sounds as you point to them.
- Then have the students say the whole word.
- Ask the students to use the word in a sentence and then to extend the sentence.
- When all of the words have been blended, point to words randomly and ask individuals to read them.

Blending Syllables

In reading the ***Student Anthologies,*** students will often encounter multisyllabic words. Some students are intimidated by long words, yet many multisyllabic words are easily read by reading and blending the syllables rather than the individual sounds. Following a set of rules for syllables is difficult since so many of the rules have exceptions. Students need to remember that each syllable in a word contains one vowel sound.

- Have students identify the vowel sounds in the word.
- Have students blend the first syllable sound by sound if necessary or read the first syllable.
- Handle the remaining syllables the same way.
- Have students blend the syllables together to read the word.

Blending Sentences

Blending sentences is the logical extension of blending words. Blending sentences helps students develop fluency, which is critical to comprehension. Encourage students to reread sentences with phrasing and natural intonation.

- Write the sentence on the board or on a transparency, underlining any high-frequency sight words—words that the students cannot decode either because they are irregular or because they contain sounds or spellings that the students have not yet learned or reviewed. If the students have not read these words before, write the words on the board or an overhead transparency and introduce them before writing the sentence. These words should not be blended but read as whole words.

Building for Success

A primary cause of students' blending failure is their failure to understand how to use the **Sound/Spelling Cards**. Students need to practice sounds and spellings when the **Sound/Spelling Cards** are introduced and during initial blending. They also need to understand that if they are not sure of how to pronounce a spelling, they can check the cards.

Early blending may be frustrating. You must lead the group almost constantly. Soon, however, leaders in the group will take over. Watch to see whether any students are having trouble during the blending. Include them in small-group instruction sessions. At that time you may want to use the vowel-first procedure described below to reteach blending lines.

Extra Help

In working with small groups during **Workshop**, you may want to use some of the following suggestions to support students who need help with blending.

Vowel-First Blending

Vowel-first blending is an alternative to sound-by-sound and whole-word blending for students who need special help. Used in small-group sessions, this technique helps students who have difficulty with the other two types of blending to focus on the most important part of each word, the vowels, and to do only one thing at a time. These students are not expected to say a sound and blend it with another at virtually the same time. The steps to use in vowel-first blending follow:

> ***Blending is the heart of phonics instruction and the key strategy students must learn to open the world of written language.***

1. Across the board or on an overhead transparency, write the vowel spelling in each of the words in the line. For a short vowel, the line may look like this:
   a   a   a
   For a long vowel, the line may look like this:
   ee   ea   ea
2. Point to the spelling as the students say the sound for the spelling.
3. Begin blending around the vowels. In front of the first vowel spelling, add the spelling for the beginning sound of the word. Make the blending motion, and have the students blend through the vowel, adding a blank to indicate that the word is still incomplete. Repeat this procedure for each partial word in the line until the line looks like this:
   ma__   sa__   pa__
   see__   mea__   tea__
4. Have the students blend the partial word again as you make the blending motion and then add the spelling for the ending sound.
5. Make the blending motion, and have the students blend the completed word—for example, *mat* or *seed.*
6. Ask a student to repeat the word and use it in a sentence. Then have another student extend the sentence.
7. Repeat steps 4, 5, and 6 for each word in the line, which might look like this:
   mat   sad   pan
   or
   seed   meat   team

Tips

- In the early lessons, do blending with as much direction and dialogue as is necessary for success. Reduce your directions to a minimum as soon as possible. You have made good progress when you no longer have to say, "Sound—Sound—Blend," because the students automatically sound and blend as you write.
- Unless the line is used to introduce or to reinforce a spelling pattern, always ask a student to use a word in a sentence and then to extend the sentence immediately after you've developed the word. If the line is used to introduce or to reinforce a spelling pattern, however, ask the students to give sentences at the end of the line. Students will naturally extend sentences by adding phrases to the ends of the sentences. Encourage them to add phrases at the beginning or in the middle of the sentence.
- Use the vowel-first procedure in small group preteaching or reteaching sessions with students who are having a lot of trouble with blending. Remember that you must adapt the blending lines in the lessons to the vowel-first method.
- The sight words in the sentences cannot be blended. The students must approach them as sight words to be memorized. If students are having problems reading sight words, tell them the words.
- Cue marks written over the vowels may help students.
  - ✓ Straight line cue for long vowels
    EXAMPLES: *āpe, mē, fīne, sō, ūse*
  - ✓ Curved line cue for short vowels
    EXAMPLES: *căt, pět, wĭn, hŏt, tŭg*
  - ✓ Tent cue for variations of a and o
    EXAMPLES: *âll, ôff*
  - ✓ Dot cue for schwa sound with multiple-syllable words
    EXAMPLES: *salȧd, planėt, pencil, wagȯn*

Explicit, Systematic Phonics (continued)

PROGRAM APPENDIX

Dictation and Spelling

Purpose

The purpose of dictation is to teach the students to spell words based on the sounds and spellings. In addition, learning dictation gives students a new strategy for reflecting on the sounds they hear in words to help them with their own writing.

As the students learn that sounds and spellings are connected to form words and that words form sentences, they begin to learn the standard spellings that will enable others to read their writing. As students learn to encode correctly, they develop their visual memory for words (spelling ability) and hence increase their writing fluency. Reinforcing the association between sounds and spellings and words through dictation gives students a spelling strategy that provides support and reassurance for writing independently. Reflecting on the sounds they hear in words will help students develop writing fluency as they apply the strategy to writing unfamiliar words.

A dictation activity is a learning experience; it is not a test. The students should be encouraged to ask for as much help as they need. The proofreading techniques are an integral part of dictation. Students' errors lead to self-correction and, if need be, to reteaching. The dictation activities must not become a frustrating ordeal. The students should receive reinforcement and feedback.

There are two kinds of dictation: Sounds-in-Sequence Dictation and Whole-Word Dictation. The two types differ mainly in the amount of help they give the students in spelling the words. The instructions vary for each type.

Procedure

Sounds-in-Sequence Dictation

Sounds-in-Sequence Dictation gives the students the opportunity to spell words sound by sound, left to right, checking the spelling of each sound as they write. (Many students write words as they think they hear and say the words, not as the words are actually pronounced or written.)

- Pronounce the first word to be spelled. Use the word in a sentence and say the word again (word/sentence/word). Have students say the word.
- Tell students to think about the sounds they hear in the word. Ask, "What's the first sound in the word?"
- Have students say the sound.
- Point to the **Sound/Spelling Card**, and direct the students to check the card. Ask what the spelling is. The students should say the spelling and then write it.
- Proceed in this manner until the word is complete.
- Proofread. You can write the word on the board as a model, or have a student do it. Check the work by referring to the **Sound/Spelling Cards**. If a word is misspelled, have the students circle the word and write it correctly, either above the word or next to it.

Whole-Word Dictation

Whole-Word Dictation gives the students the opportunity to practice this spelling strategy with less help from the teacher.

- Pronounce the word, use the word in a sentence, and then repeat the word (word/sentence/word). Have the students repeat the word. Tell the students to think about the word. Remind the students to check the **Sound/Spelling Cards** for spellings and to write the word.
- Proofread. Write or have a volunteer write the word on the board as a model. Check the word by referring to the **Sound/Spelling Cards**.

Sentence Dictation

Writing dictated sentences. Help students apply this spelling strategy to writing sentences. Dictation supports the development of fluent and independent writing. Dictation of a sentence will also help the students apply conventions of written language, such as capitalization and punctuation.

- Say the complete sentence aloud.
- Dictate one word at a time following the procedure for Sounds-in-Sequence Dictation.

Continue this procedure for the rest of the words in the sentence. Remind the students to put a period at the end. Then proofread the sentence, sound by sound, or word by word. When sentences contain sight words, the sight words should be dictated as whole words, not sound by sound. As the students learn to write more independently, the whole sentence can be dictated word by word.

Proofreading

Whenever the students write, whether at the board or on paper, they should proofread their work. Proofreading is an important technique because it allows the students to learn by self-correction and it gives them an immediate second chance for success. It is the same skill students will use as they proofread their writing. Students should proofread by circling—not by erasing—each error. After they circle an error, they should write the correction beside the circle. This type of correction allows you and the students to see the error as well as the correct form. Students also can see what needs to be changed and how they have made their own work better.

You may want to have students use a colored pencil to circle and write in the correction. This will make it easier for them to see the changes.

Procedure for Proofreading

- Have a student write the word or sentence on the board or on an overhead transparency.
- Have students tell what is good.
- Have students identify anything that can be made better.
- If there is a mistake, have the student circle it and write it correctly.
- Have the rest of the class proofread their own work.

The Word Building Game

The major reason for developing writing alongside reading is that reading and writing are complementary communicative processes. Decoding requires that students blend the phonemes together into familiar cohesive words. Spelling requires that students segment familiar cohesive words into separate phonemes. Both help students develop an understanding of how the alphabetic principle works.

The Word Building game gives the students a chance to exercise their segmentation abilities and to practice using the sounds and spellings they are learning. The game is a fast-paced activity in which the students spell related sets of words with the teacher's guidance. (Each successive word in the list differs from the previous one by one sound.)

For the Word Building game, the students use their ***Individual Letter Cards*** (Levels K and 1) to build the words. (As an alternative they can use pencil and paper.) You will be writing at the board.

Give the students the appropriate ***Letter Cards.*** For example, if the list for the Word Building game is *am, at, mat,* they will need their *a, m,* and *t* ***Letter Cards.***

- Say the first word, such as *am.* (Use it in a sentence if you wish.) Have the students repeat the word. Say the word slowly, sound by sound. Tell the students to look at the ***Sound/Spelling Cards*** to find the letters that spell the sounds. Touch the first sound's card, in this case the Lamb card, and have students say the sound. Continue the process with the second sound. Write the word on the board while the students use their ***Letter Cards*** to spell it. Have students compare their words with your word, make changes as needed, and then blend and read the word with you.
- The students will then change the first word to make a different word. Say the next word in the list, (*at*). Segment the sounds of the word, and have students find the ***Sound/Spelling Cards*** that correspond. Write the new word (*at*) under the first word (*am*) on the board and have the students change their cards to spell the new word. Have them compare their words to yours and make changes as needed. Blend and read the word with the students. Continue in a like manner through the word list.

Spelling Strategies

Spelling

Many people find English difficult, because English sound/spelling patterns seem to have a million exceptions. The key to becoming a good speller, however, is not just memorization. The key is recognizing and internalizing English spelling patterns. Some people do this naturally as they read and develop large vocabularies. They intuitively recognize spelling patterns and apply them appropriately. Others need explicit and direct teaching of vocabulary and spelling strategies and spelling patterns before they develop spelling consciousness.

Purpose

Spelling is a fundamental skill in written communication. Although a writer may have wonderful ideas, he or she may find it difficult to communicate those ideas without spelling skills. Learning to spell requires much exposure to text and writing. For many it requires a methodical presentation of English spelling patterns.

English Spelling Patterns

A basic understanding of English spelling patterns will help provide efficient and effective spelling instruction. Just as the goal of phonics instruction is to enable students to read fluently, the goal of spelling instruction is to enable students to write fluently so they can concentrate on ideas rather than spelling.

- **Sound Patterns** Many words are spelled the way they sound. Most consonants and short vowels are very regular. Once a student learns the sound/spelling relationships, he or she has the key to spelling many words.
- **Structural Patterns** Structural patterns are employed when adding endings to words. Examples of structural patterns include doubling the final consonant, adding *–s* or *–es* to form plurals, and dropping the final *e* before adding *–ing*, *-ed*, *-er*, or *–est*. Often these structural patterns are very regular in their application. Many students have little trouble learning these patterns.
- **Meaning Patterns** Many spelling patterns in English are *morphological;* in other words, the meaning relationship is maintained regardless of how a sound may change. Prefixes, suffixes, and root words that retain their spellings regardless of how they are pronounced are further examples of meaning patterns.
- **Foreign Language Patterns** Many English words are derived from foreign words and retain those language patterns. For example, *kindergarten* (German), *boulevard* (French), and *ballet* (French from Italian) are foreign language patterns at work in English.

Developmental Stages of Spelling

The most important finding in spelling research in the past thirty years is that students learn to spell in a predictable developmental sequence, much as they learn to read. It appears to take the average student three to six years to progress through the developmental stages and emerge as a fairly competent, mature speller.

Prephonemic The first stage is the *prephonemic* stage, characterized by random letters arranged either in continuous lines or in word-like clusters. Only the writer can "read" it, and it may be "read" differently on different days.

Semiphonemic As emergent readers learn that letters stand for sounds, they use particular letters specifically to represent the initial consonant sound and sometimes a few other very salient sounds. This marks the discovery of *phonemic awareness* that letters represent speech sounds in writing.

Phonemic When students can represent most of the sounds they hear in words, they have entered the *phonemic* stage of spelling. They spell what they hear, using everything they know about letter sounds, letter names, and familiar words. Many remedial spellers never develop beyond this stage and spell a word the way it sounds whenever they encounter a word they can't spell.

Transitional or Within Word Pattern As they are exposed to more difficult words, students discover that not all words are spelled as they sound. They learn that they must include silent letters, spell past tenses with *–ed*, include a vowel even in unstressed syllables, and remember how words look. The *transitional* stage represents the transition from primarily phonemic strategies to rule-bound spelling.

Derivational The *derivational* stage occurs as transitional spellers accumulate a large spelling vocabulary and gain control over affixes, contractions, homophones and other meaning patterns. They discover that related or derived forms of words share spelling features even if they do not sound the same. As spellers gain control over these subtle word features and spell most words correctly, they become conventional spellers.

Procedures

The spelling lessons are organized around different spelling patterns, beginning with phonetic spelling patterns and progressing to other types of spelling patterns in a logical sequence. Word lists including words from the literature selection focus on the particular patterns in each lesson. In general, the sound patterns occur in the first units at each grade, followed by structural patterns, meaning patterns, and foreign language patterns in the upper grade levels.

- As you begin each new spelling lesson, have students identify the spelling pattern and how it is like and different from other patterns.
- Give the pretest to help students focus on the lesson pattern.
- Have students proofread their own pretests immediately after the test, crossing out any misspellings and writing the correct spelling.
- Have them diagnose whether the errors they made were in the lesson pattern or in another part of the word. Help students determine where they made errors and what type of pattern they should work on to correct them.
- As students work through the spelling pages from the ***Spelling and Vocabulary Skills*** book, encourage them to practice the different spelling strategies in the exercises.

Sound Pattern Strategies

✓ **Pronunciation Strategy** As students encounter an unknown word, have them say the word carefully to hear each sound. Encourage them to check the **Sound/Spelling Cards.** Then have them spell each sound. (/s/ + /i/ + /t/: *sit)*

✓ **Consonant Substitution** Have students switch consonants. The vowel spelling usually remains the same. *(bat, hat, rat, flat, splat)*

✓ **Vowel Substitution** Have students switch vowels. The consonant spellings usually remain the same. (CVC: *hit, hat, hut, hot;* CVCV: *mane, mine;* CVVC: *boat, beat, bait, beet)*

✓ **Rhyming Word Strategy** Have students think of rhyming words and the rimes that spell a particular sound. Often the sound will be spelled the same way in another word. *(cub, tub, rub)*

Structural Pattern Strategies

✓ **Conventions Strategy** Have students learn the rule and exceptions for adding endings to words (dropping *y*, dropping *e*, doubling the final consonant, and so on).

✓ **Proofreading Strategy** Many spelling errors occur because of simple mistakes. Have students check their writing carefully and specifically for spelling.

✓ **Visualization Strategy** Have students think about how a word looks. Sometimes words "look" wrong because a wrong spelling pattern has been written. Have them double-check the spelling of any word that looks wrong.

Meaning Pattern Strategies

✓ **Family Strategy** When students are not sure of a spelling, have them think of how words from the same base word family are spelled. *(critic, criticize, critical; sign, signal, signature)*

Spelling and Vocabulary Strategies (continued)

✓ **Meaning Strategy** Have students determine a homophone's meaning to make sure they are using the right word. Knowing prefixes, suffixes, and base words will also help.

✓ **Compound Word Strategy** Tell students to break a compound apart and spell each word. Compounds may not follow conventions rules for adding endings. *(homework, nonetheless)*

✓ **Foreign Language Strategy** Have students think of foreign language spellings that are different from English spelling patterns. *(ballet, boulevard, sauerkraut)*

✓ **Dictionary Strategy** Ask students to look up the word in a dictionary to make sure their spelling is correct. If they do not know how to spell a word, have them try a few different spellings and look them up to see which one is correct. *(fotograph, photograph)* This develops a spelling consciousness.

Use the Final Test to determine understanding of the lesson spelling pattern and to identify any other spelling pattern problems. Encourage student understanding of spelling patterns and use of spelling strategies in all their writing to help transfer spelling skills to writing.

Vocabulary Strategies

Purpose

Strong vocabulary skills are correlated to achievement throughout school. The purpose of vocabulary strategy instruction is to teach students a range of strategies for learning, remembering, and incorporating unknown vocabulary words into their existing reading, writing, speaking, and listening vocabularies.

Procedures

The selection vocabulary instruction in the first and second part of the lesson focuses on teaching specific vocabulary necessary for understanding the literature selection more completely. The weekly vocabulary instruction in the Language Arts part of each lesson is geared toward teaching vocabulary skills and strategies to build and secure vocabulary through word relationships or develop vocabulary strategies for unknown words.

General Strategies

There is no question that having students read and reading to students are effective vocabulary instructional strategies. Most word learning occurs through exposure to words in listening and reading. Multiple exposures to words, particularly when students hear, see, say, and write words, is also effective. Word play, including meaning and dictionary games, helps to develop a word consciousness as well.

Vocabulary Skills and Strategies

Word Relationships People effectively learn new words by relating them to words they already know. An understanding of different word relationships enables students to quickly and efficiently secure new vocabulary. The weekly vocabulary lessons are organized around these types of word groups. Word relationships include:

- **Antonyms** Words with opposite or nearly opposite meanings. *(hot/cold)*
- **Synonyms** Words with similar meanings. *(cup, mug, glass)*
- **Multiple Meanings** Words that have more than one meaning. *(run, dressing, bowl)*
- **Shades of Meaning** Words that express degrees of a concept or quality. *(like, love, worship)*
- **Levels of Specificity** Words that describe at different levels of precision. *(living thing, plant, flower, daffodil)*
- **Analogies** Pairs of words that have the same relationship. *(ball is to baseball as puck is to hockey)*
- **Compound Words** Words comprised of two or more words. *(daylight)*
- **Homographs** Words that are spelled the same but have different meanings and come from different root words. *(bear, count)*
- **Homophones** Words that sound the same but have different spellings and meanings. *(mane/main, to/two/too)*
- **Base Word Families** Words that have the same base word. *(care, careless, careful, uncaring, carefree)*
- **Prefixes** An affix attached before a base word that changes the meaning of the word. *(misspell)*
- **Suffixes** An affix attached to the end of a base word that changes the meaning of the word. *(careless)*
- **Concept Vocabulary** Words that help develop understanding of a concept. *(space, sun, Earth, satellite, planet, asteroid)*
- **Classification and Categorization** Sorting words by related meanings. *(colors, shapes, animals, foods)*

Contextual Word Lists Teaching vocabulary in context is another way to secure understanding of unknown words. Grouping words by subject area such as science, social studies, math, descriptive words, new words, and so on enables students to connect word meanings and build vocabulary understanding.

- **Figurative Language** Idioms, metaphors, similes, personification, puns, and novel meanings need to be specifically taught, especially for English language learners.
- **Derivational Word Lists** Presenting groups of words derived from particular languages or with specific roots or affixes is an effective way to reinforce meanings and spellings of foreign words and word parts.

Vocabulary Strategies for Unknown Words

Different strategies have been shown to be particularly effective for learning completely new words. These strategies are included in the ***Spelling and Vocabulary Skills*** activities.

Key Word This strategy involves providing or having students create a mnemonic clue for unknown vocabulary. For example, the word *mole* is defined in chemistry as a "gram molecule." By relating *mole* to *molecule*, students have a key to the meaning of the word.

Definitions Copying a definition from a dictionary is somewhat effective in learning new vocabulary. Combining this with using the word in writing and speaking adds to the effectiveness of this strategy. Requiring students to explain a word or use it in a novel sentence helps to ensure that the meaning is understood.

Context Clues Many words are learned from context, particularly with repeated exposure to words in reading and listening. Without specific instruction in consciously using context clues, however, unknown words are often ignored.

- **Syntax** How a word is used in a sentence provides some clue to its meaning.
- **External Context Clues** Hints about a word's meaning may appear in the setting, words, phrases, or sentences surrounding a word in text. Other known words in the text may be descriptive, may provide a definition (apposition), may be compared or contrasted, or may be used synonymously in context. Modeling and teaching students to use context to infer a word's meaning can help in learning unknown words.

Word Structure Examining the affixes and roots of a word may provide some clue to its meaning. Knowing the meaning of at least part of the word can provide a clue to its meaning. (For example, *unenforceable* can be broken down into meaningful word parts.)

Semantic Mapping Having students create a semantic map of an unknown word after learning its definition helps them to learn it. Have students write the new word and then list in a map or web all words they can think of that are related to it.

Semantic Feature Analysis A semantic feature analysis helps students compare and contrast similar types of words within a category to help secure unknown words. Have students chart, for example, the similarities and differences between different types of sports, including new vocabulary such as *lacrosse* and *cricket*.

Developing Vocabulary

Purpose

Vocabulary is closely connected to comprehension. Considerable vocabulary growth occurs incidentally during reading. A clear connection exists between vocabulary development and the amount of reading a person does, and there are strong indications that vocabulary instruction is important and that understanding the meaning of key words helps with comprehension.

In ***Open Court Reading,*** vocabulary is addressed before, during, and after reading. Before reading, the teacher presents vocabulary words from the selection. Students use skills such as context clues, apposition, and structural analysis to figure out the meaning of the words. These selection vocabulary words are not only important to understanding the text but are also high-utility words that can be used in discussing and writing about the unit theme.

During reading, students monitor their understanding of words and text. When they do not understand something, they stop and clarify what they have read. Students will use these same skills—context clues, apposition, structural elements, and the like—to clarify the meanings of additional words encountered while reading. Figuring out the meanings of words while reading prepares students for the demands of independent reading both in and out of school.

After reading, students review the vocabulary words that they learned before reading the selection. They also review any interesting words that they identified and discussed during reading. Students record in their Writer's Notebook both the selection vocabulary words and the interesting words they identified during their reading and are encouraged to use both sets of words in discussion and in writing.

Procedure

Before students read a selection, the teacher uses an overhead transparency to introduce the selection vocabulary to the class. The transparency contains two sentences for each selection vocabulary word. Students must use context clues, apposition, or word structure in the sentences to figure out the meaning of the underlined vocabulary words. If students cannot figure out the meaning of the word using one of these skills, they can consult the glossary or dictionary.

Below are suggestions for modeling the use of context clues, apposition, or word structure to figure out the meaning of a word.

Modeling Using Context Clues

Have students read the sentences on the transparency. Explain to students that they will use *context clues,* or other words in the sentence, to figure out the meaning of the underlined word. For example, if the word is "treacherous," the sentences might include:

1. Mrs. Frisby must undertake a treacherous journey to bring her son some medicine.
2. We took a treacherous walk near a swamp filled with crocodiles.

Have students look for clues in the sentences that might help them understand the meaning of the underlined word. Point out that a good clue in the second sentence is "near a swamp filled with crocodiles." This clue should help them understand that *treacherous* probably has something to do with danger. Guide students until they can give a reasonable definition of *treacherous.* To consolidate understanding of the word, ask another student to use the definition in a sentence.

Modeling Using Apposition

Have students read the sentences on the transparency. Explain to students that they will use *apposition* to figure out the meaning of the word. In apposition, the word is followed by the definition, which is set off by commas. For example, if the word is "abolitionist," the sentences might include the following:

1. The conductor thought he was an abolitionist, a person who wanted to end slavery.
2. John Brown was a famous abolitionist, a person who wanted to end slavery.

It should be pretty clear to students using apposition that the definition of the word *abolitionist* is "a person who wanted to end slavery."

Modeling Using Word Structure

Have students read the sentences on the transparency. Explain to students that they will use *word structure,* or parts of the selection vocabulary word, to figure out the meaning. For example, if the word is "uncharted," the sentences might include:

1. The strong wind blew Ivan's ship away into uncharted seas.
2. The explorers Lewis and Clark went into uncharted territory.

Have students look at the word *uncharted* and break it into parts: the prefix *un-*, *chart,* and the suffix *–ed.* Students should know that the suffix *un-* means "not," and that the suffix *–ed* usually indicates the past tense of a verb. However, you may need to remind students about the meanings of these affixes. Ask students for the meaning of the word *chart.* Students should know that a chart could be a "map" or a "table." Guide them as they put together the definitions of the word parts, *un-* (not), *charted* (mapped or tabled). They should be able to come up with the definition "not mapped" or "unmapped" or even "unknown." Have them substitute their definition in the sentences to see if the definition makes sense. So, for instance, the first sentence would read "The strong wind blew Ivan's ship away into unmapped (or unknown) seas." Confirm with students that the new sentence makes sense, and then repeat the same process for the second sentence.

Reading Comprehension

PROGRAM APPENDIX

Everything the students learn about phonemic awareness, phonics, and decoding has one primary goal—to help them understand what they are reading. Without comprehension, there is no reading.

Reading Comprehension Strategies

Purpose

The primary aim of reading is comprehension. Without comprehension, neither intellectual nor emotional responses to reading are possible—other than the response of frustration. Good readers are problem solvers. They bring their critical faculties to bear on everything they read. Experienced readers generally understand most of what they read, but just as importantly, they recognize when they do not understand, and they have at their command an assortment of strategies for monitoring and furthering their understanding.

The goal of comprehension strategy instruction is to turn responsibility for using strategies over to the students as soon as possible. Research has shown that students' comprehension and learning problems are not a matter of mental capacity but rather their inability to use strategies to help them learn. Good readers use a variety of strategies to help them make sense of the text and get the most out of what they read. Trained to use a variety of comprehension strategies, students dramatically improve their learning performance. In order to do this, the teacher models strategy use and gradually incorporates different kinds of prompts and possible student think-alouds as examples of the types of thinking students might do as they read to comprehend what they are reading.

Setting Reading Goals

Even before they begin reading and using comprehension strategies, good readers set reading goals and expectations. Readers who have set their own goals and have definite expectations about the text they are about to read are more engaged in their reading and notice more in what they read. Having determined a purpose for reading, they are better able to evaluate a text and determine whether it meets their needs. Even when the reading is assigned, the reader's engagement is enhanced when he or she has determined ahead of time what information might be gathered from the selection or how the selection might interest him or her.

Comprehension Strategies

Descriptions of strategies good readers use to comprehend the text follow.

Summarizing

Good readers sum up to check their understanding as they read. Sometimes they reread to fill in gaps in their understanding. Good readers use the strategy of summarizing to keep track of what they are reading and to focus their minds on important information. The process of putting the information in one's own words not only helps good readers remember what they have read, but also prompts them to evaluate how well they understand the information. Sometimes the summary reveals that one's understanding is incomplete, in which case it might be appropriate to reread the previous section to fill in the gaps. Good readers usually find that the strategy of summarizing is particularly helpful when they are reading long or complicated text.

Monitoring and Clarifying

Good readers constantly monitor themselves as they read in order to make sure they understand what they are reading. They note the characteristics of the text, such as whether it is difficult to read or whether some sections are more challenging or more important than others are. In addition, when good readers become aware that they do not understand, they take appropriate action, such as rereading, in order to understand the text better. As they read, good readers stay alert for problem signs such as loss of concentration, unfamiliar vocabulary, or lack of sufficient background knowledge to comprehend the text. This ability to self-monitor and identify aspects of the text that hinder comprehension is crucial to becoming a proficient reader.

Asking Questions

Good readers ask questions that may prepare them for what they will learn. If their questions are not answered in the text, they may try to find answers elsewhere and thus add even more to their store of knowledge. Certain kinds of questions occur naturally to a reader, such as clearing up confusion or wondering why something in the text is as it is. Intentional readers take this somewhat informal questioning one step further by formulating questions with the specific intent of checking their understanding. They literally test themselves by thinking of questions a teacher might ask and then by determining answers to those questions.

Predicting

Good readers predict what will happen next. When reading fiction, they make predictions about what they are reading and then confirm or revise those predictions as they go.

Making Connections

Good readers make connections between what they are reading and what they already know from past experience or previous reading.

Visualizing

Good readers visualize what is happening in the text. They form mental images as they read. They picture the setting, the characters, and the action in a story. Visualizing can also be helpful when reading expository text. Visualizing helps readers understand descriptions of complex activities or processes. When a complex process or an event is being described, the reader can follow the process or the event better by visualizing each step or episode. Sometimes an author or an editor helps the reader by providing illustrations, diagrams, or maps. If no visual aids have been provided, it may help the reader to create one.

Monitoring and Adjusting Reading Speed

Good readers understand that not all text is equal. Because of this, good readers continuously monitor what they are reading and adjust their reading speed accordingly. They skim parts of the text that are not important or relevant to their reading goals and they purposely slow down when they encounter difficulty in understanding the text.

Procedures

Modeling and Thinking Aloud

One of the most effective ways to help students use and understand the strategies good readers use is to make strategic thinking public. Modeling these behaviors and encouraging students to think aloud as they attempt to understand text can demonstrate for everyone in a class how these behaviors are put into practice. Suggestions for think-alouds are provided throughout the **Teacher's Edition.**

The most effective models you can offer will be those that come from your own reading experiences. What kinds of questions did you ask yourself? What kinds of things surprised you the first time you read a story? What kinds of new information did you learn? What kinds of things were confusing until you reread or read further? Drawing on these questions and on your students' questions and comments as they read will make the strategic reading process more meaningful to the students. Below are suggestions for modeling each of the comprehension strategies.

- **Modeling Setting Reading Goals.** To model setting reading goals, engage students in the following:

- **Activate prior knowledge.** As you approach a new text, consider aloud what you already know about the subject or what your experiences have been in reading similar material.
- **Browse the text.** To get an idea of what to expect from a text, look at the title and the illustrations. Look for potential problems, such as difficult words. Have students glance quickly at the selection, looking briefly at the illustrations and the print. Have them tell what they think they might be learning about as they read the selection.
- **Decide what to expect from the text.** Anticipate enjoying the story, the language of the text, or the new information you expect to gain from the selection.

- **Modeling Summarizing.** Just as the strategy of summarizing the plot and then predicting what will happen next can enhance a student's reading of fiction, so too can the same procedure be used to the student's advantage in reading nonfiction. In expository text, it is particularly logical to stop and summarize at the end of a chapter or section before going on to the next. One way to model the valuable exercise of making predictions and at the same time expand knowledge is to summarize information learned from a piece of expository writing and then predict what the next step or category will be. Appropriate times to stop and summarize include the following:
  - when a narrative text has covered a long period of time or a number of events
  - when many facts have been presented
  - when an especially critical scene has occurred
  - when a complex process has been described
  - any time there is the potential for confusion about what has happened or what has been presented in the text
  - when returning to a selection
- **Modeling Monitoring and Clarifying.** A reader may need clarification at any point in the reading. Model this strategy by stopping at points that confuse you or that may confuse your students. Indicate that you are experiencing some confusion and need to stop and make sure you understand what is being read. Difficulty may arise from a challenging or unknown word or phrase. It may also stem from the manner in which the information is presented. Perhaps the author did not supply needed information. As you model this strategy, vary the reasons for stopping to clarify so that the students understand that good readers do not simply skip over difficult or confusing material—they stop and figure out what they don't understand.
- **Modeling Asking Questions.** Learning to ask productive questions is not an easy task. Students' earliest experiences with this strategy take the form of answering teacher-generated questions. However, students should be able to move fairly quickly to asking questions like those a teacher might ask. Questions that can be answered with a simple yes or no are not typically very useful for helping them remember and understand what they have read. Many students find it helpful to ask questions beginning with *Who? What? When? Where? How?* or *Why?* As students become more accustomed to asking and answering questions, they will naturally become more adept at phrasing their questions. As their question-asking becomes more sophisticated, they progress from simple questions that can be answered with explicit information in the text to questions that require making inferences based on the text.

Good readers use a variety of strategies to help them make sense of the text and get the most out of what they read.

- **Modeling Predicting.** Predicting can be appropriate at the beginning of a selection—on the basis of the titles and the illustrations—or at any point while reading a selection. At first, your modeling will take the form of speculation about what might happen next, but tell students from the start what clues in the text or illustrations helped you predict, in order to make it clear that predicting is not just guessing. When a student makes a prediction—especially a far-fetched one—ask what in the selection or in his or her own experience the prediction is based on. If the student can back up the prediction, let the prediction stand; otherwise, suggest that the student make another prediction on the basis of what he or she already knows. Often it is appropriate to sum up before making a prediction. This will help students consider what has come before as they make their predictions about what will happen next. When reading aloud, stop whenever a student's prediction has been confirmed or contradicted. Have students tell whether the prediction was correct. If students seem comfortable with the idea of making predictions but rarely do so on their own, encourage them to discuss how to find clues in the text that will help them.
- **Modeling Making Connections.** To model making connections, share with students any thoughts or memories that come to mind as you read the selection. Perhaps a character in a story reminds you of a childhood friend, allowing you to better identify with interactions between characters. Perhaps information in an article on Native-American life in the Old West reminds you of an article that you have read on the importance of the bison to Native Americans. Sharing your connections will help students become aware of the dynamic nature of reading and show them another way of being intentional, active learners.
- **Modeling Visualizing.** Model visualizing by describing the mental images that occur to you as you read. A well-described scene is relatively easy to visualize, and if no one does so voluntarily, you may want to prompt students to express their own visualizations. If the author has not provided a description of a scene, but a picture of the scene would make the story more interesting or comprehensible, you might want to model visualizing as follows: "Let's see. The author says that the street was busy, and we know that this story is set during the colonial period. From what I already know about those times, there were no cars, and the roads were different from the roads of today. The street may have been paved with cobblestones. Horses would have been pulling carriages or wagons. I can almost hear the horses' hoofs going clip-clop over the stones." Remind students that different readers may picture the same scene quite differently, which is fine. Every reader responds to a story in her or his own way.
- **Modeling Monitoring and Adjusting Reading Speed.** Just as readers need to monitor for problems, they need to be aware that different texts can be approached in different ways. For example, if reading a story or novel for enjoyment, the reader will typically read at a relaxed speed that is neither so fast as to be missing information nor as slow as they might read a textbook. If on the other hand, the reader is reading a textbook, he or she will probably decrease speed to assure understanding and make sure that all important information is read and understood. When modeling this strategy, be sure you indicate why you, as the reader, have chosen to slow down or speed up. Good readers continually monitor their speed and ability to understand throughout reading.

Reading Comprehension (continued)

Reading Aloud

At the beginning of the year, students should be encouraged to read selections aloud. This practice will help you and them understand some of the challenges posed by the text and how different students approach these challenges.

Reading aloud helps students build fluency, which in turn will aid their comprehension. Students in grades K–3 can use **Decodable Books** to build fluency, while students in grades 4–6 can use the literature from the **Student Anthologies.** Fluent second graders read between 82 and 124 words per minute with accuracy and understanding, depending on the time of the year (fall/spring). Fluent third graders can be expected to read between 107 and 142 words per minute; fourth (125/143); fifth (126/151); sixth (127/153).

Make sure that you set aside time to hear each student read during the first few days of class—the days devoted to Getting Started are perfect for this—so that you can determine students' abilities and needs. **Workshop** is also a good time to listen to any students who do not get to read aloud while the class is reading the selection together.

If your students have not previously engaged in the sort of strategic thinking aloud that is promoted throughout the ***SRA/Open Court Reading*** program, you will have to do all or most of the modeling at first, but encourage the students to participate as soon as possible.

As the year progresses, students should continue reading aloud often, especially with particularly challenging text. Model your own use of strategies, not only to help students better understand how to use strategies, but also to help them understand that actively using strategies is something that good, mature readers do constantly.

Most students are unaccustomed to thinking out loud. They will typically stand mute as they try to figure out an unfamiliar word or deal with a confusing passage. When this happens, students should be encouraged to identify specifically what they are having difficulty with. A student might identify a particular word, or he or she may note that the individual words are familiar but the meaning of the passage is unclear.

Active Response

Not only are good readers active in their reading when they encounter problems, but they respond constantly to whatever they read. In this way they make the text their own. As students read they should be encouraged to:

- Make as many connections as they can between what they are reading and what they already know.
- Visualize passages to help clarify their meanings or simply to picture appealing descriptions.
- Ask questions about what they are reading. The questions that go through their minds during reading will help them to examine, and thus better understand, the text. Doing so may also interest them in pursuing their own investigations. The questions may also provide a direction for students' research or exploration.
- Summarize and make predictions as a check on how well they understand what they are reading.

Tips

- Remember that the goal of all reading strategies is comprehension. If a story or article does not make sense, the reader needs to choose whatever strategies will help make sense of it. If one strategy does not work, the reader should try another.
- Always treat problems encountered in text as interesting learning opportunities rather than something to be avoided or dreaded.
- Encourage students to think out loud about text challenges.
- Encourage students to help each other build meaning from text. Rather than telling each other what a word is or what a passage means, students should tell each other how they figured out the meanings of challenging words and passages.
- Assure students that these are not the only strategies that can be used while reading. Any strategy that they find helpful in understanding text is a good useful strategy.
- Encourage students to freely share strategies they have devised on their own. You might want to write these on a large sheet of paper and tape them to the board.
- An absence of questions does not necessarily indicate that students understand what they are reading. Be especially alert to students who never seem to ask questions. Be sure to spend tutorial time with these students occasionally, and encourage them to discuss specific selections in the context of difficulties they might have encountered and how they solved them as well as their thoughts about unit concepts.
- Observing students' responses to text will enable you to ascertain not only how well they understand a particular selection but also their facility in choosing and applying appropriate strategies. Take note of the following:

✓ Whether the strategies a student uses are effective in the particular situation.

✓ Whether the student chooses from a variety of appropriate strategies or uses the same few over and over.

✓ Whether the student can explain to classmates which strategies to use in a particular situation and why.

✓ Whether the student can identify alternative resources to pursue when the strategies she or he has tried are not effective.

✓ Whether students' application of a given strategy is becoming more effective over a period of time.

Becoming familiar and comfortable with these self-monitoring techniques gives readers the confidence to tackle material that is progressively more difficult. A good, mature reader knows that he or she will know when understanding what he or she is reading is becoming a problem and can take steps to correct the situation.

Reading Comprehension Skills

Purpose

An important purpose of writing is to communicate thoughts from one person to another. The goal of instruction in reading comprehension skills is to make students aware of the logic behind the structure of a written piece. If the reader can discern the logic of the structure, he or she will be more able to understand the author's logic and gain knowledge both of the facts and the intent of the selection. By keeping the organization of a piece in mind and considering the author's purpose for writing, the reader can go beyond the actual words on the page and make inferences or draw conclusions based on what was read. Strong, mature readers utilize these "between the lines" skills to get a complete picture of not only what the writer is saying, but what the writer is trying to say.

Effective comprehension skills include:

Author's Point of View

Point of view involves identifying who is telling the story. If a character in the story is telling the story, that one character describes the action and tells what the other characters are like. This is first-person point of view. In such a story, one character will do the talking and use the pronouns *I*, *my*, *me*. All other characters' thoughts, feelings, and emotions will be reported through this one character.

If the story is told in third-person point of view, someone outside the story who is aware of all of the characters' thoughts and feelings and actions is relating them to the reader. All of the characters are referred to by their names or the pronouns *he/she*, *him/her*, *it*.

If students stay aware of who is telling a story, they will know whether they are getting the full picture or the picture of events as seen through the eyes of only one character.

Sequence

The reader can't make any decisions about relationships or events if he or she has no idea in which order the events take place. The reader needs to pay attention to how the writer is conveying the sequence. Is it simply stated that first this happened and then that happened? Does the writer present the end of the story first and then go back and let the reader know the sequence of events? Knowing what the sequence is and how it is presented helps the reader follow the writer's line of thought.

Fact and Opinion

Learning to distinguish fact from opinion is essential to critical reading and thinking. Students learn what factors need to be present in order for a statement to be provable. They also learn that an opinion, while not provable itself, should be based on fact. Readers use this knowledge to determine for themselves the validity of the ideas presented in their reading.

Main Idea and Details

An author always has something specific to say to his or her reader. The author may state this main idea in different ways, but the reader should always be able to tell what the writing is about.

To strengthen the main point or main idea of a piece, the author provides details to help the reader understand. For example, the author may use comparison and contrast to make a point, provide examples, provide facts, give opinions, give descriptions, give reasons or causes, or give definitions. The reader needs to know what kinds of details he or she is dealing with before making a judgment about the main idea.

Compare and Contrast

Using comparison and contrast is one of the most common and easiest ways a writer uses to get his or her reader to understand a subject. Comparing and contrasting unfamiliar thoughts, ideas, or things with familiar thoughts, ideas, and things gives the reader something within his or her own experience base to use in understanding.

Cause and Effect

What made this happen? Why did this character act the way he or she did? Knowing the causes of events helps the reader to see the whole story. Using this information to identify the probable outcomes (effects) of events or actions will help the reader anticipate the story or article.

Classify and Categorize

The relationships of actions, events, characters, outcomes, and such in a selection should be clear enough for the reader to see the relationships. Putting like things or ideas together can help the reader understand the relationships set up by the writer.

Author's Purpose

Everything that is written is written for a purpose. That purpose may be to entertain, to persuade, or to inform. Knowing why a piece is written—what purpose the author had for writing the piece—gives the reader an idea of what to expect and perhaps some prior idea of what the author is going to say.

If a writer is writing to entertain, then the reader can generally just relax and let the writer carry him or her away. If, on the other hand, the purpose is to persuade, it will help the reader understand and keep perspective if he or she knows that the purpose is to persuade. The reader can be prepared for whatever argument the writer delivers.

Drawing Conclusions

Often, writers do not directly state everything—they take for granted their audience's ability to "read between the lines." Readers draw conclusions when they take from the text small pieces of information about a character or event and use this information to make a statement about that character or event.

Making Inferences

Readers make inferences about characters and events to understand the total picture in a story. When making inferences, readers use information from the text, along with personal experience or knowledge, to gain a deeper understanding of a story event and its implications.

Procedure

Read the Selection

First, have students read the selection using whatever strategies they need to help them make sense of the selection. Then discuss the selection to assure that students did, indeed, understand what they read. Talk about any confusion they may have, and make any necessary clarifications.

Reread

Revisiting or rereading a selection allows the reader to note specific techniques that authors use to organize and present information in narratives and expository genres. Once students have a basic understanding of the piece, have them reread the selection in whole or in part, concentrating on selected skills. Choose examples of how the writer organized the piece to help the reader understand.

Limit this concentration on specific comprehension/writing skills to one or two that can be clearly identified in the piece. Trying to concentrate on too many things will just confuse students and make it harder for them to identify any of the organizational devices used by the writer. If a piece has many good examples of several different aspects, then go back to the piece several times over a span of days.

Write

Solidify the connection between how an author writes and how readers make sense of a selection by encouraging students to incorporate these organizational devices into their own writing. As they attempt to use these devices, they will get a clearer understanding of how to identify them when they are reading.

Remind students often that the purpose of any skill exercise is to give them tools to use when they are reading and writing. Unless students learn to apply the skills to their own reading—in every area of reading and study—then they are not gaining a full understanding of the purpose of the exercise.

Grammar, Usage, and Mechanics

PROGRAM APPENDIX

Writing is a complicated process. A writer uses handwriting, spelling, vocabulary, grammar, usage, genre structures, and mechanics skills with ideas to create readable text. In addition, a writer must know how to generate content, or ideas, and understand genre structures in order to effectively present ideas in writing. Many students never progress beyond producing a written text that duplicates their everyday speech patterns. Mature writers, however, take composition beyond conversation. They understand the importance of audience and purpose for writing. They organize their thoughts, eliminating those that do not advance their main ideas, and elaborating on those that do so that their readers can follow a logical progression of ideas in an essay or story. Mature writers also know and can use the conventions of grammar, usage, spelling, and mechanics. They proofread and edit for these conventions, so their readers are not distracted by errors.

Purpose

The Study of English Conventions

Over the years the study of grammar, usage, and mechanics has gone in and out of favor. In the past century much research has been done to demonstrate the effectiveness of traditional types of instruction in the conventions of English. Experience and research have shown that learning grammatical terms and completing grammar exercises have little effect on the student's practical application of these skills in the context of speaking or writing. These skills, in and of themselves, do not play a significant role in the way students use language to generate and express their ideas—for example during the prewriting and drafting phases of the writing process. In fact, emphasis on correct conventions has been shown to have a damaging effect when it is the sole focus of writing instruction. If students are evaluated only on the proper use of spelling, grammar, and punctuation, they tend to write fewer and less complex sentences.

Knowledge of English conventions is, however, vitally important in the editing and proofreading phases of the writing process. A paper riddled with mistakes in grammar, usage, or mechanics is quickly discounted. Many immature writers never revise or edit. They finish the last sentence and turn their papers in to the teacher. Mature writers employ their knowledge of English language conventions in the editing phase to refine and polish their ideas.

The study of grammar, usage, and mechanics is important for two reasons.

1. Educated people need to know and understand the structure of their language, which in large part defines their culture.
2. Knowledge of grammar gives teachers and students a common vocabulary for talking about language and makes discussions of writing tasks more efficient and clearer.

Procedure

The key issue in learning grammar, usage, and mechanics is *how* to do it. On the one hand, teaching these skills in isolation from writing has been shown to be ineffective and even detrimental if too much emphasis is placed on them. On the other hand, not teaching these skills and having students write without concern for conventions is equally ineffective. The answer is to teach the skills in a context that allows students to directly apply them to a reading or writing activity. Students should be taught proper use of punctuation or subject/verb agreement at the same time they are taught to proofread for those conventions. As they learn to apply their knowledge of conventions during the final stages of the writing process, they will begin to see that *correcting* errors is an editorial, rather than a composition skill.

History of English

A basic understanding of the history and structure of the English language helps students understand the rich but complex resource they have for writing.

Old English

The English language began about AD 450 when the Angles, Jutes, and Saxons—three tribes that lived in northern Europe—invaded the British Isles. Much of their language included words that had to do with farming (*sheep, dirt, tree, earth*). Many of their words are the most frequently used words in the English language today. Because of Latin influences, English became the first of the European languages to be written down.

Middle English

In 1066 William the Conqueror invaded England and brought Norman French with him. Slowly Old English and Norman French came together, and Middle English began to appear. Today 40% of Modern English comes from French. With the introduction of the printing press English became more widespread.

Modern English

With the Renaissance and its rediscovery of classical Greek and Latin, many new words were created from Greek and Latin word elements. This continued intensively during the Early Modern English period. This rich language was used in the writings of Shakespeare and his contemporaries and profoundly influenced the nature and vocabulary of English. With dictionaries and spelling books, the English language became more standardized, although it continues to be influenced by other languages and new words and trends. These influences continue to make English a living, dynamic language.

Punctuation

Early writing had no punctuation or even spaces between words. English punctuation had its beginning in ancient Greece and Rome. Early punctuation reflected speaking, rather than reading. By the end of the eighteenth century, after the invention of printing, most of the rules for punctuation were established, although they were not the same in all languages.

The Structure of English

Grammar is the sound, structure, and meaning system of language. People who speak the same language are able to communicate because they intuitively know the grammar system of that language, the rules of making meaning. All languages have grammar, and yet each language has its own grammar.

Traditional grammar study usually involves two areas:

- **Parts of speech** (nouns, verbs, adjectives, adverbs, pronouns, prepositions, conjunctions) are typically considered the content of grammar. The parts of speech involve the *form* of English words.
- **Sentence structure** (subjects, predicates, objects, clauses, phrases) is also included in grammar study. Sentence structure involves the *function* of English.

Mechanics involves the conventions of punctuation and capitalization. Punctuation helps readers understand writers' messages. Proper punctuation involves marking off sentences according to grammatical structure. In speech students can produce sentences as easily and unconsciously as they can walk, but in writing they must think about what is and what is not a sentence.

In English there are about 14 punctuation marks (period, comma, quotation marks, question mark, exclamation point, colon, semicolon, apostrophe, hyphen, ellipsis, parentheses, brackets, dash, and underscore). Most immature writers use only three: period, comma, and question mark. The experienced writer or poet with the command of punctuation adds both flexibility and meaning to his or her sentences through his or her use of punctuation.

Usage is the way in which we speak in a given community. Language varies over time, across national and geographical boundaries, by gender, across age groups, and by socioeconomic status. When the variation occurs within a given language, the different versions of the same language are called *dialects.* Every language has a *prestige dialect* associated with education and financial success. In the United States, this *dialect* is known as Standard English and is the language of school and business.

Usage involves the word choices people make when speaking certain dialects. Word choices that are perfectly acceptable in conversation among friends may be unacceptable in writing. Usage is often the most obvious indicator of the difference between conversation and composition. Errors in word usage can make a writer seem ignorant and thus jeopardize his or her credibility, no matter how valid or important his or her overall message might be. Usage depends on a student's cultural and linguistic heritage. If the dialect students have learned is not the formal language of school settings or if it is not English, students must master another dialect or language in order to write Standard English.

The English Language Conventions lessons in ***Open Court Reading*** are structured to focus on grammar and usage or mechanics skills presented in a logical sequence. A skill is introduced on the first day of the lesson with appropriate models and then practiced in reading and writing on subsequent days to ensure that skills are not taught in isolation. Encourage students to use the focused English language convention presented in each lesson as they complete each Writing Process Strategies activity. Also encourage them to reread their writing, checking for proper use of the conventions taught. With practice, students should be able to apply their knowledge of conventions to any writing they do.

Tips

- Some of the errors students make in writing are the result simply of not carefully reading their final drafts. Many errors occur because the writer's train of thought was interrupted and a sentence is not complete or a word is skipped. These may look like huge errors that a simple rereading can remedy. Most often the writer can correct these types of errors on his or her own. A major emphasis of any English composition program should be to teach the editing and proofreading phases of the writing process so students can eliminate these types of errors themselves. This involves a shift in perception—from thinking of grammar as a set of discrete skills that involve mastery of individual rules, to understanding grammar as it applies to the act of communicating in writing.
- As students learn English language conventions, they should be expected to incorporate them into their written work. A cumulative student checklist of the grammar, usage, and mechanics skills covered in a grade level appears in the back of the ***Writer's Workbook.***
- Sometimes, students write sentences that raise grammatically complex problems that require a deep understanding of English grammar. Use the Sentence Lifting strategies outlined in the **Proofreading** part of the Appendix to identify and discuss these more sophisticated types of errors that can include:
  - **Faulty Parallelism.** Parts of a sentence parallel in meaning are not parallel in structure.
  - **Nonsequitors.** A statement does not follow logically from something said previously.
  - **Dangling Modifiers.** A phrase or clause does not logically modify the word next to it.
  - **Awkwardness.** Sentences are not written simply.
  - **Wordiness.** Thoughts are not written in as few words as possible.
  - **Vocabulary.** Precise words are not used.

Listening, Speaking, Viewing

Some people are naturally good listeners, and others have no trouble speaking in front of groups. Many people, however, need explicit instruction on how to tune in for important details and how to organize and make an oral presentation. While some people naturally critique what they read, hear, and see, many others need specific guidance to develop skills for analyzing what they encounter in images and the media. The abilities to listen appropriately and to speak in conversations and in groups, as well as to critically evaluate the information with which they are presented, are fundamental skills that will serve students throughout their lives.

Purpose

In addition to reading and writing, listening, speaking, and viewing complete the language arts picture. Through the development of these language arts skills, students gain flexibility in communicating orally, visually, and in writing. When speaking and listening skills are neglected, many students have difficulty speaking in front of groups, organizing a speech, or distinguishing important information they hear. A top anxiety for many adults is speaking in front of groups. Much of this anxiety would not exist if listening, speaking, and viewing skills were taught from the early years.

The Listening, Speaking, and Viewing instruction focuses on the literature selection or the Writing Process Strategies to provide context, reinforce other elements of the lesson, and integrate the other language arts. Many of the Listening, Speaking, and Viewing skills are very similar to reading or writing skills. For example, listening for details is the same type of skill as reading for details. Preparing an oral report employs many of the same skills as preparing a written report. Learning to use these skills effectively gives students flexibility in how they approach a task.

Procedure

Listening, speaking, and viewing skills are presented with increasing sophistication throughout every grade level of ***Open Court Reading*** in the Language Arts part of each lesson. Every unit includes at least one lesson on each of the following skills so that students encounter the skills again and again throughout a grade level:

- **Listening.** Listening skills include comprehending what one hears and listening for different purposes, such as to identify sequence or details, to summarize or draw conclusions, or to follow directions.
- **Speaking.** Speaking skills include speaking formally and conversationally, using appropriate volume, giving oral presentations, and using effective grammar. Speaking skills also include using descriptive words, using figurative language, and using formal and informal language.
- **Viewing.** Viewing skills include comprehending main ideas and messages in images, mass media, and other multimedia.
- **Interaction.** Interaction instruction focuses on a combination of listening and speaking skills. These include asking and responding to questions, nonverbal cues such as eye contact, facial expression, and posture, and contributing to and interacting in group settings.
- **Presenting Information.** The last Listening, Speaking, and Viewing lesson in every unit usually focuses on presentation skills. These include sharing ideas, relating experiences or stories, organizing information, and preparing for speeches. These lessons often parallel the Writing Process Strategies instruction, so that students can prepare their information in written or oral form.

Tips

- Point out the parallels among the language arts skills: providing written and oral directions, telling or writing a narrative, and so on. Encourage students to see that they have choices for communicating. Discuss the similarities and differences between different forms of communication, and determine whether one is preferable in a given situation.
- Ensure that all students have opportunities to speak in small groups and whole-class situations.
- Provide and teach students to allow appropriate wait time before someone answers a question.

Writing

PROGRAM APPENDIX

The ability to write with clarity and coherence is essential to students' success in school as well as in life. Communicating through writing is becoming more and more important in this age of computers. Yet, writing remains a major problem for students at all levels, as well as adults in the workplace.

Purpose

Writing is a complex process. It requires the ability to use a variety of skills (penmanship, grammar, usage, mechanics, spelling, vocabulary) fluently and appropriately at the same time one's creative and critical thinking processes create and structure an idea. Familiarity with the structures of writing and different genres, audiences, and purposes is necessary to write appropriately as well. The art of writing well also involves writer's craft, the ability to manipulate words and sentences for effect.

As strange as it may seem, the better a writer is, the *harder* he or she works at writing. The best writers are not the best because they are naturally talented. They are the best usually because they work the hardest. Good writers really do take *more* time than others in the planning and revising stages of the writing process. Poorer writers make writing look easy by writing without planning and typically build a composition sentence by sentence. They turn in their papers with little or no correction.

The goals of writing instruction have many facets:

- To model and practice writing in a variety of writing genres so that students can choose and write in an appropriate form.
- To model and practice a writing process to help students develop routines for planning their work and then revising and editing it.
- To practice using spelling, vocabulary, and English language conventions skills in writing so that students can use them fluently.
- To develop writing traits: ideas, organization, voice, word choice, sentence fluency, and presentation so that students become effective writers.

Just as the goal of phonics instruction is to teach students to read, the Writing Process Strategies instruction in ***Open Court Reading*** focuses on skills, structures, and strategies for writing. The goal of this instruction is to learn how to write, rather than to develop a particular idea. From this instruction, students will have a comprehensive bank of tools for writing, which they can then employ in the development of their Research and Inquiry investigations in each unit or in any other writing application.

Procedures

Writing Genres

There are several different genres students are typically asked to write. These usually include many creative stories and a few reports. The only narrative writing most adults do, however, is summaries of meetings. The bulk of adult writing consists of writing reports, letters, analyses, memos, and proposals. College students, as well, typically write research reports or critiques. A literate student needs to be able to choose and write in an appropriate genre.

> ***The best writers are not the best because they are naturally talented. They are the best usually because they work the hardest. Good writers really do take*** **more** ***time than others in the planning and revising stages of the writing process.***

- Narrative writing is story writing, which has a beginning, middle, and end. It includes myth, realistic fiction, historical fiction, biography, science fiction, fantasy, folktale, and legend.
- Expository writing is informational writing. It includes research reports, scientific investigation, summaries, and explanations of a process.
- Descriptive writing is observational writing that includes details. It has descriptive paragraphs that may be part of narrative or expository writing.
- Poetry writing involves particular attention to word choice and rhythm. Poetry may be free form, ballad, rhyming, or a variety of other forms.
- Personal writing is functional writing to help record ideas, thoughts, or feelings or to communicate with others and may include E-mail, journals, lists, and messages.
- Persuasive writing involves the development of a persuasive argument. It includes posters, persuasive essays, and advertisements.

In ***Open Court Reading*** the first unit of every grade teaches the writing process and traits of writing. Each subsequent unit focuses on a particular genre appropriate for the unit content. Expository and persuasive writing are typically in the units with research themes such as medicine or business; personal, narrative, descriptive, and poetry writing are in units with universal themes, such as friendship and courage. Exemplary models of each form of writing are included either in the literature selection, on the ***Language Arts Transparencies,*** or in the ***Language Arts Handbook.***

Each genre has its own form and function. For example:

- A personal narrative is probably best ordered as a straightforward chronological retelling of events. Dialogue may help to tell the story.
- A process description should be told in a step-by-step order. The draft should include as much information as possible; each step must be clear. If the piece needs cutting, the student can always do it later.
- A persuasive piece appeals to feelings. It requires facts as well as expert opinions.
- An interview could be written as a series of questions and answers.
- The order of details in a descriptive piece must be easy to follow—from left to right, top to bottom, or whatever order makes sense.
- A fictional story must include details describing characters, setting, and the characters' actions. Dialogue also helps to tell the story.

The goal is not to develop full-blown novels and compositions, but to experience the structures of different forms of writing.

Structures of Writing

Structures of writing involve the effective development of sentences, paragraphs, and compositions. In ***Open Court Reading*** structures of writing are taught within the context of the Writing Process Strategies activities rather than in isolation, so that students integrate their practice of writing structures as they develop different writing genres.

Writer's Craft

Writer's Craft involves the elements and choices writers make to add drama, suspense, or lightheartedness to a written work. These elements may include foreshadowing, use of figurative language, dialogue, or enhancement of setting or use of description to affect the mood and tone. In ***Open Court Reading,*** along with structures of writing, the writer's craft is pointed out in the literature selection and then taught and practiced within the context of the Writing Process Strategies activities.

Writing Traits

Writing traits are those elements and qualities in a composition that enhance the effectiveness of the writing. These include:

- Ideas/Content. Not only the quality of the idea, but the development, support, and focus of the idea makes a strong composition.

- Organization. In quality writing, the organization develops the central idea. The order and structure move the reader through the text easily. The beginning grabs the reader's attention and the conclusion adds impact.
- Voice. Voice is the overall tone of a piece of writing. Good writers choose a voice appropriate for the topic, purpose, and audience. As students develop writing skills, a unique style begins to emerge. The writing is expressive, engaging, or sincere, demonstrating a strong commitment to the topic.
- Word Choice. In quality writing words convey the intended message in an interesting, precise, and natural way appropriate to audience and purpose.
- Sentence Fluency. Sentence fluency enhances the flow and rhythm of a composition. In good writing sentence patterns are somewhat varied, contributing to ease in oral reading.
- Conventions. Good writers demonstrate consistent use and awareness of English language conventions.
- Presentation. A quality piece of writing includes an impressive presentation with attention to format, style, illustration, and clarity.

In ***Open Court Reading,*** the traits of writing are taught in the first unit and then practiced in every Writing Process Strategies activity as an integral part of the writing process.

The Writing Process

Providing a routine or process for students to follow will help them to learn a systematic approach to writing. By following the steps of the writing process, students will learn to approach everything they write with purpose and thought. They learn that although writing takes time and thought, there are steps they can take to make their writing clear, coherent, and appealing to their audience.

In ***Open Court Reading,*** the first unit of every grade provides an overview and teaching of the writing process, including strategies and examples for getting ideas, determining audience and purpose for writing, organizing writing, drafting, revising, editing, and presenting. The vehicle used to apply this instruction is a student autobiography. The autobiographies can be collected in a school portfolio to assess writing development over the course of the elementary years.

Prewriting

Purpose

Prewriting is that phase of the writing process when students think through an idea they want to write about. To improve their writing, students should think about their ideas, discuss them, and plan how they want readers to respond. It is important for students to take time before writing to plan ahead so that they can proceed from one phase of the writing process to another without spending unnecessary time making decisions that should have been made earlier. Prewriting is the most time-consuming phase of the writing process, but it may be the most important.

> ***The goal is not to develop full-blown novels and compositions, but to familiarize and practice the structures of different forms of writing.***

Procedure

Good student writers

- Listen to advice about time requirements and plan time accordingly.
- Spend time choosing, thinking about, and planning the topic.
- Spend time narrowing the topic.
- Determine the purpose for writing.
- Consider the audience and what readers already know about the topic.
- Conduct research, if necessary, before writing.
- Get information from a lot of different sources.
- Use models for different types of writing, but develop individual plans.
- Organize the resource information.
- Make a plan for writing that shows how the ideas will be organized.
- Elaborate on a plan and evaluate and alter ideas as writing proceeds.

Noting Writing Ideas

Students can make notes of writing ideas at any time, with a special time being set aside following the discussion of each reading selection. The writing ideas students get from a discussion might be concerned with the topic of the selection they just read or with an aspect of the author's style. You should keep such a list of writing ideas also, and think aloud occasionally as you make writing idea notes.

Students must make many decisions during the prewriting phase of the writing process. Most students can benefit from talking with a partner or a small group of classmates about these decisions. They may want to discuss some of the following points.

- **Genre** or format of each writing piece. Having decided to use a writing idea such as "a misunderstanding on the first day of school," the student must decide how to use it—for example, as a personal narrative, a realistic fiction story, a poem, a fantasy story, a play, a letter, and so on.
- **Audience**. Although students' writing pieces will be shared with classmates and with you, some may ultimately be intended for other audiences.
- **Writing Purpose**. Each student should write a sentence that tells the purpose of the piece he or she plans to write. The purpose statement should name the intended audience and the effect the writer hopes to have on that audience. For example, a writer may want to describe her first day in school. The intended audience is kindergarten students, and she intends her story to be humorous. Her purpose statement would read, "I want to write a funny story for other students about my first day in kindergarten."
- **Planning**. Some writers may find it helpful to brainstorm with a partner or small group to list words and phrases they might use in a piece of writing. Sometimes this list can be organized into webs of related ideas or details. This kind of prewriting activity might be particularly useful for planning a descriptive piece. For planning a comparison/contrast piece, a writer might use another kind of visual organizer, such as a Venn diagram. Students planning fiction pieces might use a story frame or plot line.

Tips

- Circulate as students make notes on writing ideas or work in small groups on prewriting activities.
- Notice which students are having difficulty coming up with writing ideas. It may help to pair these students with students who have many ideas.
- Do not worry if this phase of the process seems noisy and somewhat chaotic. Students must be allowed to let their imaginations roam in free association and to play around with words and ideas until they hit on something that seems right. They must be permitted to share ideas and help each other.
- Do not worry if, in the early sessions, the class as a whole seems to have few ideas. Through the reading and discussion of selections in the reading anthology, most students will soon have more writing ideas than they can use.

Writing (continued)

Drafting

Purpose

During the drafting phase of the writing process, students shape their planning notes into main ideas and details. They devote their time and effort to getting words down on paper. Whether students are drafting on scrap paper or on computer screens, your role is to encourage each writer to "get it all down." You must also provide a suitable writing environment with the expectation that there will be revision to the draft and to the original plan.

Good Student Writers

- Express all their ideas in the first draft.
- Stop and think about what is being written while drafting.
- Evaluate and alter ideas while drafting.
- Change or elaborate on original plans while drafting.
- Discover that they need more information about certain parts of their writing.
- Learn a lot more about the topic while drafting.

Procedure

Here are some points to share with students before they begin drafting:

- Drafting is putting your ideas down on paper for your own use. Writers do not need to worry about spelling or exact words. They just need to get their ideas down.
- Write on every other line so that you will have room to make revisions.
- Write on only one side of a page so that when you revise you can see all of your draft at once.
- As you draft, keep in mind your purpose for writing this piece and your intended audience.
- Use your plan and your notes from research to add details.

Using Word Processors for Drafting

Many students enjoy drafting on the screen of a computer more than drafting on paper. Once they have mastered the keyboard, they may find it easier to think as they write. Their first attempts look less sloppy, and they are often more willing to make changes and experiment as they draft. They will certainly find it neater to use the delete key on the word processor than to correct their mistakes by crossing out. The Basic Computer Skills instruction in the Language Arts Overview of every lesson provides instruction on using the computer.

Tips

Sometimes the hardest part of drafting is getting the first sentence down on paper. It may help a student even before she or he starts writing to begin a story in the middle or to write the word "Draft" in big letters at the top of the paper.

- If a student feels stuck during drafting, he or she may need to go back and try a different prewriting technique.
- After an initial fifteen or twenty minutes of imposed silence, some students may work better and come up with more ideas if they share as they write.
- You may find that it is difficult to get students to "loosen up" as they draft. Remember, most students have been encouraged to be neat and to erase mistakes when they write. It may help to share some of your own marked-up manuscripts with students.

Revising

Purpose

The purpose of revising is to make sure that a piece of writing expresses the writer's ideas clearly and completely. It has been said that there is no good writing, just good rewriting. A major distinction between good writers and poor writers is the amount of time and effort they put into revision. Poor writers look for spelling and grammatical errors if they do read their work.

Good Student writers

- Evaluate what has been written.
- Read the draft as a reader, not the writer.
- Identify problems with focus, giving enough information, clarity, and order.
- Think of solutions to problems and understand when solutions will and won't work.
- Recognize when and how the text needs to be reorganized.
- Eliminate sentences or paragraphs that don't fit the main idea.
- Identify ideas that need elaboration.
- Do more research if needed to support or add ideas.
- Identify and eliminate unnecessary details.
- Ask for feedback from peer and teacher conferences.
- Take advantage of classroom and outside resources.
- Check the accuracy of facts and details.
- Give credit for any ideas from other people or sources.

Procedure

Model asking questions like the following when revising various kinds of writing:

- About a narrative:
  - ✓ Does my first sentence get my readers' attention?
  - ✓ Are events in the story told in an order that makes sense?
  - ✓ Have I included dialogue to help move the story along?
  - ✓ Does the story have a clear focus?
- About a description:
  - ✓ Have I used details that appeal to the senses?
- About a comparison/contrast piece:
  - ✓ Have I made a separate paragraph for each subject discussed?
- About an explanation:
  - ✓ Will readers understand what I am saying?
  - ✓ Are the steps of the explanation in a clear order?
  - ✓ Have I made effective use of signal words?
  - ✓ Have I included enough information?
- About fiction:
  - ✓ Have I described my characters and setting?
  - ✓ Does the plot include a problem, build to a climax, and then describe the resolution of the problem?
- About persuasive writing:
  - ✓ Have I made my position clear?
  - ✓ Does my evidence support my position?
  - ✓ Have I used opinions as well as facts, and have I said whose opinions I used?
  - ✓ Have I directed my writing to my audience?

Help students understand the value of asking questions such as the following as they revise:

- About each paragraph:
  - ✓ Does each sentence belong in it?
  - ✓ Does each sentence connect smoothly with the next?
  - ✓ Does each sentence say something about the main idea?
- About each sentence:
  - ✓ Do the sentences read smoothly?
  - ✓ Have I combined sentences that were too short?
  - ✓ Have I broken sentences that were too long into two shorter sentences?
  - ✓ Have I varied the beginnings of the sentences?
- About the words:
  - ✓ Have I changed words that were repeated too often?
  - ✓ Do transition words connect ideas?

Tips

- Use the student Writing Folder to review student progress. Check first drafts against revised versions to see how each student is able to apply revision strategies.
- You may find that some students are reluctant to revise. You might then try the following:

✓ If a student doesn't see anything that needs to be changed or doesn't want to change anything, get him or her to do something to the paper—number the details in a description or the steps in a process, circle exact words, underline the best parts of the paper. Once a paper is marked, the student may not be so reluctant to change it.

✓ One reason many students do not like to revise is that they think they must recopy everything. This is not always necessary. Sometimes writers can cut and paste sections that they want to move. Or they can use carets and deletion marks to show additions and subtractions from a piece.

✓ Give an especially reluctant student a deadline by which she or he must revise a piece or lose the chance to publish it.

✓ Students will hopefully be writing in other classes and on a variety of topics. Revision techniques can be used to improve writing in any curriculum area. Stress to students the importance of focusing on their intended audience as they revise.

Proofreading

Purpose

Writing that is free of grammatical, spelling, and technical mistakes is clearer and easier for readers to understand. By proofreading their pieces, students will also notice which errors they make repeatedly and will learn not to make them in the future.

After a piece of writing has been revised for content and style, students must read it carefully line by line to make sure that it contains no errors. This activity, the fourth phase of the writing process, is called proofreading and is a critical step that must occur before a piece of writing can be published. Students can begin proofreading a piece when they feel that it has been sufficiently revised.

Good Student Writers

- Edit the work to allow the reader to understand and enjoy the words.
- Correct most errors in English language conventions.
- Use resources or seek assistance to address any uncertainties in English language conventions.

Procedure

Using What They Have Learned

Students should be expected to proofread at a level appropriate to their grade. Young authors should not be held responsible for skills they have not yet learned. Older students will be able to check for a greater variety of errors than younger students and should be expected to take greater responsibility for their proofreading. For example, students in first grade can be expected to check for and correct omitted capital letters at the beginning of sentences, but they should not necessarily be expected to understand and correct capital letters in proper nouns or in names of organizations. Older students will have mastered many more grammatical, mechanical, usage, and spelling skills and can be expected to perform accordingly. When you spot an error related to a skill beyond a student's level, make clear to the student that you do not expect her or him to be responsible for the mistake, but do explain that the error still needs to be corrected. The following suggestions may be useful as you introduce proofreading to the students and help them develop their proofreading skills.

Proofreading Checklist

Have students use a proofreading checklist similar to the one shown here to help them remember the steps for effective proofreading.

✓ Read each sentence.

✓ Does each sentence begin with a capital letter and end with correct punctuation?

✓ Do you notice any sentence fragments or run-on sentences?

✓ Are words missing from the sentence?

✓ Is any punctuation or capitalization missing from within the sentence?

✓ Do you notice any incorrect grammar or incorrect word usage in the sentence?

✓ Do you notice any misspelled words?

✓ Are the paragraphs indented?

✓ Can very long paragraphs be broken into two paragraphs?

✓ Can very short paragraphs be combined into one paragraph?

Tips

- **Proofreader's Marks** Students should use standard Proofreader's Marks to indicate the changes they wish to make. Explain to students that these marks are a kind of code used to show which alterations to make without a long explanation. Students may also be interested to know that professional writers, editors, and proofreaders use these same marks. You may want to review these marks one by one, illustrating on the board how to use them. For example, they may insert a word or a phrase by using a caret (^). If students wish to insert more text than will fit above the line, they may write in the margin or attach another sheet of paper. It may be a good idea, when such extensive corrections are made, for students to proofread their final copy carefully to make sure they have included all their alterations.
- **Sentence lifting** is a very effective method of showing students how to proofread their own work. Because students are working on their own sentences, they will be more inclined to both pay attention to what is going on and better understand the corrections that are made.

✓ Choose several pieces of student writing and look for common errors.

✓ On an overhead transparency, write several sentences. Include at least one sentence that has no errors.

✓ Tell students that you are going to concentrate on one type of error at a time. For example, first you will concentrate on spelling.

✓ Ask students to read the first sentence and point out any words they feel are spelled incorrectly. Do not erase errors. Cross them out and write the correctly spelled word above the crossed out word.

✓ Next move to a different type of error. Ask students to check for capitalization and punctuation.

✓ Continue in this way, correcting errors as you go through the sample sentences.

- **Using a Word Processor.** If the students are using a word processor to write their pieces, they may wish to run a spell check on their document. Caution them, however, that even the most sophisticated computer cannot catch every spelling error. Misuse of homophones and typographical errors may not be caught by the computer if the misused words appear in the computer's dictionary. For example, if a student types *form* instead of *from*, the computer will not register a mistake because *form* is also a word.

Circulate as students are proofreading on their own or in pairs.

✓ Are students able to check references when they are unsure of a spelling or usage?

✓ Are students criticizing each other's work constructively?

✓ Does a student no longer omit end punctuation because he or she noticed this error repeatedly during proofreading?

✓ Note students who are having difficulty. You may wish to address these difficulties during individual conferences.

Publishing

Purpose

Publishing is the process of bringing private writing to the reading public. The purpose of writing is to communicate. Unless students are writing in a journal, they will want to present their writing to the public. Such sharing helps students to learn about themselves and others, provides an opportunity for them to take pride in their hard work, and thus motivates them to further writing.

Publishing their work helps motivate students to improve such skills as spelling, grammar, and handwriting. Publishing can be as simple as displaying papers on a bulletin board or as elaborate as creating a class newspaper. Publishing will not—indeed should not—always require large blocks of class time. Students will wish to spend more time elaborately presenting their favorite pieces and less time on other works. If students take an inordinate amount of time to publish their work, you may want to coach them on how to speed up the process.

Good Student Writers

- Present the work in a way that makes it easy to read and understand.
- Consider format, style, illustration, and clarity in the presentation of the work.
- Show pride in the finished work.

Procedure

Preparing the Final Copy

When students feel that they have thoroughly proofread their pieces, they should copy the work onto another sheet of paper, using their best handwriting, or type the work on a computer or typewriter. They should then check this copy against the proofread copy to make sure that they made all the changes correctly and did not introduce any new errors. You may need to proofread and correct students' papers one final time before publishing to make sure that they have caught all errors.

Publishing Choices

In publishing, students need to decide

✓ how to prepare the piece for publication.
✓ what form the published work should take.
✓ whether to illustrate their writing with photographs, drawings, or charts with captions, as necessary.
✓ where to place any art they are using.

Publishing Checklist

The following checklist will help students when they are publishing their work. (Not every question applies to every form of publishing.)

✓ Have I revised my work to make it better?
✓ Have I proofread it carefully?
✓ Have I decided upon my illustrations?
✓ Have I recopied my piece carefully and illustrated it?
✓ Have I numbered the pages?
✓ Have I made a cover that tells the title and my name?

Tips

- Read through the piece, and tell the student if any corrections still need to be made. Also make some suggestions about the best way to publish a piece if a student has trouble coming up with an idea.
- Make suggestions and give criticism as needed, but remember that students must retain ownership of their publishing. Leave final decisions about form and design of their work up to individual students.
- Remind students to think about their intended audience when they are deciding on the form for their published piece. Will the form they have selected present their ideas effectively to the people they want to reach?

Writing Seminar

Purpose

The purpose of Writing Seminar (Levels 1–6) is for students to discuss their work in progress and to share ideas for improving it.

Writing Seminar is one of the activities in which students may choose to participate during Workshop. Students will meet in small groups to read and discuss one another's writing. One student reads a piece in progress. Other students comment on the writing and ask questions about the ideas behind the writing. The student whose work is being critiqued writes down the comments made by his or her classmates and decides how to use these comments to make the writing better.

Procedure

To begin the seminar, have one student writer read his or her revised draft as other students listen carefully. When the student has finished, invite other students to retell the story in their own words. If they have trouble retelling the story, the writer knows that he or she must make some ideas clearer.

Then have listeners who wish to comment raise their hands. The writer calls on each in turn. The listeners ask questions or make comments about the writing, telling, for example, what they like about it or what they might change to make it better. After several comments have been made, the writer notes any information that she or he might use. Another student then reads his or her piece.

Guidelines for Peer Conferencing

In an early session, work with students to establish guidelines for peer conferencing. You might suggest rules such as the following:

✓ Listen quietly while someone else is speaking.
✓ Think carefully before you comment on another person's work.
✓ Make your comments specific.
✓ Comment on something that you like about the piece before you comment on something that needs to be improved.
✓ Discuss your work quietly so as not to disturb the rest of the class.

Modeling Seminar Behavior

You may need to model meaningful comments and questions. For example:

✓ What was your favorite part?
✓ I like the part where (or when)
✓ I like the way you describe
✓ What happened after . . . ?
✓ I'd like to know more about
✓ Why did ________ happen?
✓ What do you think is the most important part?

Teacher Conferencing

During Writing Seminar, you will want to schedule individual conferences with students to help them evaluate their writing so that they can recognize problems and find ways to solve them. Teacher conferences are useful during all phases of the writing process, but they are crucial during the revising phase. Conferences give you an opportunity to observe students as they evaluate their writing, solve problems, make decisions about their work, and take responsibility for the development and completion of their work. The basic procedure for conferences is:

- Have the student read his or her work aloud.
- Review any feedback the student has received so far.
- Identify positive elements of the work.
- Use one or more of these strategies to help the student improve his or her work.
  ✓ Have students explain how they got their ideas.
  ✓ Have students think aloud about how they will address the feedback they have received.
  ✓ Ask students to help you understand any confusion you may have about their writing.
  ✓ Have the student add, delete, or rearrange something in the work and ask how it affects the whole piece.
  ✓ Think aloud while you do a part of what the student was asked to do. Ask the student to compare what you did to what he or she did.
  ✓ Have the student prescribe as if to a younger student how to revise the work.

- Ask two or three questions to guide students through revising (see below).
- Conclude by having the student state a plan for continuing work on the piece.

Writing Conference Questions

Ideas

- Who is your audience?
- What is your purpose for writing?
- How does the reader know the purpose?
- Is there enough information about the topic?
- Do you like one part of your work more than the rest? Why?
- Is your main idea clear?
- Is there a better way to express this idea?
- Is this a good topic sentence?
- Is your introduction engaging?
- Are any important details left out?
- Are any not-so-important details left in?
- Do you use specific details and examples?
- Are your ideas accurate and, if necessary, supported by research?
- Does your conclusion sum up or restate your purpose for writing?
- What might be another way to end the work?

Organization

- Is the writing organized in a way that makes the most sense based on the main idea?
- Is the structure clear for the reader? Is there a clear beginning, middle, and end?
- Are there smooth transitions from one part to the next?
- Are supporting details ordered in the most logical way?
- Can you combine any smaller paragraphs or separate larger ones?

Voice

- Do you sound confident and knowledgeable?
- Does the voice you use reflect the purpose of your writing? Does your writing sound funny or serious when you want it to be?
- Is your voice appropriate for your audience?
- Do you sound interested in the subject?
- Have you confidently stated your opinion? Have you used the pronoun "I" if appropriate?
- Does your writing sound like you?
- Is your voice too formal or informal?
- Will this writing get a strong response from the reader?
- Does your writing make the reader care about your topic?

Word Choice

- Do you use the same word/phrase repeatedly?
- Could you say the same thing with different words?
- Have you defined words your audience may not understand?
- Have you used precise words to describe or explain?
- Is there a better word to express this idea?
- Have you used your own words when summarizing information from another text?
- Do you use time and order words such as *first*, *next*, *then*, and *last* to help the reader understand when events take place?

Sentence Fluency

- Are your sentences clear and to the point?
- Have you used different kinds and lengths of sentences to effectively present your ideas?
- Could any of your sentences be combined?
- Is there a rhythm to your sentences?
- Does each sentence introduce a new idea or a new piece of information?
- Do some sentences repeat what has already been stated? If so, cut or change them.
- Have you used transition words such as *in contrast*, *however*, and *on the other hand* to move smoothly from one subject to the other?
- Have you used transitional phrases, such as *according to*, *in addition to*, or *at the same time* to link sentences?
- Have you used conjunctions such as *and*, *but*, and *or* to combine short, choppy sentences?

Tips

- Completed pieces as well as works in progress can be shared during Writing Seminar.
- Concentrate on one phase of the writing process at a time.
- Remember to keep conferences brief and to the point. If you are calling the conference, prepare your comments in advance. Be sure that you confer regularly with every student if only to check that each one is continuing to write, revise, and publish.
- During teacher conferences, you might use the following responses to student writing.
  - ✓ To open communication with the writer:
    - How is the writing going?
    - Tell me about your piece.
    - How did you get your ideas?
  - ✓ To give encouragement:
    - I like the part where . . . .
    - I like the way you open your piece by . . . .
    - I like your description of . . . .
  - ✓ To get the writer to clarify meaning:
    - I wonder about . . . .
    - What happened after . . . .
    - Why did . . . ?
  - ✓ To get the writer to think about direction and about writing strategies:
    - What do you plan to do with your piece?
    - How will you go about doing that?
    - What could I do to help you?
- As you confer with students, also recognize growth—evidence in the text that a student has applied what he or she learned in earlier conferences to another piece of writing.
- Some cues to look for when evaluating a student's growth as a writer include:
  - ✓ The writer identifies problems.
  - ✓ The writer thinks of solutions to a problem.
  - ✓ The writer recognizes when and how the text needs to be reorganized.
  - ✓ The writer identifies ideas in the text that need elaboration.
  - ✓ The writer makes thoughtful changes and pays attention to detail.
  - ✓ The writer takes advantage of peer and teacher conferences, books, and other resources to improve his or her writing.

Teaching Strategies for Writing

The teacher's role in writing instruction is critical. Certain strategies have been shown to be particularly effective in teaching writing.

Teacher Modeling Students learn best when they have good models. Models for the forms of writing appear in the literature selections, ***Language Arts Transparencies,*** and ***Language Arts Handbook.*** The Writing Process Strategies include instruction and models for all phases of the writing process. Teachers can also model the writing process for students every time they write.

Feedback. The most effective writing instruction is the feedback good teachers give to individual student work. Unfortunately many teachers simply mark errors in spelling, grammar, usage, and mechanics. The ***Routine Card*** and the ***Writer's Workbook*** provide questions that teachers can consider to offer constructive and meaningful feedback to students.

Clear Assignments. A well-written assignment makes clear to students what they are supposed to do, how they are supposed to do it, who the students are writing for, and what constitutes a successful response. When students have this information, they can plan, organize, and produce more effective work.

Instruction. Having students write a lot does not make them good writers. Few people become good writers, no matter how much they write. For many, the effect of years of practice is simply to produce increasingly fluent bad writing. Students need specific instruction and practice on different forms of writing and on different phases of the writing process, which they receive with instruction, modeling, practice, and feedback.

Classroom Discussion

PROGRAM APPENDIX

The more students are able to discuss what they are learning, voice their confusions, and compare perceptions of what they are learning, the deeper and more meaningful their learning becomes.

Purpose

It is in discussions that students are exposed to points of view different from their own, and it is through discussion that they learn how to express their thoughts and opinions coherently. Through discussion, students add to their own knowledge that of their classmates and learn to explain themselves coherently. They also begin to ask insightful questions that help them better understand what they have read and all that they are learning through their inquiry/research and explorations. The purpose of classroom discussion is to provide a sequence through which discussion can proceed.

Procedure

Reflecting on the Selection

After students have finished reading a selection, provide an opportunity for them to engage in **whole-group** discussion about the selection. Students should:

- Check to see whether the questions they asked before reading have been answered. Encourage them to discuss whether any unanswered questions should still be answered and if so have them add those questions to the Concept/Question Board.
- Discuss any new questions that have arisen because of the reading. Encourage students to decide which of these questions should go on the Concept/Question Board.
- Share what they expected to learn from reading the selection and tell whether expectations were met.
- Talk about whatever has come to mind while reading the selection. This discussion should be an informal sharing of impressions of, or opinions about, the selection; it should never take on the aspects of a question-and-answer session about the selection.
- Give students ample opportunity to ask questions and share their thoughts about the selection. Participate as an active member of the group, making your own observations about information in a selection or modeling your own appreciation of a story. Be especially aware of unusual and interesting insights suggested by students so that these insights can be recognized and discussed. To help students learn to keep the discussion student-centered, have each student choose the next speaker instead of handing the discussion back to you.

Recording Ideas

As students finish discussions about their reactions to a selection, they should be encouraged to record their thoughts, feelings, reactions, and ideas about the selection or the subject of the selection in their Writer's Notebooks. This will not only help keep the selections fresh in students' minds; it will strengthen their writing abilities and help them learn how to write about their thoughts and feelings.

Students may find that the selection gave them ideas for their own writing, or it could have reminded them of some person or incident in their own lives. Perhaps the selection answered a question that has been on their minds or raised a question they had never thought before. Good, mature writers—especially professional writers—learn the value of recording such thoughts and impressions quickly before they fade. Students should be encouraged to do this also.

Handing Off

Handing off (Levels 1–6) is a method of turning over to students the primary responsibility for controlling discussion. Often, students who are taking responsibility for controlling a discussion tend to have all "turns" go through the teacher. The teacher is the one to whom attention is transferred when a speaker finishes, and the teacher is the one who is expected to call on the next speaker—the result being that the teacher remains the pivotal figure in the discussion.

Having the students "hand off" the discussion to other students instead of the teacher encourages them to retain complete control of the discussion and to become more actively involved in the learning process. When a student finishes his or her comments, that student should choose (hand the discussion off to) the next speaker. In this way, students maintain a discussion without relying on the teacher to decide who speaks.

When handing off is in place, the teacher's main roles are to occasionally remind students to hand off and to monitor the discussion to ensure that everyone gets a chance to contribute. The teacher may say, for example, "Remember, not just boys (or girls)," or "Try to choose someone who has not had a chance to talk yet."

In order for handing off to work effectively, a seating arrangement that allows students to see one another is essential. A circle or a semicircle is effective. In addition, all of the students need to have copies of the materials being discussed.

Actively encourage this handing-off process by letting students know that they, not you, are in control of the discussion.

If students want to remember thoughts about, or reactions to, a selection, suggest that they record these in the Writing Journal section of the Writer's Notebook. Encourage students to record the thoughts, feelings, or reactions that are elicited by any reading they do.

Exploring Concepts Within the Selection

To provide an opportunity for collaborative learning and to focus on the concepts, have students form small groups and spend time discussing what they have learned about the concepts from this selection. Topics may include new information that they have acquired or new ideas that they have had.

Students should always base their discussions on postings from the Concept/Question Board as well as on previous discussions of the concept. The small-group discussions should be ongoing throughout the unit; during this time students should continue to compare and contrast any new information with their previous ideas, opinions, and impressions about the concepts. Does this selection help confirm their ideas? Does it contradict their thinking? Has it changed their outlook?

As students discuss the concepts in small groups, circulate around the room to make sure that each group stays focused upon the selection and the concepts. After students have had some time to discuss the information and the ideas in the selection, encourage each group to formulate some statements about the concept that apply to the selection.

Sharing Ideas about Concepts

Have a representative from each group report and explain the group's ideas to the rest of the class. Then have the class formulate one or more general statements related to the unit concepts and write these statements on the Concept/Question Board. As students progress through the unit, they will gain more and more confidence in suggesting additions to the Concept/Question Board.

Visual Aids During this part of the discussion, you may find it helpful to use visual aids to help students as they build the connections to the unit concepts. Not all units or concepts will lend themselves to this type of treatment; however, aids such as time lines, charts, graphs, or pictographs may help students see how each new selection adds to their growing knowledge of the concepts.

Encourage students to ask questions about the concepts that the selection may have raised. Have students list on the Concept/Question Board those questions that cannot be answered immediately and that they want to explore further.

Exploring Concepts Across Selections

As each new selection is read, encourage students to discuss its connection with the other selections and with the unit concepts. Also encourage students to think about selections that they have read from other units and how they relate to the concepts for this unit.

Ultimately, it is this ability to make connections between past knowledge and new knowledge that allows any learner to gain insights into what is being studied. The goal of the work with concepts and the discussions is to help students to start thinking in terms of connections—how is this like what I have learned before? Does this information confirm, contradict, or add a completely different layer to that which I already know about this concept? How can the others in the class have such different ideas than I do when we just read the same selection? Why is so much written about this subject?

Learning to make connections and to delve deeper through self-generated questions gives students the tools they need to become effective, efficient, lifelong learners.

Tips

- Discussions offer a prime opportunity for you to introduce, or seed, new ideas about the concepts. New ideas can come from a variety of sources: students may draw on their own experiences or on the books or videos they are studying; you may introduce new ideas into the discussion; or you may, at times, invite experts to speak to the class.
- If students do not mention an important idea that is necessary to the understanding of some larger issue, you may "drop" that idea into the conversation and, indeed, repeat it several times to make sure that it does get picked up. This seeding may be subtle ("I think that might be important here.") or quite direct ("This is a big idea, one that we will definitely need to understand and one that we will return to regularly.").

Discussion is an integral part of learning.

- In order to facilitate this process for each unit, you must be aware of the unit concepts and be able to recognize and reinforce them when they arise spontaneously in discussions. If central unit concepts do not arise naturally, then, and only then, will you seed these ideas by direct modeling. The more you turn discussions over to students, the more involved they will become, and the more responsibility they will take for their own learning. Make it your goal to become a participant in, rather than the leader of, class discussions.
- Help students to see that they are responsible for carrying on the discussion. After a question is asked, always wait instead of jumping in with a comment or an explanation. Although this wait time may be uncomfortable at first, students will come to understand that the discussion is their responsibility and that you will not jump in every time there is a hesitation.
- As the year progresses, students will become more and more adept at conducting and participating in meaningful discussions about what they have read. These discussions will greatly enhance students' understanding of the concepts that they are exploring.

Discussion Starters

- I didn't know that . . . .
- Does anyone know . . . .
- I figured out that . . . .
- I liked the part where . . . .
- I'm still confused about . . . .
- This made me think . . . .
- I agree with ____________ because . . . .
- I disagree with ____________ because . . . .
- The reason I think . . . .

Inquiry and Investigation

PROGRAM APPENDIX

Research and Investigation form the heart of the ***SRA/Open Court Reading*** program. In order to encourage students to understand how reading can enhance their lives and help them to become mature, educated adults, they are asked in each unit to use what they are learning in the unit as the basis for further exploration and research. The unit information is simply the base for their investigations.

There are two types of units in the ***SRA/Open Court Reading*** program—units based on universal topics of interest such as Friendship, Perseverance, and Courage and research units that provide students a very solid base of information upon which they can begin their own inquiry and research. Units delving into such areas as fossils, astronomy, and medicine invite students to become true researchers by choosing definite areas of interest—problems or questions to research in small cooperative groups and then to present to their classmates. In this way, students gain much more knowledge of the subject than they would have simply by reading the selections in the unit.

The selections in the units are organized so that each selection will add more information or a different perspective to students' growing bodies of knowledge.

Investigating through Reflective Activities

Purpose

The units in ***SRA/Open Court Reading*** that deal with universal topics will be explored through reflective activities. These units—such as Courage, Friendship, and Risks and Consequences—are organized to help students expand their perspectives in familiar areas. As they explore and discuss the unit concepts related to each topic, students are involved in activities that extend their experiences and offer opportunities for reflection. Such activities include writing, drama, art, interviews, debates, and panel discussions. Throughout each unit, students may be involved in a single ongoing investigative activity, or they may participate in a number of different activities. They may choose to produce a final written project or a visual aid. They will share with the rest of the class the new knowledge that they have gained from their reflective activities. During **Workshop** students will work individually or in collaborative groups on their investigation and/or projects.

The reflective activities will be activities of students' own choosing that allow them to explore the unit concepts more fully. They are free, of course, to make other choices or to devise activities of their own.

Procedure

Choosing an Area to Investigate

Students may work on activities alone, in pairs, or in small groups. They have the option of writing about or presenting their findings to the whole group upon completion. Before choosing a reflective activity, students should decide what concept-related question or problem they wish to explore. Generally, it is better for students to generate questions or problems after they have engaged in some discussion but before they have had a chance to consult source materials. This approach is more likely to bring forth ideas that students actually wonder about or wish to understand. Students may also look at the questions posted on the Concept/Question Board or introduce fresh ideas inspired by material they have just finished reading. Students who are working in pairs or in small groups should confer with one another before making a decision about what to explore. Some of the students may need your assistance in deciding upon, or narrowing down, a question or a problem so that it can be explored more easily. A good way to model this process for students is to make webs for a few of your own ideas on the board and to narrow these ideas down to a workable question or problem.

Organizing the Group

After a question or a problem has been chosen, the students may choose an activity that will help them to investigate that problem or question. The students' next responsibility is to decide who is going to investigate which facet of the question or the problem (when they are conducting a literature search, for example) or who is going to perform which task related to the particular reflective activity (when they are writing and performing an original playlet or puppet show, for example). Lastly, students need to decide how, or if, they want to present their findings. For instance, after conducting a literature search, some students may want to read and discuss passages from a book with a plot or theme that relates to a unit concept. Other students may prefer acting out and discussing scenes from the book.

Deciding How to Investigate

The following suggestions may help you and your students choose ways in which to pursue their investigations. You may want to post this list in the classroom so that groups have access to it as they decide what they want to investigate and how they want to proceed.

Investigation Activities

- Conduct a literature search to pursue a question or a problem. Discussion or writing may follow.
- Write and produce an original playlet or puppet show based on situations related to the concepts.
- Play a role-playing game to work out a problem related to the concepts.
- Stage a panel discussion with audience participation on a question or problem.
- Hold a debate on an issue related to the concept.
- Write an advice column dealing with problems related to the concepts.
- Write a personal-experience story related to the concepts.
- Invite experts to class. Formulate questions to ask.
- Conduct an interview with someone on a subject related to the concepts.
- Produce and carry out a survey on an issue or question related to the concept.
- Produce a picture or photo essay about the concept.

EXAMPLE: In the Heritage unit in grade 5 of ***SRA/Open Court Reading,*** students read "In Two Worlds: A Yup'ik Eskimo Family." This selection is about how three generations of Eskimos living in Alaska near the Arctic strive to adopt the best of modern ways without abandoning their traditional values. During the class discussion, some students may note that Alice and Billy Rivers want their students to learn both the new and the old ways of living. As the discussion continues, many students may conclude from the story that the older generations hope that future generations will continue to value their roots and their cultural traditions. Students then relate this story to their own heritage. Some students may share information about their customs or traditions.

Students choose some reflective activities that will help them learn more about family heritage and that will answer some of their questions about the unit concepts. Some students may be interested in interviewing family members or close family friends about their cultural traditions and heritages. These students review what they know about interviewing. They proceed by:

- Contacting in advance the person(s) they want to interview.
- Preparing a list of questions to ask.
- Preparing a list of subjects to discuss, deciding how to record the interview (by audiotape, videotape, or taking notes).
- Deciding whether to photograph the person and, if so, getting permission to do so in advance—collecting the equipment necessary for conducting the interview.

After they conduct the interviews, students decide how they wish to present the information that they have collected.

Investigating through reflective activities allows students to gain a wider perspective on a concept by relating it to their own experiences. Students quickly become aware that it is their responsibility to learn and to help their peers learn more about the unit concepts.

EXAMPLE: Another group of students in the same fifth-grade class may be more interested in planning a photo essay about one family or about a neighborhood with many families belonging to a particular culture. These students may decide to re-examine "In Two Worlds" to notice how the text and the photographs complement each other and what information is conveyed in each photograph. They may also decide to examine some photo essays listed in the unit bibliography. These students will need to make some advance preparations as well. They proceed by:

- Determining which neighborhood and which family or families to photograph.
- Contacting in advance the persons to be interviewed and photographed.
- Touring the neighborhood in advance of the photo shoot.
- Making a list of questions to ask the family or families about their heritage or about their neighborhood.
- Thinking about what information to include in their essay so that they can determine what photographs to take.
- Collecting the equipment necessary for conducting interviews and photographing subjects.

After students collect the information and take photographs, they may write and organize the photo essay and present it to the class. The teacher should remind students of the phases of the writing process, and encourage them to revise and proofread their work until they are completely pleased with it. Students can continue discussing family heritage and raising any new questions that they wish to investigate. The teacher should remind them that as they read further, they may think of a variety of ways to explore the unit concepts. The teacher should then ask students to post on the Concept/Question Board any new questions they have about family heritage. Students should sign or initial their questions so that they can identify classmates with similar interests and exchange ideas with them. The teacher should encourage students to feel free to write an answer or a note on someone else's question or to consult the board for ideas for their own explorations. From time to time, the teacher should post his or her own questions on the Concept/Question Board.

Tips

- The ***Leveled Classroom Library*** contains books related to the unit concepts. Remind students that these are good sources of information and that they should consult them regularly— especially when they are investigating concept-related ideas and questions.
- Some students work better within a specified time frame. Whenever they are beginning a new activity, discuss with the students a reasonable period of time within which they will be expected to complete their investigations. Post the completion date somewhere in the classroom so that students can refer to it and pace themselves accordingly. At first, you may have to help them determine a suitable deadline, but eventually they should be able to make this judgment on their own.

PROGRAM APPENDIX

Investigating through Research

Purpose

Students come to school with a wealth of fascinating questions. Educators need to capitalize on this excitement for learning and natural curiosity. A classroom in which only correct answers are accepted and students are not allowed to make errors and consider alternative possibilities to questions can quickly deaden this natural curiosity and enthusiasm. The purpose of the research aspect of this program is to capitalize on students' questions and natural curiosity by using a proven structure. This structure helps students to not get lost or bogged down but at the same time to preserve the open-ended character of real research, which can lead to unexpected findings and to questions that were not originally considered.

There is a conventional approach to school research papers that can be found, with minor variations, in countless textbooks. It consists of a series of steps such as the following: select a topic, narrow the topic, collect materials, take notes, outline, and write. By following these steps, a student may produce a presentable paper, but the procedure does not constitute research in a meaningful sense and indeed gives students a distorted notion of what research is about. We see students in universities and even in graduate schools still following this procedure when they do library research papers or literature reviews; we see their dismay when their professors regard such work as mere cutting and pasting and ask them where their original contribution is.

Even elementary school students can produce works of genuine research—research that seeks answers to real questions or solutions to real problems. This skill in collecting and analyzing information is a valuable tool in the adult world in which adults, as consumers, are constantly analyzing new information and making informed decisions on the basis of this information. Preparing students for the analytic demands of adult life and teaching them how to find answers to their questions are goals of education.

Procedure

In order to make the research productive, the following important principles are embodied in this approach:

1. Research is focused on problems, not topics.
2. Conjectures—opinions based on less than complete evidence or proof—guide the research; the research does not simply produce conjectures.
3. New information is gathered to test and revise conjectures.
4. Discussion, ongoing feedback, and constructive criticism are important in all phases of the research but especially in the revising of problems and conjectures.
5. The cycle of true research is essentially endless, although presentations of findings are made from time to time; new findings give rise to new problems and conjectures and thus to new cycles of research.

Following a Process

While working with the research units, students are encouraged to follow a set pattern or cycle in order to keep their research activities focused and on track. Students may go through these steps many times before they come to the end of their research. Certainly for adult researchers, this cycle of question, conjecture, research, and reevaluation can go on for years and in some cases lifetimes.

This cycle uses the following process:

1. **Decide on a problem or question to research.** Students should identify a question or problem that they truly wonder about or wish to understand and then form research groups with other students who have the same interests.
   - My problem or question is ___________
2. **Formulate an idea or conjecture about the research problem.** Students should think about and discuss with classmates possible answers to their research problems or questions and meet with their research groups to discuss and record their ideas or conjectures.
   - My idea/conjecture/theory about this question or problem is ___________
3. **Identify needs and make plans.** Students should identify knowledge needs related to their conjectures and meet with their research groups to determine which resources to consult and to make individual job assignments. Students should also meet periodically with the teacher, other classmates, and research groups to present preliminary findings and make revisions to their problems and conjectures on the basis of these findings.
   - I need to find out ___________
   - To do this, I will need these resources ___________
   - My role in the group is ___________
   - This is what I have learned so far ___________
   - This is what happened when we presented our findings ___________
4. **Reevaluate the problem or question based on what we have learned so far and the feedback we have received.**
   - My revised problem or question is ___________
5. **Revise the idea or conjecture.**
   - My new conjecture about this problem is ___________
6. **Identify new needs and make new plans.**
   - Based on what I found out, I still need to know ___________
   - To do this, I will need these resources ___________
   - This is what I have learned ___________
   - This is what happened when we presented our new findings ___________

Procedure for Choosing a Problem to Research

1. Discuss with students the nature of the unit. Explain to students that the unit they are reading is a research unit and that they will produce and publish in some way the results of their explorations. They are free to decide what problems or questions they wish to explore, with whom they want to work, and how they want to present their finished products. They may publish a piece of writing, produce a poster, write and perform a play, or use any other means to present the results of their investigations and research. They may work with partners or in small groups.
2. Discuss with students the schedule you have planned for their investigations: how long the project is expected to take, how much time will be available for research, when the first presentation will be due. This schedule will partly determine the nature of the problems that students should be encouraged to work on and the depth of the inquiry students will be encouraged to pursue.
3. Have students talk about things they wonder about that are related to the unit subject. For example, in the grade 3 unit, Money, students might wonder where money in the money machine comes from or how prices are determined. Conduct a free-floating discussion of questions about the unit subject.
4. Brainstorm possible questions for students to think about. It is essential that the students' own ideas and questions be the starting point of all inquiry. *Helpful hint:* For the first research unit, you might wish to generate a list of your own ideas, having students add to this list and having them choose from it.

5. Using their wonderings, model for students the difference between a research topic and a research problem or question by providing several examples. For example, have them consider the difference between the topic California and the problem, *Why do so many people move to California?* Explain to them that if they choose to research the topic California, everything they look up under the subject heading or index entry *California* will be related in some way to their topic. Therefore, it will be quite difficult to choose which information to record. This excess of information also creates problems in organizing their research. Clearly, then, this topic is too broad and general. Choosing a specific question or problem, one that particularly interests them, helps them narrow their exploration and advance their understanding. Some possible ideas for questions can be found in the unit introduction. Ideas can also be generated as you and your students create a web of their questions or problems related to the unit concept. For example, questions related to the subject California might include the following:
   - Why do so many people move to California?
   - How have the different groups of people living in California affected the state?
6. A good research problem or question not only requires students to consult a variety of sources but is engaging and adds to the groups' knowledge of the concepts. Furthermore, good problems generate more questions. Help students understand that the question, *Why do so many people move to California?* is an easy one to research. Many sources will contribute to an answer to the question, and all information located can be easily evaluated in terms of usefulness in answering the question. *Helpful hint:* Students' initial responses may indeed be topics instead of problems or questions. If so, the following questions might be helpful:
   - What aspect of the topic really interests you?
   - Can you turn that idea into a question?
7. Remember that this initial problem or question serves only as a guide for research. As students begin collecting information and collaborating with classmates, their ideas will change, and they can revise their research problem or question. Frequently, students do not sufficiently revise their problems until after they have had time to consider their conjectures and collect information.
8. As students begin formulating their research problems, have them elaborate on their reasons for wanting to research their stated problems. They should go beyond simple expressions of interest or liking and indicate what is puzzling, important, or potentially informative, and so forth, about the problems they have chosen.
9. At this stage, students' ideas will be of a very vague and limited sort. The important thing is to start them thinking about what really interests them and what value it has to them and the class.
10. Have students present their proposed problems or questions, along with reasons for their choices, and have an open discussion of how promising proposed problems are. As students present their proposed problems, ask them what new things they think they will be learning from their investigations and how that will add to the group's growing knowledge of the concepts. This constant emphasis on group knowledge building will help set a clear purpose for students' research.

Even elementary school students can produce works of genuine research—research that seeks answers to real questions or solutions to real problems.

11. Form research groups. To make it easier for students to form groups, they may record their problems on the board or on self-sticking notes. Final groups should be constituted in the way you find best for your class—by self-selection, by assignment on the basis of common interests, or by some combination of methods. Students can then meet during **Workshop** to agree on a precise statement of their research problem, the nature of their expected research contributions, and lists of related questions that may help later in assigning individual roles. They should also record any scheduling information that can be added to the planning calendar.

Using Technology

The **Research Assistant CD-ROM** (Levels 2–6), an interactive software program, supports student research by helping them plan, organize, present, and assess their research.

Students and teachers can access the Web site **www.sra4kids.com** to find information about the themes in their grade level.

Tips

- If students are careful about the problems or questions they choose to research, they should have few problems in following through with the research. If the problem is too broad or too narrow, they will have problems.
- Have students take sufficient time in assessing their needs—both knowledge needs and physical needs in relation to their research. Careful preplanning can help the research progress smoothly with great results.
- Encourage students to reevaluate their needs often so they are not wasting time finding things they already have or ignoring needs that they haven't noticed.
- Interim presentations of material are every bit as important, if not more so, than final presentations. It is during interim presentations that students have the opportunity to rethink and reevaluate their work and change direction or decide to carry on with their planned research.

Workshop

Every teacher and every student needs time during the day to organize, take stock of work that is done, make plans for work that needs doing, and finish up incomplete projects. In addition, time is needed for differentiating instruction and for peer conferencing.

Purpose

Workshop is the period of time each day in which students work independently or collaboratively to practice and review material taught in the lessons.

A variety of activities may occur during this time. Students may work on a specific daily assignment, complete an ongoing project, work on unit exploration activities, focus on writing, or choose from among a wide range of possibilities. With lots of guidance and encouragement, students gradually learn to make decisions about their use of time and materials and to collaborate with their peers.

A goal of **Workshop** is to get students to work independently. This is essential since **Workshop** is also the time during which the teacher can work with individuals or groups of students to reinforce learning, to provide extra help for those having difficulties, to extend learning, or to assess the progress of the class or of individuals.

Procedure

Initially, for many students, you will need to structure **Workshop** carefully. Eventually, students will automatically go to the appropriate areas, take up ongoing projects, and get the materials they will need. **Workshop** will evolve slowly from a very structured period to a time when students make choices and move freely from one activity to the next.

Adhere firmly to **Workshop** guidelines. By the time the students have completed the first few weeks of school, they should feel confident during **Workshop**. If not, continue to structure the time and limit options. For young students, early periods of **Workshop** may run no more than five to eight minutes. The time can gradually increase to fifteen minutes or longer as the students gain independence. Older students may be able to work longer and independently from the very beginning of the school year.

Introducing Workshop

Introduce **Workshop** to students by telling them that every day there will be a time when they are expected to work on activities on their own or in small groups. For young students in the beginning, you will assign the **Workshop** activities to help them learn to work on their own. Point out the shelf or area of the classroom where **Workshop** materials are stored. Tell students that when they finish working with the materials for one activity, they will choose something else from the **Workshop** shelf. New activity materials will be added to the shelf from time to time. Make sure that the students know that they may always look at books during **Workshop**.

Tell older students that they will have an opportunity each day to work on their unit explorations, their writing, and other projects. Students will be working independently and collaboratively during this time.

Guidelines

- Make sure each student knows what he or she needs to do during **Workshop**.
- Demonstrate for the whole group any activity assigned for **Workshop**; for example, teaching the students a new game, introducing new materials or projects, or explaining different areas.
- For young students, it is essential to introduce and demonstrate different activities and games before the students do them on their own. With games, you may want to have several students play while the others watch. Make sure that all the students know exactly what is expected of them.
- In the beginning, plan to circulate among the students providing encouragement and help as necessary.
- Once students are engaged in appropriate activities and can work independently, meet with those students who need your particular attention. This may include individual students or small groups.
- Let the students know that they need to ask questions and clarify assignments during **Workshop** introduction, so that you are free to work with small groups.
- Be sure that students know what they are to do when they have finished an activity and where to put their finished work.

Establish and discuss rules for **Workshop** with the students. Keep them simple and straightforward. You may want to write the finalized rules on the board or on a poster. You may want to review these rules each day at the beginning of **Workshop** for the first few lessons or so. You may also wish to revisit and revise the rules from time to time. Suggested rules include:

✓ Be polite.
✓ Share.
✓ Whisper.
✓ Take only the materials you need.
✓ Return materials.

Setting Up Your Classroom for Workshop

Carefully setting up your classroom to accommodate different **Workshop** activities will help assure that the **Workshop** period progresses smoothly and effectively. While setting up your classroom, keep the primary **Workshop** activities in mind. During **Workshop** the students will be doing independent and collaborative activities. In kindergarten and first grade, these activities may include letter recognition and phonemic awareness activities and writing or illustrating stories or projects. In addition, they will be working on individual or small group projects.

Many classrooms have centers that the students visit on a regular or rotating basis. Center time can be easily and efficiently incorporated into the **Workshop** concept. For example, the activities suggested during **Workshop** can be incorporated into reading and writing areas. Other typical classroom areas include an art center, math center, science table, play area, etc.

The following are suggestions for space and materials for use during **Workshop**:

1. **Reading Area** supplied with books and magazines. The materials in the Reading Area should be dynamic—changing with students' abilities and reflecting unit themes they are reading. You may wish to add books suggested in the ***Leveled Classroom Libraries*** and unit bibliographies available with each unit.
2. **Writing Area** stocked with various types and sizes of lined and unlined paper, pencils, erasers, markers, crayons, small slates, and chalk. The area should also have various **Letter Cards**, other handwriting models, and worksheets for those students who want to practice letter formation or handwriting. Students should know that this is where they come for writing supplies. In addition to the supplies described above, the Writing Area can also have supplies to encourage the students to create and write on their own:
   ✓ magazines and catalogs to cut up for pictures; stickers, paint, glue, glitter, etc. to decorate books and book covers; precut and stapled blank books for the students to write in. (Some can be plain and some cut in special shapes.)
   ✓ cardboard, tag board, construction paper, etc., for making book covers. (Provide some samples.)

✓ tape, scissors, yarn, hole punches for binding books.

✓ picture dictionaries, dictionaries, thesaurus, word lists, and other materials that may encourage independence.

3. **Listening Area** supplied with tape recorder, CD player, optional headphones, and tapes of stories, poems, and songs for the students to listen to and react to. You might also want to provide blank tapes and encourage the students to retell and record their favorite stories or make up and tell stories for their classmates to listen to on tape. You may also want to make available the ***Listening Library Audiocassettes/CDs*** that are available with the program.
4. **Workshop Activity Center** supplied with **Alphabet Flash Cards,** individual **Alphabet Sound Card** sets (Kindergarten), **Individual Sound/Spelling Cards** and **High-Frequency Word Flash Cards** (Grades 1-3), and other materials that enhance what the students are learning. Other commonly used classroom materials that enhance reading can be included (for example, plastic letters, puzzles, workbooks).

Since students will be working on their inquiry/investigations during **Workshop**, make sure there are adequate supplies to help them with their research. These might include dictionaries, encyclopedias, magazines, newspapers, and computers—preferably with Internet capability.

Workshop is the period of time each day in which students work independently or collaboratively to practice and review material taught in the lessons.

Students thrive in an environment that provides structure, repetition, and routine. Within a sound structure, the students will gain confidence and independence. This setting allows you to differentiate instruction in order to provide opportunities for flexibility and individual choice. This will allow students to develop their strengths, abilities, and talents to the fullest.

Suggestions for English Learners

Workshop affords students who are English Learners a wealth of opportunities for gaining proficiency in English. It also encourages them to share their backgrounds with peers. Since you will be working with all students individually and in small groups regardless of their reading ability, students who need special help with language will not feel self-conscious about working with you. In addition, working in small groups made up of students with the same interests rather than the same abilities will provide them with the opportunity to learn about language from their peers during the regular course of **Workshop** activities.

Some suggestions for meeting the special needs of students with diverse backgrounds follow:

- Preread a selection with English Learners to help them identify words and ideas they wish to talk about. This will prepare them for discussions with the whole group.
- Preteach vocabulary and develop selection concepts that may be a challenge for students.
- Negotiate the meaning of selections by asking questions, checking for comprehension, and speaking with English Learners as much as possible.
- Draw English Learners into small group discussions to give them a sense that their ideas are valid and worth attention.
- Pair English Learners with native English speakers to share their experiences and provide new knowledge to other students.
- Have English Learners draw or dictate to you or another student a description of a new idea they may have during **Workshop** activities.

Workshop Management Tips

Use the following **Workshop** management tips to ensure that **Workshop** runs smoothly. Note that these suggestions for a weekly unit/lesson may not exactly correspond to a particular unit/lesson in a given grade level, but will give you a sense of how **Workshop** should progress.

Unit 1, Lesson 1 Introduce **Workshop** to students. Make sure they know where materials are located. Post the rules on the board or other prominent place in the classroom. Keep **Workshop** time short (less than thirty minutes) and very directed during the first few weeks until students can work independently.

Unit 1, Lesson 2 Discuss using small groups for pre/reteaching purposes and how you will indicate who will be in the groups. Start by forming one small group randomly and having other students do something specific such as a writing assignment. When you have finished with the small group, send them to do independent work. Call another small group of students to work with you. Continue this each day until students are accustomed to forming groups and working independently.

Unit 1, Lesson 3 Reading Roundtable is a student-formed and student-run book discussion. Encourage students participating in Reading Roundtable to choose a book that they all will read and discuss. Several different Reading Roundtable groups may form on the basis of the books students choose.

Unit 1, Lesson 4 For the first few weeks of the school year, make sure each student has a plan for using **Workshop** time.

Unit 1, Lesson 5 Allot time for presentation and discussion of research activities. Use a whole **Workshop** day and have all groups present their findings, or split the presentations over several days, depending on the small-group needs of your class.

Unit 1, Lesson 6 Review how students have used **Workshop** during this unit. Have they used their time well? Do they have the materials they need? Discuss suggestions for improving their use of this time. Take a few minutes at the beginning of each **Workshop** to make sure students know what they will be doing.

Unit 2, Lesson 1 Form small extra-practice groups with the more advanced students from time to time, as they also need special attention.

Unit 2, Lesson 2 To keep the whole class informed about the independent research being done, every other day or so invite a research group to explain what it is doing, how the research is going, and any problems they are encountering.

Workshop (continued)

Unit 2, Lesson 3 Discuss the use of **Workshop** time for doing inquiry and research projects. Introduce students to the activities provided for use with this unit at **www.sra4kids.com.**

Unit 2, Lesson 4 Make sure small extra-practice groups are formed based on your observations of students' work on the different daily lessons. Small groups should be fluid and based on demonstrated need rather than becoming static and unchanging.

Unit 2, Lesson 5 One purpose of **Workshop** is to help students learn independence and responsibility. Assign students to monitor **Workshop** materials. They should alert you whenever materials are running low or missing, and they can be responsible for checking on return dates of library books and making sure the books are either returned or renewed.

Unit 2, Lesson 6 Students sometimes have difficulty starting discussions in Reading Roundtable. Try some of these discussion starters with students, and print them on a poster paper for student use.

I didn't know that . . .	I liked the part where . . .
Does anyone know . . .	I'm still confused by . . .
I figured out that . . .	This made me think . . .

I agree/disagree with ___________ because . . .

Unit 3, Lesson 1 By this time students should be accustomed to the routines, rules, expectations, and usage of **Workshop** time and be moving smoothly from small teacher-led groups to independent work. Monitor small groups occasionally to see that they are on task and making progress on their activities.

Unit 3, Lesson 2 Make a practice of reading aloud to students. All students enjoy being read to, no matter their age or grade. Encourage them to discuss the shared reading in Reading Roundtable groups and to bring books and read them aloud to their classmates.

Unit 3, Lesson 3 Encourage cooperation and collaboration by providing students with opportunities to engage in small groups.

Unit 3, Lesson 4 Spend a few minutes each day circulating around the room and monitoring what students are doing independently or in small groups. Students can then share any questions or problems they are having with you on a timely basis.

Unit 3, Lesson 5 Take note of different small groups. Make sure that quieter students are able to participate in the discussions. Often the stronger, more confident students dominate such discussions. Encourage them to give all participants a chance to share their ideas.

Unit 3, Lesson 6 If students are not productive during **Workshop**, keep them in the small group you are working with until they can successfully benefit from independent work. Discuss strategies they could use to become more independent.

Unit 4, Lesson 1 Different students can monitor **Workshop** materials and alert you when materials or supplies are running low or missing and can check that library books are either returned or renewed.

Unit 4, Lesson 2 From time to time, join a Reading Roundtable group, and take part in their discussion. Make sure students lead the discussion.

Unit 4, Lesson 3 Encourage responsibility and independence by reminding students to show respect for each other and the materials provided.

Unit 4, Lesson 4 Be sure students discuss during Reading Roundtable what they like or dislike about a book, why they wanted to read it, and how the book either lived up to their expectations or disappointed them. Discussions should not be about basic comprehension but should help students think more deeply about the ideas presented in the book.

Unit 4, Lesson 5 Make sure students continue to use the activities provided for use with this unit at **www.sra4kids.com.**

Unit 4, Lesson 6 If students are not productive in **Workshop**, keep them in the small group you are working with until they can successfully benefit from independent work. Discuss strategies they could use to become more independent.

Unit 5, Lesson 1 Students often make great tutors for other students. They are uniquely qualified to understand problems that others might be having. Encourage students to pair up during **Workshop** to help each other with their daily lessons.

Unit 5, Lesson 2 Form small extra-practice groups with the more advanced students from time to time, as they also need special attention.

Unit 5, Lesson 3 In order to keep the whole class informed about the independent research being done, every other day or so, invite a research/investigation group to explain what it is doing, how the research is going, and any problems they are encountering.

Unit 5, Lesson 4 Most of the authors of the student anthology selections are well known and have written many, many pieces of fine literature. Encourage students who enjoy the anthology selections to find other books by the same author. Encourage them to think about and discuss what about that particular author's work attracts them.

Unit 5, Lesson 5 Share your impressions of books from the ***Leveled Classroom Library*** or other reading during Reading Roundtable. Note which students initiate sharing and which are reluctant to share.

Unit 5, Lesson 6 Review with students the time they have used in **Workshop**. Have they used their time well? Do they have the materials they need? Discuss suggestions for improving the use of this time.

Unit 6, Lesson 1 Spend a few minutes each day circulating around the room and monitoring what students are doing independently or in small groups. Students can share any questions or problems they are having with you on a timely basis.

Unit 6, Lesson 2 Students should be accustomed to the routines, rules, expectations, and usage of **Workshop** time and be moving smoothly from small teacher-led groups to independent work. Make sure to monitor small groups occasionally to see that they are on task and making progress with their activities.

Unit 6, Lesson 3 Make sure students continue to use the activities provided for use with this unit at **www.sra4kids.com.**

Unit 6, Lesson 4 Allot time for presentation and discussion of research activities. You may want to use a whole **Workshop** day and have all groups present their findings or split the presentations over several days, depending on the urgency of the small-group instruction your class needs.

Unit 6, Lesson 5 Students often make great tutors for other students. The fact that they too are just learning the materials makes them uniquely qualified to understand problems that others might be having. Encourage students to pair up during **Workshop** to help each other on their daily lessons.

Unit 6, Lesson 6 If the reading selection is an excerpt from a longer piece, encourage students to read the book from which the excerpt is taken and discuss how the excerpt fits into the larger work.

Assessment can be one of your most effective teaching tools if it is used with the purpose of informing instruction and highlighting areas that need special attention.

Purpose

Assessment is a tool the teacher uses to monitor students' progress and to detect students' strengths and weaknesses. Evaluation of student learning is addressed in two ways: Informal Assessment and Formal Assessment. Informal, observational assessment, or a quick check of students' written work, is presented in the ***Teacher's Edition*** in the form of assessment suggestions. Formal Assessment consists of performance assessment (both reading and writing) and objective tests (multiple choice and essay).

Procedure

Informal Assessment

Observation

Observing students as they go about their regular classwork is probably the single most effective way to learn in depth your students' strengths and areas of need. The more students become accustomed to you jotting down informal notes about their work, the more it will become just another part of classroom life that they accept and take little note of. This gives you the opportunity to assess their progress constantly without the interference and possible drawback of formal testing situations.

In order to make informal assessment of student progress a part of your everyday classroom routine, you might want to start by preparing the materials you will need on hand.

- Enter students' names in the Teacher's Observation Log, found in ***Program Assessment.***
- Before each day's lesson begins, decide which students you will observe.
- Keep the Teacher's Observation Log available so that you can easily record your observations.
- Decide what aspect of the students' learning you wish to monitor.
- During each lesson, observe this aspect in the performances of several students.
- Record your observations.
- It may take four to five days to make sure you have observed and recorded the performance of each student. If you need more information about performance in a particular area for some of your students, you may want to observe them more than once.

Progress Assessment

Written Work

Students are writing one thing or another all day long. Each of these pieces of writing can provide you with valuable information about your students' progress. Two very helpful resources that students will work in daily are the ***Comprehension and Language Arts Skills*** (Levels 1–6) and the ***Inquiry Journal*** (Levels 2–6).

- The ***Comprehension and Language Arts Skills*** include skills practice lessons that act as practice and reinforcement for the skills lessons taught during the reading of the lesson or in conjunction with the Language Arts lesson. These skill pages give you a clear picture of students' understanding of the skills taught. Use them as a daily assessment of student progress in the particular skills taught through the program. In ***Phonemic Awareness and Phonics Skills*** (K), and ***Phonics Skills*** (1), students practice each of the skills taught in Part 1 of the program.
- The ***Inquiry Journal*** can give you invaluable information on how students are progressing in many different areas. In the ***Inquiry Journal***, students
  - ✓ Record what they know about the concepts and what they learn. You will be able to monitor their growing ability to make connections and use their prior knowledge to help them understand new concepts.
  - ✓ Keep a record of their research: what resources they need, what they have used, where they have looked, and what they have found. You can keep track of students' growing ability to find the resources and knowledge base they need to answer the questions they pose.
  - ✓ Keep track of their work with their collaborative groups. This will give you a good idea of students' growing ability to work with peers for a common goal—the acquisition of new knowledge.
  - ✓ Practice study and research skills that will help them in all of their schooling. You can easily keep track of how well they are learning to use such things as library resources, reference books, visual organizers, and much, much more.

Dictation

In grades 1–3, students use dictation to practice the sound/spelling associations they are learning and/or reviewing. Collect the dictation papers and look through them to see how the students are doing with writing and with proofreading their words. Record notes on the papers and keep them in the student portfolios.

Portfolios

Portfolios are more than just a collection bin or gathering place for student projects and records. They add balance to an assessment program by providing unique benefits to teachers, students, and families.

- Portfolios help build self-confidence and increase self-esteem as students come to appreciate the value of their work. More importantly, portfolios allow students to reflect on what they know and what they need to learn. At the end of the school year, each student will be able to go through their portfolios and write about their progress.
- Portfolios provide the teacher with an authentic record of what students can do. Just as important, portfolios give students a concrete example of their own progress and development. Thus, portfolios become a valuable source of information for making instructional decisions.
- Portfolios allow families to judge student performance directly. Portfolios are an ideal starting point for discussions about a student's achievements and future goals during teacher/family conferences.

You will find that there are many opportunities to add to students' portfolios.

Assessment (continued)

Reading

- During partner reading, during **Workshop**, or at other times of the day, invite students, one at a time, to sit with you and read a story from an appropriate ***Decodable Book*** (grades 1–3) or from the ***Student Anthology.***
- As each student reads to you, follow along and make note of any recurring problems the student has while reading. Note students' ability to decode unknown words as well as any attempt—successful or not—to use strategies to clarify or otherwise make sense of what they are reading. From time to time, check students' fluency by timing their reading and noting how well they are able to sustain the oral reading without faltering.
- If the student has trouble reading a particular **Decodable Book**, encourage the student to read the story a few times on her or his own before reading it aloud to you. If the **Decodable Book** has two stories, use the alternate story to reassess the student a day or two later.
- If after practicing with a particular **Decodable Book** and reading it on his or her own a few times, a student is still experiencing difficulty, try the following:
  - Drop back two **Decodable Books.** (Continue to drop back until the student is able to read a story with no trouble.) If the student can read that book without problems, move up one book.
  - Continue the process until the student is able to read the current Decodable Book.

Preparing for Formal Assessment

Written Tests

- Have the students clear their desks.
- Make sure the students can hear and see clearly.
- Explain the instructions and complete one or two examples with students before each test to make sure they understand what to do.
- Give students ample time to finish each test.

Observing students as they go about their regular classwork is probably the single most effective way to learn in depth your students' strengths and areas of need.

The assessment components of ***Open Court Reading*** are designed to help teachers make appropriate instructional decisions. The variety of assessments is intended to be used continuously and formatively. That is, students should be assessed regularly as a follow-up to instructional activities, and the results of the assessment should be used to inform subsequent instruction.

Program Assessment

The Program Assessment is a series of three broad measures that are meant to be administered at the beginning of the school year, at midyear, and at the end of the year.

- The Pretest gives teachers a snapshot of students' entry-level skills. This information allows the teacher to provide supplemental instruction to students who have not mastered critical skills and to offer more challenging material to students who demonstrate advanced abilities. In addition, this Pretest can serve as a baseline against which to measure students' progress throughout the year.
- The Midyear Test reviews skills that were taught in the first half of the school year, allowing teachers to determine how well students are retaining what they have learned. In addition, the Midyear Test contains "anchor items" similar to those that appeared on the pretest. These items will allow teachers to measure student progress from the beginning of the year to the middle of the year.
- The Posttest is a review of the content that was taught throughout the year and is a summative measure that reflects exit-level skills. The Posttest also contains anchor items, so it is possible to compare students' performance on specific skills at three points in the school year.

In addition to the Pretest, Midyear Test, and Posttest, the Program Assessment also contains a Teacher's Observation Log. Informal assessment is a part of the everyday classroom routine. Teachers can record information quickly on this observation sheet, and they may extend their observations over several days, until they have had a chance to observe each student's performance in a particular area.

Unit Assessments

Unit Assessments, as the name implies, reflect the instructional content and reading selections in each unit. The various measures within a unit assessment allow the teacher to see how well students have learned the skills that have recently been taught and to provide any additional instruction that is necessary.

Unit Assessments include a variety of measures that vary in form and difficulty so they are both motivating and challenging. Some of the questions are relatively easy, and most students should answer them correctly. Others are more difficult, but none are beyond the abilities of the majority of the students in a class. The skills featured on unit assessments are tied to reading success and reflect both state and national standards.

Unit Assessments include:

- Individual lesson assessments that assess the skills taught in each lesson immediately after instruction is delivered. These assessments will help you determine how well students are grasping the skills and concepts as they are taught.
- End-of-unit assessments that assess all of the skills taught throughout the unit. These assessments will help determine the students' ability and growing bank of knowledge as well as their ability to retain concepts over a limited period of time—generally six to eight weeks per unit.

Diagnostic Assessments

For the majority of the students in a class, the Program Assessment component of ***Open Court Reading*** will provide the teacher with all the information needed to make appropriate instructional decisions. In certain circumstances, however, it may be necessary to gather additional information in order to provide students with appropriate instruction. Some students, for example, may have specific skill deficits that prevent them from making adequate progress. Other students may enter the class after the beginning of the school year. A third situation is when the teacher might want to group students who have the same skill deficit. For these circumstances, we provide Diagnostic Assessments.

The Diagnostic Assessments offer a variety of measures that allow the teacher to identify students' strengths and weaknesses. The results of the assessment can help the teacher develop intervention strategies and choose the right supplemental instruction that will meet each student's needs. General and specific instructions are provided so that the teacher can use the Diagnostic Assessments efficiently without disrupting the instructional routine.

Tips

- When observing students, do not pull them aside; rather, observe students as part of the regular lesson, either with the whole class or in small groups.
- Encourage students to express any confusion they may be experiencing. The questions students ask can give you valuable insight into their progress and development.
- The more comfortable students become with standardized-test formats—usually multiple choice—the more confident you and they will be in the fact that the test is testing their knowledge of a subject rather than their test-taking skills.
- Make sure students know that the ultimate purpose of assessment is to keep track of their progress and to help them continue to do better.

Assessment

Rubrics

A rubric is an established rule or criterion. Rubrics provide criteria for different levels of performance. Rubrics established before an assignment is given are extremely helpful in evaluating the assignment. When students know what the rubrics for a particular assignment are, they can focus their energies on the key issues.

Using Comprehension Strategies Rubrics

The following rubrics can be used to gauge the students' growing knowledge of the comprehension strategies and how adept they are becoming in their use. The rubrics are simply a guide. Students may and probably will develop strategies of their own. The important thing to consider is whether or not students are becoming strategic, active readers—do they employ these and other strategies, or do they continue to simply plough through text unaware of any problems they might be having? The rubrics indicate the types of behaviors strategic readers use and will help you identify the growing facility your students can gain in dealing with text of all sorts.

Grade 1: Comprehension Strategies Rubrics

Predicting

- The student makes predictions about what the text is about.
- The student updates predictions during reading, based on information in the text.

Visualizing

- The student visualizes ideas or scenes described in the text.

Grades 2-6: Comprehension Strategies Rubrics

Summarizing

- The student paraphrases text, reporting main ideas and a summary of what is in the text.
- The student decides which parts of the text are important in his/her summary.
- The student draws conclusions from the text.
- The student makes global interpretations of the text, such as recognizing the genre.

Asking Questions

- The student asks questions about ideas or facts presented in the text and attempts to answer these questions by reading the text.

Predicting

- The student makes predictions about what the text is about.
- The student updates predictions during reading, based on information in the text.

Making Connections

- The student activates prior knowledge and related knowledge.
- The student uses prior knowledge to explain something encountered in text.
- The student connects ideas presented later in the text to ideas presented earlier in the text.
- The student notes ideas in the text that are new to him/her or conflict with what he/she thought previously.

Visualizing

- The student visualizes ideas or scenes described in the text.

Monitoring and Clarifying

- The student notes characteristics of the text, such as whether it is difficult to read or whether some sections are more challenging or more important than others are.
- The student shows awareness of whether he/she understands the text and takes appropriate action, such as rereading, in order to understand the text better.
- The student rereads to reconsider something presented earlier in the text.
- The student recognizes problems during reading, such as a loss of concentration, unfamiliar vocabulary, or a lack of sufficient background knowledge to comprehend the text.

Monitoring and Adjusting Reading Speed

The student changes reading speed in reaction to text, exhibiting such behavior as

- Skimming parts of the text that are not important or relevant.
- Purposely reading more slowly because of difficulty in comprehending the text.

Research Rubrics

Throughout each unit, students engage in research and inquiry activities based on the unit concepts. They will present the findings of their research to the class. In this way they exhibit the wealth of knowledge and understanding they have gained about that particular concept. In addition to gaining knowledge about the concepts, students will be honing their research skills. With each unit, they will progress with their research in the same manner in which professional researchers do.

With each new unit of study, students should also become more and more sophisticated in their ability to formulate questions, make conjectures about those questions, recognize their own information needs, conduct research to find that information, reevaluate their questions and conjectures as new information is added to their knowledge base, and communicate their findings effectively. In addition, they will become more and more adept at working as a team and being aware of the progress being made as individuals and as a group. The Research Rubrics will help you to assess the students' progress as researchers and as members of collaborative teams.

Formulating Research Questions and Problems

1. With help, identifies things she/he wonders about in relation to a topic.
2. Expresses curiosity about topics; with help, translates this into specific questions.
3. Poses an interesting problem or question for research; with help, refines it into a researchable question.
4. Identifies something she/he genuinely wonders about and translates it into a researchable question.

Making Conjectures

1. Offers conjectures that are mainly expressions of fact or opinion. ("I think the Anasazi lived a long time ago." "I think tigers should be protected.")
2. Offers conjectures that partially address the research question. ("I think germs make you sick because they get your body upset." "I think germs make you sick because they multiply really fast.")
3. Offers conjectures that address the research question with guesses. ("I think the Anasazi were wiped out by a meteor.")
4. Offers reasonable conjectures that address the question and that can be improved through further research.

Recognizing Information Needs

1. Identifies topics about which more needs to be learned. ("I need to learn more about the brain.")
2. Identifies information needs that are relevant though not essential to the research question. ("To understand how Leeuwenhoek invented the microscope, I need to know what size germs are.")
3. Identifies questions that are deeper than the one originally asked. (Original question: "How does the heart work?" Deeper question: "Why does blood need to circulate?")

Finding Needed Information

1. Collects information loosely related to topic.
2. Collects information clearly related to topic.
3. Collects information helpful in advancing on a research problem.
4. Collects problem-relevant information from varied sources and notices inconsistencies and missing pieces.

Assessment (continued)

5. Collects useful information, paying attention to the reliability of sources and reviewing information critically.

Revising Problems and Conjectures

1. No revision.
2. Produces new problems or conjectures with little relation to earlier ones.
3. Tends to lift problems and conjectures directly from reference material.
4. Progresses to deeper, more refined problems and conjectures.

Communicating Research Progress and Results

1. Reporting is sparse and fragmentary.
2. Report is factual; communicates findings but not the thinking behind them.
3. Report provides a good picture of the research problem, of how original conjectures were modified in light of new information, and of difficulties and unresolved issues.
4. A report that not only interests and informs the audience but also draws helpful commentary from them.

Overall Assessment of Research

1. A collection of facts related in miscellaneous ways to a topic.
2. An organized collection of facts relevant to the research problem.
3. A thoughtful effort to tackle a research problem, with some indication of progress toward solving it.
4. Significant progress on a challenging problem of understanding.

Collaborative Group Work

1. Group members work on separate tasks with little interaction.
2. Work-related decisions are made by the group, but there is little interaction related to ideas.
3. Information and ideas are shared, but there is little discussion concerned with advancing understanding.
4. The group clearly progresses in its thinking beyond where individual students could have gone.

Participation in Collaborative Inquiry

1. Does not contribute ideas or information to team or class.
2. Makes contributions to Concept/Question Board or class discussions when specifically called upon to do so.
3. Occasionally contributes ideas or information to other students' inquiries.
4. Takes an active interest in the success of the whole class's knowledge-building efforts.

Writing Rubrics

Rubrics are particularly effective for writing assignments, which do not have simple right or wrong answers. The rubrics included in the ***Unit Assessments*** for writing cover different elements of the writing. They are intended to help teachers provide criteria and feedback to students.

Open Court Reading provides four-point rubrics for writing in each of four areas. This enables teachers to clearly distinguish among different levels of performance.

1. Point score indicates that a student is performing below basic level.
2. Point score indicates that a student's abilities are emerging.
3. Point score indicates that a student's work is adequate and achieving expectations.
4. Point score indicates that a student is exceeding expectations.

Conventions

The conventions rubrics provide criteria for evaluating a student's understanding and ability to use English language conventions, which include:

- Grammar and Usage
- Mechanics: Punctuation
- Mechanics: Capitalization
- Sentence Structure
- Spelling
- Overall grammar, usage, mechanics, and spelling

Genre

Genre rubrics, found in the ***Unit Assessment***, enable evaluation of students' grasp of the different structures and elements of each of these different forms of writing:

- Descriptive Writing
- Expository Structure
- Genre
- Narrative
- Narrative Character
- Narrative Plot
- Narrative Setting
- Persuasive
- Personal
- Poetry

Writing Process

Writing process rubrics allow teachers to evaluate students' abilities in these areas:

- Getting Ideas
- Prewriting—Organizing Writing
- Drafting
- Revising
- Editing
- Presentation/Publishing
- Self-Management
- Language Resources

Writing Traits

Writing traits rubrics, found in the ***Unit Assessment***, provide criteria for different elements of written composition to identify a student's strengths and weaknesses.

- Audience
- Citing Sources
- Elaboration (supporting details and examples that develop the main idea)
- Focus
- Ideas/Content
- Organization
- Sentence Fluency
- Voice
- Word Choice

Responding to Results

Open Court Reading provides several ways to differentiate instruction based on the results of the various assessments. These include

- ***Reteach*** for students who appear to grasp a given concept but need more instruction and practice to solidify their learning.
- ***Intervention*** for students who are struggling to understand the material and need significant help and support.
- ***English Learner Support*** for students who are having difficulty with the concepts because they lack the necessary English language background.
- ***Challenge*** for those students who are doing well and would enjoy a challenge.
- ***Differentiating Instruction Support Activities*** for students who need quick alternative activities to strengthen or extend their skills.

These materials, along with informal assessment suggestions, help ensure that assessment and instruction work together to meet each student's needs.

Audiovisual and Technology Resource Directory

This directory is provided for the convenience of ordering the Technology Resources listed on the Technology pages in each Unit Overview.

100% Educational Videos, Inc.
P.O. Box 4440
El Dorado Hills, CA 95762-0018
800-483-3383
FAX: 1-888-478-1426
www.schoolvideos.com

AIMS Multimedia
9710 De Soto Avenue
Chatsworth, CA 91311-4409
800-367-2467
www.aimsmultimedia.com

Ambrose Video
145 W. 45th Street, Suite 1115
NY, NY 10036
800-526-4663
FAX: 212-768-9282
www.ambrosevideo.com

Atari, Inc. (Humongous Entertainment)
3855 Monte Villa Parkway
Bothell, WA 98021
425-486-9258
www.funkidsgames.com

Clearvue/eav
6465 North Avondale Avenue
Chicago, IL 60631
800-CLEARVU
www.clearvue.com

Communication Skills, Inc.
49 Richmondville Ave.
Westport, CT 06880
800-824-2398
FAX: 203-226-8820
www.comunicationskills.com

Devine Entertainment Corp.
2 Berkeley St., Suite 504
Toronto, Ontario M5A 2W3, CANADA
416-364-2282

Discovery Communications Incorporated
One Discovery Place
Silver Springs, MD 20910
240-662-2000
www.discovery.com

Dorling Kindersley
375 Hudson Street
New York, NY 10014
800-788-6262
FAX: 800-227-9604
www.dk.com

Dreams Come True Productions
c/o Big Kids Productions Inc.
1606 Dywer Avenue
Austin, TX 78704
800-297-8787
www.dreamscometrueprod.com

Fine Media Group
9925 S. 76th Avenue, Suites A & B
Bridgeview, IL 60455
800-FMG-2000
www.finemediagroup.com

Fort Fun Productions
Fort Wayne, IN 46802
260-423-3373
www.ftfun.com

Goldhil Home Media International
137 E. Thousand Oaks Blvd., 2nd Floor
Thousand Oaks, CA 91360
800-250-8760
www.goldhil.com

Great Plains National Instructional Television Library
University of Nebraska—Lincoln
1800 North 33rd Street
Omaha, NE 68583
402-472-4076
www.gpn.unl.edu

Grolier Incorporated
90 Sherman Turnpike
Danbury, CT 06816
800-285-3140
www.grolier.com

Home Vision Entertainment
4423 North Ravenswood Avenue
Chicago, IL 60640-5802
www.homevision.com

Innovative Educators
P.O. Box 520
Montezuma, GA 31063
1-888-252-KIDS
FAX: 888-536-8553
www.innovative-educators.com

Library Video Company
P.O. Box 580
Wynnewood, PA 19096
800-843-3630
FAX: 610-645-4040
www.libraryvideo.com

Little Mammoth Media
704-563-3304
http://www.littlemammoth.com

Live Oak Media
P.O. Box 652
Pine Plains, NY 12567-0652
800-788-1121
FAX: 866-398-1070
http://www.liveoakmedia.com

Macmillan/McGraw-Hill School Division
220 East Danieldale Road
DeSoto, TX 75115-9960
800-442-9685
FAX: 972-228-1982
www.mhschool.com

Mazon Productions, Inc.
P.O. Box 2427
Northbrook, IL 60065
800-332-4344
www.vpopmail.cx

MCA Video
MCA Records/Universal Studios
100 Universal City Plaza
Universal City, CA 91608
818-777-1000

Mindscape, Inc.
88 Rowland Way
Novato, California 94945
415-895-2000
Fax: 415-895-2102
www.mindscape.com

MPI Media Group
16101 South 108th Ave.
Orland Park, IL 60467
800-777-2223
www.mpimedia.com

Multimedia 2000 Inc.
2017 Eighth Avenue, 3rd Floor
Seattle, WA 98101
800-850-7272
Fax: 206-622-4380
www.m-2K.com

National Geographic School Publishing
P.O. Box 10579
Des Moines, IA 50340
800-368-2728
www.nationalgeographic.com/education

Orange Cherry New Media
P.O. Box 390
69 Winchester Ave.
Pound Ridge, NY 10576
914-764-4104
FAX: 914-764-0104
www.orangecherry.com

Paramount Studios
5555 Melrose Ave.
Hollywood, CA 90038
323-956-5000
www.paramount.com

PBS Home Video
800-424-7963
www.shoppbs.org

PPI Entertainment
103 Eisenhower Parkway
Roseland, NJ 07068
800-272-4214
www.peterpan.com

Phoenix Learning Group
2349 Chaffee Drive
St. Louis, MO 63146
800-221-1274
www.phoenixlearninggroup.com

Queue, Inc.
1450 Barnum Avenue
Bridgeport, CT 06610
800-232-2224
FAX: 203-336-2481
www.queueinc.com

Rainbow Educational Media
4540 Preslyn Drive
Raleigh, NC 27616
800-331-4047
FAX: 919-954-7554
www.rainbowedumedia.com

Scholastic, Inc.
P.O. Box 7503
Jefferson City, MO 65102
800-SCHOLASTIC
www.scholastic.com

Simon & Schuster Interactive
1230 Avenue of Americas
New York, NY 10020
www.simonsays.com

Sony Music Store
P.O. Box 4000
Carrollton, GA 30017
800-338-7834
www.sonymusicstore.com

SRA/McGraw-Hill
220 East Danieldale Road
DeSoto, TX 75115-2490
888-SRA-4543
FAX: 972-228-1982
www.sraonline.com

Stage Fright Productions
P.O. Box 373
Geneva, IL 60134
800-979-6800
E-mail: stagefright@bowe.ccm.net

Sunburst Technology
1550 Executive Drive
Elgin, IL 60123
800-821-7511
www.sunburst.com

Time-Life
1450 E. Parham Road
Richmond, VA 23280
800-950-7887
www.timelife.com

Tom Snyder Productions
80 Coolidge Hill Road
Watertown, MA 02472
800-342-0236
FAX: 800-304-1254
www.tomsnyder.com

Worldlink Media
2955 Clay Street, Suite 7
San Francisco, CA 94115
415-561-2141

Scope and Sequence

PROGRAM APPENDIX

Reading

	Level						
	K	1	2	3	4	5	6
Print/Book Awareness (Recognize and understand the conventions of print and books)							
Capitalization	✔	✔	✔			✔	✔
Constancy of Words						✔	
End Punctuation	✔	✔				✔	✔
Follow Left-to-right, Top-to-bottom	✔	✔					
Letter Recognition and Formation	✔	✔					
Page Numbering		✔					
Picture/Text Relationship	✔				✔		
Quotation Marks	✔	✔	✔			✔	✔
Relationship Between Spoken and Printed Language		✔					
Sentence Recognition							
Table of Contents	✔	✔					
Word Length	✔						
Word Boundaries		✔					
Phonemic Awareness (Recognize discrete sounds in words)							
Oral Blending: Words/Word Parts	✔	✔	✔				
Oral Blending: Initial Consonants/Blends	✔	✔	✔	✔			
Oral Blending: Final Consonants	✔	✔	✔	✔			
Oral Blending: Initial Vowels		✔					
Oral Blending: Syllables		✔			✔		
Oral Blending: Vowel Replacement					✔		
Segmentation: Initial Consonants/Blends	✔	✔	✔	✔		✔	
Segmentation: Final Consonants	✔	✔	✔	✔			
Segmentation: Words/Word Parts	✔	✔	✔	✔	✔	✔	
Rhyming	✔	✔			✔	✔	
How the Alphabet Works							
Letter Knowledge	✔	✔	✔	✔			
Letter Order (Alphabetic Order)	✔	✔					
Letter Sounds	✔	✔	✔	✔	✔		
Sounds in Words	✔	✔	✔	✔	✔		
Phonics (Associate sounds and spellings to read words)							
Blending Sounds into Words	✔	✔					
Consonant Clusters		✔		✔			
Consonant Digraphs		✔		✔	✔		
Consonant Sounds and Spellings	✔	✔	✔	✔			
Phonograms	✔	✔		✔			✔
Syllables	✔	✔			✔		
Vowel Diphthongs		✔		✔			✔
Vowels: Long Sounds and Spellings	✔	✔	✔	✔	✔	✔	✔
Vowels: r-controlled		✔	✔	✔	✔	✔	✔
Vowels: Short Sounds and Spellings	✔	✔	✔	✔	✔	✔	✔

[shaded box] Skills, strategies, and other teaching opportunities ✔ Formal, progress, or informal testing opportunities

Reading (continued)

	Level K	1	2	3	4	5	6
Comprehension Strategies							
Asking Questions/Answering Questions		✔	✔	✔	✔	✔	✔
Making Connections		✔	✔	✔	✔	✔	✔
Monitoring and Clarifying		✔	✔	✔	✔	✔	✔
Monitoring and Adjusting Reading Speed			✔	✔	✔	✔	✔
Predicting/Confirming Predictions	✔	✔	✔	✔	✔	✔	✔
Summarizing		✔	✔	✔	✔	✔	✔
Visualizing		✔	✔	✔	✔	✔	✔
Comprehension Skills							
Author's Point of View			✔	✔	✔	✔	✔
Author's Purpose			✔	✔	✔	✔	✔
Cause and Effect	✔	✔	✔	✔	✔	✔	✔
Classify and Categorize	✔	✔	✔	✔	✔	✔	✔
Compare and Contrast	✔	✔	✔	✔	✔	✔	✔
Drawing Conclusions	✔	✔	✔	✔	✔	✔	✔
Fact and Opinion			✔	✔	✔	✔	✔
Main Idea and Details	✔	✔	✔	✔	✔	✔	✔
Making Inferences		✔	✔	✔	✔	✔	✔
Reality/Fantasy	✔	✔		✔			
Sequence		✔	✔	✔	✔	✔	✔
Vocabulary							
Antonyms	✔	✔	✔	✔	✔	✔	✔
Comparatives/Superlatives		✔	✔	✔	✔	✔	✔
Compound Words	✔	✔	✔	✔	✔	✔	✔
Connecting Words (Transition Words)						✔	✔
Context Clues		✔	✔	✔	✔	✔	✔
Contractions			✔	✔	✔	✔	
Figurative Language				✔		✔	
Greek and Latin Roots				✔	✔		
High-Frequency Words	✔	✔	✔	✔	✔	✔	✔
Homographs			✔	✔	✔	✔	
Homophones/Homonyms		✔	✔	✔	✔	✔	✔
Idioms					✔	✔	✔
Inflectional Endings		✔	✔	✔	✔	✔	✔
Irregular Plurals				✔		✔	✔
Multiple Meaning Words			✔	✔	✔	✔	✔
Multisyllabic Words			✔	✔		✔	
Position Words	✔	✔				✔	
Prefixes			✔	✔	✔	✔	✔
Question Words		✔					
Base or Root Words		✔	✔	✔	✔	✔	✔
Selection Vocabulary	✔	✔	✔	✔	✔	✔	✔
Suffixes		✔	✔	✔	✔	✔	✔
Synonyms		✔	✔	✔	✔	✔	✔
Time and Order Words (Creating Sequence)				✔	✔	✔	✔
Utility Words (Colors, Classroom Objects, etc.)	✔	✔					
Word Families			✔	✔	✔	✔	✔

Inquiry and Research

Study Skills	Level K	1	2	3	4	5	6
Charts, Graphs, and Diagrams/Visual Aids			✔		✔	✔	✔
Collaborative Inquiry			✔	✔	✔	✔	✔
Communicating Research Progress Results			✔	✔	✔	✔	✔
Compile Notes						✔	✔
Conducting an Interview							✔
Finding Needed Information			✔	✔	✔	✔	✔
Follow Directions	✔			✔			
Formulate Questions for Inquiry and Research			✔			✔	✔
Give Reports					✔	✔	✔
Make Outlines				✔		✔	✔
Making Conjectures			✔	✔	✔	✔	✔
Maps and Globes					✔		✔
Note Taking			✔	✔	✔	✔	✔
Parts of a Book			✔	✔	✔		
Planning Investigation			✔	✔	✔	✔	✔
Recognizing Information Needs			✔	✔	✔	✔	✔
Revising Questions and Conjectures			✔	✔	✔	✔	✔
Summarize and Organize Information					✔	✔	✔
Time Lines					✔	✔	✔
Use Appropriate Resources (Media Source, Reference Books, Experts, Internet)					✔	✔	✔
Using a Dictionary/Glossary		✔	✔	✔	✔	✔	✔
Using a Media Center/Library					✔		✔
Using a Thesaurus			✔	✔	✔	✔	✔
Using an Encyclopedia					✔		✔
Using Newspapers and Magazines					✔		✔
Using Technology							

[shaded box] Skills, strategies, and other teaching opportunities ✔ Formal, progress, or informal testing opportunities

Language Arts

Writing/Composition

	Level K	1	2	3	4	5	6
Approaches							
Collaborative Writing		✔					
Group Writing							
Process							
Brainstorming/Prewriting	✔	✔		✔	✔	✔	
Drafting	✔	✔		✔	✔	✔	
Revising	✔	✔		✔	✔	✔	
Proofreading	✔	✔		✔	✔	✔	
Publishing	✔	✔		✔	✔	✔	
Forms							
Biography/Autobiography	✔	✔	✔	✔	✔	✔	✔
Business Letter				✔	✔	✔	✔
Describe a Process		✔	✔	✔	✔		✔
Descriptive Writing	✔	✔	✔	✔	✔	✔	✔
Expository/Informational Text	✔	✔	✔	✔	✔	✔	✔
Folklore (Folktales, Fairy Tales, Tall Tales, Legends, Myths)			✔	✔	✔		
Friendly Letter		✔	✔	✔	✔	✔	✔
Historical Fiction						✔	✔
Journal Writing		✔	✔	✔	✔	✔	✔
Narrative		✔	✔	✔	✔	✔	✔
Personal Writing		✔	✔	✔	✔	✔	✔
Persuasive Writing	✔	✔	✔	✔	✔	✔	✔
Play/Dramatization				✔	✔	✔	✔
Poetry		✔	✔	✔	✔	✔	✔
Realistic Story				✔			
Writer's Craft							
Characterization			✔	✔	✔	✔	✔
Descriptive Writing	✔	✔	✔	✔	✔	✔	✔
Dialogue		✔	✔	✔	✔	✔	✔
Effective Beginnings			✔	✔	✔	✔	✔
Effective Endings			✔	✔	✔	✔	✔
Event Sequence		✔	✔	✔	✔	✔	✔
Figurative Language	✔		✔	✔	✔	✔	✔
Identifying Thoughts and Feelings	✔		✔	✔	✔	✔	✔
Mood and Tone				✔	✔	✔	✔
Plot (Problem/Solutions)	✔	✔	✔	✔	✔	✔	✔
Point of View				✔	✔	✔	
Rhyme	✔	✔	✔	✔	✔	✔	
Sensory Details				✔		✔	✔
Sentence Variety				✔		✔	✔
Sentence Elaboration				✔		✔	✔
Setting	✔		✔	✔		✔	✔
Suspense and Surprise			✔	✔	✔	✔	
Topic Sentences			✔	✔	✔	✔	✔
Using Comparisons						✔	
Purposes							
Determining Purposes for Writing	✔	✔				✔	

Scope and Sequence (continued)

Language Arts

Grammar

	Level K	1	2	3	4	5	6
Parts of Speech							
Adjectives	✔	✔	✔	✔	✔	✔	✔
Adverbs			✔	✔	✔	✔	✔
Conjunctions			✔	✔	✔	✔	✔
Nouns	✔	✔	✔	✔	✔	✔	✔
Prepositions	✔			✔	✔	✔	✔
Pronouns	✔	✔	✔	✔	✔	✔	✔
Verbs	✔	✔	✔	✔	✔	✔	✔
Sentences							
Fragments					✔	✔	✔
Parts (Subjects/Predicates)		✔	✔	✔	✔	✔	✔
Subject/Verb Agreement	✔	✔	✔	✔	✔	✔	✔
Structure (Simple, Compound, Complex)				✔	✔	✔	✔
Types (Declarative, Interrogative, Exclamatory, Imperatives)	✔	✔	✔	✔	✔	✔	✔
Verb Tenses	✔	✔	✔	✔	✔	✔	✔
Verbs (Action, Helping, Linking, Regular/Irregular)	✔	✔	✔	✔	✔	✔	✔
Usage							
Adjectives	✔	✔	✔	✔	✔	✔	✔
Adverbs			✔	✔	✔	✔	✔
Articles	✔	✔	✔	✔	✔	✔	✔
Nouns	✔	✔	✔	✔	✔	✔	✔
Pronouns	✔	✔	✔	✔	✔	✔	✔
Verbs	✔	✔	✔	✔	✔	✔	✔
Mechanics							
Capitalization (Sentence, Proper Nouns, Titles, Direct Address, Pronoun "I")	✔	✔	✔	✔	✔	✔	✔
Punctuation (End Punctuation, Comma Use, Quotation Marks, Apostrophe, Colon, Semicolon, Hyphen, Parentheses)	✔	✔	✔	✔	✔	✔	✔
Spelling							
Contractions		✔	✔	✔		✔	
Inflectional Endings			✔	✔	✔	✔	
Irregular Plurals			✔	✔	✔	✔	✔
Long Vowel Patterns		✔	✔	✔	✔	✔	✔
Multisyllabic Words			✔	✔		✔	
Phonograms		✔	✔	✔			✔
r-controlled Vowel Spellings		✔	✔	✔	✔	✔	✔
Short Vowel Spellings		✔	✔	✔	✔	✔	✔
Silent Letters				✔			
Sound/Letter Relationships		✔	✔	✔			
Special Spelling Patterns (*-ough*, *-augh*, *-all*, *-al*, *-alk*, *-ion*,*-sion*, *-tion*)		✔	✔	✔	✔	✔	✔

[shaded box] Skills, strategies, and other teaching opportunities ✔ Formal, progress, or informal testing opportunities

Language Arts (continued)

Listening/Speaking/Viewing

	K	1	2	3	4	5	6
Listening/Speaking							
Analyze/Evaluate Intent and Content of Speaker's Message		✔	✔	✔	✔	✔	✔
Ask and Answer Questions	✔	✔	✔	✔	✔	✔	✔
Determine Purposes for Listening			✔	✔	✔		
Follow Directions	✔	✔	✔	✔	✔	✔	✔
Learn about Different Cultures through Discussion					✔	✔	✔
Listen for Poetic Language (Rhythm/Rhyme)	✔	✔	✔	✔			
Participate in Group Discussions		✔	✔	✔	✔	✔	✔
Respond to Speaker	✔	✔	✔	✔	✔	✔	✔
Use Nonverbal Communication Techniques	✔	✔	✔	✔	✔	✔	✔
Speaking							
Describe Ideas and Feelings	✔	✔	✔	✔	✔	✔	✔
Give Directions					✔	✔	✔
Learn about Different Cultures through Discussion				✔	✔	✔	✔
Participate in Group Discussions	✔	✔	✔	✔	✔	✔	✔
Present Oral Reports			✔	✔	✔	✔	✔
Read Fluently with Expression, Phrasing, and Intonation			✔	✔	✔	✔	✔
Read Orally		✔	✔	✔	✔	✔	✔
Share Information	✔	✔	✔	✔	✔	✔	✔
Speak Clearly at Appropriate Volume	✔	✔	✔	✔	✔	✔	✔
Summarize/Retell Stories	✔	✔	✔	✔	✔	✔	✔
Understand Formal and Informal Language	✔	✔	✔	✔	✔	✔	✔
Use Appropriate Vocabulary for Audience		✔	✔	✔	✔	✔	✔
Use Elements of Grammar in Speech				✔	✔	✔	✔
Viewing							
Analyze Purposes and Techniques of the Media				✔	✔	✔	✔
Appreciate/Interpret Artist's Techniques							
Compare Visual and Written Material on the Same Subject	✔				✔		
Gather Information from Visual Images	✔	✔	✔	✔	✔	✔	✔
View Critically		✔	✔	✔	✔	✔	✔
View Culturally Rich Materials	✔	✔	✔		✔	✔	✔
Penmanship							
Cursive Letters			✔	✔	✔	✔	✔
Manuscript Letters	✔	✔	✔				
Numbers	✔	✔	✔	✔			

Unit Themes

	LEVEL K	LEVEL 1	LEVEL 2
Unit 1	School	Let's Read!	Sharing Stories
Unit 2	Shadows	Animals	Kindness
Unit 3	Finding Friends	Things That Go	Look Again
Unit 4	The Wind	Our Neighborhood at Work	Fossils
Unit 5	Stick to It	Weather	Courage
Unit 6	Red, White, and Blue	Journeys	Our Country and Its People
Unit 7	Teamwork	Keep Trying	
Unit 8	By the Sea	Games	
Unit 9		Being Afraid	
Unit 10		Homes	

LEVEL 3	LEVEL 4	LEVEL 5	LEVEL 6
Friendship	Risks and Consequences	Cooperation and Competition	Perseverance
City Wildlife	Dollars and Sense	Astronomy	Ancient Civilizations
Imagination	From Mystery to Medicine	Heritage	Taking a Stand
Money	Survival	Making a New Nation	Beyond the Notes
Storytelling	Communication	Going West	Ecology
Country Life	A Changing America	Journeys and Quests	A Question of Value

Leveled Classroom Library Books

PROGRAM APPENDIX

LEVEL K	LEVEL 1	LEVEL 2	LEVEL 3
Unit 1 School: *Mouse Views: What the Class Pet Saw; The 100th Day of School; Billy and the Big New School; Vera's First Day of School; Bea and Mr. Jones; The Kissing Hand* **Unit 2 Shadows:** *Footprints and Shadows; Shadows Are About; I Have a Friend; My Shadow; What Makes Day and Night?; Sun Up, Sun Down* **Unit 3 Finding Friends:** *My Friends; Yo! Yes?; Will You Be My Friend?; George and Martha One Fine Day; Friends; May I Bring a Friend?* **Unit 4 The Wind:** *The Wind Blew; One Windy Wednesday; The Sun, the Wind, and the Rain; What Makes the Wind?; Millicent and the Wind; Feel the Wind* **Unit 5 Stick to It:** *The Carrot Seed; Leo the Late Bloomer; You'll Soon Grow into Them, Titch; JoJo's Flying Side Kick; Paul Bunyan: A Tall Tale; Liang and the Magic Paintbrush* **Unit 6 Red, White, and Blue:** *The Pledge of Allegiance; 'Night, America; This Land Is Your Land; Happy Birthday, America; The Flag We Love; Mr. Lincoln's Whiskers* **Unit 7 Teamwork:** *Can I Help?; Animal Orchestra; Tippy Bear Hunts for Honey; Helping Out; Stone Soup; The Great Trash Bash* **Unit 8 By the Sea:** *Oceans; In the Ocean; Tacky the Penguin; Fish Faces; The Seashore Book; Commotion in the Ocean*	**Unit 1 Let's Read!:** *America: My Land Your Land Our Land; I Read Signs; Miss Malarkey Doesn't Live in Room 10; The Old Woman Who Loved to Read; A Cake for Herbie; More Than Anything Else* **Unit 2 Animals:** *Sweet Dreams: How Animals Sleep; Moo Moo, Brown Cow; Here Is the African Savanna; Is Your Mama a Llama?; A Pinky Is a Baby Mouse; Wolf Watch* **Unit 3 Things That Go:** *I Spy a Freight Train; Wheels Around; This Plane; This Is the Way We Go to School; The Listening Walk; Firehorse Max* **Unit 4 Our Neighborhood at Work:** *Communities; Night Shift Daddy; My Town; One Afternoon; Career Day; Mommy Works, Daddy Works* **Unit 5 Weather:** *Snow; Snowballs; Rain; Red Rubber Boot Day; Twister; Snow Is Falling* **Unit 6 Journeys:** *Rosie's Walk; The Train Ride; Amelia's Fantastic Flight; I'm Not Moving, Mama!; Ferryboat Ride!; The Josefina Story Quilt* **Unit 7 Keep Trying:** *Flap Your Wings and Try; The Chick and the Duckling; One Duck Stuck; One Fine Day; The Purple Coat; The Story of a Blue Bird* **Unit 8 Games:** *This Is Baseball; Take Me Out to the Ballgame; What's What? A Guessing Game; Leon and Bob; Moongame; James and the Rain* **Unit 9 Being Afraid:** *Sheila Rae, the Brave; Henry and Mudge and the Bedtime Thumps; First Day Jitters; Let's Go Home Little Bear; Can't You Sleep, Little Bear?; Feelings* **Unit 10 Homes:** *My House Mi Casa: A Book in Two Languages; To Market, To Market; The Someday House; Homeplace; The Little House; Livingstone Mouse*	**Unit 1 Sharing Stories:** *Just Like Me; Mouse Tales; The Wednesday Surprise; Dear Annie; Jeremiah Learns to Read; Painted Words* **Unit 2 Kindness:** *Abe Lincoln's Hat; Jamaica's Find; The Bat in the Boot; The Giving Tree; Uncle Willie and the Soup Kitchen; A Chair for My Mother* **Unit 3 Look Again:** *The Trek; Who's Hiding Here?; The Mixed-Up Chameleon; A Color of His Own; What Do You Do When Something Wants to Eat You?; Hiding Out* **Unit 4 Fossils:** *Dinosaur Babies; The Day of the Dinosaur; A Boy Wants a Dinosaur; If the Dinosaurs Came Back; Archaeologists Dig for Clues; How Big Were the Dinosaurs?* **Unit 5 Courage:** *White Dynamite and Curly Kidd; What's Under My Bed?; Ruth Law Thrills a Nation; Jamaica and the Substitute Teacher; Birdie's Lighthouse; The Buffalo Jump* **Unit 6 Our Country and Its People:** *Dancing with the Indians; A Picnic in October; Amelia's Road; Dragon Parade; The Lotus Seed; Dumpling Soup*	**Unit 1 Friendship:** *Charlotte's Web; And To Think That We Thought That We'd Never Be Friends; Best Friends; Amigo; The Mountain that Loved a Bird; Alex Is My Friend* **Unit 2 City Wildlife:** *Wild in the City; Come Back, Salmon: How a Group of Dedicated Kids Adopted Pigeon Creek and Brought It Back to Life; Farewell to Shady Glade; Coyotes in the Crosswalk: True Tales of Animal Life in the Wilds of the City!; City Park; Birds, Nests and Eggs* **Unit 3 Imagination:** *Behind the Couch; My Life with the Wave; Maria's Comet; Frederick; How I Spent My Summer Vacation; Crocodile's Masterpiece* **Unit 4 Money:** *Lemonade for Sale; Round and Round the Money Goes; Saturday Sancocho; The Treasure; Our Money; Screen of Frogs* **Unit 5 Storytelling:** *Tell Me a Story, Mama; The Worry Stone; May'naise Sandwiches & Sunshine Tea; One Grain of Rice; A Storyteller's Story; Firetalking* **Unit 6 Country Life:** *The Raft; Night in the Country; Mowing; Winter Wheat; A River Ran Wild; Unseen Rainbows, Silent Songs: The World Beyond Human Senses*

LEVEL 4	LEVEL 5	LEVEL 6
Unit 1 Risks and Consequences: *The Big Balloon Race; A Day's Work; Poppy; Sarah, Plain and Tall; The Landry News; From the Mixed-Up Files of Mrs. Basil E. Frankweiler* **Unit 2 Dollars and Sense:** *Max Malone Makes a Million; What's Cooking, Jenny Archer?; The Toothpaste Millionaire; Brainstorm! The Stories of Twenty American Kid Inventors; Odd Jobs; Better Than a Lemonade Stand!* **Unit 3 From Mystery to Medicine:** *Germs Make Me Sick!; Pasteur's Fight Against Microbes; Marie Curie and the Discovery of Radium; Kids to the Rescue! First Aid Techniques for Kids; The First Woman Doctor; Fever: 1793* **Unit 4 Survival:** *Harry the Poisonous Centipede; My Grandmother's Journey; Whichaway; Frozen Fire; Island of the Blue Dolphins; The Voyage of the Frog* **Unit 5 Communication:** *Prairie Dogs Kiss and Lobsters Wave: How Animals Say Hello; Burton and Stanley; Dear Mr. Henshaw; The Chimpanzee Family Book; The Cat's Elbow and Other Secret Languages; Julie's Wolf Pack* **Unit 6 A Changing America:** *Sleds on Boston Common: A Story from the American Revolution; The Discovery of the Americas; Stranded at Plimoth Plantation, 1626; . . . If You Traveled West in a Covered Wagon; The Louisiana Purchase; Gold Rush! The Young Prospector's Guide to Striking It Rich*	**Unit 1 Cooperation and Competition:** *The Big Bike Race; The Kid Who Ran For President; The Wheel on the School; Iditarod Dream: Dusty and His Sled Dogs Compete in Alaska's Jr. Iditarod; The View From Saturday; A World in Our Hands: In Honor of the 50th Anniversary of the United Nations* **Unit 2 Astronomy:** *The Planets; Comets, Meteors, and Asteroids; Adventure in Space: The Flight to Fix the Hubble; The Young Astronomer; Edwin Hubble: American Astronomer; Tales of the Shimmering Sky: Ten Global Folktales with Activities* **Unit 3 Heritage:** *Appalachia: The Voices of Sleeping Birds; This Land Is My Land; Going Back Home: An Artist Returns to the South; In the Year of the Boar and Jackie Robinson; The Great Ancestor Hunt: The Fun of Finding Out Who You Are; Do People Grow on Family Trees?* **Unit 4 Making a New Nation:** *Samuel's Choice; Toliver's Secret; Johnny Tremain; A Young Patriot: The American Revolution as Experienced by One Boy; Mr. Revere and I; Come All You Brave Soldiers: Blacks in the Revolutionary War* **Unit 5 Going West:** *Boom Town; Striking It Rich: The Story of the California Gold Rush; Black-Eyed Susan; By the Great Horn Spoon!; Children of the Wild West; Caddie Woodlawn* **Unit 6 Journeys and Quests:** *Alicia's Treasure; Grass Sandals: The Travels of Basho; El Güero; Coast to Coast; Orphan Train Rider: One Boy's True Story; Call It Courage*	**Unit 1 Perseverance:** *The Most Beautiful Place in the World; Wilma Unlimited: How Wilma Rudolph Became the World's Fastest Woman; Littlejim's Dreams; The Circuit: Stories from the Life of a Migrant Child; Where the Lilies Bloom; The Wright Brothers: How They Invented the Airplane* **Unit 2 Ancient Civilizations:** *Androcles and the Lion; Ancient Romans at a Glance; Painters of the Caves; Pyramids!; Dig This! How Archaeologists Uncover Our Past; Religions of the World* **Unit 3 Taking a Stand:** *Aunt Harriet's Underground Railroad in the Sky; Jane Addams: Pioneer Social Worker; Number the Stars; Run Away Home; Kids at Work: Lewis Hine and the Crusade Against Child Labor; Red Scarf Girl: A Memoir of the Cultural Revolution* **Unit 4 Beyond the Notes:** *The Jazz Man; A Mouse Called Wolf; Play Me a Story: Nine Tales about Musical Instruments; The Sea King's Daughter: A Russian Legend; Dragonsong; Music* **Unit 5 Ecology:** *The Great Kapok Tree; Lifetimes; Elephant Woman: Cynthia Moss Explores the World of Elephants; The Missing 'Gator of Gumbo Limbo; Ecology for Every Kid: Easy Activities that Make Learning Science Fun; The Most Beautiful Roof in the World* **Unit 6 A Question of Value:** *Abuelita's Heart; The Golden Bracelet; Lily's Crossing; The Black Pearl; The Monkey Thief; Wringer*

Glossary of Reading Terms

PROGRAM APPENDIX

This glossary includes linguistic, grammatical, comprehension, and literary terms that may be helpful in understanding reading instruction.

acronym a word formed from the initial letter of words in a phrase, **scuba (self-contained underwater breathing apparatus)**.

acrostic a kind of puzzle in which lines of a poem are arranged so that words or phrases are formed when certain letters from each line are used in a sequence.

adjective a word or group of words that modifies a noun.

adventure story a narrative that features the unknown or unexpected with elements of excitement, danger, and risk.

adverb a word or group of words that modifies a verb, adjective, or other adverb.

affective domain the psychological field of emotional activity.

affix a word part, either a prefix or a suffix, that changes the meaning or function of a word root or stem.

affricate a speech sound that starts as a stop but ends as a fricative, the /ch/ in **catch**.

agreement the correspondence of syntactically related words; subjects and predicates are in agreement when both are singular or plural.

alliteration the repetition of the initial sounds in neighboring words or stressed syllables.

alphabet the complete set of letters representing speech sounds used in writing a language.

alphabet book a book for helping young children learn the alphabet by pairing letters with pictures whose sounds they represent.

alphabetic principle the principle that there is an association between sounds and the letters that represent them in alphabetic writing systems.

alveolar a consonant speech sound made when the tongue and the ridge of the upper and lower jaw stop to constrict the air flow, as /t/.

anagram a word or phrase whose letters form other words or phrases when rearranged, for example, **add** and **dad**.

analogy a likeness or similarity.

analytic phonics also deductive phonics, a whole-to-part approach to phonics in which a student is taught a number of sight words and then phonetic generalizations that can be applied to other words.

antonym a word that is opposite in meaning to another word.

appositive a word that restates or modifies a preceding noun. For example, **my daughter**, **Charlotte**.

aspirate an unvoiced speech sound produced by a puff of air, as /h/ in **heart**.

aspirated stop a stop consonant sound released with a puff of air, as /k/, /p/, and /t/.

auditory discrimination the ability to hear phonetic likenesses and differences in phonemes and words.

author's purpose the motive or reason for which an author writes, includes to entertain, inform, persuade, and explain how.

automaticity fluent processing of information, requiring little effort or attention.

auxiliary verb a verb that precedes another verb to express time, mood, or voice, includes verbs such as **has**, **is**, **will**.

ballad a narrative poem, composed of short verses to be sung or recited, usually containing elements of drama and often tragic in tone.

base word a word to which affixes may be added to create related words.

blank verse unrhymed verse, especially unrhymed iambic pentameter.

blend the joining of the sounds of two or more letters with little change in those sounds, for example /spr/ in **spring**, also **consonant blend** or **consonant cluster**.

blending to combine the sounds represented by letters to sound out or pronounce a word, contrast with **oral blending**.

breve the symbol placed above a vowel to indicate that it is a short vowel.

browse to skim through or look over in search of something of interest.

canon in literature, the body of major works that a culture considers important at a given time.

case a grammatical category that indicates the syntactic/semantic role of a noun phrase in a sentence.

cause-effect relationship a stated or implied association between an outcome and the conditions that brought it about, also the comprehension skill associated with recognizing this type of relationship as an organizing principle in text.

chapter book a book long enough to be divided into chapters, but not long or complex enough to be considered a novel.

characterization the way in which an author presents a character in a story, including describing words, actions, thoughts, and impressions of that character.

choral reading oral group reading to develop oral fluency by modeling.

cinquain a stanza of five lines, specifically one that has successive lines of two, four, six, eight, and two syllables.

cipher a system for writing in code.

clarifying a comprehension strategy in which the reader rereads text, uses a dictionary, uses decoding skills, or uses context clues to comprehend something that is unclear.

clause a group of words with a subject and a predicate used to form a part of or a whole sentence, a dependent clause modifies an independent clause, which can stand alone as a complete sentence.

collaborative learning learning by working together in small groups.

command a sentence that asks for action and usually ends with a period.

common noun in contrast to **proper noun**, a noun that denotes a class rather than a unique or specific thing.

comprehension the understanding of what is written or said.

comprehension skill a skill that aids in understanding text, including identifying **author's purpose**, **comprehending cause and effect relationships**, **comparing and contrasting** items and events, **drawing conclusions**, distinguishing **fact from opinion**, identifying **main ideas**, making **inferences**, distinguishing **reality from fantasy**, and understanding **sequence**.

comprehension strategy a sequence of steps for understanding text, includes asking questions, clarifying, making connections, predicting, summarizing, and visualizing.

conjugation the complete set of all possible inflected forms of a verb.

conjunction a part of speech used to connect words, phrases, clauses, or sentences, including the words **and, but, or**.

consonant a speech sound, and the alphabet letter that represents that sound, made by partial or complete closure of part of the vocal tract, which obstructs air flow and causes audible friction.

context clue information from the immediate text that helps identify a word.

contraction a short version of a written or spoken expression in which letters are omitted, for example, **can't**.

convention an accepted practice in spoken or written language, usually referring to spelling, mechanics, or grammar rules.

cooperative learning a classroom organization that allows students to work together to achieve their individual goals.

creative writing prose and poetic forms of writing that express the writer's thoughts and feelings imaginatively.

cuing system any of the various sources of information that help to identify an unrecognizable word in reading, including phonetic, semantic, and syntactical information.

cumulative tale a story, such as The Gingerbread Man, in which details are repeated until the climax.

dangling modifier usually a participle that because of its placement in a sentence modifies the wrong object.

decodable text text materials controlled to include a majority of words whose sound/spelling relationships are known by the reader.

decode to analyze spoken or graphic symbols for meaning.

diacritical mark a mark, such as a breve or macron, added to a letter or graphic character, to indicate a specific pronunciation.

dialect a regional variety of a particular language with phonological, grammatical, and lexical patterns that distinguish it from other varieties.

dialogue a piece of writing written as conversation, usually punctuated by quotation marks.

digraph two letters that represent one speech sound, for example /sh/ or /ch/.

diphthong a vowel sound produced when the tongue glides from one vowel sound toward another in the same syllable, for example /oi/ or /ou/.

direct object the person or thing that receives the action of a verb in a sentence, for example, the word **cake** in this sentence: **Madeline baked a cake**.

drafting the process of writing ideas in rough form to record them.

drama a story in the form of a play, written to be performed.

edit in the writing process, to revise or correct a manuscript.

emergent literacy the development of the association of meaning and print that continues until a child reaches the stage of conventional reading and writing.

emergent reading a child's early interaction with books and print before the ability to decode text.

encode to change a message into symbols, for example, to change speech into writing.

epic a long narrative poem, usually about a hero.

exclamatory sentence a sentence that shows strong emotion and ends with an exclamation mark.

expository writing or **exposition** a composition in writing that explains an event or process.

fable a short tale that teaches a moral.

fantasy a highly imaginative story about characters, places, and events that do not exist.

fiction imaginative narrative designed to entertain rather than to explain, persuade, or describe.

figure of speech the expressive, nonliteral use of language usually through metaphor, simile, or personification.

fluency freedom from word-identification problems that hinder comprehension in reading.

folktale a narrative form of genre such as an epic, myth, or fable that is well-known through repeated storytellings.

foreshadowing giving clues to upcoming events in a story.

free verse verse with irregular metrical pattern.

freewriting writing that is not limited in form, style, content, or purpose, designed to encourage students to write.

genre a classification of literary works, including tragedy, comedy, novel, essay, short story, mystery, realistic fiction, poetry.

grammar the study of the classes of words, their inflections, and their functions and relations in sentences; includes phonological, morphological, syntactic, and semantic descriptions of a language.

grapheme a written or printed representation of a phoneme, such as **c** for /k/.

guided reading reading instruction in which the teacher provides the structure and purpose for reading and responding to the material read.

handing off a method of turning over to the students the primary responsibility for controlling discussion.

indirect object in a sentence, the person or thing to or for whom an action is done, for example, the word **dog** in this sentence: **Madeline gave the dog a treat**.

inference a conclusion based on facts, data, or evidence.

infinitive the base form of a verb, usually with the infinitive marker, for example, **to go**.

inflectional ending an ending that expresses a plural or possessive form of a noun, the tense of a verb, or the comparative or superlative form of an adjective or adverb.

interrogative word a word that marks a clause or sentence as a question, including **interrogative pronouns who**, **what**, **which**, **where**.

intervention a strategy or program designed to supplement or substitute instruction, especially for those students who fall behind.

invented spelling the result of an attempt to spell a word based on the writer's knowledge of the spelling system and how it works, often with overemphasis on sound/symbol relationships.

irony a figure of speech in which the literal meaning of the words is the opposite of their intended meaning.

journal a written record of daily events or responses.

juvenile book a book written for children or adolescents.

legend a traditional tale handed down from generation to generation.

leitmotif a repeated expression, event, or idea used to unify a work of art such as writing.

letter one of a set of graphic symbols that forms an alphabet and is used alone or in combination to represent a phoneme, also **grapheme**.

linguistics the study of the nature and structure of language and communication.

literary elements the elements of a story such as **setting**, **plot**, and **characterization** that create the structure of a narrative.

macron a diacritical mark placed above a vowel to indicate a long vowel sound.

main idea the central thought or chief topic of a passage.

mechanics the conventions of capitalization and punctuation.

metacognition awareness and knowledge of one's mental processes or thinking about what one is thinking about.

metaphor a figure of speech in which a comparison is implied but not stated, for example, **She is a jewel**.

miscue a deviation from text during oral reading in an attempt to make sense of the text.

modeling an instructional technique in which the teacher serves as an example of behavior.

mood the literary element that conveys the emotional atmosphere of a story.

morpheme a meaningful linguistic unit that cannot be divided into smaller units, for example, **word**; **a bound morpheme** is a morpheme that cannot stand alone as an independent word, for example, the prefix **re-**; a **free morpheme** can stand alone, for example, **dog**.

myth a story designed to explain the mysteries of life.

narrative writing or **narration** a composition in writing that tells a story or gives an account of an event.

nonfiction prose designed to explain, argue, or describe rather than to entertain with a factual emphasis, includes biography and autobiography.

noun a part of speech that denotes persons, places, things, qualities, or acts.

novel an extended fictional prose narration.

onomatopoeia the use of a word whose sound suggests its meaning, for example, **purr**.

oral blending the ability to fuse discrete phonemes into recognizable words; oral blending puts sounds together to make a word, **see also segmentation**.

orthography correct or standardized spelling according to established usage in a language.

oxymoron a figure of speech in which contrasting or contradictory words are brought together for emphasis.

paragraph a subdivision of a written composition that consists of one or more sentences, deals with one point, or gives the words of one speaker, usually beginning with an indented line.

participle a verb form used as an adjective, for example, **the skating party**.

personification a figure of speech in which animals, ideas, or things take on human characteristics.

persuasive writing a composition intended to persuade the reader to adopt the writer's point of view.

phoneme the smallest sound unit of speech, for example, the /k/ in **book**.

phonemic awareness the ability to recognize that spoken words are made up of discrete sounds and that those sounds can be manipulated.

Glossary of Reading Terms (continued)

phonetic spelling the respelling of entry words in a dictionary according to a pronunciation key.

phonetics the study of speech sounds.

phonics a way of teaching reading that addresses sound/symbol relationships, especially in beginning instruction.

phonogram a letter or symbol that represents a phonetic sound.

plot the literary element that provides the structure of the action of a story, which may include rising action, climax, and falling action leading to a resolution or denouement.

plural a grammatical form of a word that refers to more than one in number; an **irregular plural** is one that does not follow normal patterns for inflectional endings.

poetic license the liberty taken by writers to ignore conventions.

poetry a metrical form of composition in which language is chosen and arranged to create a powerful response through meaning, sound, or rhythm.

possessive showing ownership either through the use of an adjective, an adjectival pronoun, or the possessive form of a noun.

predicate the part of the sentence that expresses something about the subject and includes the verb phrase; a **complete predicate** includes the principal verb in a sentence and all its modifiers or subordinate parts.

predicting a comprehension strategy in which the reader attempts to figure out what will happen and then confirms predictions as the text is read.

prefix an affix attached before a base word that changes the meaning of the word.

preposition a part of speech in the class of function words, such as **of**, **on**, **at**, that precede noun phrases to create prepositional phrases.

prewriting the planning stage of the writing process in which the writer formulates ideas, gathers information, and considers ways to organize them.

print awareness in emergent literacy, a child's growing recognition of conventions and characteristics of written language, including reading from left to right and top to bottom in English, and that words are separated by spaces.

pronoun a part of speech used as a substitute for a noun or noun phrase.

proofreading the act of reading with the intent to correct, clarify, or improve text.

pseudonym an assumed name used by an author, a pen name or nom de plume.

publishing the process of preparing written material for presentation.

punctuation graphic marks such as comma, period, quotation marks, and brackets used to clarify meaning and give speech characteristics to written language.

question an interrogative sentence that asks a question and ends with a question mark.

realistic fiction a story that attempts to portray characters and events as they actually are.

rebus the use of a picture or symbol to suggest a word or syllable.

revise in the writing process, to change or correct a manuscript to make its message more clear.

rhyme identical or very similar recurring final sounds in words, often at the ends of lines of poetry.

rime a vowel and any following consonants of a syllable.

segmentation the ability to break words into individual sounds; **see also oral blending**.

semantic mapping a graphic display of a group of words that are meaningfully related to support vocabulary instruction.

semantics the study of meaning in language, including the meanings of words, phrases, sentences, and texts.

sentence a grammatical unit that expresses a statement, question, or command; a **simple sentence** is a sentence with one subject and one predicate; a **compound sentence** is a sentence with two or more independent clauses usually separated by a comma and conjunction, but no dependent clause; a **complex sentence** is a sentence with one independent and one or more dependent clauses.

sentence combining a teaching technique in which complex sentence chunks and paragraphs are built from basic sentences.

sentence lifting the process of using sentences from children's writing to illustrate what is wrong or right to develop children's editing and proofreading skills.

sequence the order of elements or events.

setting the literary element that includes the time, place, and physical and psychological background in which a story takes place.

sight word a word that is taught to be read as a whole word, usually words that are phonetically irregular.

simile a figure of speech in which a comparison of two things that are unlike is directly stated usually with the words **like** or **as**, for example, **She is like a jewel**.

spelling the process of representing language by means of a writing system.

statement a sentence that tells something and ends with a period.

study skills a general term for the techniques and strategies that help readers comprehend text with the intent to remember, includes following directions, organizing, locating, and using graphic aids.

style the characteristics of a work that reflect the author's particular way of writing.

subject the main topic of a sentence to which a predicate refers, including the principal noun; a **complete subject** includes the principal noun in a sentence and all its modifiers.

suffix an affix attached at the end of a base word that changes the meaning of the word.

summarizing a comprehension strategy in which the reader constructs a brief statement that contains the essential ideas of a passage.

syllable a minimal unit of sequential speech sounds comprised of a vowel sound or a vowel-sound combination.

symbolism the use of one thing to represent something else in order to represent an idea in a concrete way.

synonym a word that means the same as another word.

syntax the grammatical pattern or structure of word order in sentences, clauses, and phrases.

tense the way in which verbs indicate past, present, and future time of action.

text structure the various patterns of ideas that are built into the organization of a written work.

theme a major idea or proposition that provides an organizing concept through which by study, students gain depth of understanding.

topic sentence a sentence intended to express the main idea of a paragraph or passage.

tragedy a literary work, often a play, in which the main character suffers conflicts and which presents a serious theme and has an unfortunate ending.

usage the way in which a native language or dialect is used by the members of the community.

verb a word that expresses an action or state that occurs in a predicate of a sentence; an **irregular verb** is a verb that does not follow normal patterns of inflectional endings that reflect past, present, or future verb tense.

visualizing a comprehension strategy in which the reader constructs a mental picture of a character, setting, or process.

vowel a voiced speech sound and the alphabet letter that represents that sound, made without stoppage or friction of the air flow as it passes through the vocal tract.

vowel digraph a spelling pattern in which two or more letters represent a single vowel sound.

word calling proficiency in decoding with little or no attention to word meaning.

writing also **composition** the process or result of organizing ideas in writing to form a clear message, includes persuasive, expository, narrative, and descriptive forms.

writing process the many aspects of the complex act of producing a piece of writing, including prewriting, drafting, revising, proofreading, and publishing.

Open Court Reading develops handwriting skills through weekly Penmanship lessons. The instruction for these lessons appears in the Language Arts part of the lesson in every grade level. The purpose of these lessons is to develop important handwriting skills necessary for producing legible, properly spaced documents. Penmanship practice reinforces the vocabulary in the lesson selection.

In addition to the board, the overhead projector can be a very effective device for teaching penmanship. Students can move their pencils at the same time the teacher forms letters on the transparency. It also helps to recite the descriptions or chants that go with each letter.

Penmanship in Levels K to 2

Beginning in kindergarten, the Penmanship lessons expand on the sound/spelling instruction by introducing letters the students study in Sounds and Letters. Students learn that those letters are made of four basic lines: curved lines, horizontal lines, vertical lines, and slanted lines.

Next, students learn letter and number formation. The students practice letter formation by writing the letter being studied and then words from the literature selection that contain the particular letter. This instruction continues in Level 1 and is tied to the letter formation instruction in Phonics and Fluency.

Cursive Handwriting Models

Penmanship is developed and practiced through Level 6, with cursive instruction beginning in the final unit of Level 2. Students are taught that most cursive letters are comprised of four strokes: undercurve, downcurve, overcurve, and slanted lines. These lessons teach students the essentials of cursive handwriting, such as proper slant; loops; joining; and spacing between letters, words, and sentences. As in the earlier levels, the students practice letter formation by writing the letters in the Writer's Notebook and then words from the literature selection that contain the particular letter.

The writing exercises progress with each level. Students begin writing words in kindergarten and graduate to writing sentences by the end of Level 1 and into Level 2. Level 3 eases students into cursive by having them practice words from the literature, with a transition to sentences in Level 4, and paragraphs in Levels 5 and 6.

Hand and Paper Positioning

The **hand and paper positioning** models are for teachers' reference and enhance the written instruction of positioning lessons. The diagrams give teachers a visual aid so that they may better understand and demonstrate an effective technique of positioning.

A right-handed student should hold the pencil loosely about one inch above the point, between the thumb and middle finger. A left-handed student should hold the pencil the same way, but up to one half inch farther away from the point. The index fingers of both writers should rest lightly on the top of the pencil. The wrist should be level and just slightly raised from the desk.

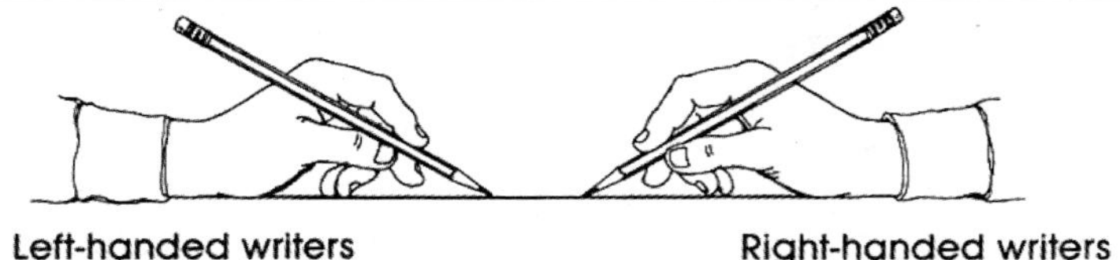

Left-handed writers Right-handed writers

For both kinds of writers, the paper should lie straight in front of the student with the edges parallel to the edges of the desk. A left-handed writer may find it easier to slant the paper slightly to the right and parallel to the left forearm. A right-handed writer's writing hand should be kept well below the writing. The left hand should hold down the paper.

Left-handed writers

Right-handed writers

Penmanship (continued)

Cursive Handwriting Models

The models of cursive handwriting provide teachers with a systematic method for teaching students to form uppercase and lowercase letters of the alphabet. The dots on the letters indicate starting points for the students. The numbered arrows show the students in what order and what direction the line should go to form the particular letter. Teachers may use the chants to describe the letter step by step as he or she models the formation on the board. Students may also say the chants in unison as they practice the formation, whether they are writing the letter or tracing it on the board.

The four basic cursive strokes diagram aids teachers by giving examples of the strokes that recur frequently in cursive handwriting. Students can form most cursive letters by using one or more of these strokes. The letters in the Penmanship lessons are grouped according to the strokes particular to each letter.

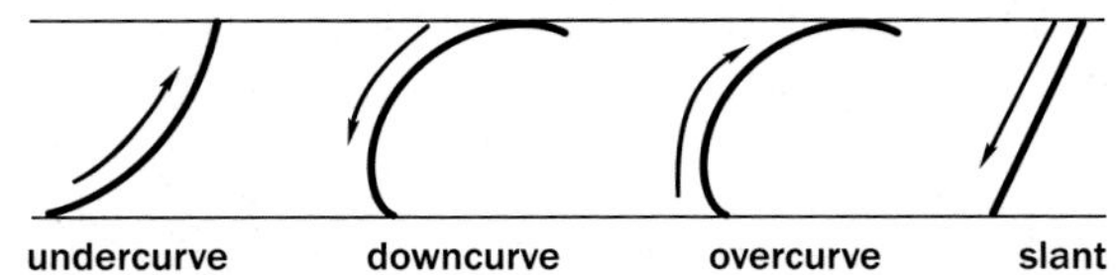

Undercurve letters

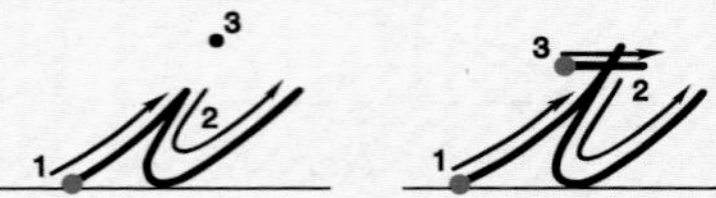

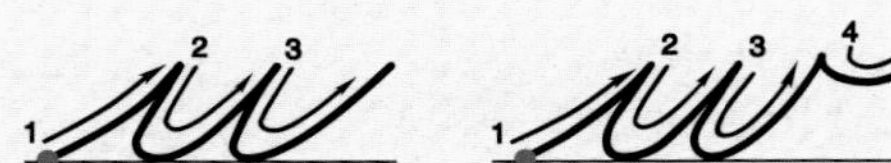

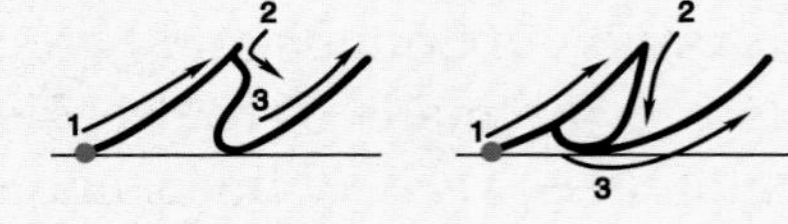

i Starting point, undercurve
Slant down, undercurve to endpoint, dot exactly above: small *i*

t Starting point, undercurve
Slant down, undercurve to endpoint
Starting point, straight across: small *t*

u Starting point, undercurve
Slant down, undercurve
Slant down, undercurve: small *u*

w Starting point, undercurve
Slant down, undercurve, slant down, undercurve, small curve to right: small *w*

r Starting point, undercurve
Slant right
Slant down, undercurve: small *r*

s Starting point, undercurve
Curve down and back, undercurve: small *s*

Downcurve letters

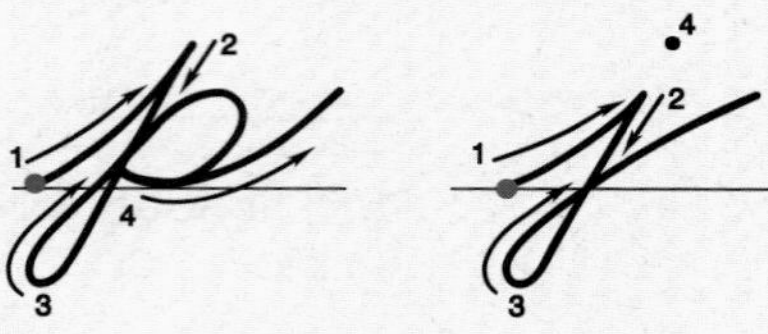

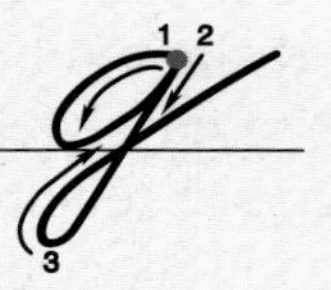

p Starting point, undercurve
Slant, loop back
Overcurve
Curve back, undercurve: small *p*

j Starting point, undercurve
Slant down
Loop back
Overcurve to endpoint
Dot exactly above: small *j*

a Starting point, downcurve
Undercurve to starting point
Slant down, undercurve: small *a*

c Starting point, downcurve
Undercurve: small *c*

d Starting point, downcurve
Undercurve past starting point
Slant down, undercurve: small *d*

q Starting point, downcurve
Undercurve to starting point
Slant down and loop forward, undercurve:
small *q*

g Starting point, downcurve
Undercurve to starting point
Slant down and loop back, overcurve: small *g*

o Starting point, downcurve
Undercurve
Small curve to right: small *o*

Cursive Handwriting Models

Overcurve letters

n Starting point, overcurve
Slant down, overcurve
Slant down, undercurve: small *n*

m Starting point, overcurve
Slant down, overcurve
Slant down, overcurve
Slant down, undercurve: small *m*

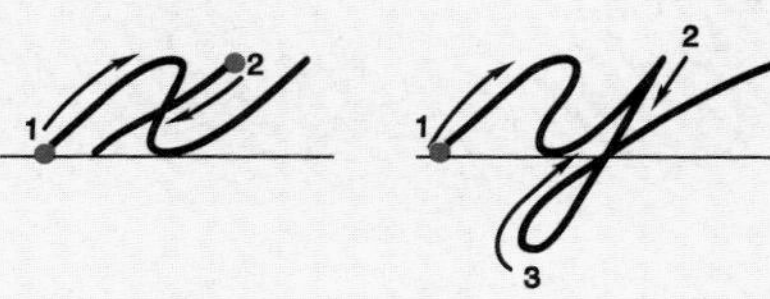

x Starting point, overcurve
Slant down, undercurve to endpoint
Starting point slant down: small *x*

y Starting point, overcurve
Slant down
Undercurve, slant down
Loop back into overcurve: small *y*

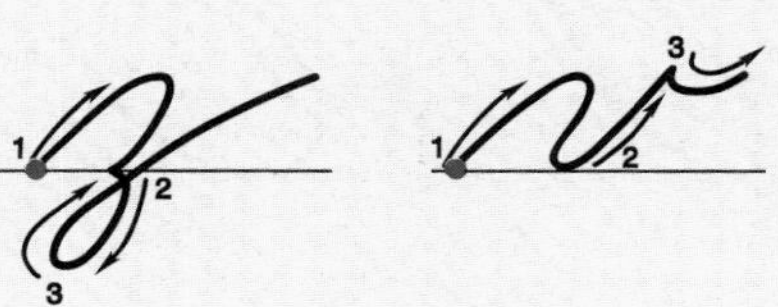

z Starting point, overcurve
Slant down, overcurve, down
Loop into overcurve: small *z*

v Starting point, overcurve
Slant down
Undercurve
Small curve to right: small *v*

Letters with loops

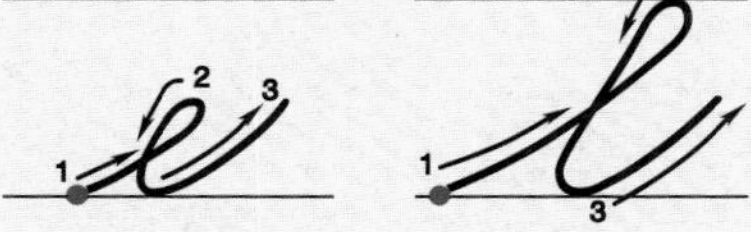

e Starting point, undercurve
Loop back, slant down
Undercurve: small *e*

l Starting point, undercurve
Loop back, slant down
Undercurve: small *l*

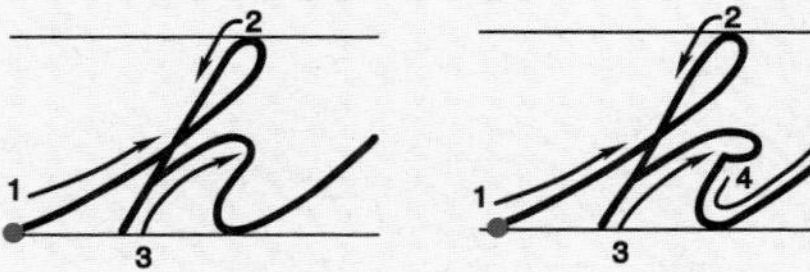

h Starting point, undercurve
Loop back, slant down
Overcurve, slant down
Undercurve: small *h*

k Starting point, undercurve
Loop back, slant down
Overcurve, curve forward and under
Slant down, undercurve: small *k*

f Starting point, undercurve
Loop back, slant down
Loop forward into undercurve: small *f*

b Starting point, undercurve
Loop back, slant down
Undercurve, small curve to right:
small *b*

Penmanship (continued)

Cursive Handwriting Models

Downcurve letters

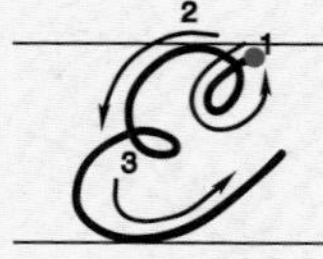

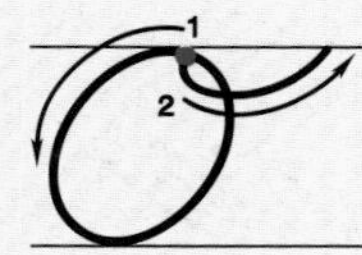

A Starting point, downcurve
Undercurve to starting point
Slant down, undercurve: capital *A*

C Starting point, loop
Downcurve, undercurve: capital *C*

E Starting point, loop
Downcurve
Loop back, downcurve
Undercurve: capital *E*

O Starting point, downcurve
left into undercurve
Loop and curve right: capital *O*

Curve forward letters

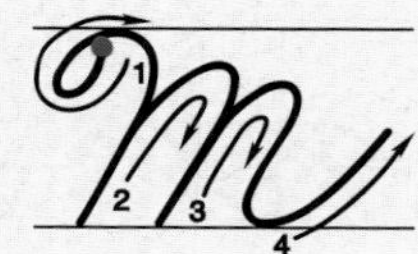

N Starting point, loop
Curve forward
Slant down
Retrace up slant
Overcurve down into undercurve:
capital *N*

M Starting point, loop
Curve forward, slant down
Retrace up slant, overcurve
Slant down, retrace up slant
Overcurve down into undercurve:
capital *M*

Curve forward letters

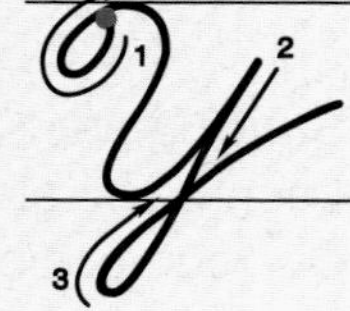

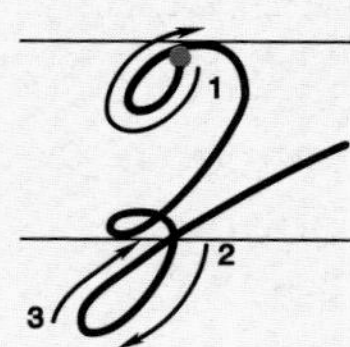

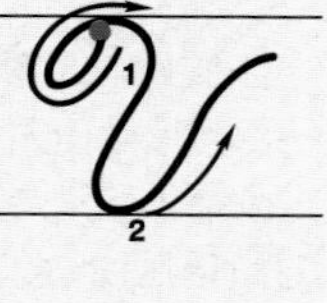

K Starting point, loop
Curve forward, slant down to end point
Starting point
Doublecurve back to slant
Curve forward
Undercurve up: capital *K*

H Starting point, loop
Curve forward, slant down to end point
Starting point
Curve back and slant down
Retrace up slant, loop left and
curve right: capital *H*

U Starting point, loop
Curve forward, slant down into
undercurve
Slant down, undercurve: capital *U*

Y Starting point, loop
Curve forward, slant down
Undercurve up, slant down
Loop back, overcurve: capital *Y*

Z Starting point, loop
Curve forward, slant down
Overcurve, curve down
Loop into overcurve: capital *Z*

V Starting point, loop
Curve forward and slant down,
undercurve up and overcurve:
capital *V*

LEVEL APPENDIX

Cursive Handwriting Models

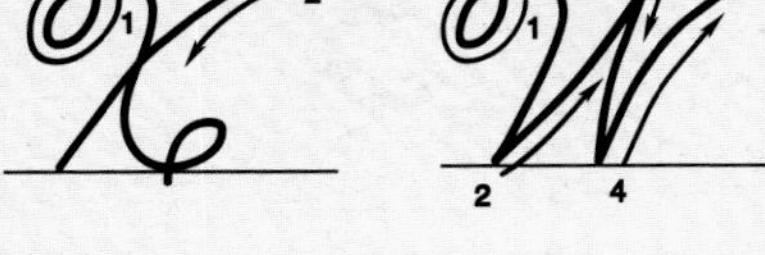

X Starting point, loop
Curve forward, slant down
Undercurve to end point
Starting point, slant down: capital *X*

W Starting point, loop
Curve forward, slant down into undercurve
Slant down into undercurve
Overcurve: capital *W*

Doublecurve letters

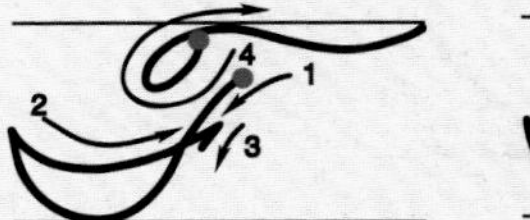

F Starting point, loop
Curve forward and right to endpoint
Starting point
Doublecurve, curve up
Curve right, slant down: capital *F*

T Starting point, loop
Curve forward to endpoint
Starting point
Doublecurve, curve up
Curve right: capital *T*

Overcurve letters

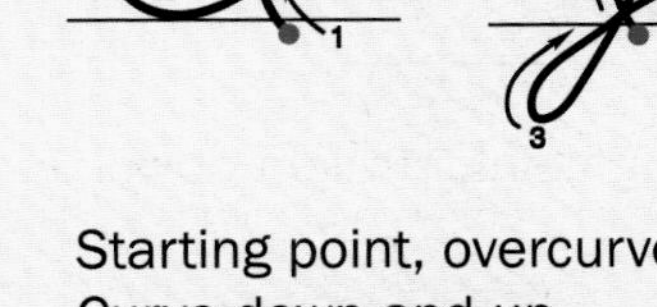

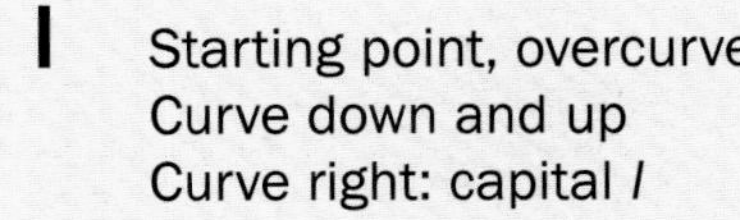

I Starting point, overcurve
Curve down and up
Curve right: capital *I*

J Starting point, overcurve
Slant down and loop back
Overcurve: capital *J*

Q Starting point, loop
Curve forward, slant down
Loop back, curve under: capital *Q*

Letters with loops

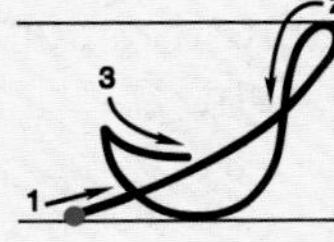

G Starting point, undercurve
Loop, curve up
Double curve, curve up
Curve right: capital G

S Starting point, undercurve
Loop, curve down and up
Curve right: capital *S*

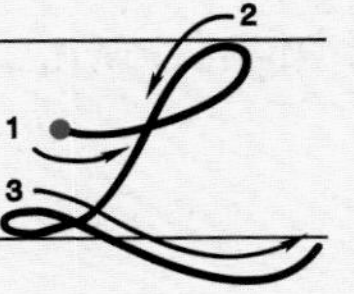

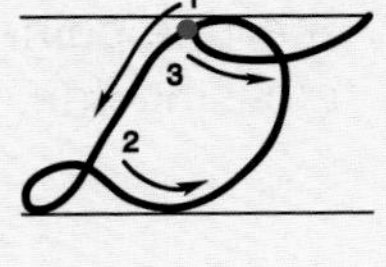

L Starting point, undercurve
Loop, curve down and loop
Curve under: capital *L*

D Starting point, slant down
Loop, curve down and up
Loop and curve right: capital *D*

Undercurve-slant letters

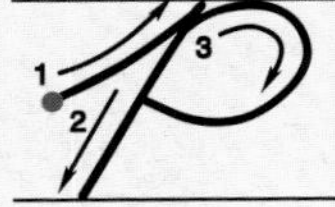

P Starting point, undercurve
Slant down, retrace up
Curve forward and back: capital *P*

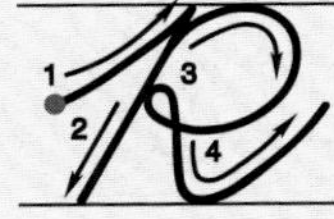

R Starting point, undercurve
Slant down, retrace up
Curve forward to slant
Curve forward
Undercurve: capital *R*

B Starting point, undercurve
Slant down, retrace up
Curve forward, loop
Curve forward and back
Curve right: capital *B*

Penmanship (continued)

Numbers

1 Starting point, straight down: *1*

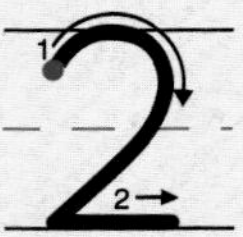

2 Starting point, around right, slanting left and straight across right: *2*

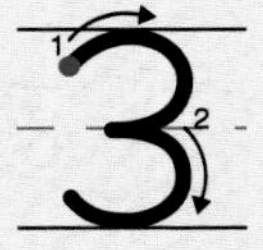

3 Starting point, around right, in at the middle, around right: *3*

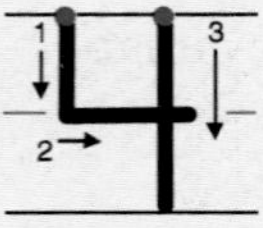

4 Starting point, straight down
Straight across right
Starting point, straight down, crossing line: *4*

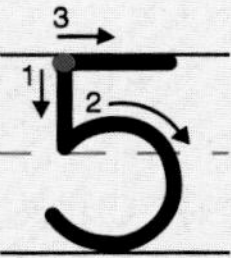

5 Starting point, curving around right and up
Starting point, straight across right: *5*

6 Starting point, slanting left, around the bottom curving up around right and into the curve: *6*

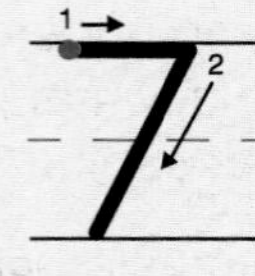

7 Starting point, straight across right, slanting down left: *7*

8 Starting point, curving left, curving down and around right, slanting up right to starting point: *8*

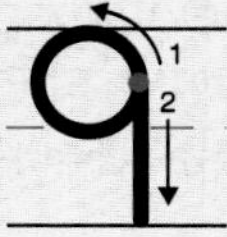

9 Starting point, curving around left all the way, straight down: *9*

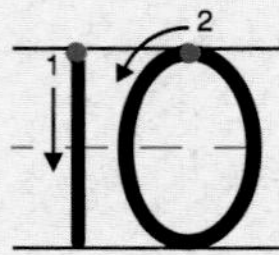

10 Starting point, straight down
Starting point, curving left all the way around to starting point: *10*

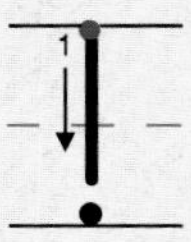

! Starting point, straight down
Dot exactly below: exclamation point

? Starting point, curving around right, straight down
Dot exactly below: question mark

A

INDEX

INDEX

D

E

F

G

INDEX

H

I

J

INDEX

M

INDEX

INDEX

Q

R

INDEX

S

INDEX

INDEX

T

U

INDEX

Y

Notes

Use this page to record lessons or elements that work well or need to be adjusted for future reference.

Lessons that work well.

Lessons that need adjustments.

Notes

Use this page to record lessons or elements that work well or need to be adjusted for future reference.

Lessons that work well.

Lessons that need adjustments.

Notes

Use this page to record lessons or elements that work well or need to be adjusted for future reference.

Lessons that work well.

Lessons that need adjustments.

Notes

Use this page to record lessons or elements that work well or need the be adjusted for future reference.

Lessons that work well.

Lessons that need adjustments.

Notes

Use this page to record lessons or elements that work well
or need the be adjusted for future reference.

Lessons that work well.

Lessons that need adjustments.

Notes

Use this page to record lessons or elements that work well or need the be adjusted for future reference.

Lessons that work well.

Lessons that need adjustments.